The New Workplace

The New Workplace
A Guide to the Human Impact of Modern Working Practices

Edited by

David Holman, Toby D. Wall and Chris W. Clegg
University of Sheffield, UK

Paul Sparrow
University of Manchester, UK

and

Ann Howard
Development Dimensions International, New Jersey, USA

WILEY

Copyright © 2003 John Wiley & Sons, Ltd, The Atrium, Southern Gate, Chichester,
West Sussex PO19 8SQ, UK

Telephone (+44) 1243 779777

Email (for orders and customer service enquiries): cs-books@wiley.co.uk
Visit our Home Page on: http://www.wileyeurope.com or http://www.wiley.com

All Rights Reserved. No part of this publication may be reproduced, stored in a retrieval system or transmitted in any form or by any means, electronic, mechanical, photocopying, recording, scanning or otherwise, except under the terms of the Copyright, Designs and Patents Act 1988 or under the terms of a licence issued by the Copyright Licensing Agency Ltd, 90 Tottenham Court Road, London W1T 4LP, UK, without the permission in writing of the Publisher. Requests to the Publisher should be addressed to the Permissions Department, John Wiley & Sons Ltd, The Atrium, Southern Gate, Chichester, West Sussex PO19 8SQ, England, or e-mailed to permreq@wiley.co.uk, or faxed to (+44) 1243 770620.

This publication is designed to provide accurate and authoritative information in regard to the subject matter covered. It is sold on the understanding that the Publisher is not engaged in rendering professional services. If professional advice or other expert assistance is required, the services of a competent professional should be sought.

Other Wiley Editorial Offices

John Wiley & Sons Inc., 111 River Street, Hoboken, NJ 07030, USA

Jossey-Bass, 989 Market Street, San Francisco, CA 94103-1741, USA

Wiley-VCH Verlag GmbH, Boschstr. 12, D-69469 Weinheim, Germany

John Wiley & Sons Australia Ltd, 33 Park Road, Milton, Queensland 4064, Australia

John Wiley & Sons (Asia) Pte Ltd, 2 Clementi Loop #02-01, Jin Xing Distripark, Singapore 129809

John Wiley & Sons Canada Ltd, 22 Worcester Road, Etobicoke, Ontario, Canada M9W 1L1

Wiley also publishes its books in a variety of electronic formats. Some content that appears in print may not be available in electronic books.

Library of Congress Cataloging-in-Publication Data

The new workplace : a guide to the human impact of modern working practices / edited by David Holman ... [et al.].
    p. cm.
    Includes bibliographical references and indexes.
    ISBN 0-471-48543-8
    1. Quality of work life. 2. Job satisfaction. 3. Psychology, Industrial. 4. Work environment. 5. Work design. 6. Human-machine systems. 7. Industrial relations. I. Holman, David.
    HD6955 .N495 2002
    331.2–dc21   2002028874

British Library Cataloguing in Publication Data

A catalogue record for this book is available from the British Library

ISBN 0-471-48543-8

Typeset in 10/12pt Times by Techbooks Electronic Services Pvt Ltd, New Delhi, India
Printed and bound in Great Britain by Biddles Ltd, Guildford and King's Lynn
This book is printed on acid-free paper responsibly manufactured from sustainable forestry in which at least two trees are planted for each one used for paper production.

Contents

List of Figures   vii

List of Tables   viii

About the Editors   ix

List of Contributors   xi

Preface   xiii

Part I   Introduction

Chapter 1   The New Workplace: An Introduction   3
David Holman and Stephen Wood

Part II   Modern Working Practices in the Workplace

Chapter 2   Workers Under Lean Manufacturing   19
Rick Delbridge

Chapter 3   The Human Side of Total Quality Management   37
Richard Cooney and Amrik Sohal

Chapter 4   Advanced Manufacturing Technology   55
Bradley Chase and Waldemar Karwowski

Chapter 5   Supply-chain Partnering   71
Máire Kerrin and Belén Icasati-Johanson

Chapter 6   Team Work   95
John Cordery

Chapter 7   Call Centres   115
David Holman

Chapter 8   Knowledge Management   135
Harry Scarbrough

Chapter 9   Employee Involvement: Utilization, Impacts, and Future Prospects   155
George S. Benson and Edward E. Lawler III

Chapter 10	Proactivity and Innovation: Promoting a New Workforce for the New Workplace *Kerry L. Unsworth and Sharon K. Parker*	175
Chapter 11	Teleworking and Virtual Organisations: The Human Impact *David Lamond, Kevin Daniels and Peter Standen*	197
Chapter 12	Performance Management Practices and Motivation *Robert D. Pritchard and Stephanie C. Payne*	219
Chapter 13	e-business: Future Prospects? *Chris W. Clegg, Belén Icasati-Johanson and Stuart Bennett*	245

Part III   Organisational Performance and Productivity

Chapter 14	Organisational Performance and Manufacturing Practices *Stephen Wood*	271
Chapter 15	Organisational Performance in Services *Rosemary Batt and Virginia Doellgast*	291
Chapter 16	The Human Resource–Firm Performance Relationship: Methodological and Theoretical Challenges *Patrick M. Wright and Timothy M. Gardner*	311

Part IV   Tools and Methods for Design and Evaluation

Chapter 17	Tools and Methods to Support the Design and Implementation of New Work Systems *Enid Mumford and Carolyn Axtell*	331
Chapter 18	Examining New Technologies and New Ways of Working: Methods for Designing Evaluation Studies *Sabine Sonnentag*	347

Part V   Reflection and Critique

Chapter 19	The Future of Work? *Paul Sparrow*	371
Chapter 20	Any Nearer a "Better" Approach? A Critical View *Karen Legge*	393
Chapter 21	The New Workplace: Taking Stock and Looking Forward *David Holman, Toby D. Wall and Ann Howard*	413

Author Index	427
Subject Index	445

List of Figures

Figure 2.1	Key organizing principles of lean manufacturing	27
Figure 4.1	A framework for competitive advanced manufacturing enterprise	65
Figure 10.1	Innovation and proactivity: summary of influential factors and good practices	180
Figure 11.1	Conceptual overview of behavioural issues in teleworking	202
Figure 12.1	A theory of motivation	221
Figure 12.2	Example of connections between different parts of the motivation theory	224
Figure 12.3	Basic practices and the theory of motivation	233
Figure 12.4	TQM and empowerment and the theory of motivation	237
Figure 12.5	Knowledge management and autonomous workgroups and the motivation model	239
Figure 12.6	ProMES and the motivation model	241
Figure 13.1	Model of e-adoption ladder	248
Figure 16.1	Architectural approach to HRM	314
Figure 16.2	Model of the HR–firm performance relationship	320

List of Tables

Table 1.1	Definition of the modern working practices covered in this book	4
Table 2.1	Ohno's comparison of production systems at Toyota and Ford	20
Table 2.2	What is lean production?	22
Table 2.3	MacDuffie's measures of work systems and HRM policies	28
Table 4.1	The HITOP framework	64
Table 5.1	Features of arm's-length contract relations and obligational contract relations	73
Table 5.2	Models of customer–supplier relations	75
Table 7.1	Characteristics of relationships and encounters	118
Table 7.2	Call centre models: "mass service" and "high commitment service"	122
Table 7.3	Individual and collective forms of CSR resistance to management control	128
Table 8.1	Perspectives on KM	139
Table 8.2	Knowledge management strategies	147
Table 8.3	The future agenda for KM	151
Table 9.1	Surveys used to research EI and organizational performance	158
Table 11.1	Types of telework and sample jobs	200
Table 11.2	Predicting forms of telework from Quinn's (1988) competing values framework	204
Table 12.1	Implication of theory to maximize motivation	226
Table 12.2	Implication of motivation theory for various practices	231
Table 13.1	Rates of uptake of e-business and related issues	249
Table 13.2	International uptake of e-business	252
Table 13.3	External barriers and enablers of e-business	254
Table 13.4	Use and effectiveness of selected modern working practices	261

About the Editors

David Holman is a Research Fellow at the Centre for Organisation and Innovation, which is part of the Institute of Work Psychology at the University of Sheffield. He obtained his degree in psychology, diploma in personnel management and doctorate from Manchester Metropolitan University. His main research interests are job design, well-being and emotions at work, learning at work, and management education and development. He is the author of *Management and Language: The Manager as a Practical Author* and has published articles in the *Journal of Occupational and Organisational Psychology, Human Relations, Management Learning, Human Factors and Ergonomics in Manufacturing* and *Applied Ergonomics*.

Toby D. Wall is Professor of Psychology at the University of Sheffield, where he is Director of the Institute of Work Psychology and the ESRC Centre for Organisation and Innovation. He obtained his first degree and his doctorate from the University of Nottingham. His main research interests have been in industrial and organisational psychology and have recently focused on the effects of advanced manufacturing technology and shop floor work organisation on work performance and strain. His research has appeared in the *Journal of Applied Psychology*, the *Academy of Management Journal* and other leading publications. He also the author of several books including *The Human Side of Advanced Manufacturing Technology* and *Job and Work Design*.

Chris W. Clegg is Professor of Organisational Psychology and Deputy Director of the Institute of Work Psychology at the University of Sheffield. He is a Co-Director of the ESRC Centre for Organisation and Innovation, and Co-Director of the BAE—Rolls-Royce University Technology Partnership for Design. He currently chairs the Sociotechnical Sub-Group of the British Computer Society. He holds a BA (Hons) in Psychology from the University of Newcastle upon Tyne and an MSc in Business Administration from the University of Bradford. He is a Fellow of the British Psychological Society and a chartered psychologist. Chris Clegg's research interests are in the areas of new technology, work organisation, information and control systems, sociotechnical theory and new management practices. He has published his work in a number of books and journals.

Paul Sparrow is the Ford Professor of International Human Resource Management at Manchester Business School. He graduated from the University of Manchester with a BSc (Hons) in Psychology and the University of Aston with an MSc in Applied Psychology and was then sponsored by Rank Xerox to study the impacts of ageing on the organisation for his Ph.D. at Aston University. He has written and edited a number of books including *European Human Resource Management in Transition, The Competent Organization: A Psychological Analysis of the Strategic Management Process* and *Human Resource Management: The New Agenda*. He has also published articles in leading journals on the future of work, human resource strategy, the psychology of strategic management, international human resource management and cross-cultural management. He is currently Editor of the *Journal of Occupational and Organisational Psychology*.

Ann Howard is Manager of Assessment Technology Integrity for Development Dimensions International (DDI), a leading provider of human resource programs and services. She has served as president of the Leadership Research Institute, a non-profit organization that she co-founded in 1987. Ann is the author of more than 85 publications on topics such as assessment centers, management selection, managerial careers, and leadership. She is the senior author (with Dr Douglas W. Bray) of *Managerial Lives in Transition: Advancing Age and Changing Times*, which received the George R. Terry Award of Excellence from the Academy of Management in 1989. She has edited two books: *The Changing Nature of Work* (1995) and *Diagnosis for Organizational Change: Methods and Models* (1994). She is a past president of the Society for Industrial and Organizational Psychology and the Society of Psychologists in Management. Ann received her Ph.D. degree from the University of Maryland and her MS degree from San Francisco State University, both in industrial-organizational psychology. She holds an honorary doctor of science degree from Goucher College, where she earned a BA degree in psychology.

List of Contributors

Carolyn Axtell, *Institute of Work Psychology, University of Sheffield, Mushroom Lane, Sheffield S10 2TN, UK*

Professor Rosemary Batt, *School of Industrial and Labor Relations, Cornell University, 387 Ives Hall, Ithaca, NY 14853, USA*

Dr Stuart Bennett, *Automatic Control and Systems Engineering, University of Sheffield, Mappin Street, Sheffield S1 3JD, UK*

Dr George S. Benson, *Department of Management, The University of Texas at Arlington, College of Business, BOC 19467, Arlington, TX 76019, USA*

Dr Bradley Chase, *Industrial and Systems Engineering, University of San Diego, 5998 Alcala Park, San Diego, CA 92110–2492, USA*

Professor Chris W. Clegg, *Institute of Work Psychology, University of Sheffield, Mushroom Lane, Sheffield S10 2TN, UK*

Dr Richard Cooney, *Department of Management, Monash University, Caulfield Campus, 900 Dandenong Road, East Caulfield, Victoria 3145, Australia*

Professor John Cordery, *Department of Organizational and Labour Studies, University of Western Australia, Nedlands, Perth, WA 6907, Australia*

Dr Kevin Daniels, *Nottingham University Business School, University of Nottingham, Wollaton Road, Nottingham NG8 1BB, UK*

Professor Rick Delbridge, *Cardiff Business School, Cardiff University, Colum Drive, Cardiff CF10 3EU, UK*

Virginia Doellgast, *School of Industrial and Labor Relations, Cornell University, 387 Ives Hall, Ithaca, NY 14853, USA*

Dr Timothy M. Gardner, *Marriott School of Management, Brigham Young University, Tanner Building, Provo, UT 84602–3113, USA*

Dr David Holman, *Institute of Work Psychology, University of Sheffield, Mushroom Lane, Sheffield S10 2TN, UK*

Dr Ann Howard, *Development Dimensions International, 21 Knoll Road, Tenafly, NJ 07670, USA*

Belén Icasati-Johanson, *Institute of Work Psychology, University of Sheffield, Mushroom Lane, Sheffield S10 2TN, UK*

Professor Waldemar Karwowski, *Center for Industrial Ergonomics, University of Louisville, Room 445, Lutz Hall, KY 40292, USA*

Dr Máire Kerrin, *Institute for Employment Studies, Mantell Building, Falmer, Brighton BN1 9RF, UK*

Professor David Lamond, *Sydney Graduate School of Management, University of Western Sydney, PO Box 6145, Paramatta Delivery Centre, NSW 2150, Australia*

Professor Edward E. Lawler III, *Center for Effective Organizations, Marshall Business School, University of Southern California, Los Angeles, CA 90089–1421, USA*

Professor Karen Legge, *Industrial Relations and Organisational Behaviour Group, Warwick Business School, University of Warwick, Coventry CV4 7AL, UK*

Professor Enid Mumford, *Manchester Business School, University of Manchester, Booth Street West, Manchester M15 6PB, UK*

Dr Sharon K. Parker, *Australian Graduate School of Management, University of New South Wales, Sydney, NSW 2052, Australia*

Dr Stephanie C. Payne, *Department of Psychology, Texas A&M University, 4235 TAMU, College Station, Texas 77843–4235, USA*

Professor Robert D. Pritchard, *Department of Psychology, Texas A&M University, 4235 TAMU, College Station, Texas 77843–4235, USA*

Professor Harry Scarbrough, *Warwick Business School, Warwick University, Coventry CV4 7AL, UK*

Professor Amrik Sohal, *Department of Management, Monash University, Caulfield Campus, 900 Dandenong Road, East Caulfield, Victoria 3145, Australia*

Professor Sabine Sonnentag, *Technical University of Braunschweig, Institute of Psychology, Spielmannstrasse 19, D-38092 Braunschweig, Germany*

Professor Paul Sparrow, *Manchester Business School, University of Manchester, Booth Street West, Manchester M15 6PB, UK*

Dr Peter Standen, *Department of Management, Edith Cowan University, Pearson St Churchlands, WA 6018, Australia*

Dr Kerrie L. Unsworth, *School of Management, Queensland University of Technology, PO Box 2434, Brisbane, Queensland 4001, Australia*

Professor Toby D. Wall, *Institute of Work Psychology, University of Sheffield, Mushroom Lane, Sheffield S10 2TN, UK*

Professor Stephen Wood, *Institute of Work Psychology, University of Sheffield, Mushroom Lane, Sheffield S10 2TN, UK*

Professor Patrick M. Wright, *Human Resource Studies, 387 Ives Hall, Cornell University, ILR School, Ithaca, NY 14853–3901, USA*

Preface

The make-up of today's workplace is characterised by the use of a wide array of modern working practices and technologies. Lean manufacturing, total quality management, advanced manufacturing technology, call centres, team working, knowledge management and e-business are just a few of the practices that organisations are using in their search for effectiveness. The introduction and use of these practices has provoked much debate and research on their nature and effects. A consistent theme within this has been that the social, psychological and organisational aspects of modern working practices and technologies must be considered in order to understand, design and manage them effectively. In order to bring this research together in one volume, we have invited leading authors from around the world to provide an up-to-date assessment of research on the main working practices that are shaping today's workplace. Where authors have been invited to write on a particular practice, we have asked them to comment on its extent, to review its impact on employees' experience of work and to consider the human resource management implications of the practice. This book also focuses on the effects that modern working practices have on performance. Thus, where possible, chapters on individual working practices consider their impact on performance. In addition, a series of chapters are devoted to examining whether modern working practices and human resource practices have an effect on organisational performance in manufacturing and service sectors. We also wanted the book to have a practical focus and so included a section on the tools and methods that can be used to jointly design and evaluate the social and technical aspects of working practices.

The breadth of working practices covered, the multi-disciplinary nature of the chapters, the focus on performance and the practical suggestions on design and evaluation distinguish this book from others. We believe that this will help the reader gain a comprehensive understanding of the social, psychological and organisational aspects of modern working practices. Ultimately, though, this book is designed to make a contribution to the understanding, design and effective management of modern working practices. The book's breadth will appeal to those with an interest in industrial/organisational psychology, human resource management, management and business studies, manufacturing, production engineering and change management, as well as those who are involved in the design, implementation and effective management of innovative working practices.

The editors would like to state that this book is part of the programme of the ESRC Centre for Organisation and Innovation, at the Institute of Work Psychology, University of Sheffield, UK. The editors therefore acknowledge the support of the Economic and Social Research Council (ESRC) (UK). David Holman would particularly like to thank the

Holman family, Curtis Wilson, David Wilson, Julia Eaton and Kate Fields for their support throughout all the stages of writing this book.

David Holman
Toby D. Wall
Chris W. Clegg
Paul Sparrow
Ann Howard

PART I
Introduction

CHAPTER 1

The New Workplace: An Introduction

David Holman and **Stephen Wood**
Institute of Work Psychology, University of Sheffield, UK

Modern working practices and technologies are typically implemented because they have a significant capacity to shape the nature of work and its effect on individuals' behaviour. They include, for example, lean manufacturing, advanced manufacturing technology, total quality management (TQM), call centres, supply-chain partnering (SCP), knowledge management and e-business. Furthermore, surveys show that these practices are increasingly prevalent in organisations in advanced industrial societies (Lawler, Mohrman & Ledford, 1995; Osterman, 1994; Waterson et al., 1999). Yet when modern working practices are implemented they can sometimes alter work in unintended ways, have deleterious effects on employees and not produce the hoped for improvements in employee and organisational performance (Clegg et al., 1997; Parker & Wall, 1998; Waterson et al., 1999). Indeed, the design, implementation and management of modern working practices often create problems for employees at all levels in the organisation. It therefore seems essential that we understand the nature of modern working practices, the effects that they have on employees, the extent of their use, their effect on organisational performance, and how they can be more effectively designed, implemented, evaluated and managed.

Needless to say, considerable research has already been conducted on these issues in disciplines such as human resource management, occupational psychology, strategic management, operations management and sociology; and one of the strongest messages to come out of this research is that the social, psychological and organisational aspects of working practices and technologies must be considered in order to understand, design and manage them effectively (Cherns, 1987; McLoughlin & Harris, 1997; Salvendy, 1997; Storey, 1994; Wall, Clegg & Kemp, 1987). As such, the main premise of this book is that the human side of workplace practices and technologies must be addressed. To do this, the book has the following five aims:

1. To examine the nature and extent of modern working practices and technologies.
2. To review and evaluate the impact modern working practices have on how people work and their experience of work.
3. To examine the human resource management implications of such practices.
4. To examine the effect that these practices have on productivity and firm performance.

The New Workplace: A Guide to the Human Impact of Modern Working Practices.
Edited by David Holman, Toby D. Wall, Chris W. Clegg, Paul Sparrow and Ann Howard. © 2003 John Wiley & Sons, Ltd.

Table 1.1 Definition of the modern working practices covered in this book

Modern working practice	Definition
Lean manufacturing	An integrated system of production with a single production flow that is pulled by the customer. Emphasis on small batch manufacture, just-in-time, team-based work and participation to eliminate non-value-adding activities and variabilities
Total quality management	A comprehensive, organisation-wide effort that is an integrated and interfunctional means of improving the quality of products and services and of sustaining competitive advantage
Advanced manufacturing technology	The application of computer-based technology to automate and integrate the different functions in the manufacturing system
Supply-chain partnering	Developing long-term, cooperative relationships with suppliers and customers
Team work	A collection of individuals who are interdependent in their tasks and outcomes, who see themselves and are seen by others as a distinct social entity within a larger social unit
Call centres	A work environment in which the main business is mediated by computer and telephone-based technologies that enable the efficient distribution of calls (or allocation of outgoing calls) to available staff, and permits customer–employee interaction to occur simultaneously with the use of display screen equipment and the instant access to, and inputting of, information
Knowledge management	The use of practices, particularly IT-based technologies and community- and network-based practices, to centralise, collectivise and create knowledge so that it can be exploited to increase the organisational performance and to develop new opportunities
Employee involvement and empowerment	The use of practices to increase employee control, participation and involvement, and the supply of personal and organisational resources necessary to do the job
Teleworking	Working remotely from the home, remote offices or other sites for all or most of the working week, and connected to the main organisation by telephone and computer technologies
Performance management	A range of practices an organisation engages in to enhance the performance of a target person or group, with the ultimate purpose of improving organisational performance
e-business	The conduct of business transactions and activities using, in large part, electronic means, and typically involving use of the internet and world wide web

5. To review different methods, tools and principles that can be used to guide the design, implementation and evaluation of modern working practices.

These aims are covered throughout the book. But Part II, Modern Working Practices in the Workplace, focuses particularly on the first three aims. The practices examined in Part II are defined in Table 1.1. They were chosen for a variety of reasons and these include being relatively new, being widely practised and having the potential to significantly impact upon the nature of work. The chapters cover the most important issues and debates pertinent to the human side of modern working practices today. Part III is primarily concerned with the fourth aim of the book, the relationship between modern working practices, human resource management and organisational performance. The first two chapters in Part III examine the impact of modern working practices in the manufacturing and service sectors, while the third considers the impact of human resource practices.

Part IV meets the fifth aim of the book by illustrating some of the tools and methods that can be used to contribute to the effective design, implementation and evaluation of new working practices. The tools and methods outlined all attempt to give explicit attention to the social, human and organisational aspects of the new ways of working, areas of concern often neglected by managers and technologists. Finally, the concluding section, Part V, looks to the future. It does this first by considering how future economic conditions and organisational forms might affect employee behaviour and human resource practice; second, by critically evaluating the research, including that covered in this book, from a Critical perspective; and third, by identifying fruitful avenues for future research.

The rest of this chapter is devoted to setting out the context in which modern working practices have been implemented, and some of the main debates and issues that have concerned researchers when examining them.

CHANGE AND CONTINUITY IN THE WORKPLACE

Most of us are now fairly well versed in the changes occurring in the economic, political and social landscape. These include: the internationalisation of the economy; a reduction in trade barriers between countries; the deregulation of markets; privatisation and the ending of state monopolies; increasing demands for greater accountability and efficiency in the public sector; demographic changes in the workforce (e.g. increased female participation, better educated workforce); and changing consumer demand (e.g. a desire for more customised products, for better quality) (Doganis, 2000; Gabriel & Lang, 1998; Katz, 1997; Pollitt, 1993). These changes have intensified competition. They have also meant that much competition has become based on cost *and* quality, innovation and customisation (Appelbaum & Batt, 1994; Piore & Sabel, 1984). Similar demands for cost efficiencies, quality and customized services are evident in the public and not-for-profit sectors (Peters, 1992). In addition, knowledge is increasingly recognised as a basis for competition and it is thought that, in many industrial sectors, competitive advantage will primarily flow from the creation, ownership and management of knowledge-based assets (see Scarbrough, Chapter 8, on Knowledge Management).

In response to these changes and the expectation of these changes (Sparrow & Cooper, 1998), it is claimed that many organisations have sought to move away from Fordist, large-scale, hierarchical bureaucracies of mass production and mass service, and towards flexible organisations that can respond quickly and efficiently to rapidly changing market and consumer demands (Amin, 1994; Kumar, 1992; Schneider & Bowen, 1995). Flexibility is seen as a key component of organisational effectiveness. Managers have sought to achieve organisational flexibility by experimenting with new organisational forms and new working practices. There are a number of flexibilities that organisations have sought (Sparrow & Marchington, 1998):

- *Structural flexibility*, by introducing, either together or in isolation, flatter hierarchies and horizontal coordination between units; modular structures that can be reconfigured as new

projects or problems arise; joint ventures; temporary alliances; and inter-organisational networks (McPhee & Poole, 2000). Team working (e.g. cross-functional teams, project-based teams, virtual teams) (Chapter 6), supply-chain partnering (Chapter 5) and e-business (Chapter 13) are working practices that can help achieve structural flexibility.
- *Functional flexibility*, by introducing working practices that enable effective responses to changes in demand, supply and work load. Advanced manufacturing technology (AMT) (Chapter 4), lean manufacturing (Chapter 2) and multi-skilled teams (Chapter 6) would help achieve this aim.
- *Numerical flexibility*, through the use of part-time and temporary employees, outsourcing and various relationships with outside partners. Supply-chain partnering (SCP) would aid the achievement of this.
- *Geographical flexibility*, so that work may be dispersed to where it can be carried out most effectively, e.g. by introducing telework and virtual teams (Chapters 6 and 11).
- *Jobs-based flexibility*, by creating jobs with greater control, broader responsibility and higher skill requirements, so that employees can control variances as they arise. This could be achieved, for example, by implementing employee empowerment and involvement initiatives (Chapter 9).

In addition to greater flexibility, different structures and practices also been used to improve quality (e.g. through TQM, SCP, call centres), to manage and exploit knowledge (e.g. through knowledge management programmes, TQM, lean manufacturing, job empowerment) and to contain and manage costs (e.g. through TQM, lean manufacturing, call centres). Management have therefore been seeking to improve organisational effectiveness on a number of fronts through the introduction of a range of working practices.

Yet the introduction of new working practices may not be sufficient to ensure success. It has often been argued that modern working practices are most effective, indeed, can only be effective, when underpinned by a highly skilled and committed workforce and when accompanied by appropriate human resource management practices (Becker & Huselid, 1998; Lawler, Mohrman & Ledford, 1995; Steedman & Wagner, 1987; Walton, 1985). Furthermore, as new technologies and practices become more widely used, the value added by the human resource becomes critical to competitive success, as the skills of the human resource may not be copied readily (Boxall, 1996; Klein, Edge & Kass, 1989; Porter, 1985).

There are a number of reasons for believing that a highly skilled and committed workforce is essential to the effective running of modern working practices. First, as modern working practices and technologies are often complex and can present the user with difficult problems, there is a need for a high level of technical skill as well as higher-order cognitive abilities, such as problem solving, critical thinking and analytical skills. Second, practices such as advanced manufacturing technology, teamwork, supply-chain partnering and job empowerment increase intra- and inter-organisational interdependencies, while social and relational networks are now viewed as crucial to the generation and sharing of knowledge (see Scarbrough, Chapter 8). This implies that interpersonal relationships must be managed effectively and that trust be developed (Hosmer, 1995; see also Chapter 5 on supply-chain partnering). To achieve this, high levels of communication and interpersonal skills are required. Third, the requirement to continuously improve processes, products and services that is embedded in much modern management (e.g. TQM) means that employees need to be creative and innovative (see Chapter 10; Amabile, 1988; West & Farr, 1990; Wolfe, 1994). Fourth, as new practices can increase the degree of discretion and responsibility, employees must be able to regulate their own behaviour (i.e. to act without close supervision and management control), respond to variances in the work process as they occur and exhibit discretionary behaviours (Susman & Chase, 1986). This means that employees need to be proactive (see Chapter 10), have the skills to deal with variances in the work process and have the skills necessary to engage in discretionary behaviour.

Given the proposed importance of a skilled and committed workforce, human resource management practices are now viewed as playing a necessarily crucial role in securing, maintaining and developing an organisation's skill base through well-resourced selection and recruitment procedures, high levels of initial and continued training, and performance management practices (see Chapter 12). The use of human resource management to secure, maintain and develop a highly skilled and committed workforce has been labelled a "high commitment" or "high involvement" approach (see Chapters 9, 14, 15, 16; Lawler, 1986; Walton, 1985). A number of surveys have documented the increasing use of human resource practices that are associated with this and the way these may be linked to modern working practices and operational management methods.

Organisational change is undoubtedly taking place but the jury is still out on the extent to which this represents a radical change across the whole economy (see Fincham & Rhodes, 1992). First, the continued influence of Taylorist and Fordist ideas would challenge such a view, e.g. in the service sector, some call centres represent an advanced form of Taylorism (Taylor & Bain, 1999) and the "McDonaldization" of service work has been well documented (Ritzer, 1998). Likewise, just-in-time (JIT), an essential component of lean manufacturing, can be viewed as an extension and revitalisation of Fordist principles, rather than a break from them (Tomaney, 1994; Wood, 1989). The "new workplace" is, so the argument would go, a mixture of "old" and "new" working practices (Blyton & Turnbull, 1994). Second, even where new practices are being introduced, this may not always be done as a package. Modern flexible working practices, in particular, may not necessarily be accompanied by high-commitment human resource practices, or vice versa. However, it is precisely the integration of these two facets that fundamentally transforms workplaces (Lawler *et al.*, 1995; Storey, 1994; see also Wood, Chapter 14). Just as there are questions about the extent and nature of workplace change, questions are also being asked about whether the effects of change are as beneficial as many imply (Philimore, 1989). Modern working practices and high commitment human resource practices are often portrayed as leading to a win–win situation for the employee and the organisation. But while there are accounts demonstrating that the introduction of modern working practices can lead to more interesting work, more highly skilled work and lower levels of stress, there is also research showing that the introduction of modern working practices can intensify work, de-skill employees and lower their well-being (Adler & Borys, 1996; Braverman, 1974; Klein, 1989; Knights, Willmott & Collinson, 1985; Parker & Wall, 1998; Sturdy, Knights & Willmott, 1992). A modern working practice can have different effects. The effects of a flexible working practice are dependent on how it is implemented, designed and managed and are not solely dependent on some intrinsic feature of the working practice itself.

In summary, as organisations have sought to adapt to changing economic and social circumstances, they have become a patchwork of "new" working practices, "old" working practices, "new" working practices that are extensions of old principles and ideas, and different types of human resource management practice. In addition, there appears to be no straightforward relationship between a working practice and its effects.

Two perspectives that have helped in understanding this complex picture are (a) job design theory and (b) research that has examined the link between human resource management and organisational performance. Job design theory is important, as the effects of a working practice are significantly affected by the job design of the working practice in question (Parker & Wall, 1998). This means that, for a full understanding of why working practices have varying effects in different contexts, it is necessary to establish the job characteristics present in a particular working practice and the processes by which job characteristics are related to specific outcomes. Job and work design is also an important factor in research examining the human resource (HR)–organisational performance link. This research is important, as it draws together two key characteristics of organisational change over the last 30 years (i.e. the movement towards flexible working practices and high-commitment HR practices), and seeks to explain their separate and joint effects on firm performance.

The following sections outline the main issues and theories in job design theory and focus on research examining the HR–organisational performance link. The issues and themes within them run throughout many of the chapters in Parts II and III. In particular, job design theory is central to many of the debates in Part II, while the issues and debates regarding the HR–performance link are central to Part III. An appreciation of these areas is therefore crucial to understanding many of the chapters in this book.

JOB AND WORK DESIGN THEORY

Historically, the main focus of job design research has been on the psychological consequences of work simplification brought about through the pervasive adoption of Taylorist and Fordist approaches to work organization. Two approaches, job characteristics and sociotechnical theories, have been particularly influential (for fuller discussion of the main job design traditions, their limitations and future prospects, see Holman *et al.*, 2002; Parker *et al.*, 2001).

The job characteristics approach to job design has been strongly influenced by Hackman & Oldham's (1976) Job Characteristics Model (JCM). They proposed five core job dimensions (autonomy, feedback, skill variety, task identity, task significance) and these are seen to be determinants of three "critical psychological states": autonomy to experienced responsibility; feedback to knowledge of results; and skill variety, task identity and task significance to experienced meaningfulness. Collectively, these critical psychological states are seen to affect work satisfaction, internal work motivation, performance, absence and turnover. Research has generally demonstrated the effect of core job characteristics on affective outcomes (satisfaction, motivation) but the effects on employee behaviour (performance, turnover, absence) are less consistent (Parker & Wall, 1998). The motivating potential of job design has been an central issue within this research tradition (Campion & McClelland, 1993; Wall & Martin, 1987), as it also has been within debates on modern working practices and high-commitment human resource practices. Pritchard & Payne address this important issue in Chapter 12. In particular, they examine how modern working practices and human resource practices affect employee motivation.

Karaseck & Theorell's (1990) control-demands model is another job characteristic approach that has been influential[1]. It predicts that "high-strain jobs" are those characterised by high work demands and low control. Although the evidence for a proposed interactive effect of control and demand is inconclusive (Van Der Doef & Maes, 1999), numerous studies have confirmed that the absence of control and the presence of high job demands are consistent predictors of job-related strain (O'Driscoll & Cooper, 1996).

The second main approach to job design has been socio-technical theory. Socio-technical theory is concerned with the design of work systems and posits that it is comprised of a technical system and a social system. These subsystems are seen as interdependent and should therefore be jointly designed in such a way that the overall system is optimal (de Sitter, den Hertog & Dankbaar, 1997). Socio-technical theory has made a number of contributions to our understanding of job design. It is best known for its articulation of a set of design principles (Cherns, 1987; Clegg, 2000); for a set of criteria of what comprises a well designed job; and for the innovation of autonomous work groups (Emery, 1964). Its design principles include: methods of working should be minimally specified; variances in work processes should be handled at source; and boundaries should not be drawn to impede the sharing of information, learning and knowledge. Desirable job characteristics are thus assumed to be a reasonable level of demand, opportunities for learning, an area of decision-making owned by the operator, and social support and recognition. These principles of design and desirable job characteristics are seen to be best expressed in autonomous work groups (AWGs), and much socio-technical research and practice has been focused at a group level. Although it has been suggested that an 'underlying lack of specificity about the nature and effects of such initiatives (i.e. AWGs) makes a coherent assessment of their outcomes difficult' (Parker, Wall & Cordery, 2001, p. 416), research demonstrates that AWGs can have positive effects on well-being and productivity (Parker & Wall, 1998).

An important focus of the job characteristic and socio-technical approaches has been job redesign (e.g. enlargement, job enrichment, AWGs) and the tools necessary to do this. Mumford & Axtell in Chapter 17 explore tools that can be used for job redesign. It can also be noted here that organisations often fail to properly evaluate the effect of interventions, and thus valuable information about how the practice could be improved may be lost. To address this, Sonnentag in Chapter 18 examines the different ways that organisations and researchers can evaluate the effectiveness of new working practices.

Another notable feature of job design research is that it has reflected many of the debates and issues concerned with the changing nature of work. For example, the recent interest in cognition and knowledge at work has focused attention on:

- Cognitive and knowledge-based job characteristics, such as problem-solving demands, attention demand, (Jackson *et al.*, 1993), non-routine knowledge work (Mohrman, Cohen & Mohrman, 1995), knowledge intensity (see Lamond, Daniels & Standen, Chapter 11) and the opportunity to develop and utilise skills (O'Brien, 1986).
- Knowledge-based job outcomes, e.g. skill, self-efficacy (Parker & Wall, 1998).
- Knowledge based-mechanisms that link job characteristics to job outcomes, i.e. jobs with high control and challenging demands promote the development of skills and knowledge

---

[1] Other job characteristic approaches include social information processing theory (Salanick & Pfeffer, 1978) and the multi-disciplinary approach of Campion and colleagues (Campion & McClelland, 1993; Medsker & Campion, 1997). The latter approach categorises job characteristics into "mechanistic" (e.g. specialisation of tools and procedures, skill simplification, repetition), "motivational" (e.g. autonomy, job feedback, social interaction, task clarity, participation), "perceptual/motor" (e.g. lighting, displays, workplace layout, information requirements), and "biological" (e.g. strength, seating, noise, wrist movement).

(Wall *et al.*, 1990). Better knowledge enhances performance, as employees are better able to deal with variances in the work process (Miller & Monge, 1986) and choose the most appropriate strategies to deal with a situation (Frese & Zapf, 1994).

In summary, job design research has coalesced around some key questions and these will be addressed throughout the book:

- What are the impacts of new technologies and new working practices on job content?
- What are the core job characteristics of modern working practices?
- What effects do the particular job designs of working practices have on psychological well-being and performance?
- Through what mechanisms do job characteristics effect job outcomes in modern working practices?
- What methods, tools and principles can be used to design and evaluate new technologies and working practices?

HUMAN RESOURCE MANAGEMENT AND ORGANISATIONAL PERFORMANCE

Key concepts in human resource management (HRM) theory are fit and synergy (Wood, 1999). Three types of fit can be identified: (a) the internal fit between human resource (HR) practices; (b) the organisational fit between HR systems—coherent sets of HR practices—and other systems within the organisations; and (c) the strategic fit between HR systems and organisational strategy.

The discussion of internal fit centred on the idea that some HR practices combine better than others, and that coherent bundles of practice will have synergistic effects. A corollary of this is that part of the explained variance in observed differences in organisational performance will be caused by the differential usage of synergistic bundles of practice. When the terms "high-commitment" and "high-involvement" have been used, authors have differed as to their precise content. But they are generally seen to include many of the following: teamwork, high control or empowered job designs; employee participation schemes; job flexibility; high quality and continued training; performance appraisal; well-resourced selection and recruitment procedures; performance-contingent incentive payment systems (including group-based pay and profit sharing); and minimal status differences (Wood, 1999). In this book, we have decided to let individual authors use their own preferred terms and constructs rather than impose a view.

A key debate is whether high commitment/involvement HR systems are universally relevant or whether their effectiveness is contingent upon its alignment with other organisational practices, i.e. an organisational fit, and whether their effectiveness is contingent upon its alignment with the organisation's strategy, i.e. the strategic fit. Universalist approaches tend to assume that high-commitment HR systems reverse features of past Tayloristic, bureaucratic and low-commitment approaches to organisation and will generally have positive effects on organisational performance. A variant of the universalist argument is that a high-commitment HR system is a necessary but not sufficient basis for high performance. Rather, there needs to be a fit or alignment between high-commitment HR systems and modern working practices, such as TQM and lean manufacturing (Kochan & Osterman,

1995; Beaumont, 1995). This "high road" approach is universalistic, as it suggests that high performance will only be attained through the synergy created by these two factors. A contingency-based approach proposes that performance will be superior when there is an organisational and strategic fit, and that the HR system chosen should flow from the organisation's strategy. It is argued that a Tayloristic/low-commitment HR system will fit a cost-minimisation strategy and that a high commitment HR system will fit an innovation/quality strategy (Batt, 2000; Hoque, 1999; Schuler & Jackson, 1987). These different approaches are presented and discussed in more depth in Part III, and also in Chapter 9, Employee Involvement.

SOCIAL AND POLITICAL PROCESSES IN THE DESIGN AND MANAGEMENT OF MODERN WORKING PRACTICES

A basic assumption of this book is that job design and human resource management are fundamental to an understanding of modern working practices. However, while much job design and HRM research accepts that modern manufacturing practices may differ in form, they have little to offer on why or how a particular practice has taken the form it has. Neither do they have much to say on the active role that employees play in shaping them. For example, interpretivist research has illuminated how the political and social assumptions of those involved in the design and introduction of new technology become embedded within the technology, in the form of prescriptive design rationales which automate a particular view of how work is undertaken (Moran & Carroll, 1996). The "final" configuration of a technology and the social practices that surround it can be seen as an outcome of social and political negotiation between various groups over time (Barley, 1990; Buchanan & Boddy, 1983; Mueller *et al.*, 1986; Orlikowski, 1992). Technologies can therefore be understood as "a frozen assemblage of practices, assumptions, beliefs [and] language" that have become "fixed" in a material form (Cooper & Woolgar, 1993, p. 2). In this way, the design and configuration process can have lasting effects on job design, productivity and the quality of working life.

Critical research within the labour process tradition has drawn attention to how management attempt to instil within workers the belief that organisational objectives are their own and to ensure that these objectives are considered when making judgements at work. Modern working practices are thus mechanisms through which the worker becomes "self-disciplined" into making "positive" productive responses (Grenier, 1988; Knights & Sturdy, 1990). Sakolosky (1992, p. 246) has concluded that control becomes "embedded not just in the machinery of production or surveillance, but in the worker's psyche". But workers are not seen as passive reactors to management initiatives. Rather, labour process theory treats workers as active agents who resist, consent and comply with managerial efforts to control them and that these resistance practices shape working conditions and working practices (Burawoy, 1979; Collinson, 1994; Knights, 1990; Sturdy, Knights & Willmott, 1992).

These two areas of research reveal the social and political processes involved in the design, introduction and management of modern working practices. They paint a more dynamic picture of organisational life, in which employees actively shape working practices and one in which there may be conflicting interests over the use and aims of modern working practices. In doing so they offer different perspectives and ask different questions about modern working practices. They include: How do the designs of modern working practices arise? How are they shaped and configured by the various actors in the process? What are the values and goals of the actors? Do these values conflict, and, if they do, how is this expressed?

CONCLUSION

The main purpose of this chapter has been to set the scene for the rest of the book by articulating the changing economic conditions, the working practices that organisations are using to respond to this changing landscape, and to cover the main issues, debates and theoretical approaches to the human side of modern working practices. Four factors are crucial for an understanding of this discussion. They are:

- The knowledge, skills and abilities of the human resource.
- The job and work design of the modern working practice.
- The human resource practices that are used in conjunction with the modern working practice.
- The social and political processes involved in the design and use of modern working practices.

These factors are recurrent themes throughout the book. Taken together, the chapters in this book present a comprehensive overview of the study of working practices, an area with a long history, whilst introducing the reader to emerging new forms of work and the perspectives that these are engendering.

REFERENCES

Adler, P. & Borys, B. (1996). Two types of bureaucracy: enabling and coercive. *Administrative Science Quarterly*, **41**, 61–89.
Amabile, T. M. (1988). A model of creativity and innovation in organizations. In B. M. Staw & L. L. Cummings (Eds), *Research in Organizational Behavior*, Vol. 10 (pp. 123–167). Greewich, CT: JAI Press.
Amin, A. (Ed.) (1994). *Post-Fordism: A Reader*. Oxford: Blackwell.
Appelbaum, E. & Batt, R. (1994). *The New American Workplace: Transforming Work Systems in the United States*. Ithaca, NY: Cornell ILR Press.
Barley, S. R. (1990). The alignment of technology and structure through roles and networks. *Administrative Science Quarterly*, **35**, 61–103.
Batt, R. (2000). Strategic segmentation in front line services: matching customers, employees and human resource systems. *International Journal of Human Resource Management*, **11**, 540–561.
Becker, B. E. & Huselid, M. A. (1998). High performance work systems and firm performance: a synthesis of research and managerial implications. In G. R. Ferris (Ed.), *Research in Personnel and Human Resources*, Vol. 16. Stamford, CT: JAI Press.
Beaumont, P. (1995). *The Future of Employment Relations*. London: Sage.
Blyton, P. & Turnbull, P. (1994). *The Dynamics of Employee Relations*. London: Macmillan.
Boxall, P. (1996). The strategic HRM debate and the resource based view of the firm. *Human Resource Management Journal*, **6**, 59–75.
Braverman, H. (1974). *Labour and Monopoly Capital*. New York: Monthly Review Press.
Buchanan, D. & Boddy, D. (1983). *Organizations in the Computer Age*. Aldershot: Gower.
Burawoy, M. (1979). *Manufacturing Consent*. Chicago: Chicago University Press.

Campion, M. A. & McClelland, C. L. (1993). Follow-up and extension of the interdisciplinary cost and benefits of enlarged jobs. *Journal of Applied Psychology*, **78**, 339–351.

Cherns, A. (1987). Principles of socio-technical design revisited. *Human Relations*, **40**, 153–162.

Clegg, C. W. (2000). Sociotechnical principles for system design. *Applied Ergonomics*, **31**, 463–477.

Clegg, C. W., Axtell, C. M., Damodaran, L., Farbey, B., Hull, R., Lloyd-Jones, R., Nicholls, J., Sell, R. & Tomlinson, C. (1997). Information technology: a study of performance and the role of human and organizational factors. *Ergonomics*, **40**, 851–871.

Collinson, D. (1994). Strategies of resistance: power, knowledge and subjectivity in the workplace. In J. Jermier, D. Knights & W. Nord (Eds), *Resistance and Power in Organizations: Agency, Subjectivity and the Labour Process* (pp. 25–68). London: Routledge.

Cooper, G. & Woolgar, S. (1993). *Software Is Society Made Malleable: the Importance of Conceptions of Audience in Software Research and Practice*. PICT Policy Research Paper 25. London: Programme in Information and Communication Technologies.

Doganis, R. (2000). *The Airline Business in the Twenty-first Century*. London: Routledge.

Emery, F. (1964). *Report of the Hunfoss Project*. Tavistock Document Series. London: Tavistock.

Fincham, R. & Rhodes, P. (1992). *The Individual, Work and Organisation*. London: Weidenfield and Nicolson.

Frese, M. & Zapf, D. (1994). Action as the core of work psychology: a German approach. In H. C. Triandis, M. D. Dunnette & L. M. Hough (Eds), *Handbook of Industrial and Organisational Psychology* (pp. 271–340). Palo Alto, CA: Consulting Psychologists Press.

Gabriel, Y. & Lang, T. (1998). *The Unmanageable Consumer: Contemporary Consumption and Its Fragmentations*. London: Sage.

Grenier, G. (1988). *Inhuman Relations: Quality circles and Anti-unionism in American Industry*, Philadelphia, PA: Temple University Press.

Hackman, J. & Oldham, G. (1976). Motivation through the design of work: test of a theory. *Organizational Behaviour and Human Performance*, **15**, 250–279.

Hoque, K. (1999). Human resource management and performance in the UK hotel industry. *British Journal of Industrial Relations*, **37**, 419–443.

Holman, D, Clegg, C. W. & Waterson, P. (2002). Navigating the territory of job design. *Applied Ergonomics*, **33**, 197–205.

Hosmer, L. T. (1995). Trust: the connecting link between organisation theory and philosophical ethics. *Academy of Management Review*, **20**, 379–403.

Jackson, P. R., Wall, T. D., Martin, R. & Davids, K. (1993). New measures of job control, cognitive demand and production responsibility. *Journal of Applied Psychology*, **78**, 753–762.

Karasek, R. & Theorell, T. (1990). *Healthy Work: Stress, Productivity, and the Reconstruction of Working Life*. New York: Basic Books.

Katz, H. C. (1997). *Telecommunications: Restructuring Work and Employment Relations Worldwide*. Ithaca, NY: ILR Press.

Klien, J. A. (1989). The human costs of manufacturing reform. *Harvard Business Review*, **67**, 60–66.

Klein, J., Edge, G. & Kass, T. (1989). Skill-based competition. *Journal of General Management*, **16**, 1–15.

Knights, D. (1990). Subjectivity, power and the labour process. In D. Knights & H. Willmott (Eds), *Labour Process Theory* (pp. 297–336). London: Macmillan.

Knights, D. & Sturdy, A. (1990). New technology and the self-disciplined worker in the insurance industry. In I. Varcoe, M. McNeil & S. Yearly (Eds), *Deciphering Science and Technology* (pp. 126–154). London: Macmillan.

Knights, D., Willmott, H. & Collinson, D. (eds) (1985). *Job Redesign: Critical Perspectives on the Labour Process*. Aldershot: Gower.

Kochan, T. & Osterman, P. (1995). *Mutual Gains*. Boston, MA: Harvard Business School.

Kumar, K. (1992). New theories of industrial society. In P. Brown & H. Lauder (Eds), *Education for Economic Survival: from Fordism to Post-Fordism*. London: Rouledge.

Lawler, E. E. (1986). *High-involvement Management*, San Fransisco, CA: Jossey-Bass.

Lawler, E. E., Mohrman, S. & Ledford, G. (1995). *Creating High Performance Organisations: Practices and Results of Employee Involvement and Total Quality Management in Fortune 1000 Companies*, San Fransisco, CA: Jossey-Bass.

McLoughlin, I. & Harris, M. (1997). *Innovation, Organizational Change and Technology*, London: Thompson Business Press.

McPhee, R. D. & Poole, M. P. (2000). Organizational Structures and Configurations. In F. M. Jablin & L. Putnam (Eds), *The New Handbook of Organizational Communication: Advances in Theory, Research and Methods*. London: Sage.

Medsker, G. J. & Campion, M. A. (1997). Job and team design. In G. Salvendy (Ed.), *Handbook of Human Factors and Ergonomics*. London: Wiley.

Mueller, W. et al. (1986). Pluralist beliefs about new technology within a manufacturing organization. *New Technology, Work and Employment*, **1**, 127–139.

Miller, K. I. & Monge, P. R. (1986). Participation, satisfaction and productivity: a meta-analytic review. *Academy of Management Journal*, **29**, 727–753.

Mohrman, S. A., Cohen, S. G. & Mohrman, A. M. Jr (1995). *Designing Team-based Organizations: New Forms for Knowledge and Work*. San Fransisco, CA: Jossey-Bass.

Moran, T. P. & Carroll, C. M. (Eds) (1996). *Design Rationale*. Hove: Erlbaum.

O'Brien, G. E. (1986). *Psychology of Work and Unemployment*. Chichester: Wiley.

O'Driscoll, M. P. & Cooper, C. L. (1996). Sources and management of excessive job stress and burnout. In P. B. Warr (Ed.), *Psychology at Work*, 4th edn. Harmondsworth: Penguin.

Orlikowski, W. (1992). The duality of technology: rethinking the concept of technology in organizations. *Organizational Science*, **3**, 398–427.

Osterman, P. (1994). How common is workplace transformation and who adopts it? *Industrial and Labour Relations Review*, **47**, 173–188.

Parker, S. K. & Wall, T. D. (1998). *Job and Work Design*. London: Sage.

Parker, S. K., Wall, T. D. & Cordery, J. L. (2001). Future work design and practice: towards an elaborated model of work design. *Journal of Occupational and Organisational Psychology*, **74**, 413–440.

Peters, M. (1992). Performance and accountability in the "Post-Industrial Society": the crisis of British universities. *Studies in Higher Education*, **17**, 123–139.

Philimore, J. (1989). Flexible specialisation, work organisation and skills. *New Technology, Work and Employment*, **4**, 79–91.

Piore, M. & Sabel, C. (1984). *The Second Industrial Divide*. New York: Basic Books.

Pollitt, C. (1993). *Managerialism and the Public Services: Cuts or Change in the 1980s*. Oxford: Blackwell.

Porter, M. (1985). *Competitive Advantage*. New York: Free Press.

Ritzer, R. (1998). *The McDonaldization Thesis: Explorations and Extensions*. Thousand Oaks, CA: Sage.

Salanick, G. & Pfeffer, J. (1978). A social information processing approach to job attitudes and task design. *Administrative Science Quarterly*, **23**, 224–253.

Salvendy, G. (Ed.) (1997). *Handbook of Human Factors and Ergonomics*, 2nd edn. New York: Wiley.

Sakolosky, G. (1992). Disciplinary power and the labour process. In A. Sturdy, D. Knights & H. Willmott (Eds), *Skill and Consent* (pp. 235–254). London: Routledge.

Schneider, B. & Bowen, D. (1995). *Winning the Service Game*. Boston, MA: Harvard Business School Press.

Schuler, R. & Jackson, S. (1987). Linking competitive strategies with human resource management practices. *Academy of Management Executive*, **1**, 207–219.

Sewell, G. & Wilkinson, B. (1992). "Someone to watch over me": surveillance, discipline and the just-in-time process. *Sociology*, **26**, 271–289.

de Sitter, L., den Hertog, J. & Dankbaar, B. (1997). From complex organizations with simple jobs to simple organizations with complex jobs. *Human Relations*, **50**, 497–534.

Sparrow, P. R. & Cooper, C. L. (1998). New organizational forms: the strategic relevance of future psychological contract scenarios. *Canadian Journal of Administrative Sciences*, **15**(4), 356–371.

Sparrow, P. R. & Marchington, M. (Eds) (1998). *Human Resource Management: the New Agenda*. London: Financial Times Pitman Publications.

Steedman, H. & Wagner, K. (1987). A second look at productivity, machinery and skills in Britain and Germany. *NI Economic Review*, **November**.

Storey, J. (1994). *New Wave Manufacturing Practices: Organizational and Human Resource Management Dimensions*. London: Chapman Paul.

Sturdy, A. Knights, D. & Willmott, H. (Eds) (1992). *Skill and Consent*. London: Routledge.
Susman, G. & Chase R. (1986). A sociotechnical systems analysis of the integrated factory. *Journal of Applied Behavioral Science*, **22**, 257–270.
Taylor, P. & Bain, P. (1999). An assembly line in the head: the call centre labour process. *Industrial Relations Journal*, **30**, 101–117.
Tomaney, J. (1994). A new paradigm of work organisation and technology? In A. Amin (Ed.), *Post-Fordism: a Reader*. Oxford: Blackwell.
Van Der Doef, M. & Maes, S. (1999). The job demand-control (-support) model and psychological well-being: a review of 20 years of empirical research. *Work and Stress*, **13**, 87–114.
Wall, T. D., Clegg, C. W. & Kemp, N. J. (Eds) (1987). *The Human Side of Advanced Manufacturing Technology*. Chichester: Wiley.
Wall, T. D., Corbett, J. M., Martin, R., Clegg, C. W. & Jackson, P. R. (1990). Advanced manufacturing technology, work design and performance: a change study. *Journal of Applied Psychology*, **75**, 691–697.
Wall, T. D. & Martin, R. (1987). Job and work design. In C. L. Cooper & I. T. Robertson (Eds), *International Review of Industrial and Organisational Psychology*. Chichester: Wiley.
Walton, R. (1985). From 'control' to 'commitment' in the workplace. *Harvard Business Review*, **63**, 77–84.
Waterson, P. E., Clegg, C. W., Bolden, R., Pepper, K., Warr, P. B. & Wall, T. D. (1999). The use and effectiveness of modern manufacturing practices: a survey of UK industry. *International Journal of Production Research*, **37**, 2271–2292.
West, M. A. & Farr, J. L. (1990). *Innovation and Creativity at Work*. Chichester: Wiley.
Wolfe, R. A. (1994). Organizational innovation: review, critique and suggested research directions. *Journal of Management Studies*, **31**, 405–431.
Wood, S. (1989). *The Transformation of Work? Skill, Flexibility and the Labour Process*. London: Unwin Hyman.
Wood, S. (1999). Human resource management and performance. *International Journal of Management Review*, **1**, 367–413.

PART II
Modern Working Practices in the Workplace

CHAPTER 2

Workers Under Lean Manufacturing

Rick Delbridge
Cardiff Business School, Cardiff University, UK

Few management ideas have been as influential in their field as lean production techniques in manufacturing industry. Initially, the interest surrounded a relatively small number of companies that were perceived to be operating in a different way to that prescribed under traditional Western manufacturing methods. Particularly since the rise of the Japanese economy in the 1980s, there has been an increasing interest in the company philosophy and management techniques utilized by such companies as Toyota (Fujimoto, 1999), Nissan (Wickens, 1995) and Toshiba (Fruin, 1997). During the 1980s, numerous authors advocated the adoption of Japanese techniques (e.g. Pascale & Athos, 1982) or the moulding of such approaches to Western contexts (e.g. Ouchi, 1981). In addition to the research on Japanese organizations in Japan, there has been an enormous amount of research undertaken to assess the activities of Japanese organizations operating overseas, e.g. in the USA (e.g. Abo, 1994; Fucini & Fucini, 1990; Kenney & Florida, 1993; Milkman, 1991), in the UK (e.g. Morris, Munday & Wilkinson, 1993; Oliver & Wilkinson, 1992) and in the Asia–Pacific region (e.g. Dedoussis, 1995; Abdullah & Keenoy, 1995). There has also been prolonged debate over the "transferability" of "Japanese" techniques by Western capital (e.g. Ackroyd *et al.*, 1988; Elger & Smith, 1994; Oliver & Wilkinson, 1992). As we will discuss, the origins of lean manufacturing lie firmly in Japanese industry. However, over the past decade the association of lean manufacturing with Japan has weakened and "lean" has become an international standard in many industry sectors.

Lean manufacturing is now understood as an integrated system of production that incorporates work organization, operations, logistics, human resource management and supply chain relations. While there is debate over whether lean manufacturing represents a "toolbox" of techniques or a "philosophy" of management (see Oliver & Wilkinson, 1992), over the past 10 years a consensus has emerged over the key organizational and operating principles of the system. This level of consensus has not been sustained when assessment has turned to the implications for workers that such a system may involve.

In this chapter, we begin with an outline of the origins of lean manufacturing, commencing with an overview of the Toyota Production System and, in particular, the ideas of Taiichi Ohno, the main architect of just-in-time (JIT). Following this we review the emergence

---

The New Workplace: A Guide to the Human Impact of Modern Working Practices.
Edited by David Holman, Toby D. Wall, Chris W. Clegg, Paul Sparrow and Ann Howard. © 2003 John Wiley & Sons, Ltd.

of "lean" with specific reference to the main work which popularized the ideas of lean production—the International Motor Vehicle Program (IMVP) and the major publication from that study, *The Machine that Changed the World* (Womack, Jones & Roos, 1990). In the next section, we distil and articulate the key organizing principles of lean manufacturing. Following this, there are two sections which review, first, competing views on the potential implications for workers and then the research evidence on the shopfloor experience of working under lean manufacturing. A final section reviews current debates and flags future issues.

THE ORIGINS OF LEAN MANUFACTURING

While there has been some debate over how "Japanese" the different components of the "Japanese manufacturing system" are (see Graham, 1988), the origins of JIT can be clearly traced to the Toyota Motor Company of Japan, and in particular the work of one of its industrial engineers during the 1960s and 1970s, Taiichi Ohno. Ohno (1988) clearly outlines his ideas in his book, *Just-in-Time: For Today and Tomorrow*. The holistic and integrative nature of lean manufacturing is to be found in his initial comments that "the business world is a trinity of the market, the factory and the company as a whole," with company strategy designed to fine-tune the factory's processes in line with the immediate and real-time needs of the marketplace. Ohno's overarching concern is the elimination of the different forms of waste, which he associates with traditional Fordist methods of production. He lists various forms of waste, including overproduction, waiting time, transportation costs, unnecessary stock, unnecessary movement and the production of defective goods. He contrasts the Toyota production system with the Fordist production system and, in particular, with the fact that Fordism is a planned production system which "pushes" products onto the market, rather than a system building to market demand (see Table 2.1 for a full comparison of the Ford and Toyota production systems).

According to Ohno, the Toyota system has two pillars—JIT and "autonomation", or "automation with a human touch". The primary focus of this is to have machines sense

Table 2.1 Ohno's comparison of production systems at Toyota and Ford

Toyota production system	Ford production system
Builds what is needed when it is needed	Planned mass production
Market "pulls" necessary items from factory	Producing to a plan "pushes" products onto the marketplace
Production of small lots of many models	Production of similar items in large lots
Emphasis on decreasing machine set-up times and increasing frequency	Emphasis on decreasing number of set-ups
Create a production flow to produce JIT	Goods pushed through with high levels of work-in-progress stock
One person attends several processes, requiring multiskilling	One person attends one process; single skill and job demarcation
Stopping work to prevent defects is encouraged	Stopping the line is discouraged
The amount produced equals the amount sold	Amount produced based on calculations in production plan

Source: Adapted from Ohno (1988).

problems and automatically stop producing when defective work arises. A fully automated machine operating smoothly does not need a worker in attendance. Only when a problem occurs is an operator summoned to the machine, generally through a light and/or alarm system. The concept of pokeyoke, or foolproofing, attempts to guard against defective production by having automatic cut-outs in a similar way. While the latter idea of autonomation impacts directly on the role of labour, e.g. in the expectation that workers will mind several machines or processes, giving rise to Ohno's prospect of multiskilling for those workers, the former pillar also has significant direct and indirect implications. In Toyota, a simple physical pull system involving coloured cards, called kanban, is utilized to try to smooth flow and tie upstream and downstream production processes. The cards cycle between processes triggering build at upstream operations to replenish those downstream. Kanban work in a number of ways to reduce the prospects of waste, e.g. by restricting the number of cards, inventories cannot build up; by acting as a work order, the cards prevent overproduction; and, since the card moves with goods in small lots, it allows a swift tracing of any goods found to be defective. The heightened visibility and close coupling of work activities have a number of implications for workers. Ohno himself describes kanban as the "autonomic nervous system" of the plant, not only making clear the role of controllers and supervisors, but also indicating to workers when operations should begin and when overtime is necessary (Ohno, 1988, p. 20).

A central feature of the Toyota production system is its close linking of supplier and customer plants, as well as work stations internal to the factory. In the advanced form of JIT adopted by Toyota and key suppliers, kanban cards flow between organizations, triggering build, managing inventory and providing identification of batches. The close linking and transparency between buyer and supplier are an important context to the activities of shopfloor employees. Ohno ascribes the successful adoption of JIT across the supplier base to the economic shock of the first oil crisis in 1973. It was at this time that both Toyota and its suppliers became convinced of the benefits of JIT. As Ohno makes clear, running a JIT system places heavy responsibility on both suppliers and customers. Customers must supply smooth and reliable schedule information upon which suppliers can depend, while the suppliers must deliver reliable quality and to tight time horizons. Organizational slack is removed both within and between members of the supply chain. It is for these reasons that right-first-time build quality is so important in lean manufacturing systems. For many years it has been common to talk of the Japanese system as a combination of JIT and total quality management (TQM).

Along with tight internal process control and the close operational integration of the supply chain, the third significant aspect of the Toyota production system, as outlined by Ohno, is "innovation". Again, Ohno is at pains to emphasize a holistic and integrated view. With regard to innovation within an organization, he comments that technological innovation is only possible when the marketplace, the factory and the research and development (R&D) department are united. He argues that:

> Workplace management does not aim simply for cost reduction through vigorous use of production management techniques. The ultimate goal must be the attainment of innovation through the aggressive development of new products and new techniques (Ohno, 1988, p. 81).

Notably, he recognizes both the importance of top-down management leadership and the bottom-up contribution of shopfloor employees in achieving improvement. Here again, the

Toyota production system represents a significant break from Western manufacturing traditions, in this instance regarding the division of labour. Under Fordist production, drawing on the ideas of Taylor's scientific management, there was a clear demarcation of responsibility between those who planned production and those who carried out the manual tasks prescribed. Under the Toyota system, it is expected that workers will make a contribution to improving how their own job is designed and organized. Moreover, Ohno argues that JIT and autonomation create a synergy between individual skill and team work. The importance of formalized team working and small-group problem solving represent a further departure from much that is commonly associated with traditional Western work organization practices.

From JIT to Lean

As we have seen, the work of Ohno provides an integrated and holistic manufacturing management template, at least with regards to the operations aspects. Concern with the human resource issues of Japanese manufacturing initially focused on the unique nature of Japan's sociocultural and historical context. Authors such as Pascale & Athos (1982) and Ouchi (1981) placed great emphasis on Japan's culture and traditions when seeking to explain the success of its manufacturing industry. However, this success soon led to debates over what could and should be learned from the Japanese and adopted by Western manufacturers. An important contribution to this transferability debate was made by the various researchers involved in the International Motor Vehicle Program (IMVP), coordinated at Massachusetts Institute of Technology (MIT).

The IMVP was a five year, $5 million study of the world's major car assemblers. The main publication from the programme, which still runs, was *The Machine that Changed the World* (Womack *et al.*, 1990). This has been perhaps the single most influential book on manufacturing management of the last 20 years and its primary objective was to "de-Japanize" the Toyota production system and argue for its efficacy and efficiency irrespective of context. The book reported data from the various projects within the IMVP, including claims that the adoption of "lean production" led to major gains in both productivity and quality performance, although some of these findings have been contested (see Williams *et al.*, 1994). As can be seen from the summary in Table 2.2, much of the substantive content of the lean production model is readily recognizable as the Toyota production system

Table 2.2 What is lean production?

- Integrated single piece production flow, with low inventories, small batches made just in time
- Defect prevention rather than rectification
- Production is pulled by the customer and not pushed to suit machine loading, and level scheduling is employed
- Team-based work organization, with flexible multiskilled operators and few indirect staff
- Active involvement in root-cause problem solving to eliminate all non-value-adding steps, interruptions and variability
- Close integration of the whole value stream from raw material to finished customer, through partnerships with suppliers and dealers

Source: Derived from Womack *et al.* (1990).

described by Ohno (1988) and others (e.g. Monden, 1983; Shingo, 1988). Womack *et al.* (1990, p. 49) themselves cite Toyota as "the birthplace" of lean production. The book itself contains relatively little about the nature or practices of lean production that is distinct from what had been reported previously, but its major success was in propagating the ideas of Toyota and advocating the wholesale adoption of what were previously seen as "Japanese" management practices.

From the outset, Womack *et al.* (1990, p. 9) distance themselves from those who attributed Japanese corporate success to the country's culture or history, "We believe that the fundamental ideas of lean production are universal—applicable anywhere by anyone—and that many non-Japanese companies have already learned this". They are also unequivocal in advocating the adoption of lean production techniques:

> Our conclusion is simple: lean production is a superior way for humans to make things ... It follows that the whole world should adopt lean production, and as quickly as possible (Womack *et al.*, 1990, p. 225).

For Womack *et al.*, the "one best way" of Fordism has been supplanted by the "one best way" of lean production. Such universalism has, of course, attracted considerable criticism (e.g. Elger & Smith, 1994; Thompson & McHugh, 1995).

The book itself concentrates primarily on the technical aspects of the system and there is little detail on the role of workers or the likely implications of adopting lean production techniques. There are stylized accounts contrasting "dispirited" General Motors' workers with the "sense of purposefulness" to be found amongst Toyota's shopfloor employees, but there is little depth to the discussion of workers' experiences under lean manufacturing. The role of labour is dealt with in a broad-brush manner:

> The truly lean plant ... transfers the maximum number of tasks and responsibilities to those workers actually adding value to the car on the line ... It is the dynamic work team that emerges as the heart of the lean factory (Womack *et al.*, 1990, p. 99).

The authors contrast the "mind-numbing stress" of mass production with the "creative tension" of lean production which is particularly engendered by the expectation for worker participation in problem solving and continuous improvement. Rather optimistically, they anticipate that shop floor work will begin to resemble that of professionals and that management will need to encourage "reciprocal obligation" in order that employees contribute to solving problems. Womack *et al.* (1990, p. 102) expect to see investment in automating repetitive tasks and thus anticipate that "... by the end of the [twentieth] century we expect that lean-assembly plants will be populated almost entirely by highly skilled problem solvers whose task will be to think continually of ways to make the system run more smoothly and productively". We will review the research evidence on the extent to which this appears an accurate prediction in a later section of the chapter. Before this, in the following sections we outline the key organizing principles of lean manufacturing and tease out the likely implications for workers.

ORGANIZING PRINCIPLES OF LEAN MANUFACTURING

Particularly in early research into Japanese manufacturing during the 1980s, the emphasis was very much upon the technical/systems aspects of practice (e.g. Schonberger, 1982; Voss & Robinson, 1987). However, increasingly the debates have turned to the organizational and work implications of lean manufacturing. Some consensus has emerged that the innovative nature of the interdependent and interorganizational nature of the system requires "new types of relationships among workers, between workers and management, and between firms and their buyers and suppliers" (Sayer, 1986, p. 43). It is the nature and implications of these new types of relationship that have been hotly debated.

Oliver & Wilkinson (1992), in their book exploring the prospects for the "Japanization" of British industry, argue that the essence of understanding Japanese methods lies in the recognition that they:

> ... dramatically increase the interdependencies between the actors involved in the whole production process, and that these heightened dependencies demand a whole set of supporting conditions if they are to be managed successfully (Oliver & Wilkinson, 1992, p. 68).

Greater interdependence is founded upon the removal of "organizational slack" or loose coupling arrangements both between processes and between firms. Organizational slack has been the traditional approach to managing uncertainty; actions consistent with coping with uncertainty tend to lead to the creation of slack or "buffers", e.g. buffers may take the form of large levels of stock between firms or between processes or of lengthy order to delivery time periods. Such buffers may be characteristic of Western manufacturers but constitute the "waste" that Ohno set out to eradicate with the Toyota production system. Thus, if firms are not to accept reduced levels of performance, managers are left to seek ways of reducing uncertainty or of coping with it in ways that do not increase slack.

In removing the buffers or safeguards against disruption typically present under traditional Fordist mass production, lean manufacturing requires that uncertainty be minimized and, where possible, eradicated. Equally, in increasing the various actors' interdependence, organizations face a greater imperative to manage these relationships, both internally and externally, so as to reduce uncertainty. For example, if inventories are minimized, then production equipment must be reliable. Similarly, while introducing internal production, flexibility can partially compensate for unpredictability in market demand; supplier performance in terms of quality and delivery must be reliable and predictable if buffers are removed. Thus, the necessity for lean manufacturers to minimize uncertainty results in a need for a fundamentally reliable and largely stable and predictable set of external relations with other actors. This has led to considerable attention being focused on the nature of supply chain relations in lean manufacturing, particularly the Japanese automotive industry (Turnbull, Oliver & Wilkinson, 1989; Sako, 1992). A number of commentators have concluded that these relationships are best characterized as "high-trust partnerships" (e.g. Lamming, 1993; Womack *et al.*, 1990).

In a very similar fashion to the mutual dependence of the supply chain, lean manufacturers are also highly dependent upon their workforce working reliably and flexibly, since a central aspect of lean is to operate with the minimum possible level of employees. This has dual implications for individual workers. The first is that, since market demand is unlikely to prove entirely predictable and stable, employees must work on tasks as they become necessary. While some workers may concentrate their efforts in a narrowly defined area, at least some workers are likely to have to rotate through different tasks as and when required by demand. Second, the desire to run at minimal levels of staffing means that absenteeism poses a particular problem for management. Under a lean system there simply is not the spare labour to cover illness or other forms of absence. Workers must themselves meet the need for reliability and predictability central to lean manufacturing. Similarly, the emphasis is on stable industrial relations. As Turnbull (1988) notes, lean production is highly susceptible to disruption through even low-cost forms of industrial action. Rather as with the buyer–supplier relations of lean manufacturers, some commentators have concluded that these demands result in high trust partnerships between labour and management (Wickens, 1987; Womack et al., 1990). We will discuss this in more detail below.

Alongside reliability of current processes, the further feature of lean manufacturing is its dynamic nature—the continual search for ways of improving performance. The drive for continuous improvement under lean manufacturing is derived from the Japanese concept of kaizen. As with the other aspects of lean manufacturing, this feature of contemporary management "best practice" has permeated widely through industry. Increasingly, contemporary manufacturing is characterized as involving (semi-) permanent innovation (Kenney & Florida, 1993; Cooke & Morgan, 1998) as managers seek to continually improve operating efficiencies and develop and introduce new products to the market. For its advocates, kaizen is the primary feature of the Japanese manufacturing model:

> KAIZEN strategy is the single most important concept in Japanese management—the key to Japanese competitive success. KAIZEN means improvement... KAIZEN means *ongoing* improvement involving *everyone*—top management, managers and workers (Imai, 1986: xxix, emphasis in original).

There are a number of organizational structures and processes that are associated with kaizen. Most notable of those involving lower-level workers are employee suggestion schemes and small group problem-solving activities, or quality circles, which involve shopfloor workers in meeting, discussing problems and generating ideas and solutions. Such activities offer the opportunity for employees to make suggestions for change. Clearly the effective operation of such activities places an emphasis on training and development of workers' skills and on engendering the appropriate employment relationship, such that workers feel willing and able to make such contributions. These further considerations compound the importance of workers and employment relations given the fragility of lean manufacturing, discussed above.

The nature of HRM and industrial relations under lean manufacturing, and particularly in Japanese firms, has been a major area of study and debate. Indeed, Japanese companies have made an influential contribution to the emergence of HRM, providing role models for the West, with their so-called "Type J" organization characterized by high levels of worker commitment and company loyalty (Ouchi, 1981; Alston, 1986). The key objectives for Japanese personnel practices, and for HRM in support of lean manufacturing more broadly, are clearly derived from the nature of the production system outlined above. Thurley (1982) identifies these as being performance, motivation, flexibility and mobility, secured through an array of complementary policies, such as self-appraisal and feedback, consultation, status/grading progress, organizational or group bonuses, job rotation and retraining, transfer policies, self-education and organizational redesign. These are portrayed as characteristic of Japanese employers, although it should be remembered that at best they refer to the employment relationship of the "permanent" staff in large Japanese corporations and that Japan has a significant duality to its economy (Chalmers, 1989). Nevertheless, the approach to HRM of lean manufacturers outside Japan has drawn heavily upon the perceived advantages of the Japanese model.

According to Peter Wickens, the Personnel Director of Nissan Motor Manufacturing UK when it was founded in the mid-1980s, the secret of Japan's success was a so-called "Japanese tripod" of team work, quality consciousness and flexibility. Wickens himself promoted Nissan's approach to HRM through published articles (Wickens, 1985) and books (Wickens, 1987). He argued that workers at Nissan regarded themselves as part of the team (and company), that quality was emphasized through work, and that the employees' genuine involvement in the company through team work and quality led naturally to flexibility. The result, according to the company, was to create a "harmonious and productive working environment" (*The Guardian*, 8 September 1987). This view of the employment relationship at Nissan was specifically criticized by research conducted with workers from the plant (Garrahan & Stewart, 1992) and the perceived harmony and mutuality of Japanese IR and HRM has been questioned more generally (e.g. Delbridge & Turnbull, 1992; Gordon, 1985).

The link between workplace harmony and manufacturing productivity has been questioned on two different but inter-related points. First, while the distinctive production methods of lean manufacturing have been linked to high productivity in Japanese plants (Oliver, Delbridge & Lowe, 1996), there has been no such clear link evident for loyalty, commitment or "corporate culture" (Dunphy, 1986). Neither do Japanese HRM policies necessarily generate higher levels of worker satisfaction (Briggs, 1988; Dunphy, 1986). As Lincoln & Kalleberg (1990, p. 60) comment, "... a striking finding, which has appeared with remarkable consistency in comparative survey research on industrial attitudes, is that the levels of job satisfaction reported by the Japanese are lower than in the Western industrialized countries". Second, as discussed above, the key role of HRM as a strategically integrated subsystem within the organizing principles of lean manufacturing is to make workers feel *obliged* to contribute to the performance of the organization and to identify with its competitive success. For this reason, Wickens' "tripod of success" has been re-labelled a "tripod of subjugation", where team work represents "management through compliance", quality consciousness results in "management through blame" and flexibility leads to "management by stress" (Delbridge & Turnbull, 1992). These competing interpretations of the HRM approach needed to underpin to lean manufacturing may be characterized as a divergence of opinion over whether workers are prepared to meet the demands of the production system because of their levels of commitment or due to their subordination to management and their subsequent coercion to comply with production requirements. Both schools of thought concur, however, that the particular technical/systems characteristics of lean manufacturing—minimal buffers, tight coupling, high quality and the drive for continuous improvement—make specific demands upon workers and consequently require supportive HR practices. A schematic representation of the key organizing principles, both within and between plants operating under lean manufacturing, is given in Figure 2.1.

The clearest research-based articulation and advocacy of these principles and their relationship to organizational performance has been provided by the work of MacDuffie (1995a), who was a researcher on the original IMVP and has subsequently further developed this work. He presents data from a survey of 62 car assembly plants in support of two related arguments: first, that what he calls "innovative HR practices" affect performance as inter-related elements in an internally consistent HR "bundle"; second, that these bundles contribute most to assembly plant productivity and quality when they are integrated with manufacturing policies under the "organizational logic" of a "flexible production

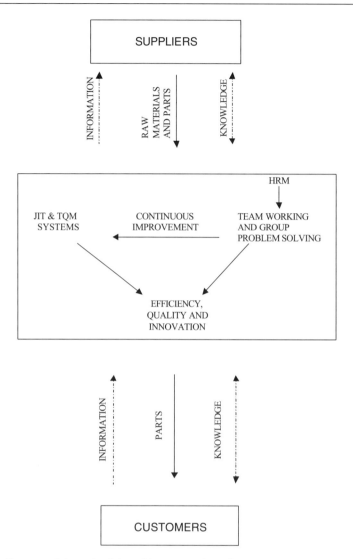

Figure 2.1 Key organizing principles of lean manufacturing

system", MacDuffie's term for lean manufacturing. His research shows that flexible production plants with team-based work systems, "high-commitment" HR practices and low inventory consistently outperformed "mass production plants".

MacDuffie (1995a, p. 198) suggests that his work "explores the role of human resources in the 'organizational logic' of a production system more deeply than previous descriptive work", such as Womack *et al.* (1990). He continues:

> Although mass and flexible (or "lean") production systems implicitly require different approaches to managing human resources, Womack *et al.* did not explain how HR practices are integrated into these different production systems, nor did they test the relationship between HR practices and performance. Indeed, the term "lean production"

Table 2.3 MacDuffie's measures of work systems and HRM policies

"High-involvement" work systems have	High percentage of workforce involved in formal work teams
	High percentage of work force involved in employee involvement groups
	Large number of production-related suggestions received per employee
	High percentage of production-related suggestions implemented
	Frequent job rotation within and across teams and departments
	Production workers responsible for quality inspection and data gathering
"High-commitment" HRM policies	Hiring criteria that emphasize openness to learning and interpersonal skills
	Pay systems contingent upon performance
	Single status workplace (common uniform, common parking, common cafeteria, no ties)
	High levels of initial training for new recruits (workers, supervisors and engineers)
	High levels of ongoing training for experienced employees

Source: Derived from MacDuffie (1995a).

used by Womack *et al.* appropriately captures the minimization of buffers but neglects the *expansion* of work force skill and conceptual knowledge required for problem solving under this approach (MacDuffie, 1995a, p. 198).

Thus, MacDuffie's work represents an attempt to capture the nature of the integrated system of operations, organization and supporting management approach and to incorporate the implications of the systemic demands made upon labour for reliable, flexible and innovative working. The main measures that he uses to identify whether a plant has "high involvement" work practices and "high commitment" practices are outlined in Table 2.3.

IMPLICATIONS FOR WORKERS

A key theme running throughout discussions of "Japanese" and lean manufacturing has been the implications that such systems of production have for the workforce. It is on this issue that the debate has polarized, with critics deeply scathing of those who anticipate beneficial working conditions. Early assessments of lean manufacturing argued that it represented "management by stress" (Parker & Slaughter, 1988; Delbridge & Turnbull, 1992) and led to "work intensification" (Dohse, Jürgens & Malsch, 1985; Delbridge, Turnbull & Wilkinson, 1992). The counter-claim was that in fact workers worked "smarter, not harder", at least if the systems were implemented appropriately (e.g. Wickens, 1995).

The critics anticipated that the system demands of just-in-time, total quality control and team working would have a severe and detrimental impact on the prospects for worker autonomy and the opportunity to exercise counter-control. Delbridge *et al.* (1992) anticipated that the likely outcome was work intensification, as a result of: (a) increased monitoring and surveillance of workers' activities; (b) heightened responsibility and individual accountability; (c) the harnessing of peer pressure within teams and via "customers"; and (d) the fostering of involvement in waste elimination and the continuous improvement of the production process. They concluded that lean factory regimes potentially consolidated and reproduced management control over the labour process in a more complete way than had been the case under traditional bureaucratic regimes. These conclusions contrast with the expectations of proponents of lean manufacturing, who have anticipated that workers will experience *increased* autonomy and involvement in decision making, primarily through their participation in problem-solving activities (e.g. Womack *et al.*, 1990). Before examining this debate in more detail, we shall consider exactly what workers are expected to do under lean manufacturing.

MacDuffie (1995b) reviews the part of workers in lean production and identifies three primary roles. These are "doing" work, "thinking" work and "team" work. As he notes, and contrary to some of the wilder speculations of Womack *et al.* (1990), under lean manufacturing "first and foremost is the provision of manual effort" and, as he further recognizes:

> Most production work at an auto assembly plant continues to require difficult and demanding physical labor... The fact that lean production shares with mass production the use of a moving assembly line and a narrow division of labor means that the *physical* experience of "doing" work is not dramatically different in these two settings (MacDuffie, 1995b, p. 55).

It is with regard to the notions of "thinking" and "team" work that MacDuffie sees a break from Taylorist traditions. For him, the key distinction surrounds the demands which stem from the drive for continuous improvement. These mean that workers must have a broader contextual knowledge of their production system so that they can link their specific, and often tacit, knowledge of their tasks to the upstream and downstream processes to which they are coupled. Further, he cites the "deliberate organization of work to encourage worker ideas to be surfaced, specified, and legitimized as an input to making changes in the production process", i.e. the process of kaizen (MacDuffie, 1995b, p. 56). However, he is realistic about where the decision-making authority lies under the system, recognizing that workers are not the dominant influence within a lean factory and that engineers still establish the initial process specifications. Moreover, worker suggestions for change are closely scrutinized and must be approved by engineers or managers before adoption. Even an advocate like MacDuffie realizes that there are important limits to the extent to which workers are empowered to take decisions and make changes within lean manufacturing. On the other hand, it is important to acknowledge that under these systems the cognitive inputs of workers are legitimized and valued; this reverses the separation of conception and execution under Taylorism.

The third role raised by MacDuffie is that of team member. This, he argues, "legitimizes the informal social network in a company as an important source of coordination and commitment" (MacDuffie, 1995b, p. 57). However, on closer inspection, MacDuffie's view is rather unitarist:

> The most important social relationship under lean production is with the company: identification with company goals around performance, competitiveness and survival pulls workers towards identifying their interests as overlapping with managers at *their* company... (MacDuffie, 1995b, p. 57; emphasis in original).

The other aspect of organizing the informal social network in the production system is aligning employee interests as closely as possible with company goals. This is vital, as MacDuffie anticipates, because of the strain that lean manufacturing can put on interworker relationships, particularly when buffers are reduced to a minimum and quality control requires a tracing of all faults to the root cause (and culpable worker). He notes that the peer controls under such circumstances can "easily turn poisonous" unless there is group cohesion, a process of close and swift dispute resolution, personal influence based on expertise rather than seniority, and incentives that align team member interests with each other and the other teams within the organization. As we will see in the following section, case evidence suggests that organizations operating a lean manufacturing system appear to have had difficulty in meeting the requirements needed to avoid the negative perception of peer pressure amongst workers themselves.

The role of workers in teams has been a major area of study across all sectors of business and industry (see Procter & Mueller, 2000). Since team working is seen to lie at the heart of the lean shopfloor, it is worth looking at the role of workers in lean teams in more detail. Delbridge, Lowe & Oliver (2000) report managerial views of the responsibilities of teams, team members and functional specialists based on an international study of lean production practices in the automotive components industry. The paper reports management responses at 30 plants using lean team working to questions regarding the distribution of responsibility for different types of shopfloor task. The findings provide something of a contrast to those of MacDuffie & Pil (1997), who concluded that lean production results in fewer functional specialists and more multiskilled workers, greater decentralization of authority and a higher degree of integration between conceptual activity and production tasks from their research into car assembly plants.

According to the managers in the study of automotive components plants, the technical role of production workers in lean manufacturing is rather limited. Operators have primary responsibility for routine quality tasks, but have not been significantly upskilled in order to play major roles in more technically complex areas, such as maintenance. Indeed, these technical tasks remain the responsibility of blue-collar skilled specialists and typically lie outside of the individual team. These results are not consistent with the findings of MacDuffie & Pil (1997). Neither is the fact that respondents report very little responsibility at operator level for the management of production activities. The findings show limited evidence of worker autonomy under lean team working. However, there is evidence to support the changing role of labour with regard to innovation and improvement activities. Managers reported significant worker responsibility for problem solving and both quality and process improvements, and this does match the findings of MacDuffie & Pil (1997) at the car assembly plants. Thus, the Taylorist separation of planning and execution appears to be partially reversed, but the position that emerges for workers is one of increasing responsibility without any increase in autonomy.

The other important finding of the research into roles under lean team working was the relative significance of the team's leader. The team leaders had primary responsibility for process improvement, the allocation of work amongst the team and the setting of work pace, as well as training and the settling of grievances. These findings suggest a pivotal role for the leaders of lean teams as the first line of management, able to contribute through both technical competence and social skills. In combination with the continuing importance of skilled blue-collar specialists, the significance of the team leader appears to have "hollowed out" the roles of middle management in the areas of engineering and quality. The findings of Delbridge *et al.* (2000) suggest that lean manufacturing may have even greater implications for the roles and work experiences of first-line supervisors, specialists and middle managers than it does for shopfloor operators. These are questions that currently remain under-researched.

In our final substantive section, we turn attention to the case study evidence regarding the experience of shopfloor workers under lean manufacturing.

CASES OF LEAN WORKING

The evidence reported in Womack *et al.* (1990), MacDuffie (1995a), MacDuffie & Pil (1997) and Delbridge *et al.* (2000) was all gathered through a similar research approach, namely, plant-level questionnaires completed with managers during plant visits by the research teams. This approach provides valuable data, but does not give the best insights into the experience of workers under lean manufacturing. For this we need a research approach that is focused on the workers and the shopfloor specifically. Of necessity, these more in-depth studies are concentrated on particular organizations and there have been a number of such case studies conducted into lean manufacturing sites over the last decade or so. Naturally enough, given the rise of lean in the motor industry, the majority of these have been centred upon car assembly plants (e.g. Fucini & Fucini, 1990; Garrahan & Stewart, 1992; Graham, 1995). Each of these studies has reported criticism of the implications of lean production for workers and has reported worker dissatisfaction and negative experiences. There has been a fair degree of consistency in these findings across different case plants.

In this section we review the work of Rinehart, Huxley & Robertson (1997) in more detail, as a good and representative example of the findings of case-based studies at car assembly plants; their research findings are reported in a book entitled *Just Another Car Factory?*, which reports a longitudinal study of the CAMI Automotive car assembly plant located in Ontario, Canada. CAMI is a joint venture between General Motors and Suzuki, which was heralded as a model of lean production when it opened in 1989. The research was jointly conducted by academics and the Canadian Auto Workers (CAW) trade union and involved worker surveys, interviews and observations conducted by a team between early 1990 and mid-1996. The authors report that, when it opened, CAMI promised workers something different from traditional plants—a humane work environment, team-based empowerment and cooperative labour–management relations—as is to be expected under the lean manufacturing model. The book systematically documents the degree to which CAMI, in the eyes of its own workers, lives up to these expectations, particularly with regard to its own "core values" of empowerment, kaizen, open communications and team spirit. According to Rinehart *et al.* (1997), the initial enthusiasm felt by workers during their recruitment and orientation steadily dissipated, as indeed did their willingness to be involved in discretionary participation activities. Workers came to describe CAMI as "just another car factory".

The authors report extensive and detailed findings on issues such as multiskilling, team working and continuous improvement and, for example, their chapter on team working confirms other work that has questioned the relative autonomy of the team, the significance and divisiveness of peer pressure and the central role of the team leader. Rinehart *et al.* (1997, p. 201) conclude that while the implementation of techniques such as JIT and kanban distinguishes CAMI from traditional mass production plants, these developments in the production system are better conceived as "refinements of Fordism" than a paradigmatic shift in organizational logic, since "The lean environment is characterized by standardized, short-cycled, heavily loaded jobs" (Rinehart et al., 1997, p. 202). Some of the findings from the researchers' worker survey are particularly striking: 88.3% viewed CAMI as no different from other companies; over 90% felt that single status trappings merely masked power differentials; and over 80% felt that the plant environment was competitive and stressful (Rinehart et al., 1997, p. 160).

Overall, the authors conclude that workers at CAMI were no more committed than workers elsewhere and report both formal and informal resistance, including strike action, as evidence of worker discontent. Graham's (1995) participant observation study of another North American car plant, Subaru-Isuzu, also reports evidence of both individual and collective worker resistance. Both studies call into serious doubt the extent to which workers are able to participate in decision making. Consistent with the plant survey findings reported in Delbridge et al. (2000), Graham (1995, p. 137) reports that the production system at Subaru-Isuzu "neither engages workers in managerial aspects of their jobs nor provides an avenue for real involvement in decision making... When workers did manage to have input into decisions affecting the quality of their lives, it was because they went outside the [Japanese/lean] model's boundaries and approached the company as its adversary". Rinehart et al. (1997) conclude from their results that lean production does not rely on committed workers and that the system works so long as everyone does his/her job competently and does not create disruptions. This position correlates with the need for reliable and flexible workers, as outlined in the earlier section on lean's key organizing principles. This conclusion, however, overlooks the discretionary contribution required of workers under kaizen activities if the lean model's innovation and continuous improvement dynamics are to be achieved.

This problem was prominent in the ethnographic study of a Japanese-owned colour television plant in the UK which was reported in Delbridge (1998). This research identifies a low trust–high surveillance shopfloor which workers find stressful and intimidating. The tight quality control in the plant results in a culture of blame and workers are actively engaged in seeking to avoid being held responsible for defects to the extent that on occasion they accuse each other, even within their own team. This fragments the notion of a shopfloor collective and undermines any suggestion that the team may provide some form of social or emotional support. Workers had responded by withdrawing from discretionary activities and did not participate in suggestion schemes nor in small group problem solving. Rinehart et al. (1997) also report the withholding of tacit knowledge by workers. If innovation and operational learning are seen as fundamental to the lean model, then these plants are failing to deliver. This suggests an essential tension in the lean model between the desire to operate without waste and at maximum efficiency, leading to stress and alienation on the part of workers, while at the same time anticipating active worker involvement in problem solving. Authors have differed in the extent to which they perceive these findings to reflect the unique history and context of the individual plants and the degree to which the problems reported are due to the inadequate or inappropriate implementation of lean production or this more deep-seated contradiction between control and commitment.

In contrast to the more critical and pessimistic accounts above, Adler's (1993) research at NUMMI, the GM–Toyota joint venture in California, found evidence of high levels of productivity, continuous improvement and employee motivation. He reported a standardized and formal set of work routines that had been designed to promote learning rather than to enforce compliance, a variation on bureaucracy which he labelled "learning bureaucracy".

Adler (1993, p. 111) shares MacDuffie's (1995b) unitarism and anticipates "a workforce assumed to share a common goal of production efficiency and quality". There may be some initial justification for this view, since the GM-Fremont plant had been closed and workers laid off in 1982 before the instigation of the joint venture which saved the operation in 1984. In his discussion, Adler (1993, p. 183) ascribes much of the situation to the "unique conditions of NUMMI's start-up". Nevertheless, the case of NUMMI is interesting in the way it appears to run contrary to the findings of other studies. The explanation may be found in Adler's own conclusion, when he comments that trust, respect, employee participation in defining key standards and policies, and the balancing of power between employees and management are "the conditions of existence" for a learning bureaucracy.

CURRENT DEBATES AND FUTURE ISSUES

Current debates surrounding the experience of working under lean manufacturing centre on the competing explanations for why case-based research, which looks in depth at the circumstances and views of shopfloor workers generally, fails to supply support for the proposition that lean systems can provide, indeed rely on, employment relations and work conditions that foster commitment and the willingness of workers to participate in discretionary activities. There are a range of views that extend from the radical critics of lean manufacturing, who argue that at its very heart lean production represents a system of management control wherein there is a false rhetoric of worker involvement, autonomy and upskilling (e.g. Parker & Slaughter, 1988), through to the more contingent view of those who ascribe the negative findings of individual case studies to failings in implementation or the strategic choices made by managers (e.g. Klein, 1989).

In a recent review of research into lean production, and in particular evidence on the impact on worker health, Landsbergis, Cahill & Schall (1999, p. 122) conclude that recent survey work has tended to confirm case evidence that lean production in auto manufacturing creates an intensified work pace, modest or temporary increases in decision authority and skill, with the decision-making latitude of workers remaining low. Such work has inherent strains, and Landsbergis et al. (1999) argue that these may lead to various health problems, such as work-related musculoskeletal disorders (e.g. tendinitis and carpal tunnel syndrome) and the potential for increases in hypertension and cardiovascular disease. However, Landsbergis et al. (1999) acknowledge the limits of current evidence and note that there have been few well-designed research studies looking specifically at the impact of lean manufacturing and worker health. This is an area where further research is overdue.

One particular avenue for fruitful further research is more systematic assessment of the psychological impact of working under lean manufacturing systems. This is the conclusion put forward in a recent article by Conti & Gill (1998), who review current understanding of work under lean manufacturing and proceed to identify a series of hypotheses regarding the potential effects of JIT and lean production on job stress. Their primary concern is to seek to generalize from the detailed case evidence that has highlighted the potentially negative effects of lean production. Their position is consistent with the contingent view, and is that there will be varying job stress effects, dependent upon the range of management choices exercised in the design and operation of a lean production system.

Conti & Gill (1998) draw upon the Karasek–Theorell model of job stress, which suggests that high levels of stress are associated with high job demands, low job control and low levels of social support. Coming from the contingent view of lean implementation, Conti & Gill (1998, p. 163) suggest that the implications for job demands are not determined and argue that, "There is nothing inherent in the structure of JIT/LP that requires the use of greater than normal pace and intensity [work] levels", but note that "there are structural characteristics of JIT/LP that inherently restrict worker control and autonomy". Thus, one of their hypotheses is that, "The stress levels exhibited in firms will increase as the proportion of production organized as JIT/LP increases" (Conti & Gill, 1998, p. 164). From this, however, they argue that management has two avenues open to it through which job stress may be alleviated: "the proper use of continuous improvement programs and providing some degree of autonomy in job design" (Conti & Gill, 1998, p. 165).

The prospect for meaningful involvement in decision making is a central component of the rhetoric of lean manufacturing but the case evidence suggests that often managers do not make available the opportunities for workers to secure any form of autonomy and/or other aspects of the employment relationship, or workers' experiences, lead them to decline from any voluntary participation. It has been argued that off-line activities, such as quality circles, give workers a degree of job control and that these may thus help to offset the low level of on-line control (e.g. Conti & Gill, 1998). The case evidence does not support this view, however, and recent analysis of the Workplace Employment Relations Survey, which has responses from 28 323 employees (see Cully et al., 1998), also indicates that workers do not perceive that narrow, "point of production" participation schemes, such as quality circles, provide meaningful opportunity for influence over their jobs (Delbridge & Whitfield, 2001). The other way, according to Conti & Gill (1998), that the stress inherent in the JIT system may be offset is through the resources and emotional support provided by working in teams. Again, this is an empirical question worthy of further investigation, but the case study evidence indicates that the particular pressures of lean manufacturing may fragment team loyalties and undermine the prospects of team-based support. At the very least, the research evidence indicates that managers seeking to ensure that innovation and improvement are a central part of their lean manufacturing system will need to reflect carefully on how they can mediate the stressful aspects inherent in such a system. In addition, they will need to integrate work, organization and supporting HR policies, such that workers perceive they have a vested interest in contributing their discretionary effort and tacit knowledge in order to make the lean shopfloor an ever more efficient and yet harmonious workplace. The current signs are that, even if managers are so inclined, this may prove beyond them.

REFERENCES

Abdullah, S. & Keenoy, T. (1995). Japanese managerial practices in the Malaysian electronics industry: two case studies. *Journal of Management Studies*, **32**(6), 747–766.

Abo, T. (1994). *The Hybrid Factory: the Japanese Production System in the United States*. Oxford: Oxford University Press.

Ackroyd, S., Burrell, G., Hughes, M. & Whitaker, A. (1988). The Japanisation of British industry. *Industrial Relations Journal*, **19**(1), 11–23.

Adler, P. (1993). The "learning bureaucracy": New United Motor Manufacturing, Inc. *Research in Organizational Behavior*, **15**, 111–194.

Alston, J. (1986). *The American Samurai: Blending American and Japanese Managerial Practices*. New York: de Gruyter.

Briggs, P. (1988). The Japanese at work: illusions of the ideal. *Industrial Relations Journal*, **19**(1), 24–30.

Chalmers, N. (1989). *Industrial Relations in Japan: the Peripheral Workforce*. London: Routledge.
Conti, R. & Gill, C. (1998). Hypothesis creation and modelling in job stress studies: the effect of just-in-time and lean production. *International Journal of Employment Studies*, **6**(1), 149–173.
Cooke, P. & Morgan, K. (1998). *The Associational Economy: Firms, Regions and Innovation*. Oxford: Oxford University Press.
Cully, M., O'Reilly, A., Millward, N., Forth, J., Woodland, S., Dix, G. & Bryson, A. (1998). *The 1998 Workplace Employee Relations Survey: First Findings*. London: HMSO.
Dedoussis, V. (1995). Simply a question of cultural barriers? The search for new perspectives in the transfer of Japanese management techniques. *Journal of Management Studies*, **32**(6), 731–745.
Delbridge, R. (1998). *Life on the Line in Contemporary Manufacturing*. Oxford: Oxford University Press.
Delbridge, R., Lowe, J. & Oliver, N. (2000). Shopfloor responsibilities under lean teamworking. *Human Relations*, **53**(11), 1459–1479.
Delbridge, R. & Turnbull, P. (1992). Human resource maximisation: the management of labour under a JIT system. In Blyton, P. & Turnbull, P. (Eds), *Reassessing Human Resource Management* (pp. 56–73). London: Sage.
Delbridge, R., Turnbull, P. & Wilkinson, B. (1992). Pushing back the frontiers: management control and work intensification under JIT/TQM factory regimes. *New Technology, Work and Employment*, **7**(2), 97–106.
Delbridge, R. & Whitfield, K. (2001). Employee perceptions of job influence and organizational participation. *Industrial Relations*, **40**(3), 472–489.
Dohse, K., Jürgens, U. & Malsch, T. (1985). From "Fordism" to "Toyotism"? The social organization of the labour process in the Japanese automobile industry. *Politics and Society*, **14**(2), 115–146.
Dunphy, D. (1986). An historical review of the literature on the Japanese enterprise and its management. In Clegg, S., Dunphy, D. & Redding, G. (Eds), *The Enterprise and Management in East Asia* (pp. 343–368). Hong Kong: Centre for Asian Studies, University of Hong Kong.
Elger, T. & Smith, C. (Eds) (1994). *Global Japanization? The Transnational Transformation of the Labour Process*. London: Routledge.
Fruin, M. (1997). *Knowledge Works: Managing Intellectual Capital at Toshiba*. Oxford: Oxford University Press.
Fucini, J. & Fucini, S. (1990). *Working for the Japanese: Inside Mazda's American Auto Plant*. New York: Free Press.
Fujimoto, T. (1999). *The Evolution of a Manufacturing System at Toyota*. Oxford: Oxford University Press.
Garrahan, P. & Stewart, P. (1992). *The Nissan Enigma: Flexibility at Work in a Local Economy*. London: Mansell.
Gordon, A. (1985). *The Evolution of Labor Relations in Japan: Heavy Industry, 1853–1945*. Boston, MA: Harvard University Press.
Graham, I. (1988). Japanisation as mythology. *Industrial Relations Journal*, **19**(1), 69–75.
Graham, L. (1995). *On the Line at Subaru-Isuzu: the Japanese Model and the American Worker*. Ithaca, NY: ILR Press.
Imai, M. (1986). *Kaizen: the Key to Japan's Competitive Success*. New York: McGraw Hill.
Kenney, M. & Florida, R. (1993). *Beyond Mass Production: the Japanese System and its Transfer to the United States*. Oxford: Oxford University Press.
Klein, J. (1989). The human cost of manufacturing reform. *Harvard Business Review*, **March–April**, 60–66.
Lamming, R. (1993). *Beyond Partnership: Strategies for Innovation and Lean Supply*, New York: Prentice Hall.
Landsbergis, P., Cahill, J. & Schall, P. (1999). The impact of lean production and related new systems of work organization on worker health. *Journal of Occupational Health Psychology*, **4**(2), 108–130.
Lincoln, J. & Kalleberg, A. (1990). *Culture, Control and Commitment*. Cambridge: Cambridge University Press.
MacDuffie, J. (1995a). Human resource bundles and manufacturing performance: organizational logic and flexible production systems in the world auto industry. *Industrial and Labor Relations Review*, **48**(2), 197–221.

MacDuffie, J. (1995b). Workers' roles in lean production: the implications for worker representation. In S. Babson (Ed.), *Lean Work: Empowerment and Exploitation in the Global Auto Industry* (pp. 54–69). Detroit: Wayne State University Press.

MacDuffie, J. & Pil, F. (1997). Changes in auto industry employment practices: an international overview. In T. Kochan, R. Lansbury, & J. MacDuffie (Eds), *After Lean Production: Evolving Employment Practice in the World Auto Industry* (pp. 9–42). Ithaca, NY: ILR Press.

Milkman, R. (1991). *Japan's California Factories: Labor Relations and Economic Globalization*. Los Angeles, CA: University of California Press.

Monden, Y. (1983). *Toyota Production System: Practical Approach to Production Management*. Norcross: Industrial Engineering and Management Press.

Morris, J., Munday, M. & Wilkinson, B. (1993). *Working for the Japanese: The Economic and Social Consequences of Japanese Investment in Wales*. London: Athlone.

Ohno, T. (1988). *Just-in-Time: For Today and Tomorrow*. Cambridge: Productivity Press.

Oliver, N., Delbridge, R. & Lowe, J. (1996). The European auto components industry: manufacturing performance and practice. *International Journal of Operations and Production Management*, **16**(11), 85–97.

Oliver, N. & Wilkinson, B. (1992). *The Japanization of British Industry: New Developments in the 1990s*. Oxford: Blackwell.

Ouchi, W. (1981) *Theory Z: How American Business Can Meet the Japanese Challenge*. Reading: Addison Wesley.

Parker, M. & Slaughter, J. (1988). *Choosing Sides: Unions and the Team Concept*. Boston, MA: Labor Notes.

Pascale, R. & Athos, A. (1982). *The Art of Japanese Management*. New York: Simon and Schuster.

Procter, S. & Mueller, F. (Eds) (2000). *Teamworking*. Basingstoke: Macmillan.

Rinehart, J., Huxley, C. & Robertson, D. (1997). *Just Another Car Factory? Lean Production and its Discontents*. Ithaca, NY: ILR Press.

Sako, M. (1992). *Prices, Quality and Trust: Inter-firm Relations in Britain and Japan*. Cambridge: Cambridge University Press.

Sayer, A. (1986). New developments in manufacturing: the just-in-time system. *Capital and Class*, **30**, 43–72.

Schonberger, R. (1982). *Japanese Manufacturing Techniques: Nine Hidden Lessons in Simplicity*. New York: Free Press.

Shingo, S. (1988). *Non-stock Production: the Shingo System for Continuous Improvement*. Cambridge: Productivity Press.

Thompson, P. & McHugh, D. (1995). *Work Organizations*. Basingstoke: Macmillan.

Thurley, K. (1982). The Japanese model: practical reservations and surprising opportunities. *Personnel Management*, **February**, 36–39.

Turnbull, P. (1988). The limits to "Japanisation"—just-in-time, labour relations and the UK automotive industry. *New Technology, Work and Employment*, **3**(1), 7–20.

Turnbull, P., Oliver, N. & Wilkinson, B. (1989). Recent developments in the UK automotive industry: JIT/TQC and information systems. *Technology Analysis and Strategic Management*, **4**(1), 409–422.

Voss, C. & Robinson, S. (1987). The application of just-in-time techniques. *International Journal of Operations and Production Management*, **7**(4), 46–52.

Wickens, P. (1985). Nissan: the thinking behind the union agreement. *Personnel Management*, **August**, 18–21.

Wickens, P. (1987). *The Road to Nissan*. Basingstoke: Macmillan.

Wickens, P. (1995). *The Ascendant Organization*. Basingstoke: Macmillan.

Williams, K., Haslam, C., Johal, S. & Williams, J. (1994). *Cars*. Providence: Berghahn Books.

Womack, J., Jones, D. & Roos, D. (1990). *The Machine that Changed the World*. New York: Rawson Macmillan.

CHAPTER 3

The Human Side of Total Quality Management

Richard Cooney and **Amrik Sohal**
Department of Management, Monash University, Victoria, Australia

Total quality management (TQM) has been a singular organizational practice. Management scholars and consultant-practitioners speak of a quality "era" and a quality "revolution" when discussing the manifold changes that have been effected under the banner of TQM. TQM programs have been implemented in a wide variety of manufacturing and service industries and they have been significant in the reshaping of public institutions and the delivery of public services. Few management practices in the modern era have been as widely disseminated as has TQM.

Within organizations, TQM has had profound effects upon the way in which senior management exercises its strategic leadership function, the way in which middle management carries out its function of supervision and control, but above all TQM has radically changed the experience of work for employees. The delegation of responsibility for quality and quality improvement has led to a dramatic expansion of the work role of employees. Employees are now directly responsible for managing manufacturing and service delivery processes to ensure that customers receive a quality product or service.

Along with this expansion of the work role to deliver quality products and services has come a reorientation on the part of employees towards their work role. Employees have been encouraged to identify more closely with the mission and values of the organization and to take a more proactive stance in achieving that mission. The implementation of TQM has, in some cases, meant that employees have assumed greater responsibility for overall organizational performance and not just quality performance. Employees have been encouraged to see themselves as, in effect, small business managers, responsible for the output of their own "business unit". It is not simply the expansion of the work role through the delegation of enhanced responsibilities for quality that has been a feature of TQM programs; equally important has been the reorientation of employees towards their work and their organization.

TQM has transformed the experience of work for employees and this chapter outlines some of the dimensions of this change. The chapter begins by investigating the multiple meanings of TQM as a management practice. TQM may be seen as a technically focused quality management program, as a philosophy of business concerned with strategic business issues, or as an organizational–behavioural intervention designed to promote the more effective use of human resources.

After outlining the elements that may appear in a TQM program, the chapter moves on to examine the impact of TQM on managers, supervisors and employees. Different kinds of TQM programs have differing effects upon the work employees and the design of jobs in contemporary work systems. The differing effects of the technical and the organizational–behavioural or, as they are often called, the "hard" and the "soft" elements of TQM, are emphasized. The chapter first analyses the effects of quality control techniques and continuous improvement activities upon employees' work design, before moving on to examine the impact of human resource practices and organizational change techniques upon employees' orientation towards their work and organization.

The chapter concludes by examining the research evidence for the efficacy of the various types of TQM program but, it transpires, the evidence is mixed. Improved enterprise competitiveness is a key goal of any TQM program but the routes to that improved performance are seemingly disparate. The available research evidence provides support for the efficacy of many varieties of TQM. Hard TQM can be effective, soft TQM can be effective and the implementation of more broadly based TQM programs can also be effective. TQM in its many guises can be an effective practice from a management perspective, but the chapter ends by questioning why seemingly little attention has been paid to the outcomes of TQM for employees.

THE VARIETIES OF TQM

TQM is a contemporary management practice that contains a number of elements and entails an number of related organizational interventions. TQM encompasses a number of themes about management itself and is an umbrella concept for a set of related organizational interventions (Hackman & Wageman, 1995). For this reason, TQM is something of a fungible concept and one that is sometimes difficult to pin down. There is not one TQM but a range of TQMs, each dependent upon the themes and the practices that are employed in the name of TQM (Dean & Bowen, 1994, Hill & Wilkinson, 1995, Wilkinson, 1995).

It is not possible to give a clear definition of TQM, but it is rather more useful to identify the major themes and practices that are said to constitute TQM. At its most basic, TQM is a program of management action to improve quality performance. Evans and Dean (2000, p. 5) define TQM as:

> A comprehensive, organization-wide effort to improve the quality of products and services

and this definition underlines both the systematic nature of TQM interventions, as well as their clear focus upon quality goals. The application of quality management and quality control tools, techniques and practices, in order to improve quality performance, is one clear focus of TQM programs (Crosby, 1980; Feigenbaum, 1983; Ishikawa, 1985).

Other writers, however, go further than this and identify TQM as a philosophy of management, as well as a management program of quality improvement. Wilkinson *et al.* (1998, p. 11) define TQM as:

A general business management philosophy, which is about the attainment of continuously improving customer satisfaction by quality-led company-wide management.

Definitions such as this highlight the fact that TQM may be about more than simple quality improvement. TQM is often about the reorientation of management thinking from a focus upon internal operational control, towards a strategic focus upon customers and markets. Increasing globalization has led to a renewed focus upon market position, and this has led to a rethinking of management approaches developed during the long post-war boom. TQM provides a philosophy of business that can guide management efforts in an uncertain business environment and it can help to reorientate management thinking about strategic business issues (Deming, 1982, 1986).

As well as being a philosophy of management, TQM may provide a focus for strategic management change efforts. Flynn, Schroeder & Sakakibara (1995, p. 660) develop this theme and state that "Quality management is an integrated, interfunctional means of achieving and sustaining competitive advantage". Such definitions emphasize the way in which quality programs can facilitate the integration of work systems, quality systems and business process systems, to develop a seamless and strategically focused organization (Dawson, 1994b). Whilst the broad quality strategy of the organization is critical, this may also serve as a catalyst for other change interventions.

Many activities are carried out in the name of TQM and not all are directly related to quality. Quality programs may entail the development of changed approaches to employee relations to encourage greater employee participation and involvement in the business; they may entail the redesign of work to establish teams and *ad hoc* work groups; they may entail greater expenditure on training and the development of human capital; they may entail significant organizational change and restructuring; and they may involve the review of business processes and product or service delivery systems. Many varied organizational interventions are conducted in the name of TQM, as part of the development of a quality strategy (Spencer, 1994).

Other scholars focusing on the strategic change initiatives entailed in a TQM program go even further and emphasize the behavioural and attitudinal elements of TQM, over and above the quality system elements and the philosophy of business elements. Cole (1998, p. 43) says that "Quality means maximizing organizational behaviour to enhance the satisfaction of present and potential customers". Here, it is the employee's orientation to work and to the company that is critical. Employees are seen as important contributors to the success of the business, capable of self-regulating their work, of monitoring performance against the goals set by management, of being accountable for that performance and of continuously improving business outcomes. Such definitions underline a new conceptualisation of the role of the employee within the enterprise, one that focuses upon their normative alignment to the organizational mission and their capacity for self-management, as work tasks are increasingly delegated to those directly producing value at the front line.

The great variety of themes and practices that fall under the banner of TQM create a perception that TQM can be all things to all people and, consequently, that it is of little conceptual value. In fact, this seeming limitation of TQM contains a practical advantage. TQM programs can be customized to suit the needs of individual enterprises and TQM practices can be selected that appeal to a range of organizational participants. Senior managers, middle managers and employees can all make sense of TQM in ways that resonate with their own experience, and they can relate to quality principles and practices that directly affect the way that they do their work.

MANAGERS, SUPERVISORS, EMPLOYEES AND TQM

For senior managers, TQM can be seen as a philosophy of management. TQM provides a coherent framework of principles and practices that can be used to steer the firm and develop its competitive position (Garvin, 1991; Schonberger, 1992). In this view, TQM is seen as providing a total approach to the problems encountered in the management of contemporary organizations. Critical themes of leadership, customer and market focus, organizational structure, management process and organizational change are all embraced by TQM. These themes give senior managers a clear interpretation of contemporary business trends and provide a structured program of management action.

Senior executive managers may also embrace TQM, as it offers them a way of managing organizational performance to improve quality, productivity and competitiveness. The tools and practices identified by TQM can assist with the identification of the organizational mission and goal setting by senior management; they can help with the planning of quality and general business improvement efforts; and they can help with the development of appropriate business metrics. As well as offering a coherent view of the purpose of management, TQM also offers a set of tools and techniques with which to guide the development of management systems in the enterprise and carry out the executive management role (Crosby, 1980; Imai, 1997; Juran & Godfrey, 1999).

TQM has both a technical and a rhetorical appeal to senior managers and this can create a dilemma for those implementing TQM. An over-emphasis on the technical elements of TQM may lead to it being seen, by employees, as a specialised technical program of marginal relevance to their work. On the other hand, an under-emphasis on the techniques of TQM, may lead to it being seen as little more than vacuous management rhetoric (Hackman & Wageman, 1995). The approach of senior managers towards TQM, the themes and practices that they choose to implement under the umbrella of TQM, is a critical factor in the success of TQM programs (Choi & Behling, 1997; Zbaracki, 1998).

For middle managers, TQM may have mixed effects, depending upon the version of TQM that is implemented. TQM, in its quality system guise, may enhance the expert power of middle managers and their ability to supervise and control subordinates. The clarification of work roles in the work system and the establishment of clear reporting systems may enhance the position of a supervisor, whilst the implementation of quality control techniques may enhance their expert power. Middle managers may thus embrace TQM because its scientific and technical practices augment their control over subordinates.

In other respects, however, TQM may pose a significant challenge to middle managers. Other versions of TQM, those that focus upon the attitudinal and behavioural elements, may challenge supervisors to relinquish their positional power and to act in new ways. Middle managers may be expected to act as facilitators, coaches, coordinators and mentors, building the lines of communication with senior management and developing trust. They may become responsible for employee skill development, for facilitating improvement activities and for championing change initiatives. These new role demands can create significant role conflict for those middle managers unwilling or unable to relinquish direct control of subordinates (Coyle-Shapiro, 1999; Dawson, 1994a; Yong & Wilkinson, 1999).

The organizational restructuring associated with the transfer of greater authority to employees has also had some dramatic effects upon middle managers and supervisors. Downsizing and delayering has drastically reduced the numbers of middle managers and it has reduced the power and influence of those remaining, as what were formerly management responsibilities are transferred to those directly producing products and services (Clinton, Williamson, & Bethke, 1994; Grant, Shani & Krishnan, 1994).

The implementation of quality programs may thus have drastic effects upon the work roles of middle managers. Middle managers may, in fact, pose the strongest point of resistance to the implementation of TQM programs, as their job security, power and authority are undermined by the changes entailed in adopting TQM. Even where TQM is embraced by middle managers, it may have a pronounced effect upon their work, making their jobs more complex and demanding as they respond to those below them in new ways (Wilkinson, Redman & Snape, 1994).

When we turn to look at employees' experience of TQM, the picture is similar to that of middle managers. The impact of TQM programs varies, depending upon whether they are implemented with a "hard" quality system/quality process orientation or with a "soft" attitudinal–behavioural orientation (Wilkinson, Godfrey & Marchington, 1997).

TQM, WORK DESIGN AND EMPLOYEES

TQM can be broadly divided into its hard and soft elements. Each of these have differing impacts upon the work of employees and it is the hard elements of TQM that have the most direct impact upon work design. Thus, TQM programs may facilitate low-skill job expansion as more tasks of the same or lesser skill levels are added to the work role. In manufacturing processes, such simple task enlargement of the work role may consist of the addition of basic tasks, such as housekeeping, simple quality inspection and quality record keeping. In such circumstances, inspection may consist of little more than visual inspection and basic gauge checking. Visual inspections may simply involve inspecting a work sample or comparing a work sample with a master sample, to check for obvious flaws. Basic gauge checking may involve the use of fixed gauges, such as "go" and "no-go" gauges, to check product attributes, and it may involve some elementary record keeping, such as the use of simple tally sheets, defect logs or defect concentration diagrams (Evans & Lindsay, 1999; Montgomery, 1991). Such simple techniques of quality control require little skill in measurement or the use of measuring instruments and demand only minimal levels of numeracy to keep and interpret quality records.

In cases where simple tools are used, operator control of quality may be supplemented by the work of quality technicians and supervisors, leading to the development of systems where limited operator control is complemented by inspection and expert control measures. Quality technicians, supervisors and middle managers may use the more sophisticated statistical quality control techniques to monitor operational processes and may take most of the decisions regarding changes to the quality control system. These quality control measures may also be supplemented by statistically-based inspection measures, such as acceptance sampling.

A similar phenomenon of limited work role expansion can be observed in the services sector, where the work of frontline service personnel may be expanded by the addition of a wider range of customer service tasks. Customer service officers may deal with a wider range of customer enquires and transactions but the interactions may be tightly scripted and organized in a lock-step sequence. In these circumstances, employees are merely called upon to deliver the scripted response, with non-routine enquiries and transactions being escalated to supervisors and senior workers. Such scripted interactions may require little product or service knowledge on the part of the frontline service personnel and may require minimal development of communicative and interpersonal skills.

The limited expansion of the work role, then, may lead to an expansion of work tasks and increased responsibility for quality, but it does not necessarily lead to any increase in skill or expansion of decisional authority. In such circumstances, operators and customer service personnel may have little or no say in the design of the quality system, little involvement in the improvement of the quality system and a limited role in the conduct of quality assurance itself.

Even this low-skill job expansion is seen, however, to be motivational, improving key work design criteria. Where frontline employees have responsibility for quality, a greater range of tasks are undertaken and so skill variety is enhanced; employees have more holistic control of the production process and so task identity is enhanced; and the work of frontline employees is more integral to the success of the enterprise, thereby enhancing task significance (Davis & Wacker, 1987, Hackman, 1977, 1991; Hackman & Oldham, 1980).

The more extensive implementation of TQM involves high-skill job enrichment, where more complex tasks requiring greater levels of skill are undertaken. Employees may be given greater responsibility for the management of quality and may be given some authority to make decisions about the operation of the quality system. Craft-like skills may be developed as employees are taught to use statistically-based tools, such as histograms, Pareto analysis, run charts and control charts. They may be authorised to take preventative and corrective actions and to deal directly with customers and customer complaints. This latter aspect is especially important in service industries, where employees may be authorised to deal with non-routine enquiries and to rectify customer complaints by providing refunds or replacement services.

Employees experiencing high-skill work redesigns may also be engaged in system design tasks. They may be involved in the design of work methods, testing and inspection methods. Employees may also be involved in the continuous redesign and improvement of both their own jobs and quality procedures. Such empowerment of employees is seen to overcome the limitations of the narrow, fragmented tasks found in routine production and service work (Adler, 1993; Adler & Borys, 1996). The high-skill redesign of work is also associated with long-term changes to employee perceptions about tasks and the work role, and thus may become the basis upon which perceptions about co-workers, managers and the firm are changed (Griffin, 1991).

The more complex work redesigns entail employees developing a broader range of skills in order to respond flexibly to changing product, service, customer and market requirements, and these increased skill demands are often reflected in greater training (Schonberger, 1994). Employees require some training in order to manage the expansion of their work role following the delegation of responsibilities for quality, but they also require some training in non-technical skills to be able to participate in quality improvement activities and the redesign of organizational systems. The provision of such training is, however, contingent, with low-skill redesigns entailing minimal training, while high-skill designs require significantly more (Gee & Nystrom, 1999).

Enhanced work motivation and the development of broad-based skills may flow from the delegation of responsibility for quality to frontline employees, but there are other effects of the implementation of hard TQM. The implementation of quality control measures improves the manufacturability or ease of manufacture of products, thus establishing a more even and steady work flow for employees. Quality problems are identified by employees and recurring quality issues are eliminated. The stress of trying to rectify defective parts and assemblies in-process may be reduced, disruptions to work flow are reduced and this may also contribute to enhanced employee satisfaction (Conti & Warner, 1997; Shingo, 1986, 1989).

Job enrichment, employee empowerment and upskilling are the positive effects of TQM programs, but such programs also have some deleterious effects upon the work of employees. The major limitation of hard TQM is that it introduces a high level of task standardization and hence limits employee discretion. Employee control of work methods is reduced as these methods are standardized, and bureaucratic procedures may have to be followed to log and record preventative, corrective and containment actions. Standardization is introduced in TQM programs to improve the consistency and reliability of processes, but the application of process disciplines, such as standardized work, limits the autonomy of employees. System standardization means that whilst employees may have a greater say in the design and improvement of the quality system, non-routine tasks are progressively eliminated and hence employee autonomy is progressively reduced. As Klein (1991) observes, whilst quality management systems encourage "task design" autonomy on the part of employees as they solve problems and improve the system, the use of TQM practices limits employees autonomy in "task execution" compared to that found in non-TQM work environments.

The standardization of work methods limits employee autonomy and it also increases the interdependencies in the processing system. Upstream and downstream processes are increasingly linked together and the increased reliance upon those in other work areas to maintain production flow and meet production targets limits employee self-regulation of work. The scope for employees in a particular work area to self-manage that area is reduced as standardized, plant-wide quality procedures and work methods are implemented (Dawson & Webb, 1989; Delbridge, Turnbull & Wilkinson, 1992).

Evidence for the deleterious effects of TQM can be found in those industries typified by the presence of routine work tasks, such as the automotive industry. Lewchuck & Robertson (1998) surveyed employees in four Canadian automotive plants and reported that 76% of employees found it difficult to make changes to aspects of their job that they did not like, 61% could not vary their work pace, and 63% reported increased monitoring of their work by management. Babson (1993) found that 73% of workers at Mazda reported changes to standardized work instructions without their involvement and consultation and 67% reported, furthermore, that these changes had made their work harder.

The implementation of hard TQM may thus have mixed effects upon the work of employees. TQM may be typified by low-skill job expansion or by high-skill job enrichment. It may contribute to employee empowerment by enhancing their decisional autonomy or it may lead to reduced autonomy in the execution of tasks, as procedures are standardized. TQM leads to an expansion of the work role of employees, but this expansion may have seemingly contradictory effects, enabling employees in some respects but constraining them in others.

CONTINUOUS IMPROVEMENT AND TQM

One element of TQM programs that is often seen as contributing to employee empowerment is employee involvement in continuous quality improvement activities. Employees in TQM programs are often called upon to identify problems and then work together in groups to analyze those problems. Employees may also be involved in generating solutions and implementing and evaluating those solutions. Involvement in these continuous improvement activities is seen to enhance employee decisional autonomy, but once again, the scope of that enhancement is contingent upon the nature of the improvement activities being undertaken (Wilkinson, Godfrey & Marchington, 1997).

When introduced in conjunction with low-skill work expansion, employee involvement in decision making may be limited to consultation rather than participation. Employees may be simply consulted by management and asked to identify quality problems or to contribute suggestions and ideas for quality improvement. The actual implementation of these ideas is then left to management and there is little further employee involvement. Employee suggestion schemes frequently operate on this basis. Employees contribute ideas for improvement, but the selection of ideas for implementation, and the work of implementation itself, remains the provenance of management alone.

Where employees participate directly in improvement activities, their authority to make decisions may also be constrained by the nature of the participative structures employed. A variety of *ad hoc* and temporary teams and work groups are often used to implement continuous improvement activities—quality circles, taskforces, problem-solving groups, improvement project groups, customer-response groups and so on—and these groups are not always well integrated into the management hierarchy of the enterprise. Such groups may in fact form parallel organizational structures established outside, but in parallel to, the decisional hierarchy. Such parallel structures are dependent upon the support of management. Projects and improvement activities are not undertaken without management support and are not implemented without management approval. If employees do not secure the approval of management for their improvement projects and, more importantly, secure from management the resources necessary to implement their projects, then the projects usually do not proceed (Cordery, 1996; Cotton, 1993; Cotton *et al.*, 1988; Hill, 1991).

The limitations of these parallel structures—involvement without decisional autonomy—go a long way towards explaining why they so often fail to secure ongoing employee interest in quality improvement activities. The use of groups such as quality circles has been found to lead to few (Marks *et al.*, 1986) or temporary (Griffin, 1988) improvements in quality performance and employee satisfaction, and consequently the use of such groups within TQM programs has often been dismissed as a fad (Lawler & Mohrman, 1985).

When introduced in conjunction with high-skill work enrichment, improvement activities may be integrated with the normal organizational structures through the delegation of responsibility for improvement to autonomous work teams. These ongoing, permanent work groups may undertake improvement activities as part of their normal work, but even here employees face the limitations of the quality improvement techniques themselves. These problem solving and data analysis techniques are frequently heavily standardized and so offer limited scope for employee initiative (Cole, 1994; Sitkin, Sutcliffe & Schroeder, 1994).

Involvement in improvement activities should emphasize information sharing between employees and management, intra- and intergroup cooperation in problem solving and the development of cross-functional work. This should lead to an emphasis upon learning and employee development, with consequent positive effects upon the organizational climate and employee satisfaction (Waldman, 1994). Employees should see improvements in quality outcomes but also in employee-related outcomes, such as improvements to the work environment and occupational health and safety. Too often, however, the scope of such benefits is limited by the constraints upon employee decision making entailed in the application of TQM improvement techniques (Wilkinson *et al.*, 1992).

TQM AND HUMAN RESOURCE MANAGEMENT

In order to make the most of TQM programs, some researchers argue that hard TQM must be combined with the extensive use of soft TQM. Innovations in quality control and employee involvement, it is argued, must be supported by innovative human resource management (HRM) practices, such as team working, performance-based compensation and single-status facilities (Kochan, Gittell & Lautsch, 1995; Schonberger, 1994).

The difficulty faced by researchers, however, is that whilst there is some overlap between TQM and HRM, the two are not identical and there is no identifiable set of HRM practices that are consistently used in TQM programs. Employee training and employee involvement are two practices that are widely accepted as part of a TQM program (Ahire, Golhar & Waller, 1996; Black & Porter, 1996; Dean & Bowen, 1994; Saraph, Benson & Schroeder, 1989) but the use of practices such as team work (Black & Porter, 1996) and performance-based rewards and recognition (Dean & Bowen, 1994) are more contentious. Some would see these practices as central to TQM programs, others not so. There is little evidence of a convergence between contemporary strategic HRM and TQM, despite some similarities.

Whilst the significance of HRM practices for TQM may be in dispute, there is wide agreement that good HRM practice is needed to support TQM initiatives and that line managers should be more highly skilled in people management, in order to facilitate employee involvement in quality management and organizational change activities.

ORGANIZATIONAL CHANGE AND TQM

The soft side of TQM may have a tenuous connection to HRM practices but it has a much stronger connection to organizational change and development practices. TQM, as a strategic management tool, often requires significant organizational structural change and it requires some broad cultural change. In the first case, change may entail reducing layers of management to improve communication and facilitate the delegation of enhanced responsibilities for quality to employees, and, in the latter case, it may entail the reorientation of employee attitudes and behaviours to enhance their focus upon customer needs and their involvement in improvement activities.

TQM entails an element of normative reorientation on the part of employees towards their work role. Employees are encouraged to embrace change as an empowering process, and to more closely identify with the firms' mission and quality values. This reorientation towards the work role is effected through the development of a quality discourse by senior management. The rhetorical presentation of quality initiatives seeks to explain change to employees, but also to shape the meaning of "quality" and the vocational identity of employees. The discourse of quality often emphasizes the unity of the work of the organization, outlining the benefits for employees, management and owners of the quality transformation. Quality is often presented as win–win change, and something that transcends sectional interests and petty organizational politics. The introduction of TQM is presented as an opportunity for employee empowerment, as a program of change that will lead to enhanced work designs, high skill development and greater decisional authority for employees (Hackman & Wageman, 1995; Tuckman, 1994; Reger *et al.*, 1994; Zbaracki, 1998).

The discourse of TQM provides for the normative orientation of employees towards change and this normative alignment is enhanced by the developmental perspective found within TQM. The development of problem solving and continuous improvement activities entails systemic learning and the development, both for employees and the organization (Adler & Cole, 1993; Cole, 1994; Sitkin, Sutcliffe & Schroeder, 1994). This learning leads to the development of new capacities amongst employees and this may influence employee attitudes (Zeitz, Mittal & McAulay, 1999).

TQM has its limitations as a model for organizational change, however, and these are fourfold. In the first instance, the TQM model is often top-down in its approach to change, and hence it is not necessarily the most effective. TQM places a strong emphasis upon senior management leadership to develop strategies and plan change initiatives. This approach leaves little room for bottom-up initiatives and little scope for broad-based participation in the change effort. The use of quality practices that promote standardisation and the use of standard procedures may also be inimical to the change effort, promoting bureaucratic inflexibility rather than an openness to change (Dawson, 1998; Dawson & Palmer, 1995; Hunter & Beaumont, 1993). TQM programs may thus be caught on the horns of a dilemma, torn between the need to standardize to improve reliability and the need to innovate and respond to changing customer requirements (Sitkin, Sutcliffe & Schroeder, 1994).

A further limitation of TQM is that the disparate nature of TQM practices can often lead to fragmented change efforts, as one failed quality initiative after another is tried and abandoned. The management literature is replete with failed quality fads, such as quality circles, quality function deployment, customer first programs and so on. These practices are often introduced in a piecemeal fashion and hence do not become embedded within the organization. Change pursued through the introduction of quality fads may be only shortterm, with high initial interest but a quick return to the *status quo ante* thereafter (Reger *et al.*, 1994; Yong & Wilkinson, 1999; Zeitz *et al.*, 1999).

The total quality approach to change also often ignores the context of that change. TQM requires the development of open communications and a high level of trust between units and departments, employees and managers, and yet it is often implemented in conjunction with major changes to operations that undermine the very preconditions for success. Total quality programs are often implemented at same time as plant closures and downsizing is occurring, for example, or as outsourcing and increased use of contingent labour to increase labour flexibility, and thus change efforts may be cynically received and perceived as little more than work intensification (Hunter & Beaumont, 1993; McCabe & Wilkinson, 1997; Parker & Slaughter, 1993).

A final limitation of the TQM model is that the quality discourse within the firm promotes the creation of a unitary organizational culture. Identification with the mission and goals of the organization by all employees leaves little room for the assertion of difference, and does not provide any recognition of the multiple identifications that employees may have with the immediate work unit, vocational peers or unions and employee representatives (Dawson, 1998; Edwards, Collinson & Rees, 1998). The quality discourse developed by senior management may also reflect management priorities and interests, and so may be perceived as self-serving by employees. The actual implementation of quality practices may in fact be perceived as an attempt to implement even greater control by management, with the consequent surfacing of withdrawal behaviours and a lack of cooperation and trust on the part of employees (Hunter & Beaumont, 1993; McCabe & Wilkinson, 1997; Zbaracki, 1998).

TQM, in its guise as a philosophy of management, offers a vision of organizational transformation, but it lacks the tools with which to implement that transformation. The TQM approach to change often fails to grasp the magnitude of change and has no clear techniques to implement change, other than the introduction of quality control techniques and employee involvement practices (Redman & Grieves, 1999). The failure of TQM as a program for organizational change may lead to the perception that it is merely rhetorical, with little workplace change and employee empowerment actually taking place (Hackman & Wageman, 1995; Reger et al., 1994; Tuckman, 1994).

TQM AND ORGANIZATIONAL PERFORMANCE

TQM is widely used and has a variety of impacts upon employees. The implementation of quality control and improvement practices leads to an expansion of the work role, whilst the development of a quality discourse leads to a reorientation on the part of employees towards that work role. How effective these changes are and what contribution they make towards improving the performance and competitive position of an enterprise, however, remains unclear. There have been a variety of attempts to assess the effectiveness of TQM, by scholars and by those promoting TQM programs, but to date a clear and comprehensive assessment remains elusive.

Some initial studies of the effect of TQM programs compared high-performing and low-performing firms to see whether there was a difference in the kind of TQM programs adopted by these firms. High-performing firms seemed to make greater use of all elements of a TQM program, and hence the inference was drawn that the adoption of comprehensive TQM programs was more efficacious than the adoption of single practices (Australian Manufacturing Council, 1994; Ferdows & De Meyer, 1990). Other studies along similar lines examined the performance of quality award winners and compared their practice with that of lower-ranked competition entrants. Once again, the main conclusion of such studies was that firms with comprehensive TQM programs seemed to perform better than firms with partially implemented TQM programs, on a range of financial and operational measures (General Accounting Office, 1991; Easton, 1995; Helton, 1995). Studies examining the longer-term impact of TQM have also found significant differences in performance between firms with comprehensive TQM programs and those with partially implemented TQM programs, adding further weight to the claims that TQM is a singularly effective management practice (Easton & Jarrell, 1998).

These general studies of TQM effectiveness, however, aggregate TQM practices together and thus do not provide much of a picture of the relationships between practices. It was the development of more sophisticated TQM frameworks that enabled researchers to examine the role of particular TQM practices in relation to organizational performance. The development of analytical frameworks that attempted to: (a) clearly specify the elements of a TQM program (Ahire, Golhar & Waller, 1996; Black & Porter, 1996; Saraph, Benson & Schroeder, 1989); (b) conceptualize the relationships between the elements of a TQM program (Flynn, Schroeder & Sakakibara, 1995); and (c) elaborate the dimensions of quality performance (Garvin, 1984), enabled scholars to develop a more detailed account of the relationship between quality practice and organizational performance. Quality was found to be a multi-dimensional construct and the strength of the relationships between the elements of a TQM program and organizational performance was found to vary. The assumption that there was a necessary interrelationship between all TQM practices began to be questioned (Dow, Samson & Ford, 1999; Powell, 1995; Samson & Terziovski, 1999).

Some studies found that it was the "hard" quality management practices that were significant in lifting performance, rather than the broader set of hard and soft TQM practices (Flynn, Schroeder & Sakakibara, 1995). These studies lend support to the view that TQM is, first and foremost, a program of management action designed to lift quality performance by using established quality control tools and techniques. The hard, technical elements of TQM, in other words, can be effective in lifting performance.

Many other studies indicated that it was senior management support for TQM programs that was critical, developing a strategic vision for the organization and providing support for the numerous change initiatives that accompany the implementation of a TQM program (Samson & Terziovski, 1999). Such findings lend support to the view that TQM can be seen as a successful philosophy of management which, if embraced whole-heartedly by senior management, can lead to significant improvements in performance.

Other studies, however, supported the view that the attitudinal and behavioural elements of a TQM program were the most critical to organizational success. These studies lend support to the view that TQM is principally an organizational–behavioural intervention and that it is the soft elements of a TQM program that have the greatest effect upon direct product quality and overall organizational performance (Ahire, Golhar & Waller, 1996; Curkovic, Vickery & Droge, 2000; Dow, Samson & Ford, 1999; Powell, 1995; Samson & Terziovski, 1999).

There is, then, some evidence that TQM is an effective management program of action. Support can be found for the effectiveness of most varieties of TQM and there is no conclusive evidence that would support the efficacy of one version of TQM over another.

CONCLUSION

This chapter has investigated the many facets of TQM. TQM may refer to simple programs of quality improvement, to a business philosophy embraced by senior management, or to a program of organizational change that focuses upon the behavioural and attitudinal aspects of organizational life. This chapter has emphasized the importance of the first and third of these aspects of TQM, for their impact upon employees. What are often referred to as the "hard" and "soft" aspects of TQM have been the focus of attention here. The hard, technical elements of TQM have been shown to have the greatest effect on work design, whilst the soft, organizational–behavioural aspects of TQM have the greatest effect upon employee orientation towards the work role.

Hard TQM has been found to lead to an expansion of the work role that enhances employee motivation and improves work design. This conception of the impact of TQM can be readily accommodated within existing work design theories and, in this respect, TQM may be seen as simply another in the long line of job redesign initiatives implemented by management (Hackman & Wageman, 1995). TQM has also been found to have effects upon the decisional autonomy given to employees, enabling or constraining their participation in workplace decision making. Once again, this change can be accommodated within existing theories of employee participation and the outcomes explained within the framework of existing work design theories (Cotton, 1993; Cotton *et al.*, 1988; Davis & Wacker, 1987; Hackman, 1977, 1991; Hackman & Oldham, 1980).

The technical elements of TQM are, however, often implemented in ways that do not challenge underlying organizational structures, social–affective systems or work cultures. Here it is the soft elements of TQM that have the greatest impact. The implementation of the soft aspects of TQM—the restructuring of hierarchical role relationships within organizations and the reorientation of employees towards their work role—introduces new dimensions to the discussion of work design, and yet this change has been little studied. The efforts within TQM programs to provide for the normative integration of employees into unitary organizational cultures have not been touched upon by previous work design theories, and there is a need to elaborate more fully a theory of work roles in contemporary work systems (Parker, Wall & Jackson, 1997).

More pragmatically, little research has focused upon the outcomes of TQM programs for employees. Few studies have examined the impact of TQM programs on employee satisfaction, employee commitment, job satisfaction or job security (Coyle-Shapiro, 1999; Cowling & Newman, 1995; Lam, 1995). TQM programs should enhance work design, and the improvements wrought by TQM should enhance the competitive position of the organization and hence job security. These effects of TQM programs are widely hypothesised, but there has been little direct study of the veracity of such claims (Edwards *et al.*, 1998).

The link between TQM and improved outcomes for employees is supported indirectly by studies of strategic HRM systems (Arthur, 1994; Becker & Gerhart, 1996; Huselid, 1995) and high-performance work systems (Brown, Reich & Stern, 1993; MacDuffie, 1995). Many of the practices examined in these studies may be said to overlap with TQM practices, but TQM is not identical to either HRM or high-performance work systems, and so direct inferences cannot be drawn. Studies of human resource management practices and employee outcomes have also been complemented by studies of advanced manufacturing practices and employee outcomes. Once again, there is some overlap with TQM; however, these studies do not look solely at TQM, but rather examine the impact of TQM practices in conjunction with advanced manufacturing technology, just-in-time flow and other new manufacturing techniques (Jayaram *et al.*, 1999; Youndt *et al.*, 1996).

There is thus a need to reconceptualise the study of employee outcomes of TQM programs. There has been some study of employee satisfaction and commitment, but little study of the impact of TQM upon employees' vocational identities or upon significant outcomes such as job security (Edwards *et al.*, 1998; Redman & Grieves, 1999). The experience of TQM, reflected here, points to the limitations of viewing such programs simply as a management initiative. The implementation of TQM has profound effects upon the work of employees and these effects need to be more extensively researched and more clearly theorised.

REFERENCES

Adler, P. S. (1993). Time-and-motion regained. *Harvard Business Review*, **January–February**, 97–108.

Adler, P. S. & Borys, B. (1996). Two types of bureaucracy: enabling and coercive. *Administrative Science Quarterly*, **41**, 61–89.

Adler, P. S. & Cole, R. E. (1993). Designed for learning: a tale of two auto plants. *Sloan Management Review*, **Spring**, 85–94.

Ahire, S. L., Golhar, D. Y. & Waller, M. A. (1996). Development and validation of TQM implementation constructs. *Decision Sciences*, **27**(1), 23–56.

Arthur, J. B. (1994). Effects of human resource systems on manufacturing performance and turnover. *Academy of Management Journal*, **37**(3), 670–687.

Australian Manufacturing Council (1994). *Leading the Way. A Study of Best Manufacturing Practices in Australia and New Zealand*. Melbourne: AMC.

Babson, S. (1993). Lean or mean: the MIT Model and lean production at Mazda. *Labour Studies Journal*, **18**(2), 3–24.

Becker, B. & Gerhart, B. (1996). The impact of human resource management on organizational performance: progress and prospects. *Academy of Management Journal*, **39**(4), 779–801.

Black, S. A. & Porter, L. J. (1996). Identification of the critical factors of TQM. *Decision Sciences*, **27**(1), 1–21.

Brown, C., Reich, M. & Stern, D. (1993). Becoming a high-performance work organization: the role of security, employee involvement and training. *International Journal of Human Resource Management*, **2**(4), 247–275.

Choi, T. Y. & Behling, O. C. (1997). Top managers and TQM success: one more look after all these years. *Academy of Management Executive*, **11**(1), 37–47.

Clinton, R. J., Williamson, S. & Bethke, A. L. (1994). Implementing total quality management: the role of human resource management. *SAM Advanced Management Journal*, **Spring**, 10–16.

Cole, R. E. (1994). Different quality paradigms and their implications for organizational learning. In M. Akoi & R. Dore (Eds), *The Japanese Firm. The Sources of Competitive Strength* (pp. 66–83). Oxford: Oxford University Press.

Cole, R. E. (1998). Learning from the quality movement: what did and didn't happen and why. *California Management Review*, **41**(1), 43–73.

Conti, R. F. & Warner, M. (1997). Technology, culture and craft: job tasks and quality realities. *New Technology, Work and Employment*, **12**(2), 123–135.

Cordery, J. L. (1996). Autonomous work groups and quality circles. In M. A. West (Ed.), *Handbook of Work Group Psychology* (pp. 225–246). Chichester: Wiley.

Cotton, J. L. (1993). *Employee Involvement. Methods for Improving Performance and Work Attitudes*. Newbury Park, CA: Sage.

Cotton, J. L., Vollrath, D. A., Froggatt, K. L., Lengnick-Hall, M. L. & Jennings, K. R. (1988). Employee participation: diverse forms and different outcomes. *Academy of Management Review*, **13**(1), 8–22.

Cowling, A. & Newman, K. (1995). Banking on people: TQM, service quality and human resources. *Personnel Review*, **24**(7), 25–41.

Coyle-Shapiro, J. A-M. (1999). Employee participation and assessment of an organizational change intervention. A three-wave study of total quality management. *Journal of Applied Behavioural Science*, **35**(4), 439–456.

Crosby, P. B. (1980). *Quality Is Free: the Art of Making Quality Certain*. New York: Mentor Books.

Curkovic, S., Vickery, S. & Droge, C. (2000). Quality-related action programs: their impact on quality performance and firm performance. *Decision Sciences*, **31**(4), 885–905.

Davis, L. E. & Wacker, G. J. (1987). Job design. In G. Salvendy (Ed.), *Handbook of Human Factors* (pp. 431–452). New York: Wiley.

Dawson, P. (1994a). *Organizational Change. A Processual Approach*. London: Paul Chapman.

Dawson, P. (1994b). Total quality management. In J. Storey (Ed.), *New Wave Manufacturing Strategies* (pp. 103–121). London: Paul Chapman.

Dawson, P. (1998). The rhetoric and bureaucracy of quality management. A totally questionable method. *Personnel Review*, **27**(1), 5–19.

Dawson, P. & Palmer, G. (1995). *Quality Management. The Theory and Practice of Implementing Change*. Melbourne: Longman.

Dawson, P. & Webb, J. (1989). New production arrangements: the totally flexible cage. *Work, Employment and Society*, **3**(2), 221–238.

Dean, J. W. Jr & Bowen, D. E. (1994). Management theory and total quality: improving research and practice through theory development. *Academy of Management Review*, **18**(3), 392–418.

Delbridge, R., Turnbull, P. & Wilkinson, B. (1992). Pushing back the frontiers: management control and work intensification under JIT/TQM factory regimes. *New Technology, Work and Employment*, **7**(2), 97–106.

Deming, W. E. (1982). *Quality, Productivity and Competitive Position*. Cambridge, MA: MIT Centre for Advanced Engineering Study.

Deming, W. E. (1986). *Out of the Crisis*. Cambridge, MA: Cambridge University Press.

Dow, D., Samson, D. & Ford, S. (1999). Exploding the myth: do all quality management practices contribute to superior performance? *Production and Operations Management*, **8**(1), 1–27.

Easton, G. S. (1995). A Baldrige Examiner's assessment of US total quality management. In R. E. Cole (Ed.), *The Death and Life of the American Quality Movement* (pp. 11–58). New York: Oxford University Press.

Easton, G. S. & Jarrell, S. L. (1998). The effects of total quality management on corporate performance: an empirical investigation. *Journal of Business*, **71**(2), 253–307.

Edwards, P., Collinson, M. & Rees, C. (1998). The determinants of employee response to total quality management: six case studies. *Organization Studies*, **19**(3), 449–475.

Evans, J. R. & Dean, J. W. Jr (2000). *Total Quality. Management, Organization and Strategy*. Cincinnati, OH: South-Western College Publishing.

Evans, J. R. & Lindsay, W. M. (1999). *The Management and Control of Quality*, 4th Edn. Cincinnati, OH: South-Western College Publishing.

Feigenbaum, A. V. (1983). *Total Quality Control*. New York: McGraw-Hill.

Ferdows, K. & De Meyer, A. (1990). Lasting improvements in manufacturing performance: in search of a new theory. *Journal of Operations Management*, **9**(2), 168–184.

Flynn, B. B., Schroeder, R. G. & Sakakibara, S. (1995). The impact of quality management practices on performance and competitive advantage. *Decision Sciences*, **26**(5), 659–691.

Garvin, D. (1984). What does product quality really mean? *Sloan Management Review*, **36**(1), 25–43.

Garvin, D. (1991). *Managing Quality: the Strategic and Competitive Edge*. New York: Free Press.

General Accounting Office (1991). *Report to the House of Representatives on Management Practices: US Companies Improve Performance Through Quality Efforts*. Washington DC: US General Accounting Office.

Gee, M. V. & Nystrom, P. C. (1999). Strategic fit between skills training and levels of quality management: an empirical study of American manufacturing plants. *Human Resource Planning*, **22**(2), 12–23.

Griffin, R. (1988). Consequences of quality circles in an industrial setting: a longitudinal assessment. *Academy of Management Journal*, **31**(2), 338–358.

Griffin, R. (1991). Effects of work redesign on employee perceptions, attitudes, and behaviours: a long-term investigation. *Academy of Management Journal*, **34**(2), 425–435.

Grant, R. M., Shani, R. & Krishnan, R. (1994). TQM's challenge to management theory and practice. *Sloan Management Review*, **Winter**, 25–35.

Hackman, R. J. (1977). Work design. In R. J. Hackman & J. L. Suttle (Eds), *Improving Life at Work. Behavioral Science Approaches to Organizational Change* (pp. 96–159). Santa Monica, CA: Goodyear.

Hackman, J. R. (1991). Work design. In R. M. Steers & L. W. Porter (Eds), *Motivation and Work Behaviour*. New York: McGraw-Hill.

Hackman, J. R. & Oldham, G. R. (1980). *Work Redesign*. The Philippines: Addison-Wesley.

Hackman, J. R. & Wageman, R. (1995). Total quality management: empirical, conceptual and practical issues. *Administrative Science Quarterly*, **40**, 309–342.

Helton, B. R. (1995). The Baldie play. *Quality Progress*, **28**(2), 43–45.

Hill, S. (1991). Why quality circles failed but total quality management might succeed. *British Journal of Industrial Relations*, **29**(4), 541–569.

Hill, S. & Wilkinson, A. (1995). In search of TQM. *Employee Relations*, **17**(3), 8–25.

Hunter, L. & Beaumont, P. B. (1993). Implementing TQM: top down or bottom up? *Industrial Relations Journal*, **24**(4), 318–327.

Huselid, M. A. (1995). The impact of human resource management practices on turnover, productivity and corporate financial performance. *Academy of Management Journal*, **38**(3), 635–672.

Imai, M. (1997). *Gemba Kaizen: A Commonsense, Low-cost Approach to Management*. New York: McGraw-Hill.

Ishikawa, K. (1985). *What Is Total Quality Control? The Japanese Way*. Englewood Cliffs, NJ: Prentice-Hall.

Jayaram, J., Droge, C. & Vickery, S. K. (1999). The impact of human resource management practices on manufacturing performance. *Journal of Operations Management*, **18**, 1–20.

Juran, J. M. & Godfrey, A. B. (Eds) (1999). *Juran's Quality Control Handbook*, 5th Edn. New York: McGraw-Hill.

Klein, J. A. (1991). A reexamination of autonomy in light of new manufacturing practices. *Human Relations*, **44**(1), 21–38.

Kochan, T. A., Gittell, J. H. & Lautsch, B. A. (1995). Total quality management and human resource systems: an international comparison. *International Journal of Human Resource Management*, **6**(2), 201–223.

Lam, S. S. K. (1995). Quality management and job satisfaction. *International Journal of Quality & Reliability Management*, **12**(4), 72–79.

Lawler, E. E. & Mohrman, S. A. (1985). Quality circles after the fad. *Harvard Business Review*, **January–February**, 64–71.

Lewchuck, W. & Robertson, D. (1998). Production without empowerment: work reorganization from the perspective of motor vehicle workers. *Capital & Class*, **63**, 37–63.

MacDuffie, J. P. (1995). Human resource bundles and manufacturing performance: organizational logic and flexible production systems in the world auto industry. *Industrial and Labor Relations Review*, **48**(2), 197–221.

McCabe, D. & Wilkinson, A. (1997). The rise and fall of TQM: the vision, meaning and operation of change. *Industrial Relations Journal*, **29**(1), 18–29.

Marks, M. L., Mirvis, P. H., Hackett, E. J. & Grady, J. F. Jr (1986). Employee participation in a quality circle program: impact on quality of work life, productivity and absenteeism. *Journal of Applied Psychology*, **71**(1), 61–69.

Montgomery, D. C. (1991). *Introduction to Statistical Quality Control*, 2dn Edn. Toronto: Wiley.

Morrow, P. C. (1997). The measurement of TQM principles and work-related outcomes. *Journal of Organizational Behaviour*, **18**(2), 363–376.

Parker, M. & Slaughter, J. (1993). Should the labour movement buy TQM? *Journal of Organizational Change Management*, **6**(4), 43–56.

Parker, S. A., Wall, T. D. & Jackson, P. R. (1997). "That's not my job": developing flexible employee work orientations. *Academy of Management Journal*, **40**(4), 899–929.

Powell, T. C. (1995). Total quality management as competitive advantage: a review and empirical study. *Strategic Management Journal*, **16**(1), 15–28.

Redman, T. & Grieves, J. (1999). Managing strategic change through TQM: learning from failure. *New Technology, Work and Employment*, **14**(1), 45–61.

Reger, R. K., Gustafson, L. T., Demarie, S. M. & Mullane, J. V. (1994). Reframing the organization: why implementing total quality is easier said than done. *Academy of Management Review*, **19**(3), 565–584.

Samson, D. & Terziovski, M. (1999). The relationship between total quality management practices and operational performance. *Journal of Operations Management*, **17**, 393–409.

Saraph, J. V., Benson, P. G. & Schroeder, R. G. (1989). An instrument for measuring the critical factors of quality management. *Decision Sciences*, **20**(4), 810–829.

Schonberger, R. J. (1992). Is strategy strategic? Impact of total quality management on strategy. *Academy of Management Executive*, **6**(3), 80–87.

Schonberger, R. J. (1994). Human resource management: lessons from a decade of total quality management and reengineering. *California Management Review*, **Summer**, 103–123.

Shingo, S. (1986). *Zero Quality Control: Source Inspection and the Poka-Yoke System* (Trans. A. P. Dillon). Cambridge, MA: Productivity Press.

Shingo, S. (1989). *A Study of the Toyota Production System from an Industrial Engineering Viewpoint* (Trans. A. P. Dillon). Cambridge, MA: Productivity Press.

Sitkin, S. B., Sutcliffe, K. M. & Schroeder, R. G. (1994). Distinguishing control from learning in total quality management: a contingency perspective. *Academy of Management Review*, **19**(3), 537–564.

Spencer, B. A. (1994). Models of organization and total quality management: a comparison and critical evaluation. *Academy of Management Review*, **19**(3), 446–471.

Tuckman, A. (1994). The yellow brick road: total quality management and the restructuring of organizational culture. *Organization Studies*, **15**(5), 727–751.

Waldman, D. A. (1994). The contributions of total quality management to a theory of work performance. *Academy of Management Review*, **19**(3), 510–536.

Wilkinson, A. (1995). Re-examining quality management. *Review of Employment Topics*, **3**(1), 187–211.

Wilkinson, A., Godfrey, G. & Marchington, M. (1997). Bouquets, brickbats and blinkers: total quality management and employee involvement in practice. *Organization Studies*, **18**(5), 799–819.

Wilkinson, A., Marchington, M., Goodman, J. & Ackers, P. (1992). Total quality management and employee involvement. *Human Resource Management Journal*, **2**(4), 1–20.

Wilkinson, A., Redman, T. & Snape, E. (1994). Quality management and the manager. *Employee Relations*, **16**(1), 62–70.

Wilkinson, A., Redman, T., Snape, E. & Marchington, M. (1998). *Managing with Total Quality Management*. Basingstoke: Macmillan Business.

Yong, J. & Wilkinson, A. (1999). The state of total quality management: a review. *International Journal of Human Resource Management*, **10**(1), 137–161.

Youndt, M. A., Snell, S. A., Dean, J. W. Jr & Lepak, D. P. (1996). Human resource management, manufacturing strategy and firm performance. *Academy of Management Journal*, **39**(4), 836–866.

Zbaracki, M. J. (1998). The rhetoric and reality of total quality management. *Administrative Science Quarterly*, **43**, 602–636.

Zeitz, G., Mittal, V. & McAulay, B. (1999). Distinguishing adoption and entrenchment of management practices: a framework for analysis. *Organization Studies*, **20**(5), 741–776.

CHAPTER 4

Advanced Manufacturing Technology

Bradley Chase
Industrial and Systems Engineering, University of San Diego, CA, USA

and

Waldemar Karwowski
Center for Industrial Ergonomics, University of Louisville, KY, USA

Contemporary manufacturing companies are exposed to tensions resulting from market demands, rapid technological development, legal provisions and social changes. Furthermore, today's customers often demand customised, high quality and competitively priced products with a timely delivery. These demands have put pressure on companies to produce products with shorter life cycles, to produce a greater variety of models, to adapt their manufacturing program to customers' wishes within short time scales, and to produce smaller batch sizes in order to keep the finished stock as low as possible (Stalk & Hout, 1990). Manufacturing organisations have responded with a wave of massive restructuring and have increased their use of advanced manufacturing technologies (AMT), such as computer-integrated manufacturing, computer-aided design and manufacture, computer-numerical-controlled machines and automated inventory systems (Storey, 1994; Waterson *et al.*, 1999).

However, the effective implementation and use of AMT has proved to be no straightforward matter (Majchrzak & Paris, 1995). In part this is due to the complexity of the technology itself, but research shows that the successful use of AMT depends on how the technology (e.g. computer-based technologies, information systems) is integrated with human factors (e.g. skill, expertise and cognition of users) and organisational factors (e.g. job design, human resource practices) (Goldman, Nagel & Preiss, 1995; Karwowski *et al.*, 1994; Karwowski & Salvendy, 1994; Kidd, 1994; Majchrzak & Wang, 1994). Conversely, a lack of integration can lead to poor outcomes, e.g. Martin (1993) reported that many manufacturing automation projects have failed because of insufficient automability (automation flexibility), inadequate user–system interfaces (i.e. human–computer integration) and an incompatibility between human needs and system requirements.

A review of recent literature by Marchrzak & Paris (1995) concluded that high failure rates in the implementation of AMT are attributable to managers and designers lacking an understanding of the organizational and human changes that are often needed with new technology. Given the importance of understanding these issues, the main aim of this chapter is to discuss the human and organizational factors that affect the operation of AMT and how these elements can be best integrated. It is important to note that space precludes a detailed discussion of all AMTs and the differences between them. This chapter therefore refers to AMT in its broadest sense and it is assumed to include computer-integrated manufacturing, computer-numerically-controlled machine tools and cellular manufacturing. Lean manufacturing can also be understood as a way of integrating AMT, people and organisation. As this practice is addressed in Chapter 2, it will not be covered in this chapter.

AMTs: COMPLEXITY AND INTEGRATION

Advanced manufacturing technology (AMT) can be defined as the application of computer-based systems to automate and integrate different functions in the manufacturing system, such as design, planning and manufacturing. Introducing AMT can significantly increase the complexity of operational systems (Majchrzak & Paris, 1995), as the technologies used often serve multiple and flexibly interchangeable functions. The different parts of the system can also be highly interdependent. This means that the removal of a disturbance is more difficult, as a solution to a problem at one machine will need to be considered in relation to other parts of the system. Designers and users of AMT therefore need to consider how best to integrate technologies by assuring effective interfacing and interactions between machines, and to consider how best to integrate different functional tasks, such as design, scheduling, maintenance and inventory control.

In addition to the integration of technological systems, the designers and users of AMT need to consider how to integrate AMT with human factors. Human factors that have been identified as being important include the skills of the operator, hardware ergonomics (e.g. safety and prevention of accidental operation), software ergonomics (e.g. provision of informative feedback to enable the correct interpretation, evaluation and diagnosis of events), operator training requirements, boredom and stress at work, and safety (Clegg & Corbett, 1987; Cummings & Blumberg, 1987; Office of Technological Assessment, 1984). However, designers of AMT systems rarely give due consideration to the paramount need for effective human integration within AMT systems and primarily focus on technological integration (Kidd, 1994). In addition, human skill is perceived as a problem and the human operator as the source of error (Bainbridge, 1983; Sanderson, 1989; Wilson *et al.*, 1994). Yet the successful operation of AMT depends upon human skill and knowledge to compensate for limitations of computer-based technology and relies on the human resource to provide a basis for the development and continuous improvement of AMT (Martin, 1990). Indeed, one of the ironies of AMT is that the role of the human becomes more important in less labour-intensive, automated AMT systems, not less (Wilson, 1991). Furthermore, it is the very fact that people are flexible, intelligent and able to solve complex novel problems that permits AMT to be used at all (Clegg & Corbett, 1987). These issues were exemplified in a study by Wobbe & Charles (1994), who concluded that:

1. The more complex products become, the more quality is dependent upon upgrading of all stages of manufacturing and demands the full dedication of employees at all levels.
2. The more sophisticated manufacturing technology becomes, the more it is vulnerable and dependent upon human skills for control and maintenance.

3. The more customized productions are, the more human intervention is necessary with regard to change-over, setting up machines, adaptation, adjustment and control.
4. If products demand a high service input and after-sales service and maintenance, skilled people are required to deal with this.
5. The shorter the life cycle of products becomes, the more innovativeness comes into play; take-off phases occur more frequently and their mastery is dependent upon experienced personnel with formal knowledge to overcome new challenges connected with the start of a new product.

In addition to being integrated with human factors, various studies have observed that AMT must be integrated with job and organizational factors. For example, the Manufacturing Studies Board (1986) in the USA concluded that realizing the full benefits of AMTs requires inter-related changes in human resource practices, planning, plant culture, plant organization, job and work design, and labour–management relations. These findings were also echoed by European studies on the fusion of flexible manufacturing systems and new information technologies (Brödner, 1987, 1991). These studies concluded that organizational factors are a key element in economic success of modern production systems, and should be valued and appreciated at the level equal to new technology.

A recurring theme in the literature on AMT is that its successful integration with human and organizational factors is fundamental to its effective use (Marchrzak, 1995). Human and organizational factors are important in AMT and must be addressed. The rest of this chapter is devoted to exploring the issues that need to be considered when attempting to integrate AMT, people and organization.

THE ROLES AND SKILLS OF THE OPERATOR IN AMT

AMT systems require operators to engage in a variety of tasks. These include: monitoring the automated system to ensure that it is functioning properly and fine-tuning it, making adjustments as necessary; detecting, diagnosing and compensating for scheduling failures, infeasible routings and other system faults; planning what should be done and specifying how it should be done; communicating with colleagues and those in other departments; making some necessary trade-offs and negotiating among alternative solutions; and learning through feedback from the plant about the impact of the above four activities (Bi & Salvendy, 1994; Sinclair, 1986). Operators need to be skilled in all these areas and from this it is apparent that, in modern manufacturing systems, the emphasis has moved away from perceptual–motor skills and towards higher-order cognitive skills (e.g. problem solving and decision making) and interpersonal skills (Goodstein, Anderson & Olsen, 1988).

Rasmussen (1983) has offered an alternative way in which to conceptualize the skills needed by human operators in AMT systems. He has classified the skills needed into three major categories. They are skill-based behaviour, rule-based behaviour and knowledge-based behaviour. Skill-based behaviour refers to sensory–motor performance during acts or activities, which take place without conscious control as smooth, automated and highly integrated patterns of behaviour. In this view, human activities are considered as a sequence of skilled acts composed for the actual situation. Rule-based behaviour is based on explicit knowledge and knowing how to employ the relevant rules in the correct situation (Goodstein et al., 1988; Johannsen, 1988). Knowledge-based behaviour refers to goal-controlled performance, where the goal is explicitly formulated, based on the knowledge of environment and aims of the person (Johannsen, 1988). The internal structure of the system is represented by a mental model. This kind of behaviour allows the operator to develop and test different plans under unfamiliar and uncertain conditions. It is particularly required when the skills and know-how of the individual are insufficient, so that conscious problem solving and planning are called for (Goodstein *et al.*, 1988). This implies that the effective use of AMT thus requires the use of higher-order cognitive knowledge-based skills.

The preceding paragraphs have shown that a range of tasks is performed in an AMT environment and that higher-order cognitive and interpersonal skills are needed to complete these tasks. Furthermore, because of the complexity and tight interdependencies of the AMT environment, it has been argued that operators need to be able to perform *all* these tasks (and have the appropriate skills) in order effectively to control variances in the work process. Only broad job roles and multiskilled operators will be able to deliver the full benefits of AMT (Marchrzak & Paris, 1995). As such, AMT has the potential to up-skill or re-skill when operators are given responsibility over a wide range of tasks, such as monitoring machines, machine maintenance, programming and problem solving (Cross, 1983; Wall *et al.*, 1990b). Yet it is not always the case that operators are given responsibility for a wide range of tasks within an AMT environment. Depending on how tasks are allocated, AMT can de-skill operators. This can occur, for example, when engineers and computer specialists rather than operators are given responsibility for maintaining machines, repairing machines and writing and fine-tuning the machines' programs. In these circumstances, not only will the operator be engaged in a restricted range of activities, but he/she may have little opportunity to use and develop high-order cognitive skills (Blumberg & Gerwin, 1983; Wall *et al.*, 1990a).

The aforementioned examples are concerned with the allocation of tasks between humans; also addressed has been task allocation between humans and machines. Attention has focused on the type of planning and scheduling tasks and the type of fault diagnosis procedures that are best carried out by either humans or machines (Nakamura & Salvendy, 1994; Karwowski *et al.*, 1997) and researchers have sought to understand the ways in which the capabilities of machines and humans can complement each other (Clegg & Corbett, 1987), e.g. a computer can generate plans or schedules far quicker than a human and, under normal conditions, can check the difference between the planned and actual schedule. However, in unusual conditions, or when a plan needs to be modified and rescheduled according to competing priorities, a human operator is normally far more effective at generating work plans and schedules. Task allocation should therefore rely on a clear understanding of the capabilities and limitations of humans and machines (see also Bi & Salvendy, 1994). It should be noted that one of the ironies of allocating human functions to machines, i.e. of automation, is that it can mystify the production process (Artandi, 1982), as operators may not be able to learn adequately about the production process as a whole. One consequence of this is that operators become unable to deal with or anticipate difficulties in the production process (Sanderson, 1989). This problem is exacerbated when the tasks of the operator are restricted and when the skills of the operator are reduced. Widening the operators' roles is one way of overcoming this problem.

JOB AND WORK DESIGN

To ensure the effective application of AMT, the following job design factors need to be addressed: job content, particularly the variety, breadth and integration of tasks (e.g. uniting planning, execution, monitoring and problem solving); job control; job demands; performance monitoring and feedback; supervisory style; social interaction; and participation in the design of technology and other work systems (Corbett, 1988; Cummings & Blumberg, 1987; Smith & Carayon, 1995).

Most emphasis has been placed on job content (e.g. task and skill variety, as discussed above) and job control. With regard to job control, much of the debate has focused on whether AMT technologies reduce or increase control. Studies indicate that the effects of AMT on operator control depend on the choices made by the designers of the technology (Clegg, 1988; Wall *et al.*, 1990a), e.g. decentralization principles can be followed to increase the control of operators (Badham & Shallock, 1991). First, operators' tasks can be widened as far as possible. Second, computer-aided planning facilities can be located at the shop floor level rather than the planning department level. Third, planning and scheduling functions can be supported at the production level, rather than the foreman/area control level. Cooley (1989) demonstrated control could be increased in a manufacturing cell by giving operators, rather than a specialist technician, control over the creation of machine programmes using high-level software tools, the improvement of software tools, machine scheduling and the programming the work handler to load and unload. Yet, while AMT may increase operator control over some aspects of work, it can reduce it with regard to other aspects. An operator may have little individual control over how he/she does his/her work, due to high levels of standardisation, but have a high degree of group or collective autonomy over the specification of these standards (Klein, 1991). Similarly, an operator may have little control over the timing of his/her work, but have a high degree of control over work methods (Wall *et al.*, 1990a).

In addition to job control, job demands, particularly cognitive demands, are likely to be affected by AMT (Jackson *et al.*, 1993; Wall *et al.*, 1990a). One of the main roles of the operator is to monitor the manufacturing process, to ensure that it is running smoothly and to be alert to problems. Attention demands are therefore likely to be high, even though little intervention in the system may be required. Furthermore, the problems that are presented to the operator may be complex and difficult to solve—although whether operators have the authority to deal with them may depend on how tasks are allocated. Another demand placed on operators has been called "production responsibility" (Jackson *et al.*, 1993). In AMT systems, machine operators may have considerable responsibility for valuable machinery and, in some cases, costly products. The failure to anticipate or identify a problem may damage the machine and lead to a costly loss of production. Furthermore, since the CNC machines used in AMT can produce a proportionally greater amount, machine downtime incurs greater costs for the firm. In total, AMT systems can increase the cognitive load on the operator.

The use of AMT also affects cognition in two other ways: hierarchically and horizontally (Sanderson, 1989). The hierarchical effect of AMT manifests itself through the process of automation, and leads to human operators acting as supervisors of the artificially intelligent manufacturing processes. The horizontal effect of AMT can be described in information-processing terms, and illustrates the situation in which the human operators have access to information about all aspects of the manufacturing system. It is clearly important that attention in the design process be given to the cognitive tasks involved when working within AMT systems, and to ensure that these are concomitant with operators' skill levels and cognitive mental models. Failure to consider an operator's skill level and mental model can increase the levels of operator error, which in an AMT environment can be costly (Reason, 1990). One approach that has sought to address this need is cognitive engineering (Harris, 1997; Hollnagel & Woods, 1983), in which human knowledge and skill are considered as an inherent part of system design requirements.

Social contact is another important work characteristic as, at a basic level, it fulfils a human need for significant social relationships (Wall & Martin, 1987). AMT can affect the extent of social contact although, as in other cases, the effect of AMT on this job characteristic is not uniform or deterministic. On the one hand, a number of studies have shown that AMT can isolate employees from each other physically and limit social interaction, due to high monitoring requirements (Argote, Goodman & Schkade, 1983; Kostecki, Mrela & Pankow, 1984). On the other hand, the interdependencies between different aspects of the AMT system can increase the need for operators to collaborate with each other and with other departments and functional roles (Blumberg & Alber, 1982; Boddy & Buchanan, 1986). In highly interdependent AMT systems, performance may therefore be enhanced by group-level re-design, such as the introduction of team work, semi-autonomous work groups and manufacturing cells, that facilitate collaboration.

Research on the effects of job characteristics on job strain and job dissatisfaction in AMT indicates that the following characteristics have the most consistent effects (Keita & Sauter, 1992; Smith *et al.*, 1992; Wall *et al.*, 1990a): a lack of control over the timing of work and the methods used (Wall & Martin, 1987); a lack of social contact and social support (Kiggundu, 1981; Warr, 1987); high problem-solving and attention/monitoring demand (Jackson *et al.*, 1993; Wall *et al.*, 1986) and high production responsibility.[1]

Given that organisations have a choice about how to organise work, a human-centred approach to AMT can be adopted to reduce employee strain. This was shown by Seppälä, Touminen & Koskinen (1992), who investigated the effects of introducing AMT and a flexible production philosophy on job contents, work demands and employee well-being in nine Finnish companies. The components of the AMT systems studied included flexible manufacturing systems, computer-numerical-controlled machine centres, and robotized machining cells. The results showed that, if management design the production system on a human-centred approach that assumes a flexible and multiskilled workforce, then AMT does not inevitably result in the impoverishment of job contents, de-skilling or employee strain.

Studies on job characteristics and well-being generally point to universal effects, whereas the effects of job design on performance appear to be contingent on factors such as operational uncertainty, e.g. Wall *et al.*, (1990b) examined whether the effect of job control on performance is greater when task uncertainty is high. The study compared two work design styles used to manage and operate CNC stand-alone systems. The work designs of interest were "specialist control" and "operator-centred control". In the specialist control mode, engineers and computer specialists maintain, repair, write and fine-tune the programs, while the operator has minimal involvement. In the operator-centred control mode, the operator is responsible for monitoring and maintenance and programming of problems as they occur. A socio-technical criterion for predicting performance through the concept of production variance was used. It was hypothesized that increasing operator control will improve performance to a greater extent in high-variance manufacturing systems than in low-variance ones. The study results revealed that introduction of enhanced operator control over CNC assembly machines led to a reduction in downtime for high-variance machines. Also of interest was the fact that work redesign improved intrinsic job satisfaction and reduced feelings of job pressure among operators. It was argued that performance improved because operators were able to immediately deal with problems and variances in the work processes

---

[1] With regard to demand characteristics and production responsibility, it is clear that extremes on any of the ranges may cause low well-being, but within the ranges found in organizations, the effects can be assumed to be linear.

in the most effective manner. It is also worth noting that several authors have proposed that AMT increases the degree of technological and operational uncertainty (Cummings & Blumberg, 1987; Majchrzak, 1988), a general implication being that job control should be high in AMT systems.

Work on the mechanisms through which job design might have its effects on AMT performance has looked at knowledge- or learning-based mechanisms and quick-response mechanisms. Evidence for these mechanisms comes from two field experiments that observed strong effects of job control on CNC machine down-time and output (Jackson & Wall, 1991; Wall et al., 1990b). The authors of these studies noticed that different measures of down-time could be used to test for different mechanisms. One measure was of the reduction in time per incident, used to examine a quick-response mechanism; and the other measure was a decrease in the number of incidents which could be used to show that operators were learning to prevent faults, i.e. a knowledge-based mechanism. The results supported the latter explanation. However, interpreting the results with regard to the quick-response mechanism is not straightforward. It could have been the case that the faults that were prevented were of shorter duration, masking a real effect on down-time per incident. Wall, Jackson & Davids (1992) addressed this problem by tracking particular types of faults on a robotics line, both before and after there had been an increase in operator control. The results were very clear. There was an instant and lasting reduction in down-time per fault, and a progressive reduction in faults. This demonstrates that both a quick-response and a knowledge-based mechanism can explain the effect of job control on performance. A more general implication is that increased job control affects performance in two ways, first by allowing the operator to use existing knowledge more effectively, e.g. to immediately rectify faults when they occur, and second, through the development of predictive knowledge and other strategies that prevents faults occurring. This clearly shows that, since AMT relies on operator knowledge and operators' use of higher-order cognitive skills, job designs that allow the opportunity to use and develop knowledge and skills are imperative for their effective use.

ADVANCED MANUFACTURING TECHNOLOGY: THE NEED FOR INTEGRATED, OPEN, HUMAN-CENTRED APPROACHES

At present, many AMT systems remain poorly integrated with the inherent capabilities of the human operators, expressed by their skills and knowledge necessary for the effective control and monitoring of these systems, and other systems within the organization (Karwowski & Rahimi, 1990; Kidd, 1994). Such incompatibility arises at all levels of the human, machine and human–machine functioning. Problems with integrating people and technology occur early at the AMT design stage. These problems can be conceptualized using the following model of the complexity of interactions (I) between contemporary manufacturing designers (D) and users (U) of AMT technology, and the AMT technology (T) itself:

$$I(U, T) = F[I(U, D), I(D, T)]$$

where: I stands for relevant interactions and F indicates functional relationships between designers (D), users (U), and technology (T).

The above model points out that the interactions between users and AMT technology are determined by the outcome of the integration of the two earlier interactions, i.e. those between the designers and potential users, and those between the designers and manufacturing technology (at the level of machines and system integration). Although strong interactions typically exist between designers and technology, only a few examples of strong connections between designers and human operators can be found.

To assure full benefits from AMT, designers need a broad vision that includes people, organization and technology (Kidd, 1991), and one in which organizational structures, work practices and technologies allow people to adapt their work strategies to the AMT systems (Kidd, 1990). As such, work practices and technologies need to be designed and developed as open systems. The term "open system" is used to describe a system that receives inputs from, and sends outputs to, the systems environment (Kidd, 1992). The term was associated in manufacturing with system architectures based on the International Standards Organization Open Systems Interconnection model (ESPRIT Consortium AMICE, 1989). The idea can be applied not only to system architectures and organizational structures, but also to work practices, human–computer interfaces and the relationship between people and technologies, such as scheduling, control systems and decision support systems (Kidd, 1990).

An open manufacturing system allows people a large degree of freedom to define the systems operation and adapt the system to the context of use. In the open, adaptable manufacturing system, the relationship between the user and the computer is determined by the user and not by the designer. The role of the designer of an open manufacturing system is to create a system that will satisfy the users' personal preferences, and allow the users to work in a way that they find most appropriate. Kidd (1990) has demonstrated the concept of an open manufacturing system for the human–computer interface in workshop-orientated computer-numerically-controlled (CNC) systems. An open human–computer interface allows the human operator to customize the interface to his/her own personal preferences by changing the dialogue, the screen layout, etc. Another example of an open system can be seen in the operator-centred work design described by Wall *et al.* (1990b), where the operator was responsible for monitoring and maintenance and programming of problems as they occurred. In a closed manufacturing system, the system designer, through hardware, software or performance constraints on the actions of the user, restricts their autonomy and, in some cases, can force the user to use the manufacturing system in a particular way. A simple example of this is where the human–computer interface of a CNC machine tool is pre-set by the manufacturing designers. Another example is where a particular task is automated but, when the manufacturing system fails, the system leaves the user without the necessary computer-based decision support.

A core feature of an open system is that it is human-centred. Corbett (1988) suggests that a human-centered AMT system should:

1. Accept the present skill of the user and provide opportunities for the user to develop new skills. Conventional technological design tends to incorporate this skill into the machine itself, with the resultant de-skilling of the human.
2. Offer a high degree of freedom to users, so that they can shape their own working behaviour and objectives.
3. Unite the planning, execution and monitoring component of work. Hence, the division of labour, which predominates present-day practice in manufacturing, is minimized.
4. Encourage social communication (both formal and informal) between users, preserving the face-to-face interaction in favour of electronically transmitted data exchange.
5. Provide a healthy, safe and efficient work environment.

The types of job and work designs and human resource practices that would support a move towards a more human-centred approach and help employees to deal with the complexity of AMT systems include the following (Liker, Fleischer & Arndorf, 1993; Marchrzak, 1988):

1. Broadening manufacturing operators' job responsibilities to include machine repair, process improvements and inspection.
2. Enlarging maintenance workers' job responsibilities to include teaching, ordering parts, scheduling and machine operations.
3. Extending supervisory job responsibilities to include working with other departments to solve problems.
4. Employing more maintenance people to compensate for increasing equipment responsibility.
5. Increased use of work teams to provide a coordinated response to broad problems.
6. Operator selection based more on human relations skills than seniority, to ensure necessary communication and coordination capabilities.
7. Increased training in problem solving and how the various manufacturing processes function to handle the increased scope of problems.

Another human-centered approach to AMT systems is based on idea of the anthropocentric production system (APS). APS are called anthropocentric because they are focused on skilled human labour instead of technology as the main resource for highly flexible, customer-orientated and quality-based production. As discussed by Wobbe & Charles (1994), the anthropocentric production system assumes that people play a central role in manufacturing, and relates the production system to work organization, the management structure and organizational culture. The defining characteristics of APS are: work in semi-autonomous groups; holistic task assignment to the groups, including both horizontal task integration (e.g. integration of technical maintenance and quality assurance into groups) and vertical task integration (e.g. integration of numerical control programming, planning and scheduling); a decentralized factory organisation, with comprehensive delegation of planning and controlling functions to semi-autonomous units; internal rotation of tasks, leading to job enlargement and job rotation for group members; and high and polyvalent skills and continuous up-skilling at work.

TOOLS AND METHODS FOR AMT JOB AND WORK RE-DESIGN

A number of different tools have been proposed as useful for the introduction and design of AMT systems. In general, these tools conform to the socio-technical principle that both the social and technical aspects of a system must be designed in congruence with each other, i.e. that they are jointly optimized. One such tool is the HITOP system, which stands for high integration of technology, organization and people (Majchrzak et al. 1991). HITOP involves the design team completing a series of checklists and forms to describe their organization, current technology and plans. It then helps the design team to consider the implications of those plans for factors such as role requirements and organizational design. A more detailed description of the HITOP framework can be seen in Table 4.1.

Table 4.1 The HITOP framework

1. *Organisational readiness*—how ready is the organisation to make the changes recommended by a HITOP analysis?
2. *Critical technical features*—those features of the technology that are most likely to impact on the integration with people and organisation
3. *Essential role requirements*—for the four primary functions in a manufacturing workforce (operators, support, supervisors and management). HITOP identifies eight role requirements, including degree and type of interdependence, information exchange, decision authority and involvement and complexity of strategic goal setting
4. *Job designs*—the HITOP analysis requires the design team to develop a set of job design values, such as "workers should have control over resources for those areas for which they are responsible"
5. *Skill requirements (including selection and training)*—the minimal skill requirements (characterized by perceptual, conceptual, manual dexterity, problem solving, technical and human relations) for each role requirement are determined in this set and a determination of which skills will be trained vs. selected
6. *Rewards systems*—forms are provided to help the design team to make three decisions about rewards: basis for pay (e.g. merit, hours, performance), basis for non-financially recognising and rewarding performance, and future career paths
7. *Organisation design*—forms are provided to help the design team work through five organisational design changes typically seen with the implementation of AMT: changes in reporting lines; procedural formality; unit grouping; cross-unit coordination mechanisms; and organisational culture

Source: After Majchrzak et al. (1991).

Another framework that has been developed for integrating technological, human and organisational factors is GOPRIST. Karwowski *et al.* (1994) proposed this conceptual framework to address the long-term issues related to competitiveness, complexity and uncertainty issues relevant to the human side of contemporary manufacturing enterprises. The GOPRIST framework (see Figure 4.1) starts with the overall company goals, the set of design principles as a basis to fulfil these goals; a set of management and organizational structures, which correspond to the given principles; and the specific techniques to implement these principles.

The "goals" refer to the desired future state of the manufacturing enterprise. Karowowski *et al.* (1994) argues that existing functional organizations of the manufacturing enterprises are too rigid to cope with external complexity and dynamics of the markets, and with rapid changes in products and processes suitable to meet the market demands. Rather, contemporary manufacturing companies should aim to create self-configurable and highly adaptive organizational structures that have a rapid response capacity and rapid product innovation. These goals are thought to be realizable if guided by a set of human factors design "principles" that include the following topics: (a) work organization; (b) job design, new forms of organizing manufacturing processes; (c) skill-orientated control and responsibility; (d) ideas for managing the change process by assessing the critical change factors and developing systems, procedures and tactics to address them; (e) evaluating change by aiming to make problems visible; (f) determining the cost/benefit of alternatives; and (g) specific tools, techniques and methods in the above-listed and other areas.

The organizational "structures" of the GOPRIST framework corresponds to the given design principles. Such structures translate these principles into specific actions by utilizing a set of available organizational design techniques. In general, the organization subsystem

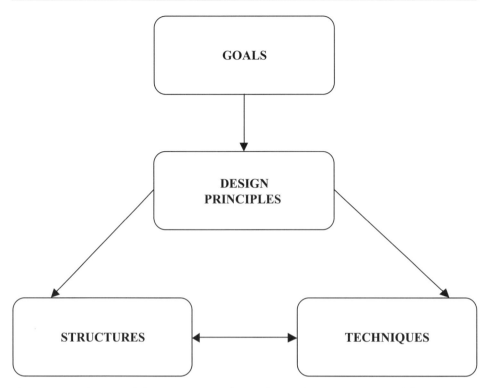

Figure 4.1 A framework for competitive advanced manufacturing enterprise (after Karwowski *et al.*, 1994)

focuses on work processes (tasks, procedures), work group design, communication and decision-making processes, and it includes the learning organization and a set of integrated organization design principles. The learning organization principle allows for the high level of cooperation, open communication and continuous improvement, and leads to an integrated organization design principle. The technology subsystem focuses on the "technology as a tool" design principle.

Finally, knowledge of the implementation process should be translated into a comprehensive set of methods and "techniques". Elements to be included into such tools are: (a) risk assessment; (b) cost-benefit analysis; (c) predictive models; (d) methods to constantly assess and modify and adjust the end state; and (e) specific application of change management theory at each stage of the change process. Examples of organizational design techniques that can be used to implement specific organizational structures include: (a) joint technical and organizational design; (b) job design principles; (c) user participation (participatory design); (d) organizationally appropriate technologies, and (e) comprehensive training and professionalization of personnel.

The use of design tools and frameworks such as HITOP and GOPRIST also needs to be seen within the wider context of the management of technology implementation. Sun & Riis (1994) have proposed the following stages for the implementation of AMT:

1. *Initiation and justification.* At this stage, a champion starts to specify the problems and to recommend the potential AMT for top management approval.

2. *Preparation and design.* The design and planning of both the physical and work organization issues related to the AMT are conducted. It is recommended that the users of the AMT are involved at this early stage and that there are early discussions with the vendor.
3. *Installation and training.* The AMT is installed and the necessary changes in work organization and human resource management practices introduced. Staff are trained in the new equipment.
4. *Routinization and learning.* All employees need to gain experience with working in the new set-up. Adjustments to the AMT and work organizations are made.

From the above, it is possible to view design and implementation as a social process, and as a process that continues after the machinery has been installed. This has a number of implications (Marchrzak, 1993). First, AMT is not best conceived as a generic model or type of equipment, but rather as a configuration of technical options, workplace decisions, human factors and socio-political factors. Second, the technological innovation process occurs continually, going to and fro between design and implementation and from one generation of technology to the next. Third, the design of technology should not be conceived as a single point in time but as an extended process that is extended in time to include post-adoption incremental design changes.

CONCLUSION

AMT technologies increase the complexity and interdependencies of the manufacturing process. One of the ironies of AMT is that human and organizational factors become more, not less, important. To successfully manage AMT, these factors must be addressed and successfully integrated with the AMT technology. Of course, AMT may be implemented and used in such a way that it reduces the skill of the operators and reduces role breadth and job control. It would appear that not only will this increase the level of employee stress, but it will not permit the efficient use of AMT. Rather, the full benefits of AMT may only be realised when accompanied by appropriate job designs that include wide job roles and high levels of operator control. This type of "empowered" job design is particularly important in uncertain conditions. Attention also needs to be given to how organizations can be designed so that they are self-adaptive to the requirements and changes in technology.

A further implication of AMT is that it increases cognitive task demands and the need for higher-order cognitive skills. As such, the cognitive demands of the workplace and cognitive characteristics of the workers need to be considered in the design and management of contemporary manufacturing systems, in order to assure their compatibility with the worker's internal models that describe the operations and functions of these systems. Using approaches such as cognitive engineering, new methods for cognitive task analysis need to be developed in order to identify the operator's model of a system. The challenge to the human factors profession is to assist in design of contemporary manufacturing systems, which incorporate the characteristics of human cognition and explicitly build into the design process both physical and cognitive images of the workers.

Acknowledgements

The authors would like to thank David Holman for his extensive work on earlier versions of this chapter.

REFERENCES

Argote, L., Goodman, P. S., & Schkade, D. (1983). The human side of robotics: how workers react to a robot. *Sloan Management Review*, **24**, 31–41.

Artandi, S. (1982). Computers and the post-industrial society: symbiosis or information tyranny? *Journal of the American Society for Information Science*, **33**, 302–307.

Badham, R. & Schallock, B. (1991). Human factors in CIM: a human-centered perspective from Europe. *International Journal of Human Factors in Manufacturing*, **1**(2): 121–141.

Bainbridge, L. (1983). Ironies of automation. *Automatica*, **19**, 775–779.

Bi, S. & Salvendy, G. (1994). Analytical modeling and experimental study of human workload in scheduling of advanced manufacturing systems. *International Journal of Human Factors in Manufacturing*, **4**, 205–234.

Blumberg, M. & Alber, A. (1982). The human element: its impact on the productivity of advanced manufacturing systems. *Journal of Manufacturing Systems*, **1**, 43–52.

Blumberg, M. & Gerwin, D. (1983). Coping with advanced manufacturing technology. *Journal of Occupational Behavior*, **5**, 113–130.

Boddy, D. & Buchanan, D. A. (1986). *Managing New Technology*. Oxford: Blackwell.

Brödner, P. (Ed.) (1987). *Strategic Options for New Production Systems—CHIM: Computer and Human Integrated Manufacturing*. FAST Occasional Papers. Brussels, Belgium: Directorate General for Science, Research and Development, Commission of the European Communities.

Brödner, P. (1991). Design of work and technology in manufacturing. *International Journal of Human Factors in Manufacturing*, **1**(1), 1–16.

Clegg, C. W. (1988). Appropriate technology for management: some management issues. *Applied Ergonomics*, **19**, 25–34.

Clegg, C. W. & Corbett, J. M. (1987). Research and development in "humanizing" advanced manufacturing technology. In T. D. Wall, C. W. Clegg & N. J. Kemp (Eds), *The Human Side of Advanced Manufacturing Technology*. Chichester: Wiley.

Cooley, M. (1989). Human-centred systems. In H. H. Rosenbrock (Ed.), *Designing Human-centred Technology* (pp.133–143). New York: Springer-Verlag.

Corbett, J. M. (1988). Ergonomics in the development of human-centered HAS. *Applied Ergonomics*, **19**, 35–39.

Corbett, J. M. (1990). Human-centered advanced manufacturing systems: from theoretics to reality. *International Journal of Industrial Ergonomics*, **5**, 83–90.

Cross, M. (1983). *Changing Requirements for Craftsmen in Process Industries. Stage 1, Interim Report*. London: Technical Change Centre.

Cummings, T. G. & Blumberg, M. (1987). Advanced manufacturing technology and work design. In T. D. Wall, C. W. Clegg & N. J. Kemp (Eds), *The Human Side of Advanced Manufacturing Technology*. Chichester: Wiley.

ESPRIT Consortium AMICE (1989). *Open System Architecture for CIM*. Berlin: Springer-Verlag.

Goldman, S. L., Nagel, R. N. & Preiss, K. (1995). *Agile Competitors and Virtual Organizations*. New York: Van Nostrand Reinhold.

Goodstein, L. P., Anderson, H. B. & Olsen, S. E. (Eds) (1988). *Tasks, Errors and Mental Models*. London: Taylor & Francis.

Harris, D. (Ed.) (1997). *Engineering Psychology and Cognitive Ergonomics, Vol. 2: Job Design and Product Design*. Aldershot: Ashgate.

Hollnagel, E. & Woods, D. (1983). Cognitive systems engineering: new wine in new bottles. *International Journal of Man–Machine Studies*, **18**, 583–600.

Jackson, P. R. & Wall, T. D. (1991). How does operator control enhance performance of advanced manufacturing technology? *Ergonomics*, **34**, 1301–1311.

Jackson, P. R., Wall, T. D., Martin, R. & Davids, K. (1993). New measures of job control, cognitive demand and production responsibility. *Journal of Applied Psychology*, **78**, 753–762.

Johannsen, G. (1988). Categories of human operator behavior in fault behavior situations. In L. P. Goodstain, H. B. Andersson & S. E. Olsen (Eds), *Tasks, Errors, and Mental Models* (pp. 251–277). London: Taylor and Francis.

Karwowski, W. & Rahimi, M. (Eds) (1990). *Ergonomics of Hybrid Automated Systems II*. Amsterdam: Elsevier.

Karwowski, W. & Salvendy, G. (Eds) (1994). *Organization and Management of Advanced Manufacturing*. New York: Wiley.

Karwowski, W., Salvendy, G., Badham, R., Brodner, P., Clegg, C., Hwang, L., Iwasawa, J., Kidd, P. T., Kobayashi, N., Koubek, R., Lamarsh, J., Nagamachi, M., Naniwada, M., Salzman, H., Seppälä, P., Schallock, B., Sheridan, T. & Warschat, J. (1994). Integrating people, organization and technology in advanced manufacturing. *Human Factors and Ergonomics in Manufacturing*, **4**, 1–19.

Karwowski, W., Warnecke, H. J., Hueser, M. & Salvendy, G. (1997). Human factors in manufacturing. In G. Salvendy (Ed.), *Handbook of Human Factors and Ergonomics*, 2nd Edn. New York: Wiley.

Keita, G. P. & Sauter, S. L. (1992). *Work and Well-being*. Washington, DC: American Psychological Association.

Kidd, P. T. (1990). An open systems human computer interface for a workshop orientated CNC lathes. In W. Karwowski & M. Rahimi (Eds), *Human Aspects of Hybrid Automated Systems II* (pp. 537–544). Amsterdam: Elsevier.

Kidd, P. T. (1991). Human and computer integrated manufacturing: a manufacturing strategy based on organization, people and technology. *International Journal of Human Factors in Manufacturing*, **1**(1), 17–32.

Kidd, P. T. (1992). Interdisciplinary design of skill-based computer-aided technologies: interfacing in depth. *International Journal of Human Factors in Manufacturing*, **2**(3), 209–228.

Kidd, P. T. (1994). *Agile Manufacturing: Forging New Frontiers*. Reading, MA: Addison-Wesley.

Kiggundu, M. N. (1981). Task interdependence and the theory of job design. *Academy of Management Review*, **6**, 499–508.

Klein, J. A. (1991). A re-examination of autonomy in light of new manufacturing practices. *Human Relations*, **44**, 21–38.

Kostecki, M. J., Mrela, K. & Pankow, W. (1984). Job design and automation in the polish machine industry: the case of non-programmed automation in a planned economy. In, F. Butera & J. Thurman (Eds), *Automation and Work Design*. Amsterdam: North-Holland.

Liker, J. K., Fleischer, M. & Arndorf, D. (1993). Fulfilling the promises. *Sloan Management Review*, **33**, 74–86.

Majchrzak, A. (1988). *The Human Side of Factory Automation*. San Francisco, CA: Jossey-Bass.

Majchrzak, A. (1993). Commentary. *International Journal of Human Factors in Manufacturing*, **3**, 89–90.

Majchrzak, A. (1995). *Tools for Analyzing Organizational Impacts of New Technology: Handbook of Technology Management*. New York: McGraw-Hill.

Majchrzak, A., Fleischer, M., Roitman, D. & Mokray, J. (1991). *Reference Manual for Performing the HITOP Analysis*. Ann Arbor, MI: Industrial Technology Institute.

Majchrzak, A. & Paris, M. L. (1995). High performing organizations match technology and management strategies: results of a survey. *International Journal of Industrial Ergonomics*, **16**, 309–326.

Majchrzak, A. & Wang, Q. (1994). The human dimension of manufacturing: results of a survey of electronics manufacturers. *Journal of Applied Manufacturing Systems*, **7**(1), 5–15.

Manufacturing Studies Board (1986). *Toward a New Era in U.S. Manufacturing: the Need for National Vision*. Washington, DC: National Academy Press.

Martin, T. (1990). The need for human skills in production: the case of CIM. *Computers in Industry*, **4**, 203–211.

Martin, T. (1993). Considering social effects in control-system design—a summary. In *Pre-prints of IFAC 12th World Congress*, Vol. 7 (pp. 325–330), Sydney, Australia, July 18–23.

Nakamura, N. & Salvendy, G. (1994). Human planner and scheduler. In G. Salvendy & W. Karwowski (Eds), *Design of Work and Development of Personnel in Advanced Manufacturing Systems* (pp. 331–354). New York: Wiley.

Office of Technology Assessment (OTA) (1984). *Computerized Manufacturing Automation: Employment, Education and the Workplace (OTA-CIT-235)*. Washington, DC: Office of Technology Assessment, US Government Printing Office.

Rasmussen, J. (1983). Skills, rules, and knowledge: signals, signs, and symbols; and other distinctions in human performance models. *IEEE Transactions on Systems, Man and Cybernetics*, *SMC* **13**(3), 257–266.

Reason, J. (1990). *Human Error*. Cambridge: Press Syndicate of the University of Cambridge.

Sanderson, P. M. (1989). The Human Planning and Scheduling Role in Advanced Manufacturing Systems (unpublished report). Urbana-Champaign, IL: Department of Mechanical and Industrial Engineering, University of Illinois.

Seppälä, P., Touminen, E. & Koskinen, P. (1992). Impact of flexible production philosophy and advanced manufacturing technology on organization and jobs. *International Journal of Human Factors in Manufacturing*, **2**, 172–192.

Sinclair, M. A. (1986). Ergonomics aspects of the automated factory. *Ergonomics*, **29**(12), 1507–1523.

Smith, M. J. & Carayon, P. (1995). New technology, automation, and work organization: stress problems and improved implementation strategies. *International Journal of Human Factors in Manufacturing*, **5**, 99–116.

Smith, M. J., Carayon, P., Sanders, K. J., Lim, S. Y. & LeGrande, D. (1992). Employee stress and health complaints in jobs with and without monitoring. *Applied Ergonomics*, **23**, 17–27.

Stalk, G. & Hout, T. M. (1990). *Competing Against Time*. New York: Free Press.

Storey, J. (1994). *New Wave Manufacturing Practices: Organizational and Human Resource Management Dimensions*. London: Paul Chapman.

Sun, H., & Riis, H. O. (1994). Organisational, technical, strategic, and managerial issues along the implementation process of advanced manufacturing technology—a general framework of implementation guide. *International Journal of Human Factors in Manufacturing*, **4**, 23–36.

Wall, T. D., Corbett, M., Clegg, C. W., Jackson, P. R. & Martin, R. (1990a). Advanced manufacturing technology and work design: towards a theoretical framework. *Journal of Organizational Behavior*, **11**, 201–219.

Wall, T. D., Corbett, J. M., Martin, R., Clegg, C. W. & Jackson, P. R. (1990b). Advanced manufacturing technology, work design and performance: a change study. *Journal of Applied Psychology*, **75**, 691–697.

Wall, T. D., Jackson, P. R. & Davids, K. (1992). Operator work design and robotics system performance: a serendipitous field study. *Journal of Applied Psychology*, **77**, 353–362.

Wall, T. D., Kemp, N. J., Jackson, P. R. & Clegg, C. W. (1986). Outcomes of autonomous work groups. *Academy of Management Journal*, **29**, 280–304.

Wall, T. D. & Martin, R. (1987). Job and work design. In C. L. Cooper & I. T. Robertson (Eds), *International Review of Industrial and Organizational Psychology*. Chichester: Wiley.

Warr, P. B. (1987). *Work, Unemployment and Mental Health*. Cambridge: Cambridge University Press.

Waterson, P. E., Clegg, C. W., Bolden, R., Pepper, K., Warr. P. B. & Wall, T. D. (1999). The use and effectiveness of modern manufacturing practices: a survey of UK industry. *International Journal of Production Research*, **37**, 2271–2292.

Wilson, J. R. (1991). Personal perspective: critical human factors contributions in modern manufacturing. *International Journal of Human Factors in Manufacturing*, **1**, 281–297.

Wilson, J. R., Koubek, R., Salvendy, G., Sharit, J. & Karwowski, W. (1994). Human factors in advanced manufacturing: a review and reappraisal. In W. Karwowski & G. Salvendy (Eds), *Organization and Management of Advanced Manufacturing* (pp. 379–415). New York: Wiley.

Wobbe, W. & Charles, T. (1994). Human roles in advanced manufacturing technology. In W. Karwowski & G. Salvendy (Eds), *Organization and Management of Advanced Manufacturing*. New York: Wiley.

CHAPTER 5

Supply-chain Partnering

Máire Kerrin
Institute for Employment Studies, Brighton, UK
and
Belén Icasati–Johanson
Institute of Work Psychology, University of Sheffield, UK

Over recent years, organisations have begun to recognise that there are strong competitive advantages and performance improvements to be gained from developing cooperative relationships with suppliers (Dyer & Ouchi, 1993; Lamming, 1993). Supply-chain partnering has therefore developed as an important trend in the context of new work practices and philosophies. It also has many links to other new working practices discussed in this section of the book, e.g. total quality management (TQM) (Chapter 3), lean manufacturing and just-in-time (JIT) (Chapter 4), and knowledge management (KM) (Chapter 8), which provide a wider context to the changes in the supply chain literature.

This chapter focuses the discussion of supply-chain partnering around the three central aims of the book. First, a review is presented of the nature and extent of supply-chain partnering. The aim is to provide a recent history of customer supplier relationships, so that the features of supply-chain partnering can be understood within a context of previous paradigms. The second aim is to explore the impact that supply-chain partnering has on the way people work and how they experience work. In particular, this section will focus on the impact and role of two psychological concepts and theories, that of trust and perspective taking. There are many concepts that could have been examined in relation to how people experience work within supply-chain partnering. However, these two were chosen as they illustrate one concept that has consistently been the focus of academic and practitioner analysis (trust), and a second that is suggested to play an important part in the future of supply-chain partnering (perspective taking).

The final part of the chapter will contemplate the implications for practice and the role of human resource management (HRM) in influencing supply-chain partnering. For example, which HRM practices might contribute to improving the experience of work within a partnership? This will be addressed generally and also in relation to the two concepts of trust and perspective taking. The chapter will also consider the design choices that are open to organisations when implementing and managing supply-chain partnering.

The New Workplace: A Guide to the Human Impact of Modern Working Practices.
Edited by David Holman, Toby D. Wall, Chris W. Clegg, Paul Sparrow and Ann Howard. © 2003 John Wiley & Sons, Ltd.

THEORETICAL APPROACHES TO CUSTOMER–SUPPLIER RELATIONSHIPS

The traditional view of customer–supplier transactions is one that is often based on the customer being passive while activity in the transaction comes from the supplier. The notion of a "relationship" between the customer and the supplier is one that has only come about in the last decade or so (Bessant, 1991; Farmer & Ploos von Amstel, 1991; Sako, 1992; Slack, 1991). The shift in focus has been away from the formal contract made between two organisations, towards a system that involves conducting multiple exchanges. This is now recognised or known as the "relationship" between two companies, and primarily recognises that buyers and sellers are both active in the transactions and hence take an *interactive* approach.

Theoretical approaches to customer–supplier relationships draw on many different academic subdisciplines, such as marketing, purchasing, economics and inter-organisational theory, to name a few. While the focus of this chapter is to explore how changes in customer–supplier relations may affect people's experience of work (through a psychological and human relations perspective), it is important to detail some of the key academic contributions to the relationship concept. For example, Williamson's (1975) transaction cost analysis (TCA) theory combines economic theory and management theory to determine the best type of relationship a firm should develop in the marketplace. The approach is based on minimising the sum of production and transaction costs by simplifying the interfaces between the stages, either by removing them completely (vertical integration) or by effectively cancelling them by creating perfectly competitive supply markets. Put another way, TCA considers how closely the purchasing organisation should become involved with its supplier. This was later developed into a model of "obligational contracting", where certain areas became the crucial factor in deciding upon how developed a relationship should be. Dore's (1987) contribution of "relational contracting" was based upon the concept of perceived and actual high levels of trust and moral trading in Japan.

Both Williamson's and Dore's concepts are brought together by Sako (1992), who constructed two ideal types of customer–supplier relationships, which are situated at either end of a continuum, and captured the complex variations in customer–supplier relationships. Any organisation can be placed on the continuum, based on the patterns of relationship with their supplier and regardless of nationality. The features of the continuum can be seen in Table 5.1 (Sako, 1992). At one extreme, organisations rely on arm's-length contract relations (ACR) if they want to retain control over their destiny. Independence is the motivating principle here, with the desire to be unaffected by the decisions of other companies. This type of company would disclose the minimum information about costings and future plans to existing and potential buyers and suppliers. The "arm's-length" nature of contracts enables the company to engage in hard commercial bargaining to obtain competitive prices. In this competitive relationship (ACR), both buyer and supplier attempt to get the best deals solely for themselves, potentially at the expense of the other party. The advantages are that the resultant insecurity ensures that suppliers are continually trying to improve their level of competitiveness, but the disadvantage is that the customer must monitor the supplier, as low trust exists. This can be carried out, for example, through heavy goods inwards inspection to ensure quality goods.

Table 5.1 Features of arm's-length contract relations (ACR) and obligational contract relations (OCR) (Sako, 1992)

	ACR←──────────── CONTINUUM ────────────→OCR

	ACR	OCR
Transactional dependence	**Customer** seeks to maintain low dependence by trading with a large number of competing suppliers within the limits permitted by need to keep down transaction costs. **Supplier** seeks to maintain low dependence by trading with a large number of customers within limits set by scale economies and transaction costs	For a **customer**, avoidance of dependence is not a high priority; it prefers to give security to few suppliers, although may still be dual or triple source for flexibility. For a **supplier**, avoidance of dependence is not a high priority, but it may well have several OCR customers
Ordering procedure	Bidding takes place; buyer does not know which supplier will win the contract before bidding. Prices negotiated and agreed before an order is commissioned	Bidding may or may not take place. With bidding, buyer has a good idea of which supplier gets the contract before bidding. Without bidding, there is a straight commission to the supplier. Prices are settled after decision about who gets contract
Projected length of trading	For the duration of the current contract. Short-term commitment by both buyer and supplier	Continued beyond the duration of the current contract. Mutual long-term commitment
Documents for exchange	Terms and conditions of contract are written, detailed and substantive	Contracts contain procedural rules, but substantive issues are decided case by case. Contracts may be oral rather than written
"Contractualism"	Contingencies are written out and followed strictly	Case-by-case resolution, with much appeal to the diffuse obligation of long-term relationships
"Contractual trust"	Supplier never starts production until written orders are received	Supplier often starts production on the basis of oral communication, before written orders are received
"Goodwill trust"	Multiple sourcing by supplier, combined with supplier's low transactional dependence	Sole sourcing by buyer, combined with supplier's transactional dependence
"Competence trust"	Thorough inspection on delivery; the principle of *caveat emptor* predominates	Little or no inspection on delivery for most parts (customer may be involved in establishing supplier's quality-control systems)
Technology transfer and training	Only the transfer, training and consultancy that can be costed and claimed for in the short run	Not always fully costed, as benefits are seen as partly intangible and/or reaped in the distant future
Communication channels and intensity	A narrow channel between the buyer's purchasing department and the supplier's sales department, with frequency kept to minimum necessary to conduct business	Extensive multiple channels, between engineers, quality assurance personnel, top managers, as well as between purchasing and sales managers. Frequent contact, often extending beyond the immediate business into socialising
Risk sharing	Little sharing of risk; how risk, resulting from price and demand fluctuations, is to be borne by each party is spelt out in explicit prior agreement	Much sharing of risk, in the sense that the relative share of unforeseen loss or gain is decided case by case, by applying some principle of fairness

Obligational contract relations (OCR) is at the other extreme of the continuum to ACR, in that it depends on high-trust cooperativeness, with a commitment to long-term trade. This commitment may include unusual requests and obligations not traditionally accepted, such as late unexpected orders. The benefits lie in good quality and service, growing or stable orders and other non-price aspects of trading (Sako, 1992). Cooperative relationships, often referred to as obligational or relational contracting, most evident in Japan, gives both parties a sense of obligation to assist one another and to protect the other's interests. It is characterised by a tightly integrated system of supply and assembly, with a minimum of waste in terms of inventories and inspection activities. In this relationship, the larger purchasing company places "trust" in its supplier's competencies only after a thorough investigation of these competencies and a lengthy probation period, and often only when financial leverage is gained through a direct stakeholding in the firm (Carr & Truesdale, 1992).

MODELS AND DEFINITIONS OF SUPPLY-CHAIN PARTNERING

Lamming's (1986, 1993) research on detailing the development of the customer–supplier relationship is a useful starting point in providing an understanding of how supply-chain partnering can take different forms. His research involved in-depth interviews in the UK, where he distinguished between three types of customer–supplier relationships. Lamming characterised these as the traditional model, the stress model and the resolved model. A fourth type was added, the partnership model, to incorporate existing best practice. The model is detailed in Table 5.2, with the key factors selected for analsing customer–supplier relationships, e.g. the nature of competition, basis of sourcing decisions, role of research and development (R&D). This original model was validated in a further 129 companies in 12 countries across four continents. As Lamming (1993) suggests, the resulting model could be said to "serve the functions of recording part of the transition from mass production to its successor (i.e. the decline of the old paradigm) and of indicating some characteristics of that successor (a new 'best practice' for customer–supplier relationships in the automotive components industry)" (p. 150).

The effective management of supply chains is said to be characterised by developing close, long-term working relationships with a limited number of supply chain partners. As is apparent in Table 5.2, mutually beneficial inter-organisational partnerships have to be developed in which information is freely shared, and where partners work together to attain common goals (Spekman, Kamauff & Myhr, 1998b). Supply-chain partnering occurs when organisations in the supply chain agree to work in a cooperative rather than an adversarial manner. Boddy *et al.* (1998) define partnering as " . . . a situation in which there is an attempt to build close long-term links between organisations in a supply chain that remain distinct, but which choose to work closely together" (p. 1004). Finally, Macbeth (1998) argues that partnering is an approach to business in which companies expect a long-term relationship, develop complementary capabilities, share more information and engage in more joint planning than is customary.

Table 5.2 illustrates the different types of customer–supplier relationships that had been developed up until the practice of supply-chain partnership in the 1990s. The purpose of this chapter is to focus on supply-chain partnering and the implications of this new way of working for employees within both the customer and supplier organisation.

Table 5.2 Models of customer–supplier relations (Lamming, 1993)

Model	Nature of competition	Basis of sourcing decision	Role of data/information exchange	Management of capacity	Delivery practice	Dealing with price changes	Attitude to quality	Role of R&D	Level of pressure
Traditional	Closed but friendly; plenty of business	Wide: enquiries; lowest bid; price-based	Very restricted—minimum necessary	Few problems: some poor scheduling	Large quantities; buyer's choice: steady	General negotiation (annual): a game (win/lose)	Inspection: arguments/laissez-faire	One-sided: either assembler or supplier	Low/medium: steady: predictable
Stress	Closed and deadly: chaotic	"Dutch Auctions": price-based	A weapon: one-way; supplier must open books	Spasmodic: no system to deal with chaos	Unstable; no control; variable; no notice of changes	Conflict in negotiation; a battle (lose/lose)	Aggressive campaigns	Shared, but only for cost reduction	High/unbearable; volatile
Resolved	Closed: some collaboration; strategic	Price, quality and delivery	Two-way: short-term, e.g. forward build	Gradually improving; linkages appearing	Smaller quantities; buyer's demands stabilizing	Annual economics plus; negotiation; (win/lose)	Joint effort towards improvements	Shared for developments	Medium: some sense of relief
Partnership	Collaboration; tiering; still dynamic	Performance history; long-term source; costs	Two-way: long-term, e.g. knowledge of costs	Coordinated and jointly planned	Small quantity; agreed basis; dynamic (JIT)	Annual economics, planned reductions (win/win?)	Joint planning for developments	Shared: some black or grey box	Very high: predictable

ADVANTAGES AND DISADVANTAGES OF SUPPLY-CHAIN PARTNERING

In today's business environment, the advantages of supply-chain partnering are becoming more evident, as conventional exchange relationships based on arm's-length transactions between independent suppliers and customers often do not allow for effective coordination of marketing activities (Anderson & Weitz, 1992). Moreover, companies that try to operate independently may be at a competitive disadvantage. This is due to the advantage in having networks of companies in supply-chain partnerships, in which more creative solutions are developed, adaptation to market changes is more speedy and services or products are brought to market in shorter periods of time (Currall & Judge, 1995). In light of this, relationships among firms are increasingly gaining importance for understanding competitive advantage at both the individual firm and network level (Dyer & Singh, 1998).

The benefits claimed for partnering are numerous, particularly when companies are operating in competitive and volatile environments and may focus multi-lateral efforts on improving areas of mutual concern, such as improved delivery, quality performance, customer service and technology sharing, as well as reduced administration costs, inventories and prices (Pagel, 1999). Furthermore, partnerships provide firms with access to new technologies, knowledge beyond the boundaries of the firm, and access to complementary skills (Mohr & Spekman, 1994). In addition, effective buyer–supplier partnerships help promote cross-functional activity within individual firms, which in turn stimulates cross-functional improvements between firms (Landeros, Reck & Plank, 1995). Indeed, because closer ties between exchange partners are usually long-term-orientated, they also help safeguard relationship-specific investments and facilitate adaptation to uncertainty (Heide & John, 1990). Sharing information during design may also support more rapid product innovation.

On the disadvantages of supply chain partnering, Cox (1998) argues that competitive advantage is more likely to come from securing direct control over strategic resources than from collaborative relationships with other suppliers. In terms of disadvantages to UK suppliers, Turnbull et al. (1993) suggest that many UK firms will struggle to meet the exacting standards required of preferred suppliers within supply-chain partnering, and that it will lead to fewer, more talented and larger suppliers that will survive. Despite all of the benefits, the problem of implementation is one which is seen as a major problem, and many partnerships fail because partners do not have processes in place to maintain the relationship.

The concerns regarding implementation make it even more crucial to examine those factors that promote success in a collaborative relationship (Boddy et al., 2000; Landeros, Reck & Plank, 1995). Case study evidence provides particular insights into how supply-chain partnering at Toyota (Langfield-Smith & Greenwood, 1998; Winfield & Kerrin, 1996) and Kodak (Ellram, Edis & Owen, 1996) was implemented successfully. These examples discuss the factors that enable an organisation to move from relationships characterised by strong buyer power and bargaining position to partnerships based on trust and cooperation. Langfield-Smith & Greenwood (1998) conclude that the factors that influence the development of a cooperative customer–supplier relationship include a consideration of similarities between the industries and technologies of the customer and supplier, prior experiences of change among suppliers, effective customer–supplier communication, and the importance of experiential learning in the acceptance of change.

In terms of uptake, early surveys into the practice in the UK of supply-chain partnering, as identified by Lamming (1993), include those reported by Oliver & Wilkinson (1992).

They found an increase in use from their 1987 data of JIT supplies and quality-assured supplies. They also reported that, "practices indicating close buyer–supplier relations—supplier involvement in design, supplier development activities and single sourcing—all show significant usage, with approximately two-thirds of companies using or planning to use each practice" (p. 191). More recently, Leverick & Cooper (1998) detailed the responses from 88 suppliers of their relationships with their customers. They found substantial levels of supplier–manufacturer partnering, based on measures of the duration and nature of the relationship, the involvement of the suppliers in design and product development, the price-setting process, the nature of supplier–manufacturer communication and the level of external awareness among suppliers. However, one survey of 100 companies that had attempted to introduce supply-chain partnering found that less than half of the respondents considered that their organisation had been successful in implementing the change (Boddy *et al.*, 1998). In a wider analysis of alliances, Spekman *et al.* (1998a) estimate that 60% of all alliances fail.

In summary, the model of customer–supplier relations (Table 5.2) illustrates that supply-chain partnering is different from previous forms of customer–supplier relationships, with different expectations of employees in both the customer and supplier organisation. Given this understanding of the shift in practices from the traditional model to supply-chain partnering, the next section will examine the impact of this new working practice on employees' work and experience of work.

IMPLICATIONS OF SUPPLY-CHAIN PARTNERING FOR EMPLOYEES' EXPERIENCE OF WORK

There are many areas where changes in the customer–supplier relationship could have an impact on the experience of work. Drawing on one of the theoretical models outlined earlier (Sako, 1992), moving away from ACR to OCR would have a major impact on the way work is carried out, particularly in areas of quality management and continuous improvement (Kerrin, in press), e.g. Table 5.1 illustrates differences in "communication channels" and "competence trust" from ACR to OCR. Both involve changes in working practices for both the customer and the supplier organisation. The recent changes in customer–supplier relationships also provide indications of changes in work practices (see Table 5.2), e.g. "management of capacity" under a partnership model is coordinated and jointly planned, while "attitude to quality" illustrates the move away from inspection towards joint planning for developments. Finally, the role of R&D involves the sharing of information for developments, requiring personnel from multiple levels within both organisations to change the way that they interact with each other.

The impact of supply-chain partnering may therefore include changes in work roles, trust, workload, innovation, perspective taking and knowledge sharing activities. For example, supply-chain partnering may increase or decrease workload, or mean that different tasks are required of employees within a supply-chain partnership. Increased workload and additional tasks may not necessarily be manual, but may relate to increasing need for communication and information to and from the suppliers, and also in increasing levels of information and communication within the organisation, e.g. in response to senior managers' requests for information on quality and costings.

Changes in workload due to demands from partnership relationships and changing job roles also affect knowledge sharing. While previous models of customer–supplier relationships encouraged individuals to retain knowledge regarding processes and products (in order to maintain a competitive edge), with supply-chain partnering knowledge sharing between organisations and individuals is vital. In the knowledge-sharing literature, there is a major debate regarding the nature of information, data and knowledge and how it is shared, and in the case of supply-chain partnering all these aspects are important. Typically, the introduction of an intranet by an organisation is predicated on an assumption by practitioners that knowledge can be codified. Roos & Von Krogh (1996) and Cook & Brown (1999) illustrate that this conception of knowledge is narrow and based on a particular epistemology. There have been criticisms in the ability of IT systems to facilitate knowledge sharing (e.g. Blackler, 1995; McDermott, 1999), which centres on the viewpoint that knowledge can never be effectively shared through a technology that involves a static repository, such as an intranet. It has been argued that as soon as the knowledge is expressed as a web page, for example, it becomes information (McDermott, 1999).

However, while information and data may be more easily transferred across organisations within the partnership (e.g. through websites, intranets and extranets), exchange of knowledge—in particular *tacit* knowledge—relating to products and processes is less straightforward (Blackler, 1995; Brown & Duguid, 1991; Cook & Brown, 1999; Lam, 1997; Lave & Wenger, 1991). Whilst there is not enough room here to discuss the issues involved in knowledge sharing, to make the most of partnerships organisations need to be able to harness this tacit knowledge so that it can be absorbed by both organisations. Questions such as how this is carried out, what resistance might there be, and what is the overall value of it, have an impact on planning HR policies and practice. The development of systems that suit both organisations in the partnership need to be developed if knowledge is to be shared at the individual, team and organizational level.

As can be seen from the examples of workload and knowledge sharing, it would be impossible to discuss the impact of supply-chain partnering on all of the issues raised above, so two areas have been selected for special analysis. The first is the impact and role of trust in supply-chain partnering. This concept has been chosen as it is often the most frequently cited issue within successful or unsuccessful partnering and yet is often poorly defined and understood in practice. The second concept is that of the role of perspective taking in supply-chain partnering. This is a concept that is less frequently discussed but it is proposed that it has potential to have a major impact on employees' experience of supply-chain partnering. Both concepts are of particular interest because of their inclusion in future developments in job and work design research and practice. For example, in a recent analysis of the future of work design research and practice, Parker, Wall & Cordery (2001), suggest that the parameters of work design, traditionally set within models such as Hackman & Oldham (1976), will be limited in explaining individuals' interactions with their workplace. In particular, they suggest an expanded model of work design which includes interpersonal trust and perspective taking as factors likely to be of importance, but yet to be considered within existing models. It is for these reasons that we now choose to concentrate on these emerging areas.

SUPPLY-CHAIN PARTNERING AND TRUST

So far, little attention has been paid to the processes needed to build and nurture effective partnerships. Given both the risks and costs associated with mismanaging a supply-chain partnership, it is crucial to explore the determinants of partnership success (Mohr & Spekman, 1994). Granovetter (1985) and Powell (1990) urge researchers to recognise the role that socially embedded personal relationships (such as those of suppliers and customers in a supply chain) play in economic exchange. In light of this, it follows that the customer–supplier relationship should be considered a key determinant of the success of the supply-chain partnership. The management and marketing literatures (e.g. Anderson & Narus, 1990; Dion, Easterling & Miller, 1995; Ganesan, 1994) have described trust as one of the key contributing factors to customer–supplier relationship success. Yet, despite the strength of the evidence linking trust to successful customer–supplier relationships and to organisational competitiveness, there is little universal agreement as to the actual definition of the trust construct. Thus, the section below will attempt to highlight the issues relating to trust as it is presently conceived in the literature.

What Is Trust?

Numerous authors (e.g. Gambetta, Ed, 1988; Powell, 1996; Williamson, 1993) have highlighted the elusiveness of the meaning of trust. A careful examination of the trust literature reveals a lack of clarity concerning the concept of trust, with probably as many definitions of the construct as there are studies examining it (e.g. Anderson & Weitz, 1989; Barney & Hansen, 1994; Crosby, Evans & Cowles, 1990; Currall & Judge, 1995; Hagen & Choe, 1998; Rotter, 1967, 1980; Schurr & Ozanne, 1985). Several authors have argued that to advance our understanding of the trust construct and usefully inform research and theory, the concept of trust requires clear contextual boundaries rather than a universal definition (Rousseau et al., 1998). They have thus called for an approach to the definition of trust that takes into account the context in which the construct is being studied, and is anchored in concrete problems (Bigley & Pearce, 1998; Rousseau et al., 1998).

The main benefit of a problem-centred focus on trust is that the construct can be limited to the context in which it is being examined. This is particularly important because, as noted by Bigley & Pearce (1998), when attempting to arrive at a universal conceptualisation of trust we run the "risk of producing constructions that are either too elaborate for theoretical purposes or relatively meaningless in the realm of empirical observation" (p. 408). Thus, the definition used here does not claim to be a universal definition of trust. Rather, it aims to define trust in a supply-chain partnering context, i.e. in the context of interpersonal relations across organisational firm boundaries in customer–supplier dyads.

Before trust in supply-chain partnering can be defined, however, there are a number of assumptions that must be made explicit (Hagen & Choe, 1998) because they relate to the many criticisms made in the past about previous attempts to define the construct.

Interpersonal Trust and Interorganisational Trust in Supply-chain Partnering

One of the key criticisms concerning the notion of trust in the inter-firm relations literature concerns the issue that ideas about inter-personal trust are transferred to inter-organisational matters (e.g. Blois, 1999). The key issue here is whether trust, which originates as an individual level construct, has meaning at the organisational level (e.g. Blois, 1999; Jensen & Meckling, 1976), e.g. some authors have suggested that "interorganisational and interpersonal trust are different, because the focal object differs" (Zaheer, McEvily & Perrone, in press, as cited in Rousseau et al., 1998).

For instance, Sako & Helper (1998) have argued that psychology's focus on interpersonal trust in the context of business organisations is "deficient". They argue that "while psychologists tend to study inter-personal trust, business firms are concerned just as much with inter-organisational trust. It is this latter construct that might survive a breakdown of interpersonal relationships due to labour turnover or personality clash, and which provides the stability necessary for firms to pursue innovative and competitive activities" (p. 389). Thus, they suggest that because of this, the determinants of interpersonal and inter-organisational trust may be different.

However, while interpersonal trust may be different from inter-organisational trust in that the focal object is different, it can be argued that interpersonal trust is one of the factors that comprises inter-firm trust. If a person in a boundary role does not trust their counterpart in the partner firm, this could ultimately influence the overall level of inter-organisational trust. For instance, if a buyer perceives his/her immediate contact at the supplier firm as untrustworthy, this may have detrimental influence upon how trustworthy that supplier's firm is. Moreover, Aulakh, Kotabe & Sahay (1996) highlight that trust can be extended to exchanges between organisations because "inter-organisational relationships are managed by individuals in each organisation" (p. 1008). So, in line with Rousseau *et al.* (1998), trust is seen here as a multilevel construct (individual, group and organisational), "integrating micro-level psychological processes and group dynamics with macro-level institutional arrangements" (p. 393). In other words, trust is "a psychological state composed of the psychological experiences of individuals, dyads and firms" (Rousseau *et al.*, 1998, p. 398). As such, interpersonal trust contributes to inter-organisational trust, which is key to the success of the supply-chain partnership (as argued below).

Multidimensional Nature of Trust

Past research has often approached the notion of trust as a unidimensional construct. Such an approach, however, fails to identify the various aspects that comprise the concept. Thus, as Blois (1999) has noted, "a person may completely trust another with regard to certain aspects of their behaviour" but "they may positively distrust them in other matters" (p. 200). In line with Blois' criticism, the stance taken here is that trust is a construct comprised of various aspects that can only be tapped into if both the definition of the concept, and the measures utilised, acknowledge this diversity. Thus, trust is here assumed to be a multidimensional construct, where trust or distrust in some aspect of the relationship does not preclude trust or distrust in other aspects of that relationship. Supply-chain partners, however, may not trust all aspects of a relationship (or indeed all of the members of the chain). Thus, distrust in some aspect of the relationship does not preclude trust in other aspects of that relationship.

Definition of Trust in Supply Chain Partnering

In light of the issues raised above, Icasati-Johanson, Clegg & Axtell (2000) conducted a study of trust in supply chains, and grounded their definitions and measures of trust on the views of relevant stakeholders. Thus, Icasati-Johanson *et al.*, (2000, p. 15) developed a definition-of-trust concept anchored in the context of supplier–buyer relationships in supply chains as:

> In an exchange relationship, under conditions of risk and interdependence, trust is the belief that a voluntarily accepted duty will prevail, ensuring that no party exploits the other's vulnerabilities.

Further, the authors noted that trust entails having optimistic expectations of positive future behaviour. Participants described a set of elements that made them trust their supply chain partners:

- An expectation that the partner will behave with *integrity*, i.e. be honest in their dealings with the partner and not take advantage or act in self-interest at the expense of the other party
- Confidence in the *competence*, dependability and reliability of the partner, i.e. a belief that a partner is capable of doing a good quality job, delivering on time and fulfilling requirements.
- An expectation the partner will be *fair* and act in a spirit of cooperation. This usually entails discussing and working through changes without imposing them, and not only taking but giving as well.
- A belief that a partner will be *loyal* and display benevolent motives towards the trustor. This involves behaving in a non-bullying manner, displaying a long-term orientation towards the relationship, and allowing partners time to react when faced with a threat to the relationship.
- An expectation of *frankness* and *openness*. This entails being straight with one another regarding issues relevant to the relationship, such as being open and direct about the fact that other market possibilities, e.g. competitors, might be approached.

Why Is Trust Important?

Numerous authors (e.g. Allison, 1999; Anderson & Weitz, 1989; Anderson & Narus, 1990; Dion, Easterling & Miller, 1995; Dwyer, Schurr & Oh, 1987; Mohr & Spekman, 1994) have highlighted the critical role of trust as a facilitator of interfirm relationships and as a key source of competitive advantage, e.g. the role of trust has been described as pivotal to the development of long-term customer–supplier relations (Dwyer *et al.*, 1987), the continuity of those relations (Anderson & Weitz, 1989; Aulakh *et al.*, 1996; Landeros *et al.*, 1995) and as one of the primary characteristics of successful trade relationships (Anderson & Narus, 1990; Corrigan, 1995; Dion *et al.*, 1995; Mohr & Spekman, 1994).

Relationships where there is greater trust can withstand greater stress and offer greater adaptability (Anderson & Weitz, 1989; Sullivan & Peterson, 1982). More specifically, trust in customer–supplier interaction influences satisfaction with profit (Mohr & Spekman, 1994), sales outcomes and performance (Dion & Banting, 1988; Dion *et al.*, 1995; Moore, 1998). In contrast, a lack of trust has been associated with partnering failure (Ellram, 1995). From this evidence it is clear that trust can facilitate interfirm relationships and act as a key source of competitive advantage to the supply chain.

How Trust Works

Trust contributes to the creation of a lasting bond and promotes cooperation in inter-organisational exchanges through a number of inter-related mechanisms (Aulakh *et al.*,

1996; Ganesan, 1994). First, trust in inter-firm exchanges reduces the perception of risk. Therefore, trust offers assurance that individual benefits will not be placed before the partnership goals, and that members of one firm will not knowingly distort information or otherwise subvert the other firm's members' interests (Crosby, Evans & Cowles, 1990). Second, trust acts as an important deterrent of opportunistic behaviour. Hill (1990, p. 51) has suggested that a trust-based approach to inter-organisational relationships reduces motivation to behave opportunistically (i.e. in a fashion that violates the cooperative spirit of agreements; Hagen & Choe, 1998), because "behavioural repertoires are biased toward cooperation rather than opportunism". Third, trust assures partners that short-term inequities, which are inevitable in any relationship, will be corrected in time, to yield a long-term benefit (Anderson & Weitz, 1989). And fourth, trust can facilitate inter-organisational relationships by lowering transaction costs in uncertain environments (Allison, 1999; Doney, Cannon & Mullen, 1998; Ganesan, 1994; Ring & Van de Ven, 1992).

This latter mechanism has been corroborated through a great deal of empirical evidence. For instance, Aulakh *et al.* (1996), found that trust was a substitute for hierarchical governance (i.e. where "formal authority structures based on ownership are used to enforce contractual obligations" p. 1009). Similarly, Gulati (1995) and Smith, Carroll & Ashford (1995) observed that trust served to replace legal relationships, like equity sharing, as a governance system (i.e. whereby partners are given formal control over each other). Moreover, Nooteboom, Berger & Noorderhaven (1997) observed that, by reducing the specification and monitoring of contracts, trust made transactions "cheaper, more agreeable and more flexible" (p. 311). Finally, McAllister (1995) found that trust was inversely and directly related to the need for monitoring, formal rules and administrative costs. This evidence lends support to the argument that trust promotes a spirit of cooperation (Smith *et al.*, 1995) that can "lower the costs of a transaction by reducing the extent of opportunism by one or more of the transacting parties, as well as the need to guard against opportunism by the other party" (Hagen & Choe, 1998, p. 589). Therefore, trust is complementary to economic factors in the governance of customer–supplier relationships in supply chains (Zaheer & Venkatraman, 1995).

How Does Trust Change People's Work Roles? Implications for Supply-chain Partnering

From the above discussion, it follows that the presence of trust in supply-chain relationships will almost inevitably lead to changes in people's work roles across the partnering organisations. The roles of boundary spanners (e.g. sales and commercial managers, buyers, account controllers, etc.) may change as awareness of the impact of inter-personal trust upon inter-organisational trust is increased (e.g. Rousseau *et al.*, 1998). Thus, people in such boundary positions may be required to actively promote and place their trust on those with whom they have perhaps had an adversarial relationship in the past, shifting the focus towards cooperation rather than opportunism. For this, however, organisations may need to use a broader range of measures to assess supply-chain partners' performance. This may in turn impact upon how one's own performance is measured, e.g. the traditionally adversarial role of the buyer, whose performance is often measured mostly in terms of lowest price obtained for purchases, may need to be reviewed to incorporate other important factors, such as reliability.

An approach to supply-chain partnering based on trust may assume a greater deal of flexibility in people's work roles and their attitude to formal contracts. Thus, employees may need to be prepared to go beyond what is stipulated in the contract (e.g. Sako, 1992). People may thus become more interdependent with partners and become less reliant on detailed written contracts. Moreover, an approach to supply-chain partnering based on trust requires that people collaborate more with their partners and take a more macro approach, whereby they take into account not only the needs of their own organisation but also the needs of the other organisations that make up the chain through to the consumer end, hence the need to see the world not only from one's own company's perspective, but also from the perspective of the other companies that make up the chain. That is, as a result of supply-chain partnering practices, a need arises for perspective taking. Just as trust in supplier–buyer relationships is crucial for inter-organisational relationship success (Anderson & Narus, 1990), so too is understanding others' points of view. Thus, before turning to discuss practical implications of how trust can be promoted in supply chains (e.g. through HR and design intervention), we will now examine the role that perspective taking in supply-chain partnering.

SUPPLY-CHAIN PARTNERING AND PERSPECTIVE TAKING

Mohrman & Cohen (1995) have argued that perspective taking will become more important given the changes in organisational structure towards a more lateral structure, where individuals no longer work within a "box". They suggest that the cognition of individuals within the emerging lateral organisational structures will be of central importance. In order to work with people across organisational interfaces and disciplines, "individuals will have to develop an understanding of ideas and frameworks different from their own" (Mohrman & Cohen, 1995, p. 381).

The activity of "perspective taking and making" has been argued to be key to organisational learning and knowledge sharing. In moving away from a focus on IT as an enabler to knowledge sharing, researchers have begun to examine other mechanisms that could facilitate knowledge sharing. For example, Boland & Tenkasi (1995) point out that, the problem of (the) integration of knowledge in knowledge-intensive firms is not a problem of simply combining, sharing or making data commonly available (*e.g. through some form of IT*). It is a problem of perspective taking in which the unique worlds of different communities of knowing are made visible and accessible to others" (p. 359).

As such, perspective taking is emerging as a concept that will have a major role to play in both employees' experience of work and managers' ability to select and develop individuals with perspective-taking abilities. Mohrman & Cohen (1995) conclude by stating that more "research is needed concerning how people working laterally can communicate across their perspectives and worldviews and learn from one another" (p. 381). In the current context of supply-chain partnering, it is important to understanding how perspective taking is operationalised at an individual level, what role might it play in the relationships within supply-chain partnering and what the implications for practice might be.

HOW IS PERSPECTIVE TAKING OPERATIONALISED AT AN INDIVIDUAL LEVEL?

Perspective taking at the individual level is not a new concept, as it has been shown to be a fundamental aspect of child development (Piaget & Inhelder, 1968). The concept of perspective taking has also been important in clinical situations, where it is often assumed that therapy can only be successful if the clinician empathises with the client (Duan & Hill, 1996). However, most of the discussion in the management literature on perspective taking and knowledge sharing has focused on the organisational or team level, e.g. the role of perspective taking is argued to be central to customer–supplier relations in order for organisational learning and knowledge-creation to occur in Japanese companies such as Hitachi (Lincoln, Ahmadjian & Mason, 1998). "Learning by taking the customer's role" enables one company to gain an intimate familiarity with one or more others. Imai, Nonaka & Takeuchi (1985) have documented learning in Fuji Xerox, where the learning process is one in which the firm "takes the role of the other", a core concept in symbolic interactionist social psychology (Stone, 1962). Within organizations, such role taking can be promoted by boundary-spanning activities, such as short-term visits, long-term transfers or stable interorganisational teams. In this way, it is interorganisational "learning by doing". The people of each firm immerse themselves in the routines of the other, thereby gaining access to the partner's stock of tacit knowledge. Learning takes place without the need to first convert tacit knowledge to explicit knowledge (Nonaka & Takeuchi, 1995).

Whilst this organisational level analysis is important to the perspective-taking process, there is a need to examine perspective taking at the level of the individual. As identified by Mohrman & Cohen (1995), there have been few studies of perspective taking in organisations, let alone in examining its impact on supply-chain partnerships.

Parker & Axtell (2001) suggest that perspective taking at the individual level is generally agreed to be a cognitive or intellectual process that results in the *affective response of empathy*. How people experience empathy depends on the level at which they cognise others. When people engage in active perspective taking they are more likely to empathise with the target, such as feeling concern at their misfortune (Betancourt, 1990; Davis, 1983), understanding or identifying with their experiences and experiencing pleasure at their achievements. Parker & Axtell (2001) argue that perspective taking is also a state that has other cognitive manifestations, such as changed attribution processes. This involves making positive attributions about another person's behaviour and outcomes, such as recognising the effects of external circumstances and acknowledging the role of internal factors such as hard work and ability when things go wrong. Often people explain the behaviour of others in more negative terms, e.g. different explanations are often given according to whether there is a positive or negative outcome. Individuals attribute their own success to internal factors (e.g. ability, hard work) and failure to external factors (e.g. task difficulty), whereas they tend to give situational explanations for others' success and dispositional explanations for others' failure. Evidence suggests that these biases are reduced when individuals take the perspective of the other (Galper, 1976; Regan & Totten, 1975).

WHAT IS THE ROLE OF PERSPECTIVE TAKING IN SUPPLY-CHAIN RELATIONSHIPS?

Although we have noted some positive organisational outcomes (e.g. increased interorganisational learning) from encouraging perspective taking between supply-chain partners (Lincoln *et al.*, 1998), this research was only based on a small number of case study organisations within Japan. One study, which has taken a more psychological approach, has tested a model of the antecedents and outcomes of supplier perspective taking at the individual level. The study, carried out by Parker & Axtell (2001), used a sample of front-line production employees within a UK-based manufacturing company. Whilst the study asked the participants to think about their "main internal supplier" (the team upstream in the process who provided materials or products for employees to work on), rather than an external supply partner, it offers some interesting findings to extrapolate to the wider supply chain.

In summary, Parker & Axtell (2001) tested a model of antecedents and outcomes of supplier perspective taking, using correlations and structural equation modelling. In terms of outcomes, they proposed that perspective taking would enhance interpersonal facilitation, or those cooperative and helping acts that support the work context. In particular, they argued that supplier perspective taking (measured by positive supplier attributions and supplier empathy) would be associated with cooperative and helping behaviours towards suppliers. They also examined the individual (experience of supplier job; production ownership; integrated understanding of the workplace) and job-related (interaction with supplier; job autonomy) antecedents that are directly or indirectly associated with perspective taking. In short, they found that supplier perspective taking was associated with team-leader ratings of employees' contextual performance. Production ownership and integrated understanding predicted supplier perspective taking, and these antecedents were in turn predicted by job autonomy. Supplier interaction contributed to supplier perspective taking directly and indirectly. Although it is only one study, it offers some support to the need to examine perspective taking as a key psychological process involved within the supply-chain relationship.

We have argued that trust and perspective taking are two important concepts within supply-chain partnering that influence the way in which employees experience work. While we have reviewed the research evidence for the impact of these concepts on employees work within this context, we now turn to examine what the implications will be for practice. What influence can human resource management practices have in supporting supply-chain partnering in general, and particularly in relation to the role of trust and perspective taking?

IMPLICATIONS FOR PRACTICE AND THE ROLE OF HUMAN RESOURCE MANAGEMENT (HRM)

Whilst we have outlined the possible impact of supply-chain partnering on employees' experience of work, it is important to consider the available mechanisms that could contribute to either improving the experience of work and/or ensuring the success of supply-chain partnering. Human resource management (HRM) policies and practices constitute one mechanism that has the potential to contribute to this area. However, although research into the mechanisms of supply-chain partnerships and alliances is beginning to be well documented, there is as yet little reference made to possible HRM implications (Partnership Sourcing, 1991; Williamson, 1985). This section will begin with a general discussion of the contribution of HRM within supply-chain partnerships, before assessing how it may impact on the issues that we have raised in relation to trust and perspective taking.

Research that has addressed the role of HRM has rightly identified that in moving towards supply-chain partnering, the management and workforce capabilities of the two organisations become paramount (Hunter, Beaumont & Sinclair, 1996). In particular, this includes each partners' ability to engage in joint development activity, to communicate effectively with each other, to participate in joint cross-functional teams and to share a common approach to problem identification and solution. These abilities highlight the contribution to the partnership of the HRM function, which for many is rarely considered. In other words, the underpinning of many of the systems that are central to supply-chain partnering depends on the capabilities, training and organisation of the human resources involved in the partnership.

Hunter *et al.* (1996) present evidence that suggests that in earlier stages of partnership development, the HRM function at the customer end is often only marginally involved. They recognise that the information gathered from the supplier is often technical in nature (e.g. quality, efficiency and productivity data) and is not concerned with matters such as employee commitment, work organisation or communication methods. Hunter *et al.* (1996) put forward two principal means by which HRM in the partner organisation can be influenced. First are the indirect effects, in which there are a number of ways that the HR department within the supplier can become involved. These might include developing training programmes in support of the business development objectives, or helping to clear away perceived industrial relations obstacles (e.g. negotiating collective agreements, permitting greater flexibility).

The second avenue that Hunter *et al.* (1996) identify is where HRM is considered as one of the major criteria for the development of a successful supply chain partnership. In this way, HRM policies and practices are central to the partnership and actually drive interventions, rather than being reactive to incompatibilities between the two organisations. Having outlined different avenues for general involvement for the HR function, we now return to the specific issues of trust and perspective taking within the supply-chain relationship and suggest areas where the HR function may contribute.

TRUST AND HRM POLICIES AND PRACTICES

It has been established that to manage supply-chain relationships better and to ensure success it is necessary to have dedicated resources to effectively manage the interface between customers and suppliers. HR practices can contribute to better aligning partners' expectations, goals and objectives. In the area of trust, there need to be measures that promote the development of trust. Although not intended as the only solution to the issues raised earlier, what follows is a set of practical recommendations that supply-chain partners may wish to consider as ways of addressing relationship problems and building trust.

Training and Development

Given the critical role that trust plays in the customer–supplier relationship, it is crucial that supply-chain partners take measures to ensure the development and/or maintenance of trust. Supply-chain partners could promote the development (or further enhance) the key characteristics of trust in their own relationships. For instance, induction programmes for newly appointed boundary role people (i.e. sales and purchasing directors and managers) could emphasise the importance of trust and its individual dimensions (e.g. integrity, competence, fairness, loyalty, and openness and frankness).

Reward Systems and Performance Measures

A way of encouraging the development of a trust approach would be, for example, the alignment of reward systems with a view to promoting close, trusting relationships. Thus, reward systems in the case of buyers should not only consider hard issues such as profit margins, but also soft aspects such as quality of the customer–supplier and inter-firm relationship. The absence of standardised or universal performance measures across the supply chain, however, is often a cause of problems arising. If supply-chain partners do not know what the goalposts are, or if these are confusing or ambiguous, the chances of effective performance across the supply chain are decreased. Thus, supply-chain partners should endeavour to identify and agree universally acceptable supply-chain performance measures. In light of the importance of trust, trust levels in the relationship should also be included as an important performance indicator. A simple tool designed to identify and measure levels of trust in interorganisational relationships may be the first step towards identifying and resolving issues that prevent trust from arising.

Communication and Information Sharing

Mohr & Spekman (1994) have suggested that to develop and maintain trust with other supply chain partners, communication both within and across organisations is crucial. Communication across different organisational functions and across organisational boundaries therefore needs to be tightly integrated, and new work roles may need to specifically and explicitly account for this. Regular review meetings, where partners voice their concerns about the relationship and update one another on order progress and business development, would ensure effective and frequent communication across businesses. Further, knowing what is going on in one's firm could impact upon the perception of competence of a particular firm (with competence being a key dimension in trust). In light of this, it is crucial that supply-chain partners evaluate their internal communication systems in an effort to identify existing areas of weakness. Moreover, such systems should ensure that clear and common objectives are agreed across departments prior to involving another member of the supply chain.

Collaboration and Commitment

The adoption of a long-term approach towards a relationship would help enhance its quality and trust levels. Indeed, relationships that were seen as difficult to substitute were described as the most trusting. In a relationship that is perceived as easily substitutable, a lower level of trust might develop. In contrast, an environment more conducive to the emergence of trust would be created by supply-chain partners approaching the relationship as one that is difficult to substitute.

Approaches to Conflict Resolution

In interorganisational relationships, such as those of a supplier and customer firm, disagreements often arise due to a conflict of interests. In such cases, buyers have traditionally resorted to threats of ending the commercial relationship if their wishes are not granted. This, however, is often described by suppliers as very harmful and counterproductive to the relationship (e.g. Icasati-Johanson et al., 2000). The use of more constructive approaches to conflict resolution should therefore be promoted. This could entail joint regular meetings where the relevant parties would raise, examine and discuss any issues and their proposed solutions.

PERSPECTIVE TAKING AND HRM POLICIES AND PRACTICES

Further studies are required in order to replicate the evidence from the above studies within the external supply chain. However, the potential implications for practice are considerable. For example, the evidence to date supports the idea that the extent to which employees see multiple viewpoints can be enhanced via organisational intervention, although Parker & Axtell (2001) do state that causality has not been firmly established. These authors suggest two ways to enhance supplier perspective taking and hence contextual performance (cooperative behaviours towards suppliers), first to increase employee interaction with suppliers and second to enrich job content. Both of these can be facilitated by HR interventions once the partnership is set up, or by taking the more direct avenue as detailed by Hunter *et al.* (1996) and designing them into the partnership agreement at the outset.

In terms of interaction, Parker & Axtell's findings suggest that the more contact employees have with their suppliers, the more likely they will be to make positive attributions about supplier behaviour and empathise with them. Regardless of the actual mechanisms involved in providing this outcome, there is major scope for HRM interventions in increasing interactions. Many of the interventions recommended to encourage perspective taking are complementary to those proposed for developing trust between supply-chain partners (e.g. training and development, collaboration and commitment, and communication). For example, training programmes or events (e.g. one-day workshops) could be devised to promote mutual understanding of the needs of customers and suppliers. Scenarios planning, a tool that helps people understand and evaluate existing ways of working and helps identify and evaluate alternative ways of working, could be used in this context. Supply-chain partners could set up a working group to explore how they currently work together and how they may work together in the future. Such an intervention would, for instance, help in promoting more interaction across companies in the chain. The perception that one member of the supply chain has different objectives to those of the remaining chain members is a source of tension that needs careful consideration. Steps therefore need to be taken to understand, and if possible align, the objectives of each member of the supply chain.

Understanding of the business of supply-chain partners can also be enhanced through the use of employee visits or exchange programmes and other events (such as meetings to discuss problems, etc.). Such collaborative programmes should be frequent enough for mutual understanding and empathy to develop. The use of cross-functional teams to work on problem-solving activities could also aid interaction and hence perspective taking. Finally, it is possible that recruitment and selection practices may also play a part in selecting individuals that have the ability to take the perspective of others. This is particularly relevant if you take a dispositional approach to empathy, which considers it as a relatively stable trait (Sawyer, 1975).

The emphasis on interaction as a facilitator to perspective taking is also relevant to the recent work in the area of knowledge sharing. Here, it is recognised that the appreciation of another's perspective (to contribute to the knowledge-sharing process) typically requires an extensive amount of social interaction and face-to-face communication (Kerrin & Currie, 2001; Lam, 1997; Leonard-Barton, 1995). It is suggested that it is this face-to-face interaction and interventions (rather than formal training courses outlining the supplier's role) that will be more successful in developing perspective taking.

Autonomy was an important predictor of employees' level of production ownership and associated with integrated understanding. Job redesign is therefore a potential perspective that can be aimed at perspective taking, in addition to traditional outcomes measures of job satisfaction and stress (Parker & Axtell, 2001). Again, the design of work tasks provides challenges for the HR function in the development of job descriptions, which allow autonomy in employees' work.

The proposals put forward here in relation to the role of the HR function provides support for many of the practices already existing in some organisations, in an attempt to encourage better customer–supplier integration through short-term visits or long-term transfers (Lincoln et al., 1998). However, what we have tried to argue here is that there is a specific role for HRM in developing trust and perspective taking within a supply-chain partnership. There are also choices for organisations to make in terms of the stages at which they involve the HR function. Given some of the interventions (e.g. training and development, job redesign), we would argue that the HR function needs to be involved directly, rather than indirectly and after the partnership has begun. This would allow the organisation to design in to the partnership key elements to provide support for perspective taking and the development of trust.

CONCLUSION

Supply-chain partnering and the mechanisms involved in its development are becoming increasingly better understood (Lamming, 1993; Sako, 1992). As a relatively new working practice, it is likely to have a significant impact on employees' experience of work in the future. This chapter has identified two areas, trust and perspective taking, where there are opportunities and choices for managers and work psychologists. It has assessed the contribution to this area by first identifying the impact of such concepts on the experience of work and second by examining practical implications for HRM. It is evident from the discussion of HR interventions that there are different design issues and different paths to follow in the structure of supply-chain partnerships that will have an impact on trust and perspective taking.

However, this chapter is not advocating a "best practice" route, which was prominent following the emergence of other new forms of working practices, such as lean production. The criticisms put forward by Lowe, Delbridge & Oliver (1997) of the "best practice" approach are recognised as relevant here. Their findings on adaptation of lean practices in the automotive components industry did not support the notion that one style of work organisation and human resource policy represents one best way. In the same way, the choices for organisations in supply-chain partnering in utilising the HR function needs to be context-specific (e.g. recognising the importance of specific organisational characteristics and choices for understanding performance). This is particularly true when dealing with issues such as trust and perspective taking. What this chapter has tried to do is to provide an indication of what is important to address within these concepts and which may then be assessed in terms of its relevance to certain contexts. Finally, given the emergence of the global organisation, contextual issues may be particularly important in considering international factors when choosing HR practices to support the development of trust and perspective taking within supply-chain partnering.

REFERENCES

Allison, D. (January 9, 1999). Making and Acting Upon Trustworthiness Assessments in Buyer–Supplier Relations. Unpublished manuscript, Center for Research on Social Organisation, University of Michigan.

Anderson, J. & Narus, J. (1990). A model of distribution firm and manufacturing firm working partnerships. *Journal of Marketing*, **54**(1), 42–59.

Anderson, E. & Weitz, B. (1989). Determinants of continuity in conventional industrial channel dyads. *Marketing Science*, **3**(4), 310–323.

Anderson, E. & Weitz, B. (1992). The use of pledges to build and sustain commitment in distribution channels. *Journal of Marketing Research*, **XXIX**(February), 18–34.

Aulakh, P. S., Kotabe, M. & Sahay, A. (1996). Trust and performance in cross-border marketing partnerships: a behavioural approach. *Journal of International Business Studies*, **27**(5), 1005–1032.

Barney, J. B. & Hansen, M. H. (1994). Trustworthiness as a source of competitive advantage. *Strategic Management Journal*, **15**: 175–190.

Bessant, J. R. (1991). *Managing Advanced Manufacturing Technology: the Challenge of the Fifth Wave*. Oxford: NCC Blackwell.

Betancourt, H. (1990). An attribution–empathy model of helping behavior: behavioral intentions and judgements of help giving. *Personality and Social Psychology Bulletin*, **16**: 573–591.

Bigley, G. A. & Pearce, J. L. (1998). Straining for shared meaning in organisation science: problems of trust and distrust. *Academy of Management Review*, **23**(3), 405–421.

Blackler, F. (1995). Knowledge, knowledge work and organisations: an overview and interpretation, *Organisation Studies*, **16**(6), 1021–1046.

Blois, K. J. (1999). Trust in business to business relationships: an evaluation of its status. *Journal of Management Studies*, **36**(2) (March), 197–215.

Boddy, D., Macbeth, D. K., Charles, M. & Fraser-Kraus, H. (1998). Success and failure in implementing partnering. *European Journal of Purchasing and Supply Management*, **4**, 143–151.

Boddy, D., Macbeth, D. K. & Wagner, B. (2000). Implementing collaboration between organizations: an empirical study of supply chain partnering. *Journal of Management Studies*, **37**(7), 1003–1017.

Boland, R. J. & Tenkasi, R. V. (1995). Perspective making and perspective taking in communities of knowing. *Organisation Science*, **6**(4) 350–363.

Brown, J. S. & Duguid, P. (1991). Organisational learning and communities of practice: toward a unified view of working, learning and innovation. *Organisation Science*, **2**(1) 40–57.

Carr, C. H. & Truesdale, T. A. (1992). Lessons from Nissan's British Suppliers. *International Journal of Operations and Production Management*, **12**(2), 49–57.

Cook, S. & Brown, J. (1999). Bridging epistemologies: the generative dance between organizational knowledge and organizational knowing. *Organization Science*, **10**(4), 381–400.

Corrigan, S. (1995). Determinants of Success in the Buyer/Supplier Relationship. Unpublished MSc Thesis, Institute of Work Psychology, University of Sheffield.

Cox, A. (1998). *Managing Business Relationships*. London: Earlsgate Press.

Crosby, L. A., Evans, K. R. & Cowles, D. (1990). Relationship quality in services selling: an interpersonal influence perspective. *Journal of Marketing*, **54**(July), 68–81.

Currall, S. C. & Judge, T. A. (1995). Measuring trust between organisational boundary role persons. *Organisational Behaviour and Human Decision Processes*, **64**(2, November), 151–170.

Davis, M. H. (1983). The effects of dispositional empathy on emotional reactions and helping: a multidimensional approach. *Journal of Personality*, **51**, 167–184.

Dion, P. A. & Banting, P. M. (1988). The purchasing agent, friend or foe to the salesperson. *Journal of Academy of Marketing Science*, **16**.

Dion, P., Easterling, D. & Miller, S. J. (1995). What is really necessary in successful buyer/seller relationships? *Industrial Marketing Management*, **24**, 1–9.

Doney, P. M., Cannon, J. P. & Mullen, M. R. (1998). Understanding the influence of national culture on the development of trust. *Academy of Management Review*, **23**(3), 601–620.

Dore, R. P. (1987). *Taking Japan Seriously*. Stanford, CT: Stanford University Press.

Duan, C. & Hill, C. E. (1996). The current state of empathy research. *Journal of Counselling Psychology*, **43**, 261–274.

Dwyer, R. F., Schurr, P. H. & Oh, S. (1987). Developing buyer–seller relationships. *Journal of Marketing*, **51**(April), 11–27.

Dyer, J. H. & Ouchi, W. G. (1993). Japanese style business partnerships: giving companies a competitive edge. *Sloan Management Review*, **35**(1), 51–63.

Dyer, J. H. & Singh, H. (1998). The relational view: cooperative strategy and sources of interorganizational competitive advantage. *Academy of Management Review*, **23**(4), 660–679.

Ellram, L. M. (1995). Partnering pitfalls and success factors. *International Journal of Purchasing and Materials Management*, **Spring**, 36–44.

Ellram, L., Edis, M. & Owen, R. V. (1996). A case study of successful partnering implementation. *International Journal of Purchasing and Materials Management*, **32**(4), 20–28.

Farmer, D. H. & Ploos von Amstel, R. (1991). *Effective Pipeline Management: How to Manage Integrated Logistics*. Aldershot: Gower.

Galper, R. E. (1976). Turning observers into actors: differential causal attributions as a function of "empathy". *Journal of Research in Personality*, **10**, 328–335.

Gambetta, D. G. (Ed.) (1988). *Trust: Making and Breaking Co-operative Relations*. New York: Basil Blackwell.

Ganesan, S. (1994). Determinants of long-term orientation in buyer–seller relationships. *Journal of Marketing*, **58**(April), 1–19.

Granovetter, M. (1985). Economic action and social structures: the problem of embeddedness. *American Journal of Sociology*, **91**(3), 481–510.

Gulati, R. (1995). Does familiarity breed trust? The implications of repeated ties for contractual choice in alliances. *Academy of Management Journal*, **38**(1), 85–112.

Hackman, J. R. & Oldham, G. (1976). Motivation through the design of work: test of a theory. *Organizational Behaviour and Human Performance*, **16**, 250–279.

Hagen, J. M. & Choe, S. (1998). Trust in Japanese interfirm relations: institutional sanctions matter. *Academy of Management Review*, **23**(3), 589–600.

Heide, J. B. & John, G. (1990). Alliances in industrial purchasing: the determinants of joint action in buyer–supplier relationships. *Journal of Marketing Research*, **XXVII**(February), 24–36.

Hill, C. W. L. (1990). Co-operation, opportunism, and the invisible hand: implications for transaction cost theory. *Academy of Management Review*, **15**(3), 500–513.

Hunter, L., Beaumont, P. & Sinclair, D. (1996). A "partnership" route to human resource management. *Journal of Management Studies*, **33**(2), 235–257.

Icasati-Johanson, B., Clegg, C. W. & Axtell, C. M. (2000). *The Role of Trust in Supplier–Buyer Relationships in Packaging Supply Chains. Feedback Report to Participating Companies*. Sheffield: ESRC Centre for Organization and Innovation. Institute of Work Psychology, University of Sheffield, April 2000.

Imai, K., Nonaka, I. & Takeuchi, H. (1985). Managing the new product development process: how Japanese companies learn and unlearn. In K. B. Clark, R. H. Hayes & C. Lorenz (Eds), *The Uneasy Alliance: Managing the Productivity–Technology Dilemma*. Boston, MA: Harvard Business School Press.

Jensen, M. C. & Meckling, W. M. (1976). Theory of the firm: managerial behaviour, agency costs, and ownership structure. *Journal of Financial Economics*, **3**, 305–360.

Kerrin, M. (in press). Continuous improvement along the supply chain: the impact of customer–supplier relations. *Integrated Manufacturing Systems*.

Kerrin, M. & Currie, G. (2001). Utilising HRM practices to mediate the impact of organizational structures and processes upon shared learning: case study evidence from a global pharmaceutical company. *Proceedings of the Managing Knowledge: Conversations and Critiques Conference*, University of Leicester Management Centre.

Lam, A. (1997). Embedded firms, embedded knowledge: problems in collaboration and knowledge transfer in global co-operative ventures. *Organization Studies*, **18**(6), 973–996.

Lamming, R. (1993). *Beyond Partnership: Strategies for Innovation and Lean Supply*. London: Prentice Hall.

Lamming, R. (1986). For better or for worse—impacts of technical change upon the UK automotive components sector. In C. Voss (Ed.), *Managing Advanced Manufacturing Technology*. Proceedings of the 1st UK Operations Management Association Conference. Bedford: IFS.

Landeros, R., Reck, R. & Plank, R. E. (1995). Maintaining buyer–supplier partnerships. *International Journal of Purchasing and Materials Management*, **Summer**, 3–11.

Langfield-Smith, K. & Greenwood, M. (1998). Developing co-operative buyer–supplier relationships: a case study of Toyota. *Journal of Management Studies*, **35**(3), 331–354.

Lave, J. & Wenger, E. (1991). *Situated Learning: Legitimate Peripheral Participation*. Cambridge: Cambridge University Press.

Leonard-Barton, D. (1995). *Wellsprings of Knowledge: Building and Sustaining the Sources of Innovation*. Boston, MA: Harvard Business School Press.

Leverick, F. & Cooper, R. (1998). Partnerships in the motor industry: opportunities and risks for suppliers. *Long Range Planning*, **31**(1), 72–81.

Lincoln, J. R, Ahmadjian, C. L. & Mason, E. (1998). Organizational learning and purchase–supply relations in Japan: Hitachi, Matsushita, and Toyota compared. *California Management Review*, **40**(3), 241–264.

Lowe, J. Delbridge, R. & Oliver, N. (1997). High-performance manufacturing: evidence from the automotive components industry. *Organization Studies*, **18**(5), 783–798.

Macbeth, D. K. (1998). Partnering—why not? *Proceedings of the 2nd Worldwide Symposium on Purchasing and Supply Chain Management* (pp. 351–362). Stamford, UK: Chartered Institute of Purchasing and Supply.

McAllister, D. J. (1995). Affect- and cognition-based trust as foundations for interpersonal co-operation in organisations. *Academy of Management Journal*, **38**(1), 24–59.

McDermott, R. (1999). Why IT inspired but cannot deliver knowledge management. *California Management Review*, **41**(4), 103–117.

Mohr, J. & Spekman, R. (1994). Characteristics of partnership success: partnership attributes, communication behavior and conflict resolution techniques. *Strategic Management Journal*, **15**, 135–152.

Mohrman, S. A. & Cohen, S. G. (1995). When people get out of the box: new relationships, new systems. In Mohrman, S. A. & Cohen, S. G. (Eds), *The Changing Nature of Work*. San Francisco, CA: Jossey-Bass.

Moore, K. R. (1998). Trust and relationship commitment in logistics alliances: a buyer perspective. *International Journal of Purchasing and Materials management*, **January**.

Nonaka, I. & Takeuchi (1995). *The Knowledge-creating Company: How Japanese Companies Create the Dynamics of Innovation*. New York: Oxford University Press.

Nooteboom, B., Berger, H. & Noorderhaven, N. G. (1997). Effects of trust and governance on relational risk. *Academy of Management Journal*, **40**, 308–338.

Oliver, N. & Wilkinson, B. (1992). *The Japanization of British Industry*. Oxford: Blackwell.

Pagel, D. (1999). Managing for optimal performance through effective coordination of the supply chain. *Production and Inventory Management Journal*, **40**(1), 66–70.

Parker, S., Wall, T. & Cordery, J. (2001). Future work design research and practice: towards an elaborated model of work design. *Journal of Occupational and Organizational Psychology*, **74**(4), 413–440.

Parker, S. & Axtell, C. (2001). Seeing another view point: antecedents and outcomes of employee perspective taking activity. *Academy of Management Journal*, **44**(6), 1085–1100.

Partnership Sourcing Ltd (1991). *Partnership Sourcing*. Reading: DTI/CBI.

Piaget, J. & Inhelder, B. (1968). *The Psychology of the Child*. New York: Basic Books.

Powell, W. W. (1990). Neither market nor hierarchy: network forms of organizations. *Research in Organizational Behavior*, **12**, 295–336.

Powell, W. W. (1996). Trust-based forms of governance. In R. M. Kramer & T. R. Tyler (Eds), *Trust in Organisations: Frontiers of Theory and Research* (pp. 51–67). Thousand Oaks, CA: Sage.

Regan, D. & Totten, J. (1975). Empathy and attribution: turning actors into observers. *Journal of Personality and Social Psychology*, **32**, 850–856.

Ring, P. S. & Van de Ven, A. H. (1992). Structuring co-operative relationships between organisations. *Strategic Management Journal*, **13**, 483–498.

Roos, J. & von Krogh, G. (1996). The epistemological challenge: managing knowledge and intellectual capital. *European Management Journal*, **14**(4), 333–337.

Rotter, J. B. (1967). A new scale for the measurement of interpersonal trust. *Journal of Personality*, **35**, 651–665.

Rotter, J. B. (1980). Interpersonal trust, trustworthiness, and gullibility. *American Psychologist* **35**(1), 1–7.

Rousseau, D. M., Sitkin, S. B., Burt, R. S. & Camerer, C. (1998). Not so different after all: a cross-discipline view of trust. Introduction to a special topic forum. *Academy of Management Review*, **23**(3), 393–404.

Sako, M. (1992). *Prices, Quality and Trust: Inter-firm Relations in Britain and Japan*. Cambridge: Cambridge University Press.

Sako, M. & Helper, S. (1998). Determinants of trust in supplier relations: evidence from the automotive industry in Japan and the United States. *Journal of Economic Behaviour & Organisation*, **34**, 387–417.

Sawyer, F. H. (1975). A conceptual analysis of empathy. *Annual of Psychoanalysis*, **3**, 37–47.

Schurr, P. H. & Ozanne, J. L. (1985). Influences on exchange processes: buyers' preconceptions of a seller's trustworthiness and bargaining toughness. *Journal of Consumer Research*, **11**, 939–953.

Slack, N. (1991). *The Manufacturing Advantage*. London: Mercury Business Books.

Smith, K. G., Carroll, S. J. & Ashford, S. J. (1995). Intra- and interorganizational co-operation: toward a research agenda. *Academy of Management Journal*, **38**(1), 7–23.

Spekman, R., Forbes, T., Isabella, L. & MacAvoy, T. (1998a). Alliance management: a view from the past and a look to the future. *Journal of Management Studies*, **35**(6), 747–772.

Spekman, R. E., Kamauff, J. W. Jr & Myhr, N. (1998b). An empirical investigation into supply chain management: a perspective on partnerships. *International Journal of Physical Distribution and Logistics Management*, **28**(8), 630–650.

Stone, G. P. (1962). Appearance and the self. In A. M. Rose (Ed.), *Human Behavior and Social Processes: an Interactionist Approach*. Boston, MA: Houghton Miffin.

Sullivan, J. & Peterson, R. B. (1982). Factors associated with trust in Japanese–American joint ventures. *Management International Review*, **22**: 30–40.

Turnbull, P., Delbridge, R., Oliver, N. & Wilkinson, B. (1993). Winners and losers—the 'tiering' of component suppliers in the UK automotive industry. *Journal of General Management*, **19**(1), 48–63.

Williamson, O. E. (1975). *Markets and Hierarchies*. New York: Free Press.

Williamson, O. E (1985). *The Economic Institutions of Capitalism*. New York: Free Press.

Williamson, O. E. (1993). Calculativenesss, trust, and economic organisation. *Journal of Law and Economics*, **36**, 453–486.

Winfield, I. J. & Kerrin M. (1996). Toyota motor manufacturing in Europe: lessons for management development. *Journal of Management Development*, **15**(4), 49–56.

Zaheer, A. & Venkatraman, N. (1995). Relational governance as an interorganizational strategy: an empirical test of the role of trust in economic exchange. *Strategic Management Journal*, **16**, 373–392.

CHAPTER 6

Team Work

John Cordery
*Department of Organizational and Labour Studies,
University of Western Australia, Perth, Australia*

The growth of interest in how groups or teams function in work settings has been nothing short of dramatic over recent decades (Ilgen, 1999; Katzell, 1994; Stewart, 2000). This reflects the fact that surveys of management practices around the globe have repeatedly shown that implementing teams is amongst the most popular initiatives aimed at improving organizational effectiveness (e.g. Clegg *et al.*, 2002; Godard, 2001; Gittleman, Horrigan & Joyce, 1998; Lawler, Mohrman & Ledford, 1995; Osterman, 2000). Why is the concept of team so popular in contemporary organizations? In this chapter, I seek to answer this question, and to describe how team working can be most effectively deployed to support the operation of modern work systems.

To understand the phenomenon, one first needs to understand what is meant by team working in a modern organizational context. The chapter thus begins by identifying the key parameters of team working, and looks at what it promises to deliver in terms of productivity and organizational effectiveness. This is followed by a review of evidence as to the actual effectiveness of team working in modern work settings, and by a discussion of contexts within which teams are more likely to be an effective work design option. This leads on to a discussion of elements of team structure and process that influence their effectiveness. Next, features of the broader management and organizational context that are needed to justify and support the use of teams are discussed. Finally, areas where our knowledge of how teams operate in real organizations is weak, along with promising avenues for further research, are identified.

THE ESSENCE OF TEAMS

If one were to identify the single most important prerequisite for describing an organisational unit as a team, it would have to be the degree to which members are truly reliant on each other's actions. This requisite reliance can take two forms (Wageman, 1995). First, there is task interdependence—the extent to which successful task performance of one team member is dependent on tasks performed by others in the team. In its simplest form, task interdependence arises where work flows sequentially from one team member to another;

The New Workplace: A Guide to the Human Impact of Modern Working Practices.
Edited by David Holman, Toby D. Wall, Chris W. Clegg, Paul Sparrow and Ann Howard. © 2003 John Wiley & Sons, Ltd.

for example, the driver of an ore truck on a minesite cannot begin the trip to the crusher until another member of his operating team has finished loading it. More complex work systems involve reciprocal forms of task interdependence, where work flows backwards and forwards between team members (as with treatment of patients by members of a primary healthcare team). A second form of reliance, outcome interdependence, refers to the extent to which team members are dependent on each other for significant outcomes or rewards. That is, members are collectively responsible for team outcomes. For example, even though task interdependence may be relatively weak, rewards to individuals within a customer service team may depend on levels of performance achieved by the team as a whole.

More than just a group of interdependent employees—after all, all organizational members are this to some degree—teams also involve an agreed collective purpose and boundaries protected by membership criteria. They are thus readily identifiable social entities that serve some legitimate organizational purpose, as well as providing a source of social identification for their members (Hogg & Terry, 2000). As a coherent social unit, they manage their interactions with others (e.g. customers, suppliers, other organizational teams) in ways that reflect their collective perspectives, interests and goals.

In summary, an organizational team may be defined as a:

> ... collection of individuals who are interdependent in their tasks, who share responsibility for outcomes, who see themselves and who are seen by others as an intact social entity embedded in one or more larger social systems (e.g. business unit or the corporation), and who manage their relationships across organizational boundaries (Cohen & Bailey, 1997, p. 242).

Of course, teams meeting the above definition can be found in many different parts of the organization, performing many different functions. For example, Cohen & Bailey (1997) offer a taxonomy of four main team types, differentiated by organizational level and function: work teams are relatively permanent groups found at the base of the operating core of the organization, and perform tasks associated with the organization's primary production or service functions, e.g. customer service team, process operator team. Parallel teams operate outside the formal authority structure, performing specific functions such as problem-solving, quality improvement and employee involvement, e.g. quality circles, process improvement teams. Project teams are temporary, and are formed for a specific time-delimited purpose, such as solving a particular problem or performing a one-off task, e.g. fighting a bushfire, designing a new building. With the increasingly rapid permeation of information technology into work organizations, there has been a rapid rise in the use of virtual project teams (Duarte & Tennant-Snyder, 2000; Majchrzak *et al.*, 2000), so-called because members are not co-located and may never meet face-to-face. Finally, management teams operate towards the strategic apex, coordinating and controlling key business processes across the organization.

THE POPULARITY OF TEAM-BASED WORK ORGANIZATION

As indicated earlier, the popularity of organizing work around teams is reflected in statistics regarding their useage. Lawler *et al.* (1995) reported that the percentage of leading US firms organizing work in their operating core around self-managing teams had risen from 28% in 1987 to 68% in 1993. At around the same time, Osterman (1994) also estimated that around

50% of US organizations were using teams, with around 40% of organizations having teams covering 50% or more of their employees. In Osterman's study, teams emerged as the single most popular work practice innovation, ahead of total quality management, job rotation and quality circles. In a follow-up study, it was also found that the use of teams had remained relatively constant over the 5 year period 1992–1997 (Osterman, 2000). More recently, in an international survey carried out 1996–1998, Clegg *et al.* (2002) have reported the use of team-based work in manufacturing organizations in the UK (35%), Japan (22%), Australia (45%) and Switzerland (50%) as significant, although at levels generally lower than in the USA.

What lies behind this level of uptake? Richard Guzzo has noted that perspectives on the importance and role of teamwork in organisations have changed over the years:

> In the 1960s teams were instruments of training and experience, thought to impart skills essential to effective management. In the 1970s teams became an antidote to worker alienation. In the 1980s teams were a solution to problems of quality and productivity that permitted foreign (especially Japanese) firms to surpass our own. And in the 1990s teams make for lean and flexible organizations (Guzzo, cited in Church, 1996).

Staw & Epstein (2000) have suggested that there is an element of fashion driving the popularity of teams. In a longitudinal study of 100 large US industrial corporations, they found no evidence to support the direct economic or efficiency benefits of management innovations such as teams. However, they did find reputational effects, namely that "companies were more admired, seen as being more innovative, and rated as having higher-quality management when they followed management trends such as quality, teams and empowerment". This, in turn, translated into higher levels of CEO remuneration.

However, Osterman (2000) argues that the rise in popularity of so-called high-performance work practices such as teams over the past two decades has occurred because they seemed to make possible benefits for both employees and employers. This idea of mutuality of benefits for organizations and employees alike stems from arguments that employees working as a team are likely to be more productive and satisfied than those working alone (Campion, Medsker & Higgs, 1993; Cohen & Ledford, 1994; Leavitt, 1975; Mohrman, Cohen & Mohrman, 1995). Three principal productivity-related advantages have been associated with team-based work structures (Pfeffer, 1998). First, the introduction of teams makes possible a shift in the nature of control processes from traditional hierarchical forms of control (e.g. through managerial supervision and direction) to more decentralized peer-based forms of control. This, in turn, leads to more direct and efficient control over performance, not simply because of the power of peer pressure to regulate individual employee behaviour (Barker, 1993) but also because key sources of performance variance may be controlled more rapidly (Cummings, 1978). When a problem arises, e.g. in relation to a production process or a customer service, the problem is more likely to be resolved quickly if a decision does not need to be referred to someone higher up in the organization. It has also been suggested that this peer-based control is associated with increased feelings of employee accountability for organizational outcomes, and that this "increased sense of responsibility stimulates more initiative and effort on the part of everyone involved" (Pfeffer, 1998, p. 75). This potential for decentralized team structures to enhance the motivational properties of work for their members has been a long-standing theme in the job design literature (e.g. Hackman, 1987; Hackman & Oldham, 1980) and also in the recent literature on psychological empowerment (e.g. Kirkman & Rosen, 2000).

The second main argument in favour of the productivity of teams relates to their potential to enhance the quality of work outcomes. For example, the range and depth of physical and cognitive resources (e.g. knowledge and skill, information-processing capacity) that can be brought to bear on a problem by the team as a whole may be considerably greater than any individual employee (including a manager or supervisor) possesses. Team working thus increases the probability of a solution to any given problem being found. Teams have also been credited with an increased likelihood of creative and innovative solutions, in the sense that synergistic outcomes may arise from the required interactions between individuals of diverse abilities, knowledge and backgrounds (Paulus, 2000).

Third, the introduction of teams has been linked to lowered operational costs associated with reductions in the levels of administrative and managerial support required. This arises as a result of improved coordination of interdependent tasks at the team level, but also because the devolution of authority and responsibility for outcomes that generally accompanies team formation means that many decisions once made by managers and supervisors are now made by team members themselves.

What about the benefits for employees themselves? Job design theory suggests that teams may offer increased scope for employees to satisfy higher-order needs and to obtain important intrinsic rewards through their work (Hackman, 1987). Psychologically significant job design characteristics, such as task autonomy and variety, can be enhanced at the team level as well as at the level of the individual job, e.g. being able to rotate between jobs within a team may increase the level of skill variety experienced by individuals. Similarly, levels of autonomy experienced by an individual can be enhanced when the team is given the responsibility to collectively manage its internal operations. Finally, teams also offer important opportunities for social interaction and also support for their members.

HOW EFFECTIVE ARE TEAMS IN PRACTICE?

Do teams actually live up to their billing as "high-performance" work systems? Is the promise of mutual benefits for employees and organizations actually realized? For some management commentators the answer is unequivocally in the affirmative, e.g. O'Reilly & Pfeffer (2000) propose that team-based people management systems are a feature of many organizations that are regarded as highly successful. They observe that:

> Even in those organizations where the work might lend itself to significant specialization... there is an emphasis on collective responsibility. This emphasis on teams as an organizing principle derives not from a current fad but from a belief in the fundamental importance of teams as a way of both getting the work done and of promoting autonomy and responsibility—of tapping the ideas and energy of everyone (p. 242).

Good empirical studies demonstrating the positive impact of teamwork on organizational and employee outcomes are relatively rare, although they do exist, e.g. Banker *et al.* (1996) reported on the impact of work teams on manufacturing performance, using a longitudinal study of employees in an electro-mechanical assembly plant. Over a period of just under 2 years, and controlling for inter-team differences resulting from differences in managerial policies (e.g. overtime, product diversity, capacity utilization), they found that the introduction of "high-performance work teams" had a significant impact on both quality and labour productivity. For example, they found that there had been a 38% reduction in defect rates from the beginning to the end of the post-implementation measurement period. They also found a 20% improvement in labour productivity, assessed as a ratio of the number of units produced to the number of hours worked, over the same period.

Batt (1999) studied self-managing teams in the customer service area of a large telecommunications firm. As in Banker et al.'s (1996) study, significant performance effects were associated with the teamwork intervention. With customer sales as the performance criterion, improvements of 10–17% were observed. Ironically, these performance gains were not regarded as sufficient by management, who abandoned the trial of teams soon after the study was completed.

Other studies, however, provide less convincing evidence of the benefits of teams to organizations and their employees. As previously indicated, Staw & Epstein (2000) could find no evidence of economic benefits associated with the implementation of teams at the organizational level, although their uptake did seem to be linked to enhancement of the firm's external reputation. Osterman (2000) has questioned the "mutual benefits" associated with introducing teams. For example, he found that the presence of teams in 1992 was positively associated with lay-offs in the same organization in subsequent years. He also found that the adoption of teams was associated with decreases in average real wages for core staff in subsequent years, and to the employment of fewer managers and fewer temporary or contract staff. Hackman's (1990) collection of 33 case studies of teams in organizations appears to contain as many instances of problematic as of successful teams, and considerable variability in research findings regarding the consequences of work teams for productivity, work attitudes and employee behaviour has been consistently noted by reviewers (e.g. Goodman, Devadas & Griffiths-Hughson, 1988; Guzzo & Dickson, 1996).

Why might teams fail to deliver in line with earlier predictions? Several possible explanations arise. First, aspects of the context may be unsuited to the introduction of teams. Second, the design of the team structures may be deficient in some way. Third, ineffective internal processes may develop within the teams themselves. Finally, teams may be poorly supported by other aspects of the organisational context. Each of these aspects are now discussed in greater detail.

CONTEXTS SUITABLE FOR TEAMS

In reviewing the evidence as to the effectiveness of teams, it should be remembered that teams form elements in larger organizational systems, interacting with other elements to influence effectiveness (Guzzo & Dickson, 1996). In addition, teams are frequently introduced along with other new work practices (Godard, 2001) and/or changes to other important influences on performance (e.g. selection and reward systems, new technology, quality management, etc.). However, it may be that there are some settings in which a team-based work design will be no more (or even less, because of potential process losses) effective than individual jobs, e.g. it seems logical to suggest that team-based work designs will only be more effective than individual job designs where (a) moderate levels of interdependence (task or goal) exist, and (b) employees have strong social needs. In some cases, it may be possible to create at least the perception of interdependence (e.g. by cross-training team members, or by providing performance feedback at the team level). However, in other cases, it may simply not be feasible (e.g. there is no natural interdependence at the level of the task or outcome, jobs are so specialized that cross-training is not possible, and team-level performance data is meaningless to team members). Similarly, giving self-management responsibilities to a team may have little effect on performance and member satisfaction where the predictability of the operating system (e.g. reliability of technology) is high, since the inherent requirement for exercising team decision-making discretion will also then be low. Each of these aspects is now discussed in more detail.

Technological Interdependence

The interdependence of tasks within a team may be seen as a fairly stable structural property of the technological system contained within the team boundaries (Thompson, 1967). This is not to say that this is the only source of task interdependence or that it is independent of managerial control (see later section on team design variables), but it is one that exerts considerable control over the way in which employees are required to interact and behave. For example, the process of refining alumina is a continuous unbuffered process, where employees performing tasks at various points in the process are directly and immediately affected by the actions of employees at other points in the sequence. To effectively perform their task of controlling the refinery operations, process operators must continually liaise over their actions. Wageman (1995) also points out that some tasks defined by the technical system may require very little interaction with others, whilst others are very interdependent, meaning that required interdependence may vary across time and tasks for the one team. In general, however, the higher the degree of task interdependence arising out of the technical system, the more likely it is that collaborative teams will offer performance advantages over employees performing alone.

Operational Uncertainty

Operational uncertainty may be defined as "a lack of knowledge about production requirements, of when problems will be met and how best to deal with them (Wall, Cordery & Clegg, 2002, p. 159). Whatever its source (it may, for example, arise as a result of interdependencies between team members), it manifests itself as variability and unpredictability in work tasks and requirements. It may be argued that the coordination and control benefits of team-based work identified earlier are likely to be most readily observed in such contexts, where the need for responsive control and coordination is intrinsically greater and the requirement for innovative decisions higher. A study by Cordery, Wright & Wall (1997) illustrates this. They investigated the effects of the introduction of self-managing work teams into a production environment concerned with the treatment of waste water prior to release into ocean and river systems. They found that where teams faced greater unpredictability associated with the process (e.g. as a consequence of using unstable biological processes to treat effluent, rather than stable mechanical processes), the reductions in the levels of pollutants in treated waste water were significantly greater. Teams in the high-uncertainty environments were able to make use of their autonomy and collective problem-solving power to effect greater improvements than those in low-uncertainty environments.

Cultural Values

It has been suggested that team-based work is likely to be less appropriate within certain cultures, specifically those where individualistic cultural values (Hofstede, 1980) predominate (Kirkman & Shapiro, 1997; Lemons, 1997; Tata, 2000). Clegg et al. (2002) found that significant cross-national differences existed in the perceived effectiveness of team-based work. It has also been found that people from countries where individualistic values predominate will tend to resist team working (Kirkman, Jones & Shapiro, 2000; Kirkman & Shapiro, 1997), and will be less influenced by group-focused training (Earley, 1994) than those from societies characterized by more collectivistic values. In a laboratory study of US and Hong Kong students, Gibson (1999) found that the impact of group efficacy (a team's belief in its capabilities) was related to features of the task (uncertainty and interdependence) and to cultural characteristics (collectivism). Where members of a team possessed low levels of collectivistic values and worked independently on uncertain tasks, no relationship was found between group efficacy and performance. Rather, the efficacy–performance relationship was maximized where collectivism and interdependence were high and task uncertainty was low.

DESIGNING A HIGH-PERFORMANCE TEAM

In general, and given a favourable context for their introduction, it is possible to identify three main variables associated with the creation of high-performing teams: team task characteristics, team composition and interdependence. These are usefully termed "team design variables", reflecting the fact that they can be engineered into the structural fabric of the team.

Team Task Characteristics

The motivational potential of the group task is the first major determinant of the level of effectiveness demonstrated by any given work team. Campion *et al.* (1993) examined the relationship between job design characteristics known to be influential in motivating task performance at the individual job level (Hackman & Oldham, 1976), particularly self-management (autonomy) and participation in decision making, and team effectiveness. Their study, which involved 80 financial services teams from the same organization, found that autonomy and self-management were amongst the most powerful predictors of team effectiveness, assessed in terms of productivity (in this case, unfinished work), employee job satisfaction, and managerial ratings of team effectiveness. Their findings are broadly consistent with other team-level research into factors that differentiate between effective and ineffective teams (Campion, Papper & Medsker, 1996; Hyatt & Ruddy, 1997). The concept of team empowerment (Kirkman & Rosen, 1999, 2000) views such task characteristics (along with group potency—see later discussion) as a powerful source of performance motivation for the team as a whole. Although there are inconsistencies in the observed strength of the autonomy–team performance relationship across studies (Cohen & Bailey, 1997; Godard, 2001; Guzzo & Dickson, 1996), as has already been observed, these most probably derive from differences in the level of operating uncertainty across different task environments. Where system variability and unpredictability is moderate to high, then it can reasonably be assumed that empowering task characteristics will be translated into increased motivation and performance by team members.

Team Composition

As would be expected, studies have demonstrated a positive relationship between team performance and constituent member abilities (Bottger & Yetton, 1987; Cohen *et al.*, 1996;

Hill, 1982; Tannenbaum, Salas & Cannon-Bowers, 1996). Researchers have also recently begun to identify a range of specific knowledge skills and abilities (KSAs) associated with effective team working (Druskat & Kayes, 1999; Stevens & Campion, 1994). Stevens & Campion (1994) proposed that effective teamwork requires five broad clusters of KSAs, namely conflict resolution, collaborative problem-solving, communication, goal setting and performance management, and planning & task coordination KSAs. Is it possible, then, to select people for effective teamworking? In a recent validation study, the same authors (Stevens & Campion, 1999) developed a pencil and paper test for identifying these KSAs. Combined results from two studies generated criterion-related validities for the test of between 0.32 and 0.40 for various aspects of team performance. Interestingly, the test correlated very highly with a battery of traditional employment aptitude tests, suggesting that the ability to work in teams is strongly related to general mental ability (g). Given the fact that teams are frequently implemented as responses to complex and uncertain task environments (Cummings & Blumberg, 1987), the finding that ability to operate effectively in teams is strongly linked to g (with its known relationship with the ability to deal with novel situations) comes as no real surprise (Barrick et al., 1998).

The personality of team members has also been linked to team effectiveness, within the framework of the "big five" model of personality (Barrick & Mount, 1991). The composition of a team in terms of average levels of agreeableness, conscientiousness, extraversion and emotional stability has been linked to predict team effectiveness in a number of recent studies (Barrick et al., 1998; Neuman & Wright, 1999). A more differentiated perspective on team personality composition has been provided by Neuman, Wagner & Christiansen (1999), who distinguish between the average level of a given personality trait within a group and the diversity of personality traits within a team. They studied teams of retail assistants, and found that the average levels of agreeableness, conscientiousness and openness to experience within a team was strongly predictive of team performance. However, heterogeneity of team personality traits was favoured when it came to predicting a positive relationship between extroversion and emotional stability and performance. In other words, too many extroverts or neurotics in a team will diminish effectiveness. What is striking about this study's findings is that, taken together, the indices of personality strength and personality diversity at the team level predicted nearly half the variance in team performance across the 82 work teams. As a well-known captain of a national sports team once put it, "seen from a distance, a successful team may look well organised and cohesive; get closer up and you see . . . the vigour and rivalries of a group of strong personalities" (Brearly, 2000, p. 1141). Reinforcing the importance of team personality composition, Neuman & Wright (1999) found that aggregate team-level agreeableness and conscientiousness predicted a range of team performance measures for human resource work teams, whilst agreeableness also predicted team interpersonal skills.

The size of a team is also a factor that has to be considered. Empirical research has failed to provide a clear-cut answer to the question of ideal team size, as a range of empirical findings attest (Cohen & Bailey, 1997). On the one hand, increasing the numbers of members in a team increases the range of resources available to the team. On the other, one might expect that group "process losses", such as arise from imperfect communication and conflict, would be magnified in large vs. small groups, leading to an inverted curvilinear relationship between size and performance (Steiner, 1972). Generally speaking, conventional wisdom suggests that the ideal team size depends on the nature of the task and the effectiveness of group processes (Wageman, 1997). Stewart's (2000) meta-analytic study reported that team size had a small negative influence on team member satisfaction and a small positive influence on team performance.

Another perspective on team composition considers the "fit" between the components of team membership. As Newman, Wagner & Christiansen's (1999) study of personalities within teams suggests, the degree of balance amongst elements of team composition may facilitate or constrain effectiveness. One of the most researched aspects of team composition relates to team heterogeneity/homogeneity. Guzzo & Dickson (1996) concluded that the relationship between team heterogeneity (in terms of the diversity of personalities, ability, gender, age, etc.) and effectiveness is "a complicated matter", with the relationship dependent on the particular focus of diversity, and with the potential interactions with other group composition variables, such as team size. Williams & O'Reilly (1998) have attempted to summarize the extensive research relating demographic diversity to group performance. Somewhat surprisingly, they concluded "that at the micro level, increased diversity typically has negative effects on the ability of the group to meet its members' needs and to function effectively over time" (p. 116). Interestingly, only functional diversity was found to be positively related to both performance and satisfaction across a range of studies.

Interdependence

As discussed earlier, task interdependence may be regarded as an inherent property of the task environment, requisite levels of which determine the need for teams in the first place. Some work processes may be regarded as inherently more interdependent than others, such that their effective control necessitates collective action. However, task interdependence can also be seen as a manipulable design feature of teams, something that arises from managerial decisions about how employees are grouped, from instructions given to employees about how to carry out their tasks, and which is reflected in the characteristic way people behave in performing their work (Wageman, 1995). For example, instead of grouping employees performing a single function together (e.g. packing, on an assembly line), teams may be formed around the complete set of functions required to manufacture a given product. Employees in a financial services team may be required to rotate through a number of positions within the team, and to check each other's work.

Other forms of interdependence can be "designed" into the team environment. Campion *et al.* (1993) refers to two such forms of interdependence as goal interdependence and interdependent feedback and rewards. Goal interdependence is the degree to which a team shares a clear engaging direction, a common sense of purpose (Wageman, 1997). As noted by Campion *et al.* (1993), the evidence relating group goals to effectiveness is less firm than it is at the individual level—nevertheless, studies do show that such a relationship exists (Hollensbe & Guthrie, 2000; O'Leary-Kelly, Martocchio & Frink, 1994; Sawyer *et al.*, 1999). Interdependence of feedback and rewards refers to the extent to which team members are dependent on each other for either (a) information on their own task performance or (b) receipt of rewards. Campion *et al.* (1993) found that interdependent feedback and rewards (also termed outcome interdependence) was significantly related to levels of employee job satisfaction within teams. Wageman's (1995) study of service technicians found that task and outcome interdependence each influenced different aspects of team effectiveness, with the former influencing cooperation amongst team members, whilst the latter influenced task motivation. Wageman's study helps confirm the primary role played by both task and outcome interdependence in determining teams effectiveness. She concluded that "The pivot, then, is how the work is structured... whenever cooperative behavior is critical to excellent task performance, it is most essential to create real task interdependence and then support the task design with interdependent rewards" (1995, p. 173).

EFFECTIVE WITHIN-TEAM PROCESSES

Interactions between team members have received a good deal of attention in the teams literature and studies have shown that intra-team processes (e.g. conflict, collaboration, communication, patterns of influence, decision-making, cohesiveness and potency) strongly influence both team performance and member satisfaction (Campion et al., 1993, 1996; Guzzo & Dickson, 1996; Stewart, 2000). However, it is important to recognise that it is not the presence or absence of processes such as conflict or communication in teams that determines team effectiveness. Cohesiveness (the level of interpersonal attraction and liking) in a group may facilitate performance (Mullen & Cooper, 1994), or it may lead to the development of dysfunctional outcomes, such as groupthink (Esser, 1998; Janis, 1982; McCauley, 1989), social loafing (Druskat & Wolff, 1999; Shepperd & Taylor, 1999), risky shift (Friedkin, 1999; Isenberg, 1986; Whyte, 1998) or encourage the development of inappropriate norms (Barker, 1993).

As a consequence, researchers have been urged to develop more fine-grained models of the sorts of process configurations associated with high levels of team performance and member satisfaction (Goodman, Ravlin & Schminke, 1987). A number of such prescriptions exist (e.g. Hackman, 1987; Katzenbach & Smith, 1993; Wageman, 1997). In this vein, Wright, Barker & Cordery (2000) contend that the ideal set of internal conditions to promote team effectiveness is approached when:

1. *Team members share responsibility and leadership, and are adaptable and flexible in task execution.* Campion et al.'s (1993) study found that participation in decision-making at the team level was consistently related to team effectiveness. Such participation is encouraged when leadership is decentralized and where it is allowed to emerge naturally, in the absence of formally assigned leadership roles. Recently, Taggar, Hackett & Saha (1999) found that teams performed best when leadership behaviours were exhibited by *all* team members, and that leadership emergence within a team was related to the general cognitive ability and personality characteristics of individual team members. Research by Cannon-Bowers et al. (1998) and Kirkman & Rosen (1999) confirms the value of flexible cross-skilling within teams. The ability of team members to communicate effectively, to empathize with others, and to respond to shifting task demands is likely to be enhanced where members of the team have a flexible orientation to who does what and when.
2. *The team as whole has clear goals and objectives and systems of control to maintain discipline in achieving those goals and objectives.* It flows from the earlier discussion of goal interdependence that teams who develop processes for setting clear and difficult collective goals for their performance are likely to expend more effort, persist longer in pursuit of that goal, and achieve higher levels of performance than groups without goals. However, it is also that case that teams need to develop internal processes to regulate behaviours in pursuit if those goals. Barker (1993, 1999) has observed that teams frequently develop powerful values-driven normative rules for behaviour within the team, designed

to ensure that all members work towards the common goal. Linked to goal-setting processes within teams is the development of collective efficacy beliefs. Collective or group efficacy refers to the aggregate belief of team members that their team can be effective in performing their overall job (Gibson, 1999; Lindsley, Brass & Thomas, 1995; Little & Madigan, 1997; Prussia & Kinicki, 1996). Sometimes this construct is referred to as group potency (Guzzo et al., 1993), and it is considered a core element in the psychological empowerment of teams (Kirkman & Rosen, 2000) Little & Madigan (1997) studied the performance of self-managing work teams in a manufacturing setting, and found that the strength of collective efficacy beliefs accounted for significant differences in performance between teams. Campion et al. (1993) found that potency was the strongest correlate of team effectiveness.

3. *The team has a sharing and supportive environment, promoting openness and trust.* One of the reasons why teams may be more effective is that their members develop an internal climate characterized by greater willingness to trust and support one another, along with a stronger sense of collective pride and commitment to the task (Wright et al., 2000). Interpersonal trust may be defined as a "willingness to be vulnerable to the actions of another party, based on the expectation that the other will perform a particular action important to the trustor, irrespective of the ability to monitor or control the other party" (Mayer, Davis & Schoorman, 1995, p. 712). Effectively, trust between team members amounts to an acceptance of the risk that comes with interdependence, the risk of others impacting negatively on one's work. Team members with a low level of trust in others (either as a result of earlier bad experiences, or because they have this predisposition) are likely to try to limit their dependence on other team members, resisting changes which might increase their reliance on other team members (Bigley & Pearce, 1998; Zand, 1972). Trust within teams is also related to team composition. For example, Mayer et al.'s (1995) model specifies a number of antecedents of trustworthiness, which include the benevolence, integrity and competence of the trustee, and the trustor's propensity to trust. The distinction between ability and both benevolence and integrity suggests that it is possible to like other team members, but not to be willing to put one's faith in their technical competence. Recent research on interpersonal trust in work teams has established that trust acts to moderate the influence of motivation on team performance, channelling motivational energy into productive group processes (Dirks, 1999). Trust has also been linked to spontaneous sociability (Fukuyama, 1995); "the myriad forms of cooperative, altruistic, and extra-role behavior in which members of a social community engage, that enhance collective well-being and further the attainment of collective goals" (Kramer, 1999, p. 583).

Related to the existence of trust in teams is the existence of positive environment characterized by openness among group members. Edmondson (1999) defined "team psychological safety" as the existence of "a shared belief that the team is safe for interpersonal risk taking" (p. 354). Similarly, West (1990) used the term "participative safety" to refer to an environment that is supportive of individuals and their contributions, such that group members feel able to participate fully in the team's affairs without fear of sanction or ridicule. West (1990) saw this particular aspect of group functioning as central to unlocking the potential of teams to generate creative and innovative solutions to problems. Edmondson's (1999) study of manufacturing teams suggests that cohesive teams that develop such shared beliefs are more likely to exhibit learning behaviours designed to improve team performance.

4. *There are systems in place to manage group knowledge, whether formal or informal.* A recent development in the study of intra-team processes has involved the study of how knowledge is accumulated, stored and accessed by teams as they perform their work. These systems for knowledge management, commonly called "team mental models", may relate to shared knowledge concerning the operation of technology and equipment, about the best way to approach a task, about team roles and responsibilities and characteristic ways of interacting, and about the personal attributes of team members (Mathieu *et al.*, 2000). Mathieu *et al.* (2000) used flight-combat simulations to demonstrate that as mental models regarding the task and other team members converged, team process improved, and so did performance. They concluded that the "knowledge organization— and the relationship among the ways various team members organize their own task knowledge—is a crucial concept" (p. 280). Recently, Stout *et al.* (1999) were able to demonstrate that pre-performance planning activities carried out by a team assisted the formation of shared mental models, which in turn led to more efficient communication and improved coordination during task performance. A related approach to describing knowledge structures in teams involves the study of transactive memory systems (Wegner, 1987). A transactive memory system (TMS) is defined as "a set of individual memory systems in combination with the communication that takes place between individuals" (Wegner, Guiliano & Hertal, 1985: 186). By means of a TMS, individuals supplement their own cognitive capacity by using other team members as units for storing knowledge. Studies carried out by Moreland and associates have indicated that the existence of TMS within work groups is associated with improved group performance (Liang, Moreland & Argote, 1995; Moreland, Argote & Krishnan, 1998; Moreland & Myakovsky, 2000).

5. *The team and its members have a proactive and innovative orientation.* The way a group frames its task is important in ensuring that team processes develop along constructive lines, e.g. Alper, Tjosvold & Law (1998) and Tjosvold & Tjosvold (1994) discuss the significance of constructive controversy, "the open-minded discussion of opposing positions" (Alper *et al.*, 1998, p. 36), to the development of group potency or efficacy, and thereby to team effectiveness. Thus, although too much intra-group conflict can hinder team effectiveness, conflict that is regulated through constructive norms relating to problem solving can give rise to beneficial outcomes. West (1996) has further proposed that the success of teams will be dependent on the extent to which they are "reflexive", i.e. they analyse and reflect on their objectives, processes, performance and environment and adapt their internal operations accordingly. According to West, Borrill & Unsworth (1998, p. 8), reflexive teams are likely to "have a more comprehensive and penetrating intellectual representation of their work; a longer time-frame; a larger inventory of environmental cues to which they respond; a better knowledge and anticipation of errors; and a more active orientation towards their work".

Finally, Kirkman & Rosen (1999) found that empowerment in teams was associated with members having a more proactive orientation to their work which, in turn, was strongly related to measures of performance effectiveness. Similarly, Wall *et al.* (2002) have suggested that empowerment practices (such as high-performance work teams) provide opportunities for both the improved application of knowledge and the development of new knowledge, alongside a more proactive employee orientation (Parker, Wall & Jackson, 1997) and improved work performance (Lawler, 1992).

A final point to note in relation to effective intra-team processes: it should be noted that some team process variables have strong relationships with some input variables, including team autonomy and individual characteristics (Stewart, 2000), indicating that it may be possible to some extent to enhance intra-team process by manipulating team design variables. For example, enhanced autonomy may encourage proactivity, potency and innovation. Similarly, the composition of the group (diversity) would also influence internal group functioning.

SUPPORTING HIGH-PERFORMANCE WORK TEAMS

Once operational, a number of key organizational supports appear necessary to maintain the operation of teams at a high level of effectiveness. Broadly speaking, these relate to the availability of requisite material resources, rewards, information, and training (Hackman, 1987; Hyatt & Ruddy, 1997). Major determinants of such supports are human resource management policies and practices within the firm, e.g. Kirkman & Rosen (1999) found that levels of team empowerment were positively related to the extent that the team was permitted to select new members, were rewarded as a team (rather than as individuals), were cross-trained to do different jobs, and evaluated the performance of their own team members. Campion et al. (1993) also found that access to training was significantly related to managerial judgements of a team's effectiveness. The importance of cross-training within teams, where members are trained to be able to take on the tasks, roles and responsibilities of their colleagues, has received particular attention from Cannon-Bowers et al. (1995, 1998). Cross-training may improve team functioning by facilitating the development of interpositional knowledge, which helps in coordination and communication within teams, particularly under conditions of high workload (Cannon-Bowers et al., 1998). Stevens & Campion's (1999) study suggests that the use of selection criteria that emphasise knowledge, skills and abilities relevant to working in teams will also help support team effectiveness. Druskat & Wolff (1999) found that developmentally-orientated peer appraisal processes, which could be expected to strengthen perceived effort–performance–outcome linkages at the team level, helped to reduce perceptions of social loafing within a team environment.

Most studies investigating the influence of these elements of organizational context on team performance have focused on the role of leaders as sources of support for effective team functioning. External team leaders (i.e. first-line supervisors, managers) can influence team effectiveness in a number of ways. First, they act as agents through which the human resource policies and practices discussed above are operationalized at the team level; for example, one supervisor might allow team members more opportunities to attend cross-training sessions than another. Second, they have the potential to act as gatekeepers, controlling the flow of informational and material resources to the work team. Leader–member exchange theory (Graen & Uhl-Bien, 1995) suggests that leaders classify subordinates as ingroup or outgroup members, and favour ingroup members when it comes to the administration of rewards (e.g. praise and recognition). Third, external team leaders ration discretion, or team autonomy. Thus, different teams may be permitted different levels of discretion by the one supervisor, or the level of direct control over team-level decisions exerted by a supervisor may vary across time (e.g. depending on production pressure). It has been pointed out that the propensity of a supervisor to allow discretion at the team level may well be related reflect that manager's characteristic leadership style (Cordery & Wall, 1985). The propensity for external leader intervention to reduce the key design element autonomy at the team level has led some to suggest that teams perform best without formal leadership (e.g. Beekun, 1989).

Fourth, the style of leader may be related to key intra-group processes, such as the development of a sense of potency. In this light, Manz & Sims (1987) identified six features of effective leadership of self-managing work teams, namely to encourage the following amongst team members: self-observation/self-evaluation; self-goal setting; self-reinforcement; self-criticism; self-expectation; and self-rehearsal Cohen, Chang & Ledford (1997) used the Self-Management Leadership Questionnaire (SMLQ) developed by Manz & Sims (1987) and were able to empirically confirm their model. Interestingly, they found only modest relationships between self-managing leader behaviours and both employee quality of work life indicators and self-rated team effectiveness. More worrying is the finding of Spreitzer, Cohen & Ledford (1999) that those teams whose leaders were perceived by team members as doing most to encourage self-management (assessed in terms of Manz & Sims' dimensions) were rated as performing worst by senior managers.

A reason for the apparently contradictory findings is provided by Wageman (1997). She has argued that the primary responsibility of a team leader is to see that the team is designed right, with a clear sense of why it exists and what it is trying to achieve, and with access to organisational supports (e.g. information, resources, etc.). Once that has occurred (and only then, she argues), the conditions are right for the leader to focus on coaching the team. Positive coaching behaviours include helping the team deal with interpersonal problems, providing feedback and reinforcement related to how effectively the team is managing its own activities, and facilitating problem-solving. Possibly because of the proposed contingency relationship with team design factors, research into the effectiveness of team coaching behaviours has produced mixed results. Thus, Druskat & Kayes (1999) found that external leadership behaviours that provided "clear and engaging direction" for the team were associated with the development of team self-management competencies; however, those that focused on more direct "coaching" of team performance were negatively associated with performance.

In another indication of the important role played by external team leadership in developing and maintaining effective teams, Stewart & Manz (1997) have suggested that teams frequently fail because supervisors resist their implementation and empowerment. They use the theory of reasoned action (Fishbein & Ajzen, 1975) to demonstrate that supervisory attitudes (e.g. empowering teams will reduce my job security; employees will take advantage of increased discretion to slack off; employees are not capable of effective self-management) and subjective norms (e.g. other supervisors do not support team empowerment) may act to impede effective team development by supervisors.

THE FUTURE FOR TEAMS

In this chapter, I have outlined the factors both within and outside teams that contribute to their internal effectiveness, and which make them a popular intervention with managers seeking to maximize the performance of work systems. The evidence suggests that, even though they sometimes fail (Hackman, 1990), they can be made to work well under the right conditions and with appropriate organizational support.

There appear to be no reasons to suggest that the existing popularity of teams in organizations will decline in future. However, as we begin the current millennium, it appears that the focus and purpose of teams is shifting once more. The combined influence of e-commerce and globalization is shifting the focus of teamwork away from physically co-located, fairly permanent work teams towards an emphasis on far more transient team structures, where interdependence is mediated via information technology, and where functioning work teams cross organizational and even national boundaries (Cascio, 2000; Duarte & Tennant-Snyder, 2000). We are also seeing transformations in the nature of work in many countries, whereby service and knowledge work is on the increase relative to manufacturing (Parker, Wall & Cordery, 2001). Developing and maintaining effective intra-team processes in teams whose membership is distributed and whose work processes are largely cognitive, centring on the development and transformation of knowledge, poses a particular challenge for managers.

There are also challenges for future research. Perhaps the most pressing is the need to develop more precise and dynamic models of how teams function. Our current input–process–output models of team effectiveness (e.g. Cohen & Bailey, 1997; Hackman, 1987; Sundstrom *et al.*, 1990) say little about the mechanisms used by teams to transform inputs into outcomes. For example, much of the previous research into team effectiveness has been framed around motivational explanations of team performance (e.g. job characteristics and empowerment theories). Yet, we also know that cognitive processes may explain some of the same transformations. Increasing team autonomy may improve collective motivation, but it may also enable learning and knowledge-based action in furtherance of improved task performance (Parker *et al.*, 2001). Interdependence may make more likely the development of transactive memory systems, leading to efficiencies in the storage and retrieval of performance-relevant knowledge. Furthermore, whilst we have a fair idea which processes are influential in team effectiveness, we still know surprisingly little about their significance, both at varying stages in task performance and for different dimensions of effectiveness (Weldon, 2000). In this respect, Marks, Mathieu & Zaccaro's (2001) conceptual model of how intra-team processes may vary over time would seem to provide a fruitful starting point for advancing our knowledge.

A second area of pressing need for research has to do with how teams perform in different contexts, particularly across different types of work. For example, some research has suggested that teams are less common (or are designed differently) in service organizations compared to manufacturing (Osterman, 1994). It is not very clear why this might be. One reason that has been suggested lies in the nature of the service task, particularly where the product is "co-produced" by employee and customer and workloads and flows are customer-driven (Hunter, 1998). Given the growth in service sector jobs over recent decades, this issue needs further investigation. Furthermore, Cohen & Bailey (1997) clearly demonstrated the value of distinguishing between teams with different strategic purposes when it comes to understanding effective team design, yet the value of having generic vs. context-specific models of team effectiveness is little understood. Finally, the issue of how effective design and processes differ between traditional physically co-acting teams and distributed computer-mediated teams must be addressed as these forms of teamwork become more common.

REFERENCES

Alper, S., Tjosvold, D. & Law, K. (1998). Interdependence and controversy in group decision making: antecedents to effective self-managing teams. *Organizational Behavior and Human Decision Processes*, **74**, 33–52.

Banker, R. D., Field, J. M., Schroeder, R. G. & Sinha, K. K. (1996). Impact of work teams on manufacturing performance: a longitudinal field study. *Academy of Management Journal*, **39**, 867–890.

Barker, J. R. (1993). Tightening the iron cage: concertive control in self-managing teams. *Administrative Science Quarterly*, **38**, 408–437.

Barker, J. R. (1999). *The Discipline of Teamwork: Participation and Concertive Control*. Newbury Park, CA: Sage.

Barrick, M. R. & Mount, M. K. (1991). The Big Five personality dimensions and job performance: a meta-analysis. *Personnel Psychology*, **44**, 1–26.

Barrick, M. R., Stewart, G. L., Neubert, M. J. & Mount, M. K. (1998). Relating member ability and personality to work-team processes and team effectiveness. *Journal of Applied Psychology*, **83**, 377–391.

Batt, R. (1999). Work organization, technology and performance in customer service and sales. *Industrial and Labor Relations Review*, **52**, 539–564.

Beekun, R. I. (1989). Assessing the effectiveness of sociotechnical interventions: antidote or fad? *Human Relations*, **47**, 877–897.

Bigley, G. A. & Pearce, J. L. (1998). Straining for shared meaning in organization science: problems of trust and distrust. *Academy of Management Review*, **23**, 405–421.

Bottger, P. C. & Yetton, P. W. (1987). Improving group performance by training in individual problem solving. *Journal of Applied Psychology*, **72**, 651–657.

Brearly, M. (2000). Teams: lessons from the world of sport. *British Medical Journal*, **321**, 1141–1143.

Campion, M. A., Medsker, G. J. & Higgs, A. C. (1993). Relations between work group characteristics and effectiveness: implications for designing effective work groups. *Personnel Psychology*, **46**, 823–850.

Campion, M. A., Papper, E. M. & Medsker, G. J. (1996). Relations between work team characteristics and effectiveness: a replication and extension. *Personnel Psychology*, **49**, 429–452.

Cannon-Bowers, J. A., Tannenbaum, S. I., Salas, E. & Volpe, C. E. (1995). Defining team competencies and establishing team training requirements. In R. A. Guzzo & E. Salas (Eds), *Team Effectiveness and Decision Making in Organizations* (pp. 333–380). San Francisco, CA: Jossey-Bass.

Cannon-Bowers, J. A., Salas, E., Blickensderfer, E. & Bowers, C. A. (1998). The impact of cross-training and workload on team functioning: a replication and extension of initial findings. *Human Factors*, **40**, 92.

Cascio, W. F. (2000). Managing a virtual workplace. *Academy of Management Executive*, **13**, 81–90.

Church, A. H. (1996). From both sides now: the power of teamwork—fact or fiction? *Industrial Psychologist*, **October**.

Clegg, C. W., Wall, T. D., Pepper, K., Stride, C., Woods, D., Morrison, D., Cordery, J., Couchman, P., Badham, R., Kuenzler, C., Grote, G., Ide, W., Takahashi, M. & Kogi, K. (2002). An international survey of the use and effectiveness of modern manufacturing practices. *Human Factors and Ergonomics in Manufacturing*, **12**(2), 171–191.

Cohen, S. G. & Bailey, D. E. (1997). What makes teams work: group effectiveness research from the shop floor to the executive suite. *Journal of Management*, **23**, 239–290.

Cohen, S. G. & Ledford, G. E. (1994). The effectiveness of self-managing teams: a quasi-experiment. *Human Relations*, **47**, 13–43.

Cohen, S. G., Ledford, G. E. & Spreitzer, G. M. (1996). A predictive model of self-managing work team effectiveness. *Human Relations*, **49**, 643–676.

Cohen, S. G., Chang, L. & Ledford, G. E. Jr (1997). A hierarchical construct of self-management leadership and its relationship to quality of work life and perceived group effectiveness. *Personnel Psychology*, **50**, 275–308.

Cordery, J. L. & Wall, T. D. (1985). Work design and supervisory practice: a model. *Human Relations*, **38**, 425–441.

Cordery, J. L., Wright, B. & Wall, T. D. (1997). Towards a more comprehensive and integrated approach to work design: production uncertainty and self-managing work-team performance. Paper presented at 12th Annual Conference of the Society for Industrial and Organisational Psychology, St. Louis, MO, April.

Cummings, T. G. (1978). Self-regulating work groups: a socio-technical synthesis. *Academy of Management Review*, **3**, 624–634.

Cummings, T. G. & Blumberg, M. (1987). Advanced manufacturing technology and work design. In T. D. Wall, C. W. Clegg & N. J. Kemp (Eds), *The Human Side of Advanced Manufacturing Technology* (pp. 37–60). New York: Wiley.

Dirks, K. T. (1999). The effects of interpersonal trust on work group performance. *Journal of Applied Psychology*, **84**, 445–455.

Druskat, V. U. & Kayes, D. C. (1999). The antecedents of team competence: toward a fine-grained model of self-managing team effectiveness. In M. A. Neale & E. A. Mannix (Series Eds) & R. Wageman (Vol. Ed.). Research on managing groups and teams: Context (Volume 2, pp. 201–231). Stanford, CT: JAI Press.

Druskat, V. U. & Wolff, S. B. (1999). Effects of timing and developmental peer appraisals in self-managing work groups. *Journal of Applied Psychology*, **84**, 58–74.

Duarte, D. L. & Tennant-Snyder, N. (2000). *Mastering Virtual Teams: Strategies, Tools, and Techniques that Succeed.* San Francisco, CA: Jossey Bass.

Earley, P. C. (1994). Self or group? Cultural effects of training on self efficacy and performance. *Administrative Science Quarterly*, **39**, 89–117.

Edmondson, A. (1999). Psychological safety and learning behavior in work teams. *Administrative Science Quarterly*, **44**, 350–383.

Esser, J. K. (1998). Alive and well after 25 years: a review of groupthink research. *Organizational Behavior and Human Decision Processes*, **73**, 116–141.

Fishbein, M. & Ajzen, I. (1975). *Belief, Attitude, Intention and Behavior: an Introduction to Theory and Research.* Reading, MA: Addison-Wesley.

Friedkin, N. E. (1999). Choice shift and group polarization. *American Sociological Review*, **64**, 856–875.

Fukuyama, F. (1995). *Trust: the Social Virtues and the Creation of Prosperity.* New York: Free Press.

Gibson, C. B. (1999). Do they do what they believe they can? Group efficacy and group effectiveness across tasks and cultures. *Academy of Management Journal*, **42**, 138–152.

Gittleman, M., Horrigan, M. & Joyce, M. (1998). 'Flexible' work practices: evidence from a nationally representative survey. *Industrial and Labor Relations Review*, **52**, 99–115.

Godard, J. (2001). High performance and the transformation of work? The implications of alternative work practices for the experience and outcomes of work. *Industrial and Labor Relations Review*, **54**, 776–805.

Goodman, P. S., Devadas, R. & Griffiths-Hughson, T. L. (1988). Groups and productivity: analyzing the effectiveness of self-managing teams. In J. P. Campbell & R. J. C. & Associates (Eds), *Productivity in Organisations* (pp. 295–327). San Francisco, CA: Jossey-Bass.

Goodman, P. S., Ravlin, E. & Schminke, M. (1987). Understanding groups in organizations. In B. M. Staw & L. L. Cummings (Eds), *Research in Organizational Behavior*, Vol. 9 (pp. 121–173). Greenwich, CT: JAI Press.

Graen G. B. & Uhl-Bien M. (1995). Development of leader–member exchange (LMX) theory of leadership over 25 years: applying a multi-level multi-domain perspective. *Leadership Quarterly*, **6**, 219–247.

Guzzo, R. A., Yost, P. R., Campbell, R. J. & Shea, G. P. (1993). Potency in groups: articulating a construct. *British Journal of Social Psychology*, **32**, 87–106.

Guzzo, R. A. & Dickson, M. W. (1996). Teams in organizations: recent research on performance and effectiveness. *Annual Review of Psychology*, **47**, 307–338.

Hackman, J. R. (1987). The design of effective work teams. In J. W. Lorsch (Ed.), *Handbook of Organizational Behavior* (pp. 316–341). Englewood Cliffs, NJ: Prentice-Hall.

Hackman, J. R. (Ed.) (1990). *Groups that Work (and Those that Don't).* San Francisco, CA: Jossey-Bass.

Hackman, J. R. & Oldham, G. R. (1976). Motivation through the design of work: test of a theory. *Organisational Behavior and Human Performance*, **15**, 250–279.

Hackman, J. R. & Oldham, G. R. (1980). *Work Redesign.* Reading, MA: Addison-Wesley.

Hill, G. W. (1982). Group vs. individual performance: are $n + 1$ heads better than one? *Psychological Bulletin*, **91**, 517–539.

Hofstede, G. (1980). *Culture's Consequences: International Differences in Work-related Values*. Newbury Park, CA: Sage.

Hogg, M. A. & Terry, D. J. (2000). Social identity and self-categorization processes in organizational contexts. *Academy of Management Review*, 25, 121–140.

Hollensbe, E. C. & Guthrie, J. P. (2000). Group pay-for-performance plans: the role of spontaneous goal setting. *Academy of Management Review*, 25, 864–872.

Hunter, L. W. (1998). Services, high-involvement management, and strategic fit. Paper presented at 1988 meeting of the Academy of Management, San Diego, CA.

Hyatt, D. & Ruddy, T. M. (1997). An examination of the relationship between work group characteristics and performance: once more unto the breach. *Personnel Psychology*, 50: 553–585.

Ilgen, D. (1999). Teams embedded in organizations: some implications. *American Psychologist*, 54, 129–139.

Isenberg, D. J. (1986). Group polarization: a critical review and meta-analysis. *Journal of Personality and Social Psychology*, 50, 1141–1151.

Janis, I. L. (1982). Groupthink: a study of foreign policy decisions and fiascos (2nd Edn). Boston, MA: Houghton Mifflin.

Katzell, R. A. (1994). Contemporary meta-trends in industrial and organizational psychology. In H. C. Triandis, M. D. Dunnette & L. M. Hough (Eds), *Handbook of Industrial and Organizational Psychology*, Vol. 4 (pp. 1–93). Palo Alto, CA: Consulting Psychologists Press.

Katzenbach, J. R. & Smith, D. K. (1993). *The Wisdom of Teams: Creating the High Performance Organization*. Boston, MA: Harvard Business School Press.

Kirkman, B. L., Jones, R. G. & Shapiro, D. L. (2000). Why do employees resist teams? Examining the "resistance barrier" to work team effectiveness. *International Journal of Conflict Management*, 11, 74–92.

Kirkman, B. L. & Shapiro, D. L. (1997). The impact of cultural values on employee resistance to teams: toward a model of self-managing work team effectiveness. *Academy of Management Review*, 22, 730–737.

Kirkman, B. L. & Shapiro, D. L. (2000). Understanding why team members won't share: an examination of factors related to employee receptivity to team-based rewards. *Small Group Research*, 31, 175–209.

Kirkman, B. L. & Rosen, B. 1999. Beyond self-management: antecedents and consequences of team empowerment. *Academy of Management Journal*, 42, 58–75.

Kirkman, B. L. & Rosen, B. (2000). Powering up teams. *Organizational Dynamics*, 28, 48–66.

Kramer, R. M. (1999). Trust and distrust in organizations: emerging perspectives, enduring questions. *Annual Review of Psychology*, 50, 569–588.

Lawler, E. E. III (1992). *The Ultimate Advantage: Creating the High Involvement Organisation*. San Francisco, CA: Jossey-Bass.

Lawler, E. E. III, Mohrman, S. A. & Ledford, G. E. (1995). *Employee Involvement and Total Quality Management: Practices and Results in Fortune 1000 Companies*. San Francisco, CA: Jossey-Bass.

Leavitt, H. J. (1975). Suppose we took groups seriously . . . In E. L. Cass & F. G. Zimmer (Eds), *Man, Work and Society*. New York: Van Nostrand Reinhold.

Lemons, M. A. (1997). Work groups or work teams? Cultural and psychological dimensions for their formation. In M. M. Beyerlein, D. A. Johnson & S. T. Beyerlein (Eds), *Advances in Interdisciplinary Studies of Work Teams*, Vol. 4 (pp. 97–113), Greenwich, CT: JAI Press.

Liang, D. W., Moreland, R. L. & Argote, L. (1995). Group vs. individual training and group performance: the mediating role of transactive memory. *Personality and Social Psychology Bulletin*, 21, 384–393.

Lindsley, D. H., Brass, D. J. & Thomas, J. B. (1995). Efficacy-performance spirals: a multilevel perspective. *Academy of Management Review*, 20, 645–678.

Little, B. L. & Madigan, R. M. (1997). The relationship between collective efficacy and performance in manufacturing work teams. *Small Group Research*, 28, 517–534.

McCauley, C. (1989). The nature of social influence in groupthink: compliance and internalization. *Journal of Personality and Social Psychology*, 57, 250–260.

Majchrzak, A., Rice, R. E., Kink, N., Malhotra, A. & Ba, S. (2000). Computer-mediated interorganizational knowledge-sharing: insights from a virtual team innovating using a collaborative tool. *Information Resources Management Journal*, 13, 44.

Manz, C. C. & Sims, H. P. Jr (1987). Leading workers to lead themselves: the external leadership of self-managing work teams. *Administrative Science Quarterly*, **32**, 106–128.

Marks, M. A., Mathieu, J. E. & Zaccaro, S. J. (2001). A temporally based framework and taxonomy of team processes. *Academy of Management Review*, **26**, 356–376.

Mathieu, J. E., Heffner, T. S., Goodwin, G. F., Salas, E. & Cannon-Bowers, J. A. (2000). The influence of shared mental models on team process and performance. *Journal of Applied Psychology*, **85**, 284–293.

Mayer, R. C., Davis, J. H. & Schoorman, F. D. (1995). An integrative model of organizational trust. *Academy of Management Review*, **20**(3), 709–734.

Mohrman, S. A., Cohen, S. G. & Mohrman, A. M. (1995). *Designing Team-based Organizations*. San Francisco, CA: Jossey-Bass.

Moreland, R. L., Argote, L. & Krishnan, R. (1998). Training people to work in groups. In R. S. Tindale, J. Edwards & E. J. Posvac (Eds), *Theory and Research on Small Groups*. New York: Plenum.

Moreland, R. L. & Myaskovsky, L. (2000). Exploring the performance benefits of group training: transactive memory or improved communication? *Organizational Behavior and Human Decision Processes*, **82**, 117–133.

Mullen, B. & Cooper, C. (1994). The relation between group cohesiveness and performance: an integration. *Psychological Bulletin*, **115**, 210–227.

Neuman, G. A., Wagner, S. H. & Christiansen, N. D. (1999). The relationship between work-team personality composition and the job performance of teams. *Group and Organization Management*, **24**, 28–45.

Neuman, G. A. & Wright, J. (1999). Team effectiveness: beyond skills and cognitive ability. *Journal of Applied Psychology*, **84**, 376–389.

O'Leary-Kelly, A. M., Martocchio, J. J. & Frink, D. D. (1994). A review of the influence of group goals on group performance. *Academy of Management Review*, **37**, 1285–1302.

O'Reilly, C. A. & Pfeffer, J. (2000). *Hidden Value: How Great Companies Achieve Extraordinary Results with Ordinary People*. Boston, MA: Harvard Business School Press.

Osterman, P. (1994). How common is workplace transformation and who adopts it? *Industrial and Labor Relations Review*, **47**, 173–188.

Osterman, P. (2000). Work reorganization in an era of restructuring: trends in diffusion and effects on employee welfare. *Industrial and Labor Relations Review*, **53**, 179–196.

Parker, S. & Wall, T. D. (1998). *Job and Work Design*. Thousand Oaks, CA: Sage.

Parker, S. K., Wall, T. D. & Jackson, P. R. (1997). "That's not my job": developing flexible employee work orientations. *Academy of Management Journal*, **40**, 899–929.

Parker, S. K., Wall, T. D. & Cordery, J. L. (2001). Future work design research and practice: an elaborated work characteristics model. *Journal of Occupational and Organizational Psychology*, **73**, 414–440.

Paulus, P. (2000). Groups, teams, and creativity: the creative potential of idea-generating groups. *Applied Psychology: an International Review*, **49**, 237–262.

Pfeffer, J. (1998). *The Human Equation*. Boston, MA: Harvard Business School Press.

Prussia, G. E. & Kinicki, A. J. (1996). A motivational investigation of group effectiveness using social cognitive theory. *Journal of Applied Psychology*, **78**, 61–72.

Sawyer, J. E., Latham, W. R., Pritchard, R. D. & Bennett, W. R. (1999). Analysis of work group productivity in an applied setting: application of a time series panel design. *Personnel Psychology*, **52**, 927–967.

Shepperd, J. A. & Taylor, K. M. (1999). Social loafing and expectancy-value theory. *Personality and Social Psychology Bulletin*, **25**, 1147–1158.

Spreitzer, G. M., Cohen, S. G. & Ledford, G. E. (1999). Developing effective self-managing work teams in service organizations. *Group and Organizational Management*, **24**, 340–366.

Staw, B. M. & Epstein, L. D. (2000). What bandwagons bring: effects of popular management techniques on corporate performance, reputation and CEO pay. *Administrative Science Quarterly*, **45**, 523–556.

Steiner, I. D. (1972). *Group Process and Productivity*. New York: Academic Press.

Stevens, M. J. & Campion, M. A. (1994). The knowledge, skill, and ability requirements for teamwork: implications for human resource management. *Journal of Management*, **20**, 503–530.

Stevens, M. J. & Campion, M. A. (1999). Staffing work teams: development and validation of a selection test for teamwork settings. *Journal of Management*, **25**, 207–228.

Stewart, G. L. (2000). Meta-analysis of work teams research published between 1977 and 1998. Paper presented at 2000 Academy of Management Conference, Organizational Behavior Division, Toronto.

Stewart, G. L. & Manz, C. C. (1997). Understanding and overcoming supervisor resistance during the transition to employee empowerment. In W. A. Pasmore & R. W. Woodman (Eds), *Research in Organizational Change and Development*, Vol. 10 (pp. 169–196). Greenwich, CT: JAI Press.

Stout, R. J., Cannon-Bowers, J. A., Salas, E. & Milanovich, D. M. (1999). Planning, shared mental models, and coordinated performance: an empirical link is established. *Human Factors*, **41**, 61.

Sundstrom, E., DeMeuse, K. P. & Futrell, D. (1990). Workteams: applications and effectiveness. *American Psychologist*, **45**, 120–133.

Taggar, S., Hackett, R. & Saha, S. (1999). Leadership emergence in autonomous work teams: antecedents and outcomes. *Personnel Psychology*, **52**, 899–926.

Tannenbaum, S. I., Salas, E. & Cannon-Bowers, J. A. (1996). Promoting team effectiveness. In M. A. West (Ed.), *Handbook of Work Group Psychology* (pp. 503–529). Chichester: Wiley.

Tata, J. (2000). The influence of national culture on work team autonomy. *International Journal of Management*, **17**, 266–271.

Thompson, J. D. (1967). *Organizations in Action*. New York: McGraw-Hill.

Tjosvold, D. & Tjosvld, M. M. (1994). Cooperation, competition, and constructive controversy: knowledge to empower self-managing teams. In M. M. Beyerlein & D. A. Johnson (Eds), *Advances in Interdisciplinary Studies of Work Teams*, Vol. 1 (pp. 119–144). Greenwich, CT: JAI Press.

Wall, T. D., Cordery, J. L. & Clegg, C. W. (2002). Empowerment, performance and operational uncertainty: a theoretical integration. *Applied Psychology: An International Review*, **51**, 146–169.

Wageman, R. (1995). Interdependence and group effectiveness. *Administrative Science Quarterly*, **40**, 145–180.

Wageman, R. (1997). Critical success factors for creating superb self-managing teams. *Organizational Dynamics*, **26**, 37–49.

Wegner, D. M. (1987). Transactive memory: a contemporary analysis of the grown mind. In B. Mullin & G. R. Goethals (Eds), *Theories of Group Behavior* (pp. 185–208). New York: Springer-Verlag.

Wegner, D. M., Giuliano, T. & Hertel, P. (1985). Cognitive interdependence in close relationships. In W. J. Ickes (Ed.), *Compatible and Incompatible Relationships* (pp. 253–276). New York: Springer-Verlag.

Weldon, E. (2000). The development of product and process improvements in work groups. *Group and Organizational Management*, **25**, 244–268.

West, M. A. (1990). The social psychology of innovation in groups. In M. A. West & J. L. Farr (Eds), *Innovation and Creativity at Work* (pp. 309–333). Chichester: Wiley.

West, M. A. (1996). Reflexivity and work group effectiveness: a conceptual integration. In M. A. West (Ed.), *Handbook of Work Group Psychology* (pp. 555–579). Chichester: Wiley.

West, M. A., Borrill, C. S. & Unsworth, K. L. (1998). Team effectiveness in organizations. In C. L. Cooper & I. T. Robertson (Eds), *International Review of Industrial and Organizational Psychology*, Vol. 13 (pp. 1–48). Chichester: Wiley.

Whyte, G. (1998). Recasting Janis's groupthink model: the key role of collective efficacy in decision fiascoes. *Organizational Behavior and Human Decision Processes*, **2**, 185–209.

Williams, K. Y. & O'Reilly, C. A. (1998). Demography and diversity in organizations. *Research in Organizational Behavior*, **20**, 77–140.

Wright, B. M., Barker, J. & Cordery, J. L. (2000). The ideal participative state: a prelude to work group effectiveness. Paper presented at the 15th Annual Conference of the Society for Industrial and Organizational Psychology, New Orleans, LA.

Zand, D. E. (1972). Trust and managerial problem solving. *Administrative Science Quarterly*, **17**, 229–239.

CHAPTER 7

Call Centres

David Holman
Institute of Work Psychology, University of Sheffield, UK

Call centres have long been part of the modern organisational landscape in one form or another. Emergency service telephone lines, operator services and customer help lines are just some of the types of call centre that have existed over the last 40–50 years, even if they have not been labelled as such. Yet, despite this historical presence, it is only recently that call centres have become of particular interest and significance. The most obvious reason for this is the recent, rapid increase in the number of call centres and those employed in them. For instance, in the UK, almost all call centre jobs have been created in the last 10 years (TUC, 2001) and a similar pattern of growth can be observed in the USA, Australia and the rest of Europe. Furthermore, it has been estimated that in 2002, 1.3% of the European working population will be employed in call centres, with the figure being 2.3% in the UK and 3% in the USA (Datamonitor, 1998). With call centres being found in almost all economic sectors, they have moved from occupying a relatively small niche to being a significant part of the global economy.

The growth in call centres is mainly attributable to technologies that combine call management systems (e.g. automatic call distribution systems) with networked information technologies (e.g. personal computers, display screen equipment, customer databases) (Waters, 1998). The use of these technologies enables the efficient distribution of incoming calls (or allocation of outgoing calls) to available staff, as well as enabling information such as customer details to be instantly accessed and/or easily inputted. Organisations have benefited because it has enabled them to rationalise and reduce the cost of existing functions (e.g. centralising back office functions in banks), to extend and improve customer service facilities (e.g. telephone banking) and to develop new avenues of revenue generation (e.g. exploiting customer databases for direct selling).

Although call centres offer organisations a number of clear benefits, the benefits for those employed in them, particularly front-line staff, are less clear. Thus, while some front-line staff enjoy call centre work, for many it is boring, demanding and stressful. It is these workplace experiences that have led some to label call centres as "electronic sweatshops" or "the dark satanic mills of the twenty-first century" (Garson, 1988; Incomes Data Services, 1997; Metcalf & Fernie, 1998).

One of the central issues, then, in the study of call centres has been how work organisation and human resource practices affect employee stress and well-being (e.g. anxiety,

---

The New Workplace: A Guide to the Human Impact of Modern Working Practices.
Edited by David Holman, Toby D. Wall, Chris W. Clegg, Paul Sparrow and Ann Howard. © 2003 John Wiley & Sons, Ltd.

depression, job satisfaction). Other key concerns relate to how call centres are organised and managed, the nature of human resources (HR) practices in call centres and call centre performance. The aim of this chapter is to review research on these topics. To meet this aim, the chapter will be split into the following sections. First, I offer a brief and basic definition of a call centre. The second section outlines those features that differentiate call centres from other work environments and those features that are less unique to call centres but still important to an understanding of them. The third section focuses on how these features affect the experiences of front-line staff, particularly their wellbeing. Research on call centre performance is then examined, followed by some concluding comments.

DEFINING CALL CENTRES

A call centre can be defined as a work environment in which the main business is mediated by computer and telephone-based technologies that enable the efficient distribution of incoming calls (or allocation of outgoing calls) to available staff, and permit customer–employee interaction to occur simultaneously with use of display screen equipment and the instant access to, and inputting of, information. It includes parts of companies dedicated to this activity, as well as the whole company (Health and Safety Executive, 1999).

This definition is useful, as it helps to distinguish a call centre environment from other working environments and it highlights two distinctive call centre features, the nature of call centre technology and the fact that customer–employee interaction is mediated by technology, particularly the telephone. However, the focus on technology tends to ignore other important but less unique call centre features, such as performance monitoring, work and job design, and human resource management practices. The following section is therefore devoted to a full exploration of these in order to delineate the distinctive and significant features of call centres.

FEATURES OF CALL CENTRES

Call Centre Technologies

Information and computer technologies are central to call centres and much of the debate among practitioners is on the technological possibilities afforded by, for example, automatic call distribution systems, interactive voice recognition, web enablement/joint browsing, E-mail and WAP mobile phone technology. Discussion often focuses on issues such as the effectiveness of call management systems, the integration of different technologies and software systems, and how customer service or revenue generation can be best promoted by technology. However, to argue that call centres are defined simply by the technologies used would be mistaken, because call centre technologies can be used in different ways, and it ignores the equally important social systems of call centres, e.g. work organisation and human resource practices. Thus, the interest here is not on the details of call centre technology *per se*, but on the relationship between the technological and social practices in call centres. In other words, our interest is in call centres as socio-technical systems (Cherns, 1987).

A good starting point when examining this socio-technical relationship is to consider how one aspect of the social system, the stakeholders who are involved in the design and implementation of call centre technology, can affect the final form of that technology (Clark et al., 1998; Orlinowski, 1992). For example, Boddy (2000) described how, during the development of a call centre, management utilised the possibilities of the IT system by opting to introduce an individualised electronic monitoring and reporting system. They chose to do this in order to further their aim of achieving greater control over the work process. The interests of management, together with the capability of the technology, shaped its final form. Other case studies have revealed how a cost minimisation strategy can shape call centre technology. One way of cutting costs is to employ cheaper, less skilled staff, a particularly attractive option in service industries where labour costs can account for up to 60% of total costs (Batt, 2000). However, to employ less skilled staff, work must be broken down into small, simple tasks (Callaghan & Thompson, 2001; Knights & McCabe, 1998; Taylor & Bain, 1999). These simple tasks then become embedded and relatively fixed within technology in the form of scripts or fixed procedures. In this way, technology has an enduring effect on other aspects of the social system, such as job design, performance appraisal and customer–employee interaction.

Call centre technology can vary according to technical factors (e.g. processing speed, call capacity, usability) and organisational and social factors (e.g. work design, monitoring). As many of these factors affect employee well-being (see later), attention to this during the design process would seem imperative. Yet, although it is increasingly recognised that the design of display screen equipment ergonomics can affect physical and psychological well-being (Vandevelde, 2001), there is little evidence that organisational and social factors are considered in relation to employee well-being during the design process. Indeed, the technologically-driven concerns of management, and a singular focus on cost minimisation, can shape technology in ways which produce deleterious effects on its users. Furthermore, the opportunity for customer service representatives (CSRs) to shape a technology according to their needs often arises only during its implementation, when, of course, the scope for change is much restricted (Boddy, 2000).

Customer–Employee Interaction

Another distinctive feature of a call centre is that customer–employee interaction is mainly mediated by the telephone (but can also be supplemented by face-to-face, letter or E-mail contact). Yet, this does not necessarily imply that customer–employee interaction in call centres is radically different to that occurring in other organisations. Indeed, customer–employee interaction in call centres differs little from customer–employee interaction in other service organisations, as defined by Gutek (1995, 1997). Gutek classified customer–employee interactions as "relationships", "encounters" or a hybrid of these, "pseudo-relationships" (see Table 7.1 for the main properties of relationships and encounters). In a relationship the participants have a shared history and attempt to know each other as individuals and as role occupants. This shared history and mutual understanding can be drawn on to make the service efficient, effective and customised. In time, this can lead to the development of trust and to increased satisfaction and loyalty for both parties (Chaudhuri & Holbrook, 2001; Singh & Sirdeshmukh, 2000).

Encounters are almost the reverse of relationships and typically involve a single, short interaction between strangers. The standardised nature of encounters makes them efficient, and it is easy to change the provider without affecting the service. In encounters, there is less room for authentic emotional expression, particularly for the service provider, and

Table 7.1 Characteristics of relationships and encounters (based on Gutek, 1997)

Relationships	Encounters
Provider and customer are known to each other	Provider and customer are strangers: can be anonymous
All providers not equivalent	Providers interchangeable, functionally equivalent
Based on trust	Based on rules
Elitist: customers treated differently	Egalitarian: all customers treated alike
Customized service	Standardized service
Difficult to start	Easy to enter
Difficult to end, loyalty is a factor	No obligation to repeat interaction
Does not need infrastructure	Is embedded in infrastructure
Fosters emotional involvement	Often requires emotional expressions not felt
Become more effective over time, e.g. therapist, lawyer, doctor, financial advisor	Designed to be operationally efficient, e.g. fast-food worker, bank teller, shop worker
Call centre example: counsellor (e.g. Samaritans, sex-lines, stockbroker)	Call centre examples: telephone banking, ticket sales, operator services

less opportunity to understand the reasons for a person's behaviour. This can lead to the customer making errors of attribution, such as attributing good service to organisational rules and bad service to individual traits.

Although relationships can be found in call centres (e.g. counselling, stock brokering or sex chat-lines!), encounters are more common (Batt, 2000). Given this, does telephone-mediated interaction prevent the development of relationships? There is some evidence that it does, because telephone-mediated interaction can reduce gestural cues, make interaction more formal, make complex problems more difficult to solve and slow down the development of trust (Grundy, 1998; Muscovici, 1967; Nohria & Eccles, 1992; Morely & Stephenson, 1970; Rutter, 1987; Rutter & Stephenson, 1979). However, people also seem to adapt readily to the medium and to regulate telephone interaction with some ease. The telephone can also make certain forms of communication easier, e.g. discussing personal issues (Short, Williams & Christie, 1976; Rosenfield, 1997). The telephone may not, therefore, significantly impede the development of relationships, which suggests that other factors are likely to account for the dominance of encounters over relationships in call centres. One reason is that, for simple services such as getting a ticket, a relationship may not be needed, possible or desired. However, it must be remembered that the simplified service on offer may be a result of choices about how a call centre is organised.

Although certain factors may prevent relationships developing, relationships "serve as a model for encounters because relationships have many positive features" for the organisation, for employees and for customers (Gutek, 1997, p. 149). Gutek (1997) suggests that, in order to emulate some of the qualities of relationships in service interactions, organisations try to develop pseudo-relationships with customers. One way is to encourage employees to develop an "instant rapport" with the customer. This might be achieved by customer-relationship management systems that track customers' interactions with the organisation and enable the employee to know a customer's service history and anticipate his/her needs. An alternative to promoting individualised relationships is to try to get the customer to feel that he/she has a trusting relationship with the organisation. The development of individual–organisational trust is supported by economic and social structures (e.g. contracts, rules expressing standards of service) rather than the quality of personal relationships (Hosmer, 1995).

Performance Monitoring

Although performance monitoring is not unique to call centres, the overt, pervasive nature of performance monitoring within many call centres is fairly distinctive. Indeed, it is the pervasiveness of performance monitoring in call centres that has provoked much debate, due to its perceived negative impact on CSRs' well-being. This impact will be discussed later, but first performance monitoring will be described.

Performance monitoring involves the observation, examination, recording and feedback of employee work behaviours and exists in both "traditional" and "electronic" forms[1] (Stanton, 2000). Traditional forms of performance monitoring encompass methods such as direct observation, listening to calls, work sampling and customer surveys. Electronic performance monitoring involves the automatic and remote collection of quantitative data (e.g. call times). The characteristics of both forms can be clustered into content or purpose (Carayon, 1993; Stanton, 2000).

The "content" of performance monitoring covers the more "objective" qualities of the monitoring process, such as its frequency, the feedback process and the type and range of performance criteria. The content of traditional monitoring in call centres is typified by a supervisor assessing call quality by listening to a call while at the side of a CSR or by listening to a call remotely (with or without the CSR's knowledge). As this is resource-rich, the monitoring of call quality is episodic, and the number of calls being assessed can vary from five times per week in some call centres to once a month in others (Frenkel et al., 1998; Holman, Chissick & Totterdell, 2001). Some call centre technologies permit every call to be recorded, meaning that every call can potentially be assessed. A call's quality is normally evaluated against a mixture of technical, social and attitudinal criteria that includes: adherence to a script; call opening and closing; accuracy of information; product knowledge; helpfulness; empathy; enthusiasm; and professional tone (Bain et al., 2001; Holman et al., 2002). Assessments are normally fed back in one-to-one discussions and summated results fed back in team meetings. In addition to call quality, CSRs are assessed against a range of non-call-related criteria, such as teamwork, helpfulness and attendance.

Electronic performance monitoring in call centres is generally conducted in a continuous manner, with the results often being fed back daily (Bain & Taylor, 2000; Frenkel et al., 1998; Holman et al., 2002). The types of performance criteria used include call length, wrap-up time (i.e. time spent in administrative duties), time spent logged-off the system and number of sales.

The purpose of performance monitoring relates to the uses to which performance data is put. For example, performance monitoring can be deployed punitively to inform disciplinary proceedings. It can also be used to improve employee performance, particularly through the identification of training needs and goal setting; to reduce costs; to ensure customer satisfaction; and, to enable the correct allocation of resources by matching employee numbers to call levels (Aiello & Kolb, 1995; Alder, 1998; Chalykoff & Kochan, 1989).

---

[1] While not ideal labels, we keep them as they are used by others in this field (cf. Stanton, 2000).

Somewhat surprisingly, there is little evidence for the assumed performance benefits of monitoring in a call centre context. Indeed, most research on monitoring and performance is laboratory-based, conducted on tasks that are quite different to those employed in call centres (e.g. non-telephone-based data-entry tasks) and has revealed no conclusive benefit to individual performance. In contrast, field research has revealed that performance monitoring can be used to improve resource allocation, i.e. balancing employee numbers to call volumes (Betts, Meadows & Walley, 2000). If the evidence linking performance monitoring to performance is so poor, why is it so pervasive in call centres? One explanation is that organisations do it because they simply *believe* that monitoring improves individual performance, and because they have some knowledge that it improves resource allocation. According to this scenario, performance monitoring has become, to management at least, an undisputed good. Another explanation is that, while performance monitoring is "dressed up" as a developmental tool for employees, this actually hides its "real" purpose, i.e. a method to enforce adherence to organisational norms. Whatever the reason, due to the effects of performance monitoring on stress levels (see later), questions should be raised about the extent to which high levels of performance monitoring are really necessary or desirable (Holman et al., 2002).

Job and Work Design

The design of a CSR's job is another salient feature of call centres that, like performance monitoring, has attracted much attention. A reason for this is that some CSR jobs do seem to be an expression of an advanced form of Taylorism (Knights & McCabe, 1998; Taylor & Bain, 1999) and, as such, have been criticised for being a primary cause of job-related stress. However, not all CSR jobs are designed in this manner, with most falling on a continuum running from "Tayloristic" to "empowered" (Batt, 2000; Frenkel et al., 1998, 1999; Holman, 2002).

At the "Taylorist" end of the continuum, jobs are unskilled, repetitive and monotonous. Calls are of a short duration, are required to be completed within a specified time and there is no choice as to whether a call can be answered or not. Calls are often conducted in accordance to a script that specifies the opening and closing of the call and, in some cases, the entire call. These factors mean that the CSRs have little control over the timing of their work, the methods they use and what they can say. CSRs also spend most of their time answering calls, a consequence being that little time is spent doing other tasks, such as administration. Variety comes from answering different call types, although actual differences may be small. The level of problem-solving demand is not high and when problems do arise there is a general expectation that these should be handed on to a supervisor. Tayloristic jobs also tend to have lower degrees of task interdependence. As a result, work is more individualised and fewer interactions with other CSRs are needed to ensure service delivery, although co-workers do interact to offer social support and help each other to learn the job (Frenkel et al., 1999).

In the "empowered" job, a semi-professional CSR has more control over how he/she works and is required to combine an extensive product or service knowledge (often of a complex product or service, such as mortgages or computer repair) with IT and customer service skills to provide a customized service (Winslow & Bramer, 1994; Frenkel et al., 1998). CSRs are engaged in a variety of calls and tasks in which problems are handled at source. Calls are longer and generally unscripted apart from the call's opening and closing. Empowered jobs tend to have higher degrees of task interdependence, as CSRs often need to draw upon others' knowledge.

It might be expected that empowered jobs would be associated with the use of self-managed teams and off-line teams, such as quality circles. Work by Batt (2000) suggests that there is little evidence of this in call centres[2]. This indicates that self-managed teams and off-line teams may be used to increase variety and participation in Tayloristic jobs when it is perceived that there is little room for achieving these aims through the redesign of the core job task.

Human Resource Management

HR practices vary considerably in call centres. To explore this variation and the reasons for it, three issues will be addressed. The first concerns whether particular HR and work organisation practices are found bundled together or whether the relationship between practices is more idiosyncratic, i.e. there is an *internal fit or alignment between* practices. The second issue focuses on whether there is an *organisational fit or alignment* between bundles of practice and a particular feature of the organisation and whether this results in performance benefits. For example, Batt (2000, p. 542) argues that "the customer–worker interface is a significant factor in defining the organisation of work and HR practices in services" and that both should be aligned to ensure maximum productivity. The third issue focuses on whether there is an alignment between the organisation's strategy and bundles of practices and whether such a *strategic fit or alignment* is beneficial.

Before these issues are explored, it is useful to note that previous work has suggested that two models of service management exist, the "mass service" model and the "high-commitment service" (HCS) model (Bowen & Schneider, 1988; Frenkel *et al.*, 1999; Levitt, 1972; Schlesinger & Heskett, 1991)[3]. In addition, a number of writers argue that, in high-performing organisations, bundles of particular work organisation and HR practices will align with other features of the organisation and with its strategic aims (Batt, 2000; Schuler & Jackson, 1995; Wright & McMahon, 1992). Applied to the call centre context, and by drawing on the work of Batt (2000), Frenkel *et al.* (1998, 1999), Holman (2002) and Kinnie, Purcell & Hutchinson (2000), two ideal models of call centre practice referred to above can be envisaged (see Table 7.2). In each model, the bundles of practice (internal alignment), the organisational alignment and strategic alignment will be as follows.

In the ideal mass service call centre, there is a strategic alignment between a mass market customer segment, a cost-minimisation strategy and a bundle of work organisation and HR practices that includes Tayloristic job designs, low rates of pay and discretionary pay, low levels of training, temporary contract in core workers and minimum recruitment criteria. An alignment of this sort is advantageous, as the small profit margins of the market served mean that costs, particularly labour costs, must be minimised. This is achieved by using

---

[2] Batt (2000) found that although 38% of organisations with empowered jobs used self-managed teams a lot, and that 18% of organisations with Tayloristic jobs used self-managed teams a lot, this difference was not significant. Batt also found that, with 90% usage of off-line teams in each, there were no differences between organisations with Tayloristic or empowered jobs.
[3] These are the functional equivalent of the mass production and high commitment/involvement models present in the manufacturing literature (Ichniowski *et al.*, 1996; Wood, 1995).

Table 7.2 Call centre models: "mass service" and "high commitment service"

Mass service	High commitment service

Customer segment
  Mass Market
	Customer Segment
	  Specialist, high-earning private customers, businesses

Market
  High-volume, low added value
	Market
	  Low-volume, high added value

Strategy
  Cost-minimisation
	Strategy
	  Customisation of service, cross-selling, bundling of services

Product/service
  Simple, one or few product or services on offers
  Standardised service
	Product/service
	  Complex and/or multiple products and services on offer
	  Customised service

Customer–worker interaction
  Encounter
	Customer–worker interaction
	  Relationship or pseudo-relationship

Job design
  Taylorist, e.g. low control and variety, low skill, high use of scripts, short call times
	Job design
	  Empowered, e.g. high control and variety, little scripting, long calls

Work design
  Low interdependence
  Work groups
  Off-line work groups
	Work design
	  High interdependence
	  High use of semi-autonomous work groups
	  Off-line work groups

Performance monitoring
  High levels of monitoring
  Emphasis on quality and quantity
  Higher tendency to use monitoring to discipline and control
	Performance monitoring
	  Low levels of monitoring
	  Emphasis on quality
	  Use of monitoring for developmental purposes

Human resource practices
  Low cost
  Recruitment—minimal criteria
  Pay—relatively low rates of pay, low percentage of total pay that is commission-based
  Training—mainly induction training
  Career—little career structure, poor promotion prospects
  Job security—low, high use of temporary contracts in core workers
	Human resource practices
	  High cost
	  Use of selection tests and competency models
	  Relatively high rates of pay, higher percentage of total pay that is commission-based, good additional benefits
	  Induction training and continuing training
	  Better promotion prospects
	  High job security, lower use of temporary contracts in core workers

Management/supervisor relations with CSRs
  Hierarchical
  Low trust
	Management/supervisor relations with CSRs
	  Supportive, facilitative
	  High trust

Tayloristic job designs, which leads to less skilled, cheaper labour being employed and fewer resources being devoted to recruiting and retaining a skilled workforce. The use of standardised products also means that it makes economic sense to ensure an organisational alignment between the customer–employee encounter, Tayloristic job designs and low-cost HR practices.

With the high-commitment service (HCS) model, the strategy is to generate high profit margins and sales revenues by providing a customised service to a specialised customer segment. To do this, the organisation needs to devote resources to recruiting, training and keeping a skilled workforce (e.g. through effective recruitment and continuous training). HR practices also reward discretionary behaviour (e.g. by the use of performance-related pay) and cultivate employee commitment to the organisation through job security and good terms and conditions. Empowered work designs permit a customised service to be provided, a relationship or pseudo-relationship between employee and customer to be developed (thus there is an organisational as well as a strategic alignment) and discretionary behaviour to be exhibited. Greater employee commitment means that less monitoring is needed to gain adherence to organisational goals and norms.

Research indicates that work organisation and HR practices in call centres do vary in a manner similar to that predicted by the models outlined above. The strongest evidence comes from Batt's (2000) study of telecommunications call centres that were serving four different customer segments and which were pursuing different strategic aims. The four customer segments were operator services (mass market), residential consumers, small businesses, and middle market (customised/specialised market). She found that empowered jobs (high control, low scripting, high skill requirements) were associated with HR practices such as low performance monitoring and high levels of discretionary pay. Moreover, this bundle was associated with relationship-type interactions and with the residential, small business and middle market customer segment. In other words, there was both an internal, organisational and strategic alignment akin to that posited in the ideal HCS call centre model. In contrast, the internal, organisational and strategic alignments akin to the mass service call centre were found in the operator services call centres. However, the match to theory was not complete, as she found little difference with regard to the use of teams, training, promotion and job security, although operator service call centres did stand out as having lower training and job security.

The respondents in the Batt (2000) survey were managers. Evidence from CSR-level data comes from Holman & Fernie (2000), who compared CSRs working in a banking call centre serving mass market customers with those in a call centre giving mortgage advice to residential and small business customers. CSRs in the banking call centre reported more encounter-type interactions, lower job control and variety, lower skill use, higher monitoring and poorer relations with managers. Thus, there were different bundles of practice and the organisational alignments were as suggested by the models. A similar pattern was reported by Frenkel *et al.* (1999) who, using case study and CSR-level survey data, found that work roles, job designs and HR practices consistent with the ideal mass service call centre were aligned with customer–employee encounters and a mass market customer segment. A case study by Hutchinson, Purcell & Kinnie (2000) also demonstrated that "the driving force for the adoption of HCM [high-commitment management] was the need to realign business strategy and organisational structure" (p. 74). In the call centre in question, HR practices were changed in response to a new strategic aim of adding value, particularly for customers, and the provision of a more complex service that combined previously distinct sales and service tasks. The HR changes included greater use of induction and continuing training, more sophisticated recruitment and selection techniques, a wider use of performance-related pay and greater involvement in quality improvement teams.

Work on HR in call centres, while limited in extent, does indicate that bundles of work organisation and HR practice do exist (i.e., there is an internal fit), that there is a degree of organisational alignment between these bundles and customer–employee interaction, and that call centres do exhibit a degree of strategic alignment to the customer segment pursued. However, the following caveats are required. First, there are many "anomalies" in the data. Some mass service call centres adopt some high commitment work practices (e.g. self-managed work teams in mass service call centres; Batt, 2000, Houlihan, 2001) and some HCS call centres adopt some mass service work practices (e.g. high levels of performance monitoring in HCS call centres; Kinnie *et al.*, 2000). Indeed, it is probable that most call centres are a hybrid of mass service call centres and HCS call centres, which Frenkel *et al.* (1998) have labelled "mass customized bureaucracies". The "anomalies" in the data also imply that managers consider other factors when choosing which practices to adopt. For example, when local labour markets are very competitive, it may not be possible to use practices such as low pay or Tayloristic job designs that exacerbate recruitment and turnover problems. Indeed, Houlihan (2001) reports that some mass service call centres use empowered job designs in response to concerns about the effects of Tayloristic jobs on employee well-being. Other factors affecting the adoption of work practices include costs, alternative organisational goals, legal requirements and problems of implementation. This implies that a true alignment or "best fit" may not be possible.

Second, a best fit may not be desirable. Internal, organisational and strategic alignments of the kind described may be easily mimicked by other organisations and may therefore fail to provide the unique organisational practices, services or products that enable the organisation to secure a niche position in the market place and to compete successfully (Boxall, 1996).

Third, any organisational or strategic alignment may not be the result of top-down strategic choice. Rather, alignment may emerge from the pragmatic choices made by managers when trying to make sense of the dynamic call centre environment (Hutchinson *et al.*, 2000; Kinnie *et al.*, 2000). Korczynski *et al.* (2000) suggest that these choices are informed by the sometimes competing rationales of "bureaucratic efficiency" and "customer orientation", which can be equated respectively with the rationale underlying the mass service call centre and that which underlies the HCS call centre. These rationales and the dynamic between them can be expressed in different ways, but include:

- Service quality vs. service quantity (Knights & McCabe, 1998; Bain *et al.* 2001).
- Ensuring employee empathy with the customer whilst also ensuring employee instrumentality, i.e. doing just enough to satisfy the customer and not waste time (Sturdy, 2000).
- Providing a customised service and having standardised procedures (Korczyniski *et al.*, 2000).
- Gaining the commitment of employees whilst ensuring adherence to organisational norms (i.e. the control of employees).

In summary, research on HR in call centres demonstrates how work organisation and HR practices vary, that they do form "messy" bundles, and that the type of bundle found is contingent upon the particular conglomeration of factors that includes customer worker interaction, the customer segment, the local labour market, the actions and views of employees, and internal organisational resources. However, it is open to question whether any organisational or strategic alignment is the result of a top-down strategy, or whether it emerges from the pragmatic choices that managers make when trying to make sense of a dynamic call centre environment.

THE EXPERIENCE OF CALL CENTRE WORK

Call centre work, particularly that of CSRs, has attracted much attention due to its perceived impact on job-related stress. In response, there is a growing literature on the causes of stress in call centres. Another body of work has focused on how CSRs actively resist managerial control and deleterious working practices. It is heavily influenced by labour process theory but not entirely disconnected from the literature on well-being.

The Experience and Causes of Stress, Stress-related Outcomes and Affect

Those factors outlined in the previous sections (e.g. job design, performance monitoring, HR practices) have a significant impact on employee stress and stress-related outcomes in call centres (Frenkel *et al.*, 1998; Holman, 2002; Incomes Data Services, 1997; Knights & McCabe, 1998; Taylor & Bain, 1999), as they do in other work settings[4].

Job design research has demonstrated that low control, lack of variety and high demands are important predictors of stress (i.e. anxiety, depression, emotional exhaustion) and stress-related outcomes (e.g. absence) (Karasek & Theorell, 1990; Spector, 1987; Terry & Jimmieson, 1999). Studies of job design in call centres report similar findings (Batt & Appelbaum, 1995; Batt & Moynihan, 2001; Zapf *et al.*, 1999), but highlight how little control CSRs have (Holman, 2001) and the impact of scripts on stress (Deery, Iverson & Walsh, 2001).

Performance monitoring is another practice that has attracted attention, due to its assumed effect on stress. Arguments in favour of monitoring are that employees benefit because they can improve their performance and develop new skills (Grant & Higgins, 1989), which in turn helps the CSR to cope better with demands (Aiello & Shao, 1993; Bandura, 1997; Stanton, 2000). Arguments against performance monitoring are that it is threatening to employees because the information gained may affect employees' remuneration or coworker relationships (Alder, 1998). Monitoring is also considered to be a demand in itself (Smith *et al.*, 1992). The threat of monitoring and the consequent feeling of increased demand are thought to negatively affect employee well-being.

Both arguments have found support. On the one hand, laboratory and field studies have reported that monitored employees (or participants) are generally found to have higher levels of stress and dissatisfaction than non-monitored employees (Aiello & Kolb; 1995; Irving, Higgins & Safeyeni, 1986; Smith *et al.*, 1992). On the other hand, in one of the few studies conducted in a call centre, Chalykoff & Kochan (1989) discovered that the performance-related content of the monitoring system (i.e. immediacy of feedback, the use of constructive feedback and the clarity of the rating criteria) was positively related to satisfaction with the monitoring system, which in turn was related to job satisfaction.

The positive and negative associations between performance monitoring and well-being suggests that various performance monitoring characteristics may be differentially related to employee well-being. This proposition found support in a study by Holman *et al.* (2002)

---

[4] Nearly all research on stress in call centres has been in relation to CSRs. The following relates to this group unless otherwise stated.

that examined the relationship between well-being and three performance monitoring characteristics in a call centre, viz. its performance-related content (i.e. immediacy of feedback, clarity of performance criteria); its beneficial purpose (i.e. does it have developmental rather than punitive aims?) and its perceived intensity (i.e. was it felt to be pervasive?). The results revealed that the performance-related content of performance monitoring reduced depression, that the beneficial purpose of monitoring reduced depression, anxiety and emotional exhaustion, whilst perceived intensity increased anxiety, depression and emotional exhaustion. Furthermore, the perceived intensity of monitoring had much stronger effects on the other two characteristics of performance monitoring. These findings support arguments both for and against performance monitoring. They show that, while performance monitoring can reduce stress if it is conducted in a developmental manner and is based on regular feedback and clear criteria, these positive effects can be wiped out if monitoring is perceived by CSRs to be too intense. Indeed, excessive monitoring may, over the long term, make employees more depressed, less enthusiastic and have the opposite effect of that intended.

Customer–employee interaction can also affect well-being. The strongest evidence comes from work on emotional labour, the regulation and expression of emotion in exchange for a wage (Grandey, 2000; Hochschild, 1983). Central to theories of emotional labour is the idea that organisations implicitly or explicitly specify what and how emotions should be expressed. Dissonance can occur when emotions felt do not match the emotional expression required. In response, the employee can either display his/her "true" emotions or he/she can try to display the required emotions. If he/she chooses the latter option, two modes of emotional regulation may be deployed, surface acting or deep acting (Hochschild, 1983). Surface acting involves displaying the required emotions, but there is little attempt to feel those emotions, e.g. an employee may "smile down the phone" (Belt, Richardson & Webster, 1999). Deep acting involves trying to feel and display the required emotions, e.g. by re-appraising the situation so that its emotional impact is lessened (Grandey, 2000). Research findings in call centres are in line with these propositions (Holman *et al.*, 2002; Zapf *et al.*, 1999) and have also revealed that emotional labour only has negative effects (i.e. anxiety, depression, emotional exhaustion) when the emotions expressed are negative and when surface acting is engaged in (Zapf *et al.*, 1999). This is because the expression of positive emotions can be pleasant in itself and lead to a sense of personal accomplishment, and because the suppression of feelings is more demanding on personal resources than other forms of regulation, such as deep acting (Holman *et al.*, 2002; Totterdell & Holman, 2002; Zapf *et al.*, 1999). These studies have also illuminated the extent to which CSRs engage in emotional regulation throughout their working day. A diary study revealed that CSRs hid negative feelings from customers for one-half of their time at work and suppressed positive feelings for one-fifth of the time (Totterdell & Holman, 2001). This suggests that surface acting may be fairly common in call centres and that customer–employee interaction may be an important cause of stress in them.

Other aspects of customer–employee interaction that can affect well-being are the provision of good customer service (Frenkel *et al.*, 1999), the expression of positive emotions, and pleasant customers (Totterdell & Holman, 2001). These can have a positive effect on well-being. In contrast, short unemotional calls may be associated with stress, although what may be more important is whether the person can control the call and whether a CSR receives a variety of calls.

Research on other causes of stress in call centres is less comprehensive. For instance, with regard to HR practices and team leader support, the perceived fairness of the payment system, the usefulness of performance appraisal and the adequacy of training, all have been linked to low anxiety, low depression and job satisfaction (Batt & Appelbaum, 1995; Frenkel et al., 1998; Holman, 2002). Technology has also been cited as a determinant of physical and psychological well-being and, although I have yet to find a study that has examined the ergonomic impact of call centre work-station design and the usability of the human–computer interface, their effect is probably little different to that elsewhere (Grieco et al., 1995, Health and Safety Executive, 1992).

While many factors have been shown to be associated with stress, those practices with the strongest associations to anxiety, depression and job satisfaction are job control, the intensity of monitoring, the adequacy of the coaching and training and team leader support (Holman, 2002). In addition to the differential effects of practices on stress, differences in levels of stress between different types of call centre have been identified. Holman & Fernie (2000) compared levels of well-being between a mass service-type call centre, an HCS-type call centre, and a hybrid type falling somewhere in between. Depression and job dissatisfaction were generally lower at the HCS and hybrid call centres. Against expectations, however, anxiety was lower at the mass service call centre. It was argued that CSRs were managing their anxiety by leaving the mass service call centre. CSRs at the other call centres, which had better terms and conditions, were more likely to stay and "sweat it out". Other studies have revealed quit rates to be lower in HCS call centres (Batt & Moynihan, 2001). Call centre work has been highlighted as particularly stressful and, by implication, more stressful than comparable forms of work. But studies show no clear pattern of findings[5]. In one study, call centre workers were found to be less satisfied than sales workers and knowledge workers (e.g. IT systems designers) (Frenkel et al., 1999). In another, call centre work compared favourably with shop floor manufacturing work and clerical work with regard to anxiety, depression and job satisfaction (Holman, 2001).

Control and Resistance in Call Centre Work: the Active Agent

Research on stress in call centres tends to paint the CSR as a rather passive figure, i.e. as someone always responding to work conditions. In contrast, studies inspired by labour process theory (Braverman, 1974; Sturdy, Knights & Willmott, 1992) have been concerned with how CSRs actively consent to, comply with and resist managers' efforts to exert control over their work. Management control practices in call centres are fairly overt and wide-ranging and include:

- The measurement of output through IT systems.
- The measurement of behaviour through call monitoring and observation.
- The inculcation of norms through training, customer awareness programmes, socialisation, coaching, performance appraisal and feedback.
- The structuring of work tasks through scripts and IT systems.

As noted, CSRs may not consent to the above control practices. CSRs may have different ideas from management on the management of the call centre or how customers should be served. CSRs are also likely to disagree with practices they view as having deleterious personal consequences. Labour process theory has illuminated the individual and collective

---

[5] Zapf et al. (1999) and Batt & Appelbaum (1995) reported differences but did not examine whether the differences were significant.

Table 7.3 Individual and collective forms of CSR resistance to management control

Individual resistance	Collective resistance
Cutting customers off	Trades union activity
Not following the script	Humour
Not selling	Sharing knowledge of how to beat the system
Deliberately cheating the IT system	
Pretending to be speaking to a customer	
Challenging targets set	
Not filling in information properly	

ways in which CSRs resist those control practices they disagree with or find deleterious. For example, at an individual level, a CSR may resist managerial exhortations to deal with calls more rapidly as a means of improving customer service. This may occur because a CSR's sense of customer service is different. The CSR may have an embodied sense of customer service, i.e. to the customer she is serving, and this makes her attend to the needs of the individual without regard to those other customers waiting in the queue (Korczynski et al., 2000; Sturdy, 2000). At a collective level, resistance may take the form of trade union activity that aims to alter job designs or performance monitoring practices (Keefe & Batt, 2001; Taylor & Bain, 2001; Trades Union Congress, 2001) (see Table 7.3 for more examples of individual and collective forms of resistance). From these different forms of resistance it can be concluded that CSRs do not passively accept their work conditions, particularly those that may decrease their well-being, and that CSRs are actively engaged in attempting to change their working conditions to ones which, in their eyes, are preferable. CSR resistance also demonstrates that, even in the most regimented call centres, total control cannot be achieved and that comparisons with panopticans are grossly overdrawn (Bain & Taylor, 2000; Metcalf & Fernie, 1998; Frenkel et al., 1999).

Finally, the labour process literature has highlighted how CSRs often use similar rationales to those used by management and that they too are faced by similar demands (e.g. quality vs. quantity, service vs. selling, etc.). What is more, whereas managers have to contend with these issues at a system level, the CSR has to balance the tensions that these demands create in every call.

CALL CENTRE PERFORMANCE

Only a small number of studies have examined performance in call centres, and they have focused on the contribution that call management, employee behaviour and work practices make to two outcomes, viz, perceptions of service quality (which includes customer satisfaction) and sales. With regard to perceptions of service quality, management's ability to regulate call volumes, and in particular their ability to reduce waiting times, is a key determinant of customer satisfaction (Evenson, Harker & Frei, 1999; Feinberg et al., 2000). Yet, managing call volumes so that demand is matched by resources has proved to be problematic with current technologies and procedures, particularly when calls are long (Betts et al., 2000). This would indicate that management's control over a key determinant of customer satisfaction is limited. Customer satisfaction has also been linked to employee behaviours, such as empathy, assurance, the authority to deal with requests, adaptiveness and displays of negative emotion (Burgers *et al.*, 2000; Doucett, 1998). Clearly the CSR needs to have the opportunity and ability to engage in such behaviours if customer satisfaction is to be achieved. Batt's (1999) work would appear to support this. She found that groups with greater self-regulation (akin to the processes involved in self-managed teams), coaching support, level of education, training and better work group relations had higher scores on an employee-reported measure of service quality. This study also showed that group–self-regulation, coaching support and level of education were also positively related to sales volume. Another study, by Batt & Moynihan (2001), showed that those call centres adopting appropriate HR practices (i.e. high-commitment practices when serving high-value customers) achieved higher sales growth.

CONCLUSION

Viewing all call centres as "electronic sweatshops" is misguided and such a simplistic view should be given short shrift. Call centres are diverse entities. This diversity is a result of the pragmatic and strategic choices made by the stakeholders involved in them. Permeating these choices are various rationales that suggest what is plausible and justifiable. From this chapter it is possible to suggest that the two most dominant rationales are the economically-based rationales of bureaucratic efficiency (which includes a focus on cost minimisation) and customer orientation (Korczynski *et al.*, 2000). Respectively, these can be seen to inform the design and running of the mass service call centre and the HCS call centre. For example, the use of a bureaucratic efficiency rationale by IT consultants and managers during the design of a call centre will often lead to standardised services and simplified job designs. Further evidence of these rationales being at work comes from those studies showing an organisational and strategic alignment of practices, although whether call centres are *explicitly* designed in accordance with these rationales is open to debate.

Yet, while these rationales enable action by suggesting what is justifiable and workable, they also constrain action by ignoring or de-legitimating other issues, such as employee well-being. The choices stakeholders make will be further constrained by the conditions in which they are made. As shown earlier, the use of Taylorist jobs can cause difficulties in labour market conditions that make high levels of labour turnover problematic. As such, the dominance or role of these two economic logics must not be overplayed. Practices may be introduced for a number of reasons and be based on alternative rationales (e.g. legal, moral), as is evidenced by mass service call centres adopting self-managed work teams to alleviate the harmful effects of Tayloristic jobs (Houlihan, 2001).

Work in the labour process tradition also shows that all stakeholders are able to use the same rationales to justify and inform their practice, although it must be said that the effect of each rationale may differ according to who uses it and when. For example, the use of a customer orientation logic by IT consultants and call centre managers may have more global effects during the design of call centre practices than the use of the same rationale by a CSR when talking to a customer. Managers also have a greater opportunity to determine the work conditions of CSRs. Ultimately, the choices of managers affect CSR well-being. This means that call centre managers can take a proactive approach to employee well-being and try to reduce stress through the design of call centre work. Furthermore, as the causes of well-being in call centres are similar to the causes in other organisations, the "old rules" still apply in a "new" setting. Call centres are not radically new forms of work organisation. As a result, many of the job redesign or system redesign methods, including socio-technical methods and the like, may be usefully applied in a call centre setting (see Chapter 17, this volume; for review, see Parker & Wall, 1998). These tools may be used most effectively on technologies, on job design and on performance monitoring systems, particularly during their design and implementation. With regard to performance monitoring, it seems imperative that it should be part of a system that aims to develop employees' skills and performance and that it should be closely linked to coaching (see Chapter 12, this volume, by Pritchard and Payne). It would also seem sensible to minimise the number of performance criteria used when monitoring to reduce the perception that it is intense.

However, in a mass service call centre, do stress-alleviating work designs and HR practices prevent the optimal alignment of work organisation, HR practices, customer–employee interaction and strategy? According to theory, the answer is yes; that in mass service call centres there must be a trade-off between effectiveness and employee well-being. Yet, although there is evidence that loose alignments occur, there is little evidence to date that aligned call centres have higher organisational or employee performance than non-aligned call centres. Furthermore, it might also be the case that employee performance, as measured by customer satisfaction, could be worse in mass service call centres, despite the best attempts of employees to engage in emotional labour, because "what employees experience, gets transmitted to customers" (Schlesinger and Heskett, 1991, p. 71). In addition, the direct and indirect costs of poor job design and extensive monitoring may prove excessive in some circumstances. This shows that there are economic as well as moral reasons which have led some "mass service" call centres to introduce empowered job designs and HR practices. These call centres have been called "compensatory", suggesting that the simple distinction between mass service and HCS call centres may be too crude (Houlihan, 2001). Therefore, not only is research needed that examines the relationship between call centre design, employee well-being, organisational performance and employee performance, but it should also examine the possibility that several types of call centre design may exist.

Research in the future should also focus on how new technologies will affect call centre employees. One current argument is that technologies will remove the more boring aspects of call centre work and make it more pleasant. This is reminiscent of previous claims about computer technologies, which subsequently turned out to have a range of impacts, positive, negative and neutral, on employee work experiences (Wood, 1982). Researchers, consultants and managers should therefore concentrate on the reasons for this variation, focus on how centre technology and its associated work practices are shaped, and take a more proactive role in shaping call centre technologies so that they do not negatively effect employee well-being.

It is evident that the causes of stress in call centres are similar to those in other organisations. Therefore, researchers in the future would do best to focus on factors particularly pertinent to a call centre environment. Such factors would include a more detailed look at performance monitoring, an examination of the effects of technology (e.g. usability, work station design) relative to other factors, and quasi-experimental redesign studies comparing the performance and well-being effects of different job designs and different performance monitoring designs.

In conclusion, this chapter has sought to demonstrate that the design and diversity of call centres emerges from the pragmatic and strategic choices made by stakeholders who, informed by various rationales, attempt to achieve their goals in the context of the unique set of contingencies with which they are faced. This dynamic understanding of call centres means that managers do have a choice in how they run and organise call centres, and that well-being can be designed into call centres. It has also demonstrated that CSRs contend with many of the same issues in their daily interactions with customers (i.e. quality vs. quantity) as those faced by managers. However, CSRs generally have little influence on how the organisation deals with these issues at a more systemic level. But the lessons from other types of organisation are that worker knowledge, when it is called upon, often improves the design of customer service, technology and HR practices (Clegg et al., 1996, 2000; Clark et al., 1998). Perhaps it is time that CSRs are given greater opportunity to engage in the design of call centre technologies and practices.

REFERENCES

Aiello, J. R. & Kolb, K. J. (1995). Electronic performance monitoring and social context: impact on productivity and stress. *Journal of Applied Psychology*, **80**, 339–353.

Aiello, J. R. & Shao, Y. (1993). Electronic performance monitoring and stress: the role of feedback and goal setting. In M. J. Smith & G. Salavendy (Eds), *Human–Computer Interaction: Applications and Case Studies* (pp. 1011–1016). Amsterdam: Elsevier Science.

Alder, G. S. (1998). Ethical issues in electronic performance monitoring: a consideration of deontological and teleological perspectives. *Journal of Business Ethics*, **17**, 729–743.

Bandura, A. (1997). *Self-efficacy: the Exercise of Control*. New York: W. H. Freeman.

Bain, P. & Taylor, P. (2000). Entrapped by the "electronic panopticon"? Worker resistance in the call centre. *New Technology, Work and Employment*, **15**, 2–18.

Bain, P., Watson, A., Mulvey, G., Taylor, P. & Gall, G. (2001). Taylorism, targets and quantity–quality dichotomy in call centres. 19th International Labour Process Conference, Royal Holloway College, University of London, March.

Batt, R. (1999). Work organization, technology and performance in customer service and sales. *Industrial and Labor Relations Review*, **52**, 539–564.

Batt, R. (2000). Strategic segmentation in front line services: matching customers, employees and human resource systems. *International Journal of Human Resource Management*, **11**, 540–561.

Batt, R. & Appelbaum, E. (1995). Worker participation in diverse settings: does the form affect the outcome, and if so, who benefits? *British Journal of Industrial Relations*, **33**, 353–378.

Batt, R. & Moynihan, L. (2001). The viability of alternative call centre production models. Paper presented at Call Centres and Beyond: the Human Resource Management Implications, Kings College, London, November.

Belt, V., Richardson, R. & Webster, J. (1999). Smiling down the phone: women's work in telephone call centres. Paper presented at RGS–IBG Annual Conference, University of Leicester, January.

Betts, A., Meadows, M. & Walley, P. (2000). Call centre capacity management. *International Journal of Service Industry Management*, **11**, 185–196.

Boddy, D. (2000). Implementing interorganizational IT systems: lessons from a call centre project. *Journal of Information Technology*, **15**, 29–37.

Bowen, D. E. & Schneider, B. (1988). Services marketing and management: implications for organizational behaviour. In B. M. Staw & L. L. Cummings (Eds) *Research in Organisational Behavior*, Vol 10 (pp. 43–80). Greenwich: JAI Press.

Boxall, P. (1996). The strategic HRM debate and the resource based view of the firm. *Human Resource Management Journal*, **6**, 59–75.

Braverman, H. (1974). *Labour and Monopoly Capital*. New York: Monthly Review Press.

Burgers, A., de Ruyter, K., Keen., C. & Streukens, S. (2000). Customer expectation dimensions of voice to voice service encounters: a scale development study. *International Journal of Service Industry Management*, **11**, 142–161.

Callaghan, G. & Thompson, P. (2001). Edwards revisited: technical control and call centres. *Economic and Industrial Democracy*, **22**, 13–37.

Carayon, P. (1993). Effects of electronic performance monitoring on job design and worker stress: review of the literature and conceptual model. *Human Factors*, **35**, 385–395.

Chalykoff, J. & Kochan, T. (1989). Computer-aided monitoring: its influence on employee job satisfaction and turnover. *Personnel Psychology*, **42**, 807–834.

Chaudhuri, A. & Holbrook, M. B. (2001). The chain effects from brand trust and brand affect to brand performance: the role of brand loyalty. *Journal of Marketing*, **65**, 81–93.

Cherns, A. (1987). Principles of socio-technical design revisited, *Human Relations*, **40**, 153–162.

Clark, J., McLoughlin, I., Rose, H. & King, J. (1998). *The Process of Technological Change: New Technology and Social Change in the Workplace*. Cambridge: Cambridge University Press.

Clegg, C. W., Axtell, C., Damodaran, L., Farby, B., Hull, R., Lloyd-Jones, R., Nicholl, J., Sell R., Tomlinson, C., Ainger A. & Stewart, T. (1996). Failing to Deliver: the IT Performance Gap. Report to Economic and Social Research Council, Institute of Work Psychology, Memo No. 64, University of Sheffield.

Clegg, C. W. (2000). Sociotechnical principles for system design. *Applied Ergonomics*, **31**, 463–477.

Datamonitor (1998). *Call Centres in Europe: Sizing by Call Centres and Agent Positions in 13 European Countries*. London: Datamonitor.

Deery, S. J., Iverson, R. D. & Walsh, J. T. (2001). Work relationships in telephone call centres: understanding emotional exhaustion and employee withdrawal. *Journal of Management Studies* (in press).

Doucett, L. (1998). Responsiveness: emotion and information dynamics in service interactions. Working Paper 98–15, Financial Institutions Center, The Wharton School, University of Pennsylvania.

Evenson, A., Harker, P. T. & Frei, F. X. (1999). Effective call center management: evidence from financial services. Working Paper 99–110, Financial Institutions Center, The Wharton School, University of Pennsylvania.

Feinberg, R. A., Kim, I-K., Hokama, L., de Ruyter, K. & Keen, C. (2000). Operational determinants of caller satisfaction in the call center. *International Journal of Service Industry Management*, **11**, 131–141.

Frenkel, S., Korczyniski, M., Shire, K. & Tam, M. (1999). *On the Front-line: Organization of Work in the Information Economy*. Ithaca, NY: Cornell University Press.

Frenkel, S., Tam, M, Korczynski, M. & Shire, K. (1998). Beyond Bureaucracy? Work organisation in call centres. *International Journal of Human Resource Management*, **9**, 957–979.

Garson, B. (1988). *The Electronic Sweatshop: How Computers are Transforming the Office of the Future into the Factory of the Past*. New York: Simon & Schuster.

Grant, R. A. & Higgins, C. A. (1989). Computerised performance monitors: factors affecting acceptance. *IEEE Transactions on Engineering Management*, **38**, 306–314.

Grieco, A., Moltini, G., Piccolo, B. & Occhipiati, E. (1995). *Work with Display Units*. Amsterdam: Elsevier Science.

Grandey, A. A. (2000). Emotion regulation in the workplace: a new way to conceptualise emotional labour. *Journal of Occupational Health*, **5**, 95–110.

Grundy, J. (1998). Trust in Organizational Teams. *Harvard Business Review*, **73**, 40–50.

Gutek, B. (1995). *The Dynamics of Service: Reflections on the Changing Nature of Customer/Provider Interactions*. San Fransisco, CA: Jossey-Bass.

Gutek, B. (1997). Dyadic interactions in organisations. In C. L. Cooper & S. E. Jackson (Eds), *Creating Tomorrows Organizations Today*. Chichester: Wiley.

Health and Safety Executive (1992). *Display Screen Equipment Regulations*. London: HMSO.

Health and Safety Executive (1999). *Initial Advice Regarding Call Centre Working Practices*. Local Authority Circular 94/1, Health and Safety Executive, Sheffield.

Hochschild, A. (1983). *The Managed Heart: the Commercialization of Human Feeling*. Los Angeles, CA: University of California Press.

Holman, D. (2001). Employee Stress in call centres. *Human Resource Management Journal* (at press).

Holman, D., Chissick, C. & Totterdell, P. (2002). The effects of performance monitoring on emotional labour on well-being in call centres. *Motivation and Emotion*, **26**(1), 57–81.

Holman, D. & Fernie, S. (2000). Employee Well-being in Call Centres. Institute of Work Psychology, Memo No. 260, University of Sheffield.

Hosmer, L. T. (1995). Trust: the connecting link between organisational theory and philosophical ethics. *Academy of Management Review*, **20**, 379–403.

Houlihan, M. (2001). Control and commitment in the call centre? More evidence from the field. Paper presented at Conference on Call Centres and Beyond: the Human Resource Management Implications, Kings College, London, November.

Hutchinson, S., Purcell, J. & Kinnie, N. (2000). Evolving high commitment management and the experience of the RAC call centre. *Human Resource Management Journal*, **10**, 63–78.

Ichniowski, C., Kochan, T., Levine, D., Olson, C. & Strauss, G. (1996). What works at work: overview and assessment. *Industrial Relations*, **35**, 299–334.

Incomes Data Services (1997). *Pay and Conditions in Call Centres*. London: Incomes Data Services.

Irving, R. H., Higgins, C. A. & Safeyeni, F. R. (1986). Computerised performance monitoring systems: use and abuse. *Communications of the ACM*, August 29, 794–801.

Karaseck, R. A. & Theorell, T. G. (1990). *Healthy Work: Stress, Productivity and the Reconstruction of Working Life*. New York: Basic Books.

Keefe, J. & Batt, R. (2001). Telecommunications services: union–management relations in an era of industry re-consolidation. In P. Clark, J. Delaney & A. Frost (Eds), *Collective Bargaining: Current Developments and Future Challenges*. IRRA Research Volume. Madison, WI: IRRA.

Kinnie, N., Purcell, J. & Hutchinson, S. (2000). Managing the employment relationship in call centres. In K. Purcell (Ed.), *Changing Boundaries in Employment* (pp. 133–159). Bristol: Bristol Academic Press.

Knights, D. & McCabe, D. (1998). What happens when the phone goes wild? Staff, stress and spaces for escape in a BPR telephone banking call regime. *Journal of Management Studies*, **35**, 163–194.

Korczynski, M., Shire, K., Frenkel, S. & Tam, M. (2000). Service work in consumer capitalism: customers, control and contradictions. *Work, Employment and Society*, **14**, 669–687.

Levitt, T. (1972). Production line approach to services. *Harvard Business Review*, **50**, 41–50.

Metcalf, D. & Fernie, S. (1998). (Not) hanging on the telephone: payment systems in the new sweatshops. *Centrepiece*, **3**, 7–11.

Morley, I. E. & Stephenson, G. M. (1970). Formality in experimental negotiations: a validation study. *British Journal of Psychology*, **61**, 383–384.

Muscovici, S. (1967). Communication processes and properties of language. In L. Berkovitz (Ed.) *Advances in Experimental Social Psychology*, Vol. 3 (pp. 225–270), Academic Press, New York.

Nohria, N. & Eccles, R. G. (Eds) (1992). *Networks and Organizations*. Boston, MA: Harvard Business School Press.

Orlinowski, W. J. (1992). The duality of technology: rethinking the concept of technology in organisations. *Organization Science*, **3**, 398–427.

Parker, S. K. & Wall, T. D. (1998). *Job and Work Design*. London: Sage.

Rosenfield, M. (1997). *Counselling by Telephone*. Sage: London.

Rutter, D. R. (1987). *Communicating by Telephone*. Oxford: Pergamon.

Rutter, D. R. & Stephenson, G. M. (1979). The role of visual communication in social interaction. *Current Anthropology*, **20**, 124–125.

Schlesinger, L. & Heskett, J. (1991). Breaking the cycle of failure in services. *Sloan Management Review*, **32**, 17–28.

Schuler, R. S. & Jackson, S. E. (1995). Linking competitive strategies with human resource management strategies. *Academy of Management Executive*, **1**, 207–219.

Short, J., Williams, E. & Christie, A. (1976). *The Social Psychology of Telecommunications*. Chichester: Wiley.

Singh, J. & Sirdeshmukh, D. (2000). Agency and trust in consumer satisfaction and loyalty judgements. *Journal of the Academy of Marketing Science*, **28**, 150–167.

Smith, M. J., Carayon, P., Sanders, K. J., Lim, S. Y. & LeGrande, D. (1992). Employee stress and health complaints in jobs with and without monitoring. *Applied Ergonomics*, **23**, 17–27.

Spector, P. E. (1987). Interactive effects of perceived control and job stressors on affective reactions and health outcomes for clerical workers. *Work and Stress*, **1**, 155–162.

Stanton, J. M. (2000). Reactions to employee performance monitoring: framework, review and research directions. *Human Performance*, **13**, 85–113.

Sturdy, A. (2000). Training in service—importing and imparting customer service culture as an interactive process. *International Journal of Human Resource Management*, **11**, 1082–1103.

Sturdy, A., Knights, D. & Willmott, H. (Eds) (1992). *Skill and Consent*. London: Routledge.

Taylor, P. & Bain, P. (1999). An assembly line in the head: the call centre labour process. *Industrial Relations Journal*, **30**, 101–117.

Taylor, P. & Bain, P. (2001). Trades unions, workers' rights and the frontier of control in UK call centres. *Economic and Industrial Democracy*, **22**, 39–66.

Terry, D. & Jimmieson, N. (1999). Work control and well-being: a decade review. In C. Cooper & I. Robertson (Eds), *International Review of Industrial and Organizational Psychology*, Vol. 14 (pp. 95–148). Chichester: Wiley.

Totterdell, P. & Holman, D. (2001). Just trying to keep my customers satisfied: a diary study of emotional dissonance in a call centre. Paper presented at European Congress of Psychology Conference, London, 3 July.

Totterdell, P. & Holman, D. (2002). Emotional regulation in customer service roles: testing a model of emotional labour. *Journal of Occupational Health Psychology* (in press).

Trades Union Congress (2001). *It's Your Call: TUC Call Centre Workers' Campaign*. London: TUC.

Vandevelde, H. (2001). Call centres don't have to be hellish. *Sunday Times*, 25 November, Public Appointments (p. 9).

Waters, R. (1998). *Computer Telephony Integration*. London: Artech House.

Winslow, C. D. & Bramer, W. L. (1994). *Futurework*. New York: Free Press.

Wood, S. (Ed.) (1982). *The Degradation of Work?* London: Hutchninson.

Wood, S. (1995). Can we speak of high commitment management on the shop floor? *Journal of Management Studies*, **32**, 215–247.

Wright, P. & McMahon, G. (1992). Theoretical perspectives for strategic human resource management. *Journal of Management*, **18**, 295–320.

Zapf, D., Vogt, C., Seifert, C., Mertini, H. & Isic, A. (1999). Emotion work as a source of stress: the concept and development of an instrument. *European Journal of Work and Organisational Psychology*, **8**, 371–400.

CHAPTER 8

Knowledge Management

Harry Scarbrough
Warwick Business School, University of Warwick, Coventry, UK

This chapter considers the impact of knowledge management (KM) on the workplace. This is still a matter of some debate, and the limited evidence currently available makes it difficult to draw any conclusive judgements. Despite this caveat, however, one of the recurring themes of this chapter will be the dramatic contrast between the level of interest and expectation surrounding KM and its concrete achievements at workplace level. The explanations for that contrast are many and various. As we will see, however, they have something to do with the inherent scope of the design of KM systems, but also the limited success of such designs, especially as they relate to the use of IT and the pursuit of management control. While KM's scope clearly extends beyond the conventional aims and criteria of work organization—being largely concerned with relationships and knowledge exchange *between*, rather than *within*, workgroups—the experience of what has been termed "first generation KM" (Blackler, 2000) has often failed to live up to the expectations that this concept has created.

To begin with the scope of KM's aspirations, however, we can observe that while KM notionally has an important impact on employee behaviour, we only have sketchy indications of the evidence for such impact. Much the greater part of the visible impact to date has been on the management community, where KM is associated with important developments in both managerial thinking and practice. In addressing KM's impact, therefore, we need to acknowledge its importance both as a discourse—a way of talking about management—and as a rationale for the use of a diverse array of tools and practices within organizations. Accordingly, this chapter is structured around the following themes: the wider context for KM; the organizational obstacles to KM; KM's impact on management thinking; KM's impact on organizational practice; and finally, KM's implications for HRM.

WIDER CONTEXT FOR KM

Before evaluating its organizational impact, it is important to place KM in a wider context. The emergence of KM can be related to a constellation of changes—some profound, some more cosmetic—in the business environment. These include:

- Long-run shifts in advanced industrial economies, which have led to the increasingly widespread perception of knowledge as an important organizational asset (Castells, 1996).
- The rise of occupations based on the creation and use of knowledge (Reich, 1991), and changes in the management of professional groups within firms (Whittington, 1991; Willcocks et al., 1995).
- The convergence of information and communication technologies, and the advent of new tools such as intranets and groupware systems (Alavi & Leidner, 1997).
- Theoretical developments, e.g. the resource-based view of the firm, which emphasize the importance of unique and inimitable assets, such as tacit knowledge (Grant, 1997).
- New wave approaches to packaging and promoting consultancy services in the wake of business process re-engineering (Willmott, 1995).

Taken together, these developments have prompted a re-thinking of conventional management approaches to knowledge. Since the development of scientific management in the early 1900s, knowledge has generally been viewed by managers not as a resource but as a cost. Indeed, the explicit aim of scientific management was to remove knowledge from the workforce altogether and concentrate it in the heads of managers. Processes of standardization, specialization and de-skilling were the bedrock of the modern organization (Clegg, 1990). Now the development of KM does not seem to signify any lessening of these economic pressures on the creation and exploitation of knowledge. Indeed, the concern to capture knowledge and to make it an organizational resource rather suggests the further intensification of such pressures. Companies seek to recycle knowledge as much as possible, ensuring that local insights and learning are made more widely available throughout the organization. Given these intensifying economic pressures, some commentators have questioned whether KM is fundamentally different to scientific management in its ultimate aims (McKinlay, 2000).

But while KM can certainly be likened to scientific management in its aim of exploiting knowledge for economic ends, it would be wrong to overstate the similarities. Not only is KM a much broader-based movement than that of scientific management, encompassing a wide range of different approaches, its emergence and practice reflect important changes in the business and organizational context, which clearly distinguish it from the narrower efficiency focus of scientific management. Arguably, the key problems that KM attempts to address are those associated with the distribution of knowledge across increasingly fluid social boundaries, e.g. hierarchical, horizontal, spatial, temporal. Firms introducing KM initiatives seek to improve their exploitation (re-use) and exploration (creation) of knowledge (March, 1991) by providing ways of interconnecting disparate knowledge domains as they restructure (e.g. into flatter, decentralized or networked forms) and reorganize (e.g. around process lines), sometimes on a global scale.

Against this backdrop, KM has become a portmanteau term to designate a number of different strands of managerial activity associated with knowledge. These include, for instance, attempts to value knowledge in financial terms; practices to exploit the intellectual property of the firm; the management of knowledge workers; and the desire to make learning and situated knowledge available throughout the organization. Despite the diversity of settings and practices, however, KM initiatives tend to share a broadly similar prospectus in terms of the utilitarian perspective they bring to the creation and diffusion of knowledge. In simple terms, this prospectus can be defined as the attempt to constitute and exploit knowledge as an organizational resource. This is reflected in many of the definitions of

KM which circulate within the literature. For example, KM is variously defined as: "an approach to adding or creating value by more actively leveraging the know-how, experience, and judgement resident within and, in many cases, outside of an organization" (Ruggles, 1998); or "the process of creating, capturing, and using knowledge to enhance organizational performance" (Bassi, 1997); or a "process of continually managing knowledge of all kinds to meet existing and emerging needs, to identify and exploit existing and acquired knowledge assets and to develop new opportunities" (Quintas *et al.*, 1997, p. 387). The view of knowledge as an asset, something to be leveraged or captured, is a recurring trope in the literature on KM.

ORGANIZATIONAL OBSTACLES TO KM

Constituting knowledge as a resource has profound implications for management and for organizational practices. These are often neglected in articles dealing with KM which tend to focus on the mechanisms for exploiting knowledge. As many studies have indicated, however, the distributed, tacit and situated character of knowledge makes it difficult to extract and transfer from specific groups and settings (Blackler, 1995; Spender, 1996; Tsoukas, 1996). Moreover, both the creation and the exploitation of knowledge is dependent on the behaviour and work practices of employees, and is thus inextricably linked to the control of labour within the firm.

This intractability and embeddedness of knowledge has long led organizations to seek to economize on its use through specialization and stratification (Grant, 1996). As noted above, the division of labour applied to that end—as reflected in existing hierarchical and functional structures—itself represents a significant obstacle to attempts to constitute knowledge as a resource for the organization as a whole. The exploitation of knowledge as an organizational resource is therefore a complex endeavour which extends across technical, social and economic dimensions, as outlined below:

- In technical terms, KM involves *centralizing* knowledge that is currently scattered across the organization and codifying tacit forms of knowledge. In this more centralized and explicit form, knowledge can be accessed by a variety of groups according to business needs. The development of centralized knowledge databases is one manifestation of this aim.
- In social and political terms, KM involves *collectivizing* knowledge, so that it is no longer the exclusive property of individuals or groups. Knowledge is abstracted from highly situated processes of social learning, such that its use is no longer so closely tied to its creation. This is reflected in the deployment of IT systems, such as intranets and groupware, which seek to enhance knowledge sharing within and between employee groups. It is also manifest in the development of "communities of practice", which seek to improve the sharing of good practice at the occupational level.
- In economic terms, KM is a response to organizations' need to intensify their creation and exploitation of knowledge. This reflects the rising competitive pressures for innovation and the more rapid turnover of new products and services. KM increases the throughput rate for converting knowledge into new products and services.

The tension between these aspirations and existing hierarchical structures and practices for managing labour helps to account for many of the initiatives associated with KM. Thus, to cite one important example, the pressures for more rapid innovation create a need for multi-functional or multi-organizational project teams, spanning organizational boundaries (Clark & Fujimoto, 1989). This in turn leads to demands for more effective ways of sharing knowledge amongst geographically and organizationally dispersed team members and of capturing the knowledge that they have generated. Such demands are aggravated, not resolved, by conventional bureaucratic and hierarchical forms of organization. The latter constrain the lateral flows of knowledge-sharing with vertical authority structures. They have few, if any, mechanisms for capturing or applying knowledge that transcend internal functional divisions.

A variety of KM initiatives, including the development of intranet technology and the cultivation of communities of practice, can be seen as attempts to address this mis-match between the pressures to exploit knowledge more intensively and prevailing hierarchical structures. As these initiatives indicate, constituting knowledge as an organizational resource involves exploiting the ability of new technologies and organizational innovations to transcend social, geographical and organizational boundaries. Their success, however, seems likely to depend not so much on the technologies or innovations *per se* as on the constraining effect of existing structures and practices predicated on the management of labour.

KM'S IMPACT ON MANAGEMENT THINKING

KM has had an important impact on the ongoing debate in the management community about the design of organizations and the use of technology. Indeed, KM has become a fashionable discourse amongst managers, academics and consultants. To present KM as a management fashion is not to understate its importance. Such fashions are, after all, now an established feature of the contemporary scene (Noon *et al.*, 2000). They represent an important vehicle for the diffusion of new ideas and practices amongst managers. As Abrahamson puts it:

> Management fashions are not cosmetic and trivial. Management fashions shape the management techniques that thousands of managers look to in order to cope with extremely important and complex managerial problems and challenges (Abrahamson, 1996, p. 279).

As a management discourse, however, KM is much more loosely defined and ambiguous than other similar concepts, such as TQM and BPR. This reflects the rich array of sources and ideas on which KM has drawn in its emergence as a discourse. The nebulous nature of "knowledge" itself empowers a wide range of approaches and tools. Much debate, for example, centres on the distinction between knowledge, information and data. Here, Earl argues that knowledge is information that is tested and validated. It may or may not be codified, depending on its tacit or explicit nature (Earl, 1996). Others adopt differing views, defining knowledge as, respectively; "a dynamic human process of justifying personal beliefs as part of an aspiration for the truth" (Nonaka, 1994); "information made actionable" (Maglitta, 1995); and "information within people's minds" (Davenport & Marchand, 1999).

KM initiatives within firms are said to focus primarily on relatively broad or intangible objectives, such as the pursuit of competitive advantage, rather than the narrower aims of improving efficiency, quality or productivity. Thus, authors argue that "KM is becoming a

Table 8.1 Perspectives on KM

Cognitive perspective	Community perspective
Knowledge is equated with objectively defined concepts and facts	Knowledge is socially constructed and based on experience
Knowledge can be codified and transferred through text: information systems have a crucial role	Knowledge can be tacit and is transferred through participation in social networks, including occupational groups and teams
Gains from knowledge management include exploitation through the recycling of existing knowledge	Gains from knowledge management include exploration through the sharing and synthesis of knowledge among different social groups and communities
The primary function of knowledge management is to codify and capture knowledge	The primary function of knowledge management is to encourage knowledge-sharing through networking
The critical success factor is technology	The critical success factor is trust and collaboration
The dominant metaphor is the human memory	The dominant metaphor is the human community

core competence that companies must develop to succeed in tomorrow's dynamic global autonomy" (Skyrme & Amidon, 1998). In keeping with this emphasis on relative competitive performance, core KM activities are said to include benchmarking and monitoring knowledge "assets" as well as processes for knowledge capture, creation and distribution (Drew, 1996).

KM's status as a fashionable discourse within the management community makes its impact on management thinking relatively visible. In addressing that impact, however, it is clear that within the diverse array of approaches to KM outlined in the literature, recent years have seen the emergence of two broad perspectives. These perspectives have been given a variety of labels, e.g. the "engineering" and the "cultivation" approaches (Markus, 2000), but here will be summarily defined as the "cognitive" and the "community" perspectives. Obviously, this distinction between two broad perspectives cannot do justice to the extensive literature relating to KM—particularly, more recent studies on "embodied interaction" (Dourish, 2001) and "embodied mind" (Clark, 1998), which not only challenge the Cartesian mind–body distinction but also help to blur the distinction between "social" and "technical" activities (Scarbrough, 1995). However, this characterization of existing thinking, which is summarized in Table 8.1, is useful in capturing the polarity in the literature between different views of knowledge, i.e. as a cognitive or a community phenomenon.

Cognitive Perspective

This approach to the management of knowledge adopts a cognitive, information-processing view of the firm, where valuable knowledge located inside people's heads or in successful organizational practices is identified, captured and processed, via the use of IT tools, so that it can be applied in new contexts. Tacit knowledge is codified into more explicit forms. The aim, then, is to make the knowledge inside employees' heads or the knowledge embedded in successful routines widely available to the rest of the organization. Indeed the practice of "knowledge management", as seen, is frequently reduced to the implementation of new IT systems for knowledge transfer, e.g. "the idea behind knowledge management is to stockpile workers' knowledge and make it accessible to others via a searchable application" (Cole-Gomolski, 1997). Knowledge is viewed metaphorically as a physical entity which can be stored, "drilled" and "mined".

Community Perspective

In contrast to the above, organizational theorists have highlighted the need to understand knowledge as also embedded in, and constructed from and through, social relationships and interactions (Blackler, 1995; Nonaka & Takeuchi, 1995). According to this view, knowledge (unlike data) cannot simply be processed; rather, it is continuously recreated and reconstituted through dynamic, interactive and social networking activity. Blackler (1995), for example, draws a categorization of forms of knowledge as: *embedded* in technologies, rules and organizational procedures; *embodied* into the practical activity-based competencies and skills of key members (i.e. practical knowledge or "know-how"); *encultured* as collective understandings, stories, values and beliefs of organizational members; or *embrained* as the conceptual understandings and cognitive skills of key members (i.e. conceptual knowledge or "know-what"). Moreover, where the cognitive perspective emphasizes the codification of knowledge into more explicit forms, here the emphasis is on the communication of knowledge on a basis of shared trust and collaboration.

The community model highlights the importance of relationships, shared understandings and attitudes to knowledge formation and sharing (Kofman & Senge, 1993). It is important to acknowledge these issues, since they help to define the likely success or failure of attempts to implement ICT-based "knowledge management" initiatives. The community model suggests that it is easier to share knowledge between individuals who have the same or similar work practices, because they share a common understanding and belief system.

In the following section, we will review the practical effects of these different approaches to KM, and seek to identify some of the reasons why they often fall short of the expectations they create.

IMPACT OF KM ON ORGANIZATIONAL PRACTICES

There is still little empirical work on the spread and impact of KM at organizational and workplace level. Much of the existing literature operates at a relatively low level of evidence, with more or less uncritical accounts of KM practices in leading firms providing the most substantive empirical material available. Firms such as BP, Skandia, Buckman Labs and Xerox continue to act as role models for the development of KM practices. Where more extensive studies have been undertaken, they have often been carried out by consultancy organizations with a vested interest in promoting KM or particular versions of it. The available evidence is therefore sketchy.

Summarising that evidence, however, leads to the following conclusions:

- KM has had only limited impact at workplace level and in the design of work organization. KM's impact on work organization and on other areas of management seems questionable. Unlike BPR or even total quality management (TQM), KM involves no explicit agenda of radical work redesign. Rather, it is often linked to investments in IT systems, such as intranets or groupware, which are designed to facilitate collaboration around existing forms of work organization. Where other discourses have sought to bring about radical changes in work practice and organizational forms, KM presents a more benign aspect. Its development is often situated *between* work groups and business units, and is frequently aimed at improving their interaction. Thus, many KM initiatives are aimed more globally at transcending existing organizational boundaries—enabling the transfer of best practice across multinational sites, for instance, or promoting knowledge-sharing amongst worldwide "communities of practice". In that sense, therefore, KM is predominantly additive rather than transformative in intent; intensifying but not fundamentally changing the existing work processes within the organization.

- KM's "discursive penetration" (Clark, 2000) into organizations is most advanced in the areas of the design and justification of IT investments. Many KM initiatives have centred on the development of IT systems such as groupware (systems which enable collaborative working between distributed groups and individuals), intranets (internal company communication systems using Internet technologies) and so-called "corporate yellow pages" (used to identify the skills of individual employees). Some evidence for this assessment of KM is provided by existing surveys of KM practice. For example, a KPMG survey in 1998 of 100 leading UK companies of £200 million plus turnover found that 90% had Internet access for employees, two-thirds had developed intranets and document-management systems, 50% had adopted groupware and one third had actually developed data warehousing and decision support systems. Against this evidence on the spread of IT systems related to KM, 43% of the sample claimed to actually have a KM initiative in place. However, only one-quarter of the latter group (i.e. only 10% of the overall sample) were said to be at the implementation stage. Moreover, only one-third of the KM adopters had developed a strategy for KM and/or a budget for KM activities. There is even evidence to suggest that in those areas where KM has penetrated, it has partly involved the relabelling of existing activities. In their study of KM practices in UK R&D functions, for instance, Coombs & Hull (1998) found that KM frequently involved the development or relabelling of existing management practices.
- The scope of KM initiatives is limited to relatively small numbers of employees—not extending beyond knowledge worker groups at the apex of the organization. For example, the CREATE study of 128 firms worldwide in 1999 found that the coverage of KM initiatives varied from 0.5–20% of the workforce.
- At the same time, and reflecting this limited coverage, many management groups are excluded from active involvement in the design of KM initiatives, with top management and Information Systems (IS) management playing the dominant roles. Thus, a survey of European businesses by the Information Systems Research Centre at Cranfield found that KM was seen as having most relevance to the R&D function and least relevance to the HR and finance functions (Cranfield School of Management, 1997). This echoed an earlier survey of 143 organizations worldwide reported in the *International Knowledge Management Newsletter* (November 1997). This found that in most organizations the responsibility for the deployment of KM lay primarily with top management and IS management.

Reflecting the different perspectives noted above, the substantive effects of KM within organizations to date seem to centre on either the IT-based extraction and concentration of knowledge or the development of communities of practice as a social arena for the sharing of knowledge. Some illustrations of these substantive effects are outlined below.

Role of IT Systems in KM

Many of the attempts to relate knowledge to information and data noted above, reflect the literature's predominant concern with the role of IT in KM. The link between IT developments and the discourse of KM is evident in the close coupling of IT and KM, which is a feature of much of the literature (Scarbrough & Swan, 2001; Raub & Ruling, 2001). Yet, despite the stress that many authors place on the use of IT, the evidence for the effective role of IT systems in creating or transferring knowledge is limited. The evidence suggests three major constraints on the use of IT for KM: the embeddedness of knowledge in social networks; the importance of face-to-face interaction for knowledge exchange; and the importance of informal settings for knowledge creation.

On the first point, this is illustrated by a study of the introduction of groupware systems (e.g. Lotus Notes). This found that such systems tend to reinforce, rather than change, the communication patterns among existing social networks. Thus, the study observed that organization members who communicated regularly and frequently before the introduction of a groupware system continued to do so using the new system. Conversely, the introduction of groupware had no impact on those members who did not communicate with each other before its introduction (Vandenbosch & Ginzberg, 1996). As Nahapiet & Ghoshal (1998) note, "The availability of electronic knowledge exchange does not automatically induce a willingness to share information and build new intellectual capital".

Similar constraints have been observed for other KM technologies. For example, a recent study of a KM initiative found that scientific employees in a pharmaceutical company made little use of a database of "lessons learned" from projects; "this was contrary to sharing tacit knowledge only with one's immediate workgroup and opened up the individual to scrutiny beyond existing structures" (McKinlay, 2000, p. 119). Likewise, a study of corporate intranet development in a global banking organization found that intranets were unsuccessful in persuading employees to share knowledge with those in other divisions (Newell *et al.*, 2001). Rather, a proliferation of intranets across business divisions only reflected and reinforced existing organizational boundaries. Moreover, the most frequent uses cited in this and other cases tend to be the provision of mundane information—inter-site bus timetables or canteen menus—rather than the sharing of knowledge.

Second, the importance of face-to-face contact has been underlined by studies which emphasize the role of trust in the sharing of knowledge (Nahapiet & Ghoshal, 1998). These studies reinforce previous research on management information systems which has highlighted the limitations of IT even for the provision of timely and valued information. One such study suggested that managers acquired two-thirds of their information from face-to-face or phone conversations and the remaining one-third from documents most of which came from outside the organization (Davenport *et al.*, 1996).

Third, the limitations of IT in knowledge creation were demonstrated in another study of the application of groupware technology (Ciborra & Patriotti, 1998). This highlighted the distinction between "above-the-line" (i.e. visible to management and colleagues in other units) and "below-the-line" activities (visible only to immediate colleagues). Below-the-line activities are where the most creative aspects of innovation projects take place as new ideas, and insights are tested and refined against the thinking of other trusted colleagues. The study found that the introduction of groupware did not remove this distinction, but rather reinforced it. Tools such as groupware were used primarily for above-the-line uses—communicating results and management reporting. Other communication tools, such as E-mail, phone, paper and fax were seen as more relevant to below-the-line activities.

The implication of these constraints on the use of IT systems in KM is not that IT has no value whatsoever in this context. Rather, a number of authors argue that IT systems need to be viewed as multi-dimensional, enabling technologies, whose use encompasses social and behavioural factors as much as technical ones (Ciborra & Patriotti, 1998). This multi-dimensional view of IT systems has been advanced, for instance, by Bressand & Distler (1995), who identify three layers within such systems: infrastructure, the hardware/software which enables the communication contact between network members; infostructure, the formal rules which govern the exchange between the actors on the network, providing a set of cognitive resources (metaphors, common language) whereby people make sense of events on the network; and infoculture, the stock of background knowledge which actors take for granted and which is embedded in the social relations surrounding work group processes.

Communities of Practice

In the 1990s a number of leading organizations identified the value of "communities of practice" as means of encouraging knowledge sharing across the organization. The origins of this approach can be traced back to studies by Lave & Wenger (1991) and Orr (1990) in the early 1990s. Orr's study of photocopier technicians, for instance, highlighted the importance of story-telling amongst this group as a means of sharing knowledge about repair problems. As Brown & Duguid (2000) put it, "The talk (i.e. amongst Orr's reps) made the work intelligible, and the work made the talk intelligible" (p. 125). "As part of this common work-and-talk, creating, learning, sharing and using knowledge appear almost indivisible" (pp. 125–126). Studies such as these were important in defining the properties of a community of practice. For example, Brown & Duguid (2000, p. 127) define such properties as follows: " . . . in getting the job done, the people involved ignored divisions of rank and role to forge a single group around their shared task, with overlapping knowledge, relatively blurred boundaries, and a common working identity". Unlike other types of social network, communities of practice are designed to support the work process directly by allowing individuals to share experience about their work. Such knowledge-sharing is seen as being facilitated by the norms of reciprocity, and levels of trust generated amongst the community.

Although the studies noted above highlight the value of a community approach, it seems to be more difficult for organizations to develop this approach. This may partly be because the cognitive approach tends to fit more neatly with established management practices; the emphasis on individuals and on the use of technology to "capture" knowledge offering a more predictable solution. Conversely, community-based approaches may seem more nebulous to managers. Such groupings do not as a rule appear in organization charts or in the different business processes designed by management (Brown & Duguid, 1998). Whereas project teams, for instance, have leaders, goals, and deliverables, communities of practice are said to be open-ended and free from directive management structures. They are said to be based on a voluntary, collaborative and egalitarian ethos.

The community of practice approach has been widely adopted in a few large organizations—notably in oil companies such as BP and Shell, where it serves to link groups of technicians and engineers who are distributed worldwide. However, the extent of its overall impact beyond these leading firms is still uncertain. There are also critical views that highlight the possible exploitative effects of this approach; McKinlay (2000) in the study noted above, analyses communities in terms of "participatory control", i.e. a form of control which requires the active engagement of participants. In his study of the UK operation of a large pharmaceutical firm, he describes the development of a "lessons learned" database encompassing tips generated by individuals and workgroup briefings at the end of a project. He describes the efforts that managers made "to socialise the digital world and to extend the reach of digital communication into the social world of the workplace" (McKinlay, 2000, p. 117). He views such efforts as an expression of the long-standing managerial desire to access tacit knowledge through the exploitation of communities of practice.

The emergence of communities of practice is seen as linked to a shift in the philosophy of management away from conventional forms of control towards what Wenger (2000) terms "cultivation" or McKinlay (2000) defines as "participatory control". These approaches involve opening up social and virtual spaces for knowledge exchange and supporting the dialogic basis of knowledge creation. They might encompass a number of activities, including the following: public events such as knowledge fairs that bring the community together; multiple forms of leadership, including "thought leaders", networkers, and people who document practice; inter-community learning projects; and the creation and dissemination of artefacts such as documents, tools, stories, websites, etc. (Wenger, 2000).

Although they proceed from a very different epistemology to that which usually informs the design of IT systems, communities of practice may still be compatible with the use of such systems. Indeed, many global organizations view them as a means of connecting geographically and culturally disparate communities. In companies such as Buckman Labs and Xerox, IT systems provide a worldwide forum through which employees can share experience and solve problems collectively. In these cases, e-mail systems or intranets allow a conversational exchange of experience about particular problems. Thus, typically, an individual might post a particular problem of practice to a discussion forum. Subsequently, a member of the worldwide community from another continent or country would respond with a suggested solution or tip for dealing with the problem, developing the thread of the exchange. Progressively, others would build on that contribution, refine it and develop it. Brown & Duguid (2000) note that an example of such a system, Xerox's "Eureka" database, currently holds about 30 000 records. They cite what they say is an example of how the database is used. In one case, an engineer in Brazil was about to replace a malfunctioning high-end colour machine at a cost of $40 000. A quick visit to the database, however, produced a tip from a Montreal photocopier representative that led him to replace a 50 cent fuse instead. Xerox were said to have quantified the savings made from this and other uses of the database at around $100 million.

HRM IMPLICATIONS OF KM

Human resource management (HRM) and KM are both broadly defined management discourses which encompass a wide variety of different perspectives. On the surface, however, they share important similarities in their aim of mobilizing important but sometimes elusive resources for the benefit of the organization's strategic goals. It may seem surprising, then, to note that relatively few articles on KM link it in any meaningful way to the HRM practices of the organization. Beyond a few cursory references to the need for employee commitment or the importance of a "supportive culture", articles on KM make few, if any, links to HRM. Substantive debate on the implications of staple HRM policies to do with recruitment, development and reward is remarkably absent from much of the existing KM literature (Scarbrough & Swan, 2001).

This myopic view certainly reflects the emphasis we find in much KM literature on IT tools and systems. It ignores a considerable body of literature which points to the formative role played by HRM practices in the development of the organization's knowledge base. The scope of this "HRM gap" in the KM debate is signalled by a variety of studies which highlight this important formative role. Under this heading, we might include studies of the impact of career systems on the development of employee knowledge (Lam, 1998), the contribution of training and development to the formation of human capital (Switzer, 1996), and the implications of reward systems for the development of team working and trust relationships within firms.

While such studies are certainly relevant to KM, relatively few studies within the HRM field itself have directly addressed the knowledge dimensions of organizations. This seems to reflect the persistence of the broad conceptual paradigm in which HRM is essentially viewed as the management of labour. This places the emphasis on the motivation and commitment of groups and individuals but neglects the impact of their contribution to the knowledge-base of the organization (Scarbrough & Carter, 2000). Of course, employee knowledge is made available through their physical interaction with their work tools and the immediate work environment. However, it is also clear that in many cases it is employees' knowledge, not their physical effort, which is critical to their relationship with the employing firm, e.g. Grant, (1991, p. 128) discusses this relationship in terms of a balance of power:

> The degree of control exercised by a firm and the balance of power between the firm and an individual employee depends crucially on the relationship between the individual's skills and organizational routines. The more deeply embedded are organizational routines within groups of individuals and the more are they supported by the contributions of other resources, then the greater is the control that the firm's management can exercise.

Some HRM studies are beginning to explore these knowledge dimensions of the employment relationship. For example, certain studies have addressed the specific problem of HRM practices for knowledge workers (Tampoe, 1993). More generally, other studies have highlighted the role of HRM practices in absorbing and retaining knowledge. The importance of such practices is underscored by the open-ended nature of the employment contract. This not only establishes the potential mobility of human resources, but also a bargaining power that may allow them to appropriate a good deal of the market value that their skills command (Kay, 1993). Existing studies suggest a variety of absorption and learning mechanisms that are available to firms. These include teamwork and firm-specific training (Kamoche & Mueller, 1998). In addition, companies can limit the bargaining power of individuals by preventing any single individual gaining access to the complete corporate stock of knowledge—an approach which is followed, for instance, by Cosworth Engineering in the UK (Kay, 1993).

Appropriating employee knowledge for the organization also involves ensuring that such knowledge is retained by the organization and not lost through turnover or delayering.

HRM practices which may enable such knowledge retention tend to centre on the creation of continuance commitment through employee status, firm-specific training and pensions. The creation of such "human resource barriers" (Capelli & Singh, 1992) may require the development of "backloaded" payment systems rewarding loyalty with seniority and status, promotion systems which lock in high performers, and attractive pension arrangements.

Studies such as these underline the extent to which the processing of knowledge within organizations is intimately linked to the way employees are recruited, developed and rewarded. Setting aside topics which have still to be adequately researched or theorized, it is possible to determine from the existing literature three major areas where KM's links to HRM are beginning to be explored; the links between KM and HRM strategy; the links to commitment and reward; and the links to organization culture.

Links to HRM Strategy

While research on knowledge absorption and retention has highlighted mechanisms and processes through which employee knowledge is appropriated by the organization, relatively few studies have analysed the relationship between such mechanisms and firm-level strategy. One study which attempts to do this, however, is a recent study of consultancy firms in the USA (Hansen et al., 1999). Although not specifically concerned with HRM, but with "knowledge management strategy", this study does identify some important relationships between HRM and KM. Hansen et al. argue that there are basically two KM strategies: "codification" and "personalization".

- *Codification:* "Knowledge is carefully codified and stored in databases where it can be accessed and used readily by anyone in the company"(p. 107).
- *Personalization:* "Knowledge is closely tied to the person who developed it and is shared mainly through direct person-to-person contacts" (p. 107).

These strategies overlap to some extent with the cognitive and community perspectives outlined earlier. However, the notion of "personalization" places a greater stress on individual rather than community knowledge, reflecting the consultancy context from which these strategies are derived. The different strategies are seen as linked to the HRM and IT management practices of the organization as outlined in Table 8.2.

This analysis does not claim that organizations pursue these strategies exclusively—firms with a codification strategy also engage in personalization to some degree. However, Hansen et al. argue that competitive success involves pursuing one strategy predominantly. Success comes from an 80–20 split in strategic emphasis. Failure comes from attempting to "straddle" both strategies equally.

As this study was based on consultancy organizations, its wider generalizability may be limited. The personalization strategy emphasizes the role of individual experts and thus reflects the relatively individualistic nature of consultancy work. However, in other settings groups and communities may play an important role in creating and sharing knowledge. At the same time, the Hansen et al. account makes several useful contributions to our understanding of the links between HRM and KM. First, it links both KM and HRM to the competitive strategy of the organization. This is a useful corrective to the many articles which imply that KM can be equated with the development of large IT databases—as if the sheer quantity of "knowledge" communicated and stored was the secret of business

Table 8.2 Knowledge management strategies

	Codification strategy	Personalization strategy
Use of IT	Invest heavily in IT—connect people with re-usable knowledge	Invest moderately in IT—facilitate conversations and exchange of tacit knowledge
Human resources		
Recruitment and selection	Hire new college graduates who are well suited to the re-use of knowledge and the implementation of solutions	Hire MBAs who like problem-solving and can tolerate ambiguity
Training and development	Train people in groups and through computer-based distance learning	Train people through one-to-one mentoring
Reward systems	Reward people for using and contributing to document databases	Reward people for directly sharing knowledge with others

Source: Adapted from Hansen *et al.* (1999).

success. Hansen *et al.* (1999) show that it is not knowledge *per se* but the way it is applied to strategic objectives which is the critical ingredient of competitiveness. Second, this account effectively demonstrates the need to align HRM practices—recruitment, training and reward—to the KM strategy in use. As they note of reward systems, for instance:

> The two knowledge management strategies call for different incentive systems. In the codification model, managers need to develop a system that encourages people to write down what they know and to get those documents into the electronic repository... companies that are following the personalization approach... need to reward people for sharing knowledge directly with other people... (Hansen *et al.*, 1999, p. 113).

The Link to Knowledge-sharing and Rewards

Writers such as Senge (1993), Kofman & Senge (1993) and Nonaka (1991, 1994) all emphasize the importance of commitment to the effective implementation of KM practices. As Nonaka notes:

> in tapping the tacit and often highly subjective insights, intuitions and hunches of individual employees... The key to this process is personal commitment, the employees' sense of identity with the enterprise and its mission (Nonaka, 1991, p. 7).

Moreover, although much of the discussion about KM adopts the perspective of the organization or its senior management, there is ample evidence to suggest that the effectiveness of KM practices ultimately hinges on the response of individual employees. The greater the commitment required of the employee, the greater the need to address the incentives that underpin such commitment. The importance of such incentives was underlined by a recent KPMG survey of 100 leading UK businesses (KPMG, 1998). This found that 39% of respondents said that their organization did not reward knowledge-sharing, and this was considered one of the most important barriers to storing and sharing knowledge (and, if anything, this figure itself seems something of an underestimate, when we consider the limited evidence of the number of firms who explicitly reward knowledge-sharing).

In addressing reward systems for KM, it is important to note that incentives can take a variety of forms, not all of them necessarily controlled by senior management. If KM systems encourage knowledge sharing between individuals and groups, for example, the rewards for commitment are provided through the *quid pro quo* of the knowledge supplied by work colleagues. There are also intangible rewards in the form of status, reputation and recognition which can be conferred on knowledge leaders in a particular field.

Turning to more tangible incentives, however, the range is equally wide in that knowledge-intensive environments, by their nature, may permit a more innovative approach to rewarding commitment. Instances of innovative rewards being used to foster KM include the example of Hewlett Packard, where free Lotus Notes licenses were distributed to encourage trainers and educators within the organization to submit comments and ideas to knowledge bases. Also, when a new knowledge base was established, 2000 free air miles were offered to the first 50 readers and another 500 miles to anyone who posted a submission. Where knowledge sharing is central to the strategy of an organization, however—as, for example, in many consultancies and R&D organizations—there may be attempts to develop a more formalized approach to incentives. This may be easier to manage where KM is focused on exploiting the expertise of individuals, e.g. long-term achievement within a particular discipline may be rewarded by promoting individuals to senior expert positions within a "dual-career" system. This practice, developed most notably at Fujitsu/ICL, for instance, avoids siphoning off knowledge leaders into mainstream management positions. Rajan *et al.* (1998) also stress the importance of "soft rewards"; it is "essential that employees can see that sharing means immediate gains, such as less hassle, or easier tasks, reducing working hours or earlier closing" (p. 14). Moreover, in terms of specific links between rewards and knowledge-sharing, they advocate the use of intranet systems, where the number of "hits" per individual employee's website may be used to influence decisions over promotion and reward.

Although a few firms have been won over by the logic of linking rewards to knowledge-sharing, it must be recognized that the vast majority of firms do not attempt to do so. A review of the existing literature, relating not only to KM but also to other management practices, suggests that there remain important constraints on managers' ability to make explicit linkages between knowledge-sharing and reward:

- Knowledge-sharing is difficult to evaluate, since the exchange of knowledge may take place in a variety of ways, many of them tacit, and the nature of what has been exchanged may be difficult to evaluate or quantify *ex ante* (von Hippel, 1990; Williamson, 1986).
- Knowledge is created and shared within communities, and much of the most important knowledge is tacit (Lave & Wenger, 1991; Orr, 1990).
- Any linkage between knowledge-sharing and rewards will encourage employees to be more reflexive and instrumental about their willingness to share knowledge with others. Where the reward system operates in an individualistic way, it may encourage individuals to withhold knowledge from others in their workgroup or community (Robertson & Swan, 1998).
- Linking rewards to knowledge means that the measures of knowledge themselves effectively become a currency. This may lead to a tokenistic emphasis on the measures, rather than the creation or sharing of knowledge *per se* (Rajan *et al.*, 1998).

- To the extent that KM is sensitive to the exchange of knowledge within informal social networks, it may be adversely affected by the introduction of reward systems which impair the operation of such networks (Kohn, 1993).

In short, differential rewards may create dissatisfaction or overly instrumental attitudes, and the reward itself may lead towards an overemphasis on the rewarded behaviour to the detriment of the task at hand. Activities relating to knowledge creation and sharing are seen to depend heavily on the participation and intrinsic motivation of the people involved. Such motivation may actually be undermined by extrinsic rewards (Deci, 1975). Given the limitations on the effectiveness of reward systems in promoting knowledge sharing, a number of authors advocate the importance of aligning the informal norms and values of the organization with the goal of knowledge-sharing. This involves giving greater attention to the role of culture and leadership in influencing behaviour.

The Role of Culture in KM

A number of writers on knowledge-intensive organizations have highlighted the attempts by managers to engineer specific forms of organizational culture, e.g. Kunda (1992, p.7) describes the manipulation of culture in one such organization:

> "Culture" is a gloss for an extensive definition of membership role in the corporate community, including rules for thought, behaviour and feeling. For some managers, culture is also the object of their work. There are specified ways of engineering it; making presentations, sending 'messages', running 'bootcamp', writing papers, giving speeches, formulating and publishing the rules....

A number of writers emphasize the role of organizational culture in fostering "normative control" over employee behaviour. This perspective highlights culture as a synthetic instrument of managerial motives, and a subtle means of manipulating meanings and identities. Knowledge-intensive firms are seen as especially prone to this form of cultural control. Although their organic structures actually involve the relaxation of individual commitment to organizational roles, this only ensures a more complete immersion of individual identity in the environing flux of tasks and projects (Alvesson, 1995).

A number of case-studies attest to the importance of culture as both an enabler and inhibitor of KM. One repeated view from the KM literature is to do with the cultural constraints that dog the initial implementation of KM systems. This operates not only in traditional, bureaucratic settings but also in dynamic knowledge-intensive organizations, where a distinct professional sub-culture has emerged. Quinn *et al.* (1996), in a study of Arthur Andersen, found that major changes in incentives and culture were required to stimulate use of its new electronic network. Similarly, there were even problems in the introduction of KM at Ernst & Young:

> The E&Y consulting culture was traditionally based on pragmatism and experience rather than a conceptual orientation; while the culture was changing there were many consultants who had entered the firm and prospered under the old model and found it difficult to aggressively pursue structured knowledge in systems and documents. (Thomas Davenport website: bus.utexas.edu).

One of the most publicized examples of successful KM also underlines the cultural dimension. The development of KM at Buckman Labs in the USA involved the introduction of a KM system, termed K'Netix, which allowed for the easy transfer of information and learning between the company's many operations worldwide. Although the technology was important, the company's CEO, Bob Buckman, believed that the company's success was "90% cultural change" (Pan & Scarbrough, 1998). To underline the value of knowledge-sharing, Buckman put in place a code of ethics which was issued on a wallet-sized laminated card to every employee. Buckman employees were asked to think about the company as a ship, with the code of ethics as the waterline of the ship.

The cultural change wrought at Buckman Labs rested on more than the issue of laminated cards, however. Leadership, and particularly the symbolic deployment of both rewards and punishments, played a critical role. In particular, Bob Buckman's ability to "manage the managers" and thus enrol them as enthusiastic practitioners of KM was of paramount importance. This helped to overcome resistance to change and dismantle barriers to communication across the organization and between different levels of management.

The role of rewards was significant, but not in an instrumental way. Buckman Labs did not formalize the link between rewards and knowledge-sharing. Incentives were offered on an occasional basis, with the explicit aim of reinforcing desired cultural norms, e.g. the group deemed to be the 150 best knowledge sharers were rewarded with a vacation at a fashionable resort. But there was also the hint of sanctions. In the early implementation period of K'Netix, top management wrote to all of those associates who were not willing to participate in the sharing activities.

CONCLUSIONS

This chapter has reviewed the implications of KM on a number of levels. Having situated the discourse within a conducive societal context, it began by acknowledging KM as a currently fashionable discourse in the management community. Setting aside the pejorative implications of management fashion, it is clear that KM has exerted an important impact on management thinking. However, KM has not presented a uniform recipe to managers so much as an array of tools and approaches. As has been noted, such approaches seem polarized between cognitive and community-based perspectives. Each of these approaches has profoundly different consequences for the way KM is practised in organizations; one emphasizing the extraction and concentration of knowledge through technocratic means, and the other stressing the importance of participation and knowledge sharing across communities.

As yet, it is difficult to gauge how far this polarization in the KM literature has affected workplaces. While there are many examples of the application of IT systems for KM, the limited empirical evidence suggests that many of these applications are relatively ineffectual in practice. At the same time, the evidence for the effects of communities of practice is more positive but is limited to a small number of leading firms. Even here, there are suggestions that such communities may be a further development of long-standing managerial interests in exploiting the tacit knowledge of employees (Contu & Willmott, 2000). The evidence on the impact of KM to date, therefore, highlights a number of challenges which still remain to be addressed before any of its variants can begin to satisfy the high expectations that have been created around it. This future agenda for KM is outlined in Table 8.3.

The reasons for the limited impact of KM in practice may be linked to the inherent difficulties confronting any attempt to constitute knowledge as an organizational resource.

Table 8.3 The future agenda for KM

Future challenges	Possible implications for KM
Overcoming the cultural and communication barriers posed by existing division of labour and organization structures	Moving away from a "technocratic" view of knowledge and relating it to the way work and employment is organized
Integrating knowledge from a variety of different contexts within the innovation process	Acknowledging the value of both the cognitive and community perspectives in deepening as well as transferring knowledge
Rewarding the sharing of knowledge as much as the application of effort	Developing KM initiatives within a framework defined by HRM strategies and systems
Linking the development of IT systems to social networks of trust and exchange	Socializing IT systems to encourage dialogue rather than centralization of knowledge
Development of corporate cultures which encourage knowledge-sharing	Linking KM to leadership and programmes of change within organizations
Development of more explicit, holistic and strategic criteria for evaluating the design and success of KM initiatives	Viewing knowledge as a means to an end, not an end in itself. Making KM a general management responsibility with associated metrics

Historically, knowledge within the firm has been fragmented and stratified by the pursuit of efficiency. The process of concentrating and collectivizing knowledge, which is the subtext of many KM initiatives, inevitably clashes with the hierarchical structures, employment practices and subcultures which have evolved within the existing division of labour. This historical legacy of management strategies for economizing on knowledge continues to constrain both the cognitive and community-based approaches to managing knowledge.

Overall, therefore, the available evidence tends to suggest that KM's influence on management thinking has been somewhat greater than its impact on organizational practices. This is partly because the discourse of KM does not empower any specific programme of work redesign. Many KM interventions are situated between work groups or business divisions and are aimed at overcoming the barriers to knowledge sharing posed by existing organizational boundaries. At the same time, KM's potential for change is often channelled through investments in IT systems which are de-coupled from any wider process of organizational change. The limited success of such systems—at least, those that have been the subject of academic research—may reflect not only the limitations of the cognitive perspective on knowledge, but also the absence of wider management involvement in their design and implementation. The relative lack of HRM involvement, in particular, seems likely to inhibit the levels of employee commitment and trust which are critical to the development of knowledge sharing amongst groups and individuals.

In this context, it seems significant that few, if any, examples of successful KM are focused on the use of IT systems. Rather, as the evidence from consultancy organizations and firms such as Buckman Labs seems to underline, successful KM initiatives proceed above all from the determination of business strategy. Whether or not they are labelled "knowledge management", such initiatives are developed at top management level and are linked to a wider programme of organizational change, encompassing HRM policies and cultural change, in which the ruthless exploitation of knowledge is the focal axis of management practice. This holistic approach empowers the kind of innovation that transcends existing internal and external boundaries and enables knowledge to be more fully appropriated as an organizational resource.

REFERENCES

Abrahamson, E. (1996). Management fashion. *Academy of Management Review*, **21**, 254–285.
Alavi, M. & Leidner, D. (1997). *Knowledge Management Systems: Emerging Views and Practices from the Field. INSEAD Working Paper Series*. Paris: INSEAD.
Alvesson, M. (1995). *Management of Knowledge-intensive Companies*. Berlin: Walter de Gruyter.
Bassi, L. J. (1997). Harnessing the power of intellectual capital. *Training and Development*, **51**, 25–30.
Blackler, F. (1995). Knowledge, knowledge work and organizations: an overview and interpretation. *Organization Studies*, **16**, 1021–1046.
Blackler, F. (2000). Knowledge management. *People Management*, **March**, 34–38.
Bressand, A. & Distler, C. (1995). *La Planete Relationelle*. Paris: Flammarion.
Brown, J. S. & Duguid, P. (1998). Organizing knowledge. *California Management Review*, **40**, 90–98.
Brown, J. S. & Duguid, P. (2000). *The Social Life of Information*. Cambridge, MA: Harvard Business School Press.
Capelli, P. & Singh, H. (1992). Integrating strategic human resources and strategic management. In D. Lewis, O. Mitchell & P. Sherer, (Eds), *Research Frontiers in Industrial Relations and Human Resources*, (Chapter 5) Washington, DC: International Industrial Relations Association.
Castells, M. (1996). *The Rise of the Network Society*. Oxford: Blackwell.
Ciborra, C. & Patriotti, G. (1998). Groupware and teamwork in R&D: limits to learning and innovation. *R&D Management*, **28**, 1–10.
Clark, A. (1998). *Being There*. Cambridge, MA: MIT Press.
Clark, K. B. & Fujimoto, T. (1989). Overlapping problem-solving in product development. In K. Ferdows (Ed.), *Managing International Manufacturing* (pp. 127–152). Amsterdam: North-Holland.
Clark, P. (2000). *Organizations in Action*. London: Routledge.
Clegg, S. (1990). *Modern Organizations*. London: Sage.
Cole-Gomolski, B. (1997). Users loathe to share their Know-how. *Computerworld*, **12**(3), 6–15.
Contu, A. & Willmott, H. (2000). Comment on Wenger and Yanow. Knowing in practice: A delicate flower in the organizational learning field. *Organization*, **7**, 269–276.
Coombs, R. H. & Hull, R. R. (1998). Knowledge management practices and path dependency. *Research Policy*, **27**, 237–253.
Cranfield School of Management (1997). *Cranfield Surveys*. Cranfield: Cranfield School of Management.
Davenport, T. H., Jarvenpaa, S. L. & Beers, M. C. (1996). Improving knowledge work processes. *Sloan Management Review*, 53–65.
Davenport T. H. & Marchand, S. (1999). Is KM just good information management? *Financial Times*, Mastering Information Management, 8 March.
Deci, E. L. (1975). *Intrinsic Motivation*. New York: Plenum.
Dourish, P. (2001). *Where the Action Is*. Cambridge, MA: MIT Press.
Drew, S. (1996). Strategy and intellectual capital. *Manager Update*, **7**, 1–11.
Earl, M. J. (1996). *Information Management: the Organizational Dimension*. Oxford: Oxford University Press.
Grant, R. M. (1991). The resource-based theory of competitive advantage: implications for strategy formulation. *California Management Review*, **34**, 114–135.
Grant, R. M. (1996). Toward a Knowledge-based theory of the firm. *Strategic Management Journal*, **17**, 109–122.

Grant, R. M. (1997). The knowledge-based view of the firm: implications for management practice. *Long Range Planning*, **30**, 450–454.
Hansen, M. T., Nohria, N. & Tierney, T. (1999). What's your strategy for managing knowledge? *Harvard Business Review*, 106–116.
Kamoche, K. & Mueller, F. (1998). Human resource management and the appropriation-learning perspective. *Human Relations*, **51**, 1033–1060.
Kay, J. (1993). *Foundation of Corporate Success: How Business Strategies Add Value*. Oxford: Oxford University Press.
Kofman, F. & Senge, P. (1993). Communities of commitment: the heart of learning organizations. *Organizational Dynamics*, **22**, 5.
Kohn, A. (1993). Why incentive plans cannot work. *Harvard Business Review*, 54–63.
KPMG Consultants (1998). *Survey Report on ICTs and KM*. KPMG web-site: www.kpmg.co.uk
Kunda, G. (1992). *Engineering Culture: Control and Commitment in a High-tech Corporation*. Philadelphia: Temple University Press.
Lam, A. (1998). Tacit knowledge, organisational learning and innovation: a societal perspective. British Academy of Management Conference, Nottingham.
Lave, J. & Wenger, E. (1991). *Situated Learning: Legitimate Peripheral Participation*. Cambridge: Cambridge University Press.
Maglitta, J. (1995). Smarten up. *Computerworld*, 4 June, 84–86.
March, J. G. (1991). Exploration and exploitation in organizational learning. *Organization Science*, **2**, 171–187.
Markus, L. (2000). Knowledge management. Warwick Business School Seminar Series, University of Warwick, August, 2000.
McKinlay, A. (2000). The bearable lightness of control. In C. Prichard, R. Hull, M. Chumner & H. Willmott (Ed.), *Managing Knowledge: Critical Investigations of Work and Learning* (pp. 107–121). Basingstoke: Macmillan.
Nahapiet, J. & Ghoshal, S. (1998). Social capital, intellectual capital and the organizational advantage. *Academy of Management Review*, **23**, 242–266.
Newell, S., Scarbrough, H. & Swan, J. (2001). From global knowledge management to internal electronic fences: contradictory outcomes of intranet development. *British Journal of Management*, **12**, 97–111.
Nonaka, I. (1991). The knowledge-creating company. *Harvard Business Review*, 96–104.
Nonaka, I. (1994). A dynamic theory of organisational knowledge creation. *Organisational Science*, **5**(1), 14–37.
Nonaka, I. & Takeuchi, H. (1995). *The Knowledge Creating Company*. New York: Oxford University Press.
Noon, M., Jenkins, S. & Lucio, M. M. (2000). Fads, techniques and control: the competing agendas of TPM and TECEX at the Royal Mail (UK). *Journal of Management Studies*, **37**, 499–520.
Orr, J. (1990). Sharing knowledge, celebrating identity: war stories and community memory in a service culture. In D. Middleton & D. Edwards (Eds), *Collective Remembering: Remembering in a Society*. London: Sage.
Pan, S. L. & Scarbrough, H. (1998). A socio-technical view of knowledge sharing at Buckman Laboratories. *Journal of Knowledge Management*, **2**, 55–66.
Quinn, J. B., Anderson, P. & Finkelstein, S. (1996). Managing professional intellect: making the most of the best. *Harvard Business Review*, **74**, 71–80.
Quintas, P., Lefrere, P. & Jones, G. (1997). Knowledge Management: a strategic agenda. *Long Range Planning*, **30**, 385–391.
Rajan, A., Lank, E. & Chapple, K. (1998). *Good Practices in Knowledge Creation and Exchange*. Tunbridge Wells: Create.
Raub, S. & Ruling, C. C. (2001). The knowledge management tussle—speech communities and rhetorical strategies in the development of knowledge management. *Journal of Information Technology*, **16**, 113–130.
Reich, R. (1991). *The Wealth of Nations: Preparing Ourselves for 21st Century Capitalism*. London: Simon and Schuster.
Robertson, M. & Swan, J. (1998). Modes of organizing in an expert consultancy: a case study of knowledge, power and egos. *Organization*, **5**, 543–564.

Ruggles, R. (1998). The state of the notion: knowledge management in practice. *California Management Review*, **40**, 80–89.

Scarbrough, H. (1995). The social engagement of social science. *Human Relations*, **48**, 1–11.

Scarbrough, H. & Carter, C. (2000). *Investigating Knowledge Management*. London: Chartered Institute of Personnel and Development.

Scarbrough, H. & Swan, J. (2001). Explaining the diffusion of knowledge management: the role of fashion. *British Journal of Management*, **12**, 3–12.

Senge, P. (1993). *The Fifth Discipline: the Art and Practice of the Learning Organization*. New York: Century Business.

Skyrme, D. J. & Amidon, D. M. (1998). New measures of sucess. *Journal of Business Strategy*, **19**(1), 20–24.

Spender, J. C. (1996). Organizational knowledge, learning and memory: three concepts in search of a theory. *Journal of Organizational Change Management*, **9**, 63–78.

Switzer, J. (1996). Managing human capital. *Banking Strategies*, **72**, 50–51.

Tampoe, M. (1993). Motivating knowledge workers: the challenge for the 1900s. *Long Range Planning*, **26**.

Tsoukas, H. (1996). The firm as a distributed knowledge system: a constructionist approach. *Strategic Management Journal*, **17**, 11–25.

Vandenbosch, B. & Ginzberg (1996). Understanding strategic learning. Academy of Management Meeting, Boston, MA.

von Hippel, E. (1990). The impact of "sticky data" on innovation and problem-solving. Cambridge, MA: Sloan School of Management, MIT.

Wenger, E. (2000). Communities of practice and social learning systems. *Organization*, **7**, 225–246.

Whittington, R. (1991). Changing control strategies in industrial R&D. *R&D Management*, **21**, 43–53.

Willcocks, L., Lacity, M. & Fitzgerald, G. (1995). IT outsourcing in Europe and the USA: assessment issues. Oxford: Oxford Institute of Information Management, Templeton College.

Williamson, O. E. (1986). *Economic Organisation: Firms, Markets and Policy Control*. Brighton: Wheatsheaf.

Willmott, H. (1995). BPR and Human Resource Management. *Personnel Review*, **23**, 34–46.

CHAPTER 9

Employee Involvement: Utilization, Impacts, and Future Prospects

George S. Benson
College of Business Administration, University of Texas at Arlington, Arlington, TX, USA

and

Edward E. Lawler III
Marshall Business School, University of Southern California, Los Angeles, CA, USA

By all accounts there has been a significant increase in the use of employee involvement practices in firms over the last 10–15 years. Practices including self-managed teams, problem-solving groups, gainsharing and cross-training have been written about by the business press and studied extensively by academics. By the mid-1990s several studies suggested some form of formal employee involvement, labeled as "innovative" or "high-performance" practices, had been embraced by a significant number of firms worldwide, including roughly half of all US firms and some two-thirds of the Fortune 1000 (Cooke, 1994; Freeman, Kleiner & Ostroff, 2000; Gittleman, Horrigan & Joyce, 1998; Kling, 1995; Lawler, Mohrman & Ledford, 1998; Locke, Kochan & Piore, 1995; Osterman, 1994). However, there is some recent evidence that the rate of growth in the adoption of employee involvement practices in the Fortune 1000 leveled off in the late 1990s (Lawler, Mohrman & Benson, 2001). This leads to the question of where the utilization of employee involvement practices is headed. Has the diffusion of employee involvement peaked and begun to decline? Have we seen the heyday of employee involvement? It also strongly raises the issue of the long-term effectiveness of employee involvement practices.

ADOPTION OF EMPLOYEE INVOLVEMENT

Employee involvement has generated a great deal of interest from organizational researchers and theorists for decades. Employee involvement has a history going back to the 1950s with some notable early experiments in Europe and the USA. From its beginnings in "industrial democracy" and "participative management", employee involvement has evolved into an

---

The New Workplace: A Guide to the Human Impact of Modern Working Practices.
Edited by David Holman, Toby D. Wall, Chris W. Clegg, Paul Sparrow and Ann Howard. © 2003 John Wiley & Sons, Ltd.

integrated approach to work system design that supports employees having decision-making authority (Argyris, 1957; Likert, 1961; McGregor, 1960). Lawler (1986, 1992, 1996) argues for the design of organizations in which employees are equipped with the skills and resources they need to make informed decisions and implement them effectively. He argues that effective employee involvement requires corporate practices that distribute power and business information, create incentive rewards and provide employees with the skills and knowledge they need in order to make decisions. He further argues that, in order for employees to feel involved, they must feel that they are in control of their work, have accurate feedback concerning their performance and be rewarded for that performance. Employee involvement theorists typically argue that lower level employees should have opportunities to make decisions concerning the conduct of their jobs and to participate in the business as a whole (Cotton, 1993; Lawler, 1992).

Employee involvement was not widely embraced by industry until the 1980s (Blasi & Kruse, 2001; Cappelli & Neumark, 2001; Parks, 1995). At that time, union-management quality of work life programs became popular, as did "greenfield" high-involvement manufacturing plants (Guest & Hoque, 1996; Katz, Kochan & Gobeille, 1983; Katz et al., 1985; Lawler, 1992; Poole, Lansbury & Wailes, 2001). Several large, multi-company studies showed a significant growth in "participative", "flexible", "high-performance" or "high-involvement" work practices in the early 1990s. In 1994, two large national representative sample surveys of establishments (actual work locations as opposed to business units or firms) estimated that work teams were being used in one-third to one-half of all establishments in the USA (Gittleman et al., 1998; Osterman, 1994). In a 1994 study of large companies, the number using self-managed teams was estimated at two-thirds (Lawler et al., 1998). Estimates of the percentage of US firms using job rotation ranged from 24% (Gittleman et al., 1998) to 43% (Osterman, 1994). Representative surveys in Europe and Australia showed similar adoption rates for employee involvement. In 1998, 42% of British establishments reported using quality circles and 65% had some sort of formally designated teams (Cully et al., 1999). An Italian survey during this same period found that 56% of firms reported some type of job rotation (Locke et al., 1995).

Part of the interest in new work systems during the 1980s and early 1990s was the result of a perceived competitiveness gap between US industry and the major Japanese manufacturing firms. A great deal of interest developed in total quality management (TQM) programs, and many companies began making use of quality circles. At the same time that foreign competition and technological changes were placing real competitive pressures on many firms, trends in re-engineering and corporate restructuring led many corporations to reassess the way they organized work (Hammer & Champy, 1988). The result was that many US firms introduced work teams and reduced their management overhead by giving more responsibility to front-line employees. In Europe and Australia the process was driven by both public policy and a transition away from traditional union-dominated industrial relations. Despite differences in national settings, increasing globalization and international competition during this time appears to have driven the adaptation of local employment practices towards employee involvement (Locke et al., 1995).

Reviewing the research on employee involvement is challenging because of the considerable number of practices that have been labeled as "high-involvement" or "high-performance"; for example, Becker & Gerhart (1996) found 27 different variables in a review of only five studies. Among the different theories of employee involvement, however, practices are commonly categorized by those that put the power to make decisions in the hands of employees, provide incentives to take responsibility for their jobs, and provide the skills or information needed to make informed decisions (Cotton, 1993; Lawler, 1986, 1992, 1996). Some also include practices that promote job security (Kochan & Osterman, 1994; Levine & Tyson, 1990). Employee involvement theory suggests that the different types of practices are complementary and need to occur together in order to create an effective work system. Research on employee involvement, therefore, is different from the vast amount of research that has been conducted on the effectiveness of the multitude of individual management practices that are part of the employee involvement approach. For example, so much academic research has examined participative decision-making that it has been the subject of more than a dozen reviews in the past 30 years (Wagner, 1995). The employee involvement research studies reviewed in this chapter involve more than decision-making power. This review focuses on the studies examining some combination of teamwork, training, job design, and contingent rewards.

Research at the work unit level confirms the importance of viewing practices as complementary. Ichniowski, Shaw & Prennushi (1995) examined steel-finishing lines and concluded that systems of practices that included work teams, flexible assignments, training and incentive pay increased productivity over plants with "traditional" control-orientated work systems. Individual practices in isolation showed no effect on productivity. However, the exact combination or "bundles" of practices required in order to create an effective high-involvement approach is uncertain and may be industry-specific (Cappelli & Neumark, 2001; Pils & MacDuffie, 1996). As a result, most of the research conducted on cross-industry data has used scales representing multiple practices, categorized by factor or cluster analysis to cope with the variation of practices used by firms and the specific interaction patterns of practices within firms (Fernie & Metcalf, 1995; Huselid, 1995; Koch & McGrath, 1996; Lawler et al., 1995, 1998, 2001; Scholarios, Ramsay & Harley, 2000; Wood & de Mensezes, 1998). While the specific practices included in these scales varies by study, they all support employee decision-making, incentive rewards, access to information on business performance, and providing workers with appropriate skills.

Table 9.1 shows the characteristics of the major surveys that have been done over the past 20 years to investigate the performance effects of employee involvement practices across a diverse group of firms or establishments in Anglophone countries around the world. In the UK and Australia, worker participation surveys have generally been conducted by government agencies. In the USA, the only government survey was conducted by the Bureau of Labor Statistics (BLS). However, surveys conducted by Columbia University, the Center for Educational Quality of the Workforce (EQW), as well as the first survey conducted by the Center for Effective Organizations (CEO) were done in cooperation with US government agencies. The remainder were conducted privately. It is not a complete list. There are several other studies that have examined adoption of practices as well as outcomes for workers, e.g. John Goddard conducted a telephone survey of Canadian establishments that examined outcomes for employees of involvement practices. In the USA, both the National Organizations Survey (NOS) conducted in 1991 and the National Longitudinal Survey of Youth (NLSY) 1992 supplement asked questions concerning workplace changes, including adoption of several employee involvement practices (for a complete summary of US studies of the adoption of practices, see Blasi & Kruse, 2001; for a bibliography of studies based on the UK Workplace Employee Relations Survey, see Millward et al., 1999).

These surveys vary significantly on a number of dimensions, making comparison of the findings across the studies that use these datasets challenging. For example, the randomness (and representativeness) of the organizations differ. The government studies are based on random or probability samples, with other studies based on all public companies or

Table 9.1 Surveys used to research EI and organizational performance

Conducted by	Year	Sample	Responses
Columbia University	1984	Public firms	495 (6%)
Michigan Industrial Training Institute	1989	20+ Establishments	2431 (70%)
Mark Huselid	1992	Public firms	968 (28%)
	1994	Public firms	740 (20%)
British Workplace Employee Relations Survey (WERS)	1990	25+ Establishments	2061 (83%)
	1998	10+ Establishments	2191 (80%)
Australian Workplace Industrial Relations Survey (AWIRS)	1995	20+ Establishments	2001 (75%)
Center for the Educational Quality of the Workforce	1994	20+ Establishments	2954 (66%)
	1997	20+ Establishments	4139 (59%)
Cheri Ostroff / SHRM	1993	SHRM members	373 (11%)
Bureau of Labor Statistics (SEPT)	1994	20+ Establishments	7895 (71%)
Center for Effective Organizations	1990	Fortune 1000 firms	313 (32%)
	1993	Fortune 1000 firms	279 (28%)
	1996	Fortune 1000 firms	212 (22%)
	1999	Fortune 1000 firms	143 (15%)

non-representative groups such as the Fortune 1000, or association membership. In terms of firm size, the government-affiliated research typically includes all establishments with more than 20 or 50 employees. Other surveys have focused on large firms, as in the case of the Fortune 1000 (Lawler *et al.*, 1995, 1998, 2001). The response rate for the studies also ranges from quite small (6% in the Columbia 1984 survey), to moderate (25–40% in the CEO Fortune 1000 surveys), to 70% for the US government-sponsored studies (e.g. BLS Survey of Employer Provided Training) and 80% for the UK and Australian government-sponsored surveys (1998 WERS and 1995 AWIRS).

Finally, each of the major surveys that have addressed employee involvement practices has idiosyncratic methods for accessing the adoption of the practices across the firms. The CEO surveys ask firms to report the percentage of all employees that are covered by individual practices in a five-point scale (0–20%, 21–40%, etc.). Some surveys asked what percentages of "core employees" are covered by practices vs. all employees in others. Some surveys have asked whether the organization has "experimented" with certain practices, while others have asked firms to report on practices that have been "adopted". These issues become particularly relevant when it comes to classifying certain firms as "high-performance". Osterman (1994) classifies an establishment as "transformed" if two practices or more (teams, quality circles, job rotation, or TQM) are used by more than 50% of "core" employees. Most others, including Huselid (1995) and Lawler *et al.* (2001), use scales to indicate the level of use of employee involvement practices within a firm.

Early Studies

Cappelli & Neumark (2001) note that the first large-scale survey of "transformed" work practices was conducted in 1982 by the New York Stock Exchange. The survey included all public firms with more than 100 employees. The survey had a 26% response rate and asked about 17 categories of practice. In 1986 the US Department of Labor and researchers at

Columbia University surveyed 7765 business units with a 6.5% response rate (Ichniowski, 1990). They estimated that 45% of firms had established some form of participation program and that 39% (unionized firms) to 54% (non-union firms) had profit sharing in place. The Michigan Industrial Training Institute (Cooke, 1994) followed this study with a survey of manufacturing firms in Michigan, which investigated teamwork and incentive compensation plans, including gainsharing and profit-sharing. Data on the adoption of practices was similar, in that approximately 45% of firms in Michigan were using teams for some portion of their workers. The proportion of firms that reported using incentive compensation was between 36% (unionized firms) and 52% (non-union firms).

The early studies differed significantly in their survey samples, but the results tended to show that employee involvement practices, including teams and incentive compensations, were in use in one-third to one-half of US firms. However, these studies also suggest that the early adopters of these practices may not have fully embraced employee participation, e.g. Delaney, Lewin & Ichniowski (1989) found that only 2% of the units surveyed in 1984 had work groups that were allowed to manage themselves.

EQW

In 1992 Paul Osterman at Wharton's Center for the Educational Quality of the Workforce (EQW) conducted a national telephone survey of manufacturing establishments with more than 50 employees that received approximately a 65% response rate. Osterman (1994) reported that one-third of organizations had an active quality program and 26% had job rotation for core employees. Approximately two-thirds of organizations at this time employed some type of contingent pay practices (e.g. gainsharing or skill-based pay). The survey also found that 40% of establishments had self-directed teams, which indicates a greater degree of employee involvement than earlier studies.

In 1994 the EQW teamed with the US Census Bureau on a national representative survey of establishments with more than 20 employees, called the National Establishment Survey (NES). This survey asked about the adoption of practices among all employees, rather than "core" employees, as was done in the original study. A follow-up to the 1994 survey was conducted in 1997. This second administration of the telephone survey was not a panel sample, but nonetheless indicated some significant increases in the adoption of certain practices. Capelli & Neumark (2001) report that a comparison of the 1994 and the 1997 data suggest growth in each of the involvement practices. Blasi & Kruse's (2001) analysis of the two surveys found that the percentage of establishments with self-managed teams had increased modestly from 31.8% to 34%. Adoption rates in the two NES surveys (1997 and 1994) are most likely to be lower than those reported by Osterman in his 1992 survey, because the NES sample includes all establishments with more than 20 employees, as opposed to the organizations with 50 or more employees that were sampled in the earlier survey. Generally, there is a relationship between organizational size and adoption. Taken together these three surveys indicate that employee involvement practices were firmly in place in the early 1990s and continued to grow slowly though the early part of the decade.

WERS and AWIRS

The 1990s also saw major survey efforts undertaken in the UK and Australia which were designed to assess the changes in industrial relations. The Workplace Employee Relations

Survey (WERS) series in the UK has addressed several aspects of employee involvement in the two most recent administrations of the survey in 1990 and 1998. Studies conducted before 1990 indicated that no more than 2% of UK establishments used quality circles or problem-solving teams and there was relatively little use of employee involvement overall (Locke *et al.*, 1995). A similar survey in Australia, called the Workplace Industrial Relations Surveys (AWIRS), was conducted in 1990 and 1995. The 1990 surveys in both countries consisted of cross-sectional samples and contained a number questions concerning communication and employee participation, but was dominated by union-representation issues. The 1998 WERS and the 1995 AWIRS present a more detailed picture of the adoption of employee involvement practices. Both of these surveys were extremely comprehensive, as they included all establishments in either the UK or Australia with more than 10 employees and had 75–80% responses. Based on these two surveys, Scholarios *et al.* (2000) reported that nearly half of workplaces in the UK (41%) and Australia (49%) have some form of contingent pay. Problem-solving teams are in place in 46% of UK establishments and 34% of Australian establishments. The latest UK and Australian establishment surveys are also unique in that they include a complement of employee surveys within a sample of establishments that measure attitudes and reactions to involvement practices.

BLS–SEPT

In 1993 the Bureau of Labor Statistics conducted the Survey of Employer Provided Training (SEPT), a comprehensive study of training practices in US establishments with 50 or more employees (Gittleman *et al.*, 1998). In addition to training data, a number of questions were asked about the establishments' work practices. This survey sample included 7500 establishments and enjoyed a 71% response rate. The survey found that 32% of establishments used team-based work for at least a portion of their employees. TQM programs were in place in 46%, and 16% used quality circles. One-quarter of the establishments had job rotation. These estimates are similar but generally smaller than the findings of the NES survey conducted around the same time.

CEO Fortune 1000 Surveys

A major research program of the Center for Effective Organizations at the University of Southern California has examined the adoption of employee involvement practices in the Fortune 1000 since 1987 with a total of five surveys (Lawler *et al.*, 1995, 1997, 2001). The first survey was conducted in conjunction with the US General Accounting Office (GAO). Mail surveys were sent to the executive office of each company and asked what percentage of employees were covered by a number of practices. These surveys provide a unique look at the adoption of practices over time. Unfortunately, the sample does not provide a true firm-by-firm longitudinal look, due to changes in the composition of the Fortune 1000. Lawler *et al.* (2001) note, however, that when they looked at a constant sample of firms their results were the same.

Findings from this series of surveys show a sharp increase in the use of many employee involvement practices in the early 1990s (Lawler *et al.*, 1998, 2001). For example, the number of companies reporting the use of self-managed teams for at least 20% of employees increased from 8% in 1987 to 32% in 1996. By the same measure, the use of individual incentive pay increased from 38% to 57% of companies (Lawler *et al.*, 1998). The findings from the most recent surveys, however, indicate that in the late 1990s growth in the adoption of employee involvement practices declined and their use may have remained constant since 1996 (Lawler *et al.*, 2001). The use of many practices, including quality circles, gainsharing and profitsharing, and cross-training, has remained relatively stable since the mid-1990s. In the case of TQM, the results indicate a significant decrease in use. In 1993, an average of 50% of employees participated in TQM activities, compared with 32% in 1999 (Lawler *et al.*, 2001).

EMPLOYEE INVOLVEMENT AND ORGANIZATIONAL PERFORMANCE

The adoption of employee involvement practices sparked dozens of research studies on their effectiveness. The relationship between employee involvement practices and firm performance has been addressed from many perspectives, including strategic management (Koch & McGrath, 1996), labor economics (Black & Lynch, 1997; Ichniowski *et al.*, 1996), human resources (Huselid, 1995; Huselid & Becker, 1996; Wright *et al.*, 2001), and industrial/organizational psychology (Vandenberg, Richardson & Eastman, 1999). The level of analysis differs between the studies, since some are based on establishment surveys, while others are firm-level surveys. This raises the question of the appropriate level of analysis for examining the relationship between practice and firm performance. Employee involvement practices, such as self-managing teams and flexible job design, are seldom applied to 100% of employees in an organization. This means that the performance benefits of employee involvement practices are localized and apply to some fraction of the total employees of a firm. Organizational performance, on the other hand, is most often measured at the firm level.

BUSINESS UNIT STUDIES

Although there have been many studies that have examined organizational performance at the business-unit or establishment level, the effort (and firm cooperation) required to collect unit level data means that these studies tend to be case study, single industry, or small sample studies (Adler, Goldoftas & Levine, 1997; Bailey, 1993; Cutcher-Gershenfeld, 1991; Ichniowski *et al.*, 1995; MacDuffie, 1995; Youndt *et al.*, 1996). Ichniowski *et al.*, (1996), Appelbaum & Batt (1995) and Appelbaum *et al.*, (2000) all provide excellent overviews of these studies. Each of these reviews finds that the results of employee involvement are generally positive. Recent studies by Appelbaum *et al.*, (2000) and Brown & Appleyard (2001) report positive effects for involvement practices through in-depth case studies and surveys in industries as diverse as steel manufacturing, apparel, medical imaging and semiconductor fabrication. Although it is dangerous to generalize from single-firm and industry studies, there have been so many studies in so many different sectors of the economy that it is safe to conclude that the productivity benefits of employee involvement are real and robust, particularly in manufacturing firms.

MULTI-INDUSTRY STUDIES

It is one thing to show that employee involvement affects productivity, it is another to show they contribute to the profitability of firms in different industries. This issue has been addressed by large-scale, multi-industry studies. The decade of the 1990s saw a significant amount of research into the effects of HR systems on firm performance, based on large cross-industry studies.

Ichniowski (1990) examined 176 firms from the Columbia University survey and found that firms that used HR practices, including training and flexible job design, had higher sales per employee and higher firm performance as measured by Tobin's Q. Tobins's Q is the difference between the market value of the firm and its total assets and has been used as a proxy for the value of the firm's intangible assets, such as human capital and managerial effectiveness (Chung & Pruitt, 1994). Ichniowski (1990) suggested that employee involvement practices have the potential to impact business performance in addition to individual productivity, but it required complementary practices being implemented together. Using data from the same survey Koch & McGrath (1996) also found a significant relationship between employee involvement practices and sales per employee. They conclude that labor productivity is positively related to a firm's willingness to invest in innovative human resource management practices.

Cooke (1994) used data on 841 manufacturing firms in Michigan and concluded that group incentives and employee participation programs had a positive effect on value-added per employee. The findings for the various practices were affected by whether or not the firm was unionized. Self-managed teams and quality circles coupled with profit-sharing and gainsharing plans had positive effects on productivity. He found that although these practices tended to increase wages, that increase was less than the value-added. Among non-unionized firms, Cooke (1994) estimated that companies with teams, incentive compensation or both pay roughly 6–7% higher wages that firms without these employee involvement practices. Even with this increase in labor costs, however, he reported that firms with employee involvement practices enjoyed 21% better net performance, as measured by value-added per employee less wage costs.

Huselid (1995) surveyed 3452 public companies and received responses from 968 firms. Based on a factor analysis of responses, he constructed two indices of work practices. The first, which he labeled "skills and work structures", includes items such as individual job design, employee participation programs, and skills training. The second index, labeled "motivation", includes measures of performance appraisals and merit-based rewards programs. Controlling industry, firm size, capital intensity, R&D concentration, sales growth, union presence, and firm-specific risk, Huselid showed significant relationships between his human resource indices, sales per employee, and firm performance, as measured by gross return on assets. He also estimated that a one standard deviation increase in practice adoption was associated with an additional $27 000 additional in sales per employee per year—a 16% increase. The same change in practice adoption was also associated with a $3800 increase in gross return on assets per employee per year. In addition, significant relationships were also found with the stock market valuation of the firm, as measured by Tobin's Q.

Around the same time, Fernie & Metcalf (1995) used data from the 1990 British Workplace Industrial Relations Survey to examine the effects of participation and contingent pay on workplace performance in nearly 1500 establishments. Performance was measured as management perception of the establishment's labor productivity relative to its competitors and perceived changes in productivity over the past 3 years. They categorized workplaces between "employee involvement", "collective bargaining" and "authoritarian", based on the levels of communication, representation and contingent pay. Fernie & Metcalf found that managers in employee involvement workplaces reported the highest productivity levels. In addition, they found that establishments that had undertaken recent efforts to increase employee involvement reported the strongest relationships with the perceptual performance measures.

For large firms, studies conducted by the Center for Effective Organizations have found consistent relationships between the adoption of employee involvement in the Fortune 1000 and several measures of financial and market performance (Lawler *et al.*, 1995, 1998, 2001). Using data on the adoption of a number of employee involvement practices, four indices were created, representing the distribution of decision-making power, access to information, level of employee training and the existence of contingent rewards. Employee involvement indices explained a small but significant amount of variance in the return on investment, return on assets and sales per employee of Fortune 1000 firms. Organizational performance was predicted in the current and following years in 1993, 1996 and, to a lesser extent, in 1999. In 1996, Fortune 1000 firms with high adoption rates of employee involvement practices (more than one standard deviation higher) had an average return on assets of 12.3%, compared with 9.2% for those firms with low adoption rates (Lawler *et al.*, 1998).

Taken together, the multi-industry studies indicate that employee involvement practices are positively correlated with firm performance, using perceptual measures, and a variety of accounting and market performance measures, including sales per employee, Tobin's Q, market returns and return on assets. However, these studies leave some important questions unanswered. Most importantly the findings from these studies raise the question of causality. Did the practices lead to the superior performance of the firms that adopted them, or did firms with the resources and flexibility provided by superior performance choose to embrace employee involvement practices? This potential problem has been labeled alternatively as a "heterogeneity bias" (Huselid & Becker, 1996) and a "self-selection bias" (Ichniowski *et al.*, 1996). Simply put, are there unmeasured management practices or other firm characteristics (such as higher quality managers and employees) that are positively related to both employee involvement and firm performance? If so, the estimates of the performance effects reviewed above may be overestimating the true impact of the employee involvement practices.

Huselid & Becker (1996) attempted to address this question with a longitudinal analysis using data from a second administration of Huselid's survey to the original sample. They used panel data collected in 1992 and 1994 to control for firm heterogeneity through a fixed effects model. In this case the estimated performance effects were substantially smaller than Huselid's (1995) original cross-sectional estimates and not statistically significant. They argue that these differences are due to measurement error common to all surveys of human resource practices; primarily that the use of a panel sample focuses the analyses on the firms that adopted employee involvement or "high-performance" practices during the study period, which in this case was only 2 years. The variance examined through this type of analysis comes from the firms that reported changes in the rates of adoption of the practices over the two survey administrations. In this case, the number of companies that reported changes was significantly smaller than those that had adopted the practices in the original survey. Although Huselid and Becker use various methods to correct this bias and conclude that the actual effects are similar to their cross-sectional estimates, their findings might also be interpreted as evidence of firm heterogeneity leading to firm performance, rather than employee involvement practices (Cappelli & Neumark, 2001).

Further evidence for the importance of firm heterogeneity in determining the performance effects of employee involvement comes from Black & Lynch (1997), who find that practices by themselves do not contribute to labor productivity, but depend on multiple contextual factors or firm contingencies for success. Using data from the National Employers Survey (NES), Black & Lynch (1997) use repeated observations of the characteristics and performance of the firm over time, rather than repeated measures of work practices. Using data collected in 1992, they assume that the use of the practices within the firms has been stable for the previous 4 years. They construct a "within estimator" using firm size, investment and labor measures for the period 1988–1993. This estimator is the residual of a regression predicting firm performance with as many firm-specific characteristics as possible. This residual is then regressed on work practices and finds that employee involvement practices explain a significant part of the variance in firm performance not explained by the control variables over time. Black & Lynch (1997) conclude that the adoption of practices alone does not contribute to productivity. They argue that the performance effects of employee involvement practices depend significantly on contextual factors, such as the educational level of workers and the use of information technology by non-managerial workers. This suggests that the effects of employee involvement depend on how practices are implemented, which in turn depends on firm characteristics, such as high-quality management and highly skilled workers. In another argument for the importance of firm heterogeneity, Wood & de Menezes (1998), in an analysis of British establishment data, found that the managers perceived the highest levels of performance in firms with either above-average or below-average use of "high-commitment" work practice, and suggest firm strategy as a critical contextual variable that might moderate the impact of these practices on firm performance.

Although the research results regarding the positive relationship between employee involvement and organizational performance have been consistent since 1990, the studies by Huselid & Becker (1996) and Lynch & Black (1998) illustrate that interpretations of these findings are not unanimous. Capelli & Neumark (2001) recently suggested that the evidence does not show conclusively that high-performance work practices contribute to the profitability of companies. They note that although the practices contribute to labor productivity, they also increase the cost of labor and wages. According to them, "The findings are suggestive of important effects but, taken as a group, remain inconclusive" (Cappelli & Neumark, 2001, p. 737). With data from two waves of the NES conducted in 1992 and 1997, they use a longitudinal design and conclude that "high-performance" work practices do not impact on labor productivity as measured by output per dollar spent on labor, and therefore have little potential effect on firm performance. These findings are supported by Freeman & Kleiner (2000), who analyzed data from the 1993 SHRM survey conducted by Ostroff to examine the performance effects of employee involvement (Freeman, Kleiner & Ostroff, 2000). They conclude, based on analysis of 273 firms, that employee involvement practices have no significant effects on output per worker. Finally, with regards to perceptual measures of performance, Addison & Belfield (2001) analyzed the 1998 British WERS and were unable find significant effects for employee involvement practices, and call into question the findings of Fernie & Metcalf (1995) and their conclusions based on the 1990 WERS.

The findings from these recent studies raise important questions regarding the true effect of employee involvement on firm performance. The theoretical and methodological problems associated with this line of research have been documented (Icknioski *et al.*, 1996; Becker & Huselid, 1998) and debated (Gerhart *et al.*, 2000; Huselid & Becker, 2000; Gerhart, Wright & McMahan, 2000). Some of these problems are particularly vexing, such as deciding on the most appropriate unit of analysis and the measurement errors associated with assessing the adoption of practices across a large and diversified organization. Data for companies is most often collected from a single respondent. Although this is less of a problem for small companies or establishments, the potential for measurement error is significant in large companies (Wright *et al.*, 2001). The contextual variables examined should be expanded and methods for research in multi-industry studies should be improved in order to address some of the problems with the existing research. However, the best approach to getting at the real effects of employee involvement may be to make a closer examination of the actual mechanisms through which these practices affect firm performance.

HOW DOES EI TRANSLATE INTO ORGANIZATIONAL PERFORMANCE?

In the organizational behavior literature, employee involvement practices are theorized to act on organizational performance through some combination of creating more efficient work processes and increasing the motivation of workers (Huselid, 1995; Ichniowski *et al.*, 1996; Lawler, 1986). Vandenberg *et al.* (1999) label these two mechanisms "cognitive" and "motivational" models. They argue that the positive effects of employee involvement on organizational performance come from the increased utilization of the knowledge and skills of employees. The increased efficacy of workers then motivates them to give extra effort, resulting in higher productivity coupled with lower absenteeism, grievances and turnover, which ultimately impact the bottom line.

From the economic efficiency perspective, employee involvement increases the value of the firm's stock of human capital that it can apply to manufacturing products or providing services. Viewing the skills and abilities of individual employees in terms of human capital has a long tradition in labor economics (Becker, 1964) and there have been multiple recent research efforts to link investment in human capital with firm performance (Bassi *et al.*, 1999; Blundell *et al.*, 1999; Bouillan, Doran & Orazem, 2001). The notion that employee involvement creates economic efficiencies in work has dominated research on the performance effects of HR practices until recently. Studies of the performance effects of employee involvement or high-performance practices have most often made arguments that employee involvement practices improve labor productivity by better use of the knowledge and skills of employee through efficient work processes. However, they have tended to look past the effects of involvement practices on employees and have focused on their attention on organizational outcomes, such as sales per employee, return on assets, and market returns. Studies of the effects of employee involvement on firms have generally taken an economic or efficiency perspective and left the individual "intervening" effects unmeasured and assumed (Ichniowski, 1990).

All of the studies reviewed above examine direct relationships between employee involvement work practices and organizational outcomes. When outcomes such as turnover (e.g. Huselid, 1995) or labor productivity (e.g. Cooke, 1994) are examined, the motivations of the workers are assumed. When organizational outcomes such as profitability and market returns are studied, the effect of the work practices on employees is left as a "black box"

(Gardner *et al.*, 2000). For example, training in TQM and statistics is assumed to lead to constant improvement of work processes and teamwork. Communication skills are thought to help identify potential problems, while cross-training and decision-making authority are thought to allow employees to act quickly when a problem does arise. Self-managed teams mean that fewer middle managers are needed to schedule and monitor individual work.

While studies of the performance impact of employee involvement have generally viewed the effects of employee involvement in terms of economic efficiencies and firm strategy, the original impetus for advocating employee involvement was based more on its effect on individual motivation and extra effort. Employee involvement is based on the notion that those closest to the actual work of the company should be responsible for as many aspects of their work as possible, because this will motivate them to perform better. That is, if employees are given challenging work that involves serving customers and contributing to the business, they will be motivated to improve their job performance. Based on a needs-satisfaction or intrinsic motivation view of the workplace, giving people responsibility and allowing them to feel part of a well-performing organization increases performance motivation.

Some of the recent research on employee involvement is moving back towards a motivation model to better explain the effects of employee involvement on firm performance. Specifically, it suggests that the link between practices and organizational performance may depend on a worker's interpretation of the practices (Meyer & Smith, 2000; Kinicki, Carson & Bohlander, 1992; Koys, 1988). Research suggests that involvement practices that promote positive employee attitudes, such as organizational commitment, may, in turn, contribute to extra-effort (Cappelli & Rogovsky, 1998), prosocial behavior (O'Reilly & Chatman, 1986), work performance (Meyer *et al.*, 1989), customer satisfaction (Oakland & Oakland, 1998; Bowen & Schneider, 1999), safety (Probst & Brubaker, 2001) and employee retention (Koys, 2001). Examining the effects of employee involvement on employee attitudes and behavior as an intermediate step between the practices and organizational performance gets back to the foundations of employee involvement as a motivational approach.

Other studies have examined different employment relationships and HR "climates" and concluded that particular configurations of HR practices (such as employee involvement systems) are associated with higher commitment and greater discretionary effort on the part of employees; specifically, those practices which invest in employees and signal long-term relationships. For example, some studies have shown significant relationships between HR strategies such as "high-performance" or "high-commitment" work systems and employee attitudes (Arthur, 1994; Lam & White, 1998; Scholarios, Ramsay & Harley, 2000; Tsui *et al.*, 1997). Employee attitudes are critical in light of other studies that indicate that positive attitudes are associated not only with organizational outcomes, such as absenteeism and turnover, but also with objective measures of performance.

A recent study by Vandenberg, Richardson & Eastman (1999) puts all of these variables together and illustrates a new approach towards examining the performance effects of employee involvement. Based on motivation theory, they predict that employee involvement leads to positive employee attitudes, which in turn leads to improved individual and organizational performance. In a study of 3500 insurance company employees in 49 organizations, they found that the level of employee involvement affected the commitment and satisfaction of workers. These attitudes, in turn, were associated with higher levels of customer satisfaction for the units, and higher individual performance rankings for the employees. Similarly, Morrison (1995) and Koys (2001) found that employee attitudes, organizational citizenship behavior and turnover mediate the effects of employee involvement and other HR practices on customer satisfaction and organizational effectiveness.

Such multi-level studies have been advocated but not widely pursued (Becker & Huselid, 1998, Gardner *et al.*, 2000; Guest, 1997). If this line of research is extended and proves to be explanatory of the relationship between employee involvement and firm performance, the implications for the future adoption and effects of work practices are significant. It means that a causal mechanism between practices and performance is their impact on employees. It may explain, in part, the differences in the success of practices across similar firms.

IMPACT ON EMPLOYEES

There is evidence that attitudes such as organizational commitment are dependent on how the employee interprets the reasons for practices. Kinicki, Carson & Bohlander (1992) found that employees only responded to certain HR practices with organizational commitment if they interpreted those practices as indications of the firm's genuine interest in their well-being. Employees who felt that the HR practices were instituted only to protect the company from lawsuits did not report higher levels of organizational commitment. In a similar study, Meyer & Smith (2000) found that the relationship between "employee-friendly" HR practices and organizational commitment was mediated by perceptions of organizational support.

This suggests that workers need to interpret employee involvement as genuine efforts to improve employee well-being in terms of job satisfaction, positive workplace relations and employee benefits, in addition to company performance. There is evidence that employees tend to respond positively to increased opportunities to share ideas and contribute on the job. In 1994 the Worker Representation and Participation Survey collected phone surveys from a representative sample of all US private sector employees regarding individual reactions to employee involvement practices. Freeman & Rogers (1999) report that 79% of non-managerial participants in employee involvement programs report having "personally benefited from [their] involvement in the program by getting more influence on how [their] job is done". Based on this survey, Freeman, Kleiner & Ostroff (2000) conclude that employee involvement practices are associated with increased job satisfaction and greater trust in management. Guest reports similar findings from two studies of a 1996 survey of 1000 British employees collected by the Institute of Personnel and Development (Guest; 1999; Guest & Conway, 1999). Goddard (2001) finds that involvement has positive relationships with satisfaction, commitment and belongingness among Canadian employees. There is also evidence that high-involvement workplaces tend to provide additional training to employees (Leigh & Gifford, 1999). Finally, Chadwick & Fister (2001) suggest that at least some employee involvement practices (including self-managed teams and job rotation) are correlated with greater fringe benefits for employees.

But are work life improvements, fringe benefits and access to training enough to sustain employee involvement practices? Models of employee involvement have generally assumed that employees are not willing to put forth the increased effort and suggestions for improvement required to make the system work if they do not feel that they are justly rewarded (Lawler, 1986) and that the firm is not committed to them over the long term (Kochan & Osterman, 1994; Levine & Tyson, 1990; Osterman, 2000). Osterman (2000) suggests that a real examination of employee welfare needs to include the effects of employee involvement on employee wages. If employees are asked to be more responsible for the performance of the firm, are they compensated for their increased involvement? However, whether or not employee involvement practices increase wages is an open question. There is some evidence that it does. Freeman & Lazear (1994) examined participative decision-making through works councils and found that it not only increased the total rent produced by the firm, but also had a positive effect on the wages of employees. Cooke (1994) also found higher wages in companies with teams and incentive pay. Chadwick & Fister (2001) found that wages were positively related to the use of self-managed teams.

Osterman (2000), on the other hand, argues that while the use of employee involvement practices dramatically increased in the 1990s, "aggregate measures of employee welfare do not show commensurate gains" (Osterman, 2000, p. 180). Osterman (2000) notes that the rise of "high-performance" practices during the 1980s and 1990s was heralded as a trend towards the "mutual-gains" enterprise, in which both companies and workers would share the benefits. However, in contrast to the findings of Freeman & Lazear (1994) and Cooke (1994), Osterman (2000) finds that there was no corresponding increase in workers' wages to reflect these gains and increased responsibilities. In addition, those companies with employee involvement practices in place were more likely to experience lay-offs in the years following. This finding suggests that employees may resist employee involvement in the future because they do not see it having a positive impact on wages or job security.

EMPLOYEE INVOLVEMENT: FUTURE PROSPECTS

What is the future of employee involvement? Employee involvement is not right for every firm, and it is becoming clearer where it fits and where it does not. It may well be that the slow-down in the adoption of employee involvement practices in the late 1990s is a very rational reaction to the popular rush towards the practices in the earlier part of the decade. In the future we are more likely to see employee involvement practices adopted by firms with employees and work processes that are suited to involvement. There will be fewer firms who adopt involvement practices because everyone is doing it, or because of pressure from investors. Because of the wealth of research and experience that exists concerning employee involvement, it is also unlikely that there will be as many naïve adopters in the future. It is now clear that what once looked like an easy route to improvement is a complex change that requires more commitment and investment than some firms are willing to make. This suggests that adoption may be less frequent but more successful in the future.

Just as relatively little is known about why employee involvement programs impact on firm performance, very little is known about why firms adopt employee involvement. There is some evidence emerging that it is more likely to be adopted by large firms and that it is particularly likely to be adopted in industries that require skilled human capital. A developed view of who adopts employee involvement and why is needed. Further understanding of adoption behavior is important because it is a precursor to organizations making intelligent adoption decisions and, ultimately, to effective implementation of employee involvement.

The future adoption of employee involvement may also be limited if it is not clear that employees gain from the practices. It is increasingly apparent that involvement practices are only successful under circumstances where employees embrace the practice and respond with increased motivation and commitment to the organization. For employees to embrace involvement practices, they need to see the benefits and react positively in terms of job satisfaction, commitment and organizational citizenship.

A clear threat to the future of employee involvement is the possibility that firms will use it in an exploitative way, i.e. they will install some of the practices, but manage them and the organization in a way that leads to gains being accrued by the organization but not by the employees. The more often this happens, the less likely it is that employees will accept involvement practices. This can be particularly problematic in unionized workplaces with a history of labor/management antagonism.

Because it is increasingly apparent that the success of employee involvement practices depends on how the practices are interpreted by employees, future research should also address the role of employee involvement in the overall employment relationship. A particularly interesting issue here concerns the importance of job security. It is not clear that employees need to have job security in order to respond favorably to involvement efforts, but some writers have suggested that it is. If it is necessary, given the turbulent economic times, this may prove to be a major limitation on the successful adoption of employee involvement programs and their survival over the long-term.

Finally, despite the large number of studies that have examined the performance effects of employee involvement, there is clearly a need for further research. A number of directions appear to be worth exploring. First and foremost, studies are needed that look at why a connection exists between the adoption of employee involvement practices and the performance of firms. More probing needs to take place to define the mechanisms at work in the "black box" between involvement and organizational performance. This probing should include a focus on how the adoption of different patterns of involvement practice affect individual attitudes and performance. Equally, we need to know how changes in individual performance changes affect organizational performance. A better understanding of the connection between practices and organizational performance should lead to a clearer understanding of how employee involvement systems should be designed and implemented, as well as where and when they are likely to be effective. It is not enough to know that involvement practices generally work; more knowledge needs to be developed concerning when, where and how they work.

Findings from several national cross-industry studies show the economic benefits of employee involvement practices, notwithstanding the well-documented limitations. However, viewing the effects of employee involvement practices from a purely economic perspective simplifies the analysis of the effects by putting the practices into a cost vs. benefits equation in terms of labor productivity and labor expense. The problem is that it may be hard to quantify the true benefits to an organization of having a highly involved workforce. Even if the costs and benefits of implementing employee involvement practices appear to cancel each other on the balance sheet, there are additional benefits in terms of positioning the firm strategically and competitively. For example, firms that use employee involvement practices may be more "agile" or "ambidextrous" (Gibson & Birkinshaw, 2001; Shafer *et al.*, 2001). In highly competitive industries, where long-term performance is determined by the ability to adapt to rapidly changing market conditions and product quality, employee involvement may prove to be an important asset that, over the long-term, is difficult to quantify. Future research should address these additional potential benefits of employee involvement.

Many questions remain concerning the future of employee involvement practices. These work practices have received a very considerable amount of attention over the past 20 years, with many large-scale studies to assess their adoption and effectiveness in industry. The bottom line, however, is that employee involvement has only been strongly embraced by a minority of firms. Given that successful work practices that yield a consistent competitive advantage are likely to be imitated by other firms, there is good reason to believe that employee involvement practices will continue to be utilized. What may change is whether they are adopted as part of a specific program. It may well be that, rather than being part of a major employee involvement change effort, practices that are associated with employee involvement may simply become standard operating procedures in companies. Ultimately, rather than being seen as part of a new approach to management, they will be seen as the right way to manage an effective organization.

REFERENCES

Adler, P., Goldoftas, B. & Levine, D. (1997). Ergonomics, employee involvement, and the Toyota production system: a case study of NUMMI's 1993 model introduction. *Industrial and Labor Relations Review*, **50**(3), 416–438.

Addison, J. & Belfield, C. (2001). Updating the determinants of firm performance: estimation using the 1998 UK Workplace Employees Relations Survey. *British Journal of Industrial Relations*, **39**(3), 341–366.

Appelbaum, E. & Batt, R. (1995). *The New American Workplace: Transforming Work Systems in the United States.* Ithaca, NY: ILR Press.

Appelbaum, E., Bailey, T., Berg, P. & Kallenberg, A. (2000). *Manufacturing Advantage: Why High-performance Work Systems Pay Off.* Ithaca, NY: ILR Press.

Argyris, C. (1957). *Personality and Organizations.* New York: Harper & Row.

Arthur, J. (1994). Effects of human resource systems on manufacturing performance and turnover. *Academy of Management Journal*, **37**(3), 670–687.

Bassi, L., Lev B., Low, J., McMurrer, D. & Seisfeld, T. (1999). Corporate investments in human capital. In M. Blair & T. Kochan (Eds), *The New Relationship: Human Capital in the American Corporation.* Washington DC: Brookings Institution Press.

Bailey, T. (1993). Organizational innovation in the apparel industry. *Industrial Relations*, **32**, 30–48.

Becker, B. & Gerhart, B., (1996). The impact of human resource management on organizational performance: progress and prospects. *Academy of Management Journal*, **39**(4), 779–801.

Becker, B. & Huselid, M. (1998). High performance work systems and firm performance: A synthesis of research and managerial implications. *Research in Personnel and Human Resources*, **16**, 53–101.

Black, S. & Lynch, L. (1997). *How to Compete: the Impact of Workplace Practices and Information Technology on Productivity.* Working Paper No. 6120. Cambridge: National Bureau of Economic Research.

Blasi, J. & Kruse, D. (2001). High performance work practices at century's end: incidence, diffusion, industry group differences and the economic environment. Unpublished manuscript, Rutgers University.

Blundell, R., Dearden, L., Meghir, C. & Sianest, B. (1999). Human capital investment: the returns from education and training to the individual, the firm, and the economy. *Fiscal Studies*, **20**(1), 1–23.

Bouillon, M., Doran, M. & Orazem, P. (2001). Human capital investment effects on firm returns. *Journal of Applied Business Research*, **12**(1), 30–41.

Bowen, B. & Schneider, D. (1999). Understanding customer delight and outrage. *Sloan Management Review*, **41**(1), 35–45.

Brown, C. & Appleyard, M. (2001). Employment practices and semiconductor manufacturing performance. *Industrial Relations*, **46**(3), 436–471.

Cappelli P. & Neumark, D. (2001). Do "high-performance" work practices improve establishment-level outcomes? *Industrial and Labor Relations Review*, **54**(4), 737–775.

Cappelli, P. & Rogovsky, N. (1998). Employee involvement and organizational citizenship: implications for labor law reform and "Lean production". *Industrial and Labor Relations Review*, **51**(4), 633–653.

Chadwick, C. & Fister, T. (2001). Innovative human resource practices and outcomes for workers. Unpublished manuscript, University of Illinois at Urbana-Champaign.

Chung, K. & Pruit, S. (1994). A simple approximation of Tobin's Q. *Financial Management*, **23**(3), 70–74.

Cooke, W. (1994). Employee participation programs, group-based incentives, and company performance: a union-nonunion perspective. *Industrial and Labor Relations Review*, **47**(4), 594–609.

Cotton, J. (1993). *Employee Involvement.* Newbury Park, CA: Sage.

Cutcher-Gershenfeld, J. (1991). The impact on economic performance of a transformation in workplace relations. *Industrial and Labor Relations Review*, **44** (January), 241–260.

Cully, M., O'Reilly, A., Millward, N., Forth, J., Woodland, S., Dix, G. & Bryson, A. (1999). *The 1998 Workplace Employee Relations Survey: First Findings.* London: Department of Trade and Industry.

Delaney, J., Lewin, D. & Ichniowski, C. (1989). *Human Resource Policies and Practices in American Firms.* Bureau of Labor–Management Relations and Cooperative Programs, US Department of Labor, BLMR 137. Washington, DC: US Government Printing Office.

Fernie, S. & Metcalf, D. (1995). Participation, contingent pay, representation and workplace performance: evidence from Great Britain. *British Journal of Industrial Relations*, **33**(3), 380–415.

Freeman, R., Kleiner, M. & Ostroff, C. (2000). *The Anatomy of Employee Involvement and Its Effects on Firms and Workers.* Working Paper No. 8050. Cambridge: National Bureau of Economic Research.

Freeman, R. & Lazear, E. (1994). *An Economic Effects of Works Councils.* Working Paper No. 4918. Cambridge: National Bureau of Economic Research.

Freeman, R. & Rogers, J. (1999). *What Workers Want.* Ithaca, NY: Cornell University Press.

Gardner, T., Moynihan, L., Park, H. & Wright, P. (2000). Unlocking the black box: examining the processes through which human resource practices impact business performance. Unpublished manuscript, Cornell University.

Gerhart, B., Wright, P., McMahan, G. & Snell, S. (2000). Measurement error in research on human resources and firm performance: how much error is there and does it influence effect size estimates? *Personnel Psychology*, **53**, 803–834.

Gerhart, B., Wright, P. & McMahan, G. (2000). Measurement error in research on the human resources and firm performance relationship: further evidence and analysis. *Personnel Psychology*, **53**, 855–872.

Gibson, C. & Birkinshaw, J. (2001). Contextual determinants of organizational ambidexterity. Unpublished manuscript, University of Southern California.

Gittleman, M., Horrigan, M. & Joyce, M. (1998). "Flexible" workplace practices: evidence from a nationally representative survey. *Industrial and Labor Relations Review*, **52**(1), 99–115.

Goddard, J. (2001). High performance and the transformation of work? The implications of alternative work practices for the experience of outcomes at work. *Industrial and Labor Relations Review*, **54**(4), 776–805.

Guest, D. (1997). Human resource management and performance: a review and research agenda. *International Journal of Human Resource Management*, **8**(3), 263–276.

Guest, D. (1999). Human resource management—the worker's verdict. *Human Resource Management Journal*, **9**(3), 5–25.

Guest, D. & Conway, N. (1999). Peering into the black hole: The downside of new employment relations in the UK. *British Journal of Industrial Relations*, **37**(3), 367–389.

Guest, D. & Hoque, K. (1996). National ownership and HR practices in UK Greenfield sites. *Human Resource Management Journal*, **6**(4), 50–74.

Hammer, M. & Champy, J. (1988). *Reengineering the Corporation.* New York: Harper Business.

Huselid, M. (1995). The impact of human resource management practices on turnover, productivity, and corporate performance. *Academy of Management Journal*, **38**(3), 635–672.

Huselid, M. & Becker, B. (1996). Methodological issues in cross-sectional and panel estimates of the human resource-firm performance link. *Industrial Relations*, **35**(3), 400–422.

Huselid, M. & Becker, B. (2000). Comment on "Measurement error in research on human resourses and firm performance: how much error is there and does it influence effect size estimates?" by Gerhart, Wright, McMahan, and Snell. *Personnel Psychology*, **53**, 835–854.

Ichniowski, C. (1990). *Human Resource Management Systems and the Performance of US Manufacturing Businesses.* Working Paper No. 3449. Cambridge: National Bureau of Economic Research.
Ichniowski, C., Shaw, K. & Prennushi, G. (1995). *The Impact of Human Resource Practices on Productivity.* Working Paper No. 5333. Cambridge: National Bureau of Economic Research.
Ichniowski, C., Kochan, T., Levine, D., Olson, C. & Strauss, G. (1996). What works at work: overview and Assessment. *Industrial Relations*, 35(3), 299–333.
Katz, H., Kochan, T. & Gobeille, K. (1983). Industrial relations performance, economic performance, and QWL programs: an inter-plant analysis. *Industrial and Labor Relations Review*, 37, 3–17.
Katz, H., Thomas, P. Kochan, T. & Weber, M. (1985). Assessing the effects of industrial relations systems and efforts to improve quality of working like on organizational effectiveness. *Academy of Management Journal*, **28**(3), 509–526.
Kinicki, A., Carson, K. & Bohlander, G. (1992). Relationship between an organization's actual human resource efforts and employee attitudes. *Group & Organization Management*, **17**(2), 135–152.
Kling. J. (1995). High performance work systems and firm performance. *Monthly Labor Review, May*, 29–36.
Koch, M. & McGrath, R. (1996). Improving labor productivity: human resource management policies do matter. *Strategic Management Journal*, **17**, 335–354.
Kochan, T. & Osterman, P. (1994). *The Mutual Gains Enterprise.* Boston: Harvard Business School Press.
Koys, D. (1988). Human resource management and a culture of respect: effects on employees' organizational commitment. *Employee Rights and Responsibilities Journal*, **1**, 57–67.
Koys, D. (2001). The effects of employee satisfaction, organizational citizenship behavior, and turnover on organizational effectiveness: a unit-level longitudinal study. *Personnel Psychology*, **54**, 101–114.
Lam, L. & White, L. (1998). Human resource orientation and corporate performance. *Human Resource Development Quarterly*, **9**(4), 351–364.
Lawler, E. (1986). *High-involvement Management: Participative Strategies for Improving Organizational Performance.* San Francisco, CA: Jossey-Bass.
Lawler, E. (1992). *The Ultimate Advantage: Creating the High Involvement Organization.* San Francisco, CA: Jossey-Bass.
Lawler, E. (1996). *From the Ground Up: Six Principles for Creating the New Logic Organization.* San Francisco, CA: Jossey-Bass.
Lawler, E., Mohrman, S. & Benson, G. (2001). *Organizing for High Performance: the CEO Report on Employee Involvement, TQM, Re-engineering, and Knowledge Management in Fortune 1000 Companies.* San Francisco, CA: Jossey-Bass.
Lawler, E. Mohrman, S. & Ledford, G. (1995). *Creating High Performance Organizations: Practice and Results of Employee Involvement and Quality Management in Fortune 1000 Companies.* San Francisco, CA: Jossey-Bass.
Lawler, E., Mohrman, S. & Ledford, G. (1998). *Strategies for High Performance Organizations: Employee Involvement, TQM, and Re-engineering Programs in Fortune 1000 corporations.* San Francisco, CA: Jossey-Bass.
Leigh, D. & Gifford, K. (1999). Workplace transformation and worker upskilling: the perspective of individual workers. *Industrial Relations*, **38**(2), 174–191.
Levine, D. & Tyson, L. (1990). Participation, productivity, and the firm's environment. In A. Blinder (Ed.), *Paying for Performance: a Review of the Evidence* (pp. 183–243). Washington, DC: Brookings Institution.
Likert, R. (1961). *New Patterns of Management.* New York: McGraw-Hill.
Locke, R., Kochan, T. & Piore, M. (1995). Reconceptualizing comparative industrial relations: Lessons from international research. *International Labour Review*, **134**(2), 139–162.
Lynch, L. & Black, S. (1998). Beyond the incidence of employer-provided training. *Industrial and Laser Relations Review*, **52**(1), 64-81.
MacDuffie, J. (1995). Human resource bundles and manufacturing performance: organizational logic and flexible production systems in the world auto industry. *Industrial and Labor Relations Review*, **48**(2), 197–222.
McGregor, D. (1960). *The Human Side of the Enterprise.* New York: McGraw-Hill.

Meyer, J., Paunonen, S., Gellatly, I., Goffin, R. & Jackson, D. (1989). Organizational commitment and job performance: it's the nature of the commitment that counts. *Journal of Applied Psychology*, **74**, 152–156.

Meyer, J. & Smith, C. (2000). HRM Practices and organizational commitment: test of a mediation model. *Canadian Journal of Administrative Sciences*, **17**(4), 319–331.

Millward, N., Woodland, S., Bryson, A., Forth, J. & Kirby, S. (1999). *A Bibliography of Research Based on the British Workplace Industrial Relations.* Survey Series. London: Department of Trade and Industry (available at http://www.dti.gov.uk/er/emar/1998wers.htm).

Morrison, E. (1995). Organizational citizenship behavior as a criticl link between HRM and service quality. *Human Resource Management*, **35**, 493–512.

Oakland, J. & Oakland, S. (1998). The links between people management, customer satisfaction and business results. *Total Quality Management*, **9**(4, 5), 185–190.

O'Reilly, C. & Chatman, J. (1986). Organizational commitment and psychological attachment: the effects of compliance, identification, and internalization on prosocial behavior. *Journal of Applied Psychology*, **71**, 492–499.

Osterman, P. (1994). How common is workplace transformation and who adopts it? *Industrial and Labor Relations Review*, **47**(2), 173–189.

Osterman, P. (2000). Work restructuring in an era of restructuring: trends in diffusion and effect on employee welfare. *Industrial and Labor Relations Review*, **53**(2), 179–196.

Parks, S. (1995). Improving workplace performance: historical and theoretical contexts. *Monthly Labor Review*, **May**, 18–28.

Pils. F. & MacDuffie, J. (1996). The adoption of high involvement work practices. *Industrial Relations*, **35**(3), 423–455.

Poole, M., Lansbury, R. & Wailes, N. (2001). A comparative analysis of developments in industrial democracy. *Industrial Relations*, **40**(3), 490–525.

Probst, T. & Brubaker, T. (2001). The effects of job insecurity on employee safety outcomes: cross-sectional and longitudinal explorations. *Journal of Occupational Health Psychology*, **6**(2), 139–159.

Scholarios, D., Ramsay, D. & Harley, B. (2000). "High-commitment" management practices and employee outcomes: evidence from Britain and Australia. Working Paper in Human Resource Management, ER, and OS, Number 9. University of Melbourne.

Shafer, R., Dyer, L., Kilty, J., Amos, J. & Ericksen, J. (2001). Crafting a human resource strategy to foster organizational agility: a case study. *Human Resource Management*, **40**(3), 197–211.

Tsui, A., Pearce, J., Porter, L. & Tripoli, A. (1997). Alternative approaches to the employee-organization relationship: does investment in employees pay off? *Academy of Management Journal*, **40**(5), 1089–1121.

Vandenberg, R., Richardson, H. & Eastman, L. (1999). The impact of high involvement work practices on organizational effectiveness: a second-order latent variable approach. *Group & Organization Management*, **24**(3), 300–339.

Wagner, J. (1995). Participation's effects on performance and satisfaction: a reconsideration of the research evidence. Academy of Management Review, **19**, 312–330.

Wood, S. & de Menezes, L. (1998). High commitment management in the UK: evidence from the Workplace Industrial Relations Survey, and Employers' Manpower and Skills Practices Survey. *Human Relations*, **51**(4), 485–515.

Wright, P., Gardner, T. M., Moynihan, L., Park, H., Gerhart, B. & Delery, J. (2001). Measurement error in research on human resources and firm performance: additional data and suggestions for future research. *Personnel Psychology*, **54**, 875–901.

Youndt, M., Snell, S., Dean J. & Lepak, D. (1996). Human resource management, manufacturing strategy, and firm performance. *Academy of Management Journal*, **39**, 836–866.

CHAPTER 10

Proactivity and Innovation: Promoting a New Workforce for the New Workplace

Kerrie L. Unsworth
School of Management, Queensland University of Technology, Brisbane, Australia
and
Sharon K. Parker
Australian Graduate School of Management, University of New South Wales, Sydney, Australia

Imagine you are running a marathon. You started at a nice, steady pace, but the speed just kept increasing. You must compete with the others in the race but they keep sprinting forward. And more and more people keep joining the race. Not only that, but things are now being thrown at you from all angles and you must duck and swerve to avoid them, and the finishing line keeps being moved. Feel the pressure? This is how many organisations today operate: in an increasingly competitive environment in which frequent changes in technologies, markets, government regulations and customers give rise to turbulence and unpredictability. So, how does an organisation deal with such pressures? How do they finish the race? We believe that one important ingredient is the proactive and innovative behaviour of employees, i.e. employees who help you to sprint forward with new ideas, and who can duck and cope with unpredictability. This chapter examines the concepts of proactivity and innovation. It is unique in that it draws together findings from these traditionally separate research streams and identifies areas of convergence and divergence.

We begin by examining why proactivity and innovation are important and show that these employee behaviours help enhance the effectiveness of organizational marathon runners. Then we look at what these concepts mean and how they relate to each other. The third section deals with the individual and environmental factors that affect proactivity and innovation. Based on these research findings, we suggest ways in which organizations can improve the proactivity and innovativeness of the workforce. Finally, we suggest some directions for future research.

The New Workplace: A Guide to the Human Impact of Modern Working Practices.
Edited by David Holman, Toby D. Wall, Chris W. Clegg, Paul Sparrow and Ann Howard. © 2003 John Wiley & Sons, Ltd.

WHY ARE PROACTIVITY AND INNOVATION IMPORTANT?

So do these behaviours help to win the race? Several sources suggest that this is, indeed, the case. For instance, the best-performing real estate agents are those who show proactivity (Crant, 1995). Zempel (1999; cited in Fay & Frese, 2001) found that the degree of firm owners' proactivity was correlated with the firms' success, in East Germany, Zimbabwe and Uganda. The UK Prime Minister, Tony Blair, said, "creativity and innovation are at the heart of a successful business" (Blair, 1999), and a study conducted on 156 small and medium manufacturing enterprises showed that organizational performance was related to the extent to which these companies used employee suggestions (Turgoose et al., 2000).

There are several reasons why employee proactivity and innovation might contribute to increasing company performance. First, many organisations are now relatively decentralized and employees need to work without close supervision. Proactive and innovative behaviours are necessary in such situations (Crant, 2000; Parker, 1998). Second, employees are closest to the coal-face: they know what is going on, what customers want and need, what inefficiencies lie in the system. Without their suggestions, organizations rely upon potentially outdated products, services and procedures and/or upon management's perceptiveness. Third, proactivity and innovation can promote organizational effectiveness through their effects on employee outcomes, such as career success (Seibert, Crant & Kramer, 1999), team commitment and team performance (Kirkman & Rosen, 1999). Finally, these behaviours are fulfilling and enjoyable (Unsworth & Wood, 2001). Such enjoyment is likely to lead to a more motivated and more productive workforce.

WHAT ARE PROACTIVITY AND INNOVATION?

These constructs represent similar, but slightly different ideas. In order to see the relationships between the two, we first discuss each separately.

Proactivity

Proactivity is about being self-starting and change-orientated in order to enhance personal or organizational effectiveness, such as by making improvements to work procedures or using one's initiative to solve a problem. In the academic literature, many constructs relate to proactivity. These constructs vary according to whether proactivity is seen as a relatively stable personality trait or as an outcome that varies across situations; as a behaviour or a psychological state; and as an individual-level construct or an organizational-level one. Here, we focus on individual-level proactive behaviours that can vary across situations. We view stable traits (e.g. proactive personality style) and psychological states (e.g. proactive motivation) as determinants, rather than defining aspects, of this behaviour.

Even restricting our focus to individual-level proactive behaviours that vary across situations, there are many related concepts with different labels and theoretical underpinnings. Crant (2000, p. 436) refers to "proactive behaviour" as "taking initiative in improving current circumstances; it involves challenging the status quo rather than passively adapting present conditions". In contrast to "spontaneous behaviours", which are voluntary extra-role behaviours (George & Brief, 1992), Crant recognized that proactive behaviour can be both in-role (e.g. agents seeking feedback about their sales techniques) or extra-role (e.g. changing the scope of one's job). The key focus of proactivity is an action orientation, rather than a passive or reactive pattern of behaviour. This action orientation is also highlighted in Frese *et al.*'s (1996; Fay & Frese, 2001) related concept of "personal initiative", which emphasises "self-starting" behaviour and action orientation. However, personal initiative is defined more stringently than proactive behaviour, as the behaviour must be consistent with the organization's mission, have a long-term focus, be goal-directed and involve persistence. "Taking charge" (Morrison & Phelps, 1999) includes voluntary behaviours related to making improvement-orientated changes in how work is executed, and is considered similar to proactivity, although it is operationalized quite differently. Other related behavioural concepts are "task revision" (Staw & Boettger, 1990), or action taken to change procedures, inaccurate job descriptions and inappropriate role expectations; "role innovation" (Schein, 1971), or employees' rejecting and re-defining their roles; and "voice" (Van Dyne & LePine, 1998), which involves challenging change-orientated behaviour, such as speaking out about gender-equity issues.

This brief review shows that there is a plethora of concepts that relate to individual-level proactive behaviour. Nevertheless, although these vary in particular ways, they have in common an emphasis on self-starting and change-orientated behaviours. For the purposes of this chapter, we therefore adopt a broad definition of proactive behaviour as:

> Proactivity is a set of self-starting, action-orientated behaviours aimed at modifying the situation or oneself to achieve greater personal or organizational effectiveness.

Innovation

While proactivity relates to self-starting change-orientated behaviours, innovation is concerned with the generation and implementation of ideas. Before further elaboration, it is important to note that there is often confusion between creativity and innovation (Drazin & Schoonhoeven, 1996; Dauw, 1969). Some researchers use the terms synonymously (e.g. Amabile, 1996), while others propose creativity to be the generation of ideas and innovation as the implementation of them (e.g. West & Farr, 1990). Others believe that creativity refers to the individual level, while innovation refers to the organizational level (Dauw, 1969; Oldham & Cummings, 1996). Nevertheless, the most widely accepted viewpoint is that creativity involves the generation of the idea, while innovation involves both the generation and the implementation of that idea (e.g. Kanter, 1983; Mumford & Gustafson, 1988; Unsworth & Clegg, 2001). Creativity is thus a part of the innovation process, and will be considered as such throughout the rest of this chapter.

One of the most commonly-cited definitions applied to innovation is the following:

> A product or response will be judged as creative to the extent that (a) it is both a novel and appropriate, useful, correct or valuable response to the task at hand, and (b) the task is heuristic rather than algorithmic (Amabile, 1983, p. 359).

As this definition makes explicit, the criterion is the production of novel and useful ideas. However, this raises some problems. First, it might not be generalisable across domains: Sprecher (1959) asked 107 engineers to define creativity and found that novelty was mentioned by only 18 people (compared to comprehensiveness, which was noted 34 times).

Both novelty and usefulness are based upon subjective judgements (Amabile, 1982), and therefore are domain- and time-specific (Ford, 1996). The degree of novelty needed is a contentious issue (relative novelty, e.g. Swan, 1995, vs. absolute novelty, e.g. Nyström, 1979). Finally, the judgement of usefulness depends upon the referent. What is useful to one stakeholder may, in fact, be detrimental or useless to another.

Therefore, the widely accepted view that innovation is defined by the production of novel and useful outcomes is problematic. In addition, Drazin, Glynn & Kazanjian (1999) recently proposed that these outcome-based definitions neglect examination of the innovation process itself. They present a definition that is based upon engagement in behaviours, regardless of the ultimate outcomes. We agree with their propositions and thus suggest that:

> Innovation is the process of engaging in behaviours designed to generate and implement new ideas, processes, products and services, regardless of the ultimate success of these new phenomena.

Linking Proactivity and Innovation

Defining innovation in terms of behaviours designed to generate and implement new ideas brings it very close to the definition of proactivity as a set of self-starting, action-orientated behaviours designed to change one's environment or oneself. However, proactivity is broader than innovation; it can result in creativity and innovation, but it can also result in other outcomes, such as effective problem-solving and coping with demands. Nevertheless, proactivity is likely to be an important driver of innovation. The self-starting component of proactivity is relevant to creativity, particularly identifying problems and generating novel solutions. Persistence and the focus on pushing change is particularly relevant to idea implementation, which involves behaviours such as seeking sponsorship for ideas and building support (e.g. Kanter, 1983).

Despite the similarities between the concepts, they have not previously been associated. Until recently, even creativity and innovation existed in separate streams of research. While proactivity and innovation are specifically orientated towards organizational domains, creativity research has been conducted predominantly in laboratories and has taken a more general orientation. In addition, creativity research emerged much earlier than proactivity and innovation research and thus is more fully developed. We feel it is important to integrate these streams and derive a synthesized model which incorporates both the shared and unique aspects of each concept. To this aim, we now discuss influences on the proactivity and innovation of employees.

HOW CAN ORGANIZATIONS IMPROVE THE PROACTIVITY AND INNOVATION OF EMPLOYEES?

When running a marathon, one wishes to know the factors that will help win the race. These factors will include the right personal characteristics (e.g. stamina, muscle tone), the right tools and context (e.g. shoes, drinks/food), the right social context (e.g. the coaching team) and the right strategy (e.g. entering into the right race). The same question regarding determinants can be applied to proactivity and innovation.

Theories of proactivity (e.g. Crant, 2000; Fay & Frese, 2001; Parker, 1999) and innovation (e.g. Amabile, 1983; Woodman, Sawyer & Griffin, 1993; Ford, 1996) generally cover three sets of antecedents: individual differences (knowledge, skills, abilities and dispositions), motivation, and context (work, social and organizational). Most theories also suggest that these factors combine in an interactive fashion: the effects of one moderate the effects of others. For instance, the effect of motivation may differ when contextual factors prohibit proactive and innovative behaviours. We now review research that has investigated the specific determinants belonging to each of these categories of individual differences, motivation and contextual factors. For each category, we look at the determinants of proactivity, then of innovation, before linking the two streams together. At the end of each section, we summarise the key messages from the research (see also Figure 10.1).

INDIVIDUAL DIFFERENCES IN KNOWLEDGE, SKILLS, ABILITIES AND DISPOSITIONS

Knowledge, Skills and Abilities

Two broad types of knowledge, skills and abilities (KSAs) are argued to be important to proactivity: job-related KSAs and context-relevant knowledge. Fay & Frese (2001) argued that taking initiative involves possessing a thorough understanding of one's work and has been shown to be positively related to job qualifications (Frese & Hilligloh, 1994). Fay & Frese (2001) also found that cognitive ability predicted personal initiative using a longitudinal analysis, and that this was independent of motivational effects.

Parker (2000) proposed two types of context-relevant knowledge antecedents. The first is "integrated understanding", or the degree to which an employee understands the wider work system and the relationships amongst its components (e.g. knowledge about customers, suppliers and other departments). The more an individual has an understanding of the wider system, the more likely he/she is to behave in a proactive manner. The second was "perspective-taking", or the extent to which employees adopt the view point of others. A recent study showed that the more employees adopted their suppliers' perspective, the more likely they were to help them (Parker & Axtell, 2001). The relationship between perspective-taking and proactivity has not been investigated, although it is likely that such a relationship will exist.

A large number of KSAs have been recognised as facilitators of innovation. Most of these are centred around idea-generation abilities, such as divergent thinking (e.g. Guastello, Bzdawka, Guastello & Rieke, 1992), experimenting (e.g. Keller & Holland, 1978) and originality and venturesomeness (e.g. Jones, 1964). Others appear to be more concerned with the "doing" of innovation: e.g. behavioural abilities (e.g. Ford, 1996), communication (e.g. Pelz & Andrews, 1966), planning skills (e.g. Sprecher, 1959), social skills (e.g. Amabile & Gryskiewicz, 1987) and organizational status (e.g. Aiken, Bacharach & French, 1980). In a related fashion, domain expertise and job-related knowledge has also been shown to be important (e.g. Amabile, 1983; Sternberg & Lubart, 1991). The relationship between creativity and intelligence has been hotly debated between those who believe there is a positive relationship (e.g. Guilford & Christensen, 1973) and those who believe this relationship is artefactual (e.g. Wallach & Kogan, 1965). The weight of evidence, however, suggests that if there is a relationship between intelligence and creativity, it is very small and probably limited to verbal or problem-solving tests (e.g. Torrance, 1967).

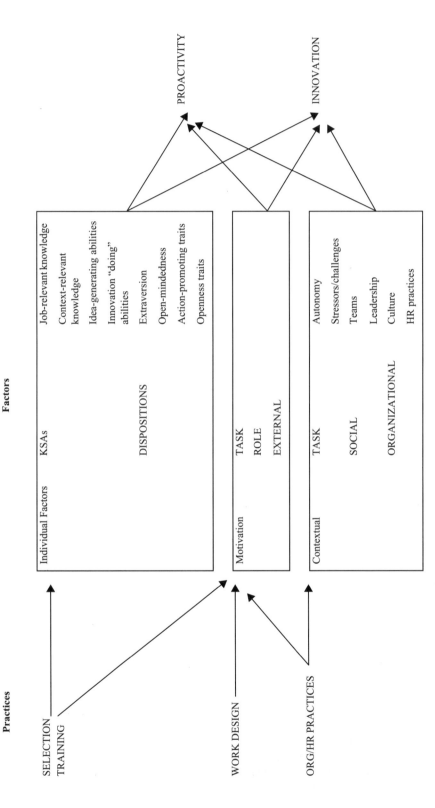

Figure 10.1 Innovation and proactivity: summary of influential factors and good practices

Thus, there are some similarities between the facilitators of proactivity and those of innovation, e.g. domain expertise and job-relevant knowledge. Nonetheless, the majority of KSAs identified in the creativity and innovation literatures relate to the ability to generate ideas. These differences are not surprising, given the different foci of the two research arenas. As noted earlier, most proactivity research has focused on work-related issues, while until recently most innovation research was focused on more general creative acts. Thus, researchers interested in proactivity concentrated mostly upon organizational determinants (e.g. the work by Frese, and by Parker), while researchers interested in innovation focused upon more general KSAs (e.g. the work by Amabile). In addition, the requirement for novelty that is inherent within innovation presumably accentuates the need for idea generation and cognitive abilities relative to proactivity.

Dispositional Influences

Dispositional influences are cross-situational and stable tendencies that exert a general influence over behaviour (Fay & Frese, 2001). Proactive personality style (Bateman & Crant, 1993), a tendency to effect environmental change, is an obvious dispositional determinant of proactive behaviour. Indeed, significant positive correlations have been shown between proactive personality and personal initiative (Fay & Frese, 2001), proactive motivation (Parker, 1998; Parker & Sprigg, 1999) and an array of other proactive outcomes, such as entrepreneurship (Crant, 1996) and career success (Siebert et al., 1999).

Two other influential predictors of proactivity are need for achievement and self-esteem. Need for achievement and action orientation have been shown to positively predict personal initiative (e.g. Frese et al., 1997; Fay & Frese, 2001) and need for achievement, along with self-esteem, also predict proactive feedback seeking (Vancouver & Morrison, 1995). Self-esteem predicts proactive coping strategies associated with job loss, such as proactive job searching (Kinicki & Latack, 1990) and role innovation (Munton & West, 1995).

In terms of the Big Five personality constructs, Fay & Frese (2001) found that personal initiative was moderately correlated with extraversion ($r = 0.33$) and conscientiousness ($r = 0.29$), but had weaker correlations with agreeableness (-0.09), openness to experience (0.13) and neuroticism (-0.14). Consistent with these results, conscientiousness and extraversion were strongly related to voice behaviour and helping/cooperative behaviour in a laboratory study, while agreeableness had a negative relationship with employee voice (LePine & Van Dyne, 2001). Collectively, these studies suggest that extraversion is an important personality factor affecting proactivity, and that the effect of conscientiousness and openness depend on the specific outcome assessed.

Piecemeal research into creativity and innovation has identified many, varied influential dispositions. Regarding the Big Five, McCrae (1987) used previously collected data and found that only open-mindedness consistently predicted creativity and innovation (correlations ranged from $r = 0.37$ to $r = 0.41$). Nevertheless, as McCrae (1987) argues, the relationship between the other factors (particularly extraversion, neuroticism and conscientiousness) and creativity and innovation may be masked by the data which were responses to laboratory-based, divergent thinking tests. In the workplace, where ideas need to be pushed and championed (e.g. Howell & Higgins, 1990), it is likely that factors such as extraversion and conscientiousness will influence the successfulness of innovation attempts.

Barron & Harrington (1981) reviewed dispositional influences on creativity and found a "fairly stable set of core characteristics" (p. 453). These traits are valuing aesthetic qualities, broad interests, attraction to complexity, high energy, independence of judgement, autonomy, intuition, self-confidence, tolerance of ambiguity and conflicts, and a creative self-identity. Other traits that have been identified as facilitating creativity include a positive attitude towards ideation (e.g. Basadur & Finkbeiner, 1985), curiosity (e.g. Amabile & Gryskiewicz, 1987), discovery orientation (e.g. Csikszentmihalyi & Getzels, 1970), enthusiasm (e.g. Udell, Baker & Albaum, 1976), flexibility (e.g. Gorman & Breskin, 1969), impulsiveness (e.g. Dellas & Gaier, 1970), risk orientation (e.g. Amabile, 1983) and sensation-seeking (e.g. Davis, Peterson & Farley, 1974). Furthermore, similar to the KSAs, a number of dispositional factors appear to be concerned with the "doing" of innovation. Such factors include energy (e.g. Amabile & Gryskiewicz, 1987), an internal locus of control (e.g. Aviram & Milgram, 1977), lack of conformity (e.g. Sprecher, 1959), need for growth (e.g. Brazeal & Weaver, 1990), persistence (e.g. Amabile, 1983) and self-confidence (e.g. Keller & Holland, 1983).

Summary of Individual Difference Factors

Comparing the factors that predict proactivity with those that predict creativity and innovation shows some striking trends. Proactivity determinants tend to be those that promote action, such as need for achievement, self-esteem, extraversion and conscientiousness. Creativity determinants tend to represent openness (e.g. attraction to complexity, broad interests, curiosity, sensation-seeking, etc.), while implementation determinants are again much more action-orientated (e.g. persistence, self-confidence). These differences are perhaps indicative of the differences between proactivity and innovation. Proactive behaviours are not necessarily creative and, as such, they may not require openness. However, once an idea has been generated, one must often be proactive in order for it to be implemented.

One last comment on individual difference factors is needed. It is now obvious that much research has been conducted in this area, particularly in the prediction of creativity and innovation. The findings, therefore, are based on a broad variety of sampled populations using very different methodologies, and are both wide-ranging and disparate. Unfortunately, much of this research has been conducted in a piecemeal fashion, and it is difficult to compare the relative importance of different individual difference factors. Nevertheless, as both the theories and the statistics are now becoming more sophisticated and more integrative, we hope that future research will be able to shed some light on this issue.

MOTIVATION

Motivation is considered essential in any proactive or innovative exercise (Bejat, 1972; Miner, Smith & Bracker, 1994). However, unlike dispositions, motivational variables are states rather than traits, and are strongly influenced by the context. We identified three situational origins of motivation that differ in their breadth: the task itself (intrinsic motivation), the role (role-based proactive motivation) and external factors (rewards and recognition).

Task-Based Intrinsic Motivation

Intrinsic task motivation is motivation to perform a task for its own sake, because of enjoyment and interest in the task. This type of motivation leads to heightened concentration on the task, which helps to maintain creative behaviours rather than relying upon habitual responses (e.g. Amabile, 1996; Csikszentmihalyi, 1996).

Perhaps the biggest player in the creativity motivation stakes is Teresa Amabile. Her componential theory of creativity (1983, 1996) places intrinsic motivation in prime position. Building upon Deci & Ryan (1987), she proposes that intrinsic motivation is beneficial to creativity and that alternative forms of motivation (such as the externally-based motivation, discussed later) are detrimental (e.g. Amabile, 1985; Amabile, Hennessey & Grossman, 1986).

Role-based Motivation

Parker (2000) identified two types of role-based motivation (referred to by Parker as "proactive motivation") that are likely to promote proactive behaviours amongst employees First, employees must develop a view of their role and responsibilities that align with proactive expectations, i.e., they need a "flexible role orientation" (Parker, Wall & Jackson, 1997). For employees who have been working in simplified jobs, this means a move away from a narrow "that's not my job" mentality to an orientation in which employees see broader problems as their responsibility and recognize the importance of being proactive.

Second, employees must feel *capable* of behaving in these types of ways, or possess "role breadth self-efficacy" (RBSE; Parker, 1998). RBSE concerns the extent to which people feel capable of carrying out a range of proactive tasks (e.g. designing improved procedures, setting goals and targets, and meeting with customers or suppliers). RBSE is distinct from, although related to, proactive personality style (Parker, 1998).

Axtell *et al.*, (2000) found that flexible role orientation and role breadth self-efficacy (particularly the latter) predicted the likelihood of production employees making innovative suggestions. Similarly, Frese, Teng & Wijnen (1999) found that various role-based motivational states, especially self-efficacy, proactive orientation and higher-order need strength, predicted whether employees have ideas for improvements, which was in turn predictive of writing and submitting ideas. Other studies have also shown that self-efficacy is an important determinant of personal initiative (Fay & Frese, 2001; Frese *et al.*, 1996; Vennekel, 2000; cited in Fay & Frese, 2001) and taking charge (Morrison & Phelps, 1999).

Externally-based Motivation

Earlier, it was suggested that externally-based motivation (such as that produced by rewards and recognition) might be detrimental to innovation. However, Eisenberger and colleagues suggest that the negative findings for rewards are caused by ambiguity about which dimension of performance is being rewarded and the high salience of the reward (e.g. Eisenberger & Cameron, 1996; Eisenberger & Armeli, 1997).

Several studies have found that extrinsic motivation, and particularly rewards, either have no effect (Cox, 1977; Cox, Nash & Ash, 1976) or enhance innovation (Fromme,

Mercadal & Mercadal, 1976; Halpin & Halpin, 1973; Krop, 1969; Locurto & Walsh, 1976). Parnes' (1976) review of the literature reported that rewards helped in implementation of ideas. Indeed, even Amabile (1997) concedes that rewards may sometimes contribute to innovation.

Nevertheless, Frese *et al.* (1999) found that the motive to get a reward had only a slight positive relationship with the number of ideas individuals put forward in a suggestions scheme, and it had no relationship with writing and submitting those ideas. Other motivational and contextual factors were much more important predictors, leading the authors to conclude that financial rewards were not important in this particular context. It appears that the degree to which externally-based motivators facilitate innovation depends upon the way in which the motivator is administered and the context in which it takes place.

Summary of Motivational Factors

In summary, then, it can be seen that motivation strongly influences the engagement and successful completion of proactive and innovative endeavours, and that it can be derived from three sources: responses to the task, responses to the role, and responses to external factors. Although some argue that externally-based motivation is detrimental to innovation, we believe that these three types of motivation influence in an additive fashion. In other words, proactive and innovative behaviours are most likely to occur when an employee is intrinsically motivated by the task, has a flexible role-orientation and role breadth self-efficacy, and is appropriately incentivized and rewarded. Further inquiry is needed to establish whether this is, indeed, the case.

So, the marathon runners now have the right personal attributes and the required motivation. However, they still will not win the race unless the context supports these personal and motivational qualities. It is these contextual factors that we now discuss.

CONTEXTUAL FACTORS

We consider three groups of contextual factors: task and work factors; social interaction characteristics; and the wider organizational context.

Task and Work Factors

Job Autonomy and Complexity

One of the most important contextual factors likely to affect proactivity and innovation is work design, particularly the amount of *job autonomy* and *job complexity*.

Many studies have linked job control and complexity to proactive and innovative outcomes (e.g. Amabile *et al.*, 1996; Andrews & Gordon, 1970; Ekvall, 1993). For example, Frese *et al.* (1996), found that personal initiative was lower amongst East Germans than West Germans due to lower job autonomy and job complexity, and showed that initiative was enhanced with increases in these job characteristics (see also Frese, Garst & Fay, 2000). LePine & Van Dyne (1998) found that employees were more likely to constructively challenge the status quo to improve their work if they had greater self-management. Axtell *et al.* (2000) found that autonomy was associated with a greater likelihood of making suggestions. Amabile & Gryskiewicz (1987) found that 74% of scientists mentioned autonomy as a major factor in successfully creative incidents, while 48% reported a lack of autonomy as being a major constraint in unsuccessful incidents. An exception, however, is Frese *et al.* (1999), who found a slight negative association between job control/job complexity and having ideas for a suggestion scheme; they suggested that those with high control and complexity can change things themselves, and so may not need to participate in such a scheme.

Many have forwarded explanations for why autonomy is important to proactivity and innovation. Andrews (1975) showed that autonomy assisted in utilizing creative potential. Ekvall & Tangeberg-Andersson (1986) believed that autonomy contributed to a creative climate which affected levels of innovation. Autonomy has been shown to increase felt responsibility (Frese *et al.*, 1996; Hackman & Oldham, 1976) and intrinsic motivation (Zuckerman *et al.*, Smith & Deci, 1978), both of which affect proactivity and innovation. Autonomy also enhances self-efficacy, role orientation, control expectations and control orientations, which in turn promote proactivity (Frese *et al.*, 2000; Parker, 1998; Parker *et al.*, 1997). Finally, autonomy increases knowledge and skill acquisition, which in turn helps the conception of alternative methods (e.g. Frese *et al.*, 1996; Wall, Jackson & Davids, 1992; Parker & Axtell, 2001). It is likely that all these mechanisms play a role in the relationship.

However, the effect of autonomy may not be as straightforward as it appears. Pelz & Andrews (1966) found that an individual's level of autonomy interacted with the average level of autonomy within the group. In very loose settings, R&D scientists with more autonomy withdrew from stimulation from colleagues, which decreased their innovation. Conversely, in settings where the group on average had little autonomy, those few autonomous individuals were prevented from capitalizing on their creativity. Only in the middle-range situations was autonomy positively related to innovation. A further study suggested that employees with some degree of proactivity are most likely to make use of job autonomy afforded to them, whereas those with a more passive personality might not exploit the opportunities autonomy offers (Parker & Sprigg, 1999). These studies suggest that there might be individual and organizational contingency factors that moderate the effect of autonomy on proactive and innovative behaviour.

Stressors—Problems, Time Pressure and Role Demands

The common adage, "necessity is the mother of invention" has been tested on a number of occasions, with contradictory results. Some have found negative links between "necessity" and innovation (e.g. Drwal, 1973; Ganesan & Subramanian, 1982), mainly due to the conceptualisation of necessity as "anxiety"—a state that diverts attention away from the innovative process. It is also suggested that time pressure prohibits experimentation with collaboration and alternative ways of thinking (e.g. Hards, 1999; Miles, Snow & Miles, 2000).

On the other hand, positive relationships have also been found (e.g. Bunce & West, 1984; Drazin *et al.*, 1999; Leith, 1972). Longitudinal studies have found work stressors (time pressure, concentration demands, job ambiguity and organizational problems) to predict subsequent proactive and innovative behaviours (Andrews & Farris, 1972; Fay & Sonnentag,

2000). In these studies, the stressors are associated with challenge, and proactive and innovative behaviours become coping strategies.

Therefore, it is likely that the effect of stressors on proactivity and innovation depends upon the appraisal of the stressor as either anxiety-provoking or an achievable challenge. Interestingly, Amabile *et al.*, (1996) measured both *excessive* workload (italics added) and challenge: the first hindered innovation, while the second helped. As this finding also suggests, the appraisal, and its subsequent effects, are dependent upon the degree to which the stressor exists. This is likely to be a U-shaped curve. Without necessity or stress there is little motivation to engage in the behaviours; too much stress may lead to anxiety, which may be detrimental, but a certain amount of challenge and necessity may be beneficial to proactivity and innovation.

Social Interaction Characteristics

Colleague Communication and Teamworking

Team processes and communication influence the success of proactivity and innovation in three ways: (a) aligning expectations; (b) increasing response possibilities; and (c) enhancing motivation. First, Campbell (2000) suggested that *information sharing* may align expectations between the employee, manager and the institution and reduce the "initiative paradox": managers expect employees to use their own judgement and initiative, but then are shocked when they behave in unexpected ways. Second, diversity among team members, of both task-related and relationship-orientated characteristics, has been shown to positively affect team innovation—most probably due to the increase in potential response possibilities (e.g. Thornburg, 1991; West & Anderson, 1996). Finally, team processes such as sharing, norms, task orientation and participation significantly affect innovation levels (Burningham & West, 1995; Triandis *et al.*, 1963) and high quality communication is an important facilitator of proactive motivation (in particular, RBSE; Parker, 1998).

Leadership

There has been less investigation of the link between leadership and proactive behaviour than one might expect, given that proactive employees are an implicit end-goal in many theories of leadership (Campbell, 2000). For example, transformational leadership aims to lead employees to expend exceptional effort and go beyond the expected. One would therefore suppose this type of leadership to be associated with greater proactivity.

Research examining the role of leadership in innovation began in laboratory experiments. Participatory leadership increased the quantity of responses, while supervisory leadership increased the quality of creative responses (Anderson & Fiedler, 1964). However, this appears to be modified by group climate: under pleasant conditions, participatory leaders increased creativity, but under more stressful conditions, supervisory leaders increased creativity (Fiedler, 1962).

More recently, research has moved to the workplace. Here, it is shown that leaders who encourage and facilitate creativity increase the likelihood of innovative behaviours (e.g. Raudsepp, 1987; Redmond, Mumford & Teach, 1993). Supportive, non-controlling leadership behaviour is predictive of employee creativity (Basu & Green, 1997; Cummings & Oldham, 1997; Oldham & Cummings, 1996). However, Basu & Green (1997) found that transformational leadership inhibited innovation, possibly due to intimidation by such a powerful leader. It has also been recognized by several researchers that managers might not always welcome proactivity and innovation, either because the behaviours are incongruent with expectations or because the managers resist the change it might involve to their own roles (Campbell, 2000). The link between leadership and proactive, innovative behaviour is therefore not straightforward.

Organizational Context

At a general level, a climate for psychological safety (i.e. feeling safe to take interpersonal risks) affects proactive and innovative performance. For example, Vennekel (2000; cited in Fay & Frese, 2001) found that individuals' perceptions of psychological safety in the team context was related to personal initiative amongst hospital staff. Such psychological safety develops feelings of openness and trust amongst employees, which increases proactivity and innovation (e.g. Ekvall & Tangeberg-Anderson, 1986; Miles *et al.*, 2000; Mumford & Gustafson, 1988), while a cold and competitive work climate can reduce creative performance (McCarrey & Edwards, 1973).

At a more specific level, climates for innovation manifest the organizational policies and structures, culture and climate and, as such, strongly promote innovative behaviours (e.g. Tesluk, Farr & Klein, 1997; Tushman & Nelson, 1990). Encouraging and supporting innovation, through both words and deeds, significantly increases the chances of innovation occurring (e.g. Eisenberger, Fasolo & Davis-LaMastro, 1990; Kanter, 1983; Mohamed & Rickards, 1996; Mumford & Gustafson, 1988). Axtell *et al.* (2000) found that with low management support, the number of suggestions employees report making has little impact on the number implemented; where management support was high, the more suggestions made, the more were implemented.

Several human resource practices also potentially influence proactive and innovative behaviours. Performance monitoring that focuses on narrow aspects of task performance could be a deterrent to proactivity (Frenkel *et al.*, 1999). Fay & Frese (2001) reported that they are developing training courses to increase employee proactivity by trying to enhance self-efficacy, change orientation, active coping, and new ways of handling errors. Similarly, formal creativity training can increase the originality of ideas produced (e.g. Kabanoff & Bottger, 1991). Finally, the presence of various lateral integration devices (Mohrman & Cohen, 1995) might promote proactivity and innovation via enhanced collaboration. Miles *et al.* (2000) argued that effective collaboration lies at the heart of successful organizations in the "innovation" era, e.g. cross-functional teams break down barriers of functional silos and are likely to facilitate continuous innovation.

Summary of Contextual Factors

It can be seen, therefore, that several contextual factors may affect proactivity and innovation. These include task and work design (autonomy, complexity, stressors), social characteristics (collegial communication, teamworking, leadership), and organizational characteristics (climate/culture, human resource practices, organizational design). These factors affect proactive and innovative working through encouragement (stressors, culture and norms), support (human resource practices, design) and opportunity (autonomy, leadership). It can also be seen from this review, however, that research in this area is much less comprehensive than other areas. We discuss this deficiency further in the concluding section.

PROMOTING PROACTIVITY AND INNOVATION: IMPLICATIONS FOR MANAGERS

In the preceding discussions, we have identified many factors that predict proactive and innovative behaviours. To make a more manageable list of implications, we have distilled those findings into the following list of good practices. These are outlined in Figure 10.1.

Our analysis first showed that there are some individuals who—because of their particular knowledge, skills, abilities, or personality—are more likely to be proactive and innovative. An obvious implication for managers who require an innovative workforce, then, is for efforts to be made to recruit appropriate individuals into the organization. This will probably mean some adaptation to selecting procedures, such as by extending criteria beyond technical skills to take account of those personal factors that have been linked to proactivity and innovation.

Selection is by no means the only, or even the best, way to obtain a proactive and innovative workforce. In our experience, managers often tend to over-emphasize selection as a strategy for obtaining the appropriate workforce, to the neglect of other strategies, such as employee training and development. The knowledge, skills, abilities, and even motivations, necessary for proactive and innovative behaviour can also be enhanced via training. First, both proactivity and innovation require high levels of job knowledge and expertise. Therefore, at the most basic level, it is important to ensure training in the particular technical area. Second, as noted earlier, it also seems possible to train employees in more generic skills and motivation required for proactivity and innovation. Third, individuals can be trained in ways to support the social processes that underpin innovation, such as communication, teamworking and leadership skills.

There is little point, however, in investing great effort into recruiting and/or developing proactive and innovative individuals if the environment does not allow, encourage or support these behaviours. Therefore, attention needs to be given to the work context, both the immediate task and work design, and the wider organizational culture, structure and processes. Designing an appropriate context is a strategy that is often neglected by managers, who tend to attribute any lack of proactivity and innovation in their work force to factors outside of their control, such as the employees' non-creative personality or lack of ability. Managers often do not recognize the important role that the work context plays in affecting employees' attitudes and behaviour.

Changing the work design to create autonomous and challenging jobs will encourage proactive and innovative behaviours. The introduction of self-managing teams is an appropriate strategy when groups of employees need to coordinate interdependent tasks. If jobs are individual in nature, then work design strategies, such as job enrichment (e.g. allowing employees to make decisions traditionally made by managers) and empowerment, are appropriate. However, when enriching jobs, a manager should also make sure that the workload is managed so as not to become anxiety-provoking. The work design also needs to align with wider human resource and control systems if it is to be successfully implemented or be sustained over the longer term (Parker, Wall & Jackson, 1997). For example, financial control systems might need to be modified to reduce unnecessary blockages to employees making financial decisions, and information systems could need to be adapted to ensure that employees have high-quality access to the information they need to act autonomously without constant referral to management.

In broad terms, the organizational design needs to support both the task and work context and the selection and training of employees if proactivity and innovation are to thrive. This includes an organic organizational structure that facilitates employee self-management, combined with various lateral integration devices and systems (e.g. team working, liaison managers) to promote interteam interdepartmental and cross-functional collaboration. For example, social events, job sharing, and knowledge management data systems can help to facilitate effective communication within and across teams, and allow individuals to understand and adopt the perspective of others. Organizational design, however, is more than the presence of formal structures or systems: the development of an organization-wide culture that is open and trusting, that supports and encourages innovation, and that allows speaking out and managed risk-taking, is also vital for promoting an innovative workforce. Without such a culture, the efforts invested in recruitment, training and work redesign may be meaningless. Some organizations will therefore require quite a fundamental change in culture, which is an organizational change that requires commitment from the highest level.

These practices are not meant to be implemented alone. We noted earlier that changing one factor alone (such as selecting individuals with the appropriate KSAs) will not help proactivity and innovation if other factors are not in place (such as a supportive working environment). Having the best running shoes in the world will not help you to win the marathon if you do not have the motivation to enter the race. Enhancing the proactivity and innovation of employees will require an integrated strategy, incorporating elements of recruitment, selection, training, task and work redesign, organizational culture management, human resource systems and organizational redesign. This is by no means an easy feat, which is why organizations that do manage to succeed in building this type of organization are likely to have a sustainable competitive advantage.

CONCLUSION AND FUTURE DIRECTIONS

We know that proactivity and innovation are important behaviours for organizations, and that they are likely to become more important as organizations continue to de-centralize to cope with rapidly changing contexts, and as competitive pressures drive the demand for innovation to stay ahead. We also know that these behaviours are predicted by a wide array of individual and organizational factors, which in turn have implications for managers, who can themselves be proactive to shape and create a proactive and innovative workforce through selection, development and organizational interventions.

However, there are many things that we still do not know, and many further directions for research. For instance, we know very little about the links between proactivity and innovation. We speculated earlier about these links, but these have not been tested. Research efforts in these spheres need also to draw upon findings from each other, rather than continue as separate traditions. The proactivity literature is relatively more recent, and it is important that it does not proceed independently of the research on innovation.

One important consideration in exploring links between these concepts will be to sharpen up conceptual understanding of the individual constructs. For example, as noted in the Introduction, proactive behaviour has been assessed using a plethora of related but distinct concepts. It is not known how much empirical overlap there is between concepts such as taking charge, personal initiative and voice. Likewise, recent developments in the innovation literature suggest some important subtleties in types of innovation (Unsworth, 2001; Unsworth & Clegg, 2001): *responsive* (externally required solution to a specific problem, e.g. solutions to divergent thinking tests); *expected* (externally required solution to a discovered problem, e.g. responses to role expectations of advertising agent); *contributory* (internally driven to solve a specific problem, e.g. helping solve a colleague's problem); and *proactive* (internally driven to discover and solve a problem, e.g. suggestions in a suggestion scheme). Future research, therefore, needs to consider these different types when examining predictors and processes.

Throughout the chapter we have discussed the current condition of academic knowledge in proactivity and innovation and highlighted areas which we believe need further research. While we know a considerable amount about the specific predictors, we know little about how these factors change over time, how they interact, which are most important, and how they can successfully be changed. There are relatively few longitudinal studies, which means causality is yet to be fully established. There have been very few intervention studies in which aspects of the organization are changed and their effects on proactivity or innovation monitored. Few studies have taken a number of factors and examined how these factors interact with, or are related to each other (with some exceptions, e.g. Frese *et al.*, 2000; Oldham & Cummings, 1996; Parker & Sprigg, 1999; Scott & Bruce, 1994). In relation to the topic of dispositional antecedents in particular, the rather disparate findings can be attributed to piecemeal approach of much of this research. Future research will benefit from a more integrated approach, in which multiple dispositions are assessed simultaneously. The use of Big Five personality determinants also offers greater integrating potential.

In addition, whilst we can be relatively clear about the value of some aspects of the context, e.g. job autonomy and a supportive climate, findings are more mixed when it comes to the roles of other factors, such as stressors, collegial communication and leadership. Research to date has been relatively minimal and/or conflictual, and in-depth field studies are needed. Some questions to be answered include: what factors influence the appraisal of a stressor as a challenge or as anxiety-provoking?; through what means does collegial communication affect proactivity and innovation?; and what factors moderate the effect of leadership on proactivity and innovation? Moreover, we and others have made several speculations about potentially important influences on proactivity and innovation, such as the inhibitory effect of performance-based monitoring or the positive effect of lateral integration methods. These speculations have not been tested empirically and research on these wider organizational contexts is also needed.

Furthermore, much of the research in these areas focuses upon, and only measures, the end-product. However, when analyzing performance in a race, you don't just look at the finishing times, you also need to look at how the runners performed throughout and the reasons why they performed in this way. It is similar here. Drazin *et al.* (1999) and Unsworth & Clegg (2001) both suggest that researchers need to use methods that collect processual information, such as interviews, diaries, observations and more detailed surveys.

This information allows us to look at what happens throughout the proactivity and innovation process. In this way, we can begin to understand how people use proactivity when being innovative, how people go from having an idea to making that idea happen, how people generate ideas, how they use their colleagues and their environment to help them become proactive and innovative, and so on. Using these more novel methods also allows for a greater understanding of innovation types and will enable us to assess which factors affect which particular types.

Along similar lines, more attention needs to be paid to the mechanisms that underpin the links between the various contextual antecedents and employee proactivity/innovation. For example, we suggested that various motivational processes underpin the link between job autonomy and proactive behaviour (e.g. the development of employee self-efficacy), but there are also likely to be cognitive processes (e.g. learning, perspective-taking). For example, team working might lead to employees developing more sophisticated and complex understanding of their work, which could promote innovation. Another mechanism could be via changing employees' expectations of what is required. For example, a supportive and encouraging culture might enhance proactivity and innovation simply because it increases the expectation that every employee must behave in this way.

We know a lot about proactivity and innovation, but there is still a long way to go. The race is getting quicker, and the finishing line is still moving further away, but we are learning more and more about how to run faster. By adopting an integrated strategy to improve the proactivity and innovativeness of their employees, managers can use their entire workforce to help win the race. And, in this race, staying ahead is everything.

REFERENCES

Aiken, M., Bacharach, S. B. & French, J. L. (1980). Organizational structure, work process and proposal making in administrative bureaucracies. *Academy of Management Journal*, **23**(4), 631–652.
Amabile, T. M. (1982). Social psychology of creativity: a consensual assessment technique. *Journal of Personality and Social Psychology*, **43**(5), 997–1013.
Amabile, T. M. (1983). The social psychology of creativity: a componential conceptualization. *Journal of Personality and Social Psychology*, **45**(2), 357–376.
Amabile, T. M. (1985). Motivation and creativity: effects of motivational orientation on creative writers. *Journal of Personality and Social Psychology*, **48**(2), 393–399.
Amabile, T. M. (1996). *Creativity in Context: Update to the Social Psychology of Creativity*. Boulder, CO: Westview.
Amabile, T. M. (1997). Entrepreneurial creativity through motivational synergy. *The Journal of Creative Behaviour*, **31**(1), 18–26.
Amabile, T. M. & Conti, R. (1996). What downsizing does to creativity. *Issues & Observations*, **15**(3), 1–6.
Amabile, T. M. & Gryskiewicz, S. S. (1987). *Creativity in the R&D Laboratory* (Technical Report Number 30). Greensboro: Center for Creative Leadership.
Amabile, T. M., Conti, R., Coon, H., Lazenby, J. & Herron, M. (1996). Assessing the work environment for creativity. *Academy of Management Journal*, **39**(5), 1154–1184.
Amabile, T. M., Hennessey, B. A. & Grossman, B. S. (1986). Social influences on creativity: the effects of contracted for reward. *Journal of Personality and Social Psychology*, **50**(1), 14–23.
Anderson, L. R. & Fiedler, F. E. (1964). The effect of participatory and supervisory leadership on group creativity. *Journal of Applied Psychology*, **48**(4), 227–236.
Andrews, F. M. (1975). Factors affecting the manifestation of creative ability by scientists. *Journal of Personality*, **33**(1), 140–152.

Andrews, F. M. & Farris, G. F. (1972). Time pressure and performance of scientists and engineers: a five year panel study. *Organizational Behaviour and Human Performance*, **8**, 185–200.

Andrews, F. M. & Gordon, G. (1970). Social and organizational factors affecting innovation in research. *Proceedings of the Annual Convention of the American Psychological Association*, **5**(2), 89–90.

Aviram, A. & Milgram, R. M. (1977). Dogmatism, locus of control and creativity in children educated in the Soviet Union, United States and Israel. *Psychological Reports*, **40**(1), 27–34.

Axtell, C. M., Holman, D. J., Unsworth, K. L., Wall, T. D., Waterson, P. E. & Harrington, E. (2000). Shopfloor innovation: facilitating the suggestion and implementation of ideas. *Journal of Occupational & Organizational Psychology*, **73**, 265–285.

Barron, F. & Harrington, D. M. (1981). Creativity, intelligence and personality. *Annual Review of Psychology*, **32**, 439–476.

Basadur, M., & Finkbeiner, C. T. (1985). Measuring preference for ideation in creative problem solving training. *Journal of Applied Behavioural Science*, **21**(1), 37–49.

Basu, R. & Green, S. G. (1997). Leader member exchange and transformational leadership: an empirical examination of innovative behaviours in leader member dyads. *Journal of Applied Social Psychology*, **27**(6), 477–499.

Bateman, T. S. & Crant, J. M. (1993). The proactive component of organizational behaviour: a measure and correlates. *Journal of Organizational Behaviour*, 14, 103–118.

Bejat, M. (1972). Creativity and problem solving. *Studia Psychologica*, **14**(4), 301–308.

Blair, T. (1999). Final announcement of the Millennium Products. Speech made at the Millennium Products Awards, London, 14 December.

Brazeal, D. V. & Weaver, K. M. (1990). Differential motivating factors among intrapreneurial and traditional managers? A look at the influence of reward systems and structures on performance among intrapreneurial and traditional managers. *Journal of Creative Behaviour*, **24**(4), 263–274.

Bunce, D. & West, M. A. (1984). Innovation as a response to occupational stress. *Occupational Psychology*, **6**, 22–25.

Burningham, C. & West, M. A. (1995). Individual, climate and group interaction processes as predictors of work team innovation. *Small Group Research*, **26**(1), 106–117.

Campbell, D. J. (2000). The proactive employee: managing workplace initiative. *Academy of Management Executive*, **14**, 52–66.

Cox, R. S. (1977). Rewarding instructions vs. brainstorming on creativity test scores of college students. *Psychological Reports*, **41**, 951–954.

Cox, R. S., Nash, W. R. & Ash, M. J. (1976). Instructions for three levels of reward and creativity test scores of college students. *Psychological Reports*, **38**, 411–414.

Crant, J. M. (1995). The Proactive Personality Scale and objective job performance among real estate agents. *Journal of Applied Psychology*, **80**, 532–537.

Crant, J. M. (1996). The proactive personality scale as a predictor of entrepreneurial intentions. *Journal of Small Business Management*, **34**, 42–49.

Crant, J. M. (2000). Proactive behaviour in organizations. *Journal of Management*, **26**, 435–462.

Csikszentmihalyi, M. (1996). *Creativity: Flow and the Psychology of Discovery and Invention*. New York: Harper Collins.

Csikszentmihalyi, M. & Getzels, J. W. (1970). Concern for discovery: an attitudinal component of creative production. *Journal of Personality*, **38**(1), 91–105.

Cummings, A. & Oldham, G. R. (1997). Enhancing creativity: managing work contexts for the high potential employee. *California Management Review*, **40**(1), 22–37.

Dauw, D. C. (1969). Bridging the creativity innovation gap. *Journal of Creative Behaviour*, **3**(2), 84–89.

Davis, G. A., Peterson, J. M. & Farley, F. H. (1974). Attitudes, motivation, sensation seeking, and belief in ESP as predictors of real creative behaviour. *Journal of Creative Behaviour*, **8**(1), 31–39.

Deci, E. L. & Ryan, R. M. (1987). The support of autonomy and the control of behaviour. *Journal of Personality and Social Psychology*, **53**(6), 1024–1037.

Dellas, M. & Gaier, E. L. (1970). Identification of creativity: the individual. *Psychological Bulletin*, **73**(1), 55–73.

Drazin, R. & Schoonhoven, C. B. (1996). Community, population and organizational effects on innovation: a multilevel perspective. *Academy of Management Journal*, **39**(5), 1065–1083.

Drazin, R., Glynn, M. A. & Kazanjian, R. K. (1999). Multilevel theorizing about creativity in organizations: a sensemaking perspective. *Academy of Management Journal*, **24**(2), 286–307.
Drwal, R. L. (1973). The influence of psychological stress upon creative thinking. *Polish Psychological Bulletin*, **4**(2), 125–129.
Eisenberger, R. & Armeli, S. (1997). Can salient reward increase creative performance without reducing intrinsic creative interest? *Journal of Personality and Social Psychology*, **72**(3), 652–663.
Eisenberger, R. & Cameron, J. (1996). Detrimental effects of reward: reality or myth? *American Psychologist*, **51**(11), 1153–1166.
Eisenberger, R., Fasolo, P. & Davis LaMastro, V. (1990). Perceived organizational support and employee diligence, commitment, and innovation. *Journal of Applied Psychology*, **75**(1), 51–59.
Ekvall, G. (1993). Creativity in project work: a longitudinal study of a product development project. *Creativity and Innovation Management*, **2**(1), 17–25.
Ekvall, G. & Tangeberg Andersson, Y. (1986). Working climate and creativity: a study of an innovative newspaper office. *Journal of Creative Behaviour*, **20**(3), 215–225.
Fay, D. & Frese, M. (2000). Conservatives' approach to work: less prepared for future work demands? *Journal of Applied Social Psychology*, **30**, 171–195.
Fay, D. & Frese, M., (2001). The concept of personal initiative: an overview of validity studies. *Human Performance*, **14**, 97–124.
Fay, D. & Sonnentag, S. (2000). Stressors and personal initiative: a longitudinal study on organizational behaviour. (manuscript submitted for publication).
Fiedler, F. E. (1962). Leader attitudes, group climate and group creativity. *Journal of Abnormal and Social Psychology*, **65**(5), 308–318.
Ford, C. M. (1996). A theory of individual creative action in multiple social domains. *Academy of Management Review*, **21**(4), 1112–1142.
Frenkel, S. J., Korczynski, M., Shire, K. A. & Tam, M. (1999). *On the Front Line: Organization of Work in the Information Economy*. London: Cornell University Press.
Frese, M., Fay, D., Hilburger, T., Leng, K. *et al*. (1997). The concept of personal initiative: operationalization, reliability and validity of two German samples. *Journal of Occupational & Organizational Psychology*, **70**, 139–161.
Frese, M., Garst, H. & Fay, D. (2000). Control and complexity in work and the development of personal initiative (PI): A four-wave longitudinal structural equation model of occupational socialization (manuscript submitted for publication).
Frese, M. & Hilligloh, S. (1994). Eigeninitiative am Arbeitsplatz im Osten und Westen Deutschlands: Ergebnisse einer empirischen Untersuchung [Personal initiative at work in East and West Germany: results of an empirical study]. In G. Trommsdorf (Ed.), *Psychologische Aspekte des sozial-politischen Wandels in Ostdeutschland* (pp. 200–215). Berlin: DeGruyter.
Frese, M., Kring, W., Soose, A. & Zempel, J. (1996). Personal initiative at work: differences between East and West Germany. *Academy of Management Journal*, **39**, 37–63.
Frese, M., Teng, E. & Wijnen, C. J. D. (1999). Helping to improve suggestion systems: predictors of making suggestions in companies. *Journal of Organizational Behaviour*, **20**, 1139–1155.
Fromme, D. K., Mercadal, D. E. & Mercadal, P. L. (1976). The effects of positive and negative feedback and reward on originality. *Journal of Research in Personality*, **10**, 237–244.
Ganesan, V. & Subramanian, S. (1982). Creativity, anxiety, time pressure and innovativeness among agricultural scientists. *Managerial Psychology*, **3**(1), 40–48.
George, J. M. & Brief, A. P. (1992). Feeling good—doing good: a conceptual analysis of the mood at work—organizational spontaneity relationship. *Psychological Bulletin*, **112**, 310–329.
Gorman, B. S. & Breskin, S. (1969). Non-verbal rigidity, creativity and problem-solving. *Perceptual and Motor Skills*, **29**(3), 715–718.
Guastello, S. J., Bzdawka, A., Guastello, D. D. & Rieke, M. L. (1992). Cognitive abilities and creative behaivors: CAB 5 and consequences. *Journal of Creative Behaviour*, **26**(4), 260–267.
Guilford, J. P. & Christensen, P. R. (1973). The one way relation between creative potential and IQ. *Journal of Creative Behaviour*, **7**(4), 247–252.
Hackman, J. R. & Oldham, G. R. (1976). Motivation through the design of work: test of a theory. *Organizational Behaviour and Human Performance*, **16**, 250–279.
Halpin, G. & Halpin, G. (1973). The effect of motivation on creative thinking abilities. *Journal of Creative Behaviour*, **7**(1), 51–53.

Hards, R. (1999). *An Investigation of Barriers to Creativity in Engineering Design: a Progress Report.* Plymouth: School of Computing, University of Plymouth.

Howell, J. M. & Higgins, C. A. (1990). Champions of technological innovation. *Administrative Science Quarterly*, **35**(2), 317–341.

Jones, F. E. (1964). Predictor variables for creativity in industrial science. *Journal of Applied Psychology*, **48**(2), 134–136.

Kabanoff, B. & Bottger, P. (1991). Effectiveness of creativity training and its relation to selected personality factors. *Journal of Organizational Behaviour*, **12**, 235–248.

Kabanoff, B. & O'Brien, G. E. (1979). Cooperation structure and the relationship of leader and member ability to group performance. *Journal of Applied Psychology*, **64**(5), 526–532.

Kanter, R. M. (1983). *The Change Masters.* New York: Simon and Schuster.

Keller, R. T. & Holland, W. E. (1978). Individual characteristics of innovativeness and communication in research and development organizations. *Journal of Applied Psychology*, **63**(6), 759–762.

Keller, R. T. & Holland, W. E. (1983). Communicators and innovators in research and development organizations. *Academy of Management Journal*, **26**(4), 742–749.

Kinicki, A. J. & Latack, J. C. (1990). Explication of the construct of coping with involuntary job loss. *Journal of Vocational Behaviour*, **36**, 339–360.

Kirkman, B. L. & Rosen, B. (1999). Beyond self-management: antecedents and consequences of team empowerment. *Academy of Management Journal*, **42**, 58–75.

Krop, H. (1969). Effects of extrinsic motivation, intrinsic motivation, and intelligence on creativity: a factorial approach. *Journal of General Psychology*, **80**, 259–266.

Leith, G. (1972). The relationships between intelligence, personality and creativity under two conditions of stress. *British Journal of Educational Psychology*, **42**(3), 240–247.

LePine, J. A. & Van Dyne, L. (1998). Predicting voice behaviour in work groups. *Journal of Applied Psychology*, **83**, 853–868.

LePine, J. A. & Van Dyne, L. (2001). Voice and cooperative behaviour as contrasting forms of contextual performance: evidence of differential relationships with Big Five personality characteristics and cognitive ability. *Journal of Applied Psychology*, **86**, 326–336.

Locurto, C. M. & Walsh, J. F. (1976). Reinforcement and self reinforcement: their effects on originality. *American Journal of Psychology*, **89**(2), 281–291.

McCarrey, M. W. & Edwards, S. A. (1973). Organizational climate conditions for effective research scientist role performance. *Organizational Behaviour and Human Performance*, **9**, 439–459.

McCrae, R. R. (1987). Creativity, divergent thinking, and openness to experience. *Journal of Personality and Social Psychology*, **52**(6), 1258–1265.

Miles, R. E., Snow, C. C. & Miles, G. (2000). The future.org. *Long Range Planning*, **33**, 300–321.

Miner, J. B., Smith, N. R. & Bracker, J. S. (1994). Role of entrepreneurial task motivation in the growth of technologically innovative firms: interpretations from follow-up data. *Journal of Applied Psychology*, **79**(4), 627–630.

Mohamed, M. Z. & Rickards, T. (1996). Assessing and comparing the innovativeness and creative climate of firms. *Scandinavian Journal of Management*, **12**(2), 109–121.

Mohrman, S. & Cohen, S. G. (1995). When people get out of the box: new relationships, new systems. In A. Howard (Ed.), *The Changing Nature of Work* (pp. 365–410). San Francisco, CA: Jossey-Bass.

Morrison, E. W. & Phelps, C. C. (1999). Taking charge at work: extrarole efforts to initiate workplace change. *Academy of Management Journal*, **42**, 403–419.

Mumford, M. D. & Gustafson, S. B. (1988). Creativity syndrome: integration, application and innovation. *Psychological Bulletin*, **103**(1), 27–43.

Munton, A. G. & West, M. A. (1995). Innovations and personal change: patterns of adjustment to relocation. *Journal of Organizational Behaviour*, **16**, 363–375.

Nyström, H. (1979). *Creativity and Innovation.* London: Wiley.

Oldham, G. R. & Cummings, A. (1996). Employee creativity: personal and contextual factors at work. *Academy of Management Journal*, **39**(3), 607–634.

Parker, S. K. (1998). Role breadth self-efficacy: relationship with work enrichment and other organizational practices. *Journal of Applied Psychology*, **83**, 835–852.

Parker, S. K. (1999). The proactive workforce: a model of the antecedents and outcomes of proactive and integrative job behaviours. (unpublished working paper).

Parker, S. K. (2000). From passive to proactive motivation: the importance of flexible role orientations and role breadth self-efficacy. *Applied Psychology: An International Review*, **49**(3), 447–469.
Parker, S. K. & Axtell, C. M. (2001). Seeing another view point: antecedents and outcomes of employee perspective-taking activity. *Academy of Management Journal*, December, **44**(6), 1085–1100.
Parker, S. K. & Sprigg, C. A. (1999). Minimizing strain and maximizing learning: the role of job demands, job control, and proactive personality. *Journal of Applied Psychology*, **84**(6), 925–939.
Parker, S. K., Wall, T. D. & Jackson, P. R. (1997). "That's not my job": developing flexible employee work orientations. *Academy of Management Journal*, **40**, 899–929.
Parnes, S. J. (1976). Idea stimulation techniques. *Journal of Creative Behaviour*, **10**(2), 126–129.
Pelz, D. C. & Andrews, F. M. (1966). Autonomy, co-ordination, and stimulation in relation to scientific achievement. *Behavioural Science*, **11**(2), 89–97.
Raudsepp, E. (1987). Establishing a creative climate. *Training and Development Journal*, **44**(4), 50–53.
Redmond, M. R., Mumford, M. D. & Teach, R. (1993). Putting creativity to work: effects of leader behaviour on subordinate creativity. *Organizational Behaviour and Human Decision Processes*, **55**(1), 120–151.
Schein, E. H. (1971). Occupational socialization in the professions: the case of role innovation. *Journal of Psychiatric Research*, **8**, 521–530.
Scott, S. G. & Bruce, R. A. (1994). Determinants of innovative behaviour: a path model of individual innovation in the workplace. *Academy of Management Journal*, **37**(3), 580–607.
Seibert, S. E., Crant, J. M. & Kraimer, M. L. (1999). Proactive personality and career success. *Journal of Applied Psychology*, **84**, 416–427.
Speier, C. & Frese, M. (1997). Generalized self-efficacy as a mediator and moderator between control and complexity at work and personal initiative: a longitudinal study in East Germany. *Human Performance*, **10**, 171–192.
Sprecher, T. B. (1959). A study of engineers' criteria for creativity. *Journal of Applied Psychology*, **43**(2), 141–148.
Staw, B. M. & Boettger, R. D. (1990). Task revision: a neglected form of work performance. *Academy of Management Journal*, **33**, 534–559.
Sternberg, R. J. & Lubart, T. I. (1991). An investment theory of creativity and its development. *Human Development*, **34**, 1–31.
Swan, J. A. (1995). Exploring knowledge and cognitions in decisions about technological innovation: mapping managerial cognitions. *Human Relations*, **48**(11), 1241–1270.
Tesluk, P. E., Farr, J. L. & Klein, S. R. (1997). Influences of organizational culture and climate on individual creativity. *Journal of Creative Behaviour*, **31**(1), 27–41.
Thornburg, T. H. (1991). Group size and member diversity influence on creative performance. *Journal of Creative Behaviour*, **25**(4), 324–333.
Torrance, E. P. (1967). The Minnesota studies of creative behaviour: national and international extensions. *Journal of Creative Behaviour*, **1**(2), 137–154.
Triandis, H., Bass, A., Ewen, R. & Hall Mikesell, E. (1963). Team creativity as function of the creativity of the members. *Journal of Applied Psychology*, **47**, 104–110.
Turgoose, C., Thacker, C., Adams, M., Carmichael, C., Gray, M., Hall, L., Nadin, S. & Todd, C. (2000). *Innovation in Manufacturing SMEs in South Yorkshire*. Sheffield: Innovation Advisory Service.
Tushman, M. L. & Nelson, R. R. (1990). Introduction: technology, organizations and innovation. *Administrative Science Quarterly*, **35**, 1–8.
Udell, G. G., Baker, K. G. & Albaum, G. S. (1976). Creativity: necessary, but not sufficient. *Journal of Creative Behaviour*, **10**(2), 92–103.
Unsworth, K. L. (2001). Unpacking creativity. *Academy of Management Review*, **26**(2), 286–297.
Unsworth, K. L. & Clegg, C. W. (2001). Conceptualising and measuring employee innovation (manuscript under review).
Unsworth, K. L. & Wood, S. (2001). *Idea Capture Scheme: A Report to [company]*. Institute of Work Psychology: Sheffield.
Van Dyne, L. & LePine, J. (1998). Helping and voice extra-role behaviours: evidence of construct and predictive validity. *Academy of Management Journal*, **41**, 108–119.

Vancouver, J. B. & Morrison, E. W. (1995). Feedback inquiry: the effect of source attributes and individual differences. *Organizational Behaviour & Human Decision Processes*, **62**, 276–285.

Wall, T. Jackson, P. & Davids, K. (1992). Operator work design and robotics system perform: a serendipitous field study. *Journal Applied Psychology*, **77**, 353–362.

Wallach, M. A. & Kogan, N. (1965). A proof to distinguish between creativity and intelligence. *Megamot*, **13**(3–4), 289–294.

West, M. A. & Anderson, N. R. (1996). Innovation in top management teams. *Journal of Applied Psychology*, **81**(6), 680–693.

West, M. A. & Farr, J. L. (Eds) (1990). *Innovation and Creativity at Work: Psychological and Organizational Strategies*. New York: Wiley.

Woodman, R. W., Sawyer, J. E. & Griffin, R. W. (1993). Toward a theory of organizational creativity. *Academy of Management Review*, **18**, 293–321.

Zuckerman, M., Porac, J., Lathin, D., Smith, R. & Deci, E. L. (1978). On the importance of self determination for intrinsically motivated behaviour. *Personality & Social Psychology Bulletin*, **4**(3), 443–446.

CHAPTER 11

Teleworking and Virtual Organisations: The Human Impact

David Lamond
Sydney Graduate School of Management, University of Western Sydney, NSW, Australia
Kevin Daniels
Nottingham University Business School, UK
and
Peter Standen
Department of Management, Edith Cowan University, Western Australia

Telework[1] is a growing work practice whereby employees work at a site(s) remote from their office(s) for at least part of the week. Common arrangements include work done at home or in the field, by teleworkers in a range of sales and service occupations. As such, telework is one of the most radical departures from standard working conditions in the suite of flexible work practices now gaining widespread acceptance, and presents unique challenges to both managers and employees.

Recent figures indicate between and eight and nine million teleworkers in the USA (Glosserman, 1996; Rourke, 1996). Huws, Jagger & O'Regan (1999) conclude that 5% of the UK workforce can be classified as teleworkers. Meanwhile, Australian Bureau of Statistics (2001) figures indicate that, as of June 2000, 3% of employees mainly worked at home, with two-thirds (64%) using information technology in the job. The European Commission (1998) estimates that the number of teleworkers rose from 0.8% to 3.1% of the workforce between 1997 and 1998. The increased interest in teleworking among managers and employees is also reflected in the literature on the subject, with more than 1000 articles being published in the period 1999–2001 (Proquest, 2001). It is worthy of note that, again from examination of the database (Proquest, 2001), the term "telecommuting" appears to be almost exclusive to the articles published in the North American media, while "teleworking" appears to be the preferred term in European publications.

There are many reasons to expect organisations and their employees to experiment with this type of work organisation, particularly given the rapid growth of affordable

---

[1] Telework or teleworking is also referred to as "telecommuting" and "homeworking". The specific choice of the term "teleworking" is explained in the chapter. To avoid confusion, all references are to teleworking, even where other authors use different terms.

The New Workplace: A Guide to the Human Impact of Modern Working Practices.
Edited by David Holman, Toby D. Wall, Chris W. Clegg, Paul Sparrow and Ann Howard. © 2003 John Wiley & Sons, Ltd.

telecommunications technology. For organisations, the benefits are seen in terms of the positive impact on what are often their two largest overheads—their work force and accommodation costs: and so teleworking has been linked to improved productivity, improved employee retention, greater staffing flexibility and more efficient use of office space (e.g. Cascio, 2000). Specific individual benefits are thought to include: more flexible working hours; more time for home and family; reduced commuting; greater job autonomy; less disturbance whilst working; and the chance to remain in work despite moving home, becoming ill or taking on family care roles (IRS, 1996). Many of these direct benefits would have indirect consequences for job and life satisfaction and possibly physical health. The list of perceived societal benefits includes increased community stability; increased entrepreneurial activity; less pollution; and more efficient use of energy resources (Cascio, 2000).

While this list of perceived benefits is impressive, the potential negative consequences of teleworking, including fewer chances for development or promotion, increased conflict between work and home and social isolation have also been acknowledged (e.g. Gainey, Kelley & Hill, 1999; Gillespie, Richardson & Cornford, 1995; Hamblin, 1995). Then there are the negative organisational consequences, which may include increased selection, training and support costs, along with health and safety consequences (cf. Cascio, 2000).

The future of teleworking depends on whether employers provide the opportunity to telework and whether workers take advantage of this opportunity. As Cascio (2000) points out, for example, not all employees are suited to spend their scheduled work hours away from their primary business locations, while not all managers are suited to manage employees with telework arrangements. However, most of the literature on telework to date has involved prescriptions based heavily on the experience of individuals and does not use existing theory or recent research.

To address this issue, this chapter presents a comprehensive framework for understanding the psychology of teleworkers and telework management, based on both organisational behaviour theory and recent empirical evidence. Embedded in this framework is an examination of the relationship between organisation structure and teleworking, in order to identify the organisational structures that are most likely to support teleworking. We begin by considering teleworking in general, with a brief examination of the various uses of the term "teleworking", and present a definition and a framework that take account of its multi-dimensional nature. We then explore the organisational and individual factors that impinge on the telework process. Theoretical and empirical considerations from the literature are used to develop predictions about how these factors impact on the various forms of telework. These predictions set an agenda for future research aimed at building a body of empirical knowledge that ultimately researchers and practitioners alike can use to make informed decisions about telework and teleworking.

TELEWORKING AND TELEWORKERS: DEFINITIONS AND TYPOLOGY

Teleworking

Despite its growing popularity, there is still no "official" definition of teleworking (Baruch, 2001). As a result, discussions on the issue of teleworking tend to cover a variety of different working practices and to overlap into related areas such as homeworking, including where the term is used to refer to unskilled workers receiving piece rates for manual tasks (cf. Felstead & Jewson, 2000). Based on an extensive review of the literature, we characterise teleworking not just as a structure or function defined primarily in terms of where work is done or what equipment is used, but as a process that involves several variables (see also Daniels, Lamond & Standen, 2000, 2001; Lamond, Daniels & Standen, 1997a, 1997b):

- *Location*—the amount of time spent in the different locations: traditional office, home, remote office/telecottage, nomadic.
- *IT usage*—extent of use of telecommunications/IT links—home/mobile computer, fax, modem, phone, mobile phone, use of WWW sites.
- *Knowledge intensity*—extent of knowledge required, ease of output measures and autonomy of work.
- *Intra-organisational contact*—extent (range and intensity) of intra-organisational contact.
- *Extra-organisational contact*—extent (range and intensity) of extra-organisational contact.

This set of variables, summarised in Table 11.1 together with exemplar jobs, allows us to say that:

- Teleworking is best viewed as a process which involves a bundle of practices.
- There is no *one* form of teleworking and, as a corollary, there is no *one best way* of teleworking.
- Teleworking is best thought of as a multidimensional phenomenon, its character varying across five major variables: IT usage; knowledge intensity; intra-organisational contact; extra-organisational contact; and location.

These five variables can be used as the basis of describing and making predictions about teleworking in different organisational contexts.

Much of the literature in this area focuses on "teleworkers" rather than the process of teleworking. Following Daniels *et al.* (2001), we consider a teleworker to be someone:

1. Who spends a fraction of working time, no matter how small, within a defined period at home, at a remote office or engaged in nomadic working.
2. For whom a fraction of work tasks, no matter how small, necessitate the use of ICTs, even if this is simply a telephone.

This provides a minimum threshold for teleworking, and is less restrictive than attempts to define teleworkers by an arbitrary threshold of time spent in given locations (cf. Qvortrup, 1998). Nevertheless, the exact form of telework should be described according to levels on all five variables.

A FRAMEWORK FOR THE STUDY OF TELEWORKING

Teleworking is a set of work practices that exists at the juncture of a wide variety of organisational, social, individual and historical forces (Daniels *et al.*, 2001). In this and the following sections we present a comprehensive framework for the study of teleworking, beginning with the macro-level context set by national variations in legislation,

Table 11.1 Types of telework and sample jobs

Location	ICT usage	High knowledge intensity				Low knowledge intensity			
		Intra-organisational contact		Extra-organisational contact		Intra-organisational contact		Extra-organisational contact	
		High	Low	High	Low	High	Low	High	Low
Home-based	Low ICT usage	Sales managers	Management accountant	Lawyer	Translator	Phone operator	Bookkeeper	Phone sales	Proof-reader
	High ICT usage	Public relations	Programmer	Financial analyst	IS developer	Customer enquiries	Secretarial/clerical	Market research	Data processing
Remote office	Low ICT usage	Sales managers	Management accountant	Lawyer	Translator	Phone operator	Bookkeeper	Phone sales	Proof-reader
	High ICT usage	Public relations	Programmer	Financial analyst	IS developer	Customer enquiries	Secretarial/clerical	Market research	Data processing
Nomadic	Low ICT usage	Sales managers	Internal management consultant	Community nurse	Architect	Service persons	Bookkeeper	Sales representative	Proof-reader
	High ICT usage	Engineer	Internal IT consultant	Auditor	IS developer	Service persons	Secretarial/clerical	Delivery staff	Data processing

Source: Reproduced by permission from Daniels et al., 2001. © 2001 Blackwell Publishers.

geography, culture and industrial relations. We then move to the organisational-level factors of culture and structure, and looking within organisations to social and group factors such as socialisation and communication. Next, we consider individual factors, such as personality, the psychological character of work including the nature of the psychological contract and motivation, job characteristics and well-being, and the home/work interface. Finally, we consider the impact of human resource management practices on the social, group and individual variables, and the outcomes of teleworking programs.

Figure 11.1 captures schematically what we consider to be the major factors which impact on, and are in turn impacted by, teleworking—national characteristics, the context of organisational structure and culture, human resource management practices, group factors within organisations, and individual factors. In subsequent sections, we speculate on some of the relationships between these influences. In some cases, the factors we discuss can be seen to moderate the impact of telework on outcomes, while in others the impact of telework on outcomes is mediated through the impact on, for example, job characteristics. Although we would expect to see mediating effects more frequently, this does not preclude the possibility of moderating effects in more specific models of telework and behaviour.

National Context

It is clear that some countries are making more use of telework than others, and differential growth rates exist (Tregaskis, 2000). For example, in Europe the Scandinavian countries and the UK appear to have greater uptake than the central and southern countries (Tregaskis, 2000). There are many factors that contribute to these differences (Tregaskis, 2000), which we consider linked to four major categories of variables: legislative factors; culture and attitudes; industrial factors; and geography. The exact form of teleworking adopted by organisations will partly depend on the conflation of such national factors, with different forms of teleworking encouraged by different combinations of national context factors, operating directly on the form of teleworking adopted or in conjunction with other contextual factors linked to organisational structures and cultures (see Daniels *et al.*, 2000, 2001, for a fuller discussion).

Organisational Context—Structure and Culture

Organisational structures and cultures are likely to influence the kinds of teleworking practices adopted by organisations. However, there are two factors specific to organisations that are necessary but not sufficient conditions for the adoption of teleworking practices. The first of these, obviously, is the suitability of work tasks for teleworking. Jobs that are suitable for teleworking are those that require the interpretation, communication and manipulation of information. The number of such jobs in an organisation places an upper limit of the number of people that can engage in teleworking practices. Second, relevant decision-makers within an organisation must realise the benefits of teleworking relative to the costs, and have sufficient power over other stakeholders to allow teleworking practices (Daniels *et al.*, 2001). Teleworking is also more likely to be implemented alongside other changes, such as relocation, since implementation of teleworking is likely to be less costly where there are changes to other fixed costs (van Ommeren, 1998).

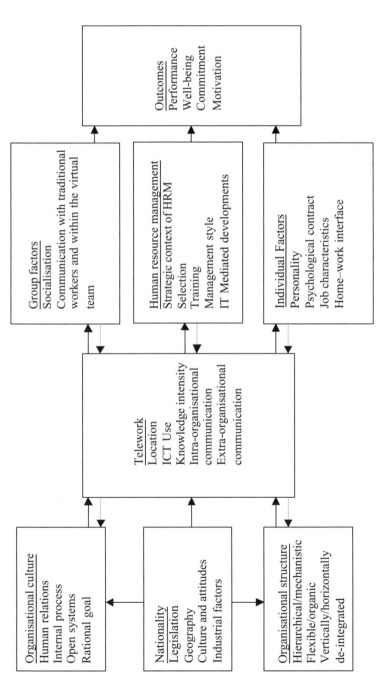

Figure 11.1 Conceptual overview of behavioural issues in teleworking. Bold lines reflect expected strong relationships; dotted lines reflect expected weak relationships

Structure

Over the last decade, we have been witnesses to a number of trends that have affected organisational structure: downsizing; delayering; process re-engineering; replacement of traditional functional departments with team-based or project-based structures; the shift to a core/periphery model with a greater role for contingent workers; growth in inter-organisational networks; and boundaryless designs (Ashkenas et al., 1995). These recent changes in organisational structure may encourage the adoption of teleworking practices (Daniels et al., 2001). The reasons appear to be twofold.

First, the rise in knowledge work and the increased sophistication of information technology make it easier for organisations to develop structures that transcend traditional space and time limits (Reich, 1992). These structures can often be characterised as loose federations of groups and individuals. Building on the contingency approach to organisational structure (e.g. Lawrence & Lorsch, 1967), it could be expected that such flexible, "organic" organisations are more likely to move towards teleworking and are more likely to have effective teleworkers. A reciprocal relationship may exist here too, as growth in teleworking encourages wider experimentation with flexible structures. For example, Travic (1998) found a positive relationship between the amount of IT usage and the existence of non-traditional organisational structures, and invoked the notion of an "organic, informated organisation" (cf. Figure 11.1 "organic/flexible").

Second, teleworking might be introduced by organisations where the primary attraction is the promised cost reductions through downsizing and delayering the organisation, and geographical relocation of the remaining employees and functions (cf. Figure 11.1 "hierarchical/mechanistic"). In this context, the impact on teleworking could be quite different to that of the organic orientation. For instance, there may be a distinct lack of interest in flexibility issues and notions of "re-engineering" may be code for cost-cutting, and teleworking introduced with stringent electronic controls and greater use of contingent workers (Daniels et al., 2001).

Culture

A number of predictions follow from the view that teleworking forms are related to organisational cultures. We have utilised Quinn's (1988) competing values framework as a basis for classifying cultures. Quinn's (1988) framework identifies organisations on two dimensions—flexibility vs. control and internal vs. external focus—creating four potential organisational archetypes. An adapted version of Quinn's (1988) framework is presented in Table 11.2, which also includes some of the predicted impacts on forms of teleworking.

HRM authorities emphasise the importance of supportive organisational cultures for flexible working practices (e.g. Guest, 1990). Accordingly, organisations whose internal processes are characterised by flexibility, trust and openness (see the Human Relations model in Table 11.2) would be expected to move towards home-based or remote office teleworking practices for all types of workers (Standen, 1997). Organisations whose cultures have an external focus (open systems) are similarly more likely to support telework when the cultures are also more flexible. These organisations are focused on expansion and

Table 11.2 Predicting forms of telework from Quinn's (1988) competing values framework

	Internal focus	External focus
	Human relations model	Open systems model
Flexibility	*Goal*: human commitment *Values*: human resources, training, cohesion, morale *Telework*: Types A and B; all types of intra- and extra-organisational contact; all locations	*Goal*: expansion and adaptation *Values*: adaptability, readiness, growth, resource acquisition, external support *Telework*: Knowledge intensive; all types of intra- and extra-organisational contact; bias towards nomadic
	Internal process model	Rational goal model
Control	*Goal*: consolidation and continuity *Values*: information management, communication, stability, control *Telework*: Limited low knowledge intensity; home, remote office, telecottage	*Goal*: maximization of output *Values*: productivity, efficiency, planning, goal setting *Telework*: Limited knowledge intensive; extra-organisational contact; mainly nomadic

adaptation and may see telework as a competitive business tool to increase flexibility and communication, and so may be biased toward forms of teleworking that emphasise flexible task completion most, e.g. high-knowledge-intensity, mobile teleworking, especially with high extra-organisational contact.

Conversely, cultures focused on flexible external goals but which have a bureaucratic control-based internal focus (rational goal), are likely to support only knowledge-intensive telework. Clerical and other non-professionals may not be considered to be trustworthy off-site, thus reducing possibilities for teleworking. Finally, organisations lacking flexibility in both internal and external perspectives (internal process) are focused on stability and would be considered least likely to experiment with radical practices like telework. With both types of control-orientated cultures, low-knowledge-intensity teleworkers may be very rare. Where such teleworkers are employed, it is likely to be only in home-based or remote office contexts, where outputs from workers can be easily monitored. For all types of workers, control-orientated organisations may only employ teleworkers where other factors (such as structure) support such practices.

As in the case of organisational structure, there are reciprocal relationships between teleworking and culture—moving towards teleworking practices necessitates changes in people's attitudes, and therefore can affect culture. It is likely, however, that most telework programs are currently small scale and that "feedback" effects will be found more in the future. At the same time, there will be limits on the influence of organisational cultures; for example, nomadic workers (sales staff and consultants) get to work off-site more from practical necessity, which may override cultural factors (Standen, 2000). Indeed, these groups were allowed to roam off-site long before telework was considered as an organising strategy.

GROUP PROCESSES, THE INDIVIDUAL, HRM PRACTICES AND TELEWORK

According to the preceding analysis, the initiation and development of a teleworking project is related, at least in part, to national contexts and the cultures and structural dynamics of the organisations in which they are initiated. The expected outcomes of these teleworking processes, summarised in Figure 11.1, are improvements in variables such as employee performance, commitment, motivation and well-being. However, as also shown in Figure 11.1, the impact of teleworking on these outcome variables will be moderated by three critical areas of organisational behaviour: (a) group and social processes that include teleworkers; (b) characteristics of individual teleworkers; and (c) human resource management practices[2]. We now examine these three areas.

Social and Group Processes

Socialising Teleworkers

In examining strategies for creating and maintaining a committed workforce, Aryee (1991) points to the importance of linking socialisation practices to business strategy. He also discusses the different types of employees and organisational roles that need to be taken into account in determining the most appropriate approach. The extent to which teleworkers participate in social networks is strongly affected by the extent of time spent off-site, but for the purposes of analysis we will consider arrangements with a high degree of off-site work (e.g. three or more days per week). Such teleworkers do not have the same opportunities for social contact as traditional workers and are not as immersed in the organisational culture. However, there are probably differences between workers engaged in different types of telework. For instance, teleworkers with high intra-organisational contact, or who regularly use real-time telecommunication media (e.g. telephones), are more likely to be socialised through natural processes. In contrast, teleworkers with low intra-organisational contact and that use non-real-time telecommunications (e.g. E-mail), are less likely to be socialised through natural means. Therefore, this group of workers is more likely to need socialisation interventions, yet many of the usual socialisation factors are not relevant.

With at least some groups of teleworkers, then, this poses an interesting problem as managers seek to use socialisation into organisational cultures as an important tool for management control of teleworkers in place of more traditional but impractical direct supervision. There are potential solutions to this problem. First, managers can begin by selecting teleworkers whose values are already close to those of the organisational culture (Billsberry, 2000). Second, it is also possible that teleworkers need less socialisation initially than a typical worker to be functional off-site. Some evidence (Omari & Standen, 1996) suggests that many teleworkers value autonomy more than other workers and resist socialisation, except where it coincides with personal values related to work achievement.

---

[2] It is recognised that, as with other organisational level variables, there is potential for feedback effects whereby there might be reciprocal relationships between teleworking and changes in social processes, some individual factors and human resource management practices more broadly in the organisation beyond the direct impact of the telework program.

Beyond initial socialisation, maintaining social networks is crucial to the success of teleworking programs. Organisations need to consider options such as regular meetings, minimum requirements for office attendance, including teleworkers in social programs, and developing off-site social events. It will be important to include teleworkers' co-workers in such events, so that contact is maintained across the team to which the teleworker belongs.

Communication between Teleworkers and Traditional Office Workers

A related issue to socialisation is the types of communication between traditional office workers and teleworkers, and the possible evolution of separate subcultures. Face-to-face communication is likely to be highest between managers and traditional workers, and lowest between managers and teleworkers. At the same time, in-group communication is likely to be highest amongst traditional workers and amongst remote office-based workers, leading to the possibility of separate and conflicting cultures emerging. Full use of information technology should overcome some barriers, supplemented by regular socialisation events that involve all workers.

Whilst teleworkers with lower intra-organisational communication requirements to perform their work tasks may experience fewer problems with task-related communication, as intimated in the previous section, communication can have an important function beyond direct facilitation of work. Therefore, it is important to be sure that managers and co-workers are happy with low levels of contact and that team cohesion is not lost. In some cases where there is otherwise little intra-organisational communication, a separate "cyberspace" subculture based on mutual support and information sharing may be beneficial to teleworkers. The next section elaborates on the issues of communication *within* the virtual team.

Communication for Decision Making within the Virtual Team

Another related but distinct problem (especially for knowledge-intensive teleworking) is the use of electronically mediated communication to make decisions. There is evidence (Hiemstra, 1982) that people prefer face-to-face communication that enables use of subtle facial and body signals in the visual channel, and the para-linguistic signals conveyed by intonation, voice, pitch, pause and pace of speech, all of which are lost in text-based media. This does not exclude the possibility that, over a period of time, teams linked by electronic media can communicate effectively (cf. Harper, 2000; Walther, 1995). Indeed, Duxbury & Nuefeld's (1999) analysis of data from two Canadian federal government departments suggests that part-time telework arrangements need not substantially change the way in which teleworkers communicate with managers, subordinates, colleagues and clients. The explosive growth of "cyberspace" as a (mostly) non-work communication medium suggests that many people will readily trade the limitations of new media for its benefits, and will find new ways to encode non-textual signals in text, e.g., the use of signs such as ":-)" (smiley face) and ";-)" (wink), or simple graphics (cf. Lea & Spears, 1992).

The optimal communication networks and the optimal media (E-mail, telephone etc.) for effective decision making need to be explored further. However, it is clear that the effectiveness of each network and medium depends on the nature of the work that is being performed and the characteristics of the organisation and the team (Harper, 2000). For example, for knowledge-work characterised by a high need for intra-organisational communication to coordinate tasks across a work team, all-channel networks and frequent and informal real-time contact (e.g. by telephone) may be more suitable for home-based or remote office teleworkers. In contrast, nomadic teleworkers who spend time working face-to-face with clients may prefer multi-channel, asynchronous (i.e. non-real time) communication via voice mail or e-mail from colleagues, so as not to disturb time spent with clients.

Individual Factors

As well as group factors, a number of individual factors will also affect the performance and satisfaction of teleworkers. These are personality, motivation and the psychological contract, job characteristics and their impact on psychological and physical health, and the home/work interface.

Personality, Competencies and Telework

Telework will not suit all workers equally. One way in which to examine the degree of fit between teleworking practices and personal characteristics is to explore personality in the context of teleworking. One popular approach to personality indicates that personalities can be summarized or classified in terms of five basic dimensions (the "Big Five")—extraversion, emotional stability, agreeableness, conscientiousness, and openness to experience (Barrick & Mount, 1991). This model, amongst others, might be suitable for making predictions about which types of people adapt better to teleworking (Lamond, 2000a).

In the teleworking context, the importance of personality may be intensified, given that the feedback and correction processes afforded by direct supervision are often not present or present to only a minimal degree. We may then expect research that indicates aspects of personality that predict good performance in non-teleworking contexts not only to generalise to teleworking contexts, but the extent of predictive relationships to be strengthened. For example, the characteristics associated with conscientiousness, such as persistence, care, capacity for hard work and being responsible, have been shown to influence the accomplishment of work tasks. We would also expect that people who work in jobs with high levels of intra- and/or extra-organisational communication are likely to be more successful if they are higher on extraversion, agreeableness and openness to experience. Personality can also be important with regard to how knowledge about aspects of teleworking is gained, since distance learning, again with minimum supervision, is an attractive training option for teleworkers for a variety of reasons (Salmon, Allen & Giles, 2000; see below). In this respect, extraversion, openness to experience and conscientiousness are important, since these dimensions are related to performance on training programs (Barrick & Mount, 1991; Behling, 1998). Behling's (1998) concurrent conclusion, that intelligence is positively related to work performance, while unsurprising, reminds us that intelligence is likely also to be a predictor in regard to teleworker training outcomes in regard to success, perhaps especially for high-knowledge-intensity, high-ICT-usage jobs.

Townsend, DeMarie & Hendrickson (1998) describe the shift to "virtual interaction"—e-mail and document sharing replaces face-to-face meetings and geographic proximity—as new ways of communicating and interacting that enable teleworking and coordination of teleworkers. They point out that virtual team members still need traditional teamwork skills—effective communication skills, goal clarity and performance orientation—but they need to learn new ways to express themselves and understand others in an environment with a "diminished sense of presence". In this sense, personality factors associated with membership of successful teams might be especially important in the context of "virtual teams", where correcting social factors might be less evident. Such personality factors include higher levels of extraversion, agreeableness, emotional stability and conscientiousness (Lamond, 2000a). Further, given the fluidity of membership of virtual teams and that they more easily transcend functional, organisational and national boundaries (Townsend et al., 1998), there is a greater need to adapt quickly to novel situations, and so the personality dimension of openness to experience may be associated with better adaptation to virtual teamworking.

As well as personality, competencies may be influential in adaptation to teleworking. Several authors have established lists of teleworking competencies (e.g. Omari & Standen, 2000; Sparrow & Daniels, 1999). These lists include competencies that can be grouped into four major clusters:

1. *Personal competencies*, such as self-discipline, self-direction, self-motivation, capacity for self-assessment, tough-mindedness, tenacity, personal integrity and self-confidence.
2. *Inter-personal competencies*, such as strong verbal and written communication skills, negotiation skills, trusting others and assertiveness.
3. *Generic task competencies*, such as organisation skills, practical orientation, basing decisions on facts, flexibility, ability to take independent decisions, time management skills, and possessing consistent, productive and organised work habits.
4. *Technical competencies*, such as information and communications technology literacy and good subject-matter knowledge.

It is reasonable to expect individual differences in adaptation to teleworking, and such individual differences have clear implications for selecting teleworkers (see below). Yet there has been very little systematic research examining the conjoint impact of different teleworking practices and personality dimensions or competencies on the performance of teleworkers or other indicators of successful adaptation. Such research is needed before any practical benefits can be truly realised.

Motivation and the Psychological Contract

Along with the broad trend towards greater flexibility in HRM, there has been a movement away from the traditional psychological contract where employers have offered career and employment stability (e.g. Sparrow & Cooper, 1998). Instead, the emerging psychological contract emphasises flexibility and mobility, where employees should expect to be flexible in their work practices, be prepared to take responsibility for their own training and career development, and be prepared to move jobs regularly. This new psychological contract brings potential problems of motivation and commitment (Sparrow & Cooper, 1998) and these could be exacerbated amongst teleworkers, who might experience hitherto unknown forms of contract violation (Sparrow, 2000) and who lack the support of office networks, unions and counselling services, along with the visibility that being in the office brings. Whilst effective socialisation may overcome some of these problems, moves towards providing clearer career paths and training opportunities may encourage employee retention and motivation without necessarily affecting the establishment of a mutually beneficial, flexible psychological contract.

Three qualifications to this picture are noted. First, although there is no clear information on the extent to which teleworking promotes non-traditional contracts, some Australian data (McClennan, 1996) does show that most home-based workers to date are in service areas where traditional employment contracts never existed, and they are on casual conditions. It is not possible to determine how many of these are engaged in telework, but one might ask whether teleworking will create a net drop in the number of traditional psychological contracts focused on career and employment stability.

The second qualification is that teleworkers may not always show the problems of their in-office counterparts with respect to psychological contracts—and telework might offer other benefits to compensate for reductions in employment and career stability. In one study (Omari & Standen, 1996), teleworkers were more likely to report feeling highly valued by the organisation and to appreciate receiving a benefit not widely available. In another study, Igbaria & Guimares (1999) found that teleworkers had lower satisfaction with promotion opportunities (and their peers), yet reported less role conflict and role ambiguity and tended to be happier with their supervisors and more committed to their organisation.

Third, and more generally, there may be differences in the experience of those engaged in knowledge-intensive and low-knowledge-intensity telework. For example, it is noted that professionals tend to show more commitment to their profession than to their employers (cf. Mintzberg, 1979) and so they may have different reactions to those with different labour market power and career involvement.

Employee Well-being and the Impact of Job Characteristics

Based on a review of current empirical knowledge in this area, Daniels (2000) has identified how different forms of teleworking might influence the development of psychologically healthy or harmful job conditions. Daniels' review was based on Warr's (1987) Vitamin Model, in which psychologically healthy jobs are characterised generally by: greater opportunities for control, through task discretion or participation in decisions; greater skill use; greater variety in work; balanced demands from work; high clarity concerning tasks, performance feedback and job security; higher wages; better physical working conditions; more support and contact with others; and greater social value accorded to the nature of the work.

Daniels considers that task discretion, skill use and variety are more likely to be reduced in telework with low knowledge intensity, possibly due to increased opportunities for electronic monitoring of outputs if such work is routinised. Lack of variety is likely to be exacerbated for home-based and satellite office teleworkers. In contrast, nomadic teleworkers at least have the opportunity to move to different locations. Daniels has suggested autonomy over scheduling of work tasks and task rotation as means of redesigning teleworking jobs to prevent these problems.

Due to remote working, opportunities for participating in decision making might be reduced in most teleworking jobs, except for jobs in which there is high extra-organisational contact and high knowledge intensity. In this latter case, contact with customers or suppliers gives access to information that other organisational members—including managers— do not have. To use this information, organisations may then require such teleworkers to participate in decisions (Daniels, 1999). Notwithstanding, frequent visits to the main organisational location to attend meetings might be one way of increasing participation, as might use of electronic means of communication between team members.

Increased demands have been reported in home-based and nomadic teleworking. In both cases, increased opportunities for workers to enact demands might lead to escalation if other contributory factors are in place. For example, any increase in demands might be accentuated for workers with high degrees of intra- and extra-organisational contact and who use several electronic media that allow many channels for information to be exchanged. Technical problems with equipment can add further to problems. One suggestion to combat these problems is for teleworkers and their line managers to establish a diary of realistic routines and tasks (Ingham, 1995). Daniels (2000) has also suggested time management and prioritisation skills training in conjunction with improvements in technology to prioritise messages.

Teleworkers often report a reduction in the quality of information they receive, especially that related to performance feedback, organisational politics and organisational strategy (Crossan & Burton, 1993), although such problems may not be as great in a satellite office with a significant number of people from the same organisation. We have discussed some ways of enhancing communication earlier in this chapter. With respect to enhancing well-being in particular, various authors have made a number of suggestions. Cox, Griffiths & Barker (1996) point to the establishment of clear goals and objectives and implementation of reporting systems as a way to prevent problems of reduced clarity for teleworkers. Daniels (2000) suggests that, provided they do not lead to information overload, establishing communication channels amongst co-workers can also provide information networks, although regular office visits provide perhaps the best access to informal networks (cf. Daniels, 1999).

Some of the strategies for improving information clarity may also help to reduce the social isolation reported by many teleworkers, especially home-based teleworkers and those with little intra- and extra-organisational contact (Daniels, 2000). Other strategies that can help reduce social isolation include social activities other than regular visits to the main office, and well-designed systems for providing managerial and technical support.

Poor physical working conditions are a problem for all teleworkers, especially low-knowledge-intensity teleworkers, who are more likely to engage in repetitive display screen work (Cox et al., 1996). Moreover, those low-knowledge-intensity teleworkers based at home are less likely to live in accommodation where a designated work-space can be easily established. Clearly, such working conditions can influence physical as well as psychological health (Huws, 1994). Gray, Hodson & Gordon (1993) suggest a number of strategies for dealing with these problems, including providing allowances for teleworkers to buy suitable equipment or adapt premises; establishing a designated space for work; inspection of premises for health and safety purposes; and health and safety training.

Daniels (2000) considers low-knowledge-intensity workers to be at risk from poor well-being caused by lower wages and lower social value attached to their work, especially as such work is more likely to be of a contingent nature (see earlier). Ensuring teleworkers' pay is comparable to traditional workers in similar jobs and establishing support networks might help prevent problems of poor well-being for low-knowledge-intensity teleworkers. Daniels also considers that most knowledge-intensive teleworking can also suffer from lower social value because of a lack of visibility that limits the opportunities for promotion often valued by knowledge-intensive workers. Again, establishing support networks might enhance visibility, as would regular visits to the main office. Regular information exchanges through remote media can also help establish greater visibility.

Home/Work Interface

Teleworkers working from home face a range of issues not met by in-office or other off-site workers. These issues derive from the ability of the worker to create physical and social conditions in the home that adequately support work. For homeworkers without family, the issues are chiefly to do with creating an appropriate physical space and restricting the impact of the wider community through regulating contacts from neighbours, friends, businesses, salespeople and so on.

Those with family or other co-residents face additional problems (Standen, Daniels & Lamond, 1999). The boundary between work and family spheres is highly permeable in the home (Ahrentzen, 1990). Consequently, "segmentation" theories of work/family relationships, which assume no interaction, are particularly inappropriate in the case of teleworkers.

Lambert (1990) has proposed, in the traditional (office) work context, that spillover from each sphere impacts on the other, in terms of both the objective and subjective conditions of work. In the case of telework, the objective impact might be where the physical conditions of work (e.g. working hours) impact on family life, either positively or negatively, or where the physical conditions of family life (e.g. need to transport children to school) impact on work performance. Subjective (psychological) effects can also be identified, such as changes in well-being and changes in the levels of work–family conflict (Standen *et al.*, 1999). Lambert (1990) contends that these impacts can cause workers to reduce their involvement in either sphere, either by compensation (e.g. where a man with a dissatisfying job becomes more orientated to the family), or accommodation (e.g. where a woman may limit her involvement in work to accommodate family; Lambert, 1990). Home-based telework may attract both these types of person.

Although research on *nomadic teleworkers* is in its infancy, one study reports more work vs. non-work conflict (Daniels, 1999). This might be reduced by interventions that allow mobile workers to filter information more effectively—so that remote contact can be established with home and managers trained to be sensitive to the demands placed on nomadic workers.

Human Resource Management

One set of management practices explicitly aimed at managing the dynamics of groups and individuals in order to achieve the organisation's goals are those subsumed under the heading of human resource management (cf. Lamond 1995, 1996). Here, we cover some of the ways in which human resource management strategies can impact on the outcomes of teleworking.

Selecting Teleworkers

Earlier observations on socialisation, personality, competencies, job features and the home–work interface suggest that teleworker selection should be a systemic process involving more than just matching personal characteristics to those of the job (Omari & Standen, 2000). From our discussion so far in this chapter, we can suggest at least three strategies for selecting teleworkers: (a) assess the congruence of personal values with organisational culture; (b) assess the likely impact of teleworking practices on the home/work interface, job characteristics and the psychological side of work (and home where relevant); (c) match personality and competencies to the requirements of the job and form of teleworking. This would entail far wider assessment of organisational, task, personal and teleworking factors than is usual for selection into more traditional forms of work.

Management Style and Management Control

There is increasing recognition of the need for managers to develop new and different skills to manage effectively into this new millennium (cf. Lamond, 1996). Management of teleworkers is no exception to this general rule. However, it is unlikely that there will emerge a uniformly effective way of managing teleworkers (Lamond, 2000b). Consequently, the usual adage of managing teleworkers by outputs—in of and by itself—may prove inappropriate for teleworkers, possibly leading to problems such as reduced well-being, reduced trust and low-quality work (Sparrow, 2000; van Ommeren, 2000). We do, however, consider it important that managers pay close attention to the social context of teleworking (Daniels *et al.*, 2000), because this is as important for establishing support networks, ensuring opportunities for communication and establishing the trust necessary for organisational learning to occur (Tregaskis & Daniels, 2000).

Likewise, telework practitioners (Gray *et al.*, 1993) recommend that managers should endeavour to provide supportive teleworking environments. Earlier, we noted the importance of congruence between organisational cultures and telework practices—human resource managers should be aware of the cultures and contexts in each area of their organisation and should endeavour to ensure that telework schemes, workers and managers suit those cultures and contexts (since changing the cultures and contexts to suit teleworking is a longer-term strategy). This necessitates selection and training of managers of teleworkers. In many ways, perhaps the best people to manage teleworkers are other teleworkers, since they are already familiar with the special circumstances of teleworking and the skills and supports needed for successful teleworking (Hilthrop, 2000).

Training and Telework

Training and development are just as important or more important for telework than more traditional forms of work (Salmon *et al.*, 2000). Indeed, there are many areas in which training may benefit teleworkers, e.g. corporate values, communication, self-management and time management, health and safety requirements off-site, company security policy, legal, tax and insurance requirements of homework, computer operation and maintenance, as well as any job-specific needs, such as the use of communications software. Counsellors, career advisers, managers and on-line support services may also help address problems that are often classified as training issues. It is likely that some of this training will itself be available off-site, particularly through CD-ROM, the Internet or traditional open learning media. Indeed, training for on-line workers might be best achieved on-line through a variety of media, as this will provide experience with the context of telework and the media that will be used eventually for work (Salmon *et al.*, 2000).

Training managers should also consider targeting telework managers or supervisors, and the colleagues of teleworkers, all of whom may need to understand office policy and the practicalities of telework, and to be aware of the need to manage by results and to maintain support, communication and socialisation. Indeed, establishing the importance of training and development may help to institutionalise greater organisational learning in itself, and make managers more aware of the need to develop the skills and working relationships necessary for organisational learning (see Tregaskis & Daniels, 2000).

Electronically-Mediated Interventions

New developments which may assist teleworkers include face-to-face (video) communication technology, on-line data bases, www sites, virtual reality, and new software capabilities found in groupware, decision-support systems, executive support systems, on-line tutors and so on. These may improve communications amongst teleworkers, assist support from other teleworkers, help the management control of telework, and deliver flexible training packages. Improving telecommunications will also make it easier to coordinate virtual teams across current boundaries set by distance and time. Improvements in ICTs may also enable greater opportunities for organisational learning, e.g. through access to electronic archives and bulletin boards (Townsend *et al.*, 1998).

CONCLUSION: THE CHALLENGE OF MANAGING TELEWORKERS

In this chapter we have examined telework as a contemporary working practice and the impact it has had on how people work and their experience of work, together with the human resource management implications of telework. How telework will evolve in the future is the subject of great speculation in the media and the academic press. However, as industries become more knowledge-intensive and telework becomes more central to business processes, there are ways to prevent the worst that the future might have to offer, or at least to buffer organisations and teleworkers against it (Daniels *et al.*, 2000).

Effective management does not mean a narrow focus on productivity. As we have noted earlier and elsewhere (Daniels *et al.*, 2000), managing teleworkers by outputs is often not a sensible option while relying purely on developments in technology to improve productivity and coordination. Indeed, the technological methods that allow managers to monitor the actions of teleworkers as closely as they could monitor on-site workers have been associated with low employee morale (Fairweather, 1999). At the same time, there is a need for an ethical approach to managing teleworkers (Fairweather, 1999; Moon & Stanworth, 1997), so that telework is *not* used to worsen employees' terms and conditions. It is clear that, instead of simply managing the outputs of teleworkers or the teleworking process, the most appropriate approach is to manage the outputs, the process and the context of teleworking.

Placing greater emphasis on the management of teleworkers can have benefits for both organisations and teleworkers, while paying attention to context and processes can help technologically-driven innovations enhance communication and organisational learning capability, through proper use of technology and creation of the right social environment. At the same time, managers must make an effort to build the supportive environments, organisational cultures and the trust needed to ensure the best results from teleworking. Managers need to confront and overcome not only the problem of trying to use organisational culture as an important tool for management control, but also the other inherent problems of alternative work arrangements—an increase in structure and flexibility, a focus on both individuals and teamwork, and an increase and decrease in control (Pearlson & Saunders, 2001).

Although it is beyond the scope of this chapter, consideration of communication for decision making for virtual teams presents some very interesting possibilities in regard to the different roles of text, voice, paper (fax, mail, courier) and video media, interactivity, manipulability (e.g. ability to enter digital communications in a database, groupware features as in Lotus Notes) and synchronicity of media. One might also ask whether new models of decision-making are emerging: do these new technologies promote more or less democratic modes, e.g. by minimising status-conferring signals of dress, voice and physical size? Do they change the type of communication and social skills needed to be a good team member?

Teleworking is most likely to be successful where teleworking forms part of a coherent and integrated human resource management system that supports organisational strategy (Daniels *et al.*, 2000). This means ensuring that telework programmes are compatible with organisational strategies, structures and cultures, and which are suited to prevailing economic and social contexts. Analysis of the organisation and its environment is important for deciding whether teleworking is appropriate for current conditions, or whether organisational structures, cultures and processes need to be changed to suit teleworking practices. Various strategies can help achieve a match between teleworking practices and the macroeconomic, organisational, social and psychological environments, including those related to technology management, socialisation processes, job design, psychological contracting and career management, selection systems, training and development practices and performance management. As noted by Hamel & Prahalad (1993), effective organisational performance comes not just from fitting the environment, but also by developing and using organisational resources in new and more effective ways. For these reasons, human resource management has wider responsibility than ensuring that teleworking fits its place in the organisation; it should also ensure that the possibilities of teleworking are explored to develop what is possible with teleworking.

This chapter has presented a framework for advancing understanding of telework, using organisational behaviour theory to fill the gaps in empirical knowledge. However, theory alone is not enough—prescriptions of "best practice" based on limited empirical knowledge and theory developed in other areas of organisational psychology must be applied in an informed, context-sensitive manner. There are, therefore, two challenges to be met in ensuring the effective management of teleworkers.

The first challenge is to practitioners. They need to reflect on the insights and prescriptions offered here and elsewhere and apply them in ways that are sensitive to their own organisational contexts. They then need to assess the impact of these prescriptions carefully and adapt them as necessary in the light of their findings. A key part of this process is to establish ongoing two-way lines of communication (in all its myriad forms) with those involved in telework, including those involved with research on this new and radical form of work.

The second challenge, then, is to researchers, to continue to develop theoretical and empirical knowledge of teleworking as a basis for reflective practice. Most of this research is in its initial phases and has, to date, been limited by what we now know to be a narrow and partial view of telework and teleworking. The presentation here of our dimensional model of telework and the overview of the attendant issues has moved us closer to a state of conceptual clarity, and so provides clear pointers for future research in all areas that we have covered in this chapter. Our framework perhaps raises as many questions as it answers, but, to the extent that it sharpens the focus of those questions, it provides a basis for developing specific theoretical models of the major issues involved in teleworking (e.g. Standen *et al.*; 1999; Daniels *et al.*, 2001). Without such detailed theoretical knowledge, research in this area will not be able to build in a cumulative fashion and empirical work will continue to be dominated by case studies and surveys that have no particular focus, other than to compare teleworkers with "traditional" workers. Consequently, the research community will not be able to inform practitioners, in any useful and generalisable way, of the circumstances in which different forms of teleworking are likely to be adopted by organisations, and the circumstances in which different forms of teleworking have specific causal effects on organisations, workers and their families.

This is not to say that initial qualitative and survey research has not been valuable in helping to inform the field. However, the emphasis should now shift from exploratory work. Surveys should incorporate longitudinal elements and test specific causal hypotheses, whilst qualitative work should be used in a reflexive way to critique and sharpen theoretical perspectives. Researchers also need to consider quasi-experimental evaluation of intelligently designed telework interventions. Given the rapid change in technology and the expected changes in work practices, new research approaches may be required and these will need to be sensitive to the multiple forms of teleworking and realities those forms encompass.

As we noted in our introduction, the future of teleworking depends on whether employers provide the opportunity to telework and whether workers take advantage of this opportunity. To realise the full benefits of telework, there must be a dialogue between teleworkers, those that manage teleworkers and researchers. The new communications media that support telework also allow researchers to interact with management and teleworker communities in new ways, bringing exciting possibilities for the research community to assist in the evolution of this new work practice[3].

REFERENCES

Ahrentzen, S. B. (1990). Managing conflict by managing boundaries: how professional home workers cope with multiple roles at home. *Environment and Behavior*, **22**, 723–752.
Aryee, S. (1991). Creating a committed workforce: linking socialisation practices to business strategy. *Asia Pacific Human Resource Management*, **29**, 102–112.
Ashkenas, R., Ulrich, D., Jick, T. & Kerr, S. (1995). *The Boundaryless Organization: Breaking the Chains of Organizational Structure*. San Francisco, CA: Jossey-Bass.
Australian Bureau of Statistics (2001). *Locations of Work, Australia*. Cat. No. 6275.0. Canberra: Australian Government Publishing Service.
Barrick, M. R. & Mount, M. K. (1991). The big five personality dimensions and job performance. *Personnel Psychology*, **44**, 1–26.
Baruch, Y. (2001). The status of research on teleworking and an agenda for future research. *International Journal of Management Reviews*, **3**, 113–129.

---

[3] An interesting aside for the reader is that all the collaboration on this chapter between the authors has been "virtual"—it has been carried out via extensive e-mail contact. Indeed, although the team now has a considerable publication record together, two of the authors have never met face to face.

Behling, O. (1998). Employee selection: will intelligence and conscientiousness do the job? *Academy of Management Executive*, **12**, 77–86.

Billsberry, J. (2000). Socialiszing teleworkers into the organization. In K. Daniels, D. Lamond & P. Standen (Eds), *Managing Telework: Perspectives from Human Resource Management and Work Psychology*. London: Thomson Learning.

Cascio, W. F. (2000). Managing a virtual workplace. *Academy of Management Executive*, **14**, 81–90.

Cox, T., Griffiths, A. & Barker, M. J. (1996). *Teleworking: Health and Safety Issues in the Member States of the European Union*. Dublin: European Foundation for the Improvement of Living and Working Conditions.

Crossan, G. & Burton, P. F. (1993). Teleworking stereotypes: a case study. *Journal of Information Science Principles & Practice*, **19**, 349–362.

Daniels, K. (1999). Home based teleworking and mobile teleworking: a study of job characteristics, well-being and negative carry-over. Work Science Report Series, *13/14* (pp. 1535–1536). Tokyo: Institute of Science of Labour.

Daniels, K. (2000). Job features and well-being. In K. Daniels, D. Lamond, & P. Standen (Eds), *Managing Telework: Perspectives from Human Resource Management and Work Psychology*. London: Thomson Learning.

Daniels, K., Lamond, D. A. & Standen, P. (Eds) (2000). *Managing Telework: Perspectives from Human Resource Management and Work Psychology*. London: Thompson Learning.

Daniels, K., Lamond, D. & Standen, P. (2001). Teleworking: frameworks for organizational research. *Journal of Management Studies*, **38**, 1151–1186.

Duxbury, L. & Nuefeld, D. (1999). An empirical evaluation of the impacts of telecommuting on intra-organizational communication. *Journal of Engineering and Technology Management*, **16**, 1–28.

European Commission (1998). *Status Report on European Telework*. Luxembourg: Office for Official Publications of the European Communities.

Fairweather, N. B. (1999). Surveillance in employment: the case of teleworking. *Journal of Business Ethics*, **22**, 39–49.

Felstead, A. & Jewson, N. (2000). *In Work, at Home*. London: Routledge.

Gainey, T. W., Kelley, D. K. & Hill, J. A. (1999). Telecommuting's impact on corporate culture and individual workers: examining the effect of employee isolation. *S.A.M. Advanced Management Journal*, **64**, 4–10.

Gillespie, A. E., Richardson, R. & Cornford, J. (1995). *Review of Teleworking in Britain: Implications for Public Policy*. London: Parliamentary Office of Science and Technology.

Glosserman, B. (1996). How green is my cyberspace? *Japan Times Weekly International Edition*, **36**(44), 15.

Gray, M., Hodson, N. & Gordon, G. (1993). *Teleworking Explained*. Chichester: Wiley.

Guest, D. (1990). Human resource management and the American dream. *Journal of Management Studies*, **27**, 377–397.

Hamblin, H. (1995). Employees' perspectives on one dimension of labour flexibility: working at a distance. *Work, Employment and Society*, **9**, 473–498.

Hamel, G. & Prahalad, C. K. (1993). Strategy as stretch and leverage. *Harvard Business Review*, **March–April**, 75–84.

Harper, R. (2000). Communication and collaboration at a distance. In K. Daniels, D. Lamond and P. Standen (Eds), *Managing Telework: Perspectives from Human Resource Management and Work Psychology*. London: Thomson Learning.

Hiemstra, G. (1982). Teleconferencing, concern for face, and organizational culture. In M. Burggon (Ed.), *Communication Yearbook 6*. Beverly Hills, CA: Sage.

Hilthrop, J. M. (2000). Preparing people and organizations for teleworking. In K. Daniels, D. Lamond, & P. Standen (Eds), *Managing Telework: Perspectives from Human Resource Management and Work Psychology*. London: Thomson Learning.

Huws, U. (1994). *Teleworking*. Brussels: European Commission's Employment Task Force (Directorate General V).

Huws, U., Jagger, N. & O'Regan, S. (1999). *Teleworking and Globalisation*. Report No. 358. Brighton: Institute for Employment Studies.

Igbaria, M. & Guimares, T. (1999). Exploring differences in employee turnover intentions and its determinants among telecommuters and non-telecommuters. *Journal of Management Information Systems*, **16**, 147–164.

Ingham, C. (1995). *Working Well at Home*. London: Thorsons.

IRS (1996). Teleworking in Europe: part three. *European Industrial Relations Review*, **271**, 18–23.

Lambert, S. J. (1990). Processes linking work and family: a critical review and research agenda. *Human Relations*, **43**, 239–257.

Lamond, D. A. (1995). The art of HRM: human relationship management. Presented at the Australian and New Zealand Academy of Management Conference, Townsville, Queensland, 3–6 December.

Lamond, D. A. (1996). Karpin on management: is that all managers should be doing? Journal of the Australian and New Zealand Academy of Management, 2(1), 21–35.

Lamond, D. (2000a). Personality and telework. In K. Daniels, D. Lamond & P. Standen (Eds), *Managing Telework: Perspectives from Human Resource Management and Work Psychology*. London: Thomson Learning.

Lamond, D. (2000b). Managerial style and telework. In K. Daniels, D. Lamond & P. Standen (Eds), *Managing Telework: Perspectives from Human Resource Management and Work Psychology*. London: Thomson Learning.

Lamond, D. A., Daniels, K. & Standen, P. (1997a). Virtual working or working virtually? an overview of contextual and behavioural issues in teleworking. *Proceedings of the Fourth International Meeting of the Decision Sciences Institute*, Part II, 477–481.

Lamond, D. A., Daniels, K. & Standen, P. (1997b). Defining telework: what is it exactly? *Proceedings of the Second International Workshop on Telework*, Amsterdam, The Netherlands.

Lawrence, P. R. & Lorsch, J. W. (1967). *Organization and Environment: Managing Differentiation and Integration*. Boston, MA: Graduate School of Business, Harvard University.

Lea, M. T. & Spears, R. (1992). Paralanguage and social perception in computer-mediated communication. *Journal of Organizational Computing*, **2**, 321–341.

McClennan, W. (1996). *Persons Employed at Home, Australia*. Australian Bureau of Statistics, Catalogue No. 6275.0. Canberra: AGPS.

Mintzberg, H. (1979). *The Structuring of Organizations*. Englewood Cliffs, NJ: Prentice Hall.

Moon, C. & Stanworth, C. (1997). Ethical issues in teleworking. *Business Ethics: A European Review*, **6**, 35–45.

Omari, M. & Standen, P. (1996). The impact of home-based work on organisational outcomes. Paper presented at the Australian and New Zealand Academy of Management Conference, Wollongong, NSW, 4–7 December.

Omari, M. & Standen, P. (2000). Selection for telework. In K. Daniels, D. Lamond, & P. Standen (Eds), *Managing Telework: Perspectives from Human Resource Management and Work Psychology*. London: Thomson Learning.

Pearlson, K. E. & Saunders, C. S. (2001). There's no place like home: managing telecommuting paradoxes. *Academy of Management Executive*, **15**(2), 117–128.

Proquest Information and Learning Company (formerly UMI Company) (2001). *ABI/Inform Global Edition, January 1999–August 2001*. Ann Arbor, MI: Proquest.

Quinn, R. (1988). *Beyond Rational Management: Mastering the Paradoxes and Competing Demands of High Performance*. San Francisco, CA: Jossey-Bass.

Qvortrup, L. (1998). From teleworking to networking: definitions and trends. In P. J. Jackson & J. M. Van der Wielen (Eds), *Teleworking: International Perspectives, from Telecommuting to the Virtual Organization*. London: Routledge.

Reich, R. (1992). *The Work of Nations*. New York: Vintage.

Rourke, J. (1996). A few good tips for telecommuters and their employers. *Rural Telecommunications*, **15**(5), 8.

Salmon, G., Allen, J. & Giles, K. (2000). Training and development for on-line working. In K. Daniels, D. Lamond & P. Standen (Eds), *Managing Telework: Perspectives from Human Resource Management and Work Psychology*. London: Thomson Learning.

Sparrow, P. (2000). Teleworking and the psychological contract: a new division of labour. In K. Daniels, D. Lamond & P. Standen (Eds), *Managing Telework: Perspectives from Human Resource Management and Work Psychology*. London: Thomson Learning.

Sparrow, P. R. & Cooper, C. L. (1998). New organizational forms: the strategic relevance of future psychological contract scenarios. *Canadian Journal of Administrative Sciences*, **15**, 356–371.

Sparrow, P. R. & Daniels, K. (1999). Human resource management and the virtual organization: mapping the future research issues. In C. L. Cooper & S. E. Jackson (Eds), *Trends in Organizational Behavior*, Vol. **6**. Chichester: Wiley.

Standen, P. (1997). Home, work and management in the information age. *Journal of the Australian and New Zealand Academy of Management*, **3**, 1–14.

Standen, P. (2000). Organizational culture and telework. In K. Daniels, D. Lamond & P. Standen (Eds), *Managing Telework: Perspectives from Human Resource Management and Work Psychology*. London: Thomson Learning.

Standen, P., Daniels, K. & Lamond, D. (1999). The home as a workplace: Work–family interaction and psychological well-being in telework. *Journal of Occupational Health Psychology*, **4**, 368–381.

Townsend, A. M., DeMarie, S. & Hendrickson, A. R. (1998). Virtual teams: technology and the workplace of the future. *Academy of Management Executive*, **12** (August), 17–29.

Travic, B. (1998). Information aspects of new organizational designs: exploring the non-traditional organization. *Journal of the American Society for Information Science*, **49**, 1224–1244.

Tregaskis, O. (2000). Telework in its national context. In K. Daniels, D. Lamond & P. Standen (Eds), *Managing Telework: Perspectives from Human Resource Management and Work Psychology*. London: Thomson Learning.

Tregaskis, O. & Daniels K. (2000). Organizational learning. In K. Daniels, D. Lamond & P. Standen (Eds), *Managing Telework: Perspectives from Human Resource Management and Work Psychology*. London: Thomson Learning.

van Ommeren, J. N. (1998). Telework in Europe. In *Teleworking Environments: Proceedings of the Third International Workshop on Telework*. Turku, Finland.

van Ommeren, J. (2000). Performance management and compensation. In K. Daniels, D. Lamond & P. Standen (Eds), *Managing Telework: Perspectives from Human Resource Management and Work Psychology*. London: Thomson Learning.

Walther, J. B. (1995). Relational aspects of computer-mediated communication: experimental observations over time. *Organization Science*, **6**, 186–202.

Warr, P. B. (1987). *Work, Unemployment and Mental Health*. Oxford: Oxford University Press.

CHAPTER 12

Performance Management Practices and Motivation

Robert D. Pritchard and **Stephanie C. Payne**
Department of Psychology, Texas A & M University, TX, USA

The overall perspective of this volume is that many new forms of work organization and approaches to improving organizational performance have gained prominence in the last 10–15 years. This chapter deals with performance management practices and the relationship between the practices and work motivation. It will describe a number of performance management practices, then present a theory of motivation and use that theory to understand the human side of these practices.

PERFORMANCE MANAGEMENT DEFINED

A number of definitions of performance management have been offered. Some authors use the terms "performance management" and "performance appraisal" interchangeably (e.g. Lepsinger & Lucia, 2001; Schay, 1993; Taylor *et al.*, 1998); however, we use a much broader definition. Consistent with the definition offered by DeNisi (2000), we define *performance management* as a range of activities or practices an organization engages in to enhance the performance of a target person or group, with the ultimate purpose of improving organizational performance. Performance management practices are change efforts that can be directed at the individual, team or organizational level of analysis.

There are a variety of performance management practices, but we can only cover some of them in this chapter. In doing this, we will make a distinction between what we call *basic practices* and the more recent *complex practices*. Basic performance management practices are simpler and have been very widely used for many decades. The basic techniques we will discuss are: training; feedback, both knowledge of results feedback and performance appraisal; goal setting; and incentives. The complex practices have been developed more recently, are less broad in their use, and often combine a number of features of the basic practices. The complex practices we will discuss are total quality management (TQM); empowerment; knowledge management (KM); autonomous work groups (AWGs); and the productivity measurement and enhancement system (ProMES). The first four of these practices were chosen because they are described in other chapters in this volume, and our

---

The New Workplace: A Guide to the Human Impact of Modern Working Practices.
Edited by David Holman, Toby D. Wall, Chris W. Clegg, Paul Sparrow and Ann Howard. © 2003 John Wiley & Sons, Ltd.

attempt to relate them to a specific theory of motivation will hopefully aid in understanding how they influence motivation, and thus behavior.

EXTENT OF USE

Performance management practices are used extensively around the world. Depending on how they are defined, the basic practices are utilized by most organizations. For example, in a survey of formal training activities conducted by organizations around the world, 582 organizations from 38 different countries reported that, on average, 71% of their employees receive formal training [American Society for Training and Development (ASTD), 2001]. Similarly, knowledge of results feedback is probably used to some degree by all organizations on some jobs, whereas performance appraisal is used by close to 80% of organizations worldwide (ASTD, 2001). Some form of goal setting, such as identifying objectives or formal setting of quantitative goals, including management by objectives (MBO), has probably been used by most organizations at some point in time. Incentive systems are the most common compensation practice worldwide, except in Japan, where profit sharing is used extensively, and in Australia and New Zealand, where knowledge- and skill-based pay are more common (ASTD, 2001).

Of the complex practices, TQM has been used by far the most frequently and continues to be a commonly used work practice across the globe (ASTD, 2001). KM systems are quickly being adopted by large consulting firms and other organizations (Bracken, 1992; Davenport & Probst, 2000; Martiny, 1998; Quinn, Anderson & Finkelstein, 1996; Scarbrough, this volume). AWGs have been used for some time (e.g. Trist, 1981), but became particularly popular in the 1990s (e.g. Geber, 1992; Kerwin, 1992; Lawler, Mohrman & Ledford, 1992). In the present era of downsizing, empowerment programs have also become quite common (Filipczak, 1993; Tosi, Rizzo & Carroll, 1990) mainly outside the USA (ASTD, 2001). ProMES (described in more detail later) has been used in approximately 150 applications in different types of organizations, for different levels of organizational personnel from entry level to top management, in seven different countries (Pritchard, 1995; Pritchard et al., 2002).

PERFORMANCE MANAGEMENT PRACTICES AND BEHAVIOR

Thus, there are a number of different techniques, interventions and procedures that are included in the area of performance management. One of the central aims of this volume is to look at the impact modern work practices like performance management have had on organizations and to also explore what we know about the human side of these work practices. This chapter focuses on the underlying mechanisms that make such interventions successful.

We can start this analysis by thinking of what the various performance management techniques have in common. One commonality is they are not specific techniques, such as lean manufacturing, nor are they specific work technologies, such as call centers. Performance management techniques can be used in virtually any work setting. Another commonality, which is even more important, is that they all deal with *changing people's behavior at work*. When we are in the area of changing people's behavior, we are dealing with motivation. So our approach to the volume's objective of exploring what we know about the human side of work practices is to start with motivation. Specifically, we will (a) present a theory of motivation, (b) derive the implications from that theory for how to maximize motivation and performance and (c) explore how each of the performance management practices deals with or incorporates these motivational implications. We will also use the implications of the theory to identify ways to optimize the effects of each practice.

A THEORY OF MOTIVATION

The theory we will use is new and is described more fully in Pritchard & Ramstad (2001). However, it is based on the theory originally described by Naylor, Pritchard & Ilgen (1980) and will be referred to as NPI. The new theory focuses on the motivational process and represents a number of revisions from the original NPI approach. As with NPI, the new theory is an example of an expectancy theory. Such theories postulate that people are motivated by the anticipation or *expectancy* of how their actions will lead to positive or negative outcomes (e.g. Campbell & Pritchard, 1976; Heckhausen, 1991; Vroom, 1964).

A basic assumption of the theory is that at any point in time, people have a certain amount of energy, which is called the "energy pool". People also have needs, e.g. for food, water, achievement, safety, power, and being with other people. These needs produce forces within the person to be satisfied. This is shown graphically in the top row of Figure 12.1. This energy pool is used to satisfy needs. Motivation is seen as the process that determines *how* this energy is used to satisfy needs. This is shown in the second row of the figure.

The motivation process itself can be broken down into a series of components, shown in the bottom row of the figure. Motivation is seen as a resource allocation process where the resource is a person's time and energy, which come from the energy pool. Time and energy are allocated across possible *actions* or tasks. Motivation includes the direction, intensity and persistence of allocating effort to tasks. Direction is which tasks effort is applied to,

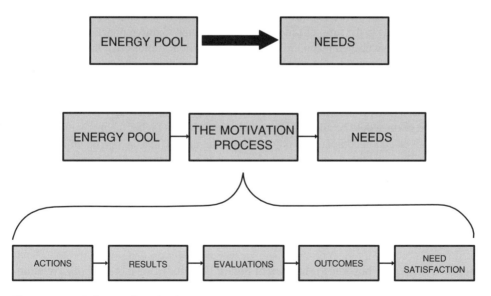

Figure 12.1 A theory of motivation

intensity is the level of effort applied to that task, and persistence is how long the effort is allocated to that task.

We will use the example of a university professor. A professor's actions include preparing lecture notes, writing manuscripts, reading, analyzing data, running, or talking with others. If energy is applied to actions, *results* are generally produced. As one sits typing (an action) one generates a manuscript (a result). Thus, a result is the person's output. When results are observed and an evaluator places the measured result on a good-to-bad evaluative continuum, this produces *evaluations*. For the professor's manuscript, evaluations are made by the professor him/herself, and also by colleagues who read the draft and give feedback, journal reviewers, and readers of the eventual published paper. So multiple evaluators assess a person's results. After these evaluations are made, *outcomes* occur. These are intrinsic outcomes, such as a feeling of accomplishment from writing a good paper, or extrinsic outcomes, such as forms of recognition, promotion, or pay raises for doing scholarly work. They can be self-administered or administered by anyone else who evaluates the result. Outcomes get their motivating power because of their ties to *need satisfaction*. Positive affect occurs when needs are satisfied and negative affect occurs when needs are not satisfied.

Motivation is seen as a future-orientated concept, in that people anticipate the amount of need satisfaction that will occur when outcomes are received. It is this anticipated satisfaction that determines behavior. As the person makes choices of how much time and effort to devote to which tasks, the goal is maximizing the total anticipated need satisfaction. Motivation is seen as being based on perceptions. It is the *perceived* relationship between applying energy to actions and need satisfaction that influences how much of the energy pool is devoted to that action. These perceptions may or may not be accurate.

Combining the Motivation Components

Actions, results, evaluations, outcomes and need satisfaction are combined into *motivational force*, which is defined as the degree to which a person believes that changes in the amount of personal resources, in the form of time and energy devoted to different actions (tasks) over time, will result in a change in anticipated need satisfaction. Actions that involve increases in effort and are expected to result in increases in need satisfaction have high motivational force, and large amounts of time and effort will be allocated to them. If variations in the amount of energy allocated to an action or set of actions produce no change in the expected amount of need satisfaction, motivational force to put energy into that action is very low, and no time and effort would be allocated to these actions. So the higher the motivational force towards a given action compared to other actions, the more effort the person will devote to that action. Thus, the theory is about *relationships*. It is the degree of relationship between amounts of the energy pool allocated to actions and the expected level of need satisfaction that determines motivation.

Connections

Between each of the boxes in the last row of Figure 12.1 are arrows that symbolize relationships called *connections*. *Action-to-result connections*, the arrow between the ACTIONS and the RESULTS boxes in the figure, describe the person's perceived relationship between the amount of effort devoted to that action and the amount of the result that is expected to be produced. Connections in the theory are actual graphic representations of the relationships in question. Examples are shown in Figure 12.2A, B. The person may see a very close connection or relationship between the level of effort devoted to an action and the amount of the result that is produced. For our professor there is probably a very close relationship perceived between the amount of effort devoted to preparing lecture notes (the action) and the amount of notes actually finished (the result). Preparing lecture notes for an experienced faculty member is a fairly straightforward task and we would expect the action-to-result connections to be quite strong. Such a connection is shown in Figure 12.2A. The horizontal axis is the amount of effort devoted to the action of preparing lecture notes, the vertical axis is the amount of the result that is completed, in this case the amount of lecture notes finished. The connection figure shows that as more and more effort is used, more notes are finished. It is only when very high levels of effort are committed and fatigue sets in that the amount of notes completed with additional effort starts to decrease.

Connections for other actions can be lower. Effort devoted to manuscript writing (the action) will have a lower relationship with the amount of the manuscript completed (the result). Sometimes the writing goes well and sometimes not so well, no matter how much time is devoted to the task. This is shown in the second action-to-results connection (Figure 12.2B). Compared to writing lecture notes, variations in effort result in fewer variations in the amount of the manuscript completed and the point of diminishing returns occurs more quickly. Other actions could have absolutely no relationship between action and results. If our professor, who has no mathematics experience, were asked to solve a series of differential equations in 1 day, no amount of effort would result in solving the equations; the action-to-result connection graphic would be a flat line intersecting the vertical axis at the 0 result level. He/She would not be motivated to solve the equations, no matter what the outcomes provided for success on the task.

The next arrow in Figure 12.1 refers to *result-to-evaluation connections*. These reflect the person's perceived relationship between the amount of the result that is produced and the level of the evaluation that is expected to occur. There would be such a connection for each different result and for each person who evaluates the result(s), such as the professor him/herself, peers, supervisors and researchers in other universities. Example graphics in Figure 12.2C, D are for the results of (C) amount of scholarly outputs (journal articles, chapters) and (D) amount of departmental service done.

The next set of connections is *evaluation-to-outcome connections*. They define the perceived relationship between the level of the evaluation and the level of an outcome. Example graphics in Figure 12.2E, F depict the contrasting connections between a department head's evaluation and a cost-of-living raise for everyone plus larger raises for higher evaluations by the department head.

The final type of connection is the *outcome-to-need satisfaction connections*. These define the relationships between how much of the outcome is received and the degree of anticipated need satisfaction that will result. If variation in the size of the raise results in large changes in the professor's need satisfaction, outcome-to-need satisfaction connections are high and this means that the outcomes of pay raises are very important to the professor (as depicted in Figure 12.2G, H). If variations in the size of the raise do not result in variations in need satisfaction, the connection is low, indicating that pay raises are not important to that professor.

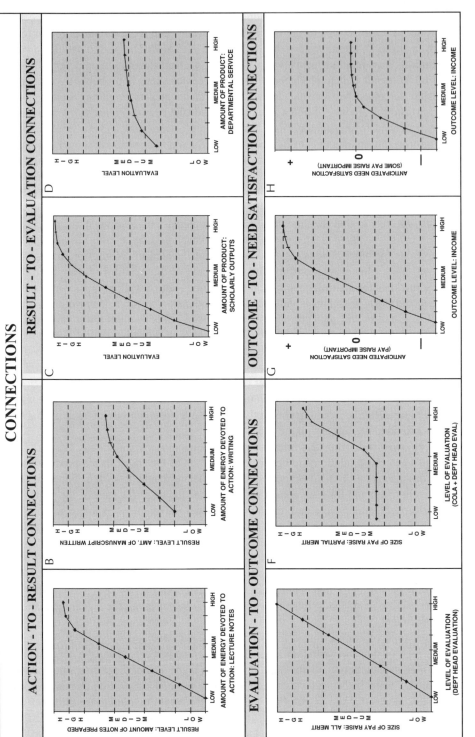

Figure 12.2 Example of connections between different parts of the motivation theory. COLA, cost of living allowance; MERIT.

Effort Allocation and Task Strategies

One of the advantages of the theory is that it predicts effort allocated *across tasks*, i.e. it does not just predict overall level of effort on the job, but also how that effort will be used for different actions. The theory conceptualizes the motivational process as one of allocating personal resources in the form of time and effort *across tasks*. Thus, the key process is a distributional process. However, most tasks are complex, like writing a manuscript. To do the task, the professor must do a whole series of actions, such as thinking, reviewing the literature, analyzing data, meeting with assistants, and writing. Each of these separate actions must be combined to produce the desired result: the manuscript. Thus, it is important to recognize that part of action-to-result connections is the *task strategy* the person uses to get the result produced. Without a good task strategy, action-to-result connections are low.

Motivation as a Process

Another key part of the theory is that motivation is viewed as a *process* and as such each stage of the process must function well for motivation, the outcome of the process, to be high. For example, if outcomes with high need satisfaction potential are tied to evaluations which are clearly tied to the level of the results, but the person does not believe that he/she can produce the results, motivation will not be high. This is an extremely important aspect of the theory that will be very useful in understanding the effects of the different performance management techniques. For motivation, and ultimately performance, to be high, *all* components of the model must be high.

IMPLICATIONS FROM THE THEORY

A number of implications about maximizing motivation can be derived from the theory. It is these implications that will guide us in understanding the motivational effects of different performance management techniques and guide us in identifying ways to maximize the effectiveness of the practices.

In the simplest terms, to maximize motivation, the connections must be maximized. That is, motivation will be high if all the following conditions are met:

- There is a strong perceived relationship between amount of energy devoted to the actions producing the results (outputs) and the amount of the results actually produced.
- There is a strong perceived relationship between how much and/or how well the results are produced and the favorableness of the evaluation by each major evaluator.
- There is a strong perceived relationship between the level of each major evaluators' evaluations and the level of outcomes that evaluator provides the person.
- The outcomes provided by the different evaluators are important in that there is a strong perceived relationship between the amount of the outcome and the level of anticipated need satisfaction.

The more specific implications for maximizing motivation are presented in Table 12.1.

Table 12.1 Implication of theory to maximize motivation

Connection		Implications to maximize motivation — Implication for motivation
Action-to-Result	1.	Changes in effort allocated to the actions must be perceived as resulting in changes in the amount of the results that are produced
	1a.	The person must have the basic ability to do all the actions required to produce the results
	1b.	The person must have the knowledge and training to do all the actions required to produce the results
	1c.	The person must have the resources (materials, tools, information, lack of other constraints, etc.) to do the actions required to produce the results
	1d.	The person must be able to control how his/her effort is allocated to different actions
	1e.	The person must have the authority to do the actions required to produce the results
	1f.	The person must have a good work strategy for producing the results
	1g.	The person must have accurate perceptions of *all* the results wanted by the different evaluators (e.g., self, peers, supervisors)
	1h.	The feedback system must measure results in a way that is valid and is perceived as valid by the person being measured
	1i.	Feedback should be based on results the person has control over
	1j.	The person must be given the opportunity to develop and test new strategies to produce the results
Result-to-Evaluation	2.	Changes in the level of results produced must be perceived as resulting in changes in the evaluations received
	2a.	Feedback should cover all the important results (all evaluated results)
	2b.	The person must have a clear understanding of the relative importance of the results needed
	2c.	The person must know what level of the results are expected. This includes what levels of the results are poor, adequate and good (evaluations)
	2d.	Evaluations must be valid and perceived as valid
	2e.	Feedback on results and evaluations must be given in a regular and timely schedule
	2f.	The person must know all the relevant evaluators
	2g.	All the important evaluators (self, peers, supervisors, management) must agree on the evaluation system
	2h.	The components of the evaluation system must be stable over reasonable amounts of time. If a change occurs, it must be clearly communicated
	2i.	Because many outcomes are awarded on the basis of overall performance, to aid in the development of evaluation-to-outcome connections, feedback should also include an overall evaluation across all the different results
	2j.	In order to develop effective work strategies, it must be clear how much improvement in evaluation will occur with improvements in each evaluated result

PERFORMANCE MANAGEMENT PRACTICES AND MOTIVATION

Table 12.1 (*continued*)

Connection		Implications to maximize motivation
		Implication for motivation
	2k.	The evaluation system for the individual and the group should be aligned with those things which provide value to the organization
Evaluation-to-Outcome	3.	Changes in the level of the evaluation(s) must be perceived as resulting in changes in amount of the outcomes received
	3a.	The outcomes for good and poor performance must be clear
	3b.	There should be as many positive intrinsic and extrinsic outcomes available as possible
	3c.	The outcomes for doing the results well or poorly must be consistent across evaluators, especially peers, supervisors, and higher level management
	3d.	The outcomes for doing the results well or poorly must be consistent across recipients and over time
Outcome-to-Need Satisfaction	4.	Changes in the levels of the outcomes received must be perceived as resulting in changes in the level of anticipated need satisfaction
	4a.	The available outcomes should satisfy important needs
	4b.	Outcomes should satisfy as many needs as possible
	4c.	The person must have an accurate expectation of the future need satisfaction of the available outcomes
Overall		*All* components of the motivational process must be positive, not just some of them

Action-to-Results (A–R) Connections

Many of these are fairly obvious implications from the theory. However, discussion of some of them will aid clarity. To have clear and strong A–R connections, (Table 12.1; 1) the person must have the ability (1a), the knowledge and training (1b) and the resources (1c) to produce the results. The design of work setting must allow for controlling how effort is applied to different actions (1d). People must have the authority to do the needed actions (1e). If the above conditions are not met, the person cannot use his/her actions to produce the needed results. A–R connections suffer and motivation is decreased. Another determinant of A–R connections is the person's work strategy (1f).

High A–R connections also suggest requirements for the feedback system. The person must know what are the important results (1g) or will be measured and evaluated by each evaluator including the self, peers, supervisors, as well as people outside the organization such as customers, suppliers and family members. The feedback system must provide valid measures of the results and these measures must be perceived as valid (1h). A–R connections cannot be formed in the absence of knowledge of results; the R part of the connection. If the measures of results are inaccurate or seen as inaccurate, A–R connections suffer because inaccurate measures mean that the same actions produce unpredictable results, thus weakening the A–R relationship. Feedback must also be based on results over which the person has a reasonable amount of control (1i). Finally, to maximize A–R connections over time, the person must regularly have the opportunity to develop and test new work strategies (1j).

Results-to-Evaluation (R–E) Connections

Developing good R–E connections (Table 12.1; 2) also has implications for feedback systems. The feedback system should include all the results that are important to evaluators who control valuable outcomes for the person (2a). To optimize work strategies, the person must know the relative importance of the different results (2b) so as to give more attention to those that are more valuable to the organization.

Providing accurate descriptive measures of all the important results is critical for the feedback system and for forming good R–E connections. However, the feedback system must also provide evaluative information. This means the person must be able to translate the amount (how much; 2a) of the result is being generated into the level of evaluation (how good; 2c). These evaluations must be valid and be perceived as valid (2d). Accurate R–E connections are enhanced when feedback on both results and evaluations is given on a regular, established schedule as close in time as possible to when the results were produced (2e).

We have mentioned the issue of multiple evaluators. To maximize R–E connections the person must know who all the important evaluators are (2f). Different evaluators may think different results are important or give different evaluations for the same level of results. This is essentially an issue of role conflict. To minimize role conflict and maximize the R–E connections, all the important evaluators should agree (2g). It is also important that these components of the evaluation system remain stable over time and, if a change is needed, that it is clearly communicated (2h).

Virtually all jobs produce multiple results. From a motivational perspective, it is valuable for the feedback system to combine the evaluations from these multiple results into an overall evaluation (2i). One reason is that many important outcomes such as salary, raises, promotions, recognition and a personal feeling of accomplishment are primarily tied to this overall evaluation. The overall score makes it easier to form clear Evaluation-to-Outcome connections.

A major reason to focus on motivation is to improve it and thereby improve performance. An especially important way a higher level of motivation improves performance is through the enhancement of work strategies. In order to optimally make improvements in results and the corresponding evaluations, the job incumbent must focus on those results where the maximum improvements in evaluations can be made. This means that the feedback system must indicate how much improvement can be made in the evaluations with gains in each result (2j).

Finally, how results are evaluated should be consistent with how much value they create for the organization (2k). If the evaluation system does not have this line-of-sight with the broader organizational goals, individuals and units will be evaluated in a way that is not consistent with what actually has value. This means they will develop suboptimal results for the organization (Ramstad, Pritchard & Bly, 2002).

Evaluation-to-Outcome (E–O) Connections

Developing good E–O connections (Table 12.1, 3) deals with the reward system in the organization. Good E–O connections mean that the consequences of good and poor performance must be clear (3a). To maximize motivation, there should be as many intrinsic and extrinsic outcomes as possible (3b) that can be tied to the evaluations (performance). Adding outcomes that are tied to evaluations can increase motivation, but the fairness of the reward system is also important. Fairness means the outcomes received for doing the results well or poorly must be consistent across evaluators, especially peers, supervisors and higher level management (3c). They should also be consistent across recipients and over time (3d).

Outcome-to-Need Satisfaction Connections

Having good O–NS connections (4) is also part of the reward system. The primary implication for motivation is that powerful outcomes mean that O–NS connections must be high. The outcomes that are available in that work setting must be able to satisfy important needs of the people there (4a), and outcomes should satisfy as many needs as possible (4b). Finally, as with all the connections, O–NS connections are perceived relationships about how well outcomes are *expected* to satisfy needs. It is important that these expectations are accurate (4c).

Overall

The last implication is one we stressed before. All the components of the motivational process must be high for the resulting motivation to be high. If any of the connections are low, this sets an upper limit on the resulting level of motivation. If A–R, R–E and O–NS connections are all very high, but the people doing the work see that evaluations are not tied to outcomes (E–O connections), motivation will be low.

PERFORMANCE MANAGEMENT PRACTICES AND THE MOTIVATION THEORY

This next section of the chapter focuses on relating the performance management practices to the motivation theory. In order to do this, we must define each practice rather clearly. The practices can be implemented in many different ways, and whether a given implication from the theory is met depends on *how* that practice is implemented. For example, performance appraisal may be feedback from just the supervisor or also include peers and subordinates. The feedback may or may not contain an overall score; it may or may not include an indication of priorities for improvement. So to relate the practice to the theory we must decide on one "form" of that practice. This is not meant to suggest these are somehow the best or only ways the practice can be implemented. However, we have tried, where possible, to pick the form of the practice that is most common.

We will follow a common format in dealing with each of the practices. We will (a) define the practice, (b) describe where it influences motivation according to the theory, and (c) show how it operationalizes the implications listed on Table 12.1.

Basic Practices

Training

We define training as a planned effort by an organization to facilitate employees' learning of job-related competencies (Noe, 2002). It is formal in that it is planned, rather than the more informal learning that occurs from experience in doing the job or from casual on-the-job training. It can be focused on specific skills directly related to doing the work, such as welding, preparation for sales calls, or using the organization's information system. It can also be focused on more general skills, such as supervision or communication. It is normally done on only a subset of the results that are important for that job.

The way training impacts motivation is shown in Figure 12.3. Training teaches what results the organization values. Whether it is welding, using a new technology, or training in emotional intelligence, the fact that the organization is providing the training clearly demonstrates that the results of being trained are important. Thus, it directly clarifies results, as shown by the arrow going from the TRAINING box to RESULTS. Training also teaches people how to combine actions to produce the results and thus clarifies the A–R connections.

We can also compare training to the implications of the motivation theory summarized in Table 12.1. If the training is done well, it will satisfy some of the implications from the theory. It clarifies at least some of the important results (1g), gives the person the knowledge and training to do the actions required to produce those results (1b) and helps the person have a good work strategy (1f).

A summary of which motivation implications training operationalizes is summarized in Table 12.2. We do this summary for each of the practices we will be discussing in this chapter. The implications from the theory are listed in the left column and each of the practices is shown across the top. If the cell contains an "X", it means that this practice formally attempts to operationalize this implication. If it contains a "P" this indicates that there is a partial operationalization of the implication. One example of a partial operationalization is where a practice formally identifies *some* of the important results, but does not make it a formal part of the practice to identify *all* the important results.

Table 12.2 was difficult to construct. Many of the practices could well include implications that are not indicated in the table. A given implementation of TQM could take great care to include all the important results. Results feedback could include a clear specification of what levels of these measured results are poor, adequate, good or excellent and thereby add evaluation information to the results feedback. However, we constructed the table consistent with our definitions of the practice, realizing that many variations for some of these practices are commonly used.

The implications from the theory also tell us under what conditions training will be maximally effective. Because training influences A–R connections, we can look at Table 12.1 and see what additional requirements are necessary to maximize A–R connections and thus training effectiveness. These include trainees having the needed basic abilities (1a) and

Table 12.2 Implication of motivation theory for various practices

Components and implications		Performance management practices									
		Training	Result feedback	Perf apprais	Goal setting	Incentives	TQM	Empower	KM	AWGs	ProMES
A–R	1a. Basic ability	P									P
	1b. Knowledge and training							X	X	X	
	1c. Resources (materials, tools, information, etc.)						P	X	P	X	X
	1d. Can control how effort is allocated to actions							X		X	X
	1e. Authority							X		X	X
	1f. Good work strategy	P						X	P	P	X
	1g. Know all the important results	P	P		P	P	P	P			X
	1h. Feedback measures results validly						P				X
	1i. Feedback on controllable results						P				X
	1j. Opportunity to develop and test new strategies				P		X	X	P	P	X
R–E	2a. Feedback covers all important results		P		P	P	P	P			X
	2b. Relative importance of the results clear		P	P	P	P	P	P			
	2c. Know evaluations of different results levels			P	P		P		P		X
	2d. Evaluations valid and perceived as valid						P			X	
	2e. Feedback given regular and timely		P	P	P	P	P				X
	2f. Evaluations by all evaluators known										P
	2g. All evaluators agree on evaluation system						X				P

'continues overleaf'

Table 12.2 (continued)

	Components and implications	Performance management practices								
		Training	Result feedback	Perf apprails	Goal setting	Incentives	TQM	Empower	KM	AWGs	ProMES
	2h. Evaluation system stable over time			X			X	P			X
	2i. Feedback includes overall score			X							X
	2j. Clear how results changes lead to evaluation changes			P	P	P	P	P			X
	2k. Evaluations aligned with broader organizational goals						P	P			X
E–O	3a. Outcomes for different performance levels clear					P				P	P
	3b. As many positive outcomes as possible				P	P		P			P
	3c. Outcomes awarded in fair way									P	P
	3d. Outcomes consistent across people and time									P	P
O–NS	4a. Outcomes satisfy important needs					P		P			P
	4b. Outcomes satisfy as many needs as possible										P
	4c. Accurate expectations of outcomes' need satisfaction										

PERFORMANCE MANAGEMENT PRACTICES AND MOTIVATION

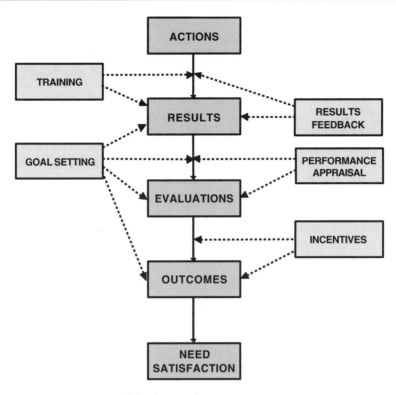

Figure 12.3 Basic practices and the theory of motivation

the resources (1c), being able to control effort allocation (1d, 1e), knowing all the important results (1g), and having the opportunity to use and evaluate new work strategies (1f, 1g).

Feedback

Feedback will be defined as the process of presenting information about one or more person's work in an effort to improve performance. We distinguish between feedback about results/outputs and formal performance appraisal.

Results Feedback

Results feedback is information about the quantity or quality of output produced by the individual, the group, or broader units of the organization. It can be provided by the job itself in the form of counts or other measures of output. External observers, such as co-workers, supervisors or customers external to the organization can also provide it. While it can sometimes be related to an individual's results, such as sales per month, it is more often group or unit level performance measures, such as the amount of scrap a steel fabricating unit has per month. The feedback occurs on a regular basis and always contains quantitative information but can also include qualitative information. However, it is primarily descriptive in nature rather than evaluative, i.e. it indicates how much output was produced but does not provide information on how that level of output compares to the expectations of the organization. Examples of such results feedback would include number of units completed per week, accidents per month, percentage of orders with defects, and company revenues for the quarter.

Figure 12.3 shows that results feedback influences results and the A–R connections. The measures of output *are* the person's or the unit's results. Because people know how much effort they are applying to which actions, clear feedback of results makes it possible to have clear A–R connections.

If we consider the implications from Table 12.1, results feedback makes the overall A–R connection more clear (1) and the feedback indicates that the results fed back are important (1g, 2a, 2b). Results feedback is normally given in a regular and timely way (2e). However, most results feedback systems do not cover *all* the important results. As with training, Table 12.1 suggests ways to maximize feedback effectiveness, e.g. 1a–c, 1e–j; 2a, 2k.

Performance Appraisal

We define performance appraisal as the formal evaluation of an employee in which multiple dimensions of performance receive ratings by the supervisor, and these quantitative ratings represent different levels of performance. In addition, a rating of overall performance is given. It is done annually, or in some cases semi-annually, and includes a face-to-face meeting with the supervisor where he/she discusses the reasons for the ratings. The same performance dimensions, rating process and discussion with the supervisor is used over time, so the system is fairly stable. The feedback focuses on behavioral dimensions, such as written communications, planning, ability to work without close supervision, and technical job knowledge. These dimensions are designed to fit a large class of jobs in the organization (e.g. all managers). The ratings represent the official ratings for that person and go into his/her personnel file. Performance appraisal differs from results feedback in that it is less frequent, less closely related to the specific outputs (results) required by that job, is always done on individuals rather than groups, and includes evaluative information on how good the performance has been.

Performance appraisal feedback, as we have defined it, influences motivation in different ways than results feedback. As Figure 12.3 shows, performance appraisal influences the R–E connections and the evaluations. The performance appraisal is by definition an evaluation, because it indicates how well the person's work compares to organizational expectations. Because the review session focuses on an action plan to improve performance (i.e. improve the evaluation), it also makes R–E connections more clear. When done well, it indicates what results need to be improved to produce a higher evaluation in the future. This further clarifies R–E connections.

It might seem as though performance appraisal should also directly influence results because it makes it clear what results are wanted. However, this is not generally the case. Performance appraisal instruments are usually designed in the way we have defined them, where the dimensions of performance are very general and can be applied to many jobs. This has the advantage of everyone being evaluated on the same set of dimensions with the same rating instrument. Examples of such dimensions are technical knowledge and supervisory skills. These are not actually results as defined by the theory. It is not a person's technical knowledge or supervisory skill that is of value to the organization, it is the *results produced* by these skills. What is valuable is solving technical problems so that the work gets done on time and supervising in a way that maximizes efficiency and keeps people satisfied. So knowing that supervisory skills and technical knowledge are important does not help to clarify what the results are. In fact, it is only in the discussion about the reasons for the ratings and the action plan that the supervisor (hopefully) gets down to the specific results on which he/she is focusing on and that are important.

Goal Setting

The term "goal setting" is used in different ways. At the most micro end of the continuum is *intention formation*. If a person forms a conscious intention to do some task, such as stop on the way home to buy milk, in this use of the term, the intention would be goal setting (e.g. Locke, 1968). Further along the continuum is the clarification of individual, group or organizational objectives (e.g. West & Anderson, 1996) or a planned attempt to improve *task strategies* (e.g. Frese & Zapf, 1994). At the most formal extreme of the goal setting continuum is what we could call *formal goal setting*. This is how we will define goal setting for our motivational analysis. This form of goal setting includes a formal, fairly public statement of a specific quantitative level of output (result) for which the subordinate will strive. It is done between a supervisor and a single subordinate or with a group of subordinates, usually in a face-to-face discussion. Part of the process is a specification of a time period after which a clear determination can be made of whether the goal was actually reached and at this time whether the goal was reached is formally discussed. The process also includes a discussion of why the goal was or was not reached, and another round of goal setting occurs with the same or different goals. It is assumed that there is quantitative feedback on the work result(s) on which the goals are set.

Figure 12.3 indicates that formal goal setting influences motivation by its effects on results, the R–E connections, evaluations and outcomes. It influences results in the same way that feedback does; if the supervisor imposes formal goal setting on a measure, it is by definition important. It influences evaluations because when the performance period is over, there is an evaluation of whether the individual or group exceeded the standard. So for those results covered by the goal setting, both the results and the evaluations become clearer, hence the R–E connections also become clearer for those results. Finally, because there is a formal evaluation when the performance period is over, outcomes in the form of recognition and achievement are added, or their opposites if the goal is not met.

Incentives

As with the other practices, incentives can be done in many different ways. For our analysis, incentive systems will be defined as a formal program of regularly occurring awards that have tangible value that are in addition to salary. The awards will most frequently be financial, but can also be vacation trips, fishing equipment or other things with some tangible value. In this definition of incentives, outcomes such as recognition or other non-tangible outcomes would be considered forms of recognition, but not incentives. These incentives are given based on level of performance. There are formally communicated, pre-defined rules by which the incentives are given. These rules are made clear to all before the performance period and the expectation is that the incentive system will continue to operate over time.

Figure 12.3 shows that the effects of incentives on motivation are through the E–O connections and outcomes. The incentive itself is an outcome. E–O connections change because a new outcome(s) is now tied to the evaluation. Because most incentives are tied to levels of results, it might seem that incentives must influence the R–E connections. However, an incentive system is actually defining what level of results is considered good and worthy of the incentive. This translation of results into what levels are good and not so good is an evaluation.

MORE COMPLEX PRACTICES

Total Quality Management

TQM became a popular practice in the mid-1980s and so many variations were developed that is now impossible to define it precisely. For the motivational analysis, we will define TQM as an approach to organizational change that involves participative management, continuous process improvement, and the use of teams to continually improve quality and productivity (Napier & Gershenfeld, 1993). Dean & Bowen (1994) identified three primary principles of TQM from Deming's (1986) 14 principles of effective management and organizational change. First, products and services must fulfill customer needs and this requires an organization-wide focus on customers. Second, consistent customer satisfaction can be attained only through continuous improvement of the processes that create products and services. Third, customer focus and continuous improvement are best achieved by collaboration throughout an organization as well as with customers and suppliers. TQM relies heavily on statistical control principles and the use of quantitative results feedback to control quality. This regularly occurring quantitative feedback, especially combined with techniques focused on reducing variation in performance (Smither, Houston & McIntire, 1996), allows managers to recognize and address variations in systems and processes that influence quality and productivity (Deming, 1986). These techniques are then translated into the plan–do–check–act cycle, which systematically assesses the effectiveness of changes introduced into a work process. However, TQM as we are defining it focuses primarily on the results that directly influence customer satisfaction and some aspects of performance. It does not formally focus on identifying all the important results. Contrary to many other performance management practices, TQM does not advocate the use of performance appraisal.

The way TQM impacts motivation is shown in Figure 12.4. TQM makes it clear that some of the important results are meeting customer needs and some aspects of performance. It also stresses feedback of results. Through its emphasis on collaboration throughout the organization and with customers and suppliers, it clarifies the actions and A–R connections needed to accomplish these results, and the A–R connections are further improved with the plan–do–check–act cycle. Statistical process control gives some information how the results will be translated into evaluations.

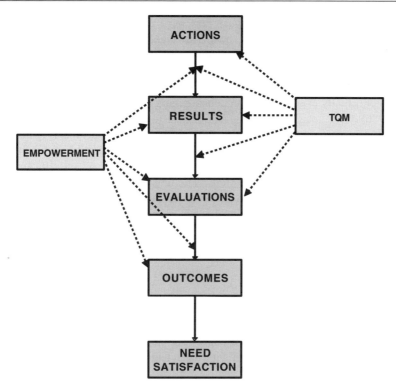

Figure 12.4 TQM and empowerment and the theory of motivation

Empowerment

Empowerment is a practice that can also mean many things. Consistent with Lawler's chapter (this volume), we define empowerment as giving employees the capacity to act in order to solve organizational problems. This involves three processes. First, empowerment means getting employees involved. This can range from a low level of involvement, entailing opportunities to offer suggestions on how to improve the organization, to a high level of involvement, where a portion of an employee's salary is determined by company stock price (Bowen & Lawler, 1992). Depending on this level of involvement, empowerment grants employees control by giving them power and decision-making authority to make organizational decisions (London, 1993), holding them accountable for their actions and rewarding them for contributing to organizational performance (e.g. share bonuses, pay for performance; see Lawler, this volume). This also means giving employees the resources they need to perform their jobs successfully, such as information about organizational performance (e.g. company reports, stock information) as well as training to ensure they have the knowledge and skills to understand and contribute to the organization (see Lawler, this volume). Second, empowerment practices enhance employees' feelings of competence (Conger & Kanungo, 1988) by building their self-efficacy or "beliefs in one's capabilities to mobilize the motivation, cognitive resources, and courses of actions needed to meet given situational demands" (Wood & Bandura, 1989, p. 408). With high levels of self-efficacy, employees believe they have the ability to do their jobs successfully and can solve problems on their own. This makes them less dependent on management to motivate them or give them direction. Finally, empowerment inspires employees to fulfill organizational goals and convinces them to internalize goals that are congruent with those of the organization (Menon, 2001). Here, management stimulates employees through intellectually exciting ideas and encouraging them to take on difficult challenges (Burke, 1986).

A major influence of empowerment is through the A–R connections (Figure 12.4) via increased authority and involvement in decision making and a formal attempt to provide people with the resources they need. Feelings of competence and self-efficacy are also directly translatable into A–R connections. The financial incentives add outcomes and, because they are tied to organizational performance, clarify the E–O connections. Because of the emphasis on making organizational goals clear and part of an individuals' goals, it clarifies what the results should be.

Knowledge Management

According to the Scarbrough chapter in this volume, KM is the attempt to constitute and exploit the intellectual property of the organization as an organizational resource in an effort to enhance organizational performance. The ultimate objective of KM is to obtain a competitive advantage (Scarbrough) with the intention of adding to the organization's resources and skills. KM practices involve the extraction and storage of knowledge, usually through technological tools, or the encouragement of knowledge sharing between employees, or both. More specifically, KM involves developing centralized knowledge databases of employee knowledge and successful organizational practices. For example, employees can document lessons learned and best practices in these databases so that others can benefit from their experiences (Quintas, Lefrere & Jones, 1997). These databases are easy to access by everyone in the organization as they are often maintained on intranets and are conducive to keyword searches. Sharing of employee knowledge is facilitated by the implementation of groupware, which also aids project management by documenting progress made on projects. Knowledge sharing can also take place face-to-face or through conference calls. Such efforts have been referred to as "learning communities" or "communities of practice", in which informal groups of people that cross organizational boundaries come together to discuss best practices, issues or skills that the group want to learn about (Martiny, 1998). Another KM practice is the development of "corporate yellow pages", or a list of individual employees and their corresponding skills (Scarbrough et al., 1999). KM initiatives are primarily designed and implemented by top management and information systems management (Scarbrough, Swan & Preston, 1999). They can also include benchmarking, or the systematic comparison of some aspect of an organization against another organization that is recognized as outstanding in that area.

As Figure 12.5 shows, the primary way that KM impacts motivation is through the A–R connections. Making information more available, more effectively sharing it, and helping people use it all help improve the translation of actions into results. It also improves peoples' ability to do the actions necessary to produce the results. The benchmarking process helps evaluate the results of one unit by comparing them to another, thus influencing R–E connections.

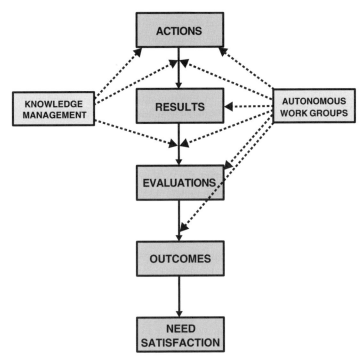

Figure 12.5 Knowledge management and autonomous work groups and the motivation model

Autonomous Work Groups

As described by Cordery in this volume, AWGs are groups of 5–15 employees who work together to accomplish an entire task or produce a complete product or service. They are also sometimes referred to as self-managed work teams, as they are primarily responsible for planning and accomplishing their work. The types of decisions delegated to AWGs range from housekeeping to making compensation decisions (Wellins, Byhan & Wilson, 1991) and can be categorized into: (a) decisions of self-regulation or decisions directly related to day-to-day processes; (b) decisions of independence or decisions concerning where, when, and in what order work will be completed; and (c) decisions of self-governance or who will be the leader and how the group will interact with one another (Susman, 1979). For the motivational analysis, we will assume that AWGs have full autonomy and the discretion to make all three types of decisions. Effective AWGs are cohesive, composed of highly skilled members, and endorse norms of learning, teamwork and quality output (Cummings, 1981). Implementing AWGs can require major structural changes to the organization and can be a difficult and demanding transition (Wellins *et al.*, 1991), yet organizations that adopt them report high levels of success (Lawler *et al.*, 1992).

AWGs have a major influence on motivation by their effects on actions and A–R connections. They control which actions are performed and the work strategy that is used. They also have considerable influence on identifying what are their important results and, because they influence how these results are translated into evaluations, they influence R–E connections. If they also make compensation decisions, they influence E–O connections as well.

ProMES

Unlike the other complex practices we have discussed, ProMES is a very specific intervention with clearly defined steps. It is described more fully in Pritchard (1990, 1995) and Pritchard *et al.* (2002). It is typically done on a group, which makes up a work unit, but can be done on individuals as well. The first phase is the development of the measurement and feedback system. The second phase uses the new system as feedback in a way designed to improve performance. To develop the system a design team is selected which includes members of the unit being measured, one or two supervisors, and a facilitator to guide them through the process. This design team identifies the overall objectives of the unit and then identifies indicators that show how well the unit is meeting these objectives. This and the subsequent steps in the process are done through discussion to consensus. The facilitator stresses the importance of measuring all aspects (results) of the work, with valid measures over which the unit has control. These objectives and measures are then reviewed by upper management to insure they are consistent with the broader organizational objectives. The design team then constructs the actual R–E connections in graphic form (called "contingencies" in ProMES), which relate the amount of the result produced to the value that amount of result contributes to the overall organization. These graphics are similar to the R–E graphics in Figure 12.2, but in ProMES actual numbers are used for both the result value and the evaluation level. The evaluation is called the "effectiveness score". These connection graphics are reviewed by higher levels of management, as were the objectives and indicators.

The second phase of ProMES is to use this information for the feedback system. Data are collected on each of the results. The feedback report for the prior period (most typically a month) includes how the unit did on each measure (result). The effectiveness scores for each result is calculated by determining what the connection graphic indicates is the effectiveness score for that level of the result. These effectiveness scores are then summed to produce an overall effectiveness score. For each performance period, the entire unit meets with the supervisor to review the feedback report. They examine their performance over this last period and discuss ideas for better ways of doing the work. In later feedback meetings, they evaluate how well these new work strategies actually resulted in improved results.

The ways ProMES influences motivation is shown in Figure 12.6. Because the design of ProMES was based on the earlier version of the motivation theory described here (Naylor *et al.*, 1980), it is not surprising that this intervention influences most of the components of the theory. The left side of the figure shows the motivational components influenced by the development of the system. Identifying objectives and indicators defines the results, the contingencies are literally the R–E connections, and management approval helps to insure that the objectives, indicators, and contingencies/connections are accurate. The implementation of ProMES is shown on the right side of the figure. Reviewing the feedback reports clarifies the actual results and the evaluations coming from them. The feedback report provides new outcomes, in that knowing their results and the evaluations coming from them influences feelings of accomplishment and recognition. Because the measurement and evaluation systems are seen as accurate, the value of these outcomes of accomplishment and recognition

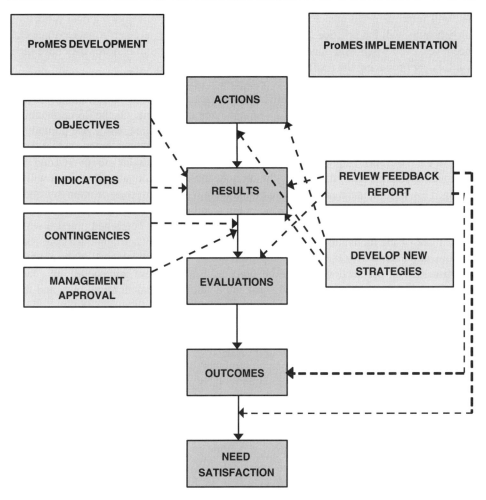

Figure 12.6 ProMES and the motivation model

is greater than it would be with a system seen as less accurate. This influences the O–NS connections between these outcomes and need satisfaction. The process of developing and evaluating new ways of doing the work changes how much energy is allocated to different actions, changing the results. When this happens, the A–R connections are also improved and clarified.

CONCLUSIONS

There are a number of important conclusions that can be drawn from this comparison of performance management practices to motivation. A major point in the motivation theory that we have made several times is that all the components of the motivational process must be strong for motivation to be high. This has important implications for any performance management practice because such practices are designed to change behavior in a way that will improve performance. However, only where the entire motivational process is fairly healthy will the practice improve motivation and ultimately performance. Financial incentives, even when well done, will have little effect if the unit believes they have little control over producing the results needed to earn the incentives.

There are several ways performance management can deal with this issue. It is clear that some practices cover more of the motivational components and the implications deriving from the theory than others. Table 12.2 summarizes this clearly. Of the 28 implications from the theory, some practices only partially operationalize three, while one partially or completely operationalizes 26. So one approach is to focus on those practices that cover more of the motivation implications. The more of the implications that are covered and thus improved by the practice, the greater the chances the entire motivational process will be strong. This, in turn, increases the chances that there will be performance improvement.

Another approach is to combine practices. For example, one could combine good results feedback with performance appraisal and goal setting. Such a combined practice would cover more of the motivational chain than any one alone. A related approach is to focus on how individual practices could be improved. Ideas for optimizing each of the practices are discussed in the section under each practice. Both of these approaches are geared to maximizing the number of motivational implications the practice improves and thus increasing the chances of improving performance.

Another, and probably the best, approach is to diagnose the motivational health of the unit before doing any performance management practice. Such a diagnosis should indicate the motivational health of the unit on each of the components and implications. If a given unit is weak in the motivation areas the practice should improve and strong in the others, that practice should be effective in that situation. In contrast, if the motivational health of the unit is not good in areas the practice does not improve, that practice will most likely not have the intended performance effects. For example, there are a number of implications from the theory on the characteristics of a good feedback system. A practice such as AWGs does very little to improve the feedback system. So if the feedback system was diagnosed as good, AWGs would likely be more effective in that unit than if the diagnosis indicated that the feedback system needed significant improvements.

This suggests that the development of valid and cost-effective ways of assessing the motivational health of organizational units is important and should be a priority in performance management. If we had good assessment devices that would identify the health of each of the elements in the motivational chain, this information could be translated directly into the appropriate practice that would be effective in that situation. This would make the job of deciding which practice or combination of practices would be most effective in different situations easier.

At a broader level, this chapter also suggests that we have learned a good deal about different performance management practices and have ideas on how they work and how to improve them. On the other hand, there is still much to learn. While the theory presented here has considerable research to support many of its components and implications, it is a new theory and needs research to assess its validity. Development and validation of good assessment instruments would also be of great aid in understanding and using performance management practices effectively. If this research can be done successfully, large improvement in performance and in the quality of work life can be made.

REFERENCES

American Society for Training and Development (2001). *International Comparisons: Report 2001.* Alexandria, VA: American Society for Training and Development.
Bowen, D. E. & Lawler, E. E., III. (1992). The empowerment of service workers: what, why, how, and when. *Sloan Management Review*, Spring, 31–39.
Bracken, D. W. (1992). Benchmarking employee attitudes. *Training and Development*, **June**, 49–53.
Burke, W. W. (1986). Leadership as empowering others. In S. Srivastva (Ed.), *Executive Power* (pp. 51–77). San Francisco, CA: Jossey-Bass.
Campbell, J. P. & Pritchard, R. D. (1976). Motivation theory in industrial and organizational psychology. In M. D. Dunnette (Ed.), *Handbook of Industrial and Organizational Psychology* (pp. 63–130). Chicago: Rand-McNally.
Conger, J. A. & Kanungo, R. N. (1988). The empowerment process: integrating theory and practice. *Academy of Management Review*, **12**, 637–647.
Cummings, T. G. (1981). Designing effective work groups. In P. Nystrom & W. Starbuck (Eds), *Handbook of Organizational Design: Remodeling Organizations and Their Environments*, Vol. 2 (pp. 250–271). New York: Oxford University Press.
Davenport, T. & Probst, G. (Eds) (2000). *Knowledge Management Case Book: Siemens Best Practices.* New York: Wiley.
Dean, J. W. Jr & Bowen, D. W. (1994). Management theory and total quality: improving research and practice through theory development. *Academy of Management Review*, **19**(3), 392–418.
Deming, W. E. (1986). *Out of the Crisis.* Cambridge, MA: MIT.
DeNisi, A. S. (2000). Performance appraisal and performance management: a multilevel analysis. In K. J. Klein & S. W. J. Kozlowski (Eds), *Multilevel Theory, Research, and Methods in Organizations: Foundations, Extensions, and New Directions* (pp. 121–156). San Francisco, CA: Jossey-Bass.
Filipczak, B. (1993). Ericsson General Electric: the evolution of empowerment. *Training*, **September**, 21–27.
Frese, M. & Zapf, D. (1994). Action as the core of work psychology: a German approach. In H. C. Triandis, M. D. Dunnette & L. M. Hough (Eds), *Handbook of Industrial/ Organizational Psychology*, 2nd Edn, Vol. 4 (pp. 271–340). Palo Alto, CA: Consulting Psychologists Press.
Geber, B. (1992). Saturn's grand experiment. *Training*, **June**, 27–35.
Heckhousen, H. (1991). *Motivation and Action.* Berlin: Springer.
Kerwin, K. (1992). Saturn. GM finally has a winner. But success is bringing a fresh batch of problems. *Business Week*, **August**, 86–91.
Lawler, E. E. III, Mohrman, S. A. & Ledford, G. E. Jr (1992). *Employee Involvement and Total Quality Management: Practices and Results in Fortune 1000 Companies.* San Francisco, CA: Jossey-Bass.
Lepsinger, R. & Lucia, A. D. (2001). Performance management and decision making. In D. W. Bracken, C. W. Timmreck & A. H. Church (Eds), *The Handbook of Multisource Feedback: the Comprehensive Resource for Designing and Implementing MSF Processes* (pp. 318–334). San Francisco, CA: Jossey-Bass.
Locke, E. A. (1968). Toward a theory of task motivation and incentives. *Organizational Behavior and Human Performance*, **3**, 157–189.
London, M. (1993). Relationships between career motivation, empowerment, and support for career development. *Journal of Occupational and Organizational Psychology*, **66**, 55–69.
Martiny, M. (1998). Knowledge management at HP Consulting. *Organizational Dynamics*, **27**(2), 71–77.
Menon, S. T. (2001). Employee empowerment: an integrative psychological approach. *Applied Psychology: an International Review*, **50**(1), 153–180.
Napier, R. & Gershenfeld, M. (1993). *Group Theory and Experience*, 5th Edn. Boston, MA: Houghton Mifflin.
Naylor, J. C., Pritchard, R. D. & Ilgen, D. R. (1980). *A Theory of Behavior in Organizations.* New York: Academic Press.
Noe, R. A. (2002). *Employee Training and Development*, 2nd Edn. Boston, MA: McGraw-Hill.
Pritchard, R. D. (1990). *Measuring and Improving Organizational Productivity: a Practical Guide* (p. 248). New York: Praeger.

Pritchard, R. D. (Ed.) (1995). *Productivity Measurement and Improvement: Organizational Case Studies* (p. 380). New York: Praeger.

Pritchard, R. D., Paquin, A. R., DeCuir, A. D., McCormick, M. J. & Bly, P. R. (2002). Measuring and improving organizational productivity: an overview of ProMES, the Productivity Measurement and Enhancement System. In R. D. Pritchard, H. Holling, F. Lammers & B. D. Clark (Eds), *Improving Organizational Performance with the Productivity Measurement and Enhancement System: an International Collaboration* (pp. 3–50). Huntington, NY: Nova Science.

Pritchard, R. D. & Ramstad, P. M. (2002). Managing Motivation (unpublished manuscript).

Quinn, J. B., Anderson, P. & Finkelstein, S. (1996). Managing professional intellect: making the most of the best. *Harvard Business Review*, **74**, 71–80.

Quintas, P., Lefrere, P. & Jones, G. (1997). Knowledge management: a strategic agenda. *Long Range Planning*, **30**(3), 385–391.

Ramstad, P. M., Pritchard, R. D. & Bly, P. R. (2002). The economic validity of ProMES components. In R. D. Pritchard, H. Holling, F. Lammers & B. D. Clark (Eds) *Improving Organizational Performance with the Productivity Measurement and Enhancement System: an International Collaboration* (pp. 167–194). Huntington, NY: Nova Science.

Scarbrough, H., Swan, J. & Preston, J. (1999). *KM and the Learning Organization: a Review of the Literature*. London: Institute of Personnel and Development.

Schay, B. W. (1993). In search of the Holy Grail: lessons in performance management. *Public Personnel Management*, **22**(4), 649–668.

Smither, R. D., Houston, J. M. & McIntire, S. A. (1996). *Organization Development: Strategies for Changing Environments*. New York: Harper Collins.

Susman, G. I. (1979). *Autonomy at Work: a Sociotechnical Analysis of Participative Management*. New York: Praeger.

Taylor, M. S., Masterson, S. S., Renard, M. K. & Tracy, K. B. (1998). Managers' reactions to procedurally just performance management systems. *Academy of Management Journal*, **41**(5), 568–579.

Tosi, H. L., Rizzo, J. R. & Carroll, S. J. (1990). *Managing Organizational Behavior*, 2nd Edn. New York: Harper Collins.

Trist, E. L. (1981). The evolution of socio-technical systems as a conceptual framework and an action research program. In A. H. Van de Ven & W. F. Joyce (Eds), *Perspectives on Organization and Behavior*. New York: Wiley.

Vroom, V. H. (1964). *Work and Motivation*. New York: Wiley.

Wellins, R. S., Byham, W. C. & Wilson, J. M. (1991). *Empowered Teams: Creating Self-directed Work Groups that Improve Quality, Productivity, and Participation*. San Francisco, CA: Jossey-Bass.

West, M. A. & Anderson, N. R. (1996). Innovation in top management teams. *Journal of Applied Psychology*, **81**(6), 680–693.

Wood, R. & Bandura, A. (1989). Impact of conceptions of ability on self-regulatory mechanisms and complex decision making. *Journal of Personality and Social Psychology*, **56**, 407–415.

CHAPTER 13

e-business: Future Prospects?

Chris W. Clegg, Belén Icasati-Johanson and **Stuart Bennett**
University of Sheffield, UK

It is easy to forget how recent is the phenomenon of e-business. For example, the Oxford Dictionary of Business, published in 1996, makes no mention of e-business or e-commerce. In the last 6 years a great deal has happened. Given the recency of the phenomenon, it is not surprising perhaps that there has been relatively little research in this area, and clearly there is a real danger that research follows slowly in the wake of rapidly evolving practice. Furthermore, what research has been undertaken has largely been in the technological, economic and market domains, as opposed to those that form the focus of this book, i.e. concerning the human and organisational issues (see e.g. Hendry, 1995; Herman, 1996; Thompson, 1997; Dedman, 1998; Ody, 1998; Stewart, 1998; Timmers, 1999; Shaw et al., 2000). For all these reasons, we are interested in trying to understand the topic. In our view, the practice of e-business is not yet well understood and has not yet stabilised—as such, research and development work in this area may have the opportunity to influence practice, and this itself presents interesting challenges.

Our aims in this chapter are to:

- Define and describe what is meant by e-business.
- Summarise existing research on the uptake of e-business, and on the main barriers to, and enablers of, adoption.
- Review the anticipated impacts of e-business, including the potential implications for the human resource function.
- Speculate on aspects of the performance of e-business.
- Propose some ways forward in this domain.

We consider these issues in the following sections, reviewing the evidence available and offering some personal views and interpretations. In some areas these can only be speculative. We note that the bulk of the evidence we have reviewed relates to UK experiences—where more international data has been obtained we report it.

DEFINITION AND DESCRIPTION

We define e-business as the conduct of business transactions and activities using, in large part, electronic means, and typically involving use of the internet and world wide web.

We include both business to customer (b2c), and business to business (b2b) transactions. These transactions are usually conducted online and in real time, and it is this that helps distinguish them from the more traditional forms of electronic data interchange (EDI). For the purposes of this chapter we make no distinction between e-business and e-commerce. Whilst the latter term is often applied to b2c type activities, this is not universal, and, for simplicity, we will use the generic term e-business throughout the chapter.

To illustrate some of the components of e-business, consider a large supermarket chain. Many such businesses now allow their customers to order and pay for their goods over the internet, and will deliver orders direct to the customer's home (b2c). At the same time, these supermarkets are increasingly developing their b2b activities through their supply chains, enabling them to order and pay for goods electronically. This may currently extend to their main suppliers, but increasingly companies are interested in extending these processes further back up the supply chains (to the suppliers of their suppliers and so on), with a view to reducing overall costs and lead times.

There are a number of different ways in which such activities can be characterised. The most common distinction is the one already made between b2b and b2c transactions. The consensus of research appears to be that b2b is potentially a much larger field, and the usual proportions of activity are cited as around 8:1 or 9:1 (b2b: b2c) (see Merrill Lynch, 2000; Wright & Dyer, 2001). Thus, around 80–90% of transactions are between businesses, in comparison with those between businesses and the final customer. This is not solely a reflection of the relative rates of actual uptake. In part, it reflects the logical point that the service or product used by a final customer will usually have worked its way through several members of a supply chain. Thus, for example, the packet of tomatoes delivered to the customer's home will have involved transactions along a supply chain incorporating the tomato grower, a packaging supplier, a label supplier, a paper supplier, and a sawmill. Several transactions precede the final one.

There have been other descriptions of the different approaches to e-business used by organisations. These sometimes place companies in one of a number of discrete categories, largely based on their (apparent) level of motivation and commitment to e-business. For example, distinctions are made between: the resistors or e-business phobics, a group that has done nothing; the reactors, the companies that have done a little, and what they have done has been under pressure from a major customer, sometimes called the "peekers"; the experimenters, the more proactive companies, sometimes termed the "pokers"; and the enthusiasts, the trailblazers who are leading the way, sometimes called the "plungers". (see e.g. Wright & Dyer, 2001; Hawkins & Prencipe, 2000).

A more operational perspective is offered by Wright & Dyer (2001). They distinguish four different models of e-business. The first they term "e-commerce", by which they mean b2c links, and this typically involves customers visiting the website of a company for information, to place orders and to pay for goods and services. The second comprises enterprise resource planning (ERP), and involves use of a company intranet to improve internal integration and coordination. The third they characterise as supply-chain management (i.e. b2b activities), through which companies may attempt to improve relationships with their suppliers, reduce inventories, increase the speed of meeting orders, and cut costs. The fourth they call "integrated e-business", in which all three of the above activities are utilised in an integrated manner.

A similar set of distinctions has been developed by CISCO, one of the leading developers and users of e-business systems and models, and used by UK Online for business (part of the UK Department of Trade and Industry). This includes the notion of an adoption ladder, implying a progressive development of e-business activities from exchanging information using e-mails, to transformed organisations involving new ways of working within and between organisations. In this model, greater business benefits accrue the further up the adoption ladder one progresses, as does the extent of organisational change and sophistication. The core model is summarised in Figure 13.1. Although presented as a progressive ladder, it is not assumed that all companies should proceed step by step, or that all business functions and activities in a company should necessarily be at the same level, or that "transformation" is the logical end-point for all companies. We have found these distinctions useful in our work and use them in the rest of this chapter.

UPTAKE AND RELATED ACTIVITIES

Sources of Information

In the sections that follow we draw heavily on three recent sets of studies, two conducted in the UK and one internationally. All were commissioned by the Department of Trade and Industry in the UK. The first set involved nine separate sector-based studies of e-business, and these were conducted in 1999–2000 in the following sectors: aerospace; automobiles; chemicals; electronics; gas downstream distribution; metal forming and manufacturing; oil and gas supplies; steel; and telecommunications. These studies were reviewed and summarised by Hawkins & Prencipe in 2000.

The second set of studies involved 14 separate sector-based investigations examining the uptake, impacts and various other aspects of e-business in the UK. The sectors were: bio-industry; book-selling; chemicals; clothing (including made-to-order clothing, fashion design and branded clothing, and knitwear); electrical retailing; exhibitions and conferences; heating, ventilation, air conditioning and refrigeration (HEVACR); management consultancy; marketing and communication; sports goods; supermarkets and convenience stores; upstream oil and gas; automotive logistics and afterparts; and automotive supply chain. These studies were undertaken in 2000–2001 and were reviewed and summarised by Clegg (2001).

The third set of studies involves an annual international benchmarking study of e-business. Here we focus on the results obtained in 2001. In this case, data were gathered from over 3000 companies in the UK and from 500 companies in France, Germany, Italy, Sweden, USA, Canada, Australia, Japan and Ireland (see Foley, 2001). Thus, the survey covered 10 countries and in each case samples were generated randomly and stratified by size and geographical region.

Uptake

We begin with the results from the 14 sector studies summarised by Clegg (2001). The main findings are summarised in Table 13.1.

Looking initially at the first seven rows in the table, we can see what percentage of companies in each sector place themselves at different points on a version of the UK Online for business adoption ladder. The main patterns are clear. In several sectors, a substantial

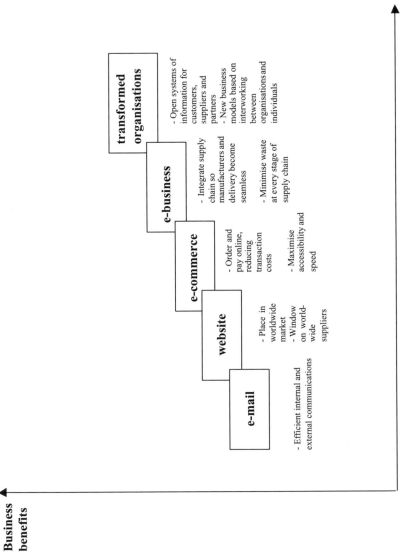

Figure 13.1 Model of e-adoption ladder. From UK Online for Business

Table 13.1 Rates of uptake of e-business and related issues

	Book selling	Clothing	Electrical retailing	Exhibitions and conferences	Management consultancy	Marketing and communication	Sports goods	Supermarkets and convenience stores	Bio-Industry	Chemicals	Heating, ventilation, air-conditioning, and refrigeration	Upstream oil and gas	Automotive logistics and afterparts	Automotive supply chain
0. No action	24%	20%	7%	0%	0%	0%	17%	27%	"Relatively immature"	23%	c.10%	3 Groups: 1. Small minority—no interest 2. Vast majority confused + reactive 3. Small minority—proactive traders	Extensive use of EDI. Some leading edge examples in new and aftermarket Limited use of online services	20% (?)
1. Messaging	27%	38%	34%	33%	28%	15%	26%	52%	"Few, if any, major Bio-industry-specific e-commerce Initiatives"	64%				53%
2. Online marketing	27%	31%	39%	42%	45%	54%	26%	14%						
3. Online ordering	5%	5%	4%	16%	24%	20%	19%	5%						27%
4. Online payment	15%	6%	16%	6%	3%	8%	10%	2%		c.10%	35%			
5. Order progress/online	2%	0%	0%	0%	0%	0%	0%	0%						
6. E-business	0%	0%	0%	3%	0%	3%	3%	0%		3%				B2C > B2B
Website	59%	53%	68%	75%	84%	83%	67%	30%	Most 100%	67%	87%	90%		87%
E-mail	80%	73%	89%	97%	100%	94%	79%	57%			90%	100%		
Strategy	20%	25% 31% 32%	18%	22%	32%	42%	31%	27%		43%				37%
Budget	10%	7% – 8%	11%	8%	21%	21%	12%	9%		46%				Majority have very small budgets
Formal	3%	25% 6%	15%	14%	16%	16%	3%	14%		39%				33%
Evaluation Informal	58%	9%	29%	42%	42%	33%	33%	22%		—	11/12			
Priority	6/7	7/8 8/8 -	3/7	4/7	3/7	3/7	3/7	6/7						

Source: Reproduced from Clegg (2001).

minority of companies have done nothing (i.e. can be placed at level 0). The scores range from 0% to 27%, with a median value of 17%. The majority of companies place themselves at level 1 (messaging) or level 2 (online marketing). At these levels the companies are exchanging information. The numbers vary, but around 53–75% fall in this range, with a median score of 66–69%. A further substantial minority of companies place themselves at level 3 (ordering online) or level 4 (paying online)—scores here range from 7% to 35% with a median score of 22%. This reflects the approximate number of companies who are undertaking some transactions online. In most sectors (although not all), there is more evidence of online ordering than there is of online paying. Unfortunately, in this study, no data are available to indicate the relative amounts of electronic as opposed to traditional transactions. Thus, whilst we know that some companies are transacting online, we have no information on the relative value of these transactions in comparison with those undertaken in more traditional ways. We return to this issue later. Very few companies report themselves at level 5 (online progress/sales) or level 6 (full e-business).

Looking now at rows 8 and 9 in Table 13.1, the most common technologies in use are websites and external e-mail. Website use varies from 30% to 90%, with a median score of 68–75%. In nine of the 12 sectors where quantified data is available, the rates of use exceed 66%. The picture is similar for external e-mail usage, with scores ranging from 57% to 100% and a median score of 90%.

The picture is broadly the same across all 14 sectors in this study. For example, the bio-industry is described as "relatively immature", with "few, if any, sector-specific initiatives". The chemical industry reports an emphasis on communications and "brochureware" (i.e. online marketing). Upstream oil and gas are in the "very early stages" with the vast majority of companies "confused and reactive". The automotive supply chain sector reports "little evidence of overall vision".

To date, across these 14 sectors, e-business largely comprises messaging and online marketing. These are information, rather than transaction-based activities. A small but significant minority of companies are undertaking some transactions electronically, and we can take 20–25% of companies as a crude average. On the other hand, another significant minority (ca. 17%) have done nothing in this area. Very few companies have adopted what might be termed "full e-business".

Managerial Commitment?

Some other important data from these same sector studies are also presented in Table 13.1. Row 10 reports the percentage of companies claiming to have a formal plan or strategy for the development of e-business in their company. Scores range from 18% to 43%, with a median of 31%. The percentages of those having a budget for their activities in this area are presented in row 11. The figures here are lower, ranging from 7% to 46%, median score 10–11%. Row 12 presents the data on the percentages having formal and informal evaluations in place. The data for formal evaluations range from 3% to 39% of companies, with a median score of 14–15%. The figures for informal evaluations, as one might expect, are higher, with a median score of 33%. Some of the sectors report that the low scores for evaluation plans reflect the relative recency of the phenomenon. This is likely to be a factor. However, we should also recall that investments in new technologies and new ways of working are not often formally evaluated (and there are many organisational and political reasons for this; see Chapter 19, this volume, by Sabine Sonnentag, and also Clegg *et al.*, 1997). In that broader context, lack of evaluation is not unusual. Finally, in Table 13.1, row 13 reports the order of priority accorded to e-business in companies. Whilst the common finding is that e-business is largely the responsibility of senior managers, it typically scores half-way down their list of priorities or lower.

Of course, one could argue that having a strategy, a budget, a formal evaluation, senior management responsibility and e-business as a high priority, do not necessarily guarantee success in this area. But taken together, one could hypothesize that they would contribute to successful uptake. Certainly, having all these things in place would at least provide evidence that the topic is being taken seriously, and is commanding managerial attention and action. These activities could be interpreted as signs of managerial commitment—if so, it would seem there is still much to do, especially on the part of senior managers.

There do appear to be some differences across these 14 sectors, e.g. book-selling, supermarkets and convenience stores, as sectors, report higher than average incidences of "no activity" (i.e. level 0). The reports describe these sectors as lagging behind the rest of the UK. But more interesting, perhaps, is the finding that there appear to be larger differences within sectors as opposed to between them. This range of activity is mentioned in several of the studies. Nor is this simply a matter of company size, whereby the smaller companies are seen as laggards. Whilst this may be a factor in some sectors, it is also the case that some smaller companies (particularly in relatively high-technology areas) are relatively advanced users of e-business. Of course, it should also be acknowledged that there may well be niches within sectors where e-business uptake is simply not appropriate because of the nature of the market, product or service. In this view, an apparent lack of progress up any so-called adoption ladder is an appropriate managerial choice, rather than evidence of a failure of managerial vision.

Consistency

Thus far we have focused heavily on one set of studies commissioned by the DTI in the UK, in part because the data is recent, and also because it is relatively comprehensive. Whilst the findings are clear, we now consider whether or not these are consistent with other data in the UK, and indeed with international data. We look first at the earlier study of nine sectors in the UK, as summarised by Hawkins & Prencipe (2000). This work focused on b2b activities and concluded that:

> Most companies now have some form of internet access, but it is limited to the exchange of e-mails or the posting of "static" company websites (offering little interactive capability beyond e-mail links). The sector studies showed that, as yet, very few firms use the internet as a fully interactive e-commerce platform. At the moment, use of the internet is confined mostly to the provision of product information—online catalogues, etc.—and to general communications within and between firms. (Hawkins and Prencipe, 2000, p. 4).

Our interpretation is that the results of these two separate studies, covering 14 and 9 sectors, respectively, are broadly consistent. Turning now to the international benchmarking survey conducted in 2001, some of the key findings are summarised in Table 13.2 (see Foley, 2001).

Table 13.2 International uptake of e-business*

	UK	France	Germany	Italy	Sweden	Ireland	USA	Canada	Australia	Japan
Connectivity	87	64	86	74	87	75	84	82	73	67
Website	80	56	78	58	80	64	77	73	60	58
Trading online	24	10	23	11	18	21	20	24	25	9
SUPPLYING										
Allowing customers to order online	29	19	43	30	38	30	29	30	32	27
Of those that do, value cf. total	12	13	11	11	17	15	20	16	19	21
Allowing customers to pay online	16	8	17	8	12	19	15	15	20	6
Of those that do, value cf. total	14	21	25	18	30	16	11	13	29	28
PURCHASING										
Ordering online	33	20	30	18	25	29	54	46	28	17
Of those that do, value cf. total	23	24	27	30	29	25	26	26	28	34
Paying online	16	5	20	9	14	16	13	17	21	7
Of those that do, value cf. total	27	25	59	49	28	31	28	24	36	64

* Showing percentages in each country.
Source: From data in Foley (2001).

To deal first with the issue of consistency between the sector-based studies described above and the results from the benchmarking survey, the results are encouraging. Thus, looking at column 1 (rows 2 and 3) in Table 13.2, we can see that 80% of UK companies have a website (rising from 66% in 2000) and 24% are transacting. The nearest equivalent data (i.e. the median scores) from the 14 sector studies were 68–75% and 22%, respectively. Our interpretation is that the findings from the sector-based studies are broadly consistent with other data, and that there are no reasons to believe they are systematically unreliable in any particular way. If there were to be biases in the data, our prediction would be that these are likely to be in the direction of over-estimates. Thus, there is some evidence from other studies (see Holman et al., 2000) that senior managers are more likely to be positive in their evaluations of new technologies and techniques than are researchers and consultants. Furthermore, such surveys may be more likely to attract higher response rates from people who are interested and enthusiastic about e-business than from people who are more neutral or indeed sceptical.

International Comparisons

We now turn to the comparative aspects of the data in Table 13.2. Rather than dwell on individual findings, we focus on the overall patterns in the data. The first obvious pattern is that there is no evidence, in these data, that the USA outstrips the rest of the world on these issues. They score highest on only one issue (i.e. 54% ordering on line). This is somewhat surprising, for example in comparison with the study by Merrill Lynch (2000), which claimed that the USA were substantially ahead of European countries. Indeed, from these data, there is no single overall world leader.

Second, the UK scores relatively highly for connectivity and websites (equal first with Sweden in both cases), but is mid-range on most indicators regarding transactions. Third, as argued above, it is apparent that the data on the adoption of e-transactions in the UK is consistent with that reported in the sector-based studies. But this survey also presents new data. Thus, whilst in the UK approximately 20–25% of companies are transacting electronically, there is data here on the relative value of such transactions. The relative values of e-transactions, where they are undertaken, range from 12% to 27% of the total value of transactions. Thus, for example, for those companies that purchase goods online, the relative value of their electronic orders is 23% of their total value of orders (see column 1, row 9). Very crudely, if we assume that around 20% of companies are transacting electronically, and that the relative value of such transactions is around 20%, then this would mean, very approximately, that 4% (i.e. 20% of 20%) of the total value of orders and payments in UK companies is transacted electronically. Of course, this does involve making a number of assumptions, not least that the values of transactions for users and non-users are broadly similar. It is probably safest to assume that this represents an overestimate of current practice.

Fourth, if we draw a distinction between the number of companies undertaking electronic transactions (and call this the *breadth* of transactions), and the relative value of those transactions (and call this the *depth* of transactions), we can draw a number of interesting conclusions. Thus, we can see that the UK scores upper mid-range on breadth, but lower mid-range on depth of transactions. For its part, Australia scores high on breadth, whilst Japan scores high on depth. For example, only 7% of Japanese companies pay online, but for those that do, this represents 64% of the value of their payments. Why this should be the case is not clear from these data, but is certainly worthy of further research.

BARRIERS TO, AND ENABLERS OF, CHANGE

Main Findings

The review by Clegg (2001) of the 14 UK sector studies will also be used as the main vehicle for addressing these issues. This reveals a consistent set of findings. The reliability and generalisability of the findings will be considered at the end of this section. First, it is clear that the main barriers and enablers are seen as internal to companies, as opposed to external. This may be regarded as encouraging if we also assume that these factors are more likely to be perceived as within the control of individual companies. Second, almost universally across the sectors, attention is drawn to the critical role of three interrelated factors: senior management understanding of e-business; their attitudes towards it; and vision within the companies.

In eight of the 14 studies these are amongst the most significant enablers. They also figure largely in the other studies, but here they are usually interpreted as barriers. Thus, the bio-industry report refers to a large number of barriers, almost all of which are the result of a "distinct lack of understanding". The heating, ventilation, air conditioning and refrigeration report points to lack of knowledge and understanding, whilst the upstream oil and gas report describes "no clear understanding at board level". The automotive logistics and afterparts sector reports a lack of conviction of benefits, and the automotive supply chain report describes a lack of expertise and understanding. Across all these sector studies, these are consistently seen as the most important success factors. Where they are present and positive, they are seen as enablers; where they are absent or deficient in some way, they are seen as barriers.

Of course, these are not the only factors. The other most common internal barriers to emerge are concerned with: the costs of investment (including disruption to normal working); the lack of e-business skills within companies; and the lack of availability of in-house technologies. The main external barriers are concerned with the availability of skills in the market place and system compatibility.

Telecommunications and Security

Some of the sector studies included consideration of the role of other issues, and these are especially interesting because some of these are often cited as critical success factors. These are concerned with: telecommunications (cost, reliability, flexibility and range of services); security and legal issues (transaction security, authentication, legal issues and intellectual property issues); and the role of government (tax regime, R&D, promotion, online services and education/training). The data from eight sectors are presented in Table 13.3, and these represent the average scores across the sectors on each of the 13 issues identified. Company respondents were asked to rate the extent to which each factor had hindered, had encouraged or had had no effect on their company's uptake of e-business over the previous 2 years.

These data are interesting. First, it is apparent that the "no effect" scores are highest in all cases. Second, in most instances, the "encourage" and "hinder" scores are similar. Third, the

Table 13.3 External barriers and enablers of e-business

		Hindered (a little or a lot) (%)	Encouraged (a little or a lot) (%)	No effect (%)
Telecoms	Cost	27	21	53
	Reliability	19	24	57
	Flexibility	19	25	55
	Range of services	16	26	58
Security/legal	Transaction security	22	16	62
	Authentication	16	15	69
	Legal issues	17	11	72
	IPR	16	11	74
Government	Tax regime	14	13	74
	R&D	15	15	69
	Government promotion	9	18	73
	Online services	13	14	74
	Education/training	11	14	75

Source: Reproduced from Clegg (2001).

cost of telecommunications, a factor often cited as a major barrier, figures less prominently than one might have anticipated—on average only 27% counted this as a barrier. And finally, a similar picture emerges for transaction security, another oft-cited barrier. We conclude that these factors generally, and the cost of telecommunications and the security of transactions in particular, are not seen as the key factors impacting upon uptake and use, at least at the present time.

Of course, we must acknowledge that such a pattern is not necessarily fixed. One could reasonably argue that senior management understanding, commitment and leadership are the main factors in these relatively early stages of adoption. But once companies develop their understanding and strategies, and focus more on implementations higher up the adoption ladder, then other factors may begin to play a more important role. In this view, some of these factors may be seen as issues waiting to happen. This, however, is speculative.

Consistency

We now turn to consider whether or not these findings are consistent with those from other studies. Again we draw on two main sources of data, the earlier sector-based summary by Hawkins & Prencipe (2000) and the international benchmarking survey (Foley, 2001).

The study by Hawkins & Prencipe (2000) lists several important barriers, but unfortunately these are not ordered in any way. They identify: organisational inertia; knowledge and skill gaps; costs; uncertainties about the needs of clients and the market; technical asymmetries; the nature of the market; regulatory and legal frameworks; and technical problems and standards. However, they do conclude that:

> On the balance of evidence in the reports, technical problems appear not to be major inhibitors of e-commerce adoption in most sectors (Hawkins & Prencipe, 2000, p. 9).

For its part, the international benchmarking study (Foley, 2001) found that the three main barriers were concerns about confidentiality, risk of fraud, and there not being enough customers online. These were the biggest three barriers for the UK sample and for the international sample as a whole, and this was true whether surveying users or non-users. The costs of technology and lack of skills, and the lack of time to understand the issues all scored lower in this regard. At first sight these findings are not as clean and consistent as one might hope. The two UK sector-based studies are not inconsistent, but it is impossible to assess the relative importance of the various factors, whereas the data from the international study do indicate a different emphasis, one not confirmed in the latest UK sector-based study. It may be that part of this arises because the international benchmarking study did not include senior management understanding and leadership as part of its investigation, although this remains a speculative explanation.

ANTICIPATED EFFECTS

Main Findings

The findings described thus far are relatively clear. They are based on empirical studies, and whilst we may debate their reliability and generalisability, at least there is some grounded empirical data to discuss. In this section we are more concerned with the impacts and effects of e-business. Given that most companies are in the early stages of adoption, most of the work here is predictive. Inevitably we draw on a range of literature that is largely speculative and must be interpreted in that regard. Nevertheless, a relatively consistent pattern of findings emerges and appears to cohere around some key points.

We begin by summarising the impacts reported in the 14 sector studies described above (see Clegg, 2001). To date the impacts have been broadly positive but rather low-key. Given the nature of the uptake, this is largely unsurprising. Where impacts have been observed, these have been in the areas of improved relationships and improved communications. This reflects the focus on information exchange as opposed to transaction-based activity. In the detailed case studies that were included in these sector studies, more significant outcomes were observed, as we would expect of more fundamental changes higher up the adoption ladder. For example, case studies undertaken in Renault (automotive logistics), Fisher Scientific (chemicals), Tibard (clothing) and anonymous companies (in the automotive supply chain) reveal significant reductions in stock levels, savings in administration costs, improved customer relations, increased sales turnover, reduced new product development time, and improved communications. Regarding the future, several predictions are made. In general, e-business activity is set to increase—it is seen as having a role of increasing importance and potential. The dominant view is that the future will see an increase in rivalry between existing competitors, along with some transformation at industry level. Thus, companies will be able to enter new markets and sectors, competing outside their traditional domains of expertise.

Future Scenarios

Looking more widely at the future of e-business, it seems useful to try to set this in a broader context regarding the future of work. Most of the writers and experts in this area believe that e-business has the capability to alter radically how we organise and conduct our work (see e.g. Andersen Consulting and Investors in People UK, 1998; KPMG, 1998; Coyle, 1999; Leadbetter, 1999; Cairncross, 2000; Economist Intelligence Unit, 2000). Some go as far as to argue that the e-business model will be the dominant way of working, and that failure to adopt such practices will result in company failure and bankruptcy. For example, Bloor (2000) argues, "You need to act and you need to act today, if not sooner. Your ship is on a collision course with an iceberg" (p. ix). The Electronic Commerce Task Force (2000), a group reporting to the Foresight Directorate in the UK, argues that e-business represents a paradigm shift on how we work, that the old business models are no longer appropriate, and that those who do not embrace the new ways will go bankrupt. Even those with less strident views argue that the potential is massive, and that we are collectively at the beginning of an interesting learning curve. Beyond that, however, opinions differ on the extent to which this capability will be realised, and over the extent to which e-business will, in practice, become the dominant business paradigm. This is as one might expect and mirrors existing debates on the changing nature of work. We can summarise aspects of this debate by drawing a distinction between two alternative scenarios (see also Holman, Clegg & Waterson, 2002).

In one view, we now have the opportunity to be much more flexible in our working arrangements, and we have the technological capability to overcome some of the previous constraints of time and place. We can work remotely (from home, hotels, whilst travelling, etc.), and we can organise work in dispersed teams. We can shift work around the globe, to speed up the process, to utilise skills and expertise in other locations, and to reduce costs (Andersen Consulting and Investors in People UK, 1998; Franklin, 1997). We can develop new relationships and new ways of working with partners, with members of our supply chain and with our customers. In this view, b2b and b2c, along with other new technology-enabled ways of working, are set to help revolutionise how companies and supply chains work, and how companies and their customers interact (IRS, 2000; KPMG, 1998; Merrill Lynch, 2000; Price Waterhouse Coopers, 1999). Underlying this scenario is the notion of flexibility, that we have the opportunity to be more flexible regarding time, place and relationship (Cairncross, 1998). In this scenario, the pattern of working is set to change. The underlying stability whereby most of us travel to the office or factory to undertake the same sort of job for the same employer for several years, and bound by the same set of underlying internal and external relationships, is changing. Furthermore, the mix of work is also changing, away from traditional blue collar manufacturing type work towards a more service and knowledge-based economy (Leadbetter, 1999). Within companies, these changes may well be driven by a largely managerial agenda that we collectively need to work "cheaper, faster, better and smarter", but underlying this rhetoric is a shift towards globalisation and global competition, enabled in part by the new information and communications technologies.

A second scenario exists, one that is much more cautious. In this, the rate and scope of change are much less dramatic—yes, there are changes afoot, but the picture is one of underlying stability and relatively slow rates of change (Trades Union Congress, 2000). The majority of employees continue to travel to a fixed place of work, where they work for around 35–40 hours a week in full-time, permanent jobs. The introduction of home-working, tele-working, flexible contracts, teamworking, new technology and e-business, to name but a selection of new initiatives, is less common and less radical than one might expect (Clegg *et al.*, 2002; Waterson *et al.*, 1999). Furthermore, much of the evidence appears to show that these innovations, when they are introduced, are usually less effective than their proponents would wish (Clegg *et al.*, 1997, 2002; Gibbs, 1997; Holman *et al.*, 2000). Their impact is less than their advocates would have us believe because they are less common, and less effective than is often widely appreciated. To the sceptics in this camp, changes are taking place, but the appropriate mindset is one of evolution, in part because of the systemic complexities involved. We have heard talk of revolutionary changes in the nature of work before—but, whatever happened to "light-less factories" and "paper-less offices"?

We have dwelt on this issue because various shades of opinion can be found in the emerging literature about e-business. Ultimately, of course, these are empirical questions and time will tell! Thus far, however, some scepticism and caution may be appropriate. We return to this issue later when discussing performance issues. Relating the above specifically to e-business, some are anxious to demystify this whole topic, arguing that, whilst it represents a departure from traditional ways of working, it is not a revolution, at least in part because the same "old" business rules apply. Thus, companies still need to develop and deliver products and services that meet the needs of their customers. They still need to manage their resources carefully, to invest in the future, to take regard of cash flow and liquidity, etc. In this perspective, e-business is just a tool, a further route to market that needs to be understood, developed and capitalised upon.

What is Different about e-business?

The debate above leads us to this question, raised by Wright & Dyer (2001) in their report on e-business. They recognise that many of the issues raised by e-business are not new, and these would include, for example, the themes of senior management leadership, vision, understanding and commitment, as already discussed in this chapter.

So, what is different? Wright & Dyer (2001) identify two factors. The first is concerned with the speed at which events happen, and at which organisations need to respond. A major aim for companies attempting to develop their e-business capability is often to reduce lead times and to take slack out of the process of fulfilling orders and providing services. Electronic messaging and transacting enable people to work in real time, and this can be problematic. Organisations need to be geared up to work in this way, and this is not simply a technological capability. The second factor identified by Wright & Dyer (2001) is concerned with uncertainty. In part this arises from the speed at which things happen, but it is also created because no-one fully understands what are the appropriate business models for the new ways of working.

Wright & Dyer (2001) argue that e-business represents a shift because it increases speed and uncertainty. Together these require that organisations become more agile, and this will lead to the need for new organisational forms (e.g. more adaptable business processes), new organisational capabilities (e.g. to create and capitalise upon opportunities in the market place), and new employee competencies (e.g. to be proactive).

Systemic Thinking

Many commentators and experts have begun to comment on the systemic nature of e-business, and this perspective appears to exist independently of whether or not they view e-business as revolutionary or evolutionary. Some examples illustrate the point. Merrill Lynch (2000) argues that economic benefits from new technology only arise when combined with organisational changes. Bray (2000) argues for the harmonisation of technology and business practices, opining that "business practices may need as much attention as technology" (p. 13). For her part, Cairncross (2000) points to the need to make a host of human and organisational changes in a coordinated fashion, and this includes the need for intelligent and empowered employees. In part, this follows logically from the recognition that timescales are speeded up and uncertainty is higher—in such circumstances, empowering employees to take responsibility for local decision-making is a better model for work organisation than is the more traditional command and control option (see also Wall, Cordery & Clegg, 2002). Several reflect on the need for a re-alignment of technology, business processes and supply-chain relationships (Richmond et al., 1998; Price Waterhouse Coopers, 1999; Timmers, 1999). In similar vein, Clegg, Icasati-Johanson & Bennett, (2001) have argued that effective e-business working will require the successful adoption of what they term "some core building blocks". Thus, e-business will require the adoption of new information and communications technologies, the careful management of integrated supply chains, the adoption of new business processes that cut through organisations in the chain, and the empowerment of employees to react rapidly to changes in real time.

We return to this argument later in the chapter. It is interesting however, that the systemic issues raised by the experts did not feature significantly in the studies of uptake and barriers/enablers described earlier. There is no evidence, at least that we have seen, that the user and provider communities of e-business hold this systemic orientation. It could be that these are issues that will become more relevant as more organisations invest in more advanced forms of e-business.

The Role of the Human Resources Function

Wright & Dyer (2001) also propose that the function of human resources (HR) will change, in terms of its focus, roles and delivery. The core argument is that:

> HR professionals have to view themselves as providing solutions to business problems in real time. They must have the competence and confidence to provide expertise in these solutions that focus on delivering satisfactory, rather than optimal improvement in the short term, with the goal of delivering optimal solutions over the long term through an iterative experimental process (Wright & Dyer, 2001, p. 69).

HR professionals will be strategic partners in the business, whilst also working as change agents. Furthermore, there will be major changes in the focus of attention and delivery, in part enabled by e-working. In particular, three predictions are made (Wright & Dyer, 2001). First, there will be less attention within HR on core transactional tasks (e.g. benefits administration), and indeed these activities will be increasingly outsourced. Second, many of the traditional HR activities (such as recruitment, selection, training) will be delivered electronically. And finally, the more transformational activities (such as knowledge management, strategic redirection, cultural change, and management development) will become increasingly important. In this view, technology and e-working can free HR professionals from transactional activities to focus on more strategic concerns.

However, another less optimistic scenario may also develop. It may well be that transactional tasks are outsourced, and that traditional HR-type activities are conducted electronically. One real danger is that these traditional activities become seen as IT-based, bureaucratic functions, with relatively low levels of input from, and ownership by, HR experts (see also Kearney, 2002). In addition, it could be that the transformational activities are not owned by the HR function. We are in no doubt that there should be a role for HR in these areas, but this may not be a view shared by other professions and power groups in organisations. In this view, e-working will not necessarily free the HR function from low-level activities and empower them in a more strategic role. Rather, e-working may allow outsourcing of basic transactional tasks, the deskilling of traditional HR functions and their transfer to other functions, and the dislocation of HR from the core strategic domains.

A third scenario can also be developed, and this involves little change. In this view, e-working will happen slowly and in an evolutionary way. For the vast majority of companies, it will be several years before changes of this scope begin to have direct impact on the HR function. In part, this is because there are other parts of the company where e-working investments have the capability to have more fundamental impacts on relationships with customers and suppliers, and thereby more direct influence on sales and profitability.

We ourselves are not especially sanguine on this topic. In one sense, e-working provides another arena within which the role of the HR function must be played out. The widespread failure of the HR function to become actively involved in new technologies and new working arrangements thus far, as it seems to us, does not bode especially well for its future.

PERFORMANCE ISSUES

Building Blocks

Given the earlier findings on levels of adoption, it is too early to make realistic assessments of the impact of e-business activity on overall company performance. Our focus here is different, and involves offering ideas about the extent to which e-business ventures will meet their objectives, and identifying what may be the preconditions for success.

E-business involves a number of key activities, critical to its overall success. Thus, e-business requires the adoption and use of some new information and communications technologies, most obviously involving the internet and world wide web; e-business working also involves the development of new relationships and ways of working through the supply chain and with customers. This requires the adoption of core business process thinking that will cut across organisations, allowing the unit of analysis to be the chain or the network, rather than the single organisation. And finally, as we have argued above, it seems likely that the employees working in these new systems will need to be empowered such that they can react and respond to changing circumstances in real time. Old-fashioned "command and control"-style bureaucracies seem an unlikely organisational model for e-business working.

Our claim, then, is that these may be regarded as the core building blocks of e-business working—if companies fail to get these working well, then their chances of effective e-working become more remote. Whilst such a proposition is novel in this precise form, the underlying logic is one shared by a number of others. Our interpretation, then, is that e-business requires the successful management of at least four critical building blocks, as identified above. Unfortunately, our track record in the UK in these areas is not good (for a fuller development of this argument, see Clegg, Icasati-Johanson & Bennett, 2001). Table 13.4 provides a summary of some results from an international survey of the use and effectiveness of management practices, including the four that are the focus of this argument (i.e. information and communications technologies, supply-chain partnering, business process re-engineering and empowerment). The table presents the rates of use of these four practices within random stratified samples of manufacturing companies within the UK, Australia, Japan and Switzerland, and also their overall rates of effectiveness (see Clegg *et al.*, 2002).

We can see that rates of substantial uptake of the four practices are not as high as one might have expected, and are between one-quarter and one-third of companies in the UK for three of the four practices. Uptake for the practices is similar to Japan but lower than for Australia and Switzerland. A similar pattern emerges for rates of substantial success against three criteria (improving quality, increasing responsiveness to customers, and reducing costs). For the UK, the rates of substantial success vary between 35% and 55%. These scores are not high. On most of the effectiveness indices (for 10 out of 12), the UK scores are either bottom or second from bottom. This is consistent with the wider results in that international survey, from which Clegg *et al.* conclude:

> Companies in the UK have been using these practices for less time than the other three countries, use them less well, and report less effectiveness with them (Clegg *et al.*, 2002, p. 186).

Table 13.4 Use and effectiveness of selected modern working practices*

	UK	Japan	Australia	Switzerland
ICBT				
Use	34	40	39	61
Effectiveness				
Quality	41	52	49	49
Responsiveness	52	56	53	52
Cost	40	46	53	42
Empowerment				
Use	23	21	34	47
Effectiveness				
Quality	35	27	40	45
Responsiveness	47	24	54	59
Cost	35	31	30	34
SCP				
Use	44	44	47	55
Effectiveness				
Quality	43	49	50	53
Responsiveness	55	47	62	56
Cost	38	52	53	48
BPR				
Use	26	22	28	51
Effectiveness				
Quality	37	38	38	43
Responsiveness	48	35	45	60
Cost	53	58	54	48

*Showing percentages reporting "substantial" use and "substantial" effectiveness, in each country.
Source: From data in Clegg et al. (2002).

Furthermore, only around 2% of the UK sample had had substantial experience of all four of these practices at the same time. Our conclusion is that UK companies, as a whole, are not experienced in these areas, and are not especially effective at managing their introduction and use. If that is the case, what are the prospects of the successful introduction and adoption of e-business working? Overall, there are grounds for scepticism.

We take our argument one step further. We believe that the successful adoption of e-business will require systemic understanding and improvement. Furthermore, we believe this will get harder as e-business systems become more inter-organisational and international (i.e. as they become more complex), as companies come under pressure to reduce lead times (i.e. as they take out slack), and as new ways of working involve more complex interactions between people and technology. As such, these systems will get harder to understand and thereby to manage effectively.

Propositions and Predictions

For the sake of clarity, we summarise our propositions and predictions as follows (from Clegg, Icasati-Johanson & Bennett, 2001):

- *Proposition 1:* success at e-business working will require the effective management of new technology, supply chains, business processes and empowered employees.
- *Proposition 2:* there is little evidence that UK companies in general are strong in these areas.
- *Proposition 3:* effectiveness in these areas requires a systemic view.
- *Proposition 4:* companies find this way of thinking and managing difficult, even within their own organisational boundaries.
- *Prediction 1:* many companies will experience great difficulty in coordinating and managing these core building blocks of e-business effectively.
- *Prediction 2:* managing e-business will be more difficult than traditional management activities, as the systems become potentially more complex, more tightly coupled, and increasingly involve complex interrelations between people, organisations and technology.
- *Prediction 3:* based on the above, the majority of e-business ventures will fail to meet their objectives, at least in the short to medium term.

SUMMARY AND WAYS FORWARD

Main Findings

Our main findings can be summarised as follows:

- The majority of companies (around 66%) in the UK are in the early stages of e-business, using e-mail and online marketing facilities—primarily they are exchanging information.
- A significant minority of UK companies (around 20%) are transacting, with online ordering, in most cases, exceeding online payment.
- For those transacting online in the UK, the value of electronic trading relative to total trading is in the approximate range 12–27%. We can estimate that the value of e-transactions, as a percentage of total transactions in the UK, is of the order of 3–4%, although this is likely to be an overestimate.
- On the other hand, a significant minority of companies (around 17%) have done nothing in this area.
- The majority of companies in the UK do not have a formal e-business strategy, do not have a separate budget, are not evaluating their activities in this area, and do not see e-business as a high priority. We interpret these as indicators of a lack of practical managerial commitment to e-business.
- Looking at international comparisons, the UK scores relatively highly for connectivity and websites, i.e. for information exchange. It is in the upper mid-range on the breadth of transactions, but is in the lower mid-range on the depth of transactions.
- No single country can be seen as the world leader in e-business; e.g. Australia scores highly on the breadth of transactions, whilst Japan scores highest on depth of transactions.
- The major barriers to, and enablers of, e-business are seen as internal to the companies.
- The most important barriers and enablers are concerned with the understanding by, and leadership of, senior managers. This is consistent with the earlier finding that it is not yet apparent that e-business is commanding the serious attention and commitment of senior managers.

- Other important barriers include the cost of investing in e-business, the availability of skills, both in companies and in the market place, the availability of in-house technologies, and system compatibility.
- Some commonly cited barriers, in particular concerning transaction security and the costs of telecommunications, are not seen currently as significant in the UK.
- We can speculate, however, that the pattern of barriers and enablers may well change as more and more companies invest further in developing their e-business capabilities.
- The impacts of e-business working thus far have been relatively low-key and are primarily in the areas of improved communications and relationships—these are consistent with the early stages of uptake and the dominant focus on information rather than transaction-based activities.
- More fundamental impacts have been reported in some case studies undertaken in companies working higher up the adoption ladder. These include significant reductions in stock level, increased sales turnover, and reduced new product development time.
- Whilst most people seem to believe that e-business has vast potential, there are differences in perceptions of the extent to which this will be realised.
- At one extreme are those who believe that e-business, in tandem with other changes, will radically alter the landscape of work, allowing for much greater flexibility in time, place and relationships.
- At the other extreme are those who believe its impact will be more muted, preferring a model based on underlying continuity and stability.
- To some, e-business is simply another route to market, whilst others argue that it is qualitatively different, particularly in terms of speed and uncertainty. If the latter is true, this will require that organisations become more agile and this will have implications for organisational structures, capabilities and competencies.
- Many experts agree that e-business is a systemic change, involving new technologies, new supplier and customer relationships, new business processes and new ways of working.
- It is not clear, however, that this is necessarily fully appreciated by the user and provider communities.
- There is a debate on what will be the impact of e-working on the HR function. In one view, e-working will free up HR professionals from some of their transactional and traditional roles, and enable them to become involved in more strategic issues.
- Another view is that there is a real danger that e-working encourages the outsourcing of basic transactional tasks, the de-skilling and transfer of traditional HR roles, and the further dislocation of HR from strategic activities.
- A further view is that it may well be some time before these new ways of working begin to impact on HR, largely because there are other areas where investment is likely to be focused.
- We are not sanguine. We believe that e-working can be seen as providing a new arena within which the role of HR must be played out. The existing contribution of HR professionals to new technologies and new ways of working does not, in our view, bode well.
- There are some core building blocks which we believe must be managed well for e-business to work effectively—these involve information and communications technologies, business processes that cut through and across organisations, supply-chain and customer relationships, and new ways of working incorporating high levels of empowerment.

- Unfortunately our track record in the UK with the development, implementation and use of these new technologies and ways of working is not good—insofar as data are available, it seems that we use these practices less, and use them less effectively than some of our international competitors.
- This leads us to make a number of predictions regarding the future of e-business in the UK, and these are listed below.
- Many companies will experience great difficulty in coordinating and managing these core building blocks of e-business effectively.
- Managing e-business will be more difficult than traditional management activities, as the systems become potentially more complex, more tightly coupled, and increasingly involve complex interrelations between people, organisations and technology.
- The majority of e-business ventures will fail to meet their objectives, at least in the short to medium term.

Grounds for Scepticism?

It is clear that substantial changes are taking place in the development of e-business models and ways of working, both in the UK and elsewhere, and these should be acknowledged. A great deal is happening. Nevertheless, we ourselves are somewhat sceptical with regard to a number of issues, and it is worth trying to be clear over what these are. Thus, it is clear that the majority of companies in the UK are using the internet and world wide web to swap information. This is not trivial, but it does not, as yet, represent a fundamental transformation in working practices and relationships for most companies. Furthermore, there are doubts that senior managers in the UK fully understand the opportunities of e-business, are providing leadership and vision in this area, and are, through their actions, displaying their commitment to it. Whilst many commentators point to the systemic qualities of e-business working, this serves to highlight the difficulties of managing these changes, and at the same time, draws attention to the apparent lack of this appreciation by the user and provider communities. Our track record in the UK with managing change in these and related areas leads us to predict widespread failure of e-business initiatives. Furthermore, we believe that managing e-business working will get harder as systems become more complex, more tightly coupled, and increasingly involve more complex interactions. Thus, our scepticism surrounds the uptake, management, understanding and future performance of e-business.

Ways Forward

In considering the ways forward, we can distinguish a number of different perspectives. From a research and development view, we need to conduct some detailed case studies of companies and supply chains that are introducing relatively advanced forms of e-business. We need to understand what these levels and types of activity actually mean for companies, their employees, their partners and their customers. We need research on a number of inter-related topics, and here we identify five of particular importance. First, we need to understand what different e-business models may be appropriate for different situations (types of organisation, product/service and market). For example, under what circumstances is it appropriate to organise for short-term relationships (using auctions and changing suppliers on this basis), as opposed to developing and maintaining long-term trust-based relationships? Second, we need to research what are the main interdependencies between the various systemic components of e-business. How do they interact to enable successful (or otherwise) ways of working? Third, we need to examine the performance of e-business ways of working and try to understand the ways in which these can be improved. Fourth, we should attempt to understand better the dynamics of mixed modes of working. Thus, it seems likely that many organisations will be utilising a range of routes to market, adopting the new electronic-based ways, along with the more traditional modes. Providing redundancy in the modes of developing and fulfilling customer needs may well prove a way forward. And finally here, we need to develop research-based methods and tools that companies can use to develop, benchmark and evaluate their e-business models and systems.

From a national policy perspective, there are a number of important issues to address. These include the continuing need to benchmark and learn from what is happening nationally and internationally regarding the uptake of e-business, and what factors may be enabling and inhibiting progress. At present it is clear that the role of senior managers is critical, most especially regarding their understanding and leadership. Action needs to be taken in these areas. But we also need to understand what may be the critical success factors as more and more companies develop their experiences and evolve their way up their own versions of the adoption ladder. This implies much more detailed understanding of how fuller versions of e-business and organisational transformation actually operate and function in practice, and how these may coexist with more traditional ways of working. This includes the need to develop tools which reveal the dynamic effects of short time scales (Riddalls & Bennett, 2002) and which support coordination across companies involved in supply chains.

At company and supply-chain level, there is a need to develop local and specific understanding and expertise. Many companies would benefit from the availability of benchmarking tools, evaluation tools, good practice guidelines and some indicators of the skills and competencies needed to make progress in this area. But such developments are likely to be beyond the scope of all but the largest companies—this implies a role for national bodies involved in research, development, education and consultancy.

Our interpretation is that e-business has a future—it is unlikely that companies will be able to ignore the issues it raises, even if they wished. But it seems likely that developments will follow an evolutionary, rather than revolutionary, path.

REFERENCES

Andersen Consulting and Investors in People UK (1998). *Nil by Mouth? Management and Communication in the e-economy*. Joint report by Andersen Consulting and Investors in People UK, London.

Bloor, R. (2000). *The Electronic B@zaar: from the Silk Road to the E Road*. London: Nicholas Brealey.

Bray, P. (2000). Harmonise the technology and the process. *Sunday Times* (London), **3 December**, B2B Section, p. 13.

Cairncross, F. (1998). Communications and distance. *Royal Society of Arts Journal*, **2**(4), 53–59.

Cairncross, F. (2000). A survey of e-management. *The Economist* (London), **19 November**.

Clegg, C. W. (2001). *E-commerce Impacts: a Review of 14 Sector Studies*. A report to UK Online for business, December 2001.

Clegg, C. W., Icasati-Johanson, B. & Bennett, S. (2001). E-business: boom or gloom? *Behaviour and Information Technology*, **20**, 293–298.

Clegg, C. W., Axtell, C. M., Damodaran, L., Farbey, B., Hull, R., Lloyd-Jones, R., Nicholls, J., Sell, R. & Tomlinson, C. (1997). Information technology: a study of performance and the role of human and organizational factors. *Ergonomics*, **40**, 851–871.

Clegg, C. W., Wall, T. D., Pepper, K., Stride, C., Woods, D., Morrison, D., Cordery, J., Couchman, P., Badham, R., Kuenzler, C., Grote, G., Ide, W., Takahashi, M. & Kogi. K. (2002). An international study of the use and effectiveness of modern manufacturing practices. *Human Factors and Ergonomics in Manufacturing*? **12**(2), 171–191.

Coyle, D. (1999). A new model of thought is needed to understand the networked e-economy. *The Independent* (London), **14 December**, p. 17.

Dedman, R. D. (1998). *Business Processes for Electronic Commerce: Profiting from the New Value Chains. An FT Management Report*. FT Media & Telecoms: London.

Economist Intelligence Unit (2000). *E-business Transformation*. EIU: London.

Electronic Commerce Task Force (2000). *Smoke on the Water. A Fire in the Sky*. A report to the UK Foresight Directorate. London: Department of Trade and Industry.

Foley, P. (2001). *Annual International Benchmarking Survey on e-business*. London: Department of Trade and Industry.

Franklin, T. (1997). *Electronic Commerce: How Soon? How? How Much?* Norwalk: Business Communications Co. Inc.

Gibbs, W. W. (1997). Taking computers to task. *Scientific American*, **277** (July), 64–71.

Hawkins, R. & Prencipe, A. (2000). Business to business e-commerce in the UK: a synthesis of sector reports commissioned by the Department of Trade and Industry, London, December 2000.

Hendry, M. (1995). *Improving Retail Efficiency through EDI*. An FT Management Report. London: Pearson Professional.

Herman, G. (1996). *IT and the Future of Retail: Integrating New Technologies and Processes*. An FT Management Report. London: Financial Times Retail and Consumer Publishing.

Holman, D., Axtell, C., Clegg, C., Pepper, K., Waterson, P., Cantista, I. & Older-Gray, M. (2000). Change and innovation in modern manufacturing practices: an expert panel survey of UK companies. *Human Factors and Ergonomics in Manufacturing*, **10**, 121–137.

Holman, D., Clegg, C. W. & Waterson, P. (2002). Navigating the territory of job design. *Applied Ergonomics* (in press).

IRS (2000). *e-commerce*. London: Industrial Relations Services.

Kearney, V. (2002). Don't leave the HR out of E-HR. *People Management*, **7 February**, 25.

KPMG (1998). *Electronic Commerce*. Research Report. London: KPMG Management Consulting.

Leadbetter, C. (1999). *Living on Thin Air*. Harmondsworth: Penguin.

Merrill Lynch (2000). *Benchmarking the New Economy*. London: Merrill Lynch.

O'Connor, J. & Galvin, E. (1998). *Creating Value through e-commerce*. Management briefings: general management. London: Financial Times Management.

Ody, P. (1998). *Non-store Retailing: Exploiting Interactive Media and Electronic Commerce*. Financial Times Retail and Consumer. London: Pearson Professional.

Oxford Dictionary of Business (1996). Oxford: Oxford University Press.

Price Waterhouse Cooper (1999). *Guide to the Use of Information Technology in the Supply Chain: Making Technology Pay*. London: Price Waterhouse Cooper.

Richmond, C., Power, T. & O'Sullivan, D. (1998). *e-business in the Supply Chain: Creating Value in a Networked Marketplace*. London: IBM.

Riddalls, C. E. & Bennett, S. (2002). The stability of supply chains. *International Journal of Production Research*, **40**(2), 459–475.

Shaw, M., Blanning, Strader, T. & Whinston, A. (Eds) (2000). *Handbook on Electronic Commerce*. International Handbooks on Information Systems. Springer: New York.

Stewart, A. (1998). *The Business Impact of Network Computing. Cutting Costs—Myth or Reality?* An FT Management Report. London: Financial Times Media & Telecoms.

Thompson, I. (1997). *The Infrastructure of Electronic Commerce: Building the New Digital Marketplace*. An FT Market Briefing. London: Financial Times Media & Telecoms, Pearson Professional Ltd.

Timmers, P. (1999). *Electronic Commerce: Strategies and Models for Business-to-Business Trading*. Chichester: Wiley.

Trades Union Congress (2000). The future of work. A report by Ian Birnkley of the TUC. Available at http://www.tuc.org.uk/em_research/tuc-2397-fo.cfm.

Wall, T. D., Cordery, J. & Clegg, C. W. (2002). Empowerment, performance, and operational uncertainty. *Applied Psychology: An International Review*. **51**(1), 146–169.

Waterson, P. E., Clegg, C. W., Bolden, R., Pepper, K., Warr, P. B. & Wall, T. D. (1999). The use and effectiveness of modern manufacturing practices: a survey of UK industry. *International Journal of Production Research*, **37**, 2271–2292.

Wright, P. M. & Dyer, L. (2001). People in the e-business: new challenges, new solutions. Working paper. Ithaca, NY: Center for Advanced Human Resource Studies, Cornell University.

PART III
Organisational Performance and Productivity

CHAPTER 14

Organisational Performance and Manufacturing Practices

Stephen Wood
Institute of Work Psychology, University of Sheffield, UK

Total quality management, just-in-time, total preventive management and supply-chain partnership are all seen as modern manufacturing practices. They are often subsumed under umbrella concepts, such as Womack, Jones & Roos's (1990) lean production, Dean & Snell's (1991) integrated manufacturing, and Schonberger's (1986) world class manufacturing. Total quality management (TQM) may itself be one such umbrella concept (Cooney & Sohal, this book). Within social theory they have been viewed as a vital part of the post-Fordist model, "Toyotaism" in some people's terms (Wood, 1989). The contrast is often drawn between this new approach to management and the excessively rigid Fordist system, which was based on Taylorist principles of job design, with a narrow division of labour, highly functional management and low role demands for the mass of workers. Womack et al. (1990) encouraged the differentiation of lean production from mass production, while TQM has been portrayed by some as a major cultural force—an enterprise lifestyle (McCloskey & Collett, 1993)—which represents a radical change in the way organisations operate.

Portrayed in such terms, lean production and TQM became in the late 1980s panaceas for management and the ills of Western economies: the low productivity, poor quality and industrial conflict. Their extension to all fields of industry and commerce was urged. Womack et al. (1990, p. 277), indeed, proclaimed that lean production would become "the standard global production system of the twenty-first century", seemingly taking it for granted that their exhortations would be heeded. Having conceived the management methods of lean production literally as a machine, they effectively turned it into a juggernaut that would eliminate in one fell swoop many, if not all, of the production, organisational and personnel problems associated with post-war Western economies.

Prescriptive packages of practices tend to be all-embracing concepts that offer a fresh way of thinking, as well as urgently needed practices. In the case of lean production, the emphasis is on viewing the organisation in the context of its suppliers and customers and in terms of a flow of activities pulled by the customer. The aim is to eliminate all elements of this system that add no value to the customer. Lean production and other such approaches were part of a movement to elevate operational management within the overall concerns of management (Abernathy, Clark & Kantrow, 1984). Prior to this, the over-riding emphasis of corporate strategy, in theory and practice, was on the development of products and markets, with some consideration given to technology. As an antidote to this, lean production and TQM have often been presented as if they could (and should) become the business strategy of the organisation.

Nonetheless, they are perhaps more limited than their architects imply. First, within them certain practices are given prominence, e.g. just-in-time (JIT) in lean production, decentralisation of quality control in TQM. Second, the practices themselves are likely to be orientated towards specific objectives, e.g. JIT to reducing costs and customer responsiveness. Third, they have evolved as reactions to past omissions in operational management theory and the problems that arose in its application. Problems of inventory management and integration were ill-considered within the Fordist and Taylorist theories of mass production. In practice, Fordist mass production was plagued by certain nagging and recurring problems: poor quality, bottlenecks, rigidities, difficulties of balancing the work of operators, and the unreliability of suppliers. Lean production was a novel way of addressing the loose ends of Fordism in theory (Walker, 1989, p. 65) and in practice (Wood, 1993). Similarly, TQM emerged to overcome the quality problems that the functional approach to quality control had either created or failed to address.

Finally, there is a tendency for the proponents of the packaged programmes of manufacturing practices to concentrate on the technology to the neglect of human and social issues. This means they under-consider two things: (a) the vital role of employee involvement in their programmes, and (b) the problems of implementation. What are sometimes called the "soft" or "people-orientated" practices, such as teamworking or continuous improvement methods, are integral to the programmes but often presented in a sanitised way, on a par with a measurement instrument, when in fact they are the conduits through which the techniques are applied. Moreover, the problems of implementation run deeper than getting people to administer the techniques competently. They involve overcoming the existing forms of commitment, control and conflict that the past system(s) of management, and particularly their functional roots, have created. In the quest to present manufacturing practices as the means of achieving leanness, total quality or world class status, authors skate over whether they can fully resolve the tensions within organisations, between groups, and between job demands and employee satisfaction (see Delbridge, Chapter 2, this volume).

The fundamental question then raised by the portrayal of manufacturing practices as the saviour of Western economies is: how are they faring? This involves at least three issues: (a) to what extent are they diffusing?; (b) to what extent do the practices associated with lean production, TQM and high involvement coexist, or is there a mirroring of the theorists' over-emphasis on techniques of operational management to the neglect of the organisational and personnel practices?; (c) is their use leading to the superior performance prophesied? No one study has thus far addressed all these questions together. Indeed, the number of studies that includes operational and human resource practices is very small. My purpose in this chapter is to overview these studies in order to take stock of what we have by way of answers to the three questions.

The literature discussed is from two areas: production management and human resource management. In the former, primacy is given to the operational practices, JIT and TQM, and the human and organisational elements are conceived as infrastructrual supports for the successful adoption of these, while in the latter, the emphasis is placed on employee involvement and then the issues are: (a) the extent to which the operational management models have spurred and shaped their development; and (b) whether "employee involvement without TQM practices is less likely to affect performance positively and vice versa" (Lawler et al., 1995, p. 144). If successful, the combined use of modern manufacturing and involvement methods should result in employees being flexible, expansive in their perceptions and willing to contribute proactively to innovation. Their main effect on performance is thus through work restructuring, innovation and learning, not through employee commitment.

THE DIFFUSION OF MANUFACTURING PRACTICES

Bolden et al. (1997, p. 1114), at the Institute of Work Psychology (IWP), Sheffield, developed a list of 70 modern manufacturing practices based on the literature and experts' views. They range from the very specific (e.g. computer-aided design) to the abstract (e.g. company vision and organisational culture). The studies thus far have, though, concentrated on those most connected with lean production, integrated manufacturing and TQM, such as JIT, decentralised quality control and computer-integrated manufacturing.

Following directly from Bolden et al.'s (1997) conceptual work, the IWP team (Waterson et al., 1999) investigated the use of some of the key practices that they identified in this. The survey, conducted in 1996, was based on a sample of 564 UK manufacturing companies with more than 150 employees. It confirmed that most of the practices were "new", as most of them had been introduced recently. In over 75% of the companies that used business process re-engineering, TQM, team-based working, empowerment and a learning culture, the practice had been introduced in the 1990s, While in the case of all other practices—JIT production, integrated computer-based technology, supply-chain partnering, total productive maintenance, concurrent engineering, manufacturing cells—the figure was over 60%, with one exception, outsourcing, where only 39% of the users had introduced it in the 1990s.

In 2000, the IWP team conducted a follow-up study of 126 of those in the 1996 study. In this, only the seven most prevalent practices in 1996 were included—TQM, JIT production, integrated computer-based technology, supply-chain partnering and team-based working, empowerment and learning culture. The use of all seven had increased significantly but their relative use had not changed significantly. Learning culture and empowerment remained the least used[1]. The most significant increases were in the usage of integrated computer manufacturing and supply-chain partnerships. There was also no evidence that the practices inevitably wane over time.

A more limited study by Wood & Albanese (1995, p. 234) showed an increasing use of practices between 1986 and 1990 in a sample of 135 manufacturing plants in the UK. The percentage of plants where operators were responsible for their quality and inspection, a key TQM practice, had increased from 51% to 76% in that period, while those having flexible job descriptions had increased from 38% to 69%, working in teams from 41% to 62%, and participating in quality circles from 8% to 16%

For the USA we also have similar evidence. In Osterman's (1994) data set of 871 establishments with 50 or more employees in both manufacturing and services, there was information on the date of introduction for four key practices—teams, job rotation, cross-training and statistical process control. Analysis showed that their usage for the core occupational

---

[1] This is based on the author's own analysis of the 2000 data.

grouping in workplaces had increased considerably in the 10 years prior to the survey, which was conducted in 1992[2].

Lawler, Mohrman & Ledford (1998, p. 60), using samples ranging from 32% to 22% of the Fortune 1000 largest manufacturing and service companies, also reported a similar trend. The use of key modern manufacturing practices—self-inspection, statistical process control for front-line employees, JIT deliveries, cell-production, employee participation groups—increased both across the economy and within these firms in the 1990s. Quality circles, however, decreased slightly in this period.

THE COMBINED USAGE OF MANUFACTURING PRACTICES

If the operational and human resource practices form a system we would expect them to coexist and, perhaps more importantly, for this coexistence to reflect an underlying managerial orientation toward integrated manufacturing. Studies addressing this question are limited in number and scope, as they concentrate simply on the association between the usage of practices. Wood (1999) and his colleagues (de Menezes, Wood & Lasaosa, 2002) have, however, made the examination of whether any association between them reflects an underlying integrated approach to management a core concern. The research thus far has mainly concentrated on TQM, JIT and high-commitment practices, with some attention being given to computer-based manufacturing.

Osterman

Osterman (1994) attempted to gain a picture of the combined use of TQM and human resource practices by aggregating their usage. Four practices were measured: TQM, quality circles, teams and job rotation. Osterman examined all possible combinations of the four practices constituting his measure and found that 36% of the workplaces used none of these, while 14% used only teams and 7% used only job rotation. All the other subsets, including the use of all four practices, were each to be found in less than 5% of the establishments. From this, Osterman concluded that no single major dominant cluster of practices emerged from the data and, by implication, that the HR and TQM practices do not necessarily go together.

Lawler, Mohrman & Leford

Lawler, Mohrman & Ledford (1995) acquired information on both TQM and employee involvement practices in their 1993 company-level survey. TQM practices were grouped into two main categories: core- and production-oriented. Core practices included quality improvement teams, cross-functional planning and customer satisfaction monitoring; while production-orientated practices consisted of self-inspection, JIT deliveries and work or manufacturing cells. Information was collected for four types of employee involvement practices, grouped under the following headings: information-sharing, training and skills, reward systems, and power-sharing.

---

[2] This is based on the author's own analysis of Osterman's data.

Lawler et al. used simple pair-wise correlations to examine the relationship between the individual TQM measures and the four indices of employee involvement, as well as an overall index based on the average scores across the indices. The correlations on a high proportion of all pairs involving the information-sharing, skills, and power-sharing indices were all significantly above zero, but the rewards index was only (weakly) related to one of the TQM practices, self-inspection. The correlations on the three other indices ranged from 0.47 to 0.08. Lawler et al. (1995, p. 58), somewhat over-zealously, concluded that "most companies have both employee involvement and TQM initiatives" and that they "are most frequently coordinated or managed as one integrated program". The size of the correlations between the use of particular TQM practices and the employee involvement indices was not consistently high enough to suggest that the dominant pattern is a fully integrated TQM and employee involvement. Neither was the frequency of use of many of them: while most firms used at least some of the practices, the typical firm used most of the practices with only 1–20% of its employees. In the absence of multivariate analysis, it is not in fact possible to conclude that TQM and employee involvement practices tend to coexist or form a unified package. In a second survey in 1996, the correlations were again varied and not especially high (Lawler et al., 1998, p. 68).

Patterson, West & Wall

For the UK, Patterson et al. (2002), in another study at the Institute of Work Psychology, went beyond the focus on TQM or JIT by including computer-based manufacturing—a form of advanced manufacturing technology (AMT)—in their study. Following Dean & Snell (1991), they took these to be the core of integrated manufacturing. They investigated these three practices in relation to two dimensions of empowerment, job enrichment and skill enhancement.

Patterson et al. collected their data in a sample of 80 manufacturing firms in the UK, drawn mainly from metal goods, mechanical engineering and the plastics and rubber sectors. They were all single-site companies selected on this basis in order to get performance data from publicly available accounts which would tally with the best level for collecting data on practices, namely the workplace. Patterson et al. did not simply rely on the responses to structured questions of the managers or employees in the firms. They first collected data from interviews conducted on site that typically involved the chief executive, the production director, the finance director and the personnel director. Different respondents were used for different practices. Patterson and his colleagues then supplemented this with information from relevant company documents and their own observations of work practices. Given this "wide array of information" (Patterson et al., 2002, p. 14), the researchers scored the practices on the basis of their own ratings, using the information from all three sources.

None of the five measures—AMT, JIT, TQM, job enrichment and skill enhancement—were heavily correlated. Patterson et al. (2002, p. 20) concluded that this does not justify treating any of them as "composite constructs" i.e. as part and parcel of the same phenomenon. Nonetheless, subsequent multiple regression analysis of the association between the three manufacturing techniques and the two human resource practices revealed that TQM and JIT were significantly related to both job enrichment and skill enhancement, while AMT was related to skill enhancement but not enrichment. This adds support, within the limits of cross-sectional data, for the idea that production concepts drive the human resource practices, as well as that they enhance jobs, rather than de-skill them.

Sakakibara et al.

From the production management literature, Sakakibara *et al.* (1997) investigated in the USA a set of practices that they viewed as either constituting JIT manufacturing or its infrastructure. For JIT, six practices were identified: set-up time reduction, scheduling flexibility, maintenance, equipment layout, *kanban*, and JIT supplier relationships; while five types of infrastructure practices were identified: product design for manufacturability, workforce practices geared towards flexibility, organisation characteristics relating to the reallocation of decision rights, quality management and manufacturing strategy.

Forty-one plants were sampled (representing a 60% response rate) and within each of them 21 questionnaires were completed by a variety of managers and workers in three industries (transport components, electronics and machinery). The average of the scores for each sub-practice was taken as the plant usage of the practice. To create the overall super-scales, the average score over the sub-practices for each type of practice was calculated. So the JIT score was based on the above six practices. The reliability of each scale was over the conventional 0.60 level, which suggests that the various practices tend to coexist. In investigating their coexistence, Sakakibara *et al.* (1997) adopted a correlational analysis similar to that of Lawler *et al.* (1995). The JIT scale was significantly correlated with the infrastructure scales—product design, workforce management, organisational characteristics, quality management and manufacturing strategy. They were all at the 0.45–0.51 level, with the exception of workforce management, which was 0.61. The weakest correlations involved product design and quality management. The correlations between the infrastructure scales were however, generally higher, these ranging from 0.52 (product design and workforce management) to 0.85 (product design and manufacturing strategy). Sakakibara *et al.* (1997) concluded that this "implies that a plant that shows strengths in quality management and manufacturing strategy is very likely to have good practices in other areas".

Wood

In making the examination of the relationship between practices a core concern, Wood went beyond correlational analysis since, for him, this alone is not the defining criterion of a system. Rather, coexistence implies a need to investigate further and assess the nature of any underlying orientation that explains the associations between the practices. Addressing this amounts to an investigation of whether umbrella concepts like lean production and integrated manufacturing represent identifiable phenomenon. In the absence of confirmation of this, they remain simply part of the discourse of management thought, not of reality, and practices may simply be being used in an *ad hoc* way. The central research question Wood addresses is, then, whether the relations amongst a set of operational and human resource practices reflect one of three possibilities:

1. Differing degrees of usage of an integrated management system combining both types of practices.
2. The operational and human resource dimensions are separate and thus, for example, TQM or JIT and high-involvement management are pursued as distinct approaches.
3. Practices are adopted in an *ad hoc* way rather than as part of a systematic approach.

Having earlier concentrated on human resource practices (Wood & Albanese, 1995; Wood, 1996; Wood & de Menezes, 1998), Wood (1999) examined the link between these and manufacturing practices using Osterman's data. It appeared to Wood that, on the basis that there was a wide diversity of combinations of practices in use in his sample of firms, Osterman's conclusion that there was no dominant system was too hasty. This diversity does not necessarily mean that there was no underlying pattern to the data.

Wood examined the pattern of association that existed between the set of total quality and human resource practices in Osterman's data set to see if it reflected an integrated quality and human resource approach, using latent variable modelling, as developed by Bartholomew (1987) and others. This assesses whether any association between items (i.e. the use of practices in a workplace) can be explained by a common factor or factors. Factor analysis is the most well-known latent variable model, but in this case the practices were binary and thus Wood attempted to fit latent trait models, in which the latent variable is, as in factor analysis, continuous, but the manifest variables are binary or categorical. Wood used more than the four practices that Osterman used as, in addition to quality circles, teamworking and job rotation, there was data on cross-training, human relations skills as a selection criterion, internal recruitment, employment security policy and statistical process control. He also excluded TQM, as the question treated it as a generic concept, not a practice.

Initially, a two-factor model fitted the data best. One factor loaded on quality circles, statistical process control and teamworking, all practices associated with TQM, and the other loaded on the two practices associated with labour flexibility, job rotation and cross-training, and to a lesser extent teamworking. This suggested that the first measure was a quality dimension and the second a human resource one, and that the use of quality and human resource practices reflected distinct approaches. This was supported by the fact that the first was correlated with the reported use of TQM but the second was not.

An examination of the distribution of the workplaces in the sample on the two scales revealed, however, that the workplaces divided into clearly recognisable groupings, and that the two groups were separated by whether or not they had quality circles. Given that quality circles were an important source of differentiation between establishments, a further latent trait analysis was conducted without this item being included. This time a one-factor model fitted the data well and the average score on this one-factor latent scale was significantly higher for those establishments claiming to use TQM than it was for those not pursuing it. The results of this second stage of analysis suggested that the two-factor model in the first stage was a false resolution and was misleading. Wood thus concluded that the latent variable is measuring an integrated high-involvement quality management.

Wood's re-analysis of Osterman's data revealed a picture that is more complicated than the three possibilities that he conceived at the outset. There was no fragmentation between quality and human resource practices. But quality circles have been shown to be distinct from the other practices, which Wood suggested is likely to be a reflection of the ambiguity towards them within management circles. Overall, the results suggest that something akin to an integrated total quality high involvement is an identifiable phenomenon.

De Menezes, Wood & Lasaosa

Wood's work has been extended, with his colleagues de Menezes and Lasaosa (de Menezes et al., 2002), through an analysis of the UK Workplace Employee Relations Survey of 1998

(WERS98). The focus was on high-involvement management in the context of TQM. First, their definition of high involvement as a task-centred approach to participation reflected the lean production/TQM model. It involved:

1. The combined use of managerial practices for working flexibly and producing innovation.
2. An orientation on the part of employers to develop and harness the human capital of the organisation.

At its core were task-level practices, such as quality circles, job flexibility and team working. But it involved two types of support practices:

1. Individual supports, through which individuals are given training and information to engage successfully in such practices.
2. Organisational-level supports—practices such as minimal status differences and job security, which are directed at the recruitment and retention of people who are able to work in a high-involvement manner.

Second, there should be a relationship between high-involvement management (HIM) and modern operational management methods, and particularly TQM. Consequently, de Menezes *et al.* (2002) examined the pattern of relationships amongst core HIM practices, the two types of supports and TQM techniques.

The WERS98, which they used, consists of a sample of 2191 workplaces with 10 or more employees across the whole economy, representing a response rate of 80% of the targeted sample. From WERS98 de Menezes *et al.* developed four measures of the task HIM practices—team working, functional flexibility, quality circles and suggestion schemes; five individual supports—induction procedures, team briefing, information disclosure, appraisal, and training in human relations; and six organisational supports—survey feedback method, commitment as a major selection criterion, internal recruitment, single status between managers and non-managers, job security guarantees, and variable pay. They measured TQM by seven practices: self-inspection; quality monitored by records of faults and complaints; quality monitored through customer surveys; records on quality of product or service that are not confidential to management, quality targets set; training on quality control; and training in problem solving. In addition, they used a measure of the use of JIT procedures.

A number of the variables were dichotomous by nature (e.g. single status) or recorded as binary in WERS98 data. The others were based on questions that asked for the percentage of employees covered by the practice, and de Menezes *et al.* (2002) found that the distributions of these practices were either multi-modal or skewed, so the variables were redefined as binary. Again adopting latent variable modelling, de Menezes *et al.* fitted latent trait and latent class models to the data. Motivation as a selection criterion and JIT were not related to any great extent to the other practices and were excluded from their main analysis. Initial stages of a step-wise procedure produced models that did not fit well and the source of the problems was diagnosed to be all the organisational supports. These practices were consequently not crucial for an integrated high-involvement quality system that is grounded on an underlying managerial orientation, and therefore were excluded from the final analysis. Latent class models, which included different combinations of the high-involvement and total quality practices, fitted the data better than any latent trait model. This means that the orientation underlying their use was best measured in terms of three grades, i.e. on a discontinuous, not continuous, scale. The population was divided into three homogeneous groups, which were identified as low, medium and high, i.e. on a discontinuous, not continuous, scale.

However, four such models were identified which were equally valid statistically. One model simply contained all the high-involvement practices. The three others incorporated elements of TQM and thus supported a broader and integrated concept of high-involvement management. These varied in emphasis; one was very biased towards TQM, another gave more weight to information dissemination, and the third favoured a more integrated (involvement–quality) approach. Within these models, the common core practices were self-inspection and customer surveys, and their likelihood of usage clearly increased from the low through the medium to the high class. All four classifications correlated with a measure of the degree to which employee involvement was embedded in an organisation, based on the manager's self-report.

The existence of four observationally equivalent models is not a problem. But there is uncertainty about what underlies the findings. On the one hand, the diversity may be indicative of different managerial orientations, i.e. just as in academia, there may be no consistent perspective on the high involvement–TQM link, there are differences between managements across the economy. Some managements may see them as distinct, while those that see a connection may view this link in different ways. On the other hand, the diversity of models may simply reflect the sparseness of the data, for even with seemingly a large data set like WERS98 there was a large number of patterns of responses that are observed only once. While de Menezes *et al.* (2002) could not say which of the two possibilities explained the variety of models, they did suggest that there were signs that, with a larger data set, the integrated high-involvement–quality management (HIQM) model might very well outperform others. Their study certainly implies that high involvement management (HIM) and TQM are overlapping concepts. So, despite the indeterminacy in the results, this study points to the value of the TQM–HIM model and suggests that:

1. The task practices are being used in conjunction with quality practices and may well be part of TQM.
2. The core of high involvement in the UK are the task practices associated with TQM carrying with it the implication of an underlying management orientation centred on continuous improvement.

The evidence thus far on the nature of the relationships amongst modern manufacturing practices is limited. Correlations alone may be misleading. However, there is sufficient in the results, particularly in the results of the latent variable studies, to suggest that the usage of practices is not *ad hoc*. The extent to which they are combined under one truly integrating concept is unclear, but it would appear that if any one such concept underlies management's use of these practices, it extends across the operational and human resource boundaries.

MANUFACTURING PRACTICES AND PERFORMANCE

Most of the research linking manufacturing practices to performance has concentrated on assessing which, if any, of TQM, JIT, HIM or other human resource practices have the most effect. Each of these has typically been measured by a number of sub-practices. Researchers have also attempted to see whether any performance effects depend on other practices being used, or at least are enhanced when they are present, i.e. to test for any synergistic relations amongst practices. If this is the case, it is the interaction effect between practices, and not the practices themselves, that should explain most of the variation in performance. In this way, a system could be identified as the set of practices that has strong performance effects. Since any reactive effect between the practices will occur regardless of whether they tend in general to coexist, it is an alternative concept to that underlying the latent variable analysis of Wood and his colleagues. Their notion, that integrated management is ultimately an underlying orientation, implies that the practices form a coherent system that reflects management's use of them as a package, albeit to varying degrees, and does not imply synergistic effects between practices but rather, as we have seen, that this coexistence will be explained by a common factor. Moreover, it may well be that although the practices form an integrated set, their collective use may not result in superior performance to other packages that reflect other integrated approaches. It is thus necessary to differentiation between synergistic and orientation-type arguments. We shall review the literature, first presenting the research which has attempted to examine synergy, ordering this according to the extent to which it has found any, before concluding with the one study based on orientations.

Patterson, West & Wall

Patterson, West & Wall (2002), uniquely, used official accounting data to measure performance. Two indices were used, labour productivity and profit. Labour productivity was measured as the logarithm of the financial value of net sales per employee, divided by labour productivity for the sector, to make it relative to the sector. Profit (before tax) was measured as the financial value of sales less costs per employee. Both productivity and profit were measured for a period of 3 financial years prior to the collection on the data on practices and for the financial year in the year following this. Patterson *et al.* (2002) were able to assess the association between five practices—TQM, JIT, AMT, job enrichment and skill enhancement—and the level and rate of change of both productivity and profits.

Using multiple regression analysis, the study showed that of the three operational practices, only AMT was significantly related to productivity. It was not, however, related to profits, the implication being that the effect of AMT on productivity is countered by investment costs. But both job enrichment and skill enhancement were related to both. Close examination of this revealed that the effect on profits of these two human resource practices was accounted for by its effects on productivity. Similar results were found when the change in productivity and profit was considered. Analysis of the interaction between the practices revealed no significant or meaningful results. There was thus no evidence of any synergistic relationship between integrated manufacturing and empowerment practices.

Lawler, Mohrman & Ledford

Lawler *et al.* (1995, pp. 87–92) examined the issue of synergy at the company level, using their data from the Fortune 1000 largest manufacturing and service companies. They analysed the effects of employee involvement (EI) and TQM on measures of economic and financial performance. The measures were total productivity, sales per employee, return on sales, return on assets, return on investment, and total return to investors. They conducted multiple regression analysis of the effects of EI and TQM, controlling for industrial sector and capital. EI and TQM variables were most strongly related to return of equity and return on assets, while all of the other outcome measures were significantly, but weakly, related to their usage, with the exception of the total return on investment. The percentage of corporate performance variance that was accounted for by EI and TQM practices was, however, relatively small; nonetheless, because of the wide range of performance, small movements in these practices could have translated into a relatively large effect on performance. A one standard deviation increase in EI and TQM practices would, Lawler *et al.* (1995) estimated, mean an additional 30% of employees within a company being covered by them, and this would have had quite big effects on five of the six performance indicators.

For the 1996 data, Lawler *et al.* (1998, pp. 142–153) did not report the results of a regression analysis on the effects of the combined use of EI and TQM on financial performance, as they did in 1993. It was, however, shown to be the case that the high users of both EI and TQM did in fact perform better on return on sales, return on assets, return on investment, and return on equity. A regression analysis of EI usage on its own showed that it was related to sales per employee and return on assets, as it was in 1993. Additionally, it was related to return on investment. However, it was not, as was the case in 1993, related to return on sales and return on equity. TQM usage, when assesssed in isolation of EI, was related to return on sales, return on assets and return on equity, which was not the case for 1993. The strength of the overall conclusion of the studies, that financial performance was affected by the use of EI and TQM, was enhanced by time-lagged analysis which showed that the use of practices in 1993 was related to financial performance in 1996, although no information was given to show that financial performance in 1993 was unrelated to the use of practices in 1996. So overall, Lawler's research, within the limits of its methodology, offers some support for the argument that HIM and TQM both constitute what Lawler *et al.* want to see as the high-performance system.

MacDuffie

MacDuffie (1995) conducted a single-industry study based on the 62 final assembly plants in the major car-producing countries, using data from the MIT Future of the Auto Industry project, the birthplace of the lean production concept. His work was a major attempt within the programme to investigate the human resource or high-involvement (Pil & MacDuffie, 1996) side of lean production. He measured the extent to which the production regime was lean, or bufferless, by the percentage of total assembly area space dedicated to final assembly repair, the average number of vehicles in the work-in-process buffer between the paint and assembly areas (as a percentage of one shift's production), and the average level of inventory stocks for a sample of eight key parts (weighted by the cost of each part). MacDuffie differentiated two types of HR practices, which he labelled "innovative work system practices" and "innovative HRM practices/policies". He measured the former by practices that are often associated with TQM: the existence of work teams, problem-solving groups, job rotation, decentralisation of quality-related tasks and an effective system for employee suggestions. The HRM policies included such high-involvement practices as selection criteria geared towards openness to learning, interpersonal and teamworking skills, a contingent pay system, and minimum status differentials.

Through cluster analysis, he identified three discrete types of plants. At the extremes were lean plants or flexible production systems with few buffers and the characteristics of both innovative work systems and human resource systems, and traditional buffered plants, which made little use of innovative work or high-involvement practices, hired on the basis of a simple match to the job requirements and trained very little. Between these was an intermediate group, which used buffers and innovative human resource practices to an extent that was half-way between the two other systems, but its usage of innovative work systems was at a similar low level to the traditional "mass" plant.

MacDuffie assessed the relative performance of plants within the three clusters on productivity, measured by the number of hours taken to build a vehicle (adjusted to allow for factors such as size of vehicle, number of welds and absenteeism) and quality, measured by consumer reports of defects per vehicles, as collected by a market-research company. Lean production plants were superior on both performance criteria, while the intermediate plants also performed better than the traditional ones on both these measures, although their quality levels were far closer to the traditional than they were to the lean plants. All the three elements of the lean production system, the non-use of buffers, the work system and human resource management, were related to productivity, and moreover, there was a strong interactive effect between them. The results for quality were less strong. For while work system and human resource practices were related to quality, the low use of buffers was not, neither was there an interaction effect between work system and human resource practices. Nevertheless, there was an interaction effect between having low buffers and the work system practices, suggesting that JIT was only working when work organisation was based on TQM principles. The interaction between buffers and human resource practices was significant but negative, not as expected, the implication being that lean production was working best when not allied with high-involvement practices.

Taking the work system practices as indicative of TQM, the evidence on both performance criteria could be taken as support for the argument that there is a synergistic relationship between TQM and JIT. The added effect of human resource practices on productivity may add credence to MacDuffie's claim that the three practices should be treated as part of the same phenomenon. The evidence of the effects on quality, however, was not so clear-cut as it implies that human resource practices have the opposite effect to those expected or even intended by those introducing them. The factor analysis of the practices that MacDuffie reported also implies these can not be seen as an integrated set of practices on the basis of their joint usage. The limited number of plants with the bufferless system and high-commitment practices in the sample may have affected the results.

Flynn, Sakakibara & Schroder

Flynn, Sakakibara & Schroder (1995) evaluated the effects of JIT and TQM on what they called JIT performance and TQM performance. In their study, JIT practices were of four types: *kanban*; lot size reduction practices; JIT scheduling; and set-up time reduction practices. TQM practices are classified into three types: statistical process control (SPC); product design for quality; and customer focus practices. Infrastructure practices were practices which have typically been seen as "supporting both JIT and TQM" (Flynn *et al.*, 1995, p. 328). They pertained to five domains of manufacturing: information feedback, plant maintenance, management support, supplier relationships, and workforce management.

Flynn *et al.* (1995) started from the premise that TQM practices should be the prime determinant of TQM performance and JIT on JIT performance, but they also argued that TQM will affect JIT performance and JIT, TQM performance. For example, TQM can reduce manufacturing process variance, which will reduce the need for inventory and shorten cycle times, and these are the key measure of JIT performance. Similarly, JIT practices may be used to reduce lot sizes and this may impact on quality performance, since the potential rework and scrap resulting from process failure will affect batches of smaller sizes.

Flynn et al. (1995) tested two sets of related hypotheses, one for JIT performance and one for TQM performance. They ordered the sets hierarchically. Since common infrastructure practices lay the foundation for the use of the unique practices, they formed the first tier of both hierarchies: common infrastructure practices are positively related to TQM or JIT performance. The second rung was the practice that corresponds to the performance outcome, thus TQM for the TQM performance equation and JIT for the JIT performance one. Finally, the last step was the inclusion of the less proximal practice: JIT positively affects TQM performance and TQM is positively related to JIT performance.

Flynn et al. (1995) tested these hypotheses using data from a stratified sample of 75 manufacturing plants in the US electronics, transportation components and machinery industries. They acquired information on the practices from a range of selected informers in the plants—operatives and managers—using questionnaires. Information was acquired on a number of practices falling under the 12 dimensions that Flynn et al. (1995) identified, e.g. three in the case of customer focus, statistical process control and most JIT methods, and nine for workforce management. They omitted two infrastructure sets of practices (information feedback and work management) and one JIT practice (set-up time reduction practices) on the grounds that they were relatively highly correlated with other independent variables, which might not have been necessary on statistical grounds as the correlations were not above 0.60.

Reflecting the way that they had organised the hypotheses, Flynn et al. (1995) conducted hierarchical regression analysis on the data. The first stage of the analysis of JIT performance revealed that a significant part of the variance could be explained by the infrastructure practices, the second stage that JIT practices added significantly to this, but the third stage revealed that the TQM measures had no significant effect. The final equation showed that management support had by far the greatest effect, while lot size was weakly related. A third factor, supportive plant environment, was also significantly related to JIT performance but the relationship was negative, not positive as expected.

Tests for interaction effects between practices suggested that having a supportive plant environment did, however, enhance the effects of (a) statistical process control, (b) JIT scheduling, and (c) lot size reduction practices. In addition, having supportive management and a customer focus both also strengthened the effect of JIT scheduling. The interaction between supportive management and *kanban* was negative, suggesting that they were operating as substitutes.

The analysis of TQM performance revealed even stronger effects from infrastructure practices ($R^2 = 0.51$ for stage one). The additional R^2 for the next two stages was not, however, significant. In the final model only the infrastructure practices were significant, management support and supplier relationship both were more strongly related to TQM performance than the third practice, plant environment, which was positively, albeit weakly, related to it. The sign of JIT scheduling was in fact negatively related to quality. Interaction analysis revealed that supportive management enhanced the effect of JIT scheduling and that supplier relations, likewise, intensified the effect of product design and JIT scheduling.

The few significant interaction effects between the supports and TQM (and JIT) practices did not suggest that they have joint effects. The research in fact showed that infrastructural supports have important effects on performance in their own right. Managerial support was especially significant. JIT scheduling was especially important for both JIT and TQM performance but its effects were not realisable without the infrastructural supports. Overall,

TQM practices appear to have little effect on the basis of this study. But statistical process control will, in the context of a supportive plant environment, affect JIT performance, while product design, when coupled with supplier relations, has an effect on TQM.

Nonetheless, the conclusion that Flynn *et al.* (1995, p. 1354) draw from their study is "that there is a relationship between TQM and JIT practices and performance" and "that although TQM and JIT function effectively in isolation, their combination yields synergies that lead to further improvements". Given that no unconditional effects of either JIT or TQM were found, nor were any significant synergies between any two types of JIT or TQM practices, this is clearly wrong. Moreover, it appears that the infrastructural practices had an independent effect in isolation of the existence of JIT or TQM practices[3]. Since the managerial support measures were biased towards quality rather than JIT, it would appear from this study that it is having a philosophy geared to quality and not the practices *per se* which is crucial for quality and JIT.

Cua, McKone & Schroeder

Cua, McKone & Schroeder (2001) investigated the effects of three operational practices, TQM, JIT and total productive maintenance (TPM). In a similar vein to Flynn *et al.* (1995), they distinguished the key practices that are uniquely associated with each of these from those that are common to them, and which in their terms are "supporting" mechanisms (Cua *et al.* 2001, p. 680) that strengthen the impact of operational practices on performance.

In their study, unique TQM practices were cross-functional product design, process management, supplier quality management, and customer involvement; unique JIT practices were set-up time reduction, pull system production, JIT delivery by suppliers, equipment layout, and daily schedule adherence; and TPM practices were autonomous and planned maintenance, technology emphasis and proprietary equipment development. The common practices were, in Cua *et al.*'s (2001, p. 679) terms, human- and strategic-orientated practices, and were: committed leadership, strategic planning, cross-functional training, employee involvement and information and feedback. Data was gathered from a survey of 163 manufacturing plants in five countries (USA, Japan, Italy, Germany and the UK), which were randomly selected in each country from three industries, electronic, machinery and transportation parts suppliers. In each plant, 26 respondents completed a questionnaire (12 were direct labourers and 14 were managers) and multiple observations of a practice were averaged to form a score for each practice. The data on performance was collected from one source, the plant manager. He/she was asked to rate the plant's performance relative to its competitors on four dimensions: cost efficiency, quality of product conformance, on-time delivery and volume flexibility. In addition, a composite performance measure based on a

---

[3] Flynn *et al.* (1995, p. 1351) appear to have concluded that there is an effect of TQM on the grounds that the results reflect the ordering that the variables were inserted in the hierarchical regression analysis. So, while the inclusion of TQM practices in the TQM performance equation, for example, added little to the starting model that just included infrastructure supports, had these formed the first stage they may well have been significant. But this is insufficient to justify a TQM effect. While the R^2 associated with TQM practices may be greater if they were included first, any significant regression coefficients for TQM at this stage would not survive the inclusion of the other variables. Flynn *et al.* (1995, p. 1350) also argued that the low addition to the R^2 following the inclusion of the TQM set may have reflected the fact that there is an overlap between the unique TQM variables and the common infrastructure. The precise meaning of this in substantive terms was, however, unclear, especially as it was being gauged from an analysis of the practices' effects.

weighted sum of the four performance measures is developed, where the weights reflect the strategic importance that the plant places on the performance dimension.

Cua *et al.* (2001) first divided the plants into high and low performance and then conducted discriminant analysis to assess which practices discriminated between the two groups. First, they created four composite measures of all the four types of practices, TQM, JIT, TPM and common or support practices, and then investigated their relative importance in discriminating between the high and low performers. The discriminant loadings for all four composite measures were all high, 0.53–0.85, over all five performance indicators, and the overall model fit was good for all equations. JIT was most significant for cost efficiency, and TQM was more important for quality and volume flexibility and even for on-time delivery. TPM was the least significant for all measures, except for the weighted measure, where JIT was slightly less significant than it, the implication being that cost efficiency was weighted highly in the measure. The discriminant loadings for the common practices were either the top or very close to the top rated practices for all the performance measures.

Second, the authors conducted a similar analysis using the individual practices that made up the TQM, JIT, TPM and support practices. The results confirmed that at least one practice from each of these "sets" had an impact on all the performance measures. For TQM, all four were important for on-time delivery, all but customer involvement was important for quality and the overall performance measure, customer involvement was the only practice significant for volume flexibility, while it and supplier management were important for cost efficiency. For JIT practices, JIT delivery from suppliers was the only important item for all the performance measures, but set-up time reduction and pull production were also significant in the case of cost efficiency. Technology emphasis was the only TPM practice which was important for all performance measures, while planned maintenance was significant for cost efficiency and on-time delivery. In the case of the supports, committed leadership was a highly significant practice in all performance models. In the case of volume flexibility, it was the only such practice of any significance. For on-time delivery all the other supports were significant; for cost efficiency all but strategic planning were; for quality, only strategic planning and employer involvement were significant common practices. Finally, for weighted performance, only strategic planning was significant.

Overall the study suggests that high performance is dependent on the use of practices across the range of JIT, TQM and TPM, as well as social and strategic mechanisms. The authors concluded that these practices are mutually supporting. But this is straying too far from their analysis, since their methodology did not allow them to test for interaction effects between the common practices and hence to see whether the common practices were complementing the operational practices. In fact, the common practices appear to be playing a main role. Moreover, their second analysis implied that the main effects on performance were from the use of specific practices within each program, not all elements.

Wood, de Menezes & Lasaosa

Wood and his colleagues (de Menezes *et al.*, 2002) investigated whether the three different classes identified in their latent class model using WERS98 data are associated with different levels of performance. They considered three performance indicators: financial performance, labour productivity, and change in labour productivity. De Menezes *et al.* (2002) ran regression models in which there were two dummy variables indicating membership of particular latent classes, the minimal and partial high-involvement quality management, or high-involvement management (depending on the model). In each regression model de Menezes et al. (2002) controlled for all other types of practice that were not included in the specific latent class model being tested, e.g. in the model based on high-involvement practices only, all the organisational supports and a measure total quality management were included. Other control variables such as the size of the establishment were also included.

Membership of the high (third) class resulted in a significant increase in the change in labour productivity in the case of all four models. There were no significant effects on labour productivity. The results are consistent with the TQM/lean production theory, since it is centred on the importance of continuous improvement and thus the performance variable that is most significant to it is the rate of productivity change. This is itself not strongly linked to the other outcomes.

Finally, de Menezes et al. (2002) tested a key element of the theory of lean production, namely that it will reverse the tendency for there to be a trade-off between productivity and quality, that chasing high quality will result in low productivity (see Womack et al., 1990). Analysis of whether high-involvement–quality management produced this virtuous combination of high productivity and quality revealed that it did, as it had the greatest effect on the relationship between the level of both. The effect was more pronounced for the integrated model than for high involvement management alone (the model that excluded quality practices).

DISCUSSION AND CONCLUSIONS

There is little doubt that the studies reviewed here are addressing important issues for our understanding of the new workplace. But when taken together, they do not offer any conclusive evidence of the diffusion, nature and effects of modern manufacturing practices. The limited studies of the changing use present a consistent picture of increased use over the past decade, and they suggest that this is not largely, if at all, reflecting faddism. Whether it is sufficient to represent the institutionalisation of lean production, TQM and high-involvement management implied by Womack et al.'s (1990) forecast is impossible to tell on the basis of the studies to date.

The evidence on the integrated use of the practices that we have reviewed is uneven. It is first uneven in quality, reflecting different methods of analysis; and second, in results, as some of the correlational analysis points to a limited coexistence between practices, while some of it implies a stronger collective use. The most systematic studies of the inter-relationship between practices by Wood and his colleagues have yielded promising results. In the case of the US (Osterman) data, Wood's analysis suggests that TQM (albeit with a limited number of measures) and HR practices may reflect some underlying integrated orientation on the part of management. In the UK (WERS98) case, the results are less clear-cut but certainly suggest that TQM and HIM are not unrelated phenomena and may well be (or even more than likely are) inseparable. This study suggests though that JIT may not be so integrated across the whole economy or even within manufacturing.

The findings on the performance effects are even more mixed. First, we have the Patterson et al. (2002) study, showing that it is the high-involvement (empowerment) elements of integrated manufacturing that are affecting labour productivity. Second, the evidence of the Lawler *et al.* (1995, 1998) and MacDuffie (1995) studies imply—more strongly in the case of the latter—that the various types of practices have positive synergistic effects on performance. Third, we have the two studies by Cua *et al.* (2001) and Flynn *et al.* (1995), which conclude that similar synergistic effects have been found, when in fact either their statistical model does not test for this or the results do not support this conclusion. At best, Cua *et al.* show that that all three of TQM, JIT and HRM practices have effects. In the case of Flynn *et al.* (1995), consistent with Patterson *et al.*, it is the human resource elements that are important, and seemingly the managerial philosophy, not the use of specific practices, that has the most effect. Finally, de Menezes *et al.* (2002), in suggesting that the combined use of TQM and HIM may well reflect an underlying "holistic" orientation on the part of management, also put emphasis on management's approach rather than the practices *per se*, these being reflections of this.

Aside from the different results, the studies vary on a range of dimensions. First, they differ according to which practices they included. Second, they differ in the way that the practices were measured, some being measured continuously, others dichotomously. Third, some have relied on a single respondent for the measures of practices, others have used multiple respondents. Fourth, studies differ according to whether or not they attempted to assess the relationship between the practices before they measured their performance effects. Fifth, the unit of analysis differs between studies, and in particular whether they were conducted at the company or workplace/establishment level. Finally, the type of performance measures used in the studies varies, with some concentrating on manufacturing measures, others productivity or financial performance data. There is also a difference between the types of measurement of these indices, as most studies relied on the assessment of relative performance by a representative of the organisation, while only Patterson *et al.* (2002) used published company data.

Since the studies vary so markedly between each other, it is not possible to do any systematic comparison of them. Nonetheless, it is clear, even without this, that the marked differences between the results of the studies does not reflect in any systematic way the underlying concepts or designs of the studies.

A number of lessons can be drawn from this review. First, the minimum that we can take from it is that the study of operational and human resource practices are best not separated. Second, if we are to progress this area of study, it seems that we need a greater consistency of concepts and research design. At the same time we need to design studies which allow us clearly to test between alternative possible ways in which the practices may be used and having an effect. The two-stage strategy followed in some studies, and most strongly by de Menezes *et al.* (2002), seems vital. We need to: (a) investigate the association between practices to assess whether they are in fact used in concert and their use is indicative of an underlying management orientation, and if so what is the nature of this and, if their use is found to be systematic; then (b) measure whether the underlying orientation(s) can be correlated with performance, to see whether it is linked. Testing for synergy between practices is a separate activity. It clearly makes less sense if the practices form part of the same phenomenon.

Third, there are a number of limitations in all the studies, which will need to be addressed as research progresses. In many ways these mirror the limitations of the HRM–performance studies that Wood & Wall (2002, pp. 263–270) highlight. The main methodological one is that they are cross-sectional, although in the case of Patterson *et al.* (2002) they do link practices to future performance. All but Patterson *et al.* (2002) are based on performance data that relied on the judgements of managers, and in some cases of a single manager, and the samples have been small and in many cases not representative. Only the WERS98 study used weights to correct any bias. Yet, the uncertainty in the results of the WERS98 study provide a salutary lesson in relying on small samples. Even with what would seemingly appear to be a large sample, we are not able to decide conclusively in favour of the integrated high-involvement quality model.

Conceptual limitations in the studies include a lack of attention to: (a) the mechanisms that link the practices to performance; (b) the effectiveness or depth of the use of the practices; and (c) the contingent nature of any use on performance effects. Attending to these issues will inevitably take us to the nuances underlying the theoretical discussions surrounding manufacturing methods. Four seem especially important.

First is the possible existence of different managerial perspectives on the relationship between the various types of practices. Even if it is subsequently discovered that, for the UK, the integrated high-involvement–quality model does reflect the UK situation best, this still leaves open two possibilities: (a) that managers differ in their view of its links to JIT and other practices not included in the study, and (b) there are different perspectives between countries. Second, there is the possibility of different types of lean production, TQM or high-involvement systems, in theory and practice, e.g. Sitken, Sutcliffe & Schroeder (1994) distinguish between TQM systems that are focused on controlling processes and add little involvement and those orientated towards organisational learning. Or there is the distinction between team-based systems which rely on heavy supervision and those based on self-managed teams (Appelbaum & Batt, 1994; Wood, 1990, p. 181). Third, there is also the question of the link between manufacturing practices and job enrichment, so central to this book. The research (Dean & Snell, 1991; Wood, 1993) specifically on this supports an additional conclusion of de Menezes *et al.*'s (2002) study, that core high involvement practices are being used alongside non-enriched jobs and that re-design of the basic tasks of a job does not seem to be central to integrated manufacturing. It also found that there were no extra performance gains from enriching the jobs when using high-involvement quality management. This analysis is tentative and needs much more research and conceptual thought. Finally, while incorporating the high-involvement practices in the analysis of operational techniques goes some way to addressing the human resource issues associated with their implementation, the focus and the methodology adopted in the studies may need to be extended if all the issues of conflict within organisations are to be addressed.

The burden of this review is that the limitations of the studies reviewed reflect, as much as anything, the fact that the debate is still in its infancy. So, while the methodological problems point to the need for a "big science" model for future research in this area, the conceptual limitations imply "little science" will also play a decisive role.

Acknowledgements

I would like to thank David Holman and Malcolm Patterson for their comments on an earlier draft of this chapter; Lilian de Menezes and Ana Lasaosa for their contribution to my ideas and the joint work I have reported above; and the Economic and Social Research Council of the UK's support for that work (Grant No. R000238112).

REFERENCES

Abernathy, W. J., Clark. K. B. & Kantrow, A. H. (1984). *Industrial Renaissance: Producing a Competitive Future for America*. New York: Basic Books.

Appelbaum, E. & Batt, R. (1994). *The New American Workplace: Transforming Work Systems in the United States*. Ithaca, NY: Cornell IR Press.

Bartholomew, D. (1987). *Latent Variable Models and Factor Analysis*. London: Charles Griffin.

Bolden, R., Waterson, P. E., Warr, P. B., Clegg, C. W. & Wall, T. D. (1997). A new taxonomy of modern manufacturing practices. *International Journal of Operations and Production Management*, **17**(11), 1112–1130.

Cua, K. O., McKone, K. E. & Schroeder, R. (2001). Relationships between implementation of TQM, JIT, and TPM and manufacturing performance. *Journal of Operations Management*, **19**(6), 675–694.

Dean, J. W. & Snell, S. A. (1991). Integrated manufacturing and job design: moderating effects of organizational inertia. *Academy of Management Journal*, **34**(4), 774–804.

Flynn, B., Sakakibara, S. & Schroeder, R. (1995). Relationship between JIT and TQM: practices and performances. *Academy of Management Journal*, **38**(5), 1325–1360.

Lawler, E. E., Mohrman S. A. & Ledford, G. E. Jr (1995). *Creating High Performance Organizations*. San Francisco, CA: Jossey-Bass.

Lawler, E. E., Mohrman, S. A. and Ledford, G. E. Jr (1998). *Strategies for High Performance Organizations*. San Francisco, CA: Jossey-Bass.

McCloskey, L. A. & Collett, D. N. (1993). *TQM*. Methuen, MS: Coal/OPC.

MacDuffie, J. P. (1995). Human resource bundles and manufacturing performance: organizational logic and flexible production systems in the world auto industry. *Industrial and Labor Relations Review*, **48**(2), 197–221.

de Menezes, L., Wood, S. & Lasaosa, A. (2002). The Foundations of Human Resource Management in the UK. Mimeo, Institute of Work Psychology, University of Sheffield.

Osterman, P. (1994). How common is workplace transformation and who adopts it? *Industrial Relations and Labour Relations Review*, **47**(2), 173–188.

Patterson, M., West, M. A. & Wall, T. D. (2002). Integrating Manufacturing, Empowerment and Company Performance. Mimeo, Institute of Work Psychology, University of Sheffield.

Pil, F. K. & MacDuffie, J. P. (1996). The adoption of high-involvement work practices. *Industrial Relations*, **35**(3), 423–455.

Sakakibara, S., Flynn, B. B., Schroeder, R. G. & Morris, W. T. (1997). The impact of just-in-time manufacturing and its infrastructure on manufacturing performance. *Management Science*, **43**(9), 1246–1257.

Schonberger, R. J. (1986). *World Class Manufacturing: the Lessons of Simplicity Applied*. New York: Free Press.

Sitken, S. B., Sutcliffe, K. M. & Schroeder, R. G. (1994). Distinguishing control from learning in total quality management: a contingency perspective. *Academy of Management Journal*, **19**(3), 537–564.

Walker, R. (1989) Machinery, labour and location. In S. Wood (Ed.), *The Transformation of Work* (pp. 1–43). London: Unwin Hyman.

Waterson, P. E., Clegg, C. W., Bolden, R., Pepper, K., Warr, P. B. & Wall, T. D. (1999). The use and effectiveness of modern manufacturing practices: a survey of UK industry. *International Journal of Production Research*, **37**(10), 2271–2292.

Womack, J., Jones, D. & Roos, D. (1990). *The Machine that Changed the World*. New York: Rawson.

Wood, S. (1989). The transformation of work. In S. Wood (Ed.), *The Transformation of Work*, (pp. 1–43). London: Unwin Hyman.

Wood, S. (1990). Tacit skills: the Japanese management model and new technology. *Applied Psychology*, **39**(20), 169–190.

Wood, S. (1993). The Japanization of Fordism. *Economic and Industrial Democracy*, **14**(4), 535–555.

Wood, S. (1996). High commitment management and payment systems. *Journal of Management Studies*, **32**(11), 83–77.

Wood, S. (1999). Getting the measure of the transformed high-performance organization. *British Journal of Industrial Relations*, **37**(2), 391–417.
Wood, S. & Albanese, M. (1995). Can you speak of a high commitment management on the shop floor? *Journal of Management Studies*, **32**(2), 215–247.
Wood, S. & De Menezes, L. (1998). High commitment management in the UK: evidence from the Workplace Industrial Relations Survey, and Employers' Manpower and Skills Practices Survey. *Human Relations*, **51**(4), 485–515.
Wood, S. & Wall, T. D. (2002). Human Resource Management and Business Performance. In P. Warr (Ed.), *The Psychology of Work* (pp. 351–374). Harmondsworth: Penguin.

CHAPTER 15

Organizational Performance in Services

Rosemary Batt and **Virginia Doellgast**
School of Industrial and Labour Relations, Cornell University, NY, USA

Competition in service activities has intensified over the last two decades and corporations have responded by fundamentally restructuring their organizations. On the demand side, national product market deregulation has encouraged price competition and facilitated the internationalization of service activities. On the supply side, advances in information technologies have expanded remote service options and automated processes, while heightened international immigration has increased the availability of labor for traditionally low-wage service jobs.

In this context, the quest for more efficient and effective service delivery systems has become a central topic among academics as well as industry practitioners. While leading management theorists in the 1970s advocated competing on price by applying industrial models of production to services (Levitt, 1972), quality service and customer relationship management have emerged as dominant themes since the mid-1980s (Heskett, Sasser & Schlesinger, 1997).

The question of performance in service activities and occupations is important for several reasons. First, over two-thirds of employment in advanced economies is in service activities. Second, productivity growth in services is historically low, lagging far behind manufacturing, and as a result, wages in production-level service jobs remain low. In addition, labor costs in service activities are often over 50% of total costs, whereas in manufacturing they have fallen to less than 25% of costs. This raises the question of whether management practices that have improved performance in manufacturing, such as investment in the skills and training of the workforce, may be more difficult or costly to apply to service activities. At the same time, these practices may be even more important for organizational performance in these labor-intensive activities. Third, the role of the customer in production makes the process of service delivery fundamentally different than that found in goods production. Thus, it is useful to focus on the factors affecting performance in services, the topic of this chapter.

To understand competition and performance in services, we first briefly review the nature and extent of change in market institutions, technologies and business strategies. We conclude that while there is variation within and across service industries and across

---

The New Workplace: A Guide to the Human Impact of Modern Working Practices.
Edited by David Holman, Toby D. Wall, Chris W. Clegg, Paul Sparrow and Ann Howard. © 2003 John Wiley & Sons, Ltd.

countries, overall intensified price competition has led firms to focus more on cost reduction than on quality-enhancing strategies. Where quality and relationship management strategies are adopted, they are typically reserved for business or high-valued added customers. To understand the predictors of performance, we turn to empirical studies within organizations regarding the link between management practices and performance outcomes, and then to empirical studies of causal mechanisms. Our literature review covered quantitative studies from 22 journals between 1995 and 2001. Conclusions follow.

CHANGING MARKETS, TECHNOLOGIES AND BUSINESS STRATEGIES

Competition in services has intensified as markets that were once local and regional have become national and international in scope. This expansion has been facilitated by a growing demand for services as inputs into global manufacturing, advances in information technology that have increased the speed and volume of electronic transactions, and political movements to deregulate and privatize service industries. We reviewed changes in markets, technologies and business strategies in five industries—airlines, financial services, telecommunications, hotels and health care. We found common patterns with respect to heightened price competition, increased scope of the market, increased concentration in ownership structures, a focus on cost cutting and the use of customer segmentation strategies.

Price competition has accelerated in airlines, financial services and telecommunications, primarily due to deregulation and privatization of national product markets. In airlines, deregulation began in the USA in 1978 and spread to the UK, New Zealand, Chile, Canada and Australia, among others (Oum & Yu, 1998). Most European nations began to deregulate in the mid-1980s and progressed more gradually (Doganis, 2000). In financial services, deregulation and privatization began in most OECD countries in the 1970s and early 1980s in response to high inflation, the internationalization of banking and the abandonment of fixed foreign exchange rates. It continued in the 1980s due to international debt crises and the entrance of new financial actors such as mutual funds and credit card companies. In telecommunications, the UK and US undertook deregulation and privatization in the early 1980s, and within a decade almost all other countries around the globe were doing the same (Katz, 1997).

The hotel industry, by contrast, experienced economic difficulties due to overbuilding of capacity in the late 1980s and early 1990s. In the USA, in particular, thousands of hotels were foreclosed and several major chains filed for bankruptcy. Competition has intensified as national and global chains have gobbled up more traditional, independently owned and operated hotels (Lattin, 1998, pp. 96–98). In health care, rising costs have threatened funding systems in most countries, although there is great variation due to the variety of national systems of funding and the high level of government involvement in health care. The USA faces the greatest crisis, with health care costs rising at two or three times the rate of inflation in recent years, due to factors such as new technology, an aging population, the rise of medical malpractice suits, overspecialization, and the cost of poor quality (Gaucher & Coffey, 1993).

Regardless of the source of pressure, organizations in these industries have responded by focusing heavily on cost-cutting strategies. In industries undergoing deregulation, new entrants to the market typically have lower cost structures and a non-union workforce, while established companies have sunk costs in obsolete technologies and a higher-waged, unionized workforce. The established firms have responded by cutting labor costs. In airlines, for example, US companies focused heavily on cutting labor costs, and European airlines followed suit by the late 1980s and early 1990s. Strategies included: downsizing; two-tier wage structures; concessions in work rules; establishing low-cost subsidiaries with lower wage scales and more flexible terms; and outsourcing activities, such as aircraft cleaning and maintenance, passenger handling, in-flight catering and accounting (Doganis, 2000, pp. 112–119).

In banking, companies began offering a range of new products, such as insurance, credit cards, cash management, and pension and mutual funds. US banks led the way in shifting the business focus from service to sales maximization and reducing labor costs through labor-saving technologies, such as automatic teller machines, new back-office data-processing technologies, and telephone and Internet banking. Banks in other OECD countries have followed many of these practices. There is some evidence that these changes have had a negative impact on customer satisfaction, as in a Norwegian study that found that cost-cutting and restructuring led to significant declines in service quality and to customer defection (Lewis & Gabrielson, 1998).

In telecommunications, the old monopolies responded by investing heavily in digital technologies and slashing labor costs through downsizing. With deregulation, sales maximization replaced the historic goal of providing a universal service to the public. These patterns varied by country, with more market-driven strategies in the USA, UK, and Australia and more union-mediated strategies in the European countries and Japan (Katz, 1997).

In the hotel industry, globalization has allowed firms to maintain low labor costs through the utilization of large numbers of low-wage immigrant workers. Labor-saving technologies in this industry also include property management systems, Internet booking, and automated check-in and check-out. In health care, organizations have attempted to constrain spending and seek more efficient organizational and funding strategies (Howard & MacFarlan, 1994). The USA has shifted from "patient-driven" to "payer-driven" competition, which has led to a decline of the influence of the medical profession and the rise of for-profit financial interests (Dranove & White, 1999). This market-orientated strategy distinguishes the USA from other industrialized nations, which responded to increases in health care costs by adopting more centralized, budget-driven strategies (Dranove & White, 1999, p. 34). While the USA appears to be experiencing the greatest crisis in health care, restructuring to reduce costs is occurring in most countries (Sochalski, Aiken & Fagin, 1997).

Some studies show that cost cutting has had negative results in health care. For example, a study of re-engineering at a large US hospital found that it had extremely negative results for employees and patients. Using three waves of employee surveys, researchers found significant increases in depression, anxiety, emotional exhaustion, job insecurity, workloads and team work. Workers also reported significant declines in the overall quality of care they gave (Woodward *et al.*, 1999). A survey of nurses from over 700 hospitals in the USA, Canada, England, Scotland and Germany in 1998–1999 found a high rate of dissatisfaction and experiences of job-related strain in all countries except Germany (Aiken *et al.*, 2001). They found a high level of discontent associated with negative perceptions of staffing adequacy and workforce management policies.

In addition to cutting labor costs and investing in labor-saving technologies, service companies have responded to heightened competition by consolidating organizations and ownership structures. While deregulation is designed to increase the number of industry players, it has led to rising concentration of ownership across OECD countries in airlines (Oum & Yu, 1998), banking (Hunter, 1999) and telecommunications (Katz, 1997). In the hotel industry, concentration has also increased, with the USA leading the way with new forms of chains, franchising, hotel development and management. Hotels in other countries are replicating US practices as international franchising and alliances increase (Lattin, 1998, pp. 54–56). The USA also has led the world in the consolidation of health care facilities, as managed care organizations assume a growing role and independent hospitals are incorporated into for-profit chains (Dranove & White, 1999).

Another service management strategy is the use of customer segmentation, in which companies stratify customers by their ability to pay. Segmentation allows companies to compete on quality and relationship management for high value-added customers, such as business clients, but to adopt a cost-minimizing or industrial model of service provision in the mass market. In airlines, for example, business customers pay a premium for quality service, while the bulk of consumers register complaints regarding cramped seating arrangements, poor baggage handling and automated reservation systems. Banks distinguish between high net worth and mass-market sectors in personal banking; and large, medium and small sectors in business banking. Segmentation strategies are problematic in banking, however, because of the difficulty of identifying the future value of customers (Hunter, 1999). In telecommunications, customer segmentation strategies have become widespread, with different levels of customer service and labor strategies for workers serving various tiers of business customers and the mass market (Batt, 2000). Similarly, hotels are typically classified into three basic strata: upscale, mid-scale, and budget/economy. Management practices and labor strategies differ across the strata, with some attention to recruitment, training and compensation at upscale hotels, but little or none in mid-scale or economy hotels. The "mass market" approach in the lower tier of the market emphasizes rationalization and intensification of work for the bulk of low-wage workers. Nonetheless, even at the high end, labor investment strategies tend to focus on front office employees and managers, not the three-quarters of hotel workers who occupy "low-level" service occupations, such as maid, janitor, food server or hotel clerk (Cobble & Merrill, 1994, pp. 455–457).

The use of workplace innovations or human resource strategies that invest in the workforce are relatively undeveloped in service organizations. Exceptions, such as Southwest Airlines, are notable. More generally, where companies have experimented, it is with a particular type of innovation. In airlines, for example, employee stock ownership plans (ESOPs) have become popular since their introduction by United Airlines. They are designed to motivate workers to have a stake in the company by offering equity in exchange for pay and work rule concessions. All major US airlines now have ESOPs and employee representation on their boards (Doganis, 2000, pp. 121–122). In banking, the literature has noted examples of work reorganization in branches to provide workers with a broader set of skills for service and cross-selling of a variety of products (Baethge, Kitay & Regalia, 1999, pp. 7–14). In telecommunications, a handful of US companies experimented with TQM and self-directed teams in the 1980s, but soon after abandoned them (Katz, 1997). And in health care, there is widespread interest in the application of TQM principles to hospitals, a trend that began in the USA in the 1980s but which is spreading throughout OECD countries. However,

Ennis & Harrington (2001) found that only 25% of the hospitals they surveyed had formal TQM programs, and half of those had started in the year prior to the survey.

In sum, service companies have paid relatively little attention to competing through high-commitment work practices that invest in the skills of the workforce and provide opportunities for employee participation and collaboration in teams. National surveys show that service industries have lagged behind manufacturing in the use of high-commitment work practices, at least in the USA. For example, a 1993 national survey of establishments by the US Bureau of Labor Statistics found that 56% of manufacturing plants used at least one innovative practice (use of teams, TQM, job rotation or quality circles), but only 36% of retail firms and 41% of all service firms did (Gittleman, Horrigan & Joyce, 1998). Hunter's (2000) analysis of a US national establishment survey found that service establishments were roughly half as likely as manufacturing establishments to use TQM and self-managed teams.

Our brief review of several major service industries suggests that firms have responded to intensified competition primarily by cutting costs and using new technologies to compete on product and process innovation. They have made relatively little use of innovative human resource practices, and where they have, these are in workplaces serving business or high-value-added customers. The question, then, is how and why quality service strategies and high-commitment practices can lead to better performance in a broader array of service activities, particularly in the mass market.

MANAGEMENT PRACTICES AND PERFORMANCE OUTCOMES

We identified a range of models for service management that vary on a continuum from those designed to focus exclusively on cost to those focused on quality professional service. Industrial models of service production are designed to maximize volume and minimize cost by emphasizing mechanization, individually designed jobs with low skills and discretion, and intense monitoring and rule enforcement (Levitt, 1972). At the other end of the spectrum are relationship management strategies modeled after professional service (Gutek, 1995; Heskett et al., 1997). They are characterized by high levels of specialization and education, independent judgment, long-term personal relationships between providers and consumers, and intense focus on quality, loyalty and customization. Between these two extremes is a range of strategies characterized by some mix of attention to cost and quality—what some have termed "mass customization" (Pine, 1993; Frenkel et al. 1999). They involve some level of automation and process re-engineering found in industrial models, coupled with some level of attention to service quality and customer loyalty found in the professional model.

Implicit in these models is the assumption of an inverse relationship between cost and quality, an assumption contrary to that found in TQM, which assumes that costs and quality may be jointly maximized. Under TQM, costs are reduced by involving workers in problem-solving to lower defect rates. However, the investments in training and high relative pay for skilled workers under TQM, lean production, or other high-commitment production models, means that labor costs are higher in these systems (Cappelli & Neumark, 2001). Thus, whether there is a net performance gain from high-commitment systems is an empirical question that is likely to vary with the relative labor intensity of an activity. The labor-intensive nature of services coupled with tight profit margins may limit the utility of high-commitment practices in mass markets.

However, evidence that the effectiveness of high-commitment practices is contingent on a quality or up-market strategy is inconclusive. On the one hand, a study of 209 hotels in the UK showed that investment in HRM was ineffective where cost control was the business strategy, but effective for hotels pursuing a quality strategy (Hoque, 1999). On the other hand, Delery & Doty (1996) studied banks in the USA and found that while some HR practices had some contingent effects, universal effects were stronger. Batt (2002) similarly found that an index of high-commitment practices had significant positive effects overall, and that the effects were *more* powerful in the mass market, where price competition dominates. Finally, using archival data from 525 US nursing homes, Mukamel & Spector (2000) found that the relationship between cost and quality was not linear. Rather, they found an inverted U relationship between quality and costs, suggesting that there are quality regimens in which higher quality is associated with lower costs. This evidence from a highly labor-intensive and cost-constrained industry supports the idea that cost and quality can be jointly maximized in mass market service activities, as TQM theory predicts.

In the remainder of this section, we first review the evidence on management practices and performance in three areas: the use of technology and skills, the organization of work, and HR incentive and control systems. We then turn to studies that integrate these dimensions and examine the processes linking management practices to organizational performance. Most of the studies included use objective measures of operational outcomes, such as productivity and quality, defined in contextually-specific ways or measured by managers or customer reports. We also included some studies of employee attitudes and behaviors that shed light on explanatory mechanisms and the limits of current research.

Information Technology and Skills

In the 1980s, service firms began investing heavily in information technology to improve historically low productivity levels in services. However, in the USA where technology investments in service industries outpaced other countries, aggregate data revealed no productivity gains in the 1980s and early 1990s (compared to manufacturing, where technology-related productivity grew significantly). Researchers referred to this phenomenon as the productivity paradox (National Research Council, 1994). By the mid-1990s, however, evidence began to shift. In a major review of the literature, Brynjolfsson & Yang (1996) concluded that the main benefits from using computers appear to be improved quality, variety, timeliness and customization—none of which are well measured in official productivity statistics. These findings held across manufacturing and service industries. In recent research, Brynjolfsson and colleagues surveyed over 400 large firms and found that greater levels of IT are significantly associated with higher skill levels, investments in training and the reorganization of work to emphasize decentralization and the use of teams. These factors, both independently and interacting with each other, lead to higher productivity. These findings, however, were not disaggregated by sector (Bresnahan, Brynjolfsson & Hitt, 2002).

Other studies specific to service industries reach similar conclusions. Pennings (1995), for example, examined 10 years of data from 107 banks on product and process innovations (ATMs, computers). He found that both had a significant positive effect on efficiency and effectiveness indicators, with computer innovations having a stronger effect on internal measures of performance and ATMs on external measures. He also found that mimetic adopters (adopting IT when many others already have done so) enjoyed fewer performance advantages than their innovating competitors who "left the pack early". Reardon, Hasty & Coe (1996) found that IT contributes as much on the margin towards the creation of output as spending on additional selling space in retail establishments. They concluded that retailers are underutilizing IT. Quinn (1996) reviewed government and service industry data and presented alternative benefits from investments in IT that do not show up in "productivity" data: maintaining market share, avoiding catastrophic losses, creating greater flexibility and adaptability, handling complexity, improving service quality, creating an attractive work environment, and increasing responsiveness and predictability of operations. However, Nielsen & Host (2000) found that IT support was not significantly associated with measures of service quality.

The Organization of Work

Choices regarding technology may influence, but not entirely predict, the design of work. One set of choices concerns the extent to which individual jobs are designed to enhance employees' use of skills through greater decision-making discretion or breadth and variety of tasks. A second set of choices concerns the organization of work as an individual or interdependent function. While most manufacturing technologies imply task interdependence, the extent of technically-required interdependence is more varied and less obvious in service settings where "products" are more intangible. Managers, therefore, have considerable choice in the extent to which they emphasize work as an individual or collaborative function in such areas as customer service, banking, retail sales, airline reservations and service, hotels and health care.

Discretion, Participation and TQM

Prior reviews of the literature on job design have shown that individual employee autonomy, "empowerment", or participation in off-line teams are generally associated with better employee attitudes, such as satisfaction, but either modest positive or no objective performance outcomes (Cotton, 1993). Findings from our review of articles since 1995 are consistent with this evidence. On the one hand, Harel & Tzafir (1999) found a positive correlation between participation and manager-reported performance in a study of service organizations in Israel. Similarly, Hunter & Hitt (2001) found that higher levels of worker discretion in retail banks were associated with significantly higher objective productivity and sales. On the other hand, King & Garey (1997) reported that empowerment had no significant correlation with guest satisfaction ratings in hotels. Rodwell, Kienzle & Shadur (1998) found no evidence that employee participation in decision-making predicts self-rated performance in a study of an Australian IT company. Other research showed that participation in off-line quality teams had no relationship to subjective and objective performance criteria for field technicians (Batt, 2001) or call center workers (Batt, 1999). In fact, in the latter case, greater autonomy was significantly negatively associated with self-reported quality. Preuss (1997, 2001) studied similar issues in hospitals, and found that greater discretion for nursing assistants led to higher rates of patient errors, while greater discretion for nurses led to lower rates. Employee involvement in personnel decisions such as scheduling, training and assignments had no effect on patient error rates.

TQM generally includes two dimensions of job redesign. One is delegation of decision-making discretion to lower organizational levels, so that employees with tacit knowledge closest to the "the point of production" can make operational decisions. The second is the use of off-line quality improvement groups (quality circles and the like) to solve problems. Several organizational studies of TQM also have shown mixed results. Douglas & Judge (2001) found a significant positive relationship between performance and the degree of implementation of TQM in a study of financial performance in 193 hospitals. Hospitals that implemented a comprehensive array of TQM practices outperformed those that had less well-developed programs. Lammers *et al.* (1996) found that commitment to TQM philosophy and the number of active teams explained 41% of the variance in perceived quality improvement in 36 medical centers. However, in another study of TQM involving 3000 patients in 16 hospitals, Shortell and colleagues (2000) observed that while there were two- to four-fold differences in all major clinical outcomes, little of the variation was explained by TQM. Patients in hospitals scoring high on TQM were more satisfied but also more likely to have hospital stays greater than 10 days. And in a study of TQM in 61 hotels in the UK, Harrington & Akehurst (1996) found that only 22% of those that had a formal quality policy reported return on capital rates of more than 10% in a 3 year period (1989–1992). There was no evidence of a statistically significant relationship between company adoption of a quality orientation and their rates of return on net assets. These inconsistent results suggest that the value of individual worker discretion, participation or TQM must be examined in contextually specific ways.

Teams and Group Collaboration

With respect to the use of groups or collaborative forms of work organization, prior reviews have found fairly consistent positive performance outcomes associated with semi-autonomous work groups or self-managed teams (Cohen & Bailey, 1997). Cohen & Bailey's review, however, contained only a handful of studies of work teams in services, and these showed inconsistent results. Since that review, new studies of semi-autonomous teams in frontline services have found more positive performance results. In a study of knowledge workers in financial services, Campion, Papper & Medsker (1996) found that Hackman & Oldham's (1980) model of job characteristics, measured at the work group level, significantly predicted better self-reported and managerial ratings, and archival data on performance. Similarly, Batt (1999) found that self-directed teams of customer service representatives had 9.2% higher monthly sales and higher self-reported quality than traditionally supervised groups. Langfred (2000) studied 1000 workers at two service workplaces: a social service agency and the Denmark military. He found that both group and individual autonomy predicted the quality and accuracy of group outcomes as reported by managers. Uhl-Bien & Graen (1998) studied 400 public sector workers and found that individual self-management showed a strong, positive relationship with team effectiveness (as reported by managers) in functional work units, but a weak, negative relationship with effectiveness in cross-functional teams.

Other research has examined the importance of inter-group relations in services, particularly among project and product development teams, where much of the original research on this topic emerged (Cohen & Bailey, 1997). More recent research, however, has shown the importance of inter-group coordination among frontline service workers, e.g. Gittell found that cross-functional coordination is a significant predictor of objective performance measures in airline (Gittell, 2001) and health care settings (Gittell *et al.*, 2000). In sum, there is growing evidence that opportunities for group work and collaboration are associated with better performance in frontline service work.

Similar to the literature on technology, researchers increasingly recognize that group effectiveness depends not only on the design of groups, but on a series of supportive management practices that create a coherent set of directions and incentives. Arguably, these management practices are more important in service workplaces, because the justification for group-based work rests less on interdependent task characteristics and more on intangible aspects, like information sharing and learning. Most of the studies of service teams, discussed above, found that group effectiveness was enhanced by supportive management practices, such as training, supervisory support, rewards and work group relations.

Cohen, Ledford & Spreitzer (1996) tested a structural equation model of performance as predicted by four dimensions of the work environment: group work design; encouraging supervisor behavior; group characteristics, such as coordination and expertise; and "employee involvement" context (information, feedback, training, resources and recognition). They found some significant relationships between all four dimensions and four outcome variables: satisfaction, self-rated and manager ratings of performance, and absenteeism. Among their strongest findings are that the context variables significantly predicted employee satisfaction and manager ratings of performance, but encouraging supervisor behavior was significantly negatively related to manager ratings. They attribute the latter finding to the possibility that supervisors interfere in worse-performing teams or that supervisors who intervene in teams may indeed undermine performance, because workers are better situated to know what to do.

HR Incentive and Control Systems

Incentive and control systems may be usefully classified as either behavior-based or outcome-based, and these may be viewed as substitutes (Eisenhardt, 1985). Behavior-based systems rely on supervisory monitoring and enforcement of rules and are typically utilized for jobs that are defined as low-skilled or routine and relatively easy to monitor. Outcome-based systems rely more on performance-based pay and are typically utilized for jobs that do not have easily programmable tasks and are difficult to monitor.

Classic mass production control systems are usually behavior-based, and thus rely heavily on monitoring and rules. High-commitment systems, in which jobs are defined as more complex and less programmed, typically rely on some type of performance-based pay. If work systems require group work, then group-based pay is the logical concomitant. If firms adopt outcome-based systems, then, in theory, supervisory responsibilities should change, from disciplining employees and enforcing rules to facilitating support, resources, employee development and coordination across work groups.

Service jobs that involve customer interaction—the bulk of employment in services—should in theory have outcome-based control systems because the customer introduces uncertainty and variability into the production process. Tasks are not easily programmed.

Sales jobs, for example, have historically relied heavily on commission pay. In reality, however, many firms have adapted mass production models to services, from call centers to fast food. In these settings, behavior-based controls are viewed as even more important than in manufacturing, because current technology limits the extent to which standardization can be accomplished through machine-pacing. Thus, service managers also must set standardized routines for interacting with customers, coupled with supervisory monitoring. In recent years, technological advances have allowed electronic monitoring systems to be used in a much broader array of service jobs, reducing the number of supervisors while maintaining high levels of surveillance.

Empirical research on the performance effects of alternative incentive systems is quite undeveloped. For example, there is limited research on the relationship between electronic monitoring, supervisory monitoring, and performance. On the one hand, electronic monitoring may replace supervisors, thereby reducing indirect labor costs and improving organizational efficiency. On the other hand, intense electronic monitoring causes emotional exhaustion and burnout (Carayon, 1993; Holman, Chissick & Totterdell, in press), which may negatively affect productivity. In addition, supervisors may be a complement to electronic monitoring, as in research by Holman et al. (in press), who found that supervisor support moderated the negative effects of electronic monitoring.

Similarly, the research on supervisors is theoretically and empirically undeveloped. Often researchers include a measure of supervisor support (positive feedback, fair treatment of workers) when they study management practices, but what supervisors actually do is unexamined. These studies typically show that supervisors influence employee attitudes but not necessarily performance, e.g. Cunningham & MacGregor (2000) found that supervisor support was a significant predictor of employee satisfaction, intention to quit, and absenteeism in a study of 750 telephone and service station workers. However, in an international survey of 400 call center workers, supervisor support and team member support had a significant relationship with job satisfaction but not employees' commitment or reported capacity to satisfy customers (Sergeant & Frenkel, 2000). Singh (2000) found that task control was more important than supervisor support as a resource for call center workers in financial services, and King & Garey (1997) found that positive supervision and leadership in hotels had little correlation to guest ratings of responsiveness and slight negative correlations to welcoming and helpfulness.

A second set of issues concerns the ratio of supervisors to workers: are new forms of work organization a complement to or substitute for supervision? One group of studies has shown that self-managed teams are a substitute for supervisors. A meta-analysis of research on self-managed teams, for example, found that teams without supervisors performed better than those with supervisors (Beekun, 1989). In a recent study of call center workers, Fernie & Metcalf (1999) found that team-based pay systems and low supervisor:worker ratios were associated with higher self-reported productivity and financial performance. Batt (2001) found that field technicians in self-managed teams absorbed the monitoring and coordination tasks of supervisors in one-third of the time required by supervisors, thereby reducing indirect labor costs without adversely affecting objective quality and productivity. In theory, teams that develop the capacity to be self-regulating and to do without supervisors will perform better. Cohen et al. (1997) tested this idea using data from 900 employees in self-managed and traditionally supervised work groups in a telecommunications firm. They found that self-managed teams scored higher on these dimensions and that these dimensions predicted employee satisfaction and self-rated effectiveness. They also found that these leadership behaviors were applicable to traditionally supervised groups.

Other researchers say that supervisors are a complement to new forms of work organization. In a study of an airline company, for example, Gittell (2002a) found that higher supervisor:worker ratios predicted better performance, and that the supervisory effect acted through its positive impact on workers' cross-functional communication. She attributes this effect to the fact that small spans of control allow supervisors to provide intensive coaching.

The empirical research on alternative pay systems also provides relatively little clarity about what predicts better outcomes, in part because of the many different types of plans and the fact that outcomes are contingent on the specifics of the plan (the fairness of the formula for payouts, the tightness of the link to performance, the type of behavior rewarded, and the combination of individual and group-level criteria, etc.). Outcomes also are contingent on the relationship between the pay system and other factors (such as the design of work and performance management). Recent comprehensive reviews of the compensation literature provide some evidence that linking pay to performance leads to better individual and organizational performance (Milkovich & Newman, 2002; Gerhart & Rynes, 2000). The strength and persuasiveness of the empirical evidence, however, varies considerably by the type of compensation plan. A few reliable studies show that gainsharing or work group-based plans produce higher performance, but the findings depend importantly on the formula for payouts. The few studies of skill-based pay plans suggest that they encourage more learning, which in turn positively affects quality. A handful of reliable studies on merit pay provide some evidence that it leads to better performance (Milkovich & Newman, 2002). Some research also shows that firms have better financial performance when they link pay to operational or financial goals (Gerhart & Rynes, 2000). However, a meta-analysis of research on financial incentives found that they were unrelated to performance quality, but significantly related to performance quantity (Jenkins, Mitra, Gupta, & Shaw, 1998).

A particularly relevant study for service and sales workplaces is a 6 year study of performance-based pay at 34 outlets of a large retail organization in the USA. The researchers tracked an experiment in which roughly half of the retail stores switched to an incentive plan that rewarded workers with individual bonuses for sales over a given target. Notably, it also threatened termination if they failed to meet the target for two successive quarters. Supervisory monitoring declined in the experimental stores; and sales, customer service and profits grew significantly. This provides some support for the idea that behavior-based and outcome-based systems are inversely related. Performance outcomes were higher in stores serving higher-valued customer markets, also consistent with the idea that outcome-based systems are more appropriate for more unprogrammed service interactions (Banker *et al.*, 1996). However, it is unclear whether the improved performance in this case was due to the pay plan or the threat of termination.

In sum, there is some evidence that investments in information technology, coupled with high relative skills and collaborative work design, yield better performance in frontline services. There is also evidence that some types of performance-based pay are associated with better performance. The evidence is not overwhelming, however, and appears to be quite contingent on the nature of the industry, occupation and organizational context.

SYSTEMS AND MECHANISMS LINKING MANAGEMENT PRACTICES AND OUTCOMES

Explanations regarding how and why management practices lead to better performance may be classified as primarily psychological and affective, on the one hand, or economic and sociological on the other. While studies in organizational behavior historically focused on worker satisfaction and commitment, more recent research considers a broader array of emotional and affective outcomes, including positive responses, such as pro-social or citizenship behaviors, and trust; and negative responses, such as emotional exhaustion, stress, withdrawal (quits, absences) and other forms of resistance. Research based in economic and sociological explanations has focused on the importance of human capital, social capital and knowledge-sharing and learning on the job.

Psychological Explanations

Affective models build on the large literature on work design, which has shown systematic relationships between enhanced job characteristics (e.g. autonomy, variety, ability to complete a whole task; Hackman & Oldham, 1980) and worker satisfaction, as have the studies of autonomous teams (Cohen & Bailey, 1997). However, these studies have failed to find that happier workers are more productive. More recently, a study of over 500 Canadian workers found that the use of high-commitment practices had contradictory effects on workers, bringing greater intrinsic rewards, such as satisfaction and commitment, but also greater reported stress (Godard, 2001). An analysis of the 1998 UK Workplace Employee Relations Survey by Ramsay, Scholarios & Harley (2000) casts doubt on the idea that the HR–performance link is mediated through workers' emotional and affective reactions. They found significant positive relationships between a comprehensive measure of high-performance work practices and several performance outcomes as reported by managers, including labor productivity, quality, financial performance, absenteeism and turnover. They then tested whether worker perceptions of discretion, management relations, pay satisfaction, commitment, security and job strain mediated the relationship between management practices and performance. They report mixed and modest mediating effects, and conclude that there is no strong evidence that performance outcomes flow via workers' attitudinal outcomes. Neither of these studies differentiated between manufacturing and service organizations, however.

Several management theorists, nonetheless, have pursued this line of research on the hunch that worker attitudes are more important in customer-contact jobs because they can more readily spill over into customer interactions—positively or negatively. The most elaborate theory (the service profit chain) links human resource practices to employee satisfaction and loyalty, which in turn inspires customer satisfaction and loyalty, ultimately resulting in higher profits (Heskett *et al.*, 1997). Loveman (1998) is the first to empirically demonstrate correlations along several links in this chain (HR practices; employee satisfaction and loyalty; and customer satisfaction, loyalty and profits), based on employee and customer data from 479 branches of a multi-site regional bank.

Schneider and his colleagues have taken a similar approach by measuring workers' reports of management practices and the extent to which they support a positive "service climate" (Schneider *et al.*, 1980). The measures in Schneider's service climate survey have parallels with the measures used in the high-commitment literature. Recent studies provide support for a significant positive relationship between worker perceptions of service climate, worker attitudes, and customer reports of service quality (Schmit & Allscheid, 1995; Johnson, 1996; Peccei & Rosenthal, 2000; Borucki & Burke, 1999) and financial performance (Borucki & Burke, 1999). In a longitudinal study of 134 bank branches, Schneider,

White & Paul (1998) found that their measure of service climate was significantly associated with higher customer reports of service quality. Moreover, in cross-lagged analyses of data over 3 years, they found a reciprocal effect for service climate and customer perceptions of quality. However, the causal relationships are not entirely clear in this line of research, as some researchers have found that customer satisfaction leads to worker satisfaction (Ryan, Schmit & Johnson, 1996). Moreover, other studies have found no relationship between commitment and objective measures of performance among hospital employees (Somers & Birnbaum, 1998).

A growing area of research concerns the boundary-spanning role of service workers as they are positioned between management and the customers. One study of a Canadian bank, for example, found that the employee–customer interface was the most important predictor of a worker's prosocial behavior (Chebat & Kolias, 2000). This boundary-spanning position, however, is vulnerable to role ambiguity and conflict because management and customers may place contradictory demands on workers. A good example is in call centers, where management may seek to limit call-handling time, while customers demand more time. Similarly, "service workers" increasingly play a dual role of service and selling— roles that require opposite skill sets and approaches to customers. In a study of restaurant workers, Babin & Boles (1998) found that role stress negatively affected customer–server interactions and increased workers' intentions to quit. Hartline & Ferrell (1996) surveyed several hundred managers, workers and customers at 279 hotels and found that role conflict contributed significantly to employees' frustration in their attempt to fulfill their jobs. In a major meta-analysis of research on role ambiguity and role conflict, Tubre & Collins (2000) found a significant negative relationship between role ambiguity and performance. However, the analysis found a negligible relationship between role conflict and performance.

Another emerging line of research seeks to understand the relationship between management practices, worker well-being and performance. Several studies of call center workers have found that routinized work design and high levels of electronic monitoring lead to stress, anxiety, depression, emotional exhaustion and burnout (Carayon, 1993; Holman, 2001; Holman, Chissick & Totterdell, 2002; Deery, Iverson & Walsh, 1999; Singh, 2000). Deery *et al.* (1999) found that customer interactions, scripts, routinization, workloads and managerial emphasis on quantity predicted emotional exhaustion, which in turn predicted absenteeism. Singh (2000) found that worker burnout with customers is associated with lower self-reported service quality. With increasing levels of burnout, call center workers were able to maintain their productivity levels, but their self-reported quality was lower. Other organization-level studies also show that electronic monitoring predicts higher quit rates (Shaw *et al.*, 1998; Batt, Colvin & Keefe, 2002).

Economic and Sociological Explanations

A second set of explanations focuses on how management practices influence the use of human capital and knowledge at work. Implicit or explicit in these approaches is Gary Becker's work on human capital (1964) and the idea that productivity hinges on the effective use of the skills and abilities of workers. Human capital theory predicts that high-commitment or high-performance systems should produce better organizational performance and wages because they provide opportunities and incentives for employees to use their skills more effectively.

In customer contact settings, firm-specific human capital is particularly important, because employees manage the boundary between the firm and the customer and their behavior shapes customers' buying behavior. Employees need to manage a range of firm-specific information and knowledge in at least three domains: products, customers and processing protocols. Product knowledge covers specific features, service agreements, pricing, packaging and legal regulations. Customer-specific knowledge includes an understanding of demand characteristics of particular individuals or segments and the ability to use that knowledge to customize service or sales. Workflow and processing protocols require specific knowledge of information processing systems and capabilities and how these affect each customer and product offering.

Research supports the idea that firm-specific human capital positively affects service performance. In a study of a department store chain, for example, Sharma, Levy & Kumar (2000) found a significant positive relationship between sales experience and performance, and they attributed this finding to the knowledge structures of workers with greater expertise. In a meta-analysis of 22 studies of job experience, Quinones, Ford & Teachout (1995) found a 0.27 correlation between experience and performance.

One study of high-commitment practices in service and sales centers found that they influenced organizational performance in two ways: directly, via the effect on employee performance, and indirectly, via employee attachment to the firm (Batt, 2002). High quit rates not only increased the costs of recruitment and selection but also negatively affected performance, because new employees face a learning curve. Long-term employees have the tacit firm-specific skills and knowledge—and often personal relationships with customers—to be more effective. In a micro-level follow-up study, Moynihan & Batt (2001) found that the design of group-based work, recognition and rewards led to greater knowledge sharing among workers, which in turn was correlated with objective service quality in call centers.

Another study in this vein focused on the importance of the quality of information in health care settings, where uncertainty is high and the quality of information is extremely important (Preuss, 1997, 2001). Preuss found that information quality is critical in this setting because patients' health status changes constantly. As a result, information on each patient's status must be updated regularly. Based on a sample of 1100 nursing employees on 50 acute care hospital units, Preuss found that units with lower medical errors were those that relied on nurses with higher levels of formal education, higher levels of experience and broader task responsibilities. Units that gave more responsibilities to lower-skilled employees had significantly higher medical errors. The quality of information mediated the relationship between work design and staffing decisions and medical errors.

A similar approach, developed by Gittell (2000b), focuses on the importance of communication and relationships among employees in service settings, particularly in settings characterized by high levels of uncertainty and time constraints. Based on her fieldwork in airlines and health care, Gittell developed a measure, "relational coordination"—the extent to which employees communicate and have positive relationships with one another within and across departments. She found that several management practices, including selection, cross-functional and flexible work design and supervisor support, shape the extent of coordination among workers. In a study of orthopedic hospital units, the extent of relational coordination predicted significantly lower post-operative pain, shorter lengths of stay and better patient-reported care (Gittell *et al.*, 2000). In airlines, relational coordination led to lower gate time, staff time, customer complaints, lost bags and late arrivals (Gittell, 2001). In her study of hospitals, Gittell (2002b) also found that stronger relationships among providers and between providers and customers produced higher levels of customer satisfaction. However, Rodwell, Kienzle & Shadur (1998) studied communication among IT employees and found that it related positively to teamwork, job satisfaction and commitment but negatively to performance.

Another recent study has focused on the knowledge-creation capability of firms. Drawing on a sample of managers and employees from 78 high-technology firms, Collins, Smith & Stevens (2001) found that four types of management practices (effective acquisition, employee development, commitment-building and networking practices) significantly improved sales growth through their effect on knowledge-creation capability. They defined this capability along three dimensions—human capital, employee motivation, and information combination and exchange—and found that these interacted to positively affect sales growth. Collins & Clark (2001) also studied internal and external networks of top management teams in high-technology companies and found that the size and range of networks significantly predicted sales growth and stock returns.

Together, these studies point to the importance not only of individual human capital, but also of networks of human capital, or organizational social capital (Leana & Van Buren, 1999). Organizational social capital may be thought of as an asset embedded in the relationships among employees. While these ideas are at initial stages of conceptual and methodological development, recent research points to the importance of communication networks and relationships of trust among employees as important sources of organizational performance.

DISCUSSION AND CONCLUSIONS

In this chapter, we have reviewed the literature on the restructuring of service industries and concluded that organizations have focused much more attention on cost-cutting strategies and investments in technology than on work redesign or human resource strategies. We then examined quantitative studies of the predictors of performance in services. This research has been conducted in a wide range of contexts and levels of analysis—across industries, firms, establishments and work groups.

At the most general level, researchers across many disciplines—from economics to psychology to sociology—have concluded that various dimensions of management practices must be understood in relation to one another, or as systems. Students of IT, for example, have demonstrated that investments in IT, when coupled with complementary high-commitment practices, are associated with higher productivity, innovation, customization and quality in services. Researchers in organizational behavior have similarly determined that group effectiveness is contingent on the presence of complementary management practices. However, despite this recognition, most studies do a poor job of understanding relationships among management practices. For example, with a few exceptions, students of organization studies and human resources have not integrated an understanding of IT into their work. As a result, at the level of work groups and organizations, we know relatively little about how the differentiated uses of IT (such as electronic monitoring or the availability of software programs and databases) interact with the organization of work and human resource management practices to produce different results. Similarly, our understanding of the relationship between alternative forms of work organization and incentive systems is undeveloped.

Our review of work organization revealed that a growing number of studies show that collaborative forms of work organization predict better performance in service contexts. Service organizations that create opportunities and incentives for collaboration within and across groups appear to perform better than those that do not. This finding is important, because in many service settings the relationship between employees and customers appears to be more salient than the relationship among employees. Sales work, for example, has typically been defined as individual. Field technicians usually work alone. However, the service process frequently depends on coordination among workers who are located in different job classifications, work groups, locations or functional departments, as in airlines, hotels or telecommunications. It also depends on collaboration across hierarchically-defined occupational groups, as in health care. In these settings, where interdependence is important but not self-evident or necessarily in the self-interest of employees, managers must self-consciously create mechanisms and incentives for employees to collaborate and cooperate. However, the specific type of coordinating mechanism—whether more or less autonomous work groups, cross-functional groups, or virtual teams—is likely to depend on the nature of work, technology, and industry setting.

The search for general findings with respect to incentive and control systems is more elusive. There are two quite different theories about whether supervisors are substitutes or complements to new forms of work organization. While some research suggests that electronic monitoring and team-based systems are substitutes for supervision, other studies suggest the opposite. It could be that both alternatives produce equally good outcomes or it could be that contingency perspectives prevail. Supervision in the form of coaching and support may be particularly important in service settings because of high levels of uncertainty and emotional labor in customer–provider relations. Further research is needed to untangle the answers to these questions.

Empirical research on pay systems is also undeveloped. While some form of performance-based pay appears to be associated with better organizational performance, the devil is in the details. We know relatively little about the differentiated effects of incentive vs. at-risk pay, about systems that combine different types of incentives or about how these systems affect employees at different income levels.

Finally, research on causal mechanisms linking management practices to outcomes is only beginning. Scholars in organizational behavior have moved from a focus on satisfaction and commitment to a wider array of worker attitudes and emotional outcomes. This work needs to move to the next step of linking worker outcomes to objective performance. The research on human capital, knowledge sharing and social capital is particularly promising, but needs to be developed theoretically and expanded empirically to cover a wider array of occupations and work settings.

In sum, while researchers have begun to identify the ways in which work organization and human resource practices influence service performance, our theoretical models are undeveloped and our empirical evidence is piecemeal. Without clear evidence to the contrary, managers have little reason to shift from tried and true strategies of competing on cost. Interdisciplinary research projects over the next decade must do a much better job of explicating the relationship between management practices and service performance in more systematic and contextually-specific studies of industries and occupations.

REFERENCES

Aiken, L. H., Sean P. Clarke, S. P., Sloane, D. M. & Sochalski, J. A. (2001). Nurses' reports on hospital care in five countries. *Health Affairs*, **20**(3), 43–53.

Babin, B. J. & Boles, J. S. (1998). Employee behavior in a service environment: a model and test of potential differences between men and women. *Journal of Marketing*, **62**, 77–91.

Baethge, M., Kitay J. & Regalia, I. (1999). Managerial strategies, human resources practices, and labor relations in banks: a comparative view. In M. Regini, J. Kitay & M. Baethge (Eds), *From Tellers to Sellers: Changing Employment Relations in Banks* (pp. 3–30). Cambridge, MA: MIT Press.

Banker, R. D., Lee, S. Y., Potter, G. & Srinivasan, D. (1996). Contextual analysis of performance impacts of outcome-based incentive compensation. *Academy of Management Journal*, **39**(4), 920–949.

Batt, R. (2000). Strategic segmentation in front-line services: matching customers, employees and human resource systems. *International Journal of Human Resource Management*, **11**(3), 540–561.

Batt, R. (1999). Work organization, technology, and performance in customer service and sales. *Industrial and Labor Relations Review*, **52**(4), 539–564.

Batt, R. (2001). The economics of teams among technicians. *British Journal of Industrial Relations*, **39**(1), 1–24.

Batt, R. (2002). Managing customer services: human resource practices, turnover, and sales growth. *Academy of Management Journal*, **45**(3): 587–59.

Batt, R., Colvin, A. & Keefe, J. (2002). Employee voice, human resource practices, and quit rates: evidence from the telecommunications industry. *Industrial and Labor Relations Review*, **55**(4): 573–591.

Becker, G. (1964). *Human Capital*. New York: Columbia University Press.

Beekun, R. I. (1989). Assessing the effectiveness of sociotechnical interventions: antidote or fad? *Human Relations*, **42**(10), 877–898.

Borucki, C. C. & Burke, M. J. (1999). An examination of service-related antecedents to retail store performance. *Journal of Organizational Behavior*, **20**, 943–962.

Bresnahan, T. F., Brynjolfsson, E. & Hitt, L. M. (2002). Information technology, workplace organization, and the demand for skilled labor: firm-level evidence. *Quarterly Journal of Economics*, **117**(1), 339–376.

Brynjolfsson, E. & Hitt, L. (2000). Beyond computation: information technology, organizational transformation, and business performance. *Journal of Economic Perspectives*, **14**(4), 23–48.

Brynjolfsson, E. & Yang, S. (1996). Information technology and productivity: a review of the literature. *Advances in Computers*, **43**, 179–214.

Campion, M. A., Papper, E. M. & Medsker, G. J. (1996). Relations between work team characteristics and effectiveness: a replication and extension. *Personnel Psychology*, **49**(2), 429–459.

Cappelli, P. & Neumark, D. (2001). Do "high-performance" work practices improve establishment-level outcomes? *Industrial and Labor Relations Review*, **54**(4), 737–772.

Carayon, P. (1993). Effect of electronic performance monitoring on job design and worker stress: review of the literature and conceptual model. *Human Factors*, **35**, 385–395.

Chebat, J. & Kollias, P. (2000). The impact of empowerment on customer contact employees' role in service organizations. *Journal of Service Research*, **3**(1), 66–81.

Cobble, D. S. & Merrill, M. (1994). Collective bargaining in the hospitality industry in the 1980s. In Voos, P. B. (Ed.), *Contemporary Collective Bargaining in the Private Sector*. Industrial Relations Research Association Series, Madison, Wisconsin.

Cohen, S. G., Cheng, L. & Ledford, G. E. (1997). A hierarchical construct of self-management leadership and its relationship to quality of work life and perceived work group effectiveness. *Personnel Psychology*, **50**(2), 275–308.

Cohen, S. G. & Bailey, D. E. (1997). What makes teams work: group effectiveness research from the shop floor to the executive suite. *Journal of Management*, **23**(3), 239–290.

Cohen, S. G., Ledford, G. E Jr. & Spreitzer, G. M. (1996). A predictive model of self-managing work team effectiveness. *Human Relations*, **49**(5), 643–676.

Collins, C. J. & Clark, K. D. (2001). Strategic human resource practices and the development of top management team social capital (draft).

Collins, C. J., Smith, K. G. & Stevens, C. K. (2001). Human resource practices, knowledge-creation capability, and performance in high technology firms. Center for Advanced Human Resources Studies Working Paper 01–02.

Cotton, J. L. (1993). *Employee Involvement: Methods for Improving Performance and Work Attitudes*. Newbury Park, CA: Sage.

Cunningham, J. B. & MacGregor, J. (2000). Trust and the design of work: complementary constructs in satisfaction and performance. *Human Relations*, **53**(12), 1575–1591.

Deery, S., Iverson, R. & Walsh, J. (2002). Work relationships in telephone call centers: understanding emotional exhaustion and employee withdrawal. *Journal of Management Studies*, **39**(4), 471–497.

Doganis, R. (2000). *The Airline Business in the Twenty-first Century*. London: Routledge.

Douglas, T. J. & Judge, W. Q. Jr (2001). TQM implementation and competitive advantage: the role of structural control and exploration. *Academy of Management Journal*, **44**(1), 158–169.

Dranove, D. & White, W. D. (1999). *How Hospitals Survived: Competition and the American Hospital*. Washington, DC: AEI Press.

Eisenhardt, K. (1985). Control: organizational and Economic Approaches. *Management Science*, **31**, 134–149.

Ennis, K. & Harrington, D. (2001). Quality management in Irish healthcare. *Service Industries Journal*, **21**(1), 149–168.

Fernie, S. & Metcalf, D. (1999). *Agent Don't Lose that Number . . . Payment Systems, Monitoring, and Performance in Call Centers*. London: Centre for Economic Performance, London School of Economics.

Frenkel, S., Korczynski, M., Shire, K. & Tam, M. (1999). *On the Front Line: Organization of Work in the Information Economy*. Ithaca, NY: Cornell University Press.

Gaucher, E. J. & Coffey, R. J. (1993). *Total Quality in Healthcare: From Theory to Practice*. San Francisco, CA: Jossey-Bass.

Gerhart, B. & Rynes, S. (eds) (2000). *Compensation in Organizations: Progress and Prospects*. San Francisco, CA: New Lexington Press.

Gittell, J. H. (2000a). Paradox of coordination and control. *California Management Review*, **42**(3), 1–17.

Gittell, J. H. (2000b). Organizing work to support relational coordination, *International Journal of Human Resource Management*, **11**(3), 517–534.

Gittell, J. H. (2001). Relational coordination: communicating and relating for the purpose of task integration (Unpublished draft).

Gittell, J. H. (2002a). Supervisory span, relational coordination and flight departure performance: a reassessment of post-bureaucracy theory. *Organization Science*, **12**(4), 367–82.

Gittell, J. H. (2002b). Relationships among service providers and their impact on customers. *Journal of Service Research*, **4**(4) (in press).

Gittell, J. H., Fairfield, K. M., Bierbaum, B., Head, W., Jackson, R., Kelly, M., Laskin, R., Lipson, S., Siliski, J., Thornhills, T. & Zuckerman, J. (2000). Impact of relational coordination on quality of care, postoperative pain and functioning, and length of stay. *Medical Care*, **38**(8), 807–819.

Gittleman, M., Horrigan, M. & Joyce, M. (1998). "Flexible" workplace practices: evidence from a nationally representative survey. *Industrial and Labor Relations Review*, **52**(1), 99–114.

Godard, J. (2001). High performance and the transformation of work? The implications of alternative work practices for the experience and outcomes of work. *Industrial and Labor Relations Review*, **54**(4), 776–805.

Gutek, B. (1995). *The Dynamics of Service: Reflections on the Changing Nature of Customer/Provider Interactions*. San Francisco, CA: Jossey-Bass.

Hackman, J. R. & Oldham, G. (1980). *Work Redesign*. Boston, MA: Addison-Wesley.

Harel, G. & Tzafir, S. (1999). The effect of human resource management practices on the perceptions of organizational and market performance of the firm. *Human Resource Management*, **38**(3), 185–200.

Harrington, D. & Akehurst, G. (1996). Service quality and business performance in the UK hotel industry. *International Journal of Hospitality Management*, **15**(3), 283–298.

Hartline, M. D. & Ferrell, O. C. (1996). The management of customer-contact service employees: an empirical investigation. *Journal of Marketing*, **60**(4), 52–70.

Heskett, J. L., Sasser, E. W. & Schlesinger, L. A. (1997). *The Service Profit Chain.* New York: Free Press.

Holman, D., Chissick, C. & Totterdell, P. (2002). The effects of performance monitoring on emotional labour and well-being in call centres. *Motivation and Emotion,* **26**(1): 57–81.

Holman, D. (2001). Employee stress in call centres. Conference on Call Centres and Beyond: the Human Resource Management Implications, Kings College, London, 6 November.

Hoque, K. (1999). Human resource management and performance in the UK hotel industry. *British Journal of Industrial Relations,* **37**(3), 419–443.

Howard, O. & MacFarlan, M. (1994). Health care reform: controlling spending and increasing efficiency. Economics Department Working Paper No. 149. Paris: OECD.

Hunter, L. W. (1999). Transforming retail banking. In Peter Cappelli (Ed.), *Employment Practices and Business Strategy* (pp. 53–192). New York: Oxford University Press.

Hunter, L. W. (2000). The adoption of innovative work practices in service establishments. *International Journal of Human Resource Management,* **11**(3), 477–496.

Hunter, L. W. & Hitt, L. (2001). What makes a high-performance service workplace? Evidence from retail bank branches (Unpublished draft).

Jenkins, G. D. Jr, Mitra, A., Gupta, N. Shaw, J. D. (1998). Are financial incentives related to performance? A meta-analytic review of empirical research. *Journal of Applied Psychology,* **83**(5), 777–787.

Johnson, J. W. (1996). Linking employee perceptions of service climate to customer satisfaction. *Personnel Psychology,* **49**(4), 831–851.

Katz, H. C. (1997). Introduction and comparative overview. In Harry Katz (Ed.), *Telecommunications: Restructuring Work and Employment Relations Worldwide* (pp. 1–30). Ithaca, NY: ILR Press.

King, C. A. & Garey, J. G. (1997). Relational quality in service encounters. *International Journal of Hospitality Mangement,* **16**(1), 39–63.

Lammers, J. C., Cretin, S., Gilman, S. & Calingo, E. (1996). Total quality management in hospitals: the contributions of commitment, quality councils, teams, budgets, and training to perceived improvement at veterans health administration hospitals. *Medical Care,* **34**(5), 463–478.

Langfred, C. W. (2000). The paradox of self-management: individual and group autonomy in work groups. *Journal of Organizational Behavior,* **21**, 563–585.

Lattin, G. W. (1998). *The Lodging and Food Service Industry,* 4th Edn. Lansing: Educational Institute of the American Hotel and Motel Association.

Leana, C. R. & Van Buren III, H. J. (1999). Organizational social capital and employment practices. *Academy of Management Review,* **24**, 538–555.

Levitt, T. (1972). Production-line approach to service. *Harvard Business Review,* **September–October**, 41–52.

Lewis, B. R. & Gabrielsen G. O. S. (1998). Intra-organization aspects of service quality management: the employees' perspective. *Service Industries Journal,* **18**(2), 64–89.

Loveman, G. W. (1998). Employee satisfaction, customer loyalty, and financial performance: an empirical examination of the service profit chain in retail banking. *Journal of Service Research,* **1**(1), 18–31.

Milkovich, G. & Newman, J. (2002). *Compensation,* 7th Edn (pp. 279–304). Boston, MA: McGraw Hill.

Moynihan, L. & Batt, R. (2001). Knowledge sharing and performance of teams in call centers. Paper presented at the 2000 Academy of Management meetings, Toronto, Ontario, August 6–9.

Mukamel, D. & Spector, W. D. (2000). Nursing home costs and risk-adjusted outcome measures of quality. *Medical Care,* **38**(1), 78–89.

National Research Council (1994). *Information Technology in the Service Sector: a 21st Century Lever.* Washington, DC: National Academy Press.

Nielsen, J. F. & Host, V. (2000). The path to service encounter performance in public and private 'bureaucracies'. *Service Industries Journal,* **20**(1), 40–60.

Oum, T. H. & Yu, C. (1998). *Winning Airlines: Productivity and Cost Competitiveness of the World's Major Airlines.* Boston: Kluwer Academic.

Peccei, R. & Rosenthal, P. (2000). Front-line responses to customer orientation programs: a theoretical and empirical analysis. *International Journal of Human Resource Management,* **11**(3), 562–590.

Pennings, J. M. (1995). Information technology and organizational effectiveness. In Harker P. T. (Ed.), *The Service Productivity and Quality Challenge.* Boston, MA: Kluwer Academic.

Pine, B. (1993). *Mass Customization*. Cambridge, MA: Harvard Business School Press.

Preuss, G. (1997). Labor, skills, and information in service delivery: an examination of hospital care. *Proceedings of the 57th Annual Meeting of the Academy of Management* (pp. 282–286). Boston, MA: Academy of Management.

Preuss, G. A. (2002). Work practices and outcome quality: Information quality in organizations. *Industrial and Labor Relations Review*, in press.

Quinn, J. B. (1996). The productivity paradox is false: Information technology improves services performance. In T. A. Swartz, D. E. Bowen & S. W. Brown (Eds), *Advances in Services Marketing and Management*, Vol. 5 (pp. 71–84). Greenwich, CT: JAI Press.

Quinones, M. A., Ford, K. J. & Teachout, M. S. (1995). The relationship between work experience and job performance: a conceptual and meta-analytic review. *Personnel Psychology*, **48**(4), 887–911.

Ramsay, H., Scholarios, D. & Harley, B. (2000). Employees and high-performance work systems: testing inside the black box. *British Journal of Industrial Relations*, **38**(4) 501–531.

Reardon, J., Hasty, R. & Coe, B. (1996). The effect of information technology on productivity in retailing. *Journal of Retailing*, **72**(4), 445–461.

Rodwell, J. J., Kienzle, R. & Shadur, M. A. (1998). The relationships among work-related perceptions, employee attitudes, and employee performance: the integral role of communication. *Human Resource Management*, **37**(3 and 4), 277–293.

Ryan, A. M., Schmit, M. J. & Johnson, R. (1996). Attitudes and effectiveness: examining relations at an organizational level. *Personnel Psychology*, **49**(4), 853–882.

Schmit, M. J. & Allscheid, S. P. (1995). Employee attitudes and customer satisfaction: making theoretical and empirical connections. *Personnel Psychology*, **48**(3), 521–537.

Schneider, B., Parkington, J. & Buxton, V. (1980). Employee and customer perceptions of service in banks. *Administrative Science Quarterly*, **25**, 252–267.

Schneider, B., White, S. S. & Paul, M. C. (1998). Linking service climate and customer perceptions of service quality: test of a causal model. *Journal of Applied Psychology*, **83**(2), 150–163.

Sergeant, A. & Frenkel, S. (2000). When do customer contact employees satisfy customers? *Journal of Service Research*, **3**(1), 18–34.

Sharma, A., Levy, M. & Kumar, A. (2000). Knowledge structures and retail sales performance: An empirical examination. *Journal of Retailing*, **76**(1), 53–69.

Shaw, J. D., Delery, J. E., Jenkins, G. D. Jr & Gupta, N. (1998). An organization-level analysis of voluntary and involuntary turnover. *Academy of Management Journal*, **39**(5), 1–15.

Shortell, S., Jones, R. H., Rademaker, A. W., Gillies, R. R., Dranove, D. S., Hughes, E. F. X., Budetti, P. P., Reynolds, K. S. E. & Huang, C. (2000). Assessing the impact of total quality management and organizational culture on multiple outcomes of care for coronary artery bypass graft surgery patients. *Medical Care*, **38**(2), 207–217.

Singh, J. (2000). Performance productivity and quality of frontline employees in service organizations. *Journal of Marketing*, **64**(2), 15–34.

Sochalski, J., Aiken, L. H. & Fagin, C. M. (1997). Hospital restructuring in the United States, Canada, and Western Europe: an outcomes research agenda. *Medical Care*, **35**(10, Suppl.), OS13–OS25.

Somers, M. J. & Birnbaum, D. (1998). Work-related commitment and job performance: it's also the nature of the performance that counts. *Journal of Organizational Behavior*, **19**, 621–634.

Tubre, T. C. & Collins, J. M. (2000). Jackson and Schuler (1985) revisited: a meta-analysis of the relationships between role ambiguity, role conflict, and job performance. *Journal of Management*, **26**(1), 155–169.

Uhl-Bien, M. & Graen, G. B. (1998). Individual self-management: analysis of professionals' self-managing activities in functional and cross-functional work teams. *Academy of Management Journal*, **41**(3), 340–350.

Woodward, C. A., Shannon, H. S., Cunningham, C., McIntosh, J., Lendrum, B., Rosenbloom, D. & Brown, J. (1999). The impact of re-engineering and other cost reduction strategies on the staff of a large teaching hospital. *Medical Care*, **37**(6), 556–569.

CHAPTER 16

The Human Resource–Firm Performance Relationship: Methodological and Theoretical Challenges

Patrick M. Wright
Cornell University, Ithaca, NY, USA
and
Timothy M. Gardner
Marriott School of Management, Brigham Young University, UT, USA

The increasingly competitive global economy pushes firms to exploit all of their available resources as a means of achieving competitive advantage. One resource recently recognized as providing a source of competitive advantage is the human resources of the firm, and this recognition has resulted in an expansion of the field of strategic human resource management (SHRM). Wright & McMahan defined SHRM as "the pattern of planned human resource deployments and activities intended to enable an organization to achieve its goals" (1992, p. 298). Because firm performance stands out as one major organizational goal, much of the recent SHRM research has been directed at understanding the relationship between human resource (HR) practices and firm performance.

Two different but related streams of research examine the relationship between HR practices and firm performance. One stream of research examines the impact of individual HR practices on relevant organizational outcomes. For example, Konrad & Mangel (2000) examined the relationship between quality of work life (QWL) programs and productivity. Shaw, Gupta & Delery (2001) examined the impact of pay systems on firm outcomes in the concrete pipe industry. Cappelli & Neumark (2001), using an extensive longitudinal data set and exemplary research methodology, found that employee empowerment programs increased both gross productivity and labor costs, resulting in little effect on overall labor efficiency. A second stream of research examines the relationship between sets or systems of HR practices and firm outcomes. The seminal and most frequently cited study is Huselid's (1995) study of the relationship among HR practices, turnover and organizational performance.

Scores of similar studies have been conducted in the years since the publication of this article (Huselid & Becker, 2000). MacDuffie (1995) showed that manufacturing plants with internally consistent bundles of HR practices, coupled with flexible production systems, outperformed plants lacking one or both of these features. Ostroff (2000) found that the type of business strategy moderated the impact of HR practices on firm outcomes. Finally, Shaw *et al.* (1998) found that a set of HR practices differentially explained organizational quit and discharge rates. While there have been some recent efforts to integrate these two research streams (Wright & Boswell, 2002), the latter stream examining the impact of systems of practices on firm outcomes has been considered "strategic" HRM, while the stream examining the impact of single practices has been considered "traditional" or "functional" (Mahoney & Deckop, 1986; Fisher, 1989; Wright & Boswell, 2002). The focus of this chapter will be on the stream of SHRM research.

While evidence mounts that HR practices are at least weakly related to firm performance, significant methodological and theoretical challenges exist with regard to furthering our understanding of this relationship. Methodologically, there is no consensus regarding which practices constitute a theoretically complete set of HR practices; how to conceptually categorize these practices; the relevance of business strategy; the appropriate level of analysis; or how HR practices and firm performance should be measured. In the first part of this chapter we review the current debates that inform these areas of research.

Theoretically, no consensus exists regarding the mechanisms by which HR practices might impact on firm outcomes. This lack of theoretical development has resulted in few empirical studies that explore the processes through which this impact takes place. In the second part of this chapter, we review the existing literature suggesting the links through which HR practices impact firm financial performance.

The purpose of this chapter is to identify some of the major empirical and theoretical challenges that SHRM researchers face in expanding our knowledge of the HR practice–firm performance relationship, and to provide at least some future directions for addressing these challenges. We will first address the empirical challenges and then the theoretical challenges. We will conclude with some specific recommendations for future SHRM research.

EMPIRICAL CHALLENGES IN EXAMINING THE RELATIONSHIP BETWEEN HR PRACTICES AND FIRM PERFORMANCE

Composition of Sets of HR Practices

As mentioned above, the SHRM research stream examines the impact of sets of human resource practices on various firm outcomes. There is a great deal of variation in the number and composition of each study's set of practices. In a review of the literature, Dyer & Reeves (1995) noted that 28 different practices were used across just four studies. Only one practice, formal training, showed up in all four studies. In a similar type of review, Becker & Gerhart (1996) documented 27 different practices across five studies, with no practice common to all five studies.

Although there is tremendous variation in HR system composition across studies, one notable trend is the difference between studies grounded in the management tradition and studies grounded in the industrial relations tradition. Management scholars tend to draw on the industrial–organizational psychology model of achieving optimal work performance through the use of HR practices to select, train and motivate individuals. This includes selection programs, job-specific training, performance management, incentive compensation, employee empowerment and job design (Delery, Gupta & Shaw, 1997; Huselid, 1995; Ostroff, 2000). Scholars from the industrial relations tradition tend to draw on the human relations model of enhancing the holistic welfare of workers. This includes practices consistent with improving workers' physical and psychological working conditions, decision-making authority, wages, job security and general skills (Appelbaum & Batt, 1994; Guthrie, 2001; MacDuffie, 1995).

We suggest that research from the industrial relations tradition starts with the assumption that firms should engage in worker-friendly policies on moral or ethical grounds. It then seeks to provide data demonstrating that taking care of workers can both improve the quality of their work lives and produce economic dividends for firms. Research from the management tradition, on the other hand, starts from the normative assumption that firm performance (in particular, profitability) is the ultimate goal. Consequently, it seeks to understand the mechanisms by which HR practices impact firm performance, the content and configuration of HR practices having the optimal impact on firm outcomes, and the contingencies by which these practices are more and less effective. Thus, the array of practices studied usually extends beyond those studied in the industrial relations area, including practices that might not be worker-friendly but would more directly impact firm performance. While both are legitimate and important lines of research, the examination of the broad set of HR practices, common in the management research stream, can better inform practice and theory of the means to optimize worker and organizational outcomes. It provides a greater potential for theorizing and discovering the impact of all of the practices to which workers are subject, be they positive or negative, from the perspective of both the workers and their employing firms. Thus, we suggest that future researchers should not limit themselves to studying only those HR practices that are explicitly beneficial to workers, but include the full set of practices organizations use to effectively acquire, develop and motivate their pool of human capital.

In addition to variance in the sets of HR practices, there is variation in the techniques scholars use to combine HR practices into coherent groups. Delery (1998) provides a comprehensive review of these methodologies. Techniques include exploratory factor analysis (Huselid, 1995), confirmatory factor analysis (Youndt *et al.*, 1996), conceptual clustering (Delery *et al.*, 1997) and cluster analysis (Lee & Chee, 1996). We support Delery's (1998) conclusion that the proper technique depends on the theoretical model and that additional research will be needed to further inform this issue.

Is Strategy Relevant?

Another important distinction must be made between SHRM and research examining the relationship between HR practices and firm performance. One of the basic assumptions driving SHRM research is the belief that achieving "fit" between a firm's strategy and HR practices will generate maximum organizational performance (Dyer, 1985; Wright & McMahan, 1992). In essence, this basic model has its roots in contingency theory, suggesting that a synergistic effect results from fitting two variables together, beyond that which would result from the summative effect of the two variables.

Recent debates have arisen regarding the necessity of the strategy construct in SHRM (Delery & Doty, 1996). Wright & Sherman (1999) noted that very little empirical research has supported the efficacy of the concept of "fit" between strategy and HR. A series of studies published as an edited book (Cappelli, 1999) finds only limited support for the thesis of a common link between HR practices strategy. Pfeffer (1994, 1998), comparing the paucity of research demonstrating the effectiveness of fitting HR to strategy to the plethora of research demonstrating that certain HR practices are consistently associated with firm performance, argues that it is these "best practices" that impact performance, not their fit with strategy. Such an approach has been referred to as a "universalistic" approach (Delery & Doty, 1996).

Wright & Sherman (1999) reviewed the research on fit between strategy and HR, and noted that a number of theoretical and empirical problems exist that might explain the failure to support the basic model. They argued that research that overcomes those limitations might find better support for the intuitively appealing and practically assumed relationships among these variables. Wright (1998), building upon the architectural approach of Becker & Gerhart (1996), proposed that HR practices could be classified into four levels, including guiding principles, policy alternatives (different practices), products (competencies or behaviors the practice promotes) and practice–process (the effectiveness of execution of the practices). This framework is illustrated in Figure 16.1. He noted that, while some practices

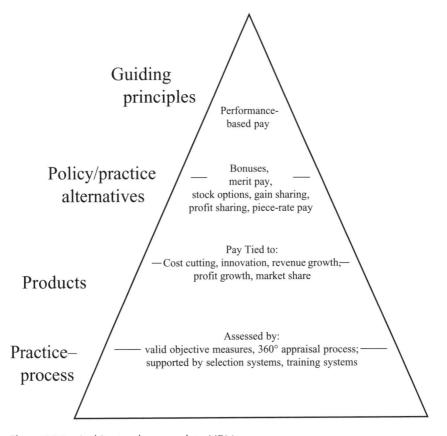

Figure 16.1 Architectural approach to HRM

(e.g. performance based pay, rigorous selection, etc.) might be universally effective, the efficacy of fit comes more at the product level (i.e. pay promoting the right kind of performance or a selection system selecting the right kinds of people, given a particularly strategy). Becker & Huselid (1998) support this idea, arguing that fit between HR and strategy might best be achieved at the level of competencies required for a strategy.

For the purposes of this paper, we consider strategy to be a legitimate, but unnecessary, variable in examining the relationship between HR practices and firm performance. We recognize the potential for HR practices to impact firm performance independent of the strategy construct. However, as we move from studying this simple relationship to SHRM we argue that infusing the strategy construct into the research stream can aid in understanding both the determinants of HR practices and also how an alignment of HR practices with strategy can provide a significant incremental effect on performance.

Levels of Analysis Issues in the HR–Firm Performance Relationship

One particularly difficult challenge in the current research stems from the variance in levels of analysis at which the HR–firm performance relationship has been studied. This literature has examined the relationship at the level of the plant, business unit and corporation. Rogers & Wright (1998) reviewed 29 empirical studies containing 80 distinct observations of an empirically tested link between HRM and organizational performance. They found reports of only five effect sizes observed at the level of the business unit, with the remaining 75 being at the corporate (56) or plant (19) level. Clearly most (in fact over two-thirds) of this research has explored the corporate level of analysis, while virtually ignoring the business unit. This, of course, begs the question as to which level provides the most appropriate test of the relationship. We explore this issue below.

Plant-level studies (e.g. Cappelli & Neumark, 2001; Ichniowski & Shaw, 1999; MacDuffie, 1995, Youndt et al., 1996) provide the advantage of measuring HR practices quite specifically and probably most accurately. Because these studies often focus only on one large job group in one location, the risk of variance in HR practices within the focal unit is minimized. Additionally, because of the close physical proximity, one could also assume that the respondent has at least somewhat accurate and first-hand experience with the enacted HR practices, thus increasing the validity of the measures. Finally, these studies have the potential of providing the most proximal measures of performance, whether they are employee (absenteeism, turnover), organizational (productivity, quality) or financial (profitability) outcomes. The major drawback of such a level stems from the fact that it often precludes assessing fit with business strategy; rather, the focus is on production strategy.

Business level studies are the optimal setting for assessing the links between HR practices and business strategy. Assessments at this level should result in the most accurate measures of business strategy, and relatively proximal measures of performance (e.g. market share, profitability, etc.). However, studying these phenomena at the business unit level creates some problems. Because businesses often have multiple locations and multiple jobs, precise assessments of HR practices become problematic. Finding a single respondent able to accurately describe HR practices across 10–20 different jobs (even if divided by exempt and non-exempt) and five or more locations seems near impossible. One can, at best, hope for rough assessments.

Finally, studying these phenomena at the corporate level provides a tremendous advantage in the assessment of financial performance, because of the publicly available databases that provide such information. One can readily access a publicly traded corporation's financial information to assess performance, such as gross rate of return on assets to compute Tobin's Q (Huselid, 1995). This explains why the bulk of SHRM research relating to firm performance has been conducted at this level. However, to consider the disadvantages of such research, take the assessment problems noted above with regard to business level studies (accurate descriptions about enacted HR practices across multiple locations and jobs) and multiply them by the number of businesses existing within the corporation. In addition, because variance exists in business strategies across businesses within some corporations, the assessment of strategy becomes problematic. Finally, because these studies often cross industries, it becomes difficult to partial out all of the industry effects.

Thus, this examination points out that no right or wrong level of analysis exists for studying the HR practice–firm performance relationship. Each level provides answers to unique questions, and each has a set of relative advantages and disadvantages. This suggests that researchers need to be quite deliberate in their choice of level of analysis, given a particular research question; or deliberate in their choice of a research question, given a level of analysis.

Measurement Issues in the HR–Firm Performance Relationship

Only recently has research begun to focus on measurement issues in this body of research. A number of recent reviews have noted some of the problems in measuring key constructs within this literature, and empirical research is beginning to appear that may have implications for measurement in future research. These measurement issues focus on the assessment of two major variables: HR practices and firm performance.

HR Practices

The accurate assessment of the relationship between HR practices and performance requires reliable and valid assessment of HR practices. Recent research points to problems in this area.

First, with regard to reliability, virtually all of the focus in this literature has been on internal consistency estimates. Huselid (1995) provided moderate internal consistency estimates as evidence of the reliability of his HR practice scales, as did others (Delery & Doty, 1996; Youndt et al., 1996). In most cases, the studies had single respondents; thus, assessments of inter-rater reliability were impossible. In the few instances where multiple respondents completed measures, Snell and his colleagues (Dean & Snell, 1991; Snell & Dean, 1992; Youndt et al., 1996) reported the r_{wg} statistic. However, Gerhart et al. (2000) recently used a multiple respondent design to examine sources of variance in the measurement of HR practices and found frighteningly low levels of overall reliability of HR practice measures. They noted that the r_{wg} statistic is inappropriate because it only assesses "agreement" within one firm, rather than "reliability" across firms. They found that with their data, a scale constructed to maximize overall reliability at best provided an estimate of 0.20. In a follow-up paper, Wright et al. (2001) found similarly low levels of reliability in HR practice measures collected from single informants in three additional studies.

Second, no agreement exists for the level of specificity with which HR practices should be measured. Specificity refers to the level of description of each practice. For example, with regard to compensation, one could assess the presence/absence of pay for performance (i.e. at the principle level). However, pay-for-performance could include profit sharing, gain sharing, merit pay, bonuses, stock options, commissions, piece-rate pay and a variety of other techniques (or policy alternatives) for tying pay to performance. One could also go so deep as to explore the variety of performance aspects to which pay could be tied such as profits, stock price growth, revenue growth, new products, cost reductions, etc. (i.e. the products). Finally, one could focus on the effectiveness of execution (practice–process) of the HR practices. Again, no consensus currently exists regarding the level of specificity at which HR practice measures should be operationalized.

Finally, scholars disagree about the proper scale of measurement. Much of the research in this area has attempted to objectify the measurement by asking respondents to indicate in some form the presence/absence of practices. Thus, scales that ask respondents to indicate the percentage of employees covered by a practice do not gather information about the effectiveness of the practice, only its presence within a percentage of the workforce (e.g. Huselid, 1995). On the other hand, some measures have a more subjective tone, through asking respondents to indicate "the extent to which" practices exist on a Likert-type scale. For example, Snell (1992) assessed HRM controls using Likert-type responses to items such as, "We have gone to great lengths to establish the best staffing procedure possible", and Snell & Dean (1992) and Youndt et al. (1996) used items such as, "How much effort is given to measuring employee performance ($1 =$ very little; $7 =$ great deal)?".

While objective measures might normally be preferred, increasing organizational size and complexity decrease respondents' ability to accurately report the use of HR practices across the organization. In other words, a Senior Vice-President of HR at a corporate headquarters for a large firm might not know the exact percentage of managers who receive formal performance appraisals, but he/she might know that performance appraisals are strongly (or weakly) emphasized in the organization. In fact, while Gerhart et al. (2000) found almost no inter-rater reliability for measures of HR practices, they found reasonable inter-rater reliability on subjective measures of the effectiveness of the HR function. It may be that HR executives/practitioners focus attention (and internal discussion) more on the goals and effectiveness of their HR practices than they do on the coverage of those practices.

This is not to call for replacing objective scales with subjective ones, but only to suggest that there may be a point of diminishing returns to objective scales, such that, at some point, measures aimed at eliciting subjective impressions provide more accurate data than those aimed at objective reporting. This is certainly an area for future research to examine.

Performance

In addition to the issues with measuring HR practices, researchers face a number of challenges in the measurement of firm performance. These challenges revolve around the relatively limited number of different performance measures that have been used in this research, and the tendency not to assess multiple performance measures in any single study.

First, regarding the variety of performance measures used in this field of research, Rogers & Wright (1998) reviewed 29 empirical studies containing 80 distinct observations of an empirically tested link between HRM and organizational performance. They categorized the performance measures into human resource (turnover being the only employee measure they found), organizational (e.g. productivity, quality, customer satisfaction), financial accounting (e.g. return on assets) and financial market (e.g. stock price or Tobin's Q). They found that only three effect sizes were reported relating HR to human resource outcomes, 34 relating to organizational outcomes, 24 to accounting outcomes and 19 to financial market outcomes. While the relative emphasis on organizational, accounting and market measures aids in convincing line executives of the value of HR, the dearth of studies on employee outcomes is disappointing for two reasons.

First, employee outcomes are those most proximal to the actual practices and, thus, more data supporting the impact of these practices on multiple employee outcomes (such as absenteeism, skills, motivation, employee attitudes, etc.) would, by itself, be interesting. For example, Wright *et al.* (1999) found that appraisal and training practices were related to workforce skills and that training and compensation practices were related to workforce motivation, as assessed by line executives in petrochemical refineries. Second, because all of our theoretical rationales for how HR impacts performance posit that the impact comes through these employee outcomes, the dearth of research in this area shows a dearth of research actually testing theory.

The second issue is that very few studies have measured firm outcomes in more than one performance category, and thus researchers are unable to examine the interrelationships among the outcomes. One noteworthy exception has been Huselid's (1995) study, which examined one employee outcome (turnover), one financial outcome (gross rate of return) and one financial market outcome (Tobin's Q). He found that at least some of the effect of HR practices on firm performance was mediated by the reduction of employee turnover.

The reasons for this failure to measure mediating variables are not surprising, and tend to boil down to lack of theoretical development and access to data. First, as will be outlined later in the chapter, there is a lack of consensus of the role and specificity of mediating variables in theoretical models. Second, across-industry studies, such as Huselid's (1995), make comparability of measures, such as customer satisfaction, quality and productivity, quite difficult. Third, within-industry studies, such as Arthur (1992) or MacDuffie (1995), may discourage competing firms from sharing certain kinds of data. In addition, within-industry studies are also fraught with comparability issues (e.g. different measures of customer satisfaction or employee satisfaction).

While empirical research on the relationship between HR and firm performance has made great strides over the past 10 years, there is still much work to be done. As we have noted, the most significant problem stems from a lack of good empirical tests of theory. Having discussed the empirical challenges in attempting to test the evolving theoretical models of the impact of HR on firm performance, we now turn our attention to the significant challenges faced by researchers in actually developing theories to be tested.

THEORETICAL CHALLENGES IN EXAMINING THE RELATIONSHIP BETWEEN HUMAN RESOURCE PRACTICES AND FIRM PERFORMANCE

A decade ago, Wright & McMahan (1992) reviewed the theoretical perspectives that had been applied to the field of SHRM. At that time, these theoretical perspectives dealt primarily with applications of existing organizational (e.g. cybernetic systems, resource dependence, institutional) and economic (e.g. agency/transaction cost, resource-based view) theories to SHRM. McMahan, Virick & Wright (1999) updated this review to include some additional theoretical perspectives, such as population ecology, strategic reference points, Foucaldian and human capital theories.

While these theoretical applications have some value in clarifying some of the determinants and consequences of HR practices, they have limited value for aiding the understanding of how HR practices impact firm performance. Rather, most of these theoretical perspectives provide extremely macro-level frameworks for explaining why certain HR practices might exist. Consequently, they do not provide a precise framework for defining the specific mechanisms through which HR practices influence firm performance.

In essence, this issue of "specific mechanisms" could be thought of as defining what's going on in the "black box" between HR practices and firm performance. One of the major challenges facing researchers lies in explicating and assessing the precise mechanisms through which HR practices influence firm performance. Facing this challenge will provide both better theoretical understanding among HR researchers and more valid tools for practitioners seeking to leverage their firm's human assets as a source of competitive advantage.

In the following section we address this "black box" issue and its associated challenges. The challenges consist of determining how many separate boxes need to be defined and how many variables should be in each box.

How Many Boxes Should Be in the Black Box?

To examine the impact of HR practices on firm outcomes, the common research design assesses a firm's HR practices and then statistically relates these practices to some financial outcome such as profitability or shareholder wealth. One of the first issues that must be settled in the effort to understand how HR practices impact performance is to theorize the means through which this relationship occurs, in essence, specifying the intervening variables between the measure of HR practices and the measure of firm performance. Virtually all authors have implicitly or explicitly treated the "black box" as a linear causal process consisting of one or more smaller boxes. For example, Becker & Huselid (1998) suggested a causal model whereby the HRM system impacts employee behaviors, which leads to strategy implementation, which consequently determines operating performance, leading to overall firm performance. Wright & Snell (1998) offer a similar model that adds employee skills between the HR practices and employee behaviors. Numerous similar models have been proposed by others (e.g. Truss & Gratton, 1994; Wright, McMahan & McWilliams, 1994). Probably the most specific to date was offered by Becker *et al.* (1997), who proposed the model depicted in Figure 16.2. The similarity among all of these models is that they all have their basis in a linear causal process.

When hypothesizing a linear causal model, one of the challenges is deciding on the appropriate number of mediating variables between the primary independent and dependent variables. The earliest models simply proposed that a fit between HR practices and firm strategy resulted in a generic outcome entitled "firm performance". Becker & Huselid (1998) increased the complexity of the model by including employee behavior, strategy implementation and operational performance as mediating variables. Becker *et al.*'s (1997) model added two layers of complexity with the inclusion of employee skills and employee

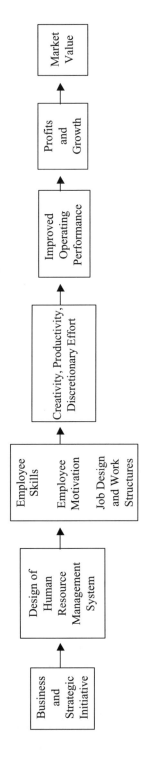

Figure 16.2 Model of the HR–firm performance relationship. Reproduced by permission from Becker *et al.* (1997)

motivation and breaking employee behaviors into productivity, creativity and discretionary effort. Wright & Snell (1998) distinguished between intended and actual HR practices, as well as intended and actual employee skills and behaviors. One could theorize even more specific linear causal models by including more and more "boxes" between HR practices and firm outcomes. The previously described models fail to include absenteeism, turnover or attitudes. The potential for additional complexity is virtually infinite.

In essence, the question of how many boxes need to be included before the model is complete has yet to be settled. It seems that consensus exists that any theoretical or empirical effort should at least specify some mediating variables, but not how many.

What Should Be in Each Box?

In addition to the number of boxes laid out in a causal order, one must also choose a level of specificity within each box. For example, Becker *et al.*'s (1997) addition of an "operating performance" box has great value, but if one is to explore this relationship empirically, on which aspect(s) of operational performance should one focus? Numerous measures of operational performance exist, such as customer satisfaction, customer retention, sales revenues, quality defects, scrap, productivity, downtime, labor costs, etc.

This leads to a multiplicative effect in determining the process of the model. If one wants to develop a specific theoretical model to unlock the "black box", in a system that might contain five main boxes with up to 10 sub-boxes in each, the task requires specification of the relationships among each of the sub-boxes. This creates a serious problem for understanding the phenomena, as the complexity becomes virtually unmanageable.

Thus, a second challenge facing SHRM researchers is to define the right level of variable specificity in the theoretical models for how HR practices impact firm performance. Again, no consensus exists regarding the right set of variables to include in our conceptual models. Researchers only seem to agree that some mediating variables must be specified, and that the more specific these variables are, the better.

What's the Causal Direction?

One particularly problematic question in the HR practice–firm performance relationship is pinpointing the causal direction. To date, all of the theoretical (cf. Figure 16.2) and empirical examinations of this relationship within the SHRM literature have assumed that the outcomes of firm performance are in some way influenced by HR practices. However, two alternative hypotheses must be considered in future research in order to determine the exact causal direction.

First, the "reverse causation" hypothesis would posit that as firms become more profitable, they invest in HR practices. These investments could stem from the belief that the practices will further increase performance, or they could stem from a simple wealth distribution process. In the first case, no requirement exists that the HR practices do, in fact, impact firm performance; only that decision-makers hold such a belief. In the second case, it may simply be that employees' share of increasing wealth is redistributed to them through increased pay, training, participation opportunities, etc. This could either be through benevolent management or through a process of bargaining. For instance, Cappelli & Neumark's

(2001) study of employee empowerment suggested that the value of productivity gains were lost to increased labor costs. However, in both cases the "true" causal model is that profits lead to HR practices, rather than the opposite. Thus, cross-sectional studies may accurately observe more progressive HR practices among higher-performing firms, but researchers might be drawing the wrong conclusions regarding the causal direction.

There exists a second possible explanation for the observed relationship between HR practices and firm performance. The "implicit theory" hypothesis suggests that the observed relationship between measures of HR practices and firm performance stems not from any true relationship, but rather from the implicit theories of organizational survey respondents. Under this hypothesis, a relationship can be observed between HR practices and performance, but this observed relationship reflects the implicit performance theory of respondents, rather than any true relationship between the variables.

Implicit performance theories have been researched in a variety of different areas, including organization–environment relations (e.g. McCabe & Dutton, 1993), strategy (Golden, 1992), corporate reputation (Brown & Perry, 1994), leadership (e.g. Eden & Leviatan, 1975) and group effectiveness (e.g. Martell & Guzzo, 1991). Consistently, this research has demonstrated that research subjects' implicit theories of relationships between variables of interest bias their responses to survey items. Gardner, Wright & Gerhart (1999) found support for implicit theories within the HR–firm performance relationship, albeit not in a field setting. Thus, there is strong direct and indirect evidence that implicit theories affect how research subjects describe HR practices; this phenomenon might account for at least some of the observed relationship between HR practices and firm performance.

CONCLUSIONS

The point of this discussion is not to suggest that past thinking and research is fatally flawed due to a lack or incorrect specification of mediating variables. Neither is the point to assert that HR has no impact on firm performance. Rather, it is to demonstrate a lack of consensus regarding the specific nature of the challenges before the field. Certainly past efforts have contributed to the knowledge base, and are worthy of attention. The past efforts undoubtedly form the foundation for future research, but if we are to move the field forward, we must move beyond what already exists to forge more complete theories of how HR impacts firm performance.

In the future, we advocate further delineation of and empirical research on processes and mechanisms through which HR practices can aid in value creation for firms. We think that, at a minimum, if profitability is the major dependent variable, such models must include at least some variables regarding operational performance (labor costs, customer satisfaction, quality, etc.), and some variables regarding the impact of HR practices on employees (skills, attitudes, behaviors, absenteeism, turnover, etc.). Such theorizing might also provide a deeper understanding of the causal direction of these relationships.

However, caution must be exercised in attempting to meet the challenge of unlocking the black box. As previously noted, no matter what the number of intervening variables posited in a theoretical framework, one can always find something that might be hypothesized to mediate between two of the intervening variables. Thus, while it is fair to say that future theory and research should propose and investigate more intervening variables, it would be unfair to criticize any one study as being inadequate because it did not recognize all of the intervening variables.

FUTURE DIRECTIONS

The recent research examining the relationship between HR practices and firm performance provides some promising results. The results seem to indicate that firms can benefit financially from the development and implementation of progressive or high-performance HR practices. However, before placing irrevocable faith in these conclusions, one must note that some problems exist in this research. The research provides enough justification to continue advocating both the increasing prevalence of these practices in organizations, and an increasing amount of research on this relationship. We have highlighted some of the problems with the past research, and in this final section we wish to lay out some suggestions for future researchers who wish to examine this relationship.

Increasing Focus on Within-industry Studies

Certainly Huselid's (1995) work using publicly traded corporations across industries has provided the empirical foundation upon which much of the future research will rely. He has been able to consistently access data on HR practices and firm performance among sufficiently large samples of firms, and this data has proved very valuable (Huselid & Becker, 1996).

While not calling for a ban on such research (continued research in this area will benefit the field), we certainly think that a next generation of HR research might benefit from an increasing use of within-industry studies. As previously noted, across-industry studies do not provide the opportunity to tease out the idiosyncratic strategies and bases for competition that exist within certain industries. Additionally, they make it difficult to find more fine-grained measures of performance, such as customer satisfaction, market share or other important performance metrics that would aid in increasing our understanding of how HR practices impact on firm performance. Studies within specific industries would enable researchers to identify the key competitive metrics that participants within the industry consider important, and to assess the unique strategies (both business and HR strategies) that firms engage in as a means of increasing their performance on those metrics.

Increasing Business and Plant Level Studies

Again, Huselid's (1995) significant research at the corporate level of analysis has provided a tremendous foundation from which this field can grow. It also is certainly the only legitimate multi-level study following the impact of HR practices through to the ultimate goal of shareholder wealth. However, again, we would call for a decrease in emphasis on the corporate level of analysis and an increase in studies of the business unit or plant level.

Corporate level studies provide the important advantage of looking at shareholder wealth as a criterion. However, they do not provide a suitable level for examining the fit between HR practices and strategy (as business level studies do) nor for precise measurement of the relationship between HR practices and employee outcomes (as plant level studies can). Thus, the recommendation to move toward more business level and plant level studies stems from the relative dearth of studies at that level, as well as the dearth of studies demonstrating the impact of HR practices on employee outcomes (Rogers & Wright, 1998).

More Reliable Measures of HR Practices

The results of Gerhart et al. (2000) and Wright et al. (2001) showed little true variance in single-informant measures of HR practices, a finding which should certainly give future researchers pause for thought. As previously noted, as organizations grow in complexity (more jobs, more locations, more divisions) and size (more employees, broader geographic/global presence), the information-processing requirements become unmanageable for a single respondent trying to accurately report enacted HR practices across an organization. This is an issue that is only recently becoming apparent in this literature.

Developing more reliable measures may entail a number and combination of alternative approaches. First, one could decrease the complexity through focusing on practices with regard to one job (or set of very similar jobs, e.g. top 10% of executives), with regard to one multi-unit business (as opposed to across businesses within an organization) or with regard to one site. One would expect that single respondents would be most able to accurately report HR practices for a single job at a single site, assuming that respondent was positioned to do so (e.g. the HR manager for that plant). As one adds levels of complexity (jobs, sites, businesses, etc.), it becomes increasingly improbable that reliable, valid measures of HR practices will be gained.

Second, assessing HR practices from multiple respondents should increase the reliability and validity of HR practice measures. Gerhart et al. (2000) noted that reliability of HR measures in their sample could have been increased to adequate levels by adding 5–10 more raters per organization. This number seems unreasonable, but the results certainly point to the need to include multiple raters. However, the addition of raters alone will not solve reliability problems if the raters are not in the position of knowing what HR practices exist. One difficult but unique avenue for future research would be to have the employees in the organization report the HR practices that exist. Since they are the focal unit the practices aim at, their assessment might provide the best (most accurate) assessment of the HR practices as they truly exist within the firm.

Finally, developing more specific measures of HR practices should increase reliability and validity as well as increase our theoretical understanding. As noted before, HR practices could be assessed at the level of principle, policy alternative, product and/or practice–process. Assessing practices at the level of principle (e.g. pay for performance, rigorous selection, extensive training, etc.) should support a universalistic or best practice approach, but will probably never adequately support a link between HR and strategy. One would expect that as our measures of HR practices become more precise, we will be better able to capture the interaction between strategy and HR in impacting firm performance.

Longitudinal Research Designs

The resolution of the question of the causal order of the relationship between HR practices and firm performance is paramount and far from resolved. One of the key criteria for establishing causal order is that the use of HR practices precedes the performance outcome (in time). Meeting this requirement requires longitudinal research designs. While there are limited examples of longitudinal research designs in past research, the vast majority of SHRM studies use cross-sectional methodology. Huselid's (1995) study provides one of the best but still not adequate examples of a longitudinal research design. Firm performance measures were collected 1 year after the collection of the HR practice data. However, one of the mediating variables, turnover, was collected at the time of the HR practice data reflecting employee exits in the year preceding the HR practice data collection effort. The only exemplary example of a strong longitudinal design comes from the single HR practice literature. Cappelli & Neumark (2001) used two different sampling frames of 16 and 19 years each. The vast majority of all other SHRM studies fall short in their use of longitudinal designs. Shaw et al. (1998) used a procedure similar to Huselid (1995) in collecting contemporary HR practice data and turnover rates from the previous year. Delery & Doty (1996), MacDuffie (1995) and Bae & Lawler (2000) used pure cross-sectional designs. Guthrie (2001) and Ichniowski, Shaw & Prennushi (1997) used what is known as a retrospective longitudinal design. Using one survey administration, Guthrie (2001) asked respondents to report HR practices in the 2 years preceding the time the survey was administered, and report turnover and subjective firm performance efforts in the year preceding the survey administration. Ichniowski et al. (1997) visited 36 steel production lines and collected approximately 4 years of retrospective HR practice data from executives and archival sources and 4 years of performance data from company archives.

A stronger case that HR practices impact organizational outcomes could be made with the use of stronger longitudinal research designs. First, we would recommend future studies avoid collecting HR practice and outcome data on one survey administration. To ensure the data is either longitudinal or at least cross-sectional, the researcher must ask the respondent to provide retrospective reports of past HR practices. This technique undoubtedly introduces excessive measurement error (Golden, 1992). Furthermore, if not designed carefully, the researcher may end up predicting outcomes that precede the use of HR practices in time (Huselid, 1995; Shaw et al., 1998). Second, we would recommend at least two separate data collection efforts. Properly timed, this will ensure that the measurement of HR practices precedes organizational outcomes in time. As we move forward, researchers should begin collecting HR practice and outcome data over multiple time periods. Such methodology will allow researchers to appropriately control for unwanted heterogeneity and possibly allow quasi-experimental designs as organizations introduce and discontinue different HR practices (Menard, 1991).

SUMMARY

The field of SHRM is still in its infancy, with its founding arguably traced to as recently as 1981 (Wright, 1998). Significant progress has been made since then, with a number of seminal articles that have demonstrated support for the relationship between HR practices and firm performance. These articles illustrated some profound truths, but, in retrospect, we may not yet know what these truths are.

This chapter has attempted to provide a critique of past research on the relationship between HR practices and firm performance, and to provide some recommendations for how future research in this area can move the field forward. This critique points to weaknesses in past research, but does so without malice. It is not intended to point fingers at past mistakes, but rather to point future research in a direction that can continue the knowledge discovery process with regard to how HR can make an impact on firm performance.

REFERENCES

Appelbaum, E. & Batt, R. (1994). *The New American Workplace: Transforming Work Systems in the United States*. Ithaca, NY: ILR Press.

Arthur, J. (1992). The link between business strategy and industrial relations systems in American steel minimills. *Industrial and Labor Relations Review*, **45**, 488–506.

Bae, J. & Lawler, J. J. (2000). Organizational and HRM strategies in Korea: impact on firm performance in an emerging economy. *Academy of Management Journal*, **43**, 502–517.

Becker, B. & Gerhart, B. (1996). The impact of human resource management on organizational performance: progress and prospects. *Academy of Management Journal*, **39**, 779–801.

Becker, B. E. & Huselid, M. A. (1998). High performance work systems and firm performance: a synthesis of research and managerial implications. In G. R. Ferris (Ed.), *Research in Personnel and Human Resource Management,* Vol. 16 (pp. 53–101). Greenwich, CT: JAI Press.

Becker, B. E., Huselid, M. A., Pickus, P. S. & Spratt, M. F. (1997). HR as a source of shareholder value: research and recommendations. *Human Resource Management*, **36**, 39–47.

Brown, B. & Perry, S. (1994). Removing the financial performance halo from Fortune's "Most Admired Companies". *Academy of Management Journal*, **37**, 1347–1359.

Cappelli, P. (Ed.) (1999). *Employment Practices and Business Strategy*. New York: Oxford University Press.

Cappelli, P. & Newmark, D. (2001). Do "high performance" work practices improve establishment level outcomes? *Industrial and Labor Relations Review*, **54**, 737–775.

Dean, J. W. & Snell, S. A. (1991). Integrated manufacturing and job design: moderating effects of organizational inertia. *Academy of Management Journal*, **34**, 776–804.

Delery, J. E. (1998). Issues of fit in strategic human resource management: implications for research. *Human Resource Management Review*, **8**, 289–309.

Delery, J. & Doty, H. (1996). Models of theorizing in strategic human resource management: tests of universalistic, contingency, and configurational performance predictions. *Academy of Management Journal*, **39**, 802–835.

Delery, J. E., Gupta, N. & Shaw, J. D. (1997). Human resource management and firm performance: a systems perspective. Paper presented at the 1997 Southern Management Association Meeting, Atlanta, GA.

Dyer, L. (1985). Strategic human resources management and planning. In G. R. Ferris (Ed.), *Research in Personnel and Human Resource Management* (pp. 1–30). Greenwich, CT: JAI Press.

Dyer, L. & Reeves, T. (1995). Human resource strategies and firm performance: what do we know and where do we need to go? *International Journal of Human Resource Management*, **6**, 656–670.

Eden, D. & Leviatan, U. (1975). Implicit leadership theory as a determinant of the factor structure underlying supervisory behavior scales. *Journal of Applied Psychology*, **60**, 736–741.

Fisher, C. D. (1989). Current and recurrent challenges in HRM. *Journal of Management*, **15**, 157–180.

Gardner, T. M., Wright, P. M. & Gerhart, B. (1999). The HR–firm performance relationship: can it be in the mind of the beholder? Working Paper, Center for Advanced Human Resource Studies, Ithaca, NY.

Gerhart, B., Wright, P. M., McMahan, G. C. & Snell, S. A. (2000). Measurement error in research on human resources and firm performance: how much error is there and how does it influence effect size estimates? *Personnel Psychology*, **53**, 803–834.

Golden, B. R. (1992). The past is the past—or is it? The use of retrospective accounts as indicators of past strategy. *Academy of Management Journal*, **35**, 848–860.

Guthrie, J. P. (2001). High involvement work practices, turnover and productivity: evidence from New Zealand. *Academy of Management Journal*, **44**, 180–190.

Huselid, M. (1995). Human resource management practices and firm performance. *Academy of Management Journal*, **38**, 635–672.

Huselid, M. A. & Becker, B. E. (1996). Methodological issues in cross-sectional and panel estimates of the human resource–firm performance link. *Industrial Relations*, **35**, 400–422.

Huselid, M. A. & Becker, B. E. (2000). Comment on "measurement error in research on human resources and firm performance: how much error is there and how does it influence effect size estimates?", by Gerhart, Wright, McMahan, and Snell. *Personnel Psychology*, **53**, 835–854.

Ichniowski, C. & Shaw, K. (1999). The effects of human resource management systems on economic performance: an international comparison of US & Japanese plants. *Management Science*, **45**, 704–721.

Ichniowski, C., Shaw, K. & Prennushi, G. (1997). The effects of human resource management practices on productivity: a study of steel finishing lines. *The American Economic Review*, **87**, 291–313.

Konrad, A. M. & Mangel, R. (2000). The impact of work-life programs on firm productivity. *Strategic Management Journal*, **21**, 1225–1237.

Lee, M. B. & Chee, Y. (1996). Business strategy, participative human resource management and organizational performance: the case of South Korea. *Asia Pacific Journal of Human Resources*, **34**, 77–94.

McCabe, D. L. & Dutton, J. E. (1993). Making sense of the environment: the role of perceived effectiveness. *Human Relations*, **46**, 623–643.

MacDuffie, J. (1995). Human resource bundles and manufacturing performance: organizational logic and flexible production systems in the world auto industry. *Industrial and Labor Relations Review*, **48**, 197–221.

Mahoney, T. A. & Deckop, J. R. (1986). Evolution of concept and practice in personnel administration/human resource management (PA/HRM). *Journal of Management*, **12**, 223–241.

Martell, R. F. & Guzzo, R. A. (1991). The dynamics of implicit theories of group performance: when and how do they operate? *Organizational Behavior and Human Decision Process*, **50**, 51–74.

McMahan, G., Virick, M. & Wright, P. (1999). Alternative theoretical perspectives for strategic human resource management: progress, problems, and prospects. In P. Wright, L. Dyer, J. Boudreau & G. Milkovich (Eds), *Research in Personnel and Human Resources Management (Supplement)*. Greenwich, CT: JAI Press.

Menard, S. (1991). *Longitudinal Research*. Newbury Park, CA: Sage.

Ostroff, C. (2000). Human resource management and firm performance: practices, systems, and contingencies. Working Paper, Arizona State University.

Pfeffer, J. (1994). *Competitive Advantage through People: Unleashing the Power of the Workforce*. Boston, MA: Harvard Business School Press.

Pfeffer, J. (1998). *The Human Equation*. Boston, MA: Harvard Business School Press.

Rogers, E. W. & Wright, P. M. (1998). Measuring organizational performance in strategic human resource management: problems, prospects, and performance information markets. *Human Resource Management Review*, **8**, 311–331.

Shaw, J. D., Delery, J. E., Jenkins, G. D. & Gupta, N. (1998). An organization-level analysis of voluntary and involuntary turnover. *Academy of Management Journal*, **41**, 511–525.

Shaw, J. D., Gupta, N. & Delery, J. E. (2001). Congruence between technology and compensation systems: implications for strategy implementation. *Strategic Management Journal*, **22**, 379–386.

Snell, S. (1992). Control theory in strategic human resource management: the mediating effect of administrative information. *Academy of Management Journal*, **35**, 292–327.

Snell, S. & Dean, J. (1992). Integrated manufacturing and human resource management: a human capital perspective. *Academy of Management Journal*, **35**, 467–504.

Truss, C. & Gratton, L. (1994). Strategic human resource management: a conceptual approach. *International Journal of Human Resource Management*, **5**, 662–686.

Wright, P. M. (1998). HR–strategy fit: does it really matter? *Human Resource Planning*, **21**(4), 56–57.

Wright, P. M. & Boswell, W. R. (2002). Desegregating HRM: a review and synthesis of micro and macro human resource management research. *Journal of Management* (in press).

Wright, P. M., Gardner, T. M., Moynihan, L. M., Park, H. J., Gerhart, B. & Delery, J. E. (2001). Measurement error in research on human resources and firm performance: additional data and suggestions for future research. *Personnel Psychology*, **54**(4), 875–901.

Wright, P. M. & McMahan, G. C. (1992). Alternative theoretical perspectives for strategic human resource management. *Journal of Management*, **18**, 295–320.

Wright, P. M., McMahan, G. C. & McWilliams, A. (1994). Human resources and sustained competitive advantage: a resource-based perspective. *International Journal of Human Resource Management*, **5**, 301–326.

Wright, P. M. & Sherman, S. (1999). The failure to find fit in strategic human resource management: theoretical and empirical considerations. In P. Wright, L. Dyer, J. Boudreau & G. Milkovich (Eds), *Research in Personnel and Human Resources Management (Supplement)*. Greenwich, CT: JAI Press.

Wright, P. M., McCormick, B., Sherman, W. S. & McMahan, G. C. (1999). The role of human resource practices in petro-chemical refinery performance. *International Journal of Human Resource Management*, **10**, 551–571.

Wright, P. M. & Snell, S. A. (1998). Toward a unifying framework for exploring fit and flexibility in strategic human resource management. *Academy of Management Review*, **23**, 756–772.

Youndt, M., Snell, S., Dean, J. & Lepak, D. (1996). Human resource management, manufacturing strategy, and firm performance. *Academy of Management Journal*, **39**, 836–866.

PART IV

Tools and Methods for Design and Evaluation

CHAPTER 17

Tools and Methods to Support the Design and Implementation of New Work Systems

Enid Mumford
University of Manchester Business School, UK
and
Carolyn Axtell
Institute of Work Psychology, University of Sheffield, UK

This chapter concerns the successful introduction of change and how it can best be achieved. Much change today is concerned with the introduction of new work systems, new technology and new organisational structures. Good practice is usually derived from good theory, and the ideas that follow are relevant to a better understanding of change, and have informed tools and methods for designing and implementing such change. Since many of these theories derive originally from two primary sources, the work of Stafford Beer and the research of the Tavistock Institute (Beer, 1975; Trist & Murray, 1993), we adopt, at least initially, a historical view of this topic. The sets of ideas from these two sources support each other. Stafford Beer has always had a great deal of contact with the Tavistock group and both he and its researchers were, and are, followers of systems theory, although they have used this theory in different ways. Beer's principle interest is operational research and cybernetics, the Tavistock group derived many of their ideas for their socio-technical systems approach from sociology and psychoanalysis.

Stafford Beer argues that a problem in all current change processes is the management of complexity (Beer, 1975). He believes that this is the major problem of our age and maintains that one way of handling complexity is through the recognition of requisite variety. The notion, or law, of requisite variety was first developed in the 1950s by Professor Ross Ashby, a cybernetician who argued that variety can only be controlled by variety (Ashby, 1956). By this he meant that the solution to a complex problem requires the problem solvers to be able to understand and influence all the variables contained in the problem. This, in turn, requires both perception and organisation—the ability to recognise, understand and manipulate the different components of the problem. Finding a solution is greatly assisted by what Beer calls "adaptive feedback". This, put simply, is the ability to learn from experience and to use this learning to rethink and adjust further action. Beer also provides us with the notion of a viable system. This is a system which contains its own problem-solving capacity because it has the capacity to adapt. It can maintain stability by responding effectively to unexpected disturbances (Espejo & Harnden, 1989). This capacity for adjustment makes it capable of a degree of self-regulation.

Once a problem is recognised and a decision taken to reduce or remove it, an understanding of its complexity will assist the choice of strategies and methods that can lead to a solution. At this stage there are always two options. One is to reduce the variety of the problem by simplifying it. This, at the same time, reduces the variety of knowledge required of the problem solver. The other is to accept that the problem cannot be simplified and to ensure that the variety it contains is recognised and matched in the knowledge of the problem solvers. This choice will be influenced by the values and skills of the problem solver and by the attitudes and interests of those affected by the solution. The danger arises when a complex problem is seen as simpler than it really is.

A major contribution of the Tavistock group is the recognition that most human systems contain technology and people. This means that the design process has to regard these as two aspects of a single socio-technical system. Both must always be catered for in any design task. Stafford Beer and the Tavistock group also believed in democracy at work, not just for ethical reasons but because it acts as a facilitator, which enables the system to work more effectively. In the light of this, the following sections provide an overview of the factors that need to be considered when undertaking socio-technical change (the environment, the nature of the change, the groups affected, the values of the organisation, communication and involvement), and a review of methods used to assist such change.

THE ENVIRONMENT

When faced with a complex problem, the first area to consider is the environment in which the problem is located. An understanding of this will assist the choice of strategies and methods that can lead to a solution. Let us suppose that the problem is the introduction of a new work system. This must be acceptable to employees, work efficiently and provide a good quality of work environment for those who have to use it. An accurate diagnosis and examination of all environmental factors that will affect the introduction of the new system, together with a ranking of these in terms of their relevance to successful change, is essential. This diagnosis will include an assessment of the stability or volatility of the situation into which the new system is to be introduced. Are the employees there used to change and unlikely to reject it, or will they find it difficult to handle? Is the company conservative and slow-moving, with major change likely to cause a severe shock? What are the reasons for change? Is the company one with a long stable history and a secure future that is accepting change to make itself even more successful? This kind of situation presents little threat to job security and is likely to be welcomed by a work force anxious to keep up-to-date with the needs of its markets. Or is the change a result of increased competition to which the company is having difficulty in responding and which may threaten its future survival? Here innovation may be a symptom of fear, rather than confidence.

The principle of requisite variety advises us that successful problem solving requires the ability to understand the situation into which change is being introduced and to recognise the factors in it that will either help or hinder successful change. This requires both a knowledge of the present and an ability to foresee the future. Many of today's work situations are complex and dynamic, employees come and go with some rapidity, competitors appear and disappear, yet the successful assimilation of change usually requires a degree of stability. How can this be achieved?

THE NATURE OF THE CHANGE

The reason for the change will greatly affect its nature. Is it a product of past success leading to a desire for more growth and diversity? Is it a result of new, and more advanced technical developments that must be taken advantage of? Or is it for negative reasons, such as economic problems that require the company to rethink its activities and options?

Change can also take many different forms. It may need to be sustainable so that it lasts a long time, or temporary to solve a short-term problem. Its size will also be a major factor. Is it small and bounded, such as a specific new system for a particular function or department? Or is it a revolutionary, all-embracing change that is going to affect everywhere and everyone? Companies that attempt to change their work cultures to make themselves more responsive to external demands or increased competition often fall into this last category. Until recently, with some exceptions, most change was not all-embracing. It was more likely to be a new computer system that affected one or two departments, or offices, or the shop floor. Today, large companies are increasingly trying to introduce change that has a major and universal impact. Shell International, under pressure to become more environmentally friendly, is an example here.

Change is also more likely to be difficult than easy. The British government has experienced serious problems with new computer systems that were introduced to improve public services yet did not fulfil the promises that were made when they were ordered. These failures greatly raised costs, alienated both staff and the public, and gave the national authority involved a reputation for incompetence. The change process was chaotic, rather than controlled. This means that right from the start of any change programme there are two different but associated influences that are likely to affect its success. These are the nature of the change that is to take place and the positive or negative success factors operating in the environment it will enter.

THE GROUPS AFFECTED

An important factor that adds to the complexity is the nature of the group, or groups, that will be affected by the change. Change is disturbing for most people, whether it is viewed as positive or negative. It moves the individual or group into unfamiliar situations, which they may see as challenging or threatening. It alters existing social relationships and it requires coping mechanisms, which not all people will have. It can greatly increase the complexity of the world we inhabit and can cause much stress and anxiety.

Employees vary greatly in terms of their personalities, needs, competencies and interests. Where the organisation and its employees have similar values and goals, and the employees are dedicated and totally immersed in its activities, the reaction to change may be different from elsewhere. Professions such as teaching and medicine may have once belonged to this group. However, unfortunately the environment of hospitals, schools and similar institutions has become increasingly unattractive and the psychological rewards have diminished. Many such employees feel increasingly exploited, as the rewards of the job no longer match the dedication and effort that is required.

Groups such as those epitomized by California's Silicon Valley and similar fast-moving environments may react differently again to change. These are typically highly entrepreneurial individuals, some of whom may be portfolio workers. They are fast thinkers, very mobile and constantly seeking new opportunities. They are looking for both mental stimulation and good financial rewards. They may prefer short-term contract work to long-term secure employment and they are risk takers. They are also usually young, clever, and with few family responsibilities. In contrast, a very different group is that made up of people working for large companies who were brought up with the expectation of a "job for life". This group may be older, with families, and its members will value job security. Other groups that may be affected differently by change are women (or men) with small children, particularly if they are single parents, who may feel great strain as they try to manage both work and family. Finally, there is the large and increasing group of workers employed by call centres and other service industries (see Chapter 7, this volume, by Holman) who have both boring work and low pay. They are possibly little different from the workers tied to the moving assembly line of 20 years ago. Each of these groups will have their own anxieties, problems and needs when faced with a change in their work situation. With the exception of the portfolio group, most are unlikely to welcome this.

Some groups, particularly if they are unionised, may want to want to fight new circumstances which are seen as having a negative effect. They may go out on strike. Other individuals will leave the situation and look for new jobs. There may be mixed reactions; some individuals prepared to wait and see what happens, others determined not to cooperate with something they do not understand. These adverse reactions will not come only from employees. Customers and suppliers may also react with hostility as the situations they are familiar with become disturbed.

A successful change programme always requires the ability to get individuals and groups working cooperatively together. This, in turn, requires an understanding of social processes: people's visions, interests, intentions, attitudes and emotions. These are much more difficult to handle than new technology or new work structures, but just as important. They will influence whether the new system is received with enthusiasm or gloom and dismay. Positive attitudes are a result of involvement, communication, motivation and good timing. They are the means for making things happen, the "levers" which enable change to be successfully introduced.

VALUES

Values are powerful principles, usually of an ethical nature, that guide our relationships with others. This means that major influences on how change is handled are the values of those in influential positions. Influential senior managers may be able to motivate employees to operate on the basis of a set of beliefs regarding what is right and wrong for the company. Some companies publicise these as a set of business principles, so that employees, customers, and any other group that has a relationship with the firm, know exactly what to expect in terms of company behaviour.

Although there have always been companies operating with strong social, if paternalistic, ethics (like Cadbury's), the command and control management philosophies of many organisations in the past meant that those at the bottom of the employee hierarchy were undervalued. The human being was not seen as an individual requiring caring and support. Rather, he/she was viewed as an operating unit that could be adjusted through training and incentives to meet the needs of the organisation. These needs were usually related to profits, costs and output. Management viewed most unskilled people as unreliable, with narrow capabilities and limited usefulness. It followed that they should therefore be tightly controlled and given small, low-discretion jobs.

Both Stafford Beer and the Tavistock group were strongly opposed to these attitudes. Stafford Beer believed that people were an important part of his requisite variety theory, therefore their needs and aspirations must be recognised and catered for. The Tavistock group made their position even more explicit. One of their design objectives was always an improvement in the quality of working life, and they believed that this was best secured through involving those on the receiving end of change in its management. Today, the Tavistock has extended its area of interest to the environment, with the hope of ensuring that that people's needs are always considered when environmental change is being introduced. Frank Heller has suggested that this approach could be called socio-ecotechnology, involving joint optimisation between socio-technology and ecology (Heller, 1997).

But, despite this continuing interest in human values, labour can still be regarded as a commodity to be acquired or removed as markets and profits require, and new technical work systems are still introduced with little account being taken of the needs of the people who have to work with them. The belief that the jobs of tomorrow will increasingly require people who have skill, independence and a good capacity for problem solving and decision taking is proving something of a myth. It is clear that many of today's new jobs are in service industries and require caring or interpersonal skills rather than 'cleverness', while the predicted small, entrepreneurial, high-tech companies of Silicon Valley are not yet commonplace. Most small companies still provide rather dull jobs for low salaries (Parker, 2001). The socio-technical philosophy has, as one of its major objectives, the provision of a learning experience for all employees that will provide challenge and enable them to increase their skills, to work cooperatively with others, and to become efficient decision takers and problem solvers.

COMMUNICATION AND INVOLVEMENT

The socio-technical school argues that the best way to achieve successful change is through accepting the importance of human motivation and involving all those likely to be affected by change in the development processes. Enid Mumford's (1995, 1996) positive personal experience of helping different groups to play a major role in the design of their own work systems highlights the success of this approach in helping to create an accepted and acceptable reorganisation of work. Stafford Beer also makes communication an important part of his viable system concept. He states that the end product, the operational system, must have outward and inward communication as well as upward and downward. Also, information must not be filtered through a number of groups before reaching its destination. It must go straight from its source of origin to the group that actually needs to use it.

In order to retain the trust and confidence of the work force and make change more acceptable, employees must be kept in the picture about what is going to happen. The question is, how best to do this? How much communicating do you do, when do you do it, how do you do it? Employees are likely to be both apprehensive and antagonistic if they get their information in an *ad hoc* manner through rumour. So, unless there are exceptional circumstances that require commercial secrecy, most companies will need to develop a communication strategy when introducing change. The next question, then, is how honest should this be? Should it focus only on positive aspects of the change, or should managers try and be totally open with their staff, especially if employee redundancy is likely to be involved? Another question is, how comprehensive should it be? Should only the group directly affected be told or should everyone be kept informed? The answer is that to support democratic participation in the design and implementation of new systems, good communication is always required and this should include both those affected by the new system and those who are merely spectators.

Experience has shown that encouraging the future users of a new work system or other major change to play a part in its development has many advantages. Participation of this kind arouses interest and assists the creation of positive attitudes. It also acts as a learning experience, so that the new system's use and functions are understood when it becomes operational. Moreover, as employees know a great deal about the work they are responsible for and the kinds of service they are expected to perform, it helps ensure that modifications are made that lead to a better fit between the system and its environment. But not everyone wants to participate in introducing change. Senior managers, when asked to do so, may take the attitude of, "I am too busy" and "It's not my job to change things, that's what the change agent should be doing!'. Groups who are reluctant to accept change or are on bad terms with their employer can also have this negative approach. It must be stressed that good communication is an essential part of democratic systems design.

The principles of good communication have not changed much over the years, even though there are now more technical aids to assist the process. Information needs to be clear, comprehensive and continuous throughout the change programme. It needs to be provided initially by senior managers who are respected and followed up by individuals who are trusted and not seen as having a particular axe to grind. Different communication media can be used, from personal talks to newsletters, videos and the Internet. The Internet is particularly useful as it enables communication to be two-way with questions asked and answered. If a new computer system is being introduced, then the manufacturer or software provider can be invited to make a presentation, although this must be seen as what it usually is, a marketing tool. Future users should be helped to identify other companies who are using the same or a similar system, and encouraged to visit them. Nothing is better at providing "the truth" than a visit to another user. Yet it is surprising how few firms do this.

METHODS FOR ASSISTING CHANGE

There are many methods to assist the technical design of new systems, and these are generally accepted because data has to be logically assembled in a computer for usable software to emerge. These methods have similar structures and steps and tend to concentrate on formal data and data-related activities (Jayaratna, 1994). However, there are very few widely accepted methods that contribute to the organisational design of the system and to the needs of the users. The methods developed by Stafford Beer and the Tavistock group have been used as the principle examples in this chapter so far because they have been widely accepted by many different companies in many different countries. This was especially true in the 1970s and 1980s, when many industries were trying to attract and develop a more skilled labour force. Both methods had the support of influential international groups. Stafford Beer was President of the Operational Research Society and had also worked with Eric Trist in the USA, and the socio-technical approach was supported by an influential international body called the Quality of Working Life Group.

Amitai Etzioni (2000) has an explanation for why other similar methods were and are neglected by industry. He argues that many subjects have become too academic and there is too great a gap between rhetoric and reality. Those who have good ideas do not understand how to apply them, and theory is not enough if it is not seen as relevant to organisational life. The result has been that, in subjects such as information technology, change can occur as a result of campaigns related to persuasion and management fashion, rather than to considered decision taking. The work of academics has only rarely been seen as relevant to concrete issues of policy and practice. Also, methods for designing and implementing change are more likely to be accepted when they are related to technical issues, or when they are launched by consultants who are good at marketing.

However, several methods have been derived from the socio-technical and systems theory traditions as well as methods that help developers become more user-centred in their approach. Although it is beyond the scope of this chapter to review all such methods, we will highlight some examples. These include soft systems analysis (Checkland, 1981); the HUFIT PAS toolset (Taylor, 1990), which arises from the perspective of "user-centred design"; the Scandanavian approaches (Ehn, 1989); the Organisational Scenarios tool (Clegg et al., 1996); ETHICS (Mumford, 1995); and Search Conferences (Emery & Purser, 1996). After a brief look at the first few methods, we will concentrate on the final two methods, as these represent the two most widely used methods for small-scale group participation (ETHICS) and large-scale group participation (Search Conferences).

Soft systems analysis (SSA: Checkland, 1981, 1999) is a method for discussing and planning change in complex systems. The method is derived from "systems theory", within which the different interpretations or viewpoints that people hold of the system they inhabit are considered "the norm" rather than "irritating noise" (Clegg & Walsh, 1998). Thus, the values of the approach are to promote participation, debate and agreement with regard to changing the system. The soft systems analyst is not a domain expert, but rather a facilitator who helps the participants analyse and approach change within the system under consideration.

SSA is organised into several iterative stages, requiring logical analysis as well as encouraging imagination and innovation. First, data is gathered about the problem situation and recorded in pictorial form by the analyst, to form a "rich picture" of the system. The participants then try looking at this system in a number of alternative ways (or from different perspectives). These perspectives are then fleshed out to develop a "root definition" (or precise description) of the implications of these perspectives and to develop conceptual models of what the system would logically have to do in order to meet the requirements of these views. So, for instance, alternative perspectives on a pub could be: a system for providing drinks; or a system for providing employment; or a system for integrating the community (Clegg & Walsh, 1998), and each resultant definition and model may shed a different light on the problem situation. Lessons for change are derived and discussed by comparing alternative models with the existing problem situation. This process can take several iterations before a set of changes are agreed and implemented.

SSA is a useful research and practical working tool that has been used extensively by researchers and some practitioners. It can be very powerful, but is fairly difficult to learn and needs a skilled facilitator. Moreover, although it is helpful for reaching agreement about a change and thus setting the goals, it does not offer guidance on how to actually implement such change.

The HUFIT/PAS toolset (Taylor, 1990) was developed at the HUSAT Research Centre at Loughborough. These tools were designed for use by developers without human factors knowledge to enable them to incorporate human factors into the design of information technology. The planning, analysis and specification (PAS) tools facilitate the incorporation of user and task needs into the system requirements specification. Participation of relevant stakeholders (from marketing, planning, development, testing, etc.) is recommended within a workshop setting. Within this workshop, the tools provide structure and support for design decisions and enable the issues and decisions to be recorded for use later in the design process.

The toolset comprises six integrated tools (Allison *et al.*, 1992): the user mapping tool (to identify users and stakeholders, the job goals for these groups, and the benefits and costs of them using the proposed product); user characteristics tool and task characteristics tool (to identify various attributes of the users, their tasks and contexts in which they work, highlighting unusual or important factors which will affect the use of the product); user requirements summary (summary of product requirements gathered from previous stages); usability specification, through drawing up an evaluation table (where product goals are cross-referenced against user tests to ensure that goals are met); and functionality matrix (integration of user requirements with proposed technical specification). Although the toolset is aimed at IT development, it has also been used in a wider range of contexts (e.g. generic office products' design).

Although the tools address individual tasks and users, they do not appear to address the environment in terms of the wider work group or organisational issues in any detail (Maclaren *et al.*, 1991). The tools are intended for use by developers to help them be "user-centred" in their approach. However, given that the tools are relatively straightforward and highly usable, it is feasible that users could use the PAS tools themselves to gather the required information (Maclaren *et al.*, 1991). According to the tools' designers, PAS has been well received in Europe, where it has made a major contribution to the design of usable IT products (Allison *et al.*, 1992).

The democratic, socio-technical Scandanavian approaches developed by Pelle Ehn and colleagues have been used in several projects in that part of the world (most notably the UTOPIA project; Bødker *et al.*, 1987). The approach is based on the strong value given to industrial democracy that exists in Scandanavia. The strategies and techniques used within these approaches have been evolving and changing since the 1970s and broadly comprise four main phases, described by Bødker, Grønbæk & Kyng, (1993). These are: workplace visits; future workshops; organisational games; and embodying ideas.

After initial workplace visits to interview employees and see demonstrations of their work practices, the next phase involves future workshops (Kensing & Halskov Madsen, 1991). These workshops involve three stages: the critique, the fantasy and the implementation phase. The critique phase involves eliciting and recording the problems experienced with the current way of working. In the fantasy phase, participants are able to explore alternatives to the current workplace situation by inverting the negative points into positive statements and brainstorming other statements. From these positive statements, participants are able to develop an outline of a Utopian future (or goal), and this in turn helps to elicit the requirements for the new computer system. During the implementation phase, these Utopian futures are evaluated as to whether they are possible to implement. Themes arising from the future workshop are then used in the organisational games phase (Sjögren & Ehn, 1991), which include the use of mock-ups and cooperative prototyping. In this workshop different scenarios and work organisations are role-played by users and evaluated using simple cardboard and paper mock-ups and collaboratively designed computer-based prototypes. In the final phase, a subset of ideas from the previous stages are embodied and developed through further mock-up design, continued cooperative prototyping, and new or modified work organisation scenarios.

The approach aims to bring together the goals of employers and trade unions, as well as integrating technical and human/organisational issues, and thus involves all groups affected by the change. The approach deals with strategic issues, task allocation, the design of employee jobs, health and safety and training needs. As such, the approach is reliant on collaboration between trade unions and employers, as well as the participation of end-users. Design is seen as a communicative and creative process and so the end-users are considered an essential part of this activity (Maclaren *et al.*, 1991) with "design by doing" being the key to a better understanding and successful design.

There are other notions using similar methods, which there is not space to describe here, e.g. the Dutch have always been followers of a socio-technical approach, as have the Italians through the pioneering work of Professor Federico Butera.

The organisational scenarios tool, which forms part of the Sheffield toolkit (Clegg *et al.*, 1996) is similar to soft systems analysis (SSA), in that it is a systematic method for developing and evaluating alternative ways that an organisation (or part of it) could work. It is influenced by both socio-technical and systems thinking. However, instead of pictures, a set of headings is used to describe the current and alternative scenarios. The method also encourages the participation of relevant stakeholders in the process and requires a facilitator. Arguably, the scenarios tool is simpler for organisations to learn and use than SSA, although some specialist knowledge is required when using the associated and more detailed job design or allocation of function tools (see Clegg *et al.*, 1996; Waterson *et al.*, in press).

First, the participants, with the help of the facilitator, describe and record the current scenario under seven main headings. Next, the participants are encouraged to consider a range of alternative visions for how the system could work and evaluate them using the same headings as before. These are: the "scope" (or boundaries) of the scenario under consideration (e.g. the production area); the "vision" of how the scenario works (e.g. empowered and multi-skilled employees); the "logic" underlying the way it works (e.g. operators need to be empowered to deal with problems as they arise when using complex machinery); the "organisational structure" that supports this way of working (e.g. self-managing teams with fewer supervisors); the "roles" that exist within that structure (e.g.

self-managing operators, who maintain the machinery, engineers and supervisors who concentrate on strategic management); the "benefits" (e.g. greater job satisfaction) and "costs" (e.g. high training costs) and finally the "implications" of keeping or moving to that scenario (e.g. a change in organisational culture from autocratic to consultative and participative).

After considering a range of options, the participants can compare the scenarios and narrow their choice down to a preferred goal. Action planning and preventative planning for change can then proceed. Depending on the system, participants may wish to examine the different tasks that employees would need to undertake within the chosen scenario using the job design tool. Additionally, if being used to design a computer system, then the allocation of tasks between humans and computers may be considered using the function allocation tool. Descriptions of these specific tools can be found in Clegg *et al.*, (1996) and Waterson *et al.*, (in press).

The organisational scenarios tool has been used in several organisations by researchers and a modified version has been used in a supply chain. The tool is flexible enough to endure some modifications to the headings, so that it fits the circumstances or language of the participants. The tool only addresses the "socio" aspects of design, but can also be used alongside other technical approaches and methods. Principally, the tool assists in organisational planning, but does not specifically aid implementation beyond encouraging preventative planning as a result of highlighting the costs and implications.

Although the tools and methods described above illustrate a range of those available, not all have gained large-scale recognition or up-take. We turn now to two socio-technical approaches that have been widely recognised and used for both small-scale and large-scale change: ETHICS and search conferences.

ETHICS

Participative methods have been Enid Mumford's principal area of interest for many years. She has acted as adviser and facilitator to many different kinds of organisation (Mumford, 1995, 1996). The ETHICS method was developed as a result of Enid Mumford's experience in working with groups. ETHICS is an acronym for effective technical and human implementation of computer-based systems. The method (as outlined below) provides a reminder of the different problem-solving stages that might be encountered as projects progress. This has been helpful to both the members of the design groups and to the person in the facilitator role. But methods can become straitjackets as well as decision aids and it was often found expedient to take a "mix-and-match approach", with design groups using those parts of the method that best fitted their particular design situations.

The organisations in which Enid Mumford has facilitated change were interested in using democratic processes to involve staff in the design and implementation of new work systems. Such processes can take many different forms. If only a single department is involved in the change, then all staff can play a part in decision-making or a small representative group can be voted into the decision-making role. In larger projects an elected user design group will be drawn from a number of departments. Although, ideally, the design group always contained a representative mix of people from different jobs, different age groups and men and women, in practice this was not always possible. In some firms, management wanted to have some influence over who were to be members, in

Ethics[1]

Stage 1—diagnosis of needs
- *Step 1.* Why do we need to change? Discuss existing problems and the improvement offered by new technology.
- *Step 2.* What are the system boundaries? Where do our design responsibilities begin and end?
- *Step 3.* Make a description of the existing work system. It is important to understand how this operates before introducing a replacement or modification
- *Step 4.* Define key objectives. Why does this department or function exist, what should it be doing?
- *Step 5.* Define key tasks and information needs. What are the tasks that must be completed, irrespective of how the department is organised or the technology it uses? What information is required to complete these tasks?
- *Step 6.* Measure pre-change job satisfaction. Here a questionnaire is used based on current theories of job satisfaction. The design group gives this to their colleagues who will be affected by the change
- *Step 7.* Measure efficiency. A second questionnaire based on the control theories of Stafford Beer is also given to everyone likely to be affected
- *Step 8.* Assess what is likely to change in the research situation in the future. Design must be for the future as well as the present

Stage 2—Setting of objectives

Clear efficiency, job satisfaction and future change objectives are now set for the new system

Stage 3—Identifying solutions

The design group now identifies and discusses in detail a range of alternative organisational and technical design options. Socio-technical solutions will be included in this but these are not necessarily the ones that are finally selected by the design group. At this stage the design options are likely to be discussed with the Steering Group and with all the future users of the new system

Stage 4—Choice and implementation of solution

Stage 5—Follow-up evaluation

Stage 6—Reports for the company and academic articles describing the theory and practice of the research

---

[1] Readers who would like more information on the practical application of ETHICS should access Enid Mumford's website: www.enid.u-net.com

others those interested in taking on a participative role put themselves forward. There was also always a steering group of departmental and senior management and, in some firms, the trade unions. Their role was to set the boundaries for the project and give guidance when this was requested. The design groups always came up with three or more options for the redesign of work so that a democratic choice could be made as to which was preferable.

Most of Enid Mumford's early projects were associated with the computerisation of customer accounts or pay and records systems that had previously been done manually. Many banks took part in these projects and they led to the redesign of bank branches and, in Lloyds Bank International, of a foreign exchange department. They were mostly initiated by progressive and democratically minded computer specialists who wished to bring together good technical and organisational design. Gradually the projects increased in size and were associated with large systems in major companies such as Rolls Royce, ICI, the Civil Service, the British Navy and a large Manchester hospital.

Many of the projects then took place outside Britain. The largest and longest was with the Digital Equipment Corporation in Boston. Here a representative group of sales staff from all over the USA helped develop the software for a new expert system (Mumford & MacDonald, 1989). This was followed by a number of projects in The Netherlands, including one that involved the participative design of a new production control system. All projects, whether British or overseas, came to a successful conclusion and resulted in technical and organisational systems that fitted well together and were liked by those who had to use them. But they all presented some challenging problems. ICI offered a range of different situations from a manufacturing plant producing salt, to the secretaries of a major research department. Rolls Royce wanted to reform a Purchase Invoice Department where an elderly labour force had become demotivated and inefficient. The Navy was introducing a new pay and records system and was nervous of anything going wrong. Sailors who did not receive the correct pay had a tradition of responding with mutiny.

The objective of all the design groups was to create socio-technical systems that worked well, met technical objectives and provided staff with opportunities for learning, high job satisfaction and well designed jobs. Social needs were also considered. These concerned staff being treated fairly, good communication, and regular consultation. Together, these variables broadly covered the variety of the system that had to be catered for in planning and design.

The design groups also tried to achieve Stafford Beer's Viable System requirements. Beer defines a viable system as having five levels. The bottom, operational, level is concerned with the basic, day-to-day tasks that achieve the system primary's purpose. This usually will be creating a product or providing a service. The next level up is the anti-oscillation level. This contains the diagnostic tools for identifying and solving problems and for preventing these problems occurring. The objective of this level is to maintain the system in a stable state, even though it is responding to external change. The third level is about optimisation. It ensures that critical success factors are recognised and achieved and that all aspects of the system work efficiently. The fourth level seeks information. This is information coming in from outside the system that it needs to understand, assimilate and respond to. The fifth and top level is the control system. This has the task of ensuring that all five systems communicate effectively with each other and with the outside world. The three bottom levels of the viable system are concerned with internal affairs. The fourth and fifth levels respond to external information and events. These ensure that strategy and goals are modified when external inputs affect the internal situation.

In these projects, the length of time required for the design task varied according to the size of the system. Systems affecting only one part of a firm could be completed in about 6 months, with the design group meeting for half a day once a fortnight or a day once a month. The Digital project, which affected all sales offices throughout the USA, took much longer and lasted several years. Here the design group continued meeting once the system was running as further modifications were required.

Although these systems were successful, a lesson learnt from the Digital project was that a participative approach to design and implementation will not help if the technical part of the system later turns out to be unsatisfactory. The project was intended to improve the configuring ability of the Digital sales force when they were quoting prices to customers. Configuring is the process of specifying the various components that a customer's proposed system needs to incorporate and costing these. Sales people had always found this a difficult task and had made mistakes. The company believed that a computer-based configuring system would provide much greater accuracy. In fact, once installed, the sales force soon got tired of using the new automated system. It was slow and complicated and they could work out components and costs more quickly in their heads, even though these were more likely to be inaccurate. Also there were no personal gains from using the system. It did not help to increase the sales people's sales figures and it was these that influenced their level of salary.

Search Conferences and Large-scale Change

Socio-technical design has never stood still. While its boom period was the 1970s and early 1980s, with economic pressures causing its decline in the early 1990s, it is now back and accelerating forward. A number of important developments have recently influenced the socio-technical design environment. One is related to the scale and speed of projects. Whereas in the past most projects were usually quite small and applied to specific groups of employees, many change programmes are now very large and affect everyone working in a company. Today's shorter business and product cycles require them to be introduced at speed to meet rapidly changing situations and demands. This has led to the development of change programmes that enable large numbers of employees to come together to gather ideas and agree on strategies for change. This approach was first developed in the 1970s by Fred and Merrelyn Emery in Australia (Emery & Purser, 1996). In recent years it has been supported, developed and marketed by the US Socio-technical Round Table, which has many consultants among its members. The approach is now extensively used by firms in Canada and the USA.

The aim of large-scale meetings of this kind is to create conditions under which complex issues can be cooperatively explored. This requires bringing together all those with an interest in a particular problem in an environment where the problem can be discussed and creative ideas provided for its solution. Most strategies are a product of large and small group interventions, with final decisions being taken by the larger group, while smaller groups identify and discuss specific problems that need to be tackled along the route to major change. The role of the employees at a meeting or "search conference" is a facilitative one. They are there to manage the learning process, not to put forward ideas of their own. Most of the conferences require 3–4 days for their completion. A search conference is future-orientated, usually taking a time period of 10–15 years as its time horizon.

These conferences all adhere to the traditional socio-technical principle of viewing an organisation as two systems, a technical system of work processes and associated technology and a social system made up of the people as individuals, as groups and as members of a complex structure (Lytle, 1998).

This comprehensive approach is often called "transformational change" because it is an attempt to alter the whole organisation at once. It enables a critical mass of people in an organisation to participate in understanding the need for change, to consider the present situation and identify what should change, to generate ideas on how to manage this change and to implement and support the change and ensure that it works (Bunker & Alban, 1997).

Involving entire groups or communities in a participative decision-making approach takes us back to the past and is very similar to the consultative process used by the Romans in the fifth century BC. Then, Roman citizens would take decisions that affected all the community at *comitia plebis*, or public meetings. Here problems would be presented to them for discussion by a magistrate. Any resolutions taken would be regarded as binding, once they had been ratified by the Senate. The day for this meeting would be carefully chosen. Signs were read to ensure that proposed courses of action had the approval of the gods and the meeting had to be held on the inaugurated site of a temple. These meetings were held regularly. Sometimes they were for all citizens, sometimes they were restricted to particular groups or communities.

The participative decisions that major industries are taking today are often organised in a similar way. They are popular with many large American firms and with sections of the British police. The West Yorkshire Force has been in the forefront of these developments, e.g. the Association of Chief Police Officers (ACPO) has met in this way to discuss the future use of information technology by the Police Service and arrive at an agreed and viable strategy. Discussions involved about 40 senior policemen, who met for 2–3 days to explore past and present experiences with IT and to jointly identify a desirable technical future. Specially trained facilitators assisted this process. They ensured that every meeting had a clear purpose, that all stakeholders, or a representative cross-section, were involved in discussions and decisions, that everyone's input was equally valued and that the process finished with the identification and description of a desired future.

Similar conferences were held by other police authorities but focused on different issues, for example agreeing plans for specific organisational change and deciding how these might be implemented. Projects are usually run as a series, with the ideas from the first turned into practice by a project team who then feed the results from this into the next project. The British police are now continuing enthusiastically with this approach, are trying to broaden the subjects for discussion and to organise events with other agencies with whom they work in partnership, e.g. the public. Like the Romans, the police have found these large group conferences helpful in creating useful ideas for change and establishing commitment to change.

There seem to be a number of reasons why these approaches are becoming popular. The challenge of global competition is forcing organisations to become more competitive. This means that they must learn how to change rapidly in order to survive in new and turbulent environments. Managers are recognising that change of this kind, to be successful, requires the acceptance and commitment of all staff. Also, many companies are trying to shift from traditional hierarchical structures to more flexible and participative networking styles. The large-scale intervention approach has many advantages if it is successful. It follows the principle of requisite variety by bringing a large multi-skilled group together to consider a multi-faceted change problem. It ensures that everyone likely to be affected not only understands the proposed change but can play a role in the form this takes. It helps to develop trust and commitment.

CONCLUSION

This chapter has tried to show that the management of change is becoming increasingly complex as much of industry rethinks its traditional way of doing things. This complexity has to be recognised and catered for in any planning and design process. The cybernetic concept of requisite variety is seen as useful here as is Stafford Beer's notion of a viable system. As the old command and control philosophy for running industry becomes obsolete, the need to involve employees, customers and other stakeholders in decision taking becomes increasingly important. There are several tools at the disposal of organisations undergoing change and we have reviewed some of these. Their use is likely to involve a shift in perspective for some organisations and a certain level of expertise and knowledge. Such methods and tools are likely to receive renewed interest as organisations deal with increasing complexity. With the challenges of a global market, complexity may extend beyond the organisation itself. For instance, in setting up inter-organisational partnerships or supply chains, socio-technical tools will need to be developed for use across organisations and networks (Clegg, 2000). Moreover, new ways or working, such as e-business, virtual teams and teleworking, make a focus on the "people" factor imperative. Concentrating solely on the technology when designing these new forms of work organisation is perilous. With increased organisational and inter-organisational complexity, the socio-technical philosophy of participative design is even more helpful and relevant today and the future than it has been in the past.

REFERENCES

Allison, G., Catteral, B., Dowd, M., Galer, M., Maguire, M. & Taylor, B. (1992). Human Factors Tools for designers of Information Technology Products. In M. Galer, S. Harker & J. Ziegler (Eds) *Methods and Tools in User-centred Design for Information Technology*. Amsterdam: Elsevier Science.
Ashby, W. R. (1956). *An Introduction to Cybernetics*. London: Chapman and Hall.
Beer, S. (1975). *Platform for Change*. London: Wiley.
Bunker, B. & Alban, B. T. (1997). *Large Group Interventions*. San Francisco, CA: Jossey-Bass.
Bødker, S., Ehn, P., Kammergaard, J., Kyng, M. & Sundblad, Y. (1987). A Utopian experience. In G. Bjerknes, P. Ehn & M. Kyng (Eds), *Computers and Democracy: a Scandinavian Challenge* (pp. 251–278) Aldershot: Avebury.
Bødker, S., Grønbæk, K. & Kyng, M. (1993). Cooperative design: techniques and experiences from the Scandinavian scene. In D. Schhuler & A. Namioka (Eds), *Participatory Design: Principles and Practices* (pp. 157–176). Hillsdale, NJ: Erlbaum.
Checkland, P. (1981). *Systems Thinking, Systems Practice*. Chichester: Wiley.
Checkland, P. (1999). Soft systems methodology: a 30 year retrospective. In P. B. Checkland & J. Scholes. *Soft Systems Methodology in Action*. Chichester: Wiley.
Clegg, C., Coleman, P., Hornby, P., Maclaren, R., Robsen, J., Carey, N. & Symon, G. (1996). Tools to incorporate some psychological and organizational issues during the development of computer-based systems. *Ergonomics*, **39**(3), 482–511.
Clegg C. W. & Walsh, S. (1998). Soft systems methodology: A critical analysis. In G. Symon & C. Cassell (Eds), *Qualitative Methods in Organizational Research* (vol. 2). London: Sage.
Clegg, C. W. (2000). Sociotechnical principles for system design. *Applied Ergonomics*, **31**, 463–477.
Ehn, P. (1989). *Work Oriented Design of Computer Artifacts*, 2nd Edn. Hillsdale, NJ: Erlbaum.
Emery, M. & Purser, R. E. (1996). *The Search Conference: Theory and Practice*. San Francisco, CA: Jossey-Bass.
Espejo, R. & Harnden, R. (1989). *The Viable Systems Model*. London: Wiley.
Etzioni, A. (2000). *The Third Way to a Good Society*. London: Demos.
Heller, F. (1997). Sociotechnology and the environment. *Human Relations*, **50**, 605–624.
Jayaratna, N. (1994). *Understanding and Evaluating Methodologies*. London: McGraw-Hill.
Kensing, F. & Halskov Madsen, K. (1991) Generating visions: future workshops and metaphorical design. In J. Greenbaum & M. Kyng (Eds), *Design at Work: Cooperative Design of Computer Systems* (pp. 155–168). Hillsdale, NJ: Erlbaum.
Lytle, W. O. (1998). *Designing High Performance Organization*. Clark, NJ: Block, Petrella, Weisbord, Inc.

Maclaren, R., Hornby, P., Robson, J., O'Brien, P., Clegg, C. & Richardson, S. (1991). *Systems Design Methods—The Human Dimension.* Reading: DEC Press.

Mumford, E. (1995). *Effective Systems Design and Requirements Analysis: the ETHICS Method.* London: Macmillan.

Mumford, E. (1996). *Systems Design: Ethical Tools for Ethical Change.* London: Macmillan.

Mumford, E. & MacDonald, W. B. (1989). *Xsel's Progress.* London: Wiley.

Parker, R. (2001). The myth of the entrepreneurial economy: employment and innovation in small firms. *Work Employment and Society,* **15**, 373–384.

Sjögren, D. & Ehn, P. (1991). From system description to scripts for action. In J. Greenbaum & M. Kyng (Eds), *Design at Work: Cooperative Design of Computer Systems* (pp. 269–280). Hillsdale, NJ: Erlbaum.

Taylor, B. (1990). The HUFIT planning analysis and specification tool set. In D. Diaper, D. Gilmore, G. Cockton & B. Shackel (Eds), *Proceedings of Interact 1990.* Amsterdam: North-Holland.

Trist, E. & Murray, H. (Eds) (1993). *The Social Engagement of Social Science. Vol. 2 The Sociotechnical Perspective.* Philadelphia, PA: University of Pennsylvania Press.

Waterson, P. E., Older Gray, M. T. & Clegg, C. W. (in press). A sociotechnical method for designing work systems. *Human Factors,* (Fall 2002).

CHAPTER 18

Examining New Technologies and New Ways of Working: Methods for Designing Evaluation Studies

Sabine Sonnentag
Institute of Psychology, Technical University of Braunschweig, Germany

Organizations spend a lot of financial resources on new technologies and on the implementation of new ways of working, such as team work or total quality programmes. Suppliers of new technologies promise better, less stressful and more efficient ways of working. Employees hope that their work becomes more interesting and that they keep their skills and knowledge up-to-date when adopting new ways of working and using new technologies. However, after having introduced a new technology or having implemented another innovation, an organization is faced with a number of questions. Did the investments pay off? Are the hopes and promises expressed by suppliers and employees fulfilled? Or are new technologies and other innovations a waste of an organization's financial resources? Do new ways of working lead to a deterioration of employees' work situation, as more pessimistic proponents expect?

To provide answers to these questions, evaluation research is necessary. In this context, evaluation research aims at a systematic examination of the processes and effects associated with the implementation of new technologies and new ways of working. Evaluation research can be done at the level of a single organization or even single organizational departments and single technologies, e.g. a company may be interested to learn whether team work introduced in some of the company's production areas results in improved product quality and higher employee satisfaction. Evaluation research also can adopt a broader scope; for example it can address the question of whether the broad implementation of computer technologies in a specific line of business results in improved economic performance throughout this line of business.

It is not only a question of whether new ways of working *per se* have an impact on how individuals and groups experience their work and how organizations perform. It is even more important to examine which features of new ways of working affect individuals, groups and organizations. As a consequence, evaluation research should not only contrast new ways of working with the "old" ways, but also compare between different types of a new technology or way of working.

The New Workplace: A Guide to the Human Impact of Modern Working Practices.
Edited by David Holman, Toby D. Wall, Chris W. Clegg, Paul Sparrow and Ann Howard. © 2003 John Wiley & Sons, Ltd.

As described throughout the chapters of this book, "new ways of working" encompasses a whole range of technological and organizational innovations. These innovations include technological implementations aiming at specific purposes, such as advanced technology in manufacturing or video-conferencing, as well as broader concepts of work organization, such as team work, lean production or total quality management (TQM). In organizational practice, these concepts are often not implemented in isolation. Rather, organizations introduce a combination of several innovations. For example, the implementation of a TQM programme might be supplemented by the introduction of team work arrangements. This strategy of simultaneously introducing multiple innovations makes sense from a practical point of view, but sometimes puts great challenges on professionals who wish to evaluate the effect of these innovations.

The purpose of this chapter is to provide an overview over main issues in evaluation research in the field of new technologies and new ways of working. A comprehensive review of the outcomes of past evaluation research, as well as a detailed discussion of specific methodological problems, is beyond the scope of the present chapter (for a more detailed discussion, see Rossi, Freeman & Lipsey, 1998). Nevertheless, to illustrate how evaluation research can be implemented in practice, this chapter incorporates many examples from past research. The first section of the chapter introduces the evaluation concept and presents basic evaluation criteria. The second section discusses benefits and costs of evaluations. The third section concentrates on different evaluation approaches. More specifically, the section presents experimental and quasi-experimental research designs and discusses how these designs can be implemented in both laboratory and field research settings. The next section describes data collection methods for various evaluation foci. The last section refers to a range of specific problems in evaluation research and discusses ways to overcome these difficulties.

Evaluations do not pursue a purely academic goal, but should directly benefit organizational practice. Therefore, evaluation is a task not only for academics but also for practitioners and consultants who wish to support organizations' performance processes. Throughout this chapter, I will use the term "evaluation researcher" for a person engaged in evaluation research, be it as an academic, a practitioner or consultant.

EVALUATION: CONCEPT AND CRITERIA

In general, evaluation research refers to the formal and systematic examination of a programme or a planned intervention. It applies scientific procedures to collect and analyze information about these programmes and interventions (Clarke & Dawson, 1999). In contrast to more basic research, it aims at providing knowledge and guidance for practical decision-making and action.

By evaluating a programme or an intervention, one intends to determine its respective merit, worth or value. This implies that programmes and interventions are evaluated against a set of criteria (House, 1993). Specifically, when assessing the effects of new technologies and new ways of working, one can think of a broad range of possible evaluation criteria, including (a) work situation factors, (b) performance, and (c) well-being. Work situation factors refer to characteristics of the work places. They comprise aspects such as job control, work demands and responsibilities, and other work stressors. Performance refers to work behavior and results of this behavior, often expressed as the outcome with respect to quantity and quality. Well-being comprises job satisfaction as well as health-related aspects, such as mental and physical health.

In the first place, the choice of evaluation criteria in a specific evaluation study is contingent on the overall goal of the intervention programme. For example, if an intervention aims at quality improvement, quality should be the core evaluation criterion. In addition, it is important to examine whether an intervention has side-effects. For example, a new technology might result in improved quality—at the cost of quantity or employee well-being. Thus, it is useful to evaluate new technologies and new ways of working against a broader set of criteria than those referring to the main objective of the intervention.

BENEFITS AND COSTS OF EVALUATION

Organizations can benefit from evaluating new technologies and new ways of working in several ways. First of all, evaluations can point to shortcomings and problems of the specific implemented technologies and innovations. Identifying such shortcomings and problems is a necessary prerequisite for an informed improvement and redesign process. For example, evaluation might show that it is necessary to adjust the user interface, to include additional functionality within the technological system, to change some features of the work organization, or to provide more training to employees so that they can better deal with the new technology and associated demands.

Second, evaluations can support decision-making processes, when organizations have to decide between competing innovations. By providing information that helps to opt for the best available solution, evaluations contribute to an organization's functioning and performance.

In addition, evaluations can support organizational learning. When well-documented and communicated, evaluation outcomes can be particularly helpful for the future implementation of innovations or innovations in other parts of the organization. Moreover, evaluations can stimulate discussions about organizational practices and procedures that go beyond the specific technological implementation or innovation evaluated at the moment. Such discussions might contribute to a broader improvement and learning process.

Despite the clear benefits of evaluation, organizations are often reluctant to initiate evaluation projects. Although it is difficult to provide exact recent figures, one can assume that only a small portion of all technology implementations and other innovations is evaluated on a sound methodological basis (Clegg, 2000; Hillam & Edwards, 2001). This reluctance to engage in evaluations is illustrated by survey data gathered in 33 large Australasian organizations: CEOs of these organizations rated "measuring information systems' effectiveness/productivity" as the most problematic issue among a total of 31 issues (Pervan, 1998). In addition, if done at all, most evaluations focus on financial issues; organizational and psychological effects of new technologies and other innovations receive far less attention in organizational practice (Doherty & King, 2001).

There are a number of reasons why many organizations are not overly enthusiastic to initiate and conduct evaluation studies. First, evaluation is not an easy task. Consultants and researchers face a number of problems. For example, often there are no ready-made instruments available or timing of measurements might be difficult. The present chapter will address typical methodological and practical problems emerging during evaluation research and will illustrate possible solutions to these problems. Second, evaluation is associated with financial costs. Among others, these costs include expenses for the researchers who accomplish the evaluation task and compensation for lost working time of employees participating as respondents in the evaluation study. It has to be noted that in most cases these evaluation costs are small compared to the costs for technology investments. Nevertheless, many organizations wish to save these expenses, particularly if they are not convinced about the benefits of evaluation.

Third, organizations are afraid of additional costs associated with evaluations. These additional costs are not primarily financial in nature, but refer to issues of organizational politics. For example, organizational stakeholders who have pushed a specific investment in technology or another innovation do not want to have such an implementation examined in detail, because identifying problems or failures might weaken their power within the organization.

Thus, it can not be taken for granted that organizations engage in careful evaluations of their investments in new technology and other innovations. However, when weighing up the costs against the benefits of evaluations, it should become evident that a sound evaluation will pay off in the long run.

EVALUATION APPROACHES

Overview

Systematic evaluation research is informed by the methodological principles of social science research. As in other fields of social science research, there is a whole range of specific methodological approaches. The major distinctions refer to (a) study design (experimental vs. quasi-experimental), (b) research setting (laboratory vs. field) and (c) data collection methods (quantitative vs. qualitative).

In an experiment, researchers examine the effect of one (or more) independent variable(s) on a dependent variable by manipulating the independent variable(s) and holding all other factors constant. Study participants are randomly assigned to the various experimental conditions. If well-planned, an experimental design allows for ruling out that other factors than the manipulation had an effect on the dependent variable. Most often, experiments are conducted in a laboratory setting, but field experiments are also possible.

A quasi-experiment differs from a "true" experiment in two core features: first, the independent variables are not manipulated, but measured as they naturally vary; second, participants are not randomly assigned to the various study conditions.

The term "laboratory setting" usually refers to a research environment within a university or another research institution, e.g. a set of rooms equipped with facilities which allow for the precise measurement of study participants' behavior, and which allow for holding all factors identical for all participants. "Field setting" refers to a "real-world setting" outside the laboratory, e.g. a business organization in which a new technology is implemented.

Quantitative data collection methods include standardized observations, standardized questionnaires or surveys, and other methods that typically result in data to be easily submitted to quantitative data analysis. For example, research following a quantitative data collection approach will ask all study participants to fill in the same questionnaire, consisting of a set of items that have been developed earlier in the research process. Qualitative data collection methods include open interviews, participatory observations, and more specific ethnographic methods. For example, a researcher following a more qualitative data collection approach will participate in a work team's daily routines and will conduct relatively unstructured interviews with individual team members, focusing on the individuals' experiences.

In recent years, researchers engaged in a lively debate about qualitative vs. quantitative methods within organizational and evaluation research (Symon & Cassell, 1998). Most authors agree that the distinction between the qualitative vs. quantitative approach refers not only to different data collection methods but also reflects two distinct research paradigms (Clarke & Dawson, 1999). The quantitative approach is based on the positivistic, deductive perspective, assuming an "objective reality" outside the observer, which can be uncovered with research methods similar to the methods used in the natural sciences. The qualitative approach is based on a constructivist, inductive perspective. It assumes that no objective reality exists outside the observer, but that "reality" is constructed by interpretative and sense-making processes of individuals and groups. Although it seems difficult to reconcile the quantitative with the qualitative research paradigm at the conceptual level, evaluation studies benefit from a pragmatic combination of quantitative and qualitative data collection methods.

In evaluation studies, there are several ways to combine these three features of study design, research setting and data collection methods. For example, experimental studies can be done both in laboratory and field settings, quantitative data can be gathered in both experimental and quasi-experimental studies. Nevertheless, some combinations are more frequent than others, e.g. experimental studies are more often done in laboratory than in field settings, and qualitative data are more often gathered in quasi-experimental field studies than in experimental laboratory studies.

In the remainder of this section, I will discuss various combinations of experimental vs. quasi-experimental studies in laboratory and field settings. I will address the advantages of the specific approaches as well as associated problems and pitfalls. I will illustrate the crucial points with examples from existing evaluation studies. Later in this chapter, I will come back to data collection methods and will describe quantitative and qualitative approaches in more detail.

Experimental and Quasi-experimental Laboratory Studies

A laboratory is a research setting which adequately meets the requirements for a true experiment, such as the manipulation of the independent variable(s), control of all other factors and random assignment of study participants to the various study conditions.

When it comes to the evaluation of new ways of working, experimental laboratory studies have been extensively used in research on technically-mediated group work. Within this area, researchers compared computer-mediated group work with face-to-face group discussions. A prototypical study is an experiment by Weisband, Schneider & Connolly (1995; study 1), who assigned participants to either a face-to-face meeting or a computer-mediated group meeting. Group members in both conditions were to "discuss" an ethical decision task. Dependent measures included participation and influence measures (for a summary on this kind of research, see McLeod, 1992). More recent studies contrasted video-conferencing with audio-conferencing settings (e.g. Daly-Jones, Monk & Watts, 1998). Also, the effects of electronic performance monitoring are addressed in experimental laboratory studies (Stanton & Barnes-Farrell, 1996).

Experimental laboratory studies offer good opportunities to examine the effects of a specific technology or to compare two or more specific technologies in a controlled setting. The majority of the study participants are students, most often not the intended target groups when it comes to the implementation of the technology in work organizations. Additionally, the time frames covered by these experiments are relatively short. Thus, changes in perceptions or performance over longer periods of time can not be addressed. Moreover, laboratory experiments keep all background variables constant. This is a clear advantage from an experimental point of view but, at the same time, it implies that the effects of organizational-level and job-level factors that might interact with the new technology can not be examined.

Laboratory settings offer good opportunities also for conducting quasi-experimental studies. In a quasi-experimental approach, the independent variables are not manipulated systematically, but assessed as they exist within the participating persons. For example, the question of how experienced vs. inexperienced computer users use a new technology is a typical research question to be examined with a quasi-experimental approach.

Because it is not always feasible to manipulate the independent variable, a quasi-experimental approach offers an alternative. However, compared to an experimental approach, a quasi-experimental design does not allow for drawing causal conclusions.

Experimental Field Studies

Experimental field studies implement an experimental procedure within a real-world context. When it comes to the evaluation of new technologies, this real-world context may be a business or public organization or a specific department within such an organization. Experimental field studies are difficult to conduct, because in real-world settings researchers often have only limited control in manipulating the independent variables, in randomly assigning study participants to the study conditions and in holding background variables constant.

Within most organizations, the introduction of new technologies and new ways of working is primarily driven not by research but for practical purposes. For example, when introducing a new way of working or a new technology, organizations often have clear reasons why a specific group of employees should work within the new work arrangement, or why a specific group of employees should start working with this technology and why other groups should join later. This makes the random assignment of participants to the various study conditions very difficult, if not impossible. Moreover, pure experimental design considerations require that study participants in the experimental group do not know what is going on in the control group, and vice versa. However, in organizations is it often not realistic to hide from other departments what is going on in the department that receives the experimental treatment, i.e. the new technology. All these aspects threaten the implementation of a proper experimental procedure. Therefore, experimental field studies are relatively rare, particularly in work settings.

A noteworthy exception is an experimental study by Martin & Wall (1989). By implementing a repeated measurement design in an electronics company, the researchers examined the effects of attentional demands and cost responsibility on employee well-being. A more recent example is a study by Chapman & Rowe (2001), who examined the effects of video-conference technology on evaluations in employment interviews.

Compared to work settings, it is somewhat easier to conduct experimental field studies in learning environments. For example, there are a substantial amount of studies that compared computer-based learning arrangements with more traditional learning designs (e.g. Benbunan-Fich & Hiltz, 1999; Remdisch, Heimbeck & Kolvenbach, 2000).

Quasi-experimental Field Studies

For evaluating new technologies and new ways of working, researchers very often use quasi-experimental field studies. They gather data in real-world settings in which individuals and groups work in new types of work arrangements or use new technologies. Researchers do not aim at doing any experimental manipulation but assess work processes and their outcomes as they occur in the natural work environment. It is a clear advantage of many of these studies that they show high external validity. Internal validity however, is a more problematic issue.

One-group Post-test-only Design

Researchers face numerous design options when conducting quasi-experimental field studies. The most simple quasi-experimental design is a one-group post-test-only design. In the context of evaluating new ways of working, such a design would imply implementation of a new technology in one department and assessment of employees' behaviors and perceptions after the implementation. There are numerous studies that relied on such a design. Often, these studies are designed as case studies (for a summary of these studies, see Wall & Davids, 1992).

For example, Nardi *et al.* (1996) studied the use of a multimedia system in a hospital context. By following an ethnographic approach, the researchers examined how members of a neurosurgical team used video in the operating room and how they communicated with one another. Edwards, Collinson, & Rees (1998) used a more quantitative approach and summarized findings on employee reactions to TQM from six case studies.

In addition to case studies, many surveys conducted in a larger number of organizations rely on the one-group, post-test-only design, e.g. Delbridge, Lowe & Oliver (2000) examined whether shop-floor responsibilities changed under lean production. More specifically, the authors assessed managers' views on employee work roles and responsibilities in production plants that had implemented a lean production concept.

Studies based on the one-group post-test-only design can offer important insights in the way employees deal with a new technology or a new way of working. Nevertheless, many of these studies do not offer unequivocal conclusions: one does not know whether the specific behaviors and perceptions reported after the implementation of the innovation were already present before this implementation. Moreover, most of these studies do not provide any information on whether any other implementation would have resulted in the same experiences and outcomes. Here, qualitative data can give some important hints but, as a whole, the one-group post-test-only design may not provide conclusive answers.

One-group, Pre-test, Post-test Design

To rule out alternative interpretations, researchers might chose a one-group, pre-test, post-test design and measure employees' behaviors and perceptions before and after the implemention of the innovation. This approach allows the researcher to observe whether any change occurred between the two measurement points. Sometimes, researchers even collect data at more than two times. For example, Järvenpää (1997) conducted a study on the introduction and use of computer technology in a district court office. Specifically, she studied how office workers and judges distributed their working time among various tasks and how they perceived their job characteristics before, 6 months after and 2 years after the implementation of the new computer technology.

Mullarkey, Jackson & Parker (1995) collected data at four measurement points and illustrated the successive implementation of several innovations within an organization. In an even more complex time series approach, comprising seven measurement periods, Wall, Jackson & Davids (1992) contrasted two types of operator work design and assessed stoppages of robotics systems. Moses & Stahelski (1999) examined the effects of problem solving teams on aluminium plant productivity by assessing data at a total of four measurement points.

Post-test Only, Non-equivalent Groups Design

Despite its clear improvement over the one-group post-test only design, the one-group, pre-test, post-test design incorporates a major shortcoming. If changes in behaviors or perceptions between the pre- and post-measures are observed, one does not know whether these changes would have occurred anyway, i.e. without implementing the innovation. This interpretation calls for including a control group in the study. A simple option is the post-test only, non-equivalent groups design. When following this option for evaluating a new way of working, a researcher measures behaviors and perceptions of a group of employees now working with a new technology and compares it to a group of employees that did not experience this innovation. For example, Jackson & Mullarkey (2000) examined autonomy, work demands and social climate in the garment industry and compared individuals working in lean production teams with individuals working under a more conventional manufacturing regime.

Similarly, a post-test-only, non-equivalent groups design allows for the comparison between two alternative ways of implementing new ways of working. This is particularly important because often there is more than one way of implementing a new technology and organizing work around the technology (Wall & Davids, 1992). For example, Wall *et al.* (1990) examined employees' psychological well-being in a group of operators working under a specialist control regime, as opposed to an operator control regime. Another example is a study by O'Conaill, Whittaker & Wilbur (1993), who compared speech processes occurring during different types of video-meditated communication.

Researchers often use this type of quasi-experimental design to study how different groups of employees respond to new technologies and new ways of working. Typical examples of such studies address differences in reactions to new technologies between men and women or between different occupational groups (Hartman, Stoner & Arora, 1992; Lindström, 1991; Long, 1993).

This approach, however, is not constrained to the comparison of two (or more) groups on one dimension but allows for including other factors into the study design. For example, Wall *et al.* (1990b) examined whether the effects of two types of manufacturing job design differed between low- and high-variance systems in the manufacturing industry.

The major shortcoming of this post-test-only, non-equivalent groups design is that employees are not randomly assigned to the implementation vs. non-implementation situation or the various implementation options. If one observes differences in behaviors and perceptions between the several study groups, one does not know whether these differences already existed before the implementation. If different groups of persons react differentially to new technologies or new ways of working, such differences might reflect not only specific reactions to the new technologies but also reactions to other aspects of a person's work situation. To rule out some of the alternative interpretations, one should control for a range of other variables, such as educational level, job control or task variety.

Pre-test, Post-test Design with a Quasi-experimental Control Group

To overcome the shortcomings of the quasi-experimental designs presented up to now, it is necessary to use a pre-test, post-test design with a quasi-experimental control group. This design compares the pre- and post-implementation measures of the implementation group with the respective measures of a control group that did not undergo the implementation.

A good example for this type of research is a study by Jackson & Martin (1996). The authors compared two production lines in the computer industry. One line was organized as a just-in-time line, the other was a conventional production line. On both lines, measures of job content, psychological strain and job satisfaction were taken before and after the intervention. This design allowed for the comparison of the two lines at both measurement points. Another typical example for this research design is a study on the implementation of TQM in a surgical clinic (Kivimaki *et al.*, 1997). In this study, the researchers compared one hospital department using TQM with two other departments not using TQM. Pre- and post-measures of well-being at work and work-related perceptions (e.g. goal clarity) were taken before and after the implementation of TQM.

The pre-test, post-test design with a quasi-experimental control group is also appropriate when evaluating the effects of two (or more) types of technology implementation. For example, Korunka, Weiss & Karetta (1993) examined two implementation process groups. At three measurement times, the researchers contrasted a group of employees participating extensively in the implementation process with a group of non-participating employees.

Variants of the Traditional Quasi-experimental Approach

It is a core feature of quasi-experimental designs not to manipulate the independent variable(s), but to compare two or more levels of the independent variable(s) as they pre-exist, independently from the researcher's intervention. As described above, typical designs refer to the comparison between a pre- and a post-implementation situation or the comparison between two or more implementation groups. Within the quasi-experimental approach, there are alternatives to the comparison of two (or more) distinct groups or two (or more) distinct points in time. It is also possible to adopt a correlational approach and to assess the independent variable(s) as continuous variable(s). For example, one might measure the degree to which a specific technology has been implemented in various organizations, and then analyse whether the degree of implementation is related to some outcome measures of interest.

For example, Dean & Snell (1991) assessed the extent to which companies had implemented various new manufacturing practices and related this degree of technology implementation to employees' job characteristics. In a study in general medical hospitals, Douglas & Judge (2001) examined the relationship between the degree of TQM implementation and organizational performance. When analyzing the data gathered in this type of studies, researchers often chose multiple regression analysis. This approach enables the researcher to control for third variables, such as demographic factors or work characteristics. For example, when analyzing the effects of telecommuting and mobile work on work outcomes and work/life balance, Hill et al., (1998) controlled for variables such as gender and presence of pre-school children.

Nevertheless, cross-sectional designs do not allow for causal conclusions. Although it is often plausible that the degree of technology implementation affects employee performance and satisfaction, there are alternative interpretations. First, it might be that employee performance or satisfaction may have an effect on technology implementation and the speed and determination with which the innovation is introduced in the organization. Second, both technology implementation and outcomes such as performance or satisfaction might be influenced by additional factors, so-called third variables. Although some of these third variables can be controlled for in cross-sectional designs (see the study by Hill et al., described above), the list of potential third variables is nearly endless. Thus, cross-sectional designs studies can never give a conclusive answer to the causality issue.

Longitudinal studies offer more possibilities for ruling out alternative interpretations. Therefore, evaluation researchers should choose a longitudinal design whenever possible. Longitudinal studies, however, are more expensive and researchers have to deal with specific problems when collecting and analyzing the data (for more detailed discussions of typical problems in longitudinal research, see Carayon, 1997; Zapf, Dormann & Frese, 1996).

There are some studies that have addressed the effects of new technologies and new ways of working in longitudinal designs. For example, Colye-Shapiro (1999) studied participation in TQM and the perceived benefit of TQM. Specifically, she examined whether supervisory participative style had an effect on employee participation in TQM. She took measures 6 months prior and 9 and 32 months after the introduction of TQM. Most important, for testing the longitudinal effect on participation in TQM, she controlled for previous participation in TQM in a multiple regression approach.

Structural equation modelling offers some advantages over the more traditional multiple regression analysis (Zapf et al., 1996). Korunka & Vitouch (1999) report a study about the effects of the new office information technology, employee strain and dissatisfaction. By using structural equation modelling, these researchers showed that it is not the implementation of the new technology *per se* but the change in context that had an effect on strain and dissatisfaction.

DATA COLLECTING METHODS

When collecting data about new ways of working, researchers can pursue various approaches. One option is to focus on the technology or innovation itself. For example, they may ask employees or managers about how they feel about a new technology or observe how employees work with the innovation. Researchers may also chose to focus on the context and outcome of the technology or innovation and examine how new ways of working affect work place characteristics, performance or employee well-being.

Methods Focusing on New Technologies and Innovations

In studies focusing directly on new technologies and new ways of working, researchers can ask employees if, how often and for which types of tasks they use a specific technology. Attitudes towards the new technology can also be measured by directly asking the employees (e.g. Edwards *et al.*, 1998).

However, when evaluating new ways of working, some researchers prefer not to ask the employees themselves but their managers or supervisors. The study by Delbridge *et al.* (2000) is a typical example of this approach. In this study on lean production, managers were asked about who was responsible for a range of shop-floor activities and how teams solved innovation and improvement problems.

At first sight, it is a promising option to concentrate on managers' reports when collecting data. Often, it seems more feasible to assess data from a few managers than from 50 or even 100 employees working with the new technology. In most cases, managers have a better overview over the technological innovations introduced in a department or organization. However, asking managers may often only show one part of the picture. Managers may lack first-hand information about specific problems associated with the use of a new technology. Additionally, managers sometimes have their own agendas and may wish to present an innovation as a success story, even when serious problems are obvious. Thus, to arrive at a more complete picture about a new technology one should aim at collecting data from both managers and employees directly working with the innovation.

Another approach for evaluating new technologies and new ways of working is to observe how employees use a new technology for accomplishing their tasks. Here, researchers may choose between qualitative and more structured quantitative approaches. Qualitative observations are often embedded in an ethnographic approach. Typically, the researchers become closely involved in the settings they study. They even might participate in the processes they are interested in, for example by becoming a team member for a limited period of time. Whether participative or not, observations within an ethnographic approach aim at collecting data about the processes and procedures as they occur in the daily routines. Such qualitative observations are often supplemented by other types of data, including interview data.

In a study on the use of communication technologies, Orlikowski & Yates (1994) analyzed e-mail messages generated by geographically dispersed project group members over a period of 25 months. In another study, Cook (1996) observed anesthesiologists working with a new computer system in the operating room. During the observation period of 14 weeks, Cook took notes on the anesthesiologists' interactions with the new devices and later transcribed and annotated his notes. In both studies, the researchers gathered supplementary interview data.

More structured observational approaches are planned as non-obtrusive observations, and often rely on video material and detailed coding schemes. Whereas in qualitative observations the precise focus of the observation often emerges during the observational process, in more structured observations observational and coding categories are developed before the onset of the observation. Examples of more structured observations include a study by

Nyerges *et al.*, (1998), who assessed interaction processes of users of a groupware system, and a study by Carletta, Anderson & McEwan (2000), who analyzed conversations in face-to-face and technically mediated meetings.

Zapf *et al.* (1992) applied observational methods for assessing errors users made when working with computerized office systems. By using such a method, the researchers gained detailed insight into the cognitive and action processes associated with the use of new technologies. Such observations are helpful when it comes to (re)designing computer systems and developing training interventions.

In the field of human–computer interaction, checklists and questionnaires are available for evaluating software systems, particularly the user interface. Typical examples include the ISONORM questionnaire (Prümper, 1993) and the IsoMetrics Usability Inventory (Gediga, Hamborg & Düntsch, 1999). These questionnaires are based on the Standard ISO 9241, and ask computer users to evaluate the computer system they work with along a number of criteria. An alternative to these questionnaires and checklists to be directly filled-in by the computer users are expert-based evaluation approaches. Here, experts (e.g. human factor professionals) give an evaluation of the system, based on their expert knowledge. For arriving at their judgment, experts may also pose a set of questions to the computer users (Oppermann & Reiterer, 1997).

Methods Focusing on the Outcomes of New Technologies and Innovations

Researchers and stakeholders within organizations might want to know whether work place characteristics change when an organization implements a new technology or a new way of working. For example, it might be of interest to examine whether job control, level of demands and social aspects of the workplace improve or deteriorate. Such workplace characteristics can be measured using questionnaire methods. In the past, researchers often used measures derived from the job characteristics model (Hackman & Oldham, 1976) to examine the effects of new technologies and new ways of working (Järvenpää, 1997; Wall & Clegg, 1981). However, new technologies might affect more and other aspects of a work situation than originally specified in the job characteristics models (Wall *et al.*, 1990a). Therefore, Jackson *et al.* (1993) suggested new measures for assessing changes in workplace characteristics associated with new technologies. These new scales comprise measures of time control, method control, monitoring demands, problem-solving demand, and production responsibility. In addition, other measures are available which assess a broader range of stressors and resources at work (Korunka & Vitouch, 1999; Zapf, 1993).

Performance data can be assessed at various levels, e.g. at organizational, departmental, team and individual levels. Generally speaking, one should evaluate the effects of a new way of working at the same level where the innovation has been implemented. For example, when a new technology has been introduced only at a few workplaces within an organization, it is most appropriate to assess the performance effects at these individual workplaces. Although there might be exceptions, it would not be realistic to expect a huge effect at the organizational level. If a new concept has been implemented organization-wide, it is advisable to assess the performance effects at the organizational level. For example, when a TQM concept has been implemented throughout the whole organization, it makes sense to measure organizational performance (Douglas & Judge, 2001).

Whenever possible, researchers should use objective performance data when evaluating the effects of new ways of working. Many organizations keep records of performance data over many years. Such records are particularly helpful because they do not cause further costs for data collection. Moreover, it is not plausible that these past performance data have been influenced by the anticipation of future innovations. A good example for a study where such objective performance data have been used is a study by Wall et al. (1990b). In this study, the amount and incident of stoppages and machine breakdowns have been analyzed. Additionally, data that have been developed in performance measurement systems can be very useful for evaluation purposes (see Pritchard et al., 1989; van Tuijl et al., 2002).

Similarly, one might think of using financial performance data. These data are easily available in many organizations and often are regarded as the "bottom line" of any intervention. However, one should be particularly careful when interpreting such data, as gains and losses may be caused not only by changes in technology but by a whole range of other events and processes. Thus, although promising at first glance, it is often difficult to come to unequivocal conclusions about new technologies and new ways of working when looking exclusively at financial performance data (for a more detailed discussion of the relationship between technology and performance, see Hesketh & Neal, 1999).

In addition to performance, employee well-being should be a core outcome variable when evaluating the effects of new technologies and new ways of working. Well-being is a broad concept referring to affective experiences and comprising aspects of satisfaction and health (Diener et al., 1999; Warr, 1990). A rather straightforward way to assess the effects of new ways of working is to measure employee job satisfaction. As job satisfaction is a multidimensional concept in itself, it is not plausible to assume that all aspects of job satisfaction will change when introducing a new way of working. For example, satisfaction with the job itself might change, but supervisory satisfaction or pay satisfaction might remain unchanged (see Wall et al., 1990b). Stated differently, researchers should not expect that all aspects of job satisfaction may change when a new technology is introduced. A change in *all* aspects of job satisfaction might rather imply that a halo effect or another bias occurred.

Often, it will be useful to supplement job satisfaction measures with other assessments of well-being, addressing mental and physical health. One measure of mental health that has been successfully used in many studies is the General Health Questionnaire (GHQ; Goldberg, 1972), but a number of other good measures are also available (Korunka et al., 1993; Warr, 1990; Warr, Cook & Wall, 1979). Measures of physical health are particularly helpful when evaluating the effects of new hardware devices.

In addition to well-being data assessed by verbal self-reports, evaluation studies can be extended by using physiological measures (Arnetz, 1997; Korunka et al., 1996). These measures are useful for assessing specific stress reactions. However, assessing physiological measures is laborious and expensive.

Taken together, there is a whole range of data collection methods available for assessing the effects of new technologies and new ways of working. The decision for a specific method is not always an easy choice. When researchers face several options, they should check whether the preferred method meets the following criteria. First of all, the method should allow for an answer to the core research question. For example, when interested in the potential objective performance benefits of a technology, objective performance indicators must be assessed; subjective performance data, including ratings will not be sufficient. Second, satisfactory objectivity, reliability and validity of the method should have been shown beforehand. Third, the application of the method should not exceed reasonable time requirements for either researchers or research participants.

Often, one single method will not be sufficient for providing an answer to all aspects of a research question and will not allow for ruling out all the major alternative interpretations of study findings. Therefore, it is a good idea to follow a multiple-method approach and to combine several data collection methods.

SPECIFIC PROBLEMS

When designing studies to evaluate new technologies and new ways of working, researchers face a number of specific problems. There problems refer to (a) the selection of the study group, (b) sample size and (c) time of measurement.

Selection of Study Groups

When interested in the effects of new technologies and new ways of working, the selection of an adequate study group is crucial. Most of the time, this selection will be rather straightforward. For example, a group of employees starts with telework. Then, it would be advisable to examine the changes in these employees' work characteristics, work behavior and attitudes—preferably by comparing these employees with a control group and by including pre-intervention measures. However, introducing telework in an organization might not only affect the employees who started with this type of work arrangement: employees who continue with the "old" work arrangement might be affected as well. One can imagine that these employees also face changes in communication requirements and patterns. Thus, it would be short-sighted to include only those persons in an evaluation study who were the core target group of an innovation and who were assumed to be directly affected by the innovation.

Studies conducted by Wall, Parker and their co-workers (Parker, Wall & Jackson, 1997; Wall et al., 1990b) illustrate this point. These studies on advanced manufacturing technologies examined the benefits of operator control, as opposed to specialist control. Operator control is characterized by giving shop-floor operators responsibility over some maintenance and programming tasks previously exclusively executed by engineers and programmers, whereas in a specialist control setting, maintenance and programming tasks are allocated to engineers and programmers. One of the studies showed that operators working under a operator control regime experienced less job pressure and more intrinsic job satisfaction than operators working under a specialist control regime (e.g. Wall et al., 1990b). Thus, operator control clearly paid off for the operators. However, this study did not include other groups of employees also affected by operator control job design. The more recent study by Parker et al. (1997) showed that specialist engineers' work was deskilled by the implementation of more control for the shop-floor operators. It turned out that only operators' but not engineers' role orientations increased after the innovation. Taken together, this example suggests that a study that includes only the primary target group of the innovation tells only half of the story. Thus, researchers should extend their evaluation efforts to those groups of employees who might be indirectly affected by a new technology or a new way of working.

Sample Size

A second issue refers to sample size. Generally speaking, the planned sample size is a function of the expected effect size, statistical power of the test, and level of significance used in significance testing. Therefore, sample size should be calculated on the basis of the expected effect size (Cohen, 1988).

Such a procedure requires some knowledge about the expected effect size of a new technology or a new way of working. Often, when it comes to the implementation of a completely new technology, such knowledge is not available by definition. However, studies evaluating a similar technology might at least provide some hints about the effects size that can be expected.

Previous research has shown that the effects of new technologies and new ways of working most times do not exceed moderate effect sizes (Hill *et al.*, 1998; Jackson & Martin, 1996; Jackson & Mullarkey, 2000). Thus, the fact that the effects are often small to moderate in size makes planning of an evaluation study more difficult. In the case of modest effect sizes, one needs a relatively large sample to detect the effect in conventional significance testing. For example, in a rather simple post-test-only design with one implementation and one control group, an effect size of $d = 0.40$ would require about 100 persons in the implementation and additionally 100 persons in the control group (with $1 - \beta = 0.90$ and $\alpha = 0.05$). However, when it comes to evaluations in real organizations, it might happen that the total number of employees who work with the new technology of interest does not reach the size needed for finding the expected effect. This might particularly be the case in small or medium-sized companies or in situations when changes cover only a small number of individuals. Thus, although there might be an effect, it will be difficult to detect it with the standard statistical procedures. The case is even more problematic when using non-parametric tests that have a more limited statistical power.

In evaluation studies, it is not unlikely that a small effect that is relevant in practical terms is not detected because of a small sample size. Therefore, researchers should take sample size issues seriously. Researchers should make a power analysis and should choose the sample size accordingly. They are relatively well off when the organization (or organizational department) is large enough and allows for an adequate sample size. In cases where the sample size requirements exceed the available population within an organization, it might be an option to combine several sub-samples in the analyses. In addition, qualitative methods might be very helpful in such instances.

Time of Measurement

Choosing adequate times of measurement is a third crucial issue. In the case of a traditional quasi-experimental design, this refers both to the pre- and post-measures. Generally, pre-measures should be taken before the onset of the implementation process. Thus, the pre-measurement should capture the state before any change occurs. Although this sounds simple in theory, it is rather difficult to implement in organizational practice. For example, before the beginning of "real" changes, management might have already informed the employees that some changes are planned. In cases where no deliberate information process might have been started, there might be rumors that changes will occur. Even the fact that a survey is held might make some respondents suspicious. Thus, if doing a measurement at this point in time, one should take into account that such an assessment does not always capture the "pure" pre-implementation state.

Often, the choice of an adequate time for the post-measurement is even more difficult. Before deciding about the exact measurement point(s), researchers should be clear about whether they are interested in the implementation's short-term or more longer-term effects. Short-term effects might reflect effects of the innovation and change process itself. On the one hand, such short-term evaluations might draw a rather negative picture of the innovation, because often the change process itself is experienced as stressful. Additionally, the technology might not yet function in an optimal way or employees' skills to handle the new technology might not yet be fully developed. On the other hand, a "honeymoon effect" might occur. More specifically, the fact that something is changing might be experienced as a positive event and might be reflected in an overly optimistic evaluation outcome. Thus, measures taken briefly after the innovation might reflect effects and biases that will not last for a longer time. However, this does not imply that early measures are useless. They can point to still-existing suboptimalities in the new technology or the way employees use this technology. Thus, such early evaluations can play an important role in iteratively improving technology or in initiating training efforts.

Longer-term measurements refer to the effects after the first problems have been overcome—or the first enthusiasm has gone. Often, researchers might be more interested in such longer-term effects. However, there are no clear indications about the adequate period for studying longer-term effects. Empirical studies often used time intervals between about 6 months (Jackson & Martin, 1996; Korunka & Vitouch, 1999) and 2–3 years (Colye-Shapiro, 1999; Huutanen & Leino, 1992) between the implementation and the post-measurement point.

When choosing measurement intervals, both theoretical and practical issues are important. With respective to the theoretical issue, measures should be taken at the point in time when the new technologies and implementations of new work concepts have exerted their effects on the individuals and groups working under these new arrangements. This sounds trivial. However, for exactly determining the optimal period for measuring such longer-term effects, we would need an understanding about how long it takes until the technological and organizational changes affect employees' behaviors and perceptions. Until now, no sound knowledge has been available about the time frame of such change processes. Moreover, the time frames might differ for the several outcome variables (Frese & Zapf, 1988).

From a practical perspective, matters become particularly problematic when extending the measurement interval. First, the longer the time frame, the greater the probability that changes other than the initial one have occurred in the organization or the environment. Second, the longer the measurement interval, the more difficult it will be to have the initial sample studied a second (or a third) time. This problem is evident in most longitudinal designs, and up to a certain point it reflects "normal" attrition in longitudinal studies. In addition, there might be selective attrition in studies evaluating new technologies and new ways of working. For example, employees who are unable or unwilling to use the new technology or work under new work arrangements might have left the organization. In addition, as in many organizations, innovation often goes hand in hand with organizational downsizing; specific groups of employees might have left the organization. Typical examples include older employees who are offered early retirement plans when leaving the organization in times of restructuring and downsizing. These processes imply that the employees studied at later measurement points are not representative of the employees initially affected by the innovation.

To cope with these theoretical and practical problems, evaluation researchers might choose a pragmatic strategy. Unless there are clear theoretically-based indications about when the technological and organizational changes affect employees, researchers should opt for more than one post-measurement point, with half a year or 1 year between sucessive measurements. Moreover, there is a great necessity to document all the events and changes going on in the organization and the organization's environment during the evaluation period, so that this information can be taken into account when interpreting data from evaluation studies. Also, changes in an organization's workforce should be documented.

CONCLUDING REMARKS

Conducting an evaluation project is not an easy task. First, researchers face a large range of study options with respect to study design, research setting and data collection methods. Choosing and implementing the most appropriate option can be a tough job. The decision among several options should be always guided by the research question to be answered and the technology or work arrangement concepts to be evaluated. For example, it might be a good option to start the evaluation of a video-conferencing system with a laboratory experiment, whereas this approach will be less suitable for evaluating the performance effects of a large advanced manufacturing system.

Second, feasibility issues come into play. Sometimes, researchers might experience frictions between high methodological standards and practicability issues. For example, researchers might want to include a control group in the study, but no group might exist within a given organization that could function as such a control group. Also, limited resources might make it difficult to follow the most appropriate research approach. Therefore, some sort of compromise will often be necessary.

Third, conducting methodologically sound evaluation studies requires effort and involvement on the part of the researchers and the organization. Often, a lot of time and financial resources have to go into an evaluation project. Therefore, it is particularly important to plan the evaluation study carefully beforehand and to pursue the approach that promises the most valuable outcome for the specific issue in question. In addition, it will be helpful to spend some effort on informing organizational members about the evaluation project and to convince them to participate. This is particularly useful when data are gathered at several points in time and employees might lose interest in the study over time.

Fourth, there might be some reluctance about initiating an evaluation project at all. For example, stakeholders within an organization might be afraid of the evaluation outcomes or might anticipate specific negative results. In other instances there might be high enthusiasm when starting the evaluation project but interest might wane over time, and the evaluation project might never get finished. Thus, it is important to inform and convince organizational stakeholders about the long-term benefits of carefully planned and completed evaluation studies. Support from the top management is particularly helpful.

Given all these difficulties, organizations might be tempted to refrain from any evaluation study or to opt for a very simple and limited approach, such as asking a small number of arbitrarily chosen employees or managers about their opinions on a new technology or a new work arrangement. However, conclusions that can be drawn from such a limited approach will be limited in themselves. Without a methodologically sound evaluation study, little information will be available that can help in improving technological innovations and their use in organizations. Thus, sound evaluation studies can support the design of better workplaces for employees. They can help organizations to ensure that their investments in new technologies and new ways of working pay off in the long run.

Acknowledgements

I am grateful to David Holman, Chris Clegg and Christian Korunka for their helpful comments on an earlier version of this chapter.

REFERENCES

Arnetz, B. B. (1997). Technological stress: psychophysiological aspects of working with modern information technology. *Scandinavian Journal of Work Environment and Health*, **23**, 97–103.

Benbunan-Fich, R. & Hiltz, S. R. (1999). Impacts of asynchronous learning networks on individual and group problem solving: a field experiment. *Group Decision and Negotiation*, **8**, 409–426.

Carayon, P. (1997). Temporal issues of quality of working life and stress in human–computer interaction. *International Journal of Human-Computer Interaction*, **9**, 325–342.

Carletta, J., Anderson, A. H. & McEwan, R. (2000). The effects of multimedia communication technology on non-collocated teams: a case study. *Ergonomics*, **43**, 1237–1251.

Chapman, D. S. & Rowe, P. M. (2001). The impact of video technology, interview structure, and interviewer gender on interviewer evaluations in the employment interview: a field experiment. *Journal of Occupational and Organizational Psychology*, **74**, 279–298.

Clarke, A. & Dawson, R. (1999). *Evaluation Research: an Introduction to Principles, Methods and Practice*. London: Sage.

Clegg, C. W. (2000). Sociotechnical principles for system design. *Applied Ergonomics*, **31**, 463–477.

Cohen, J. (1988). *Statistical Power Analysis for the Behavioral Sciences*. Hillsdale, NJ: Erlbaum.

Colye-Shapiro, J. A. M. (1999). Employee participation and assessment of an organizational change intervention: A three-wave study of total quality management. *Journal of Applied Behavioral Science*, **35**, 439–546.

Cook, R. I. (1996). Adapting to new technology in the operating room. *Human Factors*, **38**, 593–613.

Daly-Jones, O., Monk, A. & Watts, L. (1998). Some advantages of video conferencing over high-quality audi conferencing: fluency and awareness of attentional focus. *International Journal of Human–Computer Studies*, **49**, 21–58.

Dean, J. W. Jr. & Snell, S. A. (1991). Integrated manufacturing and job design: moderating effects of organizational inertia. *Academy of Management Journal*, **34**, 776–804.

Delbridge, R., Lowe, J. & Oliver, N. (2000). Shopfloor responsibilities under lean teamworking. *Human Relations*, **53**, 1459–1479.

Diener, E., Suh, E. M., Lucas, R. E. & Smith, H. L. (1999). Subjective well-being: three decades of progress. *Psychological Bulletin*, **125**, 276–302.

Doherty, N. & King, M. (2001). The treatment of organisational issues in systems development practice: the implications for the evaluation of information technology investments. *Electronic Journal of Information Systems Evaluation*. Retrieved 30 January 2002, from the World Wide Web: http://is.twi.tudelft.nl/ejise/vol4/papers/Organisational%20Issues%20Evaluation.htm

Douglas, T. J. & Judge, W. Q. J. (2001). Total quality management implementation and competitive advantage: the role of structural control and exploration. *Academy of Management Journal*, **44**, 158–169.

Edwards, P., Collinson, M. & Rees, C. (1998). The determinants of employee responses to total quality management: six case studies. *Organization Studies*, **19**, 449–475.

Frese, M. & Zapf, D. (1988). Methodological issues in the study of work stress: objective vs. subjective measurement and the question of longitudinal studies. In C. L. Cooper & R. Payne (Eds), *Causes, Coping, and Consequences of Stress at Work* (pp. 375–411). New York: Wiley.

Gediga, G., Hamborg, K.-C. & Düntsch, I. (1999). The IsoMetrics usability inventory: an operationalisation of ISO 9241-10. *Behaviour and Information Technology*, **18**, 151–164.

Goldberg, D. (1972). *The Detection of Psychiatric Illness by Questionnaire*. London: Oxford University Press.

Hackman, J. R. & Oldham, G. R. (1976). Motivation through the design of work: test of a theory. *Organizational Behavior and Human Performance*, **16**, 250–279.

Hartman, R. I., Stoner, C. R. & Arora, R. (1992). An investigation of selected variables affecting telecommuting productivity and satisfaction. *Journal of Business and Psychology*, **6**, 207–225.

Hesketh, B. & Neal, A. (1999). Technology and performance. In D. R. Ilgen & E. D. Pulakos (Eds), *The Changing Nature of Performance. Implications for Staffing, Motivation, and Development* (pp. 21–55). San Francisco, CA: Jossey-Bass.

Hill, E. J., Miller, B. C., Weiner, A. P. & Colihan, J. (1998). Influences of the virtual office on aspects of work and work/life balance. *Personnel Psychology*, **51**, 667–683.

Hillam, C. E. & Edwards, H. M. (2001). A case study approach to evaluation of information technology/information systems (IT/IS) investment evaluation processes within SMEs. *Electronic Journal of Information Systems Evaluation*. Retrieved 30 January 2002, from the World Wide Web: http://is.twi.tudelft.nl/ejise/vol4/papers/6thECITEPaper.htm.

House, E. R. (1993). *Professional Evaluation: Social Impact and Political Consequences*. Newbury Park, CA: Sage.

Huutanen, P. & Leino, T. (1992). The impact of new technology by occupation and age on work in financial firms: a 2-year follow-up. *International Journal of Human-Computer Interaction*, **4**, 123–142.

Jackson, P. R. & Martin, R. (1996). Impact of just-in-time on job content, employee attitudes and well-being: a longitudinal study. *Ergonomics*, **39**, 1–16.

Jackson, P. R. & Mullarkey, S. (2000). Lean production teams and health in garment manufacture. *Journal of Occupational Health Psychology*, **5**, 231–245.

Jackson, P. R., Wall, T. D., Martin, R. & Davids, K. (1993). New measures of job control, cognitive demand, and production responsibility. *Journal of Applied Psychology*, **78**, 753–762.

Järvenpää, E. (1997). Implementation of office automation and its effects on job characteristics and strain in a district court. *International Journal of Human–Computer Interaction*, **9**, 425–442.

Kivimaki, M., Mäki, E., Lindström, K., Alanko, A., Seitsonen, S. & Järvinen, K. (1997). Does the implementation of total quality management (TQM) change the well-being and work-related attitudes of health care personnel? Study of a TQM prize-winning surgical clinic. *Journal of Organizational Change*, **10**, 456–470.

Korunka, C., Huemer, K. H., Litschauer, B. Karetta, B. & Kafka-Lützow, A. (1996). Working with new technologies: hormone excretion as an indicator for sustained arousal: a pilot study. *Biological Psychology*, **42**, 439–452.

Korunka, C. & Vitouch, O. (1999). Effects of the implementation of information technology on employees' strain and job satisfaction: a context-dependent approach. *Work and Stress*, **34**, 341–363.

Korunka, C., Weiss, A. & Karetta, B. (1993). Effects of new technologies with special regard for the implementation process *per se*. *Journal of Organizational Behavior*, **14**, 331–348.

Lindström, K. (1991). Well-being and computer-mediated work of various occupational groups in banking and insurance. *International Journal of Human-Computer Interaction*, **3**, 339–361.

Long, R. J. (1993). The impact of new office information technology on job quality of female and male employees. *Human Relations*, **8**, 939–961.

Martin, R. & Wall, T. D. (1989). Attentional demand and cost responsibility as stressors in shopfloor jobs. *Academy of Management Journal*, **32**, 69–86.

McLeod, P. L. (1992). An assessment of the experimental literature on electronic support of group work: results of a meta-analysis. *Human–Computer Interaction*, **7**, 257–280.

Moses, T. P. & Stahelski, A. J. (1999). A productivity evaluation of teamwork at an aluminum manufacturing plant. *Group and Organization Studies*, **24**, 391–412.

Mullarkey, S., Jackson, P. R. & Parker, S. K. (1995). Employee reactions to JIT manufacturing practices: a two-phase investigation. *International Journal of Operations and Production Management*, **15**, 62–79.

Nardi, B. A., Kuchinsky, A., Whittaker, S., Leichner, R. & Schwarz, H. (1996). Video-as-Data: technical and social aspects of a collaborative multimedia application. *Computer Supported Cooperative Work (CSCW)*, **4**, 73–100.

Nyerges, T., Moore, T. J., Montejano, R. & Compton, M. (1998). Developing and using interaction coding systems for studying groupware use. *Human–Computer Interaction*, **13**, 127–165.

O'Conaill, B., Whittaker, S. & Wilbur, S. (1993). Conversations over video conferences: an evaluation of the spoken aspects of video-mediated communication. *Human–Computer Interaction*, **8**, 389–428.

Oppermann, R. & Reiterer, H. (1997). Software evaluation using the 9241 evaluator. *Behaviour & Information Technology*, **16**, 232–245.

Orlikowski, W. & Yates, J. (1994). Genre repertoire: the structuring of communicative practices in organizations. *Administrative Science Quarterly*, **39**, 541–574.

Parker, S. K., Wall, T. D. & Jackson, P. R. (1997). "That's not my job": developing flexible employee work orientations. *Academy of Management Journal*, **40**, 899–929.

Pervan, G. (1998). How chief executive officers in large organizations view the management of their information systems. *Journal of Informational Technology*, **13**, 95–109.

Pritchard, R. D., Jones, S. D., Roth, P. L., Stuebing, K. K. & Ekeberg, S. E. (1989). The evaluation of an integrated approach to measuring organizational productivity. *Personnel Psychology*, **42**, 69–115.

Prümper, J. (1993). Software-evaluation based upon ISO 9241, Part 10. In T. Grechenig & M. Tscheligi (Eds), *Human–Computer Interaction* (pp. 255–265). Berlin: Springer.

Remdisch, S., Heimbeck, D. & Kolvenbach, T. (2000). Computer-based Training als innovative Form betrieblichen Lernens: Ein Vergleich verschiedener Lernformen in der Praxis. *Zeitschrift für Arbeits- und Organisationspsychologie*, **44**, 202–208.

Rossi, P. H., Freeman, H. E. & Lipsey, M. W. (1998). *Evaluation: a Systematic Approach*. Thousand Oales, CA: Sage.

Stanton, J. M. & Barnes-Farrell, J. L. (1996). Effects of electronic performance monitoring on personal control, task satisfaction, and task performance. *Journal of Applied Psychology*, **81**, 738–745.

Symon, G. & Cassell, C. (1998). Reflections of the use of qualitative methods. In G. Symon & C. Cassell (Eds), *Qualitative Methods and Analysis in Organizational Research. A Practical Guide* (pp. 1–9). London: Sage.

van Tuijl, H. F. J. M., Kleingeld, A. Algera, J. A. & Rutten, M. L. (2002). Performance measurement and pay for performance. In S. Sonnentag (Ed.), *Psychological Management of Individual Performance* (pp. 349–370). Chichester: Wiley.

Wall, T. D. & Clegg, C. W. (1981). A longitudinal field study of group work redesign. *Journal of Occupational Behavior*, **2**, 31–49.

Wall, T. D., Corbett, J. M., Clegg, C. W., Jackson, P. R. & Martin, R. (1990a). Advanced manufacturing technology and work design: towards a theoretical framework. *Journal of Organizational Behavior*, **11**, 201–219.

Wall, T. D., Corbett, M., Martin, R., Clegg, C. W. & Jackson, P. R. (1990b). Advanced manufacturing technology, work design, and performance: a change study. *Journal of Applied Psychology*, **75**, 691–697.

Wall, T. D. & Davids, K. (1992). Shopfloor work organization and advanced manufacturing technology. In C. L. Cooper & I. R. Robertson (Eds), *International Review of Industrial and Organizational Psychology* (pp. 363–398). Chichester: Wiley.

Wall, T. D., Jackson, P. R. & Davids, K. (1992). Operator work design and robotics system performance: a serendipitous field study. *Journal of Applied Psychology*, **77**, 353–362.

Warr, P. (1990). The measurement of well-being and other aspects of mental health. *Journal of Occupational Psychology*, **63**, 193–210.

Warr, P. B., Cook, J. D. & Wall, T. D. (1979). Scales for the measurement of some work attitudes and aspects of psychological well-being. *Journal of Occupational Psychology*, **52**, 129–148.

Weisband, S. P., Schneider, S. K. & Connolly, T. (1995). Computer-mediated communication and social information: status salience and status differences. *Academy of Management Journal*, **38**, 1124–1151.

Zapf, D. (1993). Stress-oriented analysis of computerized office work. *European Work and Organizational Psychologist*, **3**, 85–100.

Zapf, D., Brodbeck, F. C., Frese, M., Peters, M. & Prümper, J. (1992). Errors in working with office computers: a first validation of a taxonomy for observed errors in a field setting. *International Journal of Human–Computer Interaction*, **4**, 311–339.

Zapf, D., Dormann, C. & Frese, M. (1996). Longitudinal studies in organizational stress research: a review of the literature with reference to methodological issues. *Journal of Occupational Health Psychology*, **1**, 145–169.

PART V
Reflection and Critique

CHAPTER 19

The Future of Work?

Paul Sparrow
University of Manchester Business School, UK

This chapter is intended to achieve three things. The first objective is to restate and then build upon the phenomenon that previous chapters have made explicit—that there is a process of fundamental organisational change in process and that this signals many important transitions in the territory in which job design psychologists will work. The second goal is to introduce some of the theoretical considerations that are currently being debated as academics try to understand and articulate the nature of the changes that are taking place. I use the latest thinking about models of high reliability organisations, knowledge management, information markets and social capital to provide insight into the new workplace and the role of people, technology and organisation within it. The third objective is to consider some of the challenges that this creates for work psychologists concerned with these issues.

To begin, however, we must ask—are we really witnessing a period of fundamental organisational change? Recently a 3 year collaborative project involving several hundred strategic management, marketing, international management and business policy specialists, organisational scientists and social psychologists, organised by the US Academy of Management and the journal *Organization Science* (see Ilinitch, Lewin & D'Aveni, 1998), concluded that we are indeed living in a period of unprecedented economic transition. The economic cycles that have created this period of turbulence are long-wave, with disorder created at the interface between the end of the cycle of economic growth based on the post-war economy and the beginning of a cycle based on new technological drivers of information, communication and biotechnology. The economic opportunities are immense and the social disruptions challenging. We are in a period of what has been termed "hypercompetition". Academics of course disagree over the *scale* of this disorder. On the one hand, business economists and strategic management researchers, such as Porter (1996), argue that these changes are constrained only to particular sectors, whilst on the other hand, organizational behaviour specialists and organisational analysts, such as Zohar & Morgan (1998), suggest that corporate anarchy will be the ultimate result of the economic and competitive forces that have been unleashed. Hypercompetition is not the force driving the changes currently experienced by many contemporary organisations; rather, it is the *expected response to these changes*. Although there is some debate over the breadth and depth of this process, there is considerable consensus about the nature of this response.

Organisations are experimenting with a range of new organisational forms and strategies to adapt to or manage this unprecedented change (Bartlett & Ghoshal, 1993; Brown & Eisenhardt, 1998; Nohria & Ghoshal, 1997). Although the structural implications of this shift towards a more information-intensive economy are often idiosyncratic and varied, it is possible to specify some of the main conceptual elements that are influencing the design choices that are being made by organisations (Child & McGrath, 2001). There is also consensus that knowledge-based assets within an organisation will form the foundation for success in the twenty-first century (Offsey, 1997). Turuch (2001) outlines four main reasons why knowledge-based competition has already assumed heightened importance in the world economy. First, the bulk of fixed costs associated with knowledge-based products and services accrue in respect of their creation, as opposed to their dissemination or distribution. Second, as knowledge grows, it tends to branch and fragment. Rapid and effective recreation of knowledge can represent a source of competitive advantage. Third, the value of investments in knowledge can be difficult to estimate, with outcomes ranging from disappointment through to extraordinary knowledge development. Fourth, even when knowledge investments create considerable economic value, it is hard to predict who will capture the lion's share of these investments. In economies based on information, competitive advantage is now presumed to result from the ability of firms to charge economic rents (defined as above-normal profits in relation to others in the industry), which are in turn gained only by those firms that can create and protect new knowledge (Child & McGrath, 2001).

For many academics, competitive advantage is now considered to flow from the creation, ownership and management of knowledge assets-based enterprises (McKeen, 2001). This view is, however, predicated on the assumption that knowledge-based enterprises are more efficient than markets at gathering information and disseminating understanding, because they have reduced communication costs and heightened capabilities to support individual learning and the management of knowledge. The effect on the employment relationship of the new forms of work organisation are still broadly unknown (Sparrow & Cooper, 1998). However, the shift towards an information-based economics of production, as opposed to a materials-based economics, is redefining what is core employment and what is peripheral employment, with "core work" increasingly felt to consist of knowledge work and professional work within the organisation that leads to the design of soft concepts and hard technologies (Child & McGrath, 2001).

Organisational sociologists place the emergence of these new organisational forms within discussion of the "new capitalism", which first emerged from the 1980s onwards and has been characterised by stiff international competition, state deregulation of industry, institutional ownership of firms, rapid technological change, smaller firm size, structural simplicity and flexibility (Budros, 1997). For Cappelli (1999), a labour economist, the "traditional" employment relationship has been ended by the variety of management practices that have brought both the external product market and the labour market inside the organisation. These have included competitive pressures to cut time to market and an acceleration in the obsolescence of fixed investments in capital (including human capital). Information technology has replaced the coordination and monitoring tasks of middle managers and has enabled a large range of business functions to be outsourced. Financial arrangements have made it possible to advance the interests of shareholders far ahead of other traditional stakeholders, increasing the squeeze of fixed costs. Finally, management techniques, such as profit centres, external benchmarking and core competences, have exposed every business process and employee to market pressures. Market principles have therefore quickly replaced the old behavioural rules of reciprocity, equity, loyalty, attachment and long-term commitment.

As HR practitioners and occupational psychologists try to find an acceptable path through the many dilemmas they face in dealing with the practical issues and concerns experienced by employees that are raised by these transitions, the fields of knowledge that will carry most weight, and that will be necessary to shape their thinking, will change rapidly (Sparrow, 1998, 2000a). We are therefore witnessing many new and informative dialogues. There is a dialogue between traditional job analysis academics (who consider the partitioning of work into manageable units), organisation design academics (who understand the coordination of work across important vertical, horizontal, and external boundaries) and human resource management (HRM) specialists (who ponder over the creation of HRM systems to control and gain commitment to the implementation of the new systems).

As the 1990s progressed, a series of *ad hoc* and opportunistic initiatives also led to a broad process of "jobs-based flexibility" (Sparrow, 1998). Organisations began—and continue—to significantly repackage the work elements, tasks, duties and positions that are together bundled into definable "jobs". They are therefore redesigning the relationship between jobs and the context into which jobs are placed. This jobs-based flexibility involves the simultaneous manipulation of four elements:

1. The components that are bundled together into definable "jobs" (through the tasks, operations, work elements and duties that are deemed still necessary).
2. Redesign of the context into which jobs are placed and the position of the new job in the broader organisation design (through the family of jobs to which it is deemed to belong, the occupation of the job holder, the career stream to which jobs belong, and the work process of which it forms a part).
3. The ways in which jobs relate to and interact with each other (through the roles assigned to jobs, the information and control systems, the relative levels of power they possess).
4. The ways in which HRM systems integrate the new bundles of jobs into the strategic process (through the re-shaping of employee competencies and commitment).

Parker & Wall (1996) have explained how this re-ordering of jobs is impacting both the content of jobs and the way in which remaining roles relate to each. The main psychological theories that the field of work design uses to understand these changes have been reviewed recently (Parker & Wall, 2001; Parker, Wall & Cordery, 2001). The historical focus has been on the job characteristics model, psychological empowerment, the demand-control model and socio-technical systems. It is also evident that many traditional concerns, such as the dangers of job simplification, remain a central focus. Moreover, new insights will also help inform debate, such as the finding that enhanced autonomy actually has greater positive impact on performance in an uncertain context; recent examination of the psychological impact of greater levels of work interdependence; and an understanding of the emotional demands created by modern work designs (Parker & Wall, 2001). However, Parker *et al.* (2001) argue that general developments in work design theory have not kept pace with organisational changes and that "existing theory is under-specified and relatively context-insensitive" (Parker *et al.*, 2001, p. 417).

Much of the theorising in this book has drawn upon psychological principles that underpin organisational changes. We are, however, also witnessing a dialogue across academic traditions, as once-unique fields of study and management disciplines are grappling with common but significant changes in the nature of work. There has also been a broad range of theorising in the organisational science literatures. Building on Parker *et al.*'s (2001) call for more analysis of the antecedents to work design, in this chapter I therefore weave together the main dialogues that are now taking place in the broader organisation theory literature. In so doing I make little comment in this chapter about the long-term sustainability of these new organisational models, or the many psychological consequences of the pursuit of strategic flexibility. At the individual level, a series of complex changes in the psychological contract at work are taking place (Sparrow, 2000b). This is a major task and an area of uncertainty in itself that has been addressed elsewhere. Indeed, Sparrow & Cooper (1998) have discussed four different outcomes (some positive, many negative) that might be expected from the continuing changes in the employment relationship. It should, therefore, be self-evident that the changes in organisational form articulated in this chapter have significant implications for almost every traditional area of work psychology.

However, the task in this chapter is not to consider such a broad agenda, but rather to convey the essence of the respective positions being taken by new organisational theorists, highlight a number of important theoretical debates that they are engaging in, and examine how these might enrich and inform the work conducted within the work and organisational psychology field. I draw attention to developments in the following *five* main areas of theorising:

1. Organisational forms in information-intensive economies.
2. Organisations as high-reliability systems.
3. Organisations designed for the management of knowledge.
4. Organisations as knowledge markets: new managerial roles.
5. Social capital theory and network-based organisations.

THEORETICAL CONSIDERATIONS

Organisational Forms in Information-intensive Economies

The first theoretical theme in the literature reviewed here—and the one that serves as the capstone for most of the other issues discussed in this chapter—is the attention that has been given to the topic of *organisational forms designed for strategic flexibility*. Organisational theory emphasises how new organisational forms are generally produced by technological innovations, although other agents of organisational form creation, such as social movements, can also play a role (Rao, Morrill & Zald, 2000). Within the academic literature, however, it has been the transition to an economy based on flows of information that has led to the debate about the challenges created for organisation design and organisational forms (Child & McGrath (2001).

Organisational form refers to the combination of strategy, structure and internal control and coordination systems that provide an organisation with its operating logic, its rules of resource allocation and its mechanism of corporate governance (Pfeffer, 1992). Managers are the primary designers of this "form", through the choices they make about the organisation and job design (Sparrow, 1998). Organisational forms serve three purposes (Aldrich, 1999):

1. They help identify and disseminate the collective aims of the organisation.
2. They regulate the flow of resources into and out of it.

3. They identify and govern the duties, rights, functions and roles of the members of the organisation.

Their impact is pervasive, notably because trust is a pervasive feature of organisational design choices (Bradach & Eccles, 1989). Trust is reflected both in the control and coordination systems, and the use of incentives to direct behaviour, that constitute part of the realisation of a new organisational form. Higher levels of trust are associated with fewer controls and therefore lower "transaction costs" incurred by the organisation. Managers make two important trust-related judgements when they redesign organisational forms:

1. Is there implicit employee "task reliability", i.e. do employees have the capabilities and potential to exercise responsible self-direction and self-control?
2. Is there sufficient "values congruence" with the purpose of the organisation, i.e. is there a dominant written and spoken philosophy that will guide the ultimate way in which employees will act?

There is a conflict between the higher levels of trust that are both implicit in and a necessary ingredient of the operating logic of many of the new organisational forms (such as network organisations) and the levels of trust as reflected in the attitudes and psychological contract of employees (Sparrow, 2000a). However, it seems that there is an even bigger conflict between the need to operate in today's hyper-competitive environment and a reliance on bureaucratic forms of organisation.

A recent special research forum on new and evolving organisational forms in the Academy of Management Journal notes that bureaucratic organisations have an inbuilt design fault in this regard (Child & McGrath, 2001). Because they are designed for the efficient allocation of resources, once knowledge is codified it becomes treated as a commodity and built into stable routines within the organisation. Control over knowledge flows becomes difficult to exert and dissemination of codified insight more open. Yet, at the same time, control and reliance on conformity to core processes "... inhibits the accidental, fortuitous and creative processes that facilitate exploratory learning" (Child & McGrath, 2001, p.1136). There has been a fragmentation of bureaucratic organisational forms.

A wide variety of terminology has been used to capture the looser set of organisational forms that have evolved as part of this fragmentation. This evolution of organisational forms itself forms part of "... the phenomenon whereby the role of a tightly integrated hierarchy is supplanted by 'loosely coupled' networks of organisational actors" (Schilling & Steensma, 2001, p. 1149). The most well-known descriptions of new organisational forms include:

- Flexible firm (Volberda, 1998).
- Re-engineered corporation (Hammer & Champy, 1993).
- Virtual organisation (Davidow & Malone, 1992).
- Boundaryless company (Ashkenas *et al.*, 1995).
- Network organisations (Castells, 1996).
- Modular organisations (Sanchez & Mahoney, 1996).
- High performance or high-commitment work system (Pfeffer, 1998).
- Knowledge-creating company (Nonaka & Takeuchi, 1995) and the firm as a distributed knowledge system (Tsoukas, 1996).

Flexibility has been considered an important issue for many years, as witnessed by the above plethora of paradigms. However, it has become much more vital in recent years, leading to a deeper examination of the above formulations. Both the technological revolution and globalisation have transformed the competitive landscape. In order to survive, firms are building core competences and developing their human capital and work systems in ways that enable strategic flexibility (Hitt *et al.*, 1998; Nadler & Tushman, 1999) and ensure that they can cope with the demands of hyper-competition (Volberda, 1996). Modularity is considered to bestow greater flexibility on a system by enabling its components to be recombined in different ways and to be tasked with different functions, with little loss of function through reconfiguration (Garud & Kumaraswamy, 1995).

Child & McGrath (2001) summarise the common features of the above prescriptions and the differences between the conventional and emerging perspectives on organisational form that they highlight, as follows:

1. *The setting of goals, identifying and disseminating aims, decision making and the exercise of power* stresses: decentralised rather than top-down goal setting; distributed rather than concentrated power; a preference for smaller units; leadership roles that provide guidance and conflict management rather than control, monitoring, exercise of formal authority and concrete objectives; vision that emerges in the organisation rather than being dictated; and team and work group structures rather than formal hierarchies.
2. *The maintenance of integrity, regulation of resources and establishment of boundaries within and between organisations* stresses: the production system or network as the primary unit of analysis, rather then the firm; permeable and fuzzy boundaries rather than durable and clearly set ones; flexibility rather than reliability and replicability; horizontal regulation rather than vertical regulation; relationship-based rather than rule-based integrity; and structures that are independent of assets rather than assets being linked to particular organisational units.
3. *Differentiation between rights and duties, functions and roles* that stresses: general and fuzzy role definitions, not specialised and clear ones; adaptation rather than the attempt to absorb uncertainty; impermanent rights and duties rather than permanent ones; and an orientation on innovation rather than efficiency.

Schilling & Steensma (2001, pp. 1149–1150) note that "... despite the wealth of attention being paid to the disaggregration of firms and the formation of interfirm networks, there are few explicitly causal models of this process and even fewer empirical tests". In an attempt to address the theoretical underpinnings of the changes taking place in organisational form, Child & McGrath (2001) identify four core theoretical issues associated with these new more loosely coupled organisational forms:

1. *Interdependence.* The scope and depth of interdependence prevalent in business today is at unprecedented levels (Whitman, 1999). Advances in information and communication technologies, coupled with changes in regulatory regimes and control over capital flows, have made interdependent operations both more desirable and cost-effective. The outcomes for all parties in a transaction are fundamentally entwined with the actions and outcomes of other parties. The management of interdependent systems becomes more complex as authority is dispersed, and coordination of changes becomes more unpredictable. The presumption that there is advantage in controlling resources within the boundaries of the firm is challenged.
2. *Disembodiment.* The traditional link between ownership and control of assets and performance has been broken. It is not necessary to physically own an asset to utilise it, and

as a consequence the definition of what should be core activities for the firm has shifted (Schilling & Steensma, 2001). Large hierarchical entities have been replaced by loosely interconnected organisational components with semi-permeable boundaries (Ashkenas *et al.*, 1995; Orton & Weick, 1990). The locus of production occurs at the nexus of relationships between these parties, rather than within the boundaries of a single firm. The presumption that efficient production is more valuable than inefficient innovation is challenged.
3. *Velocity.* From product development down to internal communications, forces such as trade liberalisation, deregulated capital movement and new communication technologies have accelerated the velocity at which the organisation has to function (Eisenhardt, 1989). This has led to hyper-competition in many sectors (D'Aveni, 1994), and a reduction in the stimulus–response time open to organisations (hence experiments with how organisations use time). Pressure is placed on vertical information and decision flows.
4. *Power.* Power has shifted in terms of both locus and concentration. Power derived from possession of tangible assets has been superseded by power derived from the possession of knowledge and information. There is growing asymmetry of power between managerial agents in charge of large global firms and most other groups in society (consumers, employees and local communities) (Whitman, 1999). Power becomes a more complex matter, with multiple stakeholders who are not organised hierarchically.

Organisations as High-reliability Systems

In order to gain insight into organizational effectiveness under trying conditions or conditions of turbulence, uncertainty and high risk (see the previous discussion of velocity), Weick, Sutcliffe & Obstfeld (1999) have forwarded the concept of high-reliability organisations (HROs) and the associated high-reliability theory (HRT) (Weick, 1987; Roberts, 1990). High-reliability organisations are adaptive organisational forms that are designed to cope with increasingly complex environments. The processes that are found within HROs provide researchers with insight into what is considered to be in effect a cognitive infrastructure that enables both reliable performance and adaptive learning. These insights are considered to be important and relevant to a number of areas that are covered in this book. It is argued by Weick *et al.* (1999) that, for example, failures in process improvement programmes built around principles of reliability (such as total quality management) occur because this cognitive infrastructure is under-developed.

The study of HROs draws largely upon the analysis of effective practice, limited failure, near-catastrophes and successes that should have been failures in nuclear power stations (Marcus, 1995; Bourrier, 1996), naval aircraft carriers (Rochlin, La Porte & Roberts, 1987) and air traffic control systems and space shuttles (Vaughan, 1996). These all operate in an "...environment rich with the potential for error, where the scale of consequences precludes learning through experimentation" (Weick *et al.*, 1999, p. 83). Researchers have concentrated on the ways in which such organisations concentrate on the strategic prioritisation of safety, how they give careful attention to the design of their procedures, consider the operation of decentralised decision making and continuous training, and create strong cultures that engender a broad sense of vigilance and a level of responsiveness towards potential accidents (LaPorte & Consolini, 1991). In studying this, they argue that we should re-appraise our views about what reliability means in modern organisational forms. It has moved beyond the development of standardised routines towards a competence that requires the ability to handle unforeseen situations in ways that actually forestall unintended consequences. In essence, this means organisational forms that allow variation in the activity being carried out, but stability in the cognitive processes (or cognitive architecture) that makes sense of this activity. Organisations concerned with reliability enact collective mental processes that are more fully developed than those that are only concerned with efficiency. An inductive analysis of studies into HROs revealed five common ways in which mindfulness was evidenced (Weick et al., 1999):

- A preoccupation with failure.
- Reluctance to simplify interpretations.
- Sensitivity to operations.
- Commitment to resilience.
- An under-specification of structures.

Weick et al. (1999) adapted Langer's (1997) concept of "mindfulness" to capture this stability in underlying cognitive process and architecture. Mindfulness is an enriched awareness that is induced by there being concern for the potential of catastrophe. It leads to the construction, discovery and correction of unexpected events that are capable of escalating into serious problems. Mindfulness is therefore concerned with both the conservation of this attention and the actual cognitive processes used (March, 1994), i.e. the interpretation of weak signals, differentiation of wisdom, and reframing understanding. In understanding such cultures, it becomes clear that culture should not just be used as a loose metaphor for organisational cognition, but also as a specific model of collective mind (Spender, 1998). Team-level cognition is more than just the result of there being a shared understanding, it can create a collective mind, and this can only be understood by paying close attention to the communication processes that have to take place between a group's members.

This kind of theorising suggests that tacit knowledge can be synthesised in ways that belie the constraints of the organisation's design (Hodgkinson & Sparrow, 2002) and that we can understand knowledge creation processes through the study of culture (Roberts, 1990; Weick, 1987). Organisational cultures can be created through which it is possible to contain the uncertainties inherent in organisational designs that combine "tight coupling" (whereby minor failures can propagate rapidly through the system) with "interactive complexity" (in which information and communication—who talks to whom—flows in multiple directions and through multiple media).

Returning briefly to the opening discussion of hypercompetition, researchers in the HRT area use the arguments by D'Aveni (1994) and his colleagues to suggest that, as environments become more competitive, uncertain, turbulent and complex, then analysis of HROs provides insights in particular to two issues. First, the operation of work practices associated with quality, in that practices have to be designed to encourage mindfulness and avoid ending up becoming routinised in the interests of efficiency. Second, the cognitive infrastructure that underlies mindfulness helps provide insight into the complex but loose coupling between centralisation and decentralisation required in modern organisational forms, as a capacity for local detection of problems is delegated, but has to exist simultaneously with a broader awareness of the vulnerability of the organisation and a coordination of its learning activity centrally.

High-reliability theory is not without its critics, in that there are some who believe that accidents are an inevitable consequence in the highly turbulent, high-risk environment that high-reliability organisations have to operate in. However, the relevance of this work to those concerned with work practices intended to engender reliability and quality, and the often paradoxical demands placed on decentralised organisations, seems clear. More importantly, it highlights the role of cognitive factors in creating a stable architecture within organisations that can assist the interpretation of weak signals, differentiation of wisdom and reframing of understanding that seem to be a central requirement in modern organisational forms.

Organisations Designed for the Management of Knowledge

Another central theme in the literature has been the pursuit of organisational forms designed for the management of knowledge. Knowledge management is subsumed under the issue of power in Child & McGrath's (2001) analysis of theoretical underpinnings to the new organisational forms. In a recent review of changes in organisational form, Pettigrew & Fenton (2000) argue that the requirement to leverage intellectual capital within the firm has placed a premium on organising around the social and relational exchanges that take place within it—a view supported by the work of Nahapiet & Ghoshal (1998). Moreover, a series of inter- and intra-organisational relationships based around the brokering of knowledge have taken over from economic transactions as the primary unit of organisational analysis (Easton & Araujo, 1994). Managers deal with a myriad of interorganisational connections that span owned and affiliated subunits, joint ventures, strategic partnerships, and political, social and professional institutions. The boundaries between organisations and their environments are progressively blurring.

The emergence of intra-organisational networks has also had a major impact on knowledge flows *within* organisations (Hedlund, 1994). Many organisations are now structures around dense sets of dispersed, differentiated but interdependent organisational units (Van Wijk & van den Bosch, 2000). These interconnected units act as distributed knowledge systems, decentralised in nature, with a tendency to differentiate, on the basis of their resources, capabilities, activities and knowledge (Galunic & Rodan, 1998; Tsoukas, 1996). Each unit pursues its own decisions rather than being guided by the centralised, top-down decisions that characterise multi-divisionalised organisations.

Knowledge-based enterprises have to convert social capital (which is examined in more detail later in this chapter) into intellectual capital, and organisational learning is central to this transformation process (Dierkes *et al.*, 2001). A number of attempts have been made to conceptualise the firm in knowledge-based terms and researchers have posited several organisational forms that might facilitate a more dynamic process of knowledge creation, capture, protection and integration. Indeed, there has been an explosion of interest in the topic of knowledge management in recent years (see e.g. reviews by Scarbrough, Swan & Preston, 1999; Staples, Greenaway & McKeen, 2001).

What cuts across the many concepts of the knowledge-creating organisation is the attention given to the series of *knowledge capabilities* deemed necessary to support such a knowledge-based enterprise. Staples, Greenaway & McKeen (2001) have grouped these knowledge capabilities into three clusters:

1. *Knowledge acquisition and creation:* the acquisition or creation of new knowledge fundamental to the long-term viability of the enterprise.

2. *Knowledge capture and storage:* the creation of an inventory of knowledge, so the organisation knows what knowledge it possesses and where it resides.
3. *Knowledge diffusion and transfer:* the subsequent mobilisation and flow of knowledge within the organisation that creates knowledge-based value within the organisation.

It must be said that at present there is no clearly accepted *knowledge-based theory of the firm*, neither are there any accepted theories of how knowledge-based assets should be *managed*. Moreover, there is also a fundamental difference in opinion amongst the strategic management theorists as to *where the knowledge-creation process fundamentally resides* within organisations (Hodgkinson & Sparrow, 2002). A useful distinction can be drawn between those theorists who view the knowledge creation as a process that primarily resides *within individuals*, and those for whom knowledge creation is primarily a process that occurs *within institutions* (Grant, 1996). Writers such as Levitt, March, Huber, Child, Spender and Nonaka see organisational knowledge creation essentially as an individual-level activity which is then directed towards the production of goods and services. Consequently, the focus is on the ways in which individual creativity and learning can be facilitated, and the ways in which the resultant knowledge can be transferred into value-added outputs, such as products and services. Attention to those mechanisms that: create superior knowledge management capabilities that foster innovation (Lubit, 2001); bring together and integrate the varied knowledge of small numbers of individuals (Fenton & Pettigrew, 2000); and act to spread tacit knowledge (knowledge that other organisations find almost impossible to copy) internally (Nonaka & Takeuchi, 1995).

When writers from the institutional perspective on new organisational forms consider the topic of knowledge creation and dissemination within organisations (see e.g. Liebeskind, 1996), they direct attention towards the ways in which the firm's administrative structure (which includes the design of the organisation and the processes that this design engenders) can itself institutionalise knowledge. When the firm is viewed as a 'knowledge-integrating institution' that must be designed and administered in ways that create, capture, protect and integrate knowledge, then we are forced to consider the management of knowledge *in its many forms*. Whilst most observers agree that knowledge has to be *managed*, we have to ask, "what does this actually mean?". Before we can talk about organisational forms designed for the effective management of knowledge, we must ask, "what is knowledge?"

The moment we do so, it becomes clear that knowledge within organisations is an exceedingly complex phenomenon. A wide number of taxonomies of knowledge have been proposed, a few of which are noted here. These taxonomies should serve to signal the challenge that we face in our efforts to create universal organisational designs that are "fit for purpose". Knowledge has been defined as information combined with experience, context, interpretation and reflection (Davenport & Prusak, 1998). It is the ability of the human mind to categorise, associate, interpret and transform that turns information into knowledge (Drott, 2001). Collins (1993) distinguishes five types of knowledge: encultured (shared understandings); embedded (systematic routines); encoded (conveyed by signs and symbols); embrained (dependent upon the conceptual skills and cognitive abilities of the organisation's members); and embodied (action-orientated). Sackmann (1991) has studied the nature of the first of the above forms of knowledge in organisations—encultured knowledge—and has in turn identified four kinds of cultural knowledge: dictionary knowledge (*definitions and classifications* of objects and events, i.e. procedural in nature); directory knowledge (information on how things *are done*, i.e. descriptive in nature); recipe knowledge (information on how things *should preferably be done*, i.e. prescriptive in nature); and axiomatic knowledge (fundamental beliefs or final causes that cannot be reduced any further).

The work that is now taking place on knowledge management systems is very diverse and no one discipline has managed to exert a dominant influence on our thinking. However, regardless of the differences of opinion regarding the locus of knowledge creation within organisations, most theorists nonetheless agree that organisations have to be designed to respond to new knowledge and be able to codify it rapidly.

Organisations as Knowledge Markets: New Managerial Roles

The recent explosion in "electronic connectivity" means that the number of "interactions" that now surround many organisations is expected to increase. It has led to attention being given to a third issue, which is *the operation of knowledge markets within firms* and the changes that this is bringing to the nature of management roles. It was noted above that intra-organisational relationships based around the brokering of knowledge should form the primary unit of organisational analysis (Easton & Araujo, 1994).

The overall "interactive capability" in developed countries is set to increase markedly over the next decade (Butler *et al.*, 1997). Workers will be able to process existing interactions in less than half of the time that it currently takes. Recent theorising has led to the view that organisations are best viewed now as *knowledge markets* (Hansen & Haas, 2001; Hansen, Nohria & Tierney, 1999). Hansen and his colleagues have studied the trading of electronic documents within these markets and highlighted the innovative ways in which managers now have to transact and compete. Although these represent just one form of information that is currently being traded within organisations, the rapidity with which they can be disseminated demonstrates the web of interactions that exist within organisations and illustrate the dynamic nature of these *"intra-organizational information markets"*, about which four theoretical assumptions are made:

1. Employees search internal databases and information media to help them complete their tasks.
2. There is a distinct set of suppliers of information, such as practice groups and business functions, that are responsible for gathering, selecting, editing, codifying and publishing codified knowledge.
3. Both information suppliers and information users receive rewards for their participation in the internal knowledge market (and the creation of documents that are attended to) through performance evaluations and social rewards such as status.
4. There is a significant problem in matching the dispersed set of users and suppliers of information documents.

These interactions within organisations have the same economic purpose, which is the exchange of goods, services or information. The central purpose of managers is to seek the right party with whom to exchange information, arrange the presentation of the information, manage its brokerage, integrate it with information from other databases, and monitor the performance of the interaction. In short, managers act as information brokers, managing a web of natural "interactions" that take place within the organisation. They act as market intermediaries or brokers, whose role is to add value to the communication or information flows, by augmenting them (Kocharekar, 2001). Paradoxically, therefore, these new organisational forms might have likely rendered organisations *more* dependent on the remaining human agents in the value chain (Hodgkinson & Sparrow, 2002), but only if in their roles as market intermediaries or brokers their competencies enable them to add value to the organisation. If they cannot add such value, then it is argued that they will be by-passed.

Not surprisingly, therefore, Van Wijk & van den Bosch (2000, p. 175) have concluded that, "... understanding the enabling and restricting factors of this knowledge sharing process is of great importance". Theoretically, suppliers of information within and between organisations are competing with one another to gain the attention of users in an internal market for knowledge. However, there are a number of sources of study that cast doubt on the efficiency of this process. From a managerial and organisational cognition perspective, concerns are being raised about the capability of managers to cope with the levels of information load the new organisational forms engender (Hodgkinson & Sparrow, 2002). The interactions described above occur in many forms and each medium is associated with a different load and richness of information. The media that are used to convey interactions place different cognitive demands on actors within the organisation, in terms of their requirements for data gathering and information search, coordination, communication, collaborative problem solving and the monitoring of transactions. In information-rich environments the most scarce resource is not information but the amount of *attention* that individuals can allocate to information search, filtration and interpretation (Ocasio, 1997). When competing for attention in knowledge markets, the real problem is that: "... a wealth of information creates a poverty of attention" (Simon, 1997, p. 40).

Moreover, the initiatives associated with these new organisational forms often demonstrate the subtle ways in which resistance and power continue to exert an influence. In their attempts to overcome problems of intra-organisational communication, organisations have exploited the potential benefits of intranets to promote information sharing across disparate sites and businesses. Indeed, intranet technology is often seen as a solution to the problems of managing knowledge (see Chapter 8, this volume, by Scarbrough). Newell, Scarbrough & Swan (2001) examined the development and impact of intranet technology within a European financial services company and demonstrated that the reality is rarely so positive. What actually happened was that a new and unforeseen series of "internal electronic fences" was created by the technology, as the users sought to defend the integrity of the social community in which their knowledge was embedded. Far from serving as an important integrating mechanism that encouraged knowledge-sharing, the technology served as a symbol and instrument "of sub-unit power and autonomy, thereby reinforcing divisions across groups" (Newell, Scarbrough & Swan, 2001, p. 107). A number of tensions were created between the desire, on the one hand, to support a diversity of knowledge through different perspective taking, and threats to the integrity of the social communities within which knowledge is embedded as access to their information was handed over. Similarly, there were tensions between a desire for a centralised and standardised IT approach and the perceived homogenisation and de-skilling of different knowledge groups.

Nonetheless, technological and work process changes seem to be reinforcing a shift towards a clearer divide between simple transactional work and higher value-added knowledge-based work. Towards the end of the 1990s, organisations consolidated many of their internal transactional systems into enterprise-level resource planning systems (ERP). Coupled with initiatives in business process re-engineering, the net effect was to streamline the organisation's back-end processes. Organisations responded broadly on two (currently unconnected) fronts (Kocharekar, 2001):

1. *Transaction efficiency:* broadly delivered through e-commerce initiatives intended to foster greater efficiency by better linking internal transactional systems and processes to the outside world. Internal and external stakeholders of the organisation are linked through different models (e.g. business-to-business and business-to-consumer).
2. *Intellectual capital effectiveness:* delivered through knowledge management initiatives, in an attempt to leverage intellectual capital by turning attention away from the pursuit of streamlined internal transactions, towards a focus on internal collaborative endeavours that facilitate the sharing of information and knowledge.

Within the popular management literature, it is argued that ultimately these two (currently unconnected) strategic drives towards transaction efficiency and intellectual capital effectiveness will need to converge, as more and more commerce itself becomes knowledge-based (Kocharekar, 2001). The above work suggests that organisations now operate as information markets and that, information load dysfunctions and electronic fences apart, managers run the risk of being by-passed if they do not have the competencies to compete effectively within these markets. But will they really be by-passed, will they really be designed out of the process, based on information-brokering capabilities? As organisations attempt to navigate their way through the complex changes taking place in the business environment, then "... social processes and interpersonal relationships are of huge importance" (Child & McGrath, 2001, p. 1144).

Social Capital Theory and Network-based Organisations

In the previous sections I have examined some of the work that has considered the role of intellectual capital, knowledge management capabilities, and the creation of information markets. I now introduce the fifth and final theoretical perspective introduced in this chapter—work that has considered the other side of the equation, i.e. the nature and role of social capital. Harryson (2000) studied knowledge management and innovation processes in a number of leading firms. He argues that the knowledge and innovation process is no longer limited to intracorporate "know-how" (the solving of problems efficiently, based on accumulated knowledge, experience and skills). Today it is leveraged more by global "know-who" (the ability to acquire, transform and apply know-how across networks). What the popular management press would call "know-who", academics label "social capital".

There are many loose definitions as to what social capital is and the most important outcomes that it leads to. In the latest review, 20 definitions are noted, but Adler & Kwon (2002, p.17) argue that the construct in general concerns "... the good-will that is engendered by the fabric of social relations and that can be mobilised to facilitate action". This goodwill that others have towards us is a valuable resource, and consequently the relevance of this social structure and its social ties is now being recognised by organisational theorists in relation to a wide range of work issues. Bourdieu & Wacquant (1992, p.119) define social capital as, "... the sum of the resources, actual or virtual, that accrue to an individual or group by virtue of possessing a durable network of more or less institutionalised relationships of mutual acceptance or recognition". It serves a powerful production role in that it makes possible the achievement of certain ends that would not be attainable in its absence (Coleman, 1990).

Social capital theory has mainly been the preserve of economists (see Woolcock, 1998) and sociologists (Portes, 1998). Its theoretical principles have been established through the analysis of networks and network mechanisms associated with the market exchange of goods or ideas necessary for the delivery of effective business performance. Social capital has become viewed as a critical business competence, and as such a critical goal for organisations. It has also been used as a loose metaphor for the principles of coordination, creativity, leadership, learning and teamwork that the new organisational forms engender (Burt, 2000).

It is distinguished from human capital theory as follows: whilst human capital theory assumes that people, groups or organisations do better (i.e. receive higher returns for their efforts) because of their personal traits and characteristics (such as intelligence and competence), social capital theory assumes that they do better because they are better "connected". This "connection" might be realised in the form of trust, obligation or dependency. Certain network structures, or certain locations in this set of exchange relationships, become an asset in their own right, and it is this asset that is the social capital.

Building upon the view outlined earlier that organisations operate as information markets, the nature of these network structures can affect or replace the flow of information and what people can do with that information (Podolny, 1993). Four mechanisms have been highlighted in the literature: contagion, dominance, closure and brokerage. Often, in the absence of quality information, actors look to the standing of a unit in the social network to infer the qualities that they seek. This may be a limitation, known as "social contagion", but it has been shown to drive strategic formulation, the diffusion of strategies or the abandonment of strategies (Greve, 1995). It is an advantage when the social structure conveys beliefs and practices that prove to be appropriate, or when the unit has a position of network dominance. Examination of the behaviour of networks (Burt, 2000) shows that:

- Prior relationships speed up communications, opportunity or insight, and therefore determine who knows early.
- Such information circulates within groups before it circulates between groups or spreads across people in a market (which may be work groups, divisions or industries).

There are, of course, risks associated with incomplete social capital. Network closure and brokerage serve to manage these risks. A network has "closure" when "... everyone is connected such that no-one can escape the notice of others" (Burt, 2000, p. 351). This is sometimes also called a "dense network". This closure results in superior access to information and removes the loss of information that usually occurs when it is transmitted through an intermediary (Baker & Iyer, 1992). It also increases the likelihood of sanctions when norms are breached and so fosters higher levels of trust (Coleman, 1988). Only in closed networks can reputation and social capital arise.

Earlier in the chapter I discussed the role of managers as information brokers. What is it that provides them with advantage in such brokering? Social capital theory addresses such questions through the concept of brokerage opportunities. For Burt (1992), brokerage opportunities exist in relation to participation in, and control of, information diffusion. Central to this process is the concept of "structural holes" (holes in the social structure of a network that might not reflect a total unawareness of the other parties but do reflect a lack of attention to them). Structural holes are implicit in the boundaries between cohorts of employees, teams and divisions, and between firms. Individuals, units or organisations that have relationships that span these holes can create a competitive advantage, depending on the nature of their brokerage. Holes act as buffers with people on either side of the hole, circulating in different flows of information. They therefore offer an opportunity to broker the flow of information between people and to control the projects that bring people together from opposite sides of the hole. A number of structural features have been measured including "network bridges", "constraints" (redundant contacts) and "betweenness" (brokerage of indirect connections).

Network time and energy can more easily be shifted by entrepreneurial roles than via bureaucracies. A wide range of research has demonstrated benefits that accrue to individuals, units and organisations that span structural holes. At the organisational level, benefits demonstrated include patent outputs, innovation levels, organisational learning and survival rates (Burt, 2000). In relation to the discussion of strategic flexibility earlier in the chapter, social capital theory has been used to examine how a firm's position in a loosely coupled web of firms can impact its ability to meet its objectives (Schilling & Steensma, 2001). Drawing a link back to the previous section and Hansen et al.'s (1999) work on knowledge markets, Hansen has used social capital theory to explain how differing network positions impact performance in the computer industry. Similar work has been conducted in the biotechnology sector (Powell, Koput & Smith-Doerr, 1996) and textiles/apparel sector (Uzzi, 1997).

Work on social networks and social capital also has some relevance for the earlier discussion of disembodied (or disaggregated) organisational forms. Its principles help explain the workings of such designs and the new organisational forms that are emerging (Nahapiet & Ghoshal, 1998) and analysis of social capital has been linked to: the formation of virtual organisations; the creation of inter-organisational linkages; and the design of knowledge-based organisations. In terms of strategic flexibility and social networks, attention has been paid recently to three important consequences of the effective (or ineffective) management of social capital at the organisational level:

- The transfer of learning within and between organisations that can be facilitated through social capital (Kogut, & Zander, 1992; Matusik & Hill, 1998; Powell, 1998).
- The implications for levels of trust and social embeddedness that arise from the exchanges that take place across network relationships (Jones & Bowie, 1998; Uzzi, 1997).
- The implications for corporate governance that arise from social capital-driven inter-organisational links and business relationships (Jones, Hesterly & Borgatti, 1997).

In concluding this section, it is clear that for work psychologists, social capital theory seems to have most relevance for the design of work teams in network forms of organisation. Social capital, for example, becomes paramount as we move towards virtual forms of organisation (Sparrow & Daniels, 1999) and analyse the behaviour of teleworkers (see Chapter 11, this volume, by Lamond, Daniels & Standen). At the individual level it also has many significant impacts. The possession of social capital has been linked to: salary values; positive peer and supervisor evaluations; promotion; information and control benefits that accrue to the teams in which high-social-capital individuals serve; and a positive relationship between team performance and the average social capital of members (Burt, 2000). It has also recently been used to understand the career behaviour of individuals pursuing a psychological contract based on employability (Adler & Kwon, 2000) and the implications of network destruction on survivor reactions to downsizing (Shah, 2000). The concept of social capital has many attractions to those interested in the design of work practices, technology and organisation. There inevitably will be important lessons to be learned about the nature of governance, coordination, creativity, leadership, learning and teamwork under such forms of work organisation.

CONCLUSION

In conclusion, this chapter has argued that organisations are operating in a period of unprecedented competition. One of the major responses to this has been to experiment with radical organisational designs and forms. A wide terminology has been used to capture these experiments, but these new organisational forms are highly relevant for work psychologists and the attention that they give to work design, because it is the over-arching organisational forms, not the work designs, that really regulate the flow of resources into and out of the organisation and govern the duties, rights, functions and roles of employees. Therefore, they *set the frame* for the various work practices and HRM developments discussed throughout this book. For example, the discussion of numerical, functional, financial, temporal, geographical, organisational and cognitive flexibility (see Chapter 1 for more detail) found throughout this book should be seen as reflections of this deeper shift towards strategic flexibility outlined at the beginning of the chapter.

There is consensus that the strategic flexibility that the new organisational forms are designed to deliver is driven by changes in inter-dependence, disembodiment, velocity and power. However, whilst there is consensus over the broad parameter of changes in what has been called "intra-firm form", there is still a rich diversity of thought about the consequences that it will have and, more specifically, about the most appropriate models that we should use to help guide our understanding.

In this chapter I have used models of high-reliability organisations, knowledge management, information markets and social capital to help provide insight into the new workplace and the role of people, technology and organisation within it. The management of knowledge has become a central driver behind many new work practices. As made clear in this chapter, there is still much confusion in this area, created largely because of the divide between those who consider the problem from a technological (IT) perspective and those who view it from a psychological perspective. However, the argument that intra-organisational relationships based around the brokering of knowledge should become the central unit of organisational analysis seems to be a fruitful one.

Similarly, work that analyses the conversion of social capital into intellectual capital, and the nature of organisational learning that is engendered by this conversion process, should become a central concern. Although there is consensus about the knowledge capabilities that facilitate this conversion (acquisition and creation, capture and storage, and diffusion and transfer) there is a fundamental difference of opinion regarding the locus of the knowledge creation process, i.e. does it primarily reside within individuals, or is it a process that resides within institutions? The truth is that both locations have a significant influence. Again, there is the opportunity for cross-fertilisation of ideas here, particularly in the debate about what is the nature of knowledge within organisations that has to be acquired, created, captured, stored, diffused and transferred in the first place. Clarification of this issue will have major implications for the design of the work practices and systems that manage knowledge. There will inevitably be subtle forms of resistance and new electronic fences created within organisations. However, work system strategies designed to improve transaction efficiency and intellectual capital effectiveness will begin to converge in future as more commerce becomes knowledge-based.

There is also much to be learned about the nature of organisations as information markets and the flows of information, and the brokerage of its value, across the structural holes that exist within organisational designs. In the immediate future, we should also expect to see the transfer of learning, the role of trust, and the nature of corporate governance across loosely coupled webs of firms (and teams and networks within firms) to become central areas of investigation.

However, this chapter has hopefully also made it clear that ultimately the new work designs and practices also imply the need to develop a new perspective on the nature of organisational or strategic competence, the type of individual competencies that are associated with this, and the need for work practices to facilitate a convergence between these two levels of analysis. In order to delineate the nature of this new competence, we need to take a multilevel perspective on the strategic management and organisational change process. The new work practices that it has spawned seem to link processes of individual, intra-organisational and inter-organisational learning and cognition with the demands on organisations for high levels of performance and creativity and effective processes of knowledge management. Hodgkinson & Sparrow (2002) argue that this places a premium on the ability of organisational members to acquire, store, recall, interpret and act upon information of relevance to the longer-term survival and well-being of the organisation. Organisations and their members have to work within their cognitive limitations, yet still engineer work and business processes in such a way that they are still able to maintain an appropriate level of responsiveness to the contingencies confronting them.

The challenge for work psychologists in the immediate future will be to develop our understanding of: the individual level factors that enable better processing within an environment of high information load and dysfunctional demands; the collective factors and work practices that facilitate sense making and sense giving; the organisational factors that reinforce the emergence of effective individual competencies and collective sense-making processes necessary to cope with the new levels of complexity; and the efficiency and effectiveness of the specific work practices detailed throughout this book in delivering strategic competence to the organisation.

REFERENCES

Adler, P. & Kwon, S. (2000). Social capital: the good, the bad, the ugly. In E. L. Lesser (Ed.), *Knowledge and Social Capital*. Boston, MA: Butterworth-Heinemann.

Adler, P. S. & Kwon, S.-W. (2002). Social capital: prospects for a new concept. *Academy of Management Review*, **27**(1), 17–40.

Aldrich, H. E. (1999). *Organizations Evolving*. Thousand Oaks, CA: Sage.

Ashkenas, R., Ulrich, D., Jick, T. & Kerr, S. (1995). *The Boundaryless Organization: Breaking the Chains of Organizational Structure*. San Francisco, CA: Jossey-Bass.

Baker, W. E. & Iyer, A. (1992). Information networks and market behavior. *Journal of Mathematical Sociology*, **16**, 305–332.

Bartlett, C. A. & Ghoshal, S. (1993). Beyond the M-form: toward a managerial theory of the firm. *Strategic Management Journal*, **14** (Special Issue): 23–46.

Bourdieu, P. & Wacquant, L. J. D. (1992). *An Invitation to Reflexive Sociology*. Chicago, IL: University of Chicago Press.

Bourrier, M. (1996). Organizing maintenance work at two nuclear power plants. *Journal of Contingencies and Crisis Management*, **4**, 104–112.

Bradach, J. L. & Eccles, R. G. (1989). Price, authority, and trust: from ideal types to plural forms. *Annual Review of Sociology*, **15**, 97–118.

Bridges, W. (1994). *Jobshift: How to Prosper in a Workplace Without Jobs*. Wokingham: Addison-Wesley.

Brown, S. & Eisenhardt, K. M. (1997). The art of continuous change: linking complexity theory and time-paced evolution in relentlessly shifting organizations. *Administrative Science Quarterly*, **42**, 1–34.

Brown, S. & Eisenhardt, K. M. (1998). *Competing on the Edge: Strategy as Structured Chaos*. Boston, MA: Harvard Business School Press.

Budros, A. (1997). The new capitalism and organizational rationality: the adoption of downsizing programs, 1979–1994. *Social Forces*, **76**(1), 229–250.

Burt, R. S. (1992). *Structural Holes*. Cambridge, MA: Harvard University Press.

Burt, R. S. (1997). The contingent value of social capital. *Administrative Science Quarterly*, **42**, 339–365.

Burt, R. S. (2000). The network structure of social capital. In B. M. Staw & R. I. Sutton (Eds), *Research in Organizational Behavior: an Annual Series of Analytical Essays and Critical Reviews*, Vol. 22. New York: JAI Press.

Butler, P., Hall, T. W., Hanna, A. M., Mendonca, L., Auguste, B., Manyika, J. & Sahay, A. (1997). A revolution in interaction. *McKinsey Quarterly*, **1997**(1) 5–24.

Cappelli, P. (1999) *The New Deal at Work: Managing the Market-driven Workforce*. Boston, MA: Harvard Business School Press.

Castells, M. (1996). *The Rise of the Network Society*. Cambridge, MA: Blackwell.

Child, J. & McGrath, R. G. (2001). Organizations unfettered: organizational form in an information-intensive economy. *Academy of Management Journal*, **44**(6), 1135–1148.

Coleman, J. S. (1988). Social capital in the creation of human capital. *American Journal of Sociology*, **94**, S95–S120.

Coleman, J. S. (1990). *Foundations of Social Theory*. Cambridge, MA: Harvard University Press.

Collins, H. (1993). The structure of knowledge. *Social Research*, **60**, 95–116.

D'Aveni, R. (1994). *Hypercompetition: Managing the Dynamics of Strategic Maneuvering*. New York: Free Press.

Davenport, T. H. & Prusak, L. (1998). *Working Knowledge: How Organisations Manage What They Know*. Boston, MA: Harvard Business School Press.

Davidow, W. H. & Malone, M. S. (1992). *The Virtual Corporation: Structuring and Revitalising the Corporation for the 21st Century*. New York: Harper Collins.

Dierkes, M., Antal, A. B. Child, J. & Nonaka, I. (Eds) (2001). *Handbook of Organizational Learning and Knowledge*. Oxford: Oxford University Press.

Drott, M. C. (2001). Personal knowledge, corporate information: the challenges for competitive intelligence. *Business Horizons*, **44**(2), 31–37.

Easton, G. & Araujo, L. (1994). Market exchange, social structures and time. *European Journal of Marketing*, **28**(3), 72–84.

Eisenhardt, K. M. (1989). Making fast strategic decisions in high-velocity environments. *Academy of Management Journal*, **32**, 543–576.

Fenton, E. M. & Pettigrew, A. (2000). Theoretical perspectives on new forms of organizing. In A. M. Pettigrew & E. M. Fenton (Eds), *The Innovating Organization*. London: Sage.

Galunic, D. C. & Rodin, S. (1998). Resource recombinations in the firm: knowledge structures and the potential for Schumpeterian innovation. *Strategic Management Journal*, **19**(12), 1193–1201.

Garud, R. & Kumaraswamy, A. (1995). Technological and organizational designs for realigning economies of substitution. *Strategic Management Journal*, **16**, 93–109.

Grant, R. M. (1996). Toward a knowledge-based theory of the firm. *Strategic Management Journal*, **17**, 109–122.

Greve, H. R. (1995). Jumping ship: the diffusion of strategy abandonment. *Administrative Science Quarterly*, **40**, 444–473.

Hammer, M. & Champy, J. (1993). *Reengineering the Corporation: a Manifesto for Business Revolution*. New York: Harper Business.

Hansen, M. T. & Haas, M. R. (2001). Competing for attention in knowledge markets: electronic document dissemination in a management consulting company. *Administrative Science Quarterly*, **46**(1), 1–28.

Hansen, M. T., Nohria, N. & Tierney, T. (1999). What's your strategy for managing knowledge? *Harvard Business Review*, **77**(2), 106–116.

Harryson, S. J. (2000). *Managing Know-Who-based Companies: a Multi-networked Approach to Knowledge and Innovation Management*. Cheltenham: Edward Elgar.

Hedlund, G. (1994). A model of knowledge management and the N-form corporation. *Strategic Management Journal*, **15**, 73–90.

Hitt, M. A., Keats, B. W. & DeMarie, S. M. (1998). Navigating in the new competitive landscape: building strategic flexibility and competitive advantage in the 21st century. *Academy of Management Executive*, **12**(4), 22–42.

Hodgkinson, G. & Sparrow, P. R (2002). *The Competent Organization: a Psychological Analysis of the Strategic Management Process*. Buckingham: Open University Press.

Ilinitch, A. Y., Lewin, A. Y. & D'Aveni, R. D. (1998). Introduction. In A. Y. Ilinitch, A. Y. Lewin & R. D'Aveni (Eds), *Managing in Times of Disorder: Hypercompetitive Organizational Responses*. London: Sage.

Jones, C., Hesterly, W. & Borgatti, S. (1997). A general theory of network governance: exchange conditions and social mechanisms. *Academy of Management Review*, **22**, 911–945.

Jones, T. & Bowie, N. (1998). Moral hazards on the road to the "virtual" corporation. *Business Ethics Quarterly*, **8**, 273–292.

Kocharekar, R. (2001). K-commerce: knowledge-based commerce architecture with convergence of e-commerce and knowledge management. *Information Systems Management*, **18**(2), 30–35.

Kogut, B. & Zander, U. (1992). Knowledge of the firm, combinative capabilities, and the replication of technology. *Organization Science*, **3**, 383–397.

Langer, E. J. (1997). *The Power of Mindful Learning*. Reading, MA: Addison-Wesley.

LaPorte, T. R. & Consolini, P. (1991). Working in practice but not in theory: theoretical challenges in high organizations. *Journal of Public Administration Research and Theory*, **1** (Winter), 19–47.

Lawler, E. E. (1994). From job-based to competency-based organizations.*Journal of Organizational Behavior*, **15**, 3–15.

Liebeskind, J. P. (1996). Knowledge strategy, and the theory of the firm. *Strategic Management Journal*, **17**, 93–107.

Lubit, R. (2001). Tacit knowledge and knowledge management: the keys to sustainable competitive advantage. *Organization Dynamics*, **29**(4), 164–178.

March, J. G. (1994). *A Primer on Decision Making: How Decisions Happen*. New York: Free Press.

Marcus, A. (1995). Managing with danger. *Industrial and Environmental Crisis Quarterly*, **9**, 139–152.

Matusik, S. & Hill, C. W. L. (1998). The utilization of contingent work, knowledge creation, and competitive advantage. *Academy of Management Review*, **22**, 974–996.

McKeen, J. D. (2001). Editorial. Special Issue on the Study of Knowledge-based Enterprises. *International Journal of Management Reviews*, **3**(1), iii–iv.

Nadler, D. & Tushman, M. (1999). The organization of the future: strategic imperatives and core competencies for the 21st century. *Organizational Dynamics*, **28**(1), 45–60.

Nahapiet, J. & Ghoshal, S. (1998). Social capital, intellectual capital, and the organization advantage. *Academy of Management Review*, **23**, 242–266.

Newell, S., Scarbrough, H. & Swan, J. (2001). From global knowledge management to internal electronic fences: contradictory outcomes of intranet development. *British Journal of Management*, **12**, 97–111.

Nohria, N. & Eccles, R. G. (Eds) (1992). *Networks and Organizations*. Boston, NA: Harvard Business School.

Nohria, N. & Ghoshal, S. (1997). *The Differentiated Network: Organizing Multinational Corporations for Value Creation*. San Francisco, CA: Jossey–Bass.

Nonaka, I. & Takeuchi, H. (1995). *The Knowledge-creating Company*. New York: Oxford University Press.

Ocasio, W. (1997). Towards an attention-based view of the firm. *Strategic Management Journal*, **18**, 187–206.

Offsey, S. (1997). Knowledge management: linking people to knowledge for bottom line results. *Journal of Knowledge Management*, **1**(2), 113–122.

Orton, J. D. & Weick, K. E. (1990). Loosely coupled systems: a reconceptualization. *Academy of Management Review*, **15**, 203–223.

Parker, S. K. & Wall, T. D. (1996). Job design and modern manufacturing. In P. Warr (Ed.), *Psychology and Work*, 4th Edn. Harmondsworth: Penguin.

Parker, S. K. & Wall, T. D. (2001). Work design: learning from the past and mapping a new terrain. In N. Anderson, D. S. Ones, H. K. Sinangil & C. Viswesvaran (Eds), *Handbook of Industrial, Work and Organizational Psychology. Vol. 1: Personnel Psychology*. London: Sage.

Parker, S. K., Wall, T. D. & Cordery, J. L. (2001). Future work design research and practice: towards an elaborated model of work design. *Journal of Occupational and Organizational Psychology*, **74**, 413–440.

Pettigrew, A. M. Fenton, E. M. (2000). Complexities and dualities in innovative forms of organizing. In A. M. Pettigrew & E. M. Fenton (Eds), *The Innovating Organization*. London: Sage.

Pfeffer, J. (1992). *Managing with Power*. Boston, MA: Harvard Business School Press.

Pfeffer, J. (1998). Seven practices of successful organizations. *California Management Review*, **40**(2), 96–124.

Podolny, J. K. (1993). A status-based model of market competition. *American Journal of Sociology*, **98**, 829–872.

Porter, M. E. (1996). What is strategy? *Harvard Business Review*, **74**(6), 61–78.

Portes, A. (1998). Social capital: its origins and applications in modern sociology. *Annual Review of Sociology*, **24**, 1–24.

Powell, W. (1998). Learning from collaboration: knowledge and networks in the biotechnology and pharmaceutical industries. *California Management Review*, **40**(3), 228–240.

Powell, W., Koput, K. & Smith-Doerr, L. (1996). Interorganizational collaboration and the locus of innovation: networks of learning in biotechnology. *Administrative Science Quarterly*, **41**, 116–146.

Rao, H., Morrill, C. & Zald, M. N. (2000). Power plays: how social movements and collective action create new organizational forms. In B. M. Staw & R. I. Sutton (Eds), *Research in Organizational Behavior: an Annual Series of Analytical Essays and Critical Reviews*, Vol. 22. New York: JAI Press.

Roberts, K. H. (1990). Some characteristics of high reliability organizations. *Organization Science*, **1**, 160–177.

Rochlin, G. I., La Porte, T. R. & Roberts, K. (1987). The self-designing high reliability organization: aircraft flight operation at sea. *Naval War College Review*, **40**, 76–90.

Sackmann, S. A. (1991). *Cultural Knowledge in Organizations: Exploring the Collective Mind*. Newbury Park, CA: Sage.

Sanchez, R. & Mahoney, J. (1996). Modularity flexibility, and knowledge management in product and organizational design. *Strategic Management Journal*, **17**, 63–76.

Scarbrough, H., Swan, J. & Preston, J. (1999). *Knowledge Management: a Literature Review*. London: Chartered Institute of Personnel and Development.

Schilling, M. A. & Steensma, H. K. (2001). The use of modular organizational forms: an industry-level analysis. *Academy of Management Journal*, **44**(6), 1149–1167.

Shah, P. P. (2000). Network destruction: the structural implications of downsizing. *Academy of Management Journal*, **43**(1), 101–112.

Simon, H. A. (1997). Designing organizations for an information-rich world. In D. M. Lamberton (Ed.), *The Economics of Communication and Information*. Cheltenham: Edward Elgar.

Sparrow, P. R. (1998). The pursuit of multiple and parallel organizational flexibilities: reconstituting jobs. *European Journal of Work and Organizational Psychology*, **7**(1), 79–95.

Sparrow, P. R. (1999). Teleworking and the psychological contract: a new division of labour? In K. Daniels, D. Lamond & P. Standen (Eds), *Managing Teleworkers*. London: Sage.

Sparrow, P. R. (2000a). New employee behaviours, work designs and forms of work organisation: what is in store for the future of work? *Journal of Managerial Psychology*, **15**(3), 202–218.

Sparrow, P. R. (2000b). The new employment contract: psychological implications of future work. In R. Burke & C.Cooper (Eds), *The Organization in Crisis: Downsizing, Restructuring, and Privatization*. London: Basil Blackwell.

Sparrow, P. R. (2001). The new employment relationship: the dilemmas of a post-downsized, socially-excluded, and low trust future. In J. Gual (Ed.), *Strategy, Organization and the Changing Nature of Work*. Cheltenham: Edward Elgar.

Sparrow, P. R. & Cooper, C. L. (1998). New organizational forms: the strategic relevance of future psychological contract scenarios. *Canadian Journal of Administrative Sciences*, **15**(4), 356–371.

Sparrow, P. R. & Daniels, K. (1999). Human resource management and the virtual organization: mapping the future research issues. In C. L. Cooper & D. Rousseau (Eds), *Trends in Organizational Behavior*, Vol. 6. London: Wiley.

Sparrow, P. R. & Marchington, M. (Eds) (1998). *Human Resource Management: the New Agenda*. London: Financial Times Pitman Publications.

Spender, J.-C. (1998). The dynamics of individual and organizational knowledge. In C. Eden and J.-C. Spender (Eds), *Managerial and Organizational Cognition: Theory, Methods and Research*. London: Sage.

Staples, D. S., Greenaway, K. & McKeen, J. D. (2001). Opportunities for research about managing the knowledge-based enterprise. *International Journal of Management Reviews*, **3**(1), 1–20.

Tsoukas, H. (1996). The firm as a distributed knowledge system: a constructionist approach. *Strategic Management Journal*, **17**, 11–25.

Turuch, E. (2001). Knowledge Management: auditing and reporting intellectual capital. *Journal of General Management*, **26**(3), 26–40.

Uzzi, B. (1997). Social structure and competition in inter-firm networks: the paradox of embeddedness. *Administrative Science Quarterly*, **22**, 587–605.

Van Wijk, R. A. & van den Bosch, F. A. J. (2000). The emergence and development of internal networks and their impact on knowledge flows: the case of Rabobank Group. In A. M. Pettigrew & E. M. Fenton (Eds), *The Innovating Organization*. London: Sage.

Vaughan, D. (1996). *The Challenger Launch Decision*. Chicago, IL: Chicago University Press.

Volberda, H. W. (1996). Towards the flexible form: how to remain vital in hypercompetitive environments. *Organization Science*, 7, 359–374.

Volberda, H. W. (1998). *Building the Flexible Firm*. Oxford: Oxford University Press.

Weick, K. E. (1987). Organizational culture as a source of high reliability. *California Management Review*, **29**, 112–127.

Weick, K. E., Sutcliffe, K. M. & Obstfeld, D. (1999). Organizing for high reliability. In R. I. Sutton & B. M. Staw (Eds), *Research in Organizational Behavior: an Annual Series of Analytical Essays and Critical Reviews*, Vol. 21. New York: JAI Press.

Whitman, M. N. (1999). *New World, New Rules: the Changing Role of the American Corporation*. Boston, MA: Harvard Business School Press.

Woolcock, M. (1998). Social capital and economic development: toward a theoretical synthesis and policy framework. *Theory and Society*, **27**, 151–208.

Zohar, A. & Morgan, G. (1998). Refining our understanding of hypercompetition and hyperturbulence. In A. Y. Ilinitch, A. Y. Lewin and R. D'Aveni (Eds), *Managing in Times of Disorder: Hypercompetitive Organizational Responses*. London: Sage.

CHAPTER 20

Any Nearer a "Better" Approach? A Critical View

Karen Legge
Warwick University Business School, Coventry, UK

The brief I was given for writing this chapter suggested that I "summarise and evaluate the previous chapters... in particular, to critically assess the evidence for the effectiveness of new working practices, discuss the extent to which they have had a positive or negative effect on the experience of work, and propose ways in which the gaps in our practice and theory may be overcome".

In responding to this brief, I intend to focus on four issues. The first issue is to consider what really is new about the organisational and work designs discussed in these chapters. Is twenty-first century teamworking much different from the semi-autonomous work groups of the 1970s or call centre work different from any 1950s factory organised on Tayloristic lines? Have issues about new technologies and work design advanced much beyond the early work of the socio-technical systems theorists of the 1950s and 1960s (Rice, 1958; Trist & Bamford, 1951; Trist et al., 1963) or even the work of the 1980s and 1990s (Clark et al., 1988; Clark, 1995)? Second, what evidence do we really have of employees' experience of work? As has been discussed elsewhere (Mabey et al., 1997), even when we purport to talk of employees' "experience", too much of our "evidence" relies at best on employees responding to highly structured questionnaires or on managers speaking on their behalf. In any case, in the globalised world to which Sparrow (Chapter 19) refers, with the extended supply chains that Kerrin & Icasati-Johanson (Chapter 5) discuss, who are the employees that we are (or should be) referring to? Surely not just those handily placed for Western researchers to access with questionnaires based on ethnocentric, Western theories of organisational psychology? Third, there is the related issue of the inadequacies of positivistic methodologies (even in their own terms) to deliver meaningful findings about the relationships between working practices and various outcome measures, notably organisational performance. Fourth, when considering gaps between theory and practice, we perhaps need to query whether some of these reflect psychology's neglect of political dimensions to behaviour at work, including the "political" behaviours of academics themselves.

In the light of the above agenda, I should declare an interest. Unlike most of the other contributors to this volume, my background is not in organisational psychology but in radical organisational theory, oscillating between sympathies for postmodernist and critical realist approaches to organisational analysis. Hence, although I will attempt to assess this work in its own terms, as a devil's advocate, I will also critique it from an agnostic—or should I say excommunicated—position.

PLUS CA CHANGE, PLUS C'EST LA MEME CHOSE?

Reading the chapters in this collection, at first sight, is like returning to debates and issues of the 1970s and 1980s. Old familiar friends raise their heads, such as those of organisational choice/technological determinism (e.g. Cooney & Sohal, Chapter 3, in relation to TQM; Holman, Chapter 7, in relation to call centres), job characteristics [e.g. discussions of autonomy, job enrichment, job enlargement and empowerment feature in Chapter 15, by Batt & Doellgast, on service sector work, Lamond and colleagues (Chapter 11) on teleworking and Benson & Lawler (Chapter 9) on employee involvement], work systems design [e.g. Cordery (Chapter 6) on team working, Unsworth & Parker (Chapter 10) on promoting a proactive and innovative workforce] and socio-technical systems analysis [e.g. Mumford & Axtell (Chapter 17) on tools and methods to support the design and implementation of new work systems]. As would be expected from organisational psychologists, concepts such as motivation, job satisfaction and stress feature heavily as dependent variables. All this is very familiar ground.

However, as Sparrow (Chapter 19) is at pains to point out, whether we use such buzz words as "disorganised capitalism", "globalisation" or "unprecedented economic transition", there is an academic discourse of "hypercompetition" which is translated into management-speak as the "search for competitive advantage". Either way, to quote Sparrow, it refers to the *response expected to these changes* and puts a different slant on *some* of the job and work system design changes that we have seen at the end of the twentieth and beginning of the twenty-first century [of course, as Grey & Mitev (1995) have suggested in relation to the "revolution" of business process re-engineering, by its advocacy and implementation of competitive techniques it *constitutes* the competition, which is then the problem that the organisation must address].

The new slant on task and work systems design, as compared to the 1970s is the backgrounding of quality of working life (QWL) issues and the foregrounding of organisational performance. In the tight Western labour markets of the 1970s, before south-east Asian competition in manufactured consumer goods began to bite in western Europe and the USA, before the ascendancy of the new right liberal economics and the demise of corporatism and Keynsianism in the Anglo-Saxon world, job and work system design "experiments", such as the famous experiments by Volvo at Kalmar and Uddevalla, were chiefly aimed at securing worker retention (and hopefully, motivation and commitment) through attention to QWL issues. Although improved performance was central to the agenda, it was conceptualised as improved *worker* performance (invariably in manufacturing industry) through enhanced motivation, resultant on job designs that adhered to the tenets of the job characteristics model, embedded in work system designs that embraced the socio-technical systems principle of joint optimisation. Although the action researchers involved in such experiments did not fall into the managerial fantasy of reverse causality, that "the happy worker is the productive worker", there was often an explicit commitment to the idea that work should be designed in such a way that workers could fulfil at least some higher-order needs and gain intrinsic satisfactions that would enhance their experience of work.

Contrast that position with work system designs and research conducted in the 1990s, generally featuring initiatives in business process engineering, JIT and TQM. Business process engineering, in theory at least, rests on the logic of cutting out anything within the organisation or along its supply chain (people, structures, technologies, materials) that does not add value. As such, it is a key ingredient of lean manufacturing. "Lean manufacturing", as Delbridge (Chapter 2) makes only too clear, is based, via JIT and its symbiotic relationship with TQM and continuous improvement (*kaizen*), on the removal of organisational slack (defined as "waste" or anything that does not add value), both within and between members of the supply chain. Removal of waste is aimed first and foremost at reducing costs and so improving productivity, while the "bottom line" may be yet further enhanced by greater responsiveness to the customer in terms of speed of delivery, price and quality competitiveness. The object of such designs (and recognised as such by employees) (Bacon & Blyton, 2000; Collinson *et al.*, 1998) is pre-eminently to improve the financial performance of the organisation or, to put it in late-1990s managerial-speak, to "increase shareholder value". Certainly there is a recognition (at least in theory and among academics) that "lean" organisations, being extremely fragile systems, need to secure a workforce that is both flexible and reliable and that this is likely to have implications for skill enhancement and the generation of employee commitment. There is recognition that this points logically to some form of "high-commitment" (in the USA, significantly termed "high-performance" HRM (Becker & Gerhart, 1996; Becker & Huselid, 1998; Delery & Doty, 1996; Huselid, 1995), which may address many of the concerns of the QWL protagonists. However, this is seen very much as a corollary of a work system design aimed at efficiency, rather than being the object of the design. Whereas the designs of the 1970s were intended to enhance worker motivation and performance and so *indirectly* organisational performance, some of the designs of the 1990s and 2000s, notably those involving BPR and "lean" manufacturing, are intended *directly* to improve financial returns, with a "high- commitment" HRM strategy being regarded by way of an ongoing servicing and insurance policy, rather as an end in itself and, as such, as a potential cost just as much as a benefit.

Of course, this is not the whole story. It could be argued that initiatives involving the adoption of "high-commitment" HRM policies, no less than the QWL experiments of the 1970s, rest on the assumption that such policies will generate highly skilled, flexible and motivated employees who will be highly productive, enabling enhanced organisational performance. But a key issue here is whether one adopts a universalistic or a contingency approach to task and work system design. Although the sociotechnical systems approach of the 1970s was contingent in the sense that organisational choices about design should match the exigencies of the context in order to achieve joint (social and technical) optimisation—the "composite shortwall" design in the British coal-mining industry being a classic example (Trist *et al.*, 1963)—it was universalistic in its concern for QWL issues and in its belief that these were best served by designing jobs high in the requisite task attributes of autonomy, variety, skill, feedback and task identity (Hackman & Oldham, 1976).

Similarly, today, there are universalistic and contingency approaches in relation to the choice of HRM policies, including task and work system design, skill levels sought, training and reward system policy. The universalistic approach maintains that there is an identifiable "bundle" of best ("high-commitment"/ "high-performance") HR policies and practices that have universal, additive, positive effects on organisational performance, irrespective of external circumstances or business strategy (e.g. Guest, 1987; Huselid, 1995; MacDuffie, 1995; Pfeffer, 1994: Walton, 1985). This is consistent with institutional theory about organisational isomorphism—that organisations survive because they identify and implement the "best" policies and practices and that, as a result, successful organisations get to look more and more like each other (DiMaggio & Powell, 1983).

In contrast, the contingency approach argues that, to achieve high organisational performance, HRM policies and practices must be congruent with other organisational characteristics, such as culture, and be in alignment with the firm's business strategy (e.g. Arthur, 1994; Purcell, 1999). The contingency approach, in contrast to the universalistic, would also argue that "high-commitment" HRM practices, while appropriate to high-skill, high-value-added activities, are inappropriate to low-skill, mass production or service activities, if the objective is to maximise profitability. The contingent assumption seems to be that designs based on the control of the workforce suit mass production or service activities, while the generation of commitment is necessary where high-value-added activities are involved. This position is consistent with resource-based theories that argue that sustained competitive advantage rests not on imitating "best" practice, but on developing unique and non-imitable competences (Barney, 1991).

A third approach to task and work system design is a muddling-through, seat- of-the-pants pragmatism guided by a concern for short-term cost-effectiveness. This lacks the coherence of either a commitment to "best" practice or to consistent strategic alignment.

Where the "one best way" philosophy of "high-commitment"/"high-performance" HRM is adopted, there is much overlap with the designs proposed by the socio-technical systems, QWL movement of the 1970s, *except* that belief in QWL values appears purely instrumental, not as an end in itself. This is consistent with the prevailing liberal economics of the late twentieth and early twenty-first century, just as adherence to QWL values for their own sake was consistent with the corporatism of the post-war decades, pre-1980s. Rather than having any position on QWL issues, a contingency approach to task and work system design, however, where strategic integration or alignment is a priority, would suggest that Tayloristic designs in some circumstances might be deemed more appropriate than those based on the investment in training, multiskilling and empowerment strategies of "high commitment" HRM. This is indeed what we find in the studies cited in many of the chapters. There is evidence of organisations taking both the "high" and the "low" road, to use Bacon and Blyton's (2000) terminology. Let us consider team working and "lean manufacturing" by way of example.

"High" road team working, as typified by Bacon & Blyton's research in the UK steel industry, is characterised by task variety (maintenance tasks integrated into production tasks, frequent job rotation, flexible job descriptions, no job classification system), identification with team tasks (skilled maintenance workers integrated into the team), expertise in teams (integration of craft expertise in teams), stability and belief in teams (workers in teams have similar skills), participative management (delayered management, teams responsible for some production targets and some measure of financial performance, team leaders selected with team input) and common rewards (few pay bands and few grades within the teams). This is very much the sort of team working discussed in Cordery's chapter and reported in the US steel industry (Ichniowski *et al.*, 1997). In contrast, "low" road team working is typified by Bacon & Blyton (2000, p. 1429) as involving a "low-skill–low-wage strategy". A key difference seems to lie in management's rationale for introducing team working. Although, irrespective of the type of team work, an economic rationale was perceived by their respondents as predominating, in the case of "high" road team working, social and cultural objectives, such as improving job satisfaction and increasing worker commitment and motivation, were scored more highly than where "low" road team working prevailed.

Clearly, the latter is a far cry from the team working Cordery appears to have in mind when he speaks of the employee benefits it may afford of increased scope to satisfy higher-order needs and to obtain important intrinsic rewards through work, such as task variety and autonomy, increased social interaction, etc. Perhaps more recognition of, and research into, situations where "low" road team working is the norm might be appropriate, at least in the UK, given the finding from the Workplace Employee Relations Survey (WERS), that, of the 65% of workplaces reporting team working, only 5% had teams with features of autonomous team working (Cully et al., 1999).

A similar story seems to emerge with respect to "lean" manufacturing. Delbridge's analysis finds evidence of a lean manufacturing that, at least in many employees' experience, falls well short of the ideal type marriage of the "hardware" of TQM, JIT and associated "Japanese" production processes with the "software" of "high-commitment" HRM (Rees et al., 1996) to provide a "tripod of success" (Wickens, 1987), where employees work "smarter not harder". Delbridge points to the down-side of "lean" manufacturing as involving labour intensification, low trust–high surveillance control, "peer controls turning poisonous" and high stress levels—a state of affairs which elsewhere has been termed the "tripod of subjugation": management-by-stress, management-through-blame and management-through-compliance (Garrahan & Stewart, 1992). This is not surprising, at least in relation to UK research evidence. For it is highly debatable to what extent the "Japanese" model of "lean" manufacturing can be applied to UK manufacturing, let alone to services.

Indeed, based on an analysis of the largest 200 British-owned firms (size measured by capitalisation), Ackroyd & Proctor (1998) suggest that a different form of lean organisation exists in the bulk of British manufacturing industry. They emphasise that the typical British manufacturing firm has grown through merger and acquisition, comprising a large number of decentralised production facilities producing a wide range of "cash cow" goods for retail in mature markets. These are firms that favour a tight control of financial performance from the centre, with a good deal of operational freedom allowed to plant management and which are characterised by the shortism of much of British industry (Storey & Sisson, 1993). In terms of production systems and working practices, there is little evidence here of high levels of investment in advanced technology or of multi-skilling or of "high-commitment" HRM practices. Rather, they argue, the characteristics of the typical British manufacturing firm are as follows:

- Production is organised as cellular manufacture as it facilitates the calculation of marginal costs and the identification of unprofitable activities, while limiting the need for employees to develop a broad spectrum of skills.
- Advanced manufacturing technology is little used, except as additions to existing configurations of equipment.
- Labour flexibility is achieved by teams of semi-skilled workers performing a range of specific tasks and given some on-the-job training.
- Employees do not enjoy privileged status or high employment security, but compete with sub-contracted labour and alternative suppliers.
- Production operations are considered as dispensable, separate segments, about which calculations of cost are regularly made.
- Management takes the form of intensified indirect control, based on the allocation of costs.

- The high-surveillance management regimes associated with "Japanese" lean manufacturing are not typical of British manufacturing, as they exaggerate the quality of information typically available and the willingness and ability of managers to appraise such information, even if available, given the much reduced ranks of middle management and supervision.

This model of lean organisation lacks the coherency and logic of the "ideal-type" "Japanese" model. Indeed, it smacks of a policy of "asset management" rather than "value-added", to use Capelli & McKersie's (1987) well-known distinction. Even where working practices are used that are associated with Japanese-style lean manufacturing, such as team working, the motivation for their introduction may be pragmatic rather than due to any concern for strategic and operational integration. This form of leanness, motivated exclusively by financial concerns, is often accused of "cutting muscle" rather than fat, of giving rise to the stressed-out anorexic organisation. In the context of this argument, it is not surprising that Cordery's chapter on team-working finds studies where it is associated with lay-offs, decreases in average real wages for core staff, with the employment of fewer managers and fewer temporary or contract staff. Cordery also finds considerable variability in the findings regarding the consequences for productivity, work attitudes and employee behaviour (Goodman *et al.*, 1988; Guzzo & Dickson, 1996; Hackman, 1990; Osterman, 2000).

One noticeable difference between job and work systems design research in the 1970s and 2000 reflects the changing structure of Western economies. In the 1970s research was focused largely on manufacturing industry and, in so far as the service sector got a look-in, the focus was on task design for office workers and computer operators (e.g. Mumford, 1972). A major concern in the late 1990s and 2000s is the "office factories" of call centres (Batt, 1999, 2000; Deery *et al.*, 2002; Frenkel *et al.*, 1999; Hutchinson *et al.*, 2000; Knights & McCabe, 1998; Taylor & Bain, 1999) and those retail services where the worker has direct contact with the customer and is involved in "emotional labour" (retail stores, fast food outlets, hotels, airlines, health care) (Hochschild, 1983). Another issue is the changing patterns of work that arise from new information and communication technologies—not just the call centres, whose very existence relies on computer and telephone-based technologies—but teleworking (see Lamond *et al.*, Chapter 11) and E-business (see Clegg *et al.*, Chapter 13) (I will consider E-business in a later section of this chapter).

Holman (Chapter 7) on call centres echoes some of the themes already discussed with reference to teamworking and lean manufacturing. In call centres, similarly, there seems to be the choice between a Tayloristic, mass service model of task design (the "low" road), aimed at cost minimisation and a high commitment, customer service-orientated model, aimed at customer satisfaction (the "high" road). The "low" road is characterised by task fragmentation, little variety or task interdependence, low autonomy (rigid adherence to set scripts) and potentially punitive performance monitoring (listening in to calls for disciplinary purposes). In contrast, the "high" road, aiming to provide a customised service, is characterised by more variety involving the use of extensive product or service knowledge, more autonomy (unscripted calls apart from the opening and closing formulae) and higher degrees of task interdependence, as staff often need to draw on others' knowledge and performance monitoring that is less intense and focused on support and development rather than sanctions. Not surprisingly, the "low" road, in particular, is often associated with stress, exacerbated by the strains of surface acting associated with emotional labour.

Furthermore, the pragmatism inherent in the UK version of lean manufacturing (Ackroyd & Proctor, 1998) also seems evident in design choices in call centres. As Holman points out, there are many anomalies in the data, in that some mass service call centres adopt some high-commitment work practices (Batt, 2000) and some high-commitment service call centres adopt some mass service work practices (Kinnie *et al.*, 2000). He argues that this implies that true alignment, consistent with contingency theory, may not be possible. For example, if local labour markets are very competitive, it may not be possible to use low pay and Tayloristic work practices, which exacerbate recruitment and turnover problems, even if the logic of a mass low cost service calls for this strategy. Pragmatic choices may emerge as managers juggle the contradictions of a call centre environment—between service quality and quantity; ensuring employee empathy with the customer and instrumentality; providing a customised service and having standardised procedures; balancing employee control and commitment.

Lamond and colleagues (Chapter 11) on teleworking again introduce the "high" road/"low" road distinction. Where teleworking involves knowledge intensive professional work and is seen as part of the creation of an "organic informated organisation" (Travic, 1998) designed to transcend, in a globalised economy, traditional time/space constraints, the outcomes may be high employee autonomy and flexible task completion combined with high intra-organisational contact and little of the reported experience of social isolation that may afflict home-based teleworkers. In contrast, where teleworking involves low knowledge intensity and is introduced to achieve cost reductions through downsizing, delayering and shedding accommodation costs, then, as the authors suggest, "notions of 're-engineering' may be code for cost-cutting, and teleworking introduced with stringent electronic controls and greater use of contingent workers".

In their broader discussion of the service sector, Batt & Doellgast (Chapter 15) interestingly, find evidence that could be interpreted as supportive of both contingency and universalistic approaches. On the one hand, similarly to Holman, they found that intensified price competition in the industries studied (airlines, financial services, telecommunications and hotels) led firms to focus more on cost reduction than on quality-enhancing strategies. Where the latter are adopted, they are typically reserved, as contingency theory would lead us to expect, for business or high-value-added customers. On the other hand, Batt & Doellgast found that investments in IT, when coupled with complementary high-commitment HR practices, are consistently associated with higher productivity, product and service innovations, customization and order-processing efficiencies. Also, fairly consistent evidence was found that collaborative forms of work "are associated with better performance in front-line service work".

THE EXPERIENCE OF WORK

I deliberately ended the preceding paragraph with a quotation that talks of *associations*. Most of the studies reviewed in these chapters are survey-based empirical research that seeks statistical associations between responses representing independent and dependent variables. The ontology is realist (measurable variables) and the epistemology is positivistic, one "which seek(s) to explain and predict what happens in the social world by searching for regularities, and causal relationships between its constituent elements" (Burrell & Morgan, 1979, p. 5). The majority of the authors in this book represent people's experience of work in these terms, e.g. "team processes such as sharing, norms, task orientation and participation significantly affect innovation levels" (Unsworth & Parker, Chapter 10); "the technological methods that allow managers to monitor the actions of teleworkers as closely as they could monitor on-site workers have been associated with low employee morale" (Lamond *et al.*, Chapter 11); "trust in buyer–seller interaction influences satisfaction with profit, sales outcomes and performance. In contrast, a lack of trust has been associated with partnering failure" (Kerrin & Icasati-Johanson, Chapter 5).

While fully accepting the importance of strong positivistic designs, such as experimental and *strong* quasi-experimental designs (such as the interrupted time series with comparison series design) in establishing the internal validity of causal attributions, and while recognising the problems of external validity associated with qualitative case-study designs, I query whether positivistic designs give us much insight into the *experience* of work (see Legge, 1984, for an extended critique of the use of positivistic designs in evaluation research). In the case of weak correlational designs, I wonder if they give us much insight into anything.

In my view, the review of positivistic studies with which the chapters are largely concerned gives rise to two problems. First, in relation to causal attributions, with respect, some of the chapters contain statements that are at best unsurprising, not to say trite, even tautological, e.g. "Too many extroverts or neurotics in a team will diminish effectiveness" (Cordery); "Proactivity determinants tend to be those that promote action, such as need for achievement, self-esteem, extraversion and conscientiousness" (Unsworth & Parker); "The provision of such training is, however, contingent, with low-skill redesigns entailing minimal training while high-skill designs require significantly more" (Cooney & Sohal); "Hill has suggested that a trust based approach to inter-organisational relationships, reduces motivation to behave opportunistically . . . because 'behavioural repertoires are biased towards cooperation rather than opportunism'" (Kerrin & Icasati-Johanson). Exceptionally, this can result in chapters arguing what may seem self-evident. For example, the message of Kerrin & Icasati-Johanson's chapter seems to be largely that trust and perspective taking (the affective response of empathy) is important in developing successful supply-chain partnering. This level of generality can exist because contextual variation is not adequately explored.

Second, many of the chapters refer to mixed or contradictory findings about outcomes (but cf. Clegg *et al.*, (Chapter 13 on e-business) who report consistent findings!). For example, Batt & Doellgast find evidence that the effectiveness of high-commitment practices on a quality or up-market service strategy is "inconclusive", that several organisational studies of TQM have shown "mixed results", as have studies on the effects of supervisory support. Holman finds that studies aimed to discover whether call centre work is more stressful than comparable forms of work "show no clear pattern of findings", while there are many "anomalies" in findings on the degree of strategic alignment of "bundles" of HR practices with customer segment. Cordery finds very mixed evidence of the benefits of teams to organisations and their employees. The fact that findings may be mixed or contradictory is hardly surprising, as the independent variables may be differently specified (e.g."high" road vs. "low" road team working) and intervening variables, such as contextual factors, may differ. Indeed, Batt & Doellgast repeatedly call for research designs that are more contextually sensitive, while Clegg *et al.*, in relation to e-business, argue for detailed case studies of companies and supply chains that are introducing relatively advanced forms of e-business and for the importance of contextual issues. A better understanding of the context to which findings refer can help explain contradictory results.

However, most importantly, an understanding of context is essential in understanding people's experience of work. "Experience of work" is not just about measurable attitudinal and behavioural responses to task and work systems design interventions, but about people's *situated* sense-making through processes of human action and interaction (Weick, 1995). Even if one rejects a fully social constructionist position, where the reality of the work context "is created afresh in each encounter of everyday life as individuals impose themselves (by language, labels, actions and routines) on their world to establish a realm of meaningful definition" (Morgan & Smircich, 1980), it must be recognised that people's experience is grounded in daily interactions that are located in specific times and spaces and which generate meaning. Most of the research studies reviewed in these chapters, given their epistemological stance, cannot access experience in these terms and hence their discussion is inevitably partial.

For example, there is no way that Cordery's discussion of positivistic studies of team working can access the subtle shades of meaning yielded by rich ethnographic data such as that of McCabe's case study of the "bewitched, bothered and bewildered" employees of an automobile company (McCabe, 2000; Knights & McCabe, 2000). Drawing on formal and informal interview data, McCabe identifies three types of employees and their experience of team working. First (by far the minority of those interviewed), there are those who seem to have been "bewitched" by the discourse of team working and who, in a wholehearted manner, have internalised its norms and values. Second, there are those who are "bothered" by team working in the sense that they are disturbed by what they perceive to be its incessant intrusion into their lives. They are concerned that some of their colleagues seem to be enthralled by the team discourse and alarmed at what they see as psychological warfare waged by management through an ideology of team working. Third, there are employees who are "bewildered" by team working, less because of its ideological overtones than because of its attack on established ways of doing things and the working practices and trade demarcations that reflect and reinforce their own sense of identity. The bewildered are ambivalent or confused because, while approving of the quality standards promoted by team working, they feel no necessity to change their practices to achieve them. Rather, such changes threaten their pride (and hence their identity) in having always worked to high standards. Knight & McCabe's (2000, p. 1489) comment on the identification of these three categories should act as a warning to those who think that the experience of work can be captured by the instruments of survey-based positivistic studies:

> These ideal types are used as a heuristic device and we recognize that there are dangers of forcing complex human experiences into simplistic constructions. Moreover, we also acknowledge that the employees we identify as bewitched or bothered may respond differently under different circumstances or at different times. Indeed, employees may disagree with our "labels" and their position in relation to them and, as such, it is important to see this typology as fluid and dynamic.

One further point. In talking of employees' experience of work, the implicit assumption in all the chapters is that we are referring to the experience of workers in the Western developed world. This seems an odd omission in the context of Sparrow's comments (Chapter 19) about globalisation and the boundaryless company, and given the recognition of the importance of supply-chain partnerships (Kerrin & Icasati-Johanson, Chapter 5). Nevertheless, this probably reflects how little research on developing countries is published in UK- and USA-refereed organisational psychology and management journals. I will return to this point in my conclusions.

ASSESSING THE OUTCOMES OF NEW WORKING PRACTICES AND "HIGH-COMMITMENT"/"HIGH-PERFORMANCE" HRM

I mentioned earlier the importance of strong positivistic designs in establishing the internal validity of causal attributions. In theory, then, they should come into their own in demonstrating the effects of new working practices and associated HRM interventions. However, Wright & Gardner's excellent chapter (Chapter 16) on the theoretical and empirical challenges in studying the HR practice–firm performance relationship casts doubts on the methodological adequacies of much of the positivistic research conducted in this area and its ability to provide cumulative knowledge. In this section I will consider their arguments, along with the doubts I have already expressed elsewhere (Legge, 2001a).

First there is the problem that there is no agreed conceptualisation of HRM ("strategic", "descriptive" or "prescriptive" approach?), little consensus about what precise practices should be included in the operationalization of "high-commitment"/ "high-performance" HRM and, even where there is some agreement on the inclusion of a particular "high-commitment/performance" working practice, none on its specification and measurement. There is concern, too, about the validity and reliability of measures of HR practices (see Legge, 2001a, pp. 23–26).

Second, there are problems in conceptualising and measuring performance. In the US studies, the measures of performance are invariably those relating to financial performance and productivity, rather than to employee outcomes (Rogers & Wright, 1998) (cf. Guest, 1999; Cully *et al.*, 1999, who *do* look at UK employee reactions to HRM initiatives). The US studies seem misguided, as all the theoretical rationales of how HRM affects performance rest on the assumption that it occurs *through* these employee outcomes. Apart from this very limited and questionable conceptualisation of organisational performance and, with the exception of Guest (1997, p. 267), no recognition that the financial and productivity measures are but social constructions, there are problems with measurement. As Wright & Gardner point out, with the notable exception of Huselid's (1995) study, there is a tendency not to assess multiple performance measures in any single study. As a result, researchers are unable to examine the interrelationships among outcomes, although Huselid's study suggests that these may be significant (at least some of the effect of HR practices on firm performance was mediated by the reduction in employee turnover).

Third, these problems pale into insignificance when compared to those associated with examining the *relationship* between HRM and performance, however conceptualised. Leaving aside the lack of agreement on the conceptualisation of the relationship between HRM and performance ("universalistic"? "contingency"?—or even "configurational"?) (Delery & Doty, 1996), Wright & Gardner raise serious methodological problems in establishing valid findings.

First, there is the practical issue of trade-offs in selecting an appropriate level of analysis in testing HRM–performance relationships. Plant-level studies have three strengths: the risk of variance in HR practices is minimised; the respondent(s) is likely to have first-hand knowledge of HR practices—both espoused and in-use—increasing the validity of the responses; and there is the potential of providing the most proximal measures of performance. The drawback is that research at this level may not allow assessing the "fit" between HR practices and business strategy and there are perennial issues about generalisability. Organisational or business level studies are optimal for assessing relationships between HR practices and business strategy, but given that businesses often have multiple locations, categories of employees and jobs, precise assessments of HR practices become problematic, especially when—as is often the case—the research design relies on just one senior management respondent. The bulk of research linking HR practices and performance has been conducted at corporate level, given the reliance on financial measures of performance, as it is at this level that much of the publicly available financial data exists. However, this exacerbates problems associated with the validity of single-respondent assessments, given the complexity of assessing HR practices over a range of businesses, the problem that there may be variance between the business strategies across businesses within some corporations (hence, identifying *a* business strategy is likely to be problematic) and, because these studies cross industries, the difficulty in partialling out all of the industry effects.

Not only are there methodological issues here, but what is worrying theoretically is that, if the majority of the research studies remains located at the corporate level, given the US obsession with measures of financial performance, this is not conducive to assessing the enacted aspects of employee behaviour that constitute the intervening variable in explaining the relationship between HR practices, operating and financial performance. It is difficult to see how such studies can *test* causal relationships, as opposed to making theory-derived inferences about the correlations they find.

This brings us to the issue of establishing causality, where Wright and Gardner's critique is trenchant. First, with some exceptions, the majority of the US studies are cross-sectional rather than longitudinal and, hence, while causality may be *inferred* from correlation, technically, it is not tested. This gives rise to three possibilities. A causal relationship may exist in the direction inferred, i.e. HRM policies and practices may give rise to positive outcomes, although as Purcell (1999, p. 30) has pointed out, this may be no more than a temporary "Hawthorne" effect [of course, it is possible, with the same direction of causality, that HRM, particularly "hard" HRM, may give rise to negative outcomes or, as Guest & Hoque (1994) report, positive outcomes on organisational performance measures but negative outcomes on HR–employee outcomes]. Or, reverse causality may exist (a possibility also recognised by Batt & Doellgast in this book). In other words, as a firm becomes more profitable or its share price rises, it may invest in "high-commitment/performance" HRM practices, such as expenditure on training or profit sharing. As Wright & Gardner point out, this may be due to a belief that such practices will further increase performance, or that they will reduce the risk of performance declines, or from a belief in the justice and efficacy of wealth distribution. However, it is the profits that generate HR practices, rather than vice versa.

A further possibility that they identify is that the observed relationship between HR practices and performance may not stem from any true relationship (i.e. "true" from a positivistic perspective), but from implicit theories of organisational survey respondents. In other words, if a respondent has little detailed knowledge of HR practices in his/her firm (highly likely if the firm is large, diverse and multi-sited), but knows the firm is performing well in terms of productivity and profitability, he/she may infer that "high-performance" HR practices *must* exist, given this level of performance, based on the implicit theory that such practices are related to high performance (Gardner *et al.*, 1999).

Finally, Wright & Gardner raise the issue of how little has been done to unlock the "black box" of the processes that link HRM (however conceptualised) with performance (however conceptualised). But unless this is done, e.g. by developing models that include theory-derived, key intervening variables, it is not possible to rule out unequivocally alternative causal models that explain empirical associations between HR practices and organisational outcomes.

The question then becomes how many and what intervening variables should there be in the "black box" (employee behaviour/skills? strategy implementation? operating performance?) and how should these variables be specified? For example, "operating performance" might be defined and measured in terms of customer satisfaction, customer retention, sales revenues, quality defects, scrap, down-time, productivity, labour costs. Then there is the issue of distinguishing between espoused and actual HR practices and employee skills and behaviours. And, as Wright & Gardner point out, the greater the number of intervening variables identified and the greater the level of specificity, the greater the multiplicative effect in determining the processes of a model, as the model building requires the specification of the relationships between each of the specifications of the major intervening variables.

If this complexity is problematic when a universalistic approach to HR practices/performance relationships is adopted, it becomes additionally so when a contingency or a configurational approach is preferred. With contingency models of HRM–performance relationships, there are issues of causal ambiguity and path-dependent contingencies that add up to idiosyncratic choices (Boxall, 1992; Collis & Montgomery, 1995; Purcell, 1999). Causal ambiguity refers to the numerous and subtle interconnections between contingent factors that make each organisation's experience, in a sense, unique. Path dependency recognises the emergent nature of strategy and the dependence of policy choices on the organisation's history and culture. Put the two together and the resultant idiosyncratic contingency suggests that each organisation has to make choices of HR policy and practice based on its judgement, not only of appropriateness to business and operational strategies but of what "suits" the history and culture of the organisation, what "feels" right (Purcell, 1999, p. 35). Such potential complexity sits uneasily with the large-scale surveys and quantitative approaches of positivistic research designs.

I have focused here on Wright & Gardner's critique of theoretical and methodological problems in researching HRM outcomes, but much of the critique could also be applied to studies about the effects of task and work system design. Certainly this must be considered in the light of the contradictory and inconsistent findings I mentioned earlier. Can the inconsistencies be explained by different contextual factors or are they methodological artefacts? Or is it a question of not "either/or", but "and/both"?

The (Absent) Political Dimension

In reading the chapters which, fundamentally, are about resource allocation and change, I was struck by a curious absence of reference to a political dimension. For example, the concept of "empowerment" is generally treated as non-problematic, although clearly it means different things to managers and mainstream organisational psychology researchers than it does to critical organisation theorists (Hardy & Leiba-O'Sullivan, 1998). In Pritchard & Payne's otherwise excellent discussion (Chapter 12) of the relationship between performance management practices and their variant of an expectancy theory of motivation, there is no questioning of the implicit managerial agenda which they appear wholeheartedly to embrace, nor a recognition of what is marginalised by a focus on "motivation". That is, to look for "performance" improvements (as defined by managerial interests) in terms of an *individual* level concept, "motivation", deflects attention from the *societal* and *organisational structures* of inequality, which not only allow the powerful (including academics from leading US business schools) to set the agenda, but to place responsibility for "poor" performance on the individual rather than on the economic and social system. Scarbrough (Chapter 8) provides a very interesting discussion of cognitive vs. community perspectives on knowledge management, of codification vs. personalization knowledge management strategies and of the constraints on the use of IT for knowledge management. Here, issues of power and politics are clearly apparent (e.g. in the tensions between knowledge sharing and career paths in bureaucratic, hierarchical structures; in general issues of the ownership and control of knowledge), but they are not highlighted. Sonnentag's chapter (Chapter 18) on designing evaluation studies contains one reference to a potentially political issue in evaluation research ("there might be some reluctance in initiating an evaluation project at all ... stakeholders within an organisation might be afraid of the evaluation outcomes or anticipate negative specific results"), but otherwise treats it as a purely technical, rationalistic exercise. Indeed, the chapter treats evaluation research as something that may present technical problems, but is otherwise unproblematic.

I would take a very different view, but admittedly from a different epistemological and from a political standpoint. Almost 20 years ago, I too was asking questions about the evaluation of organisational change (Legge, 1984). As a result of my researches, I came to very different conclusions from Sonnentag about the role of positivistic evaluation designs.

Briefly, in the 1980s, several prominent evaluation researchers (such as Patton, Guba and Lincoln) were openly sceptical about positivistic methods as a result of their tendency to produce "weak" or uninterpretable findings about change outcomes. In part the problem appeared to have resulted from difficulties in maintaining internal validity and the conflicting requirements of internal and external validity in organisation settings. Some disbelievers were more a product of the paradigm warfare that was prevalent in the 1980s and early 1990s, when debates raged about paradigm incommensurability and the need for minority, non-positivistic voices to form breakaway movements, such as the Standing Conference of Organisational Symbolism or European Group of Organization Studies to protect their epistemological positions (and careers) from US-led, functionalist imperialism (see Pfeffer, 1993, 1995; van Maanen, 1995a,b). How then do you account for the continued prevalence of positivistic designs? The imperialism of entrenched, traditionalist academic interests on both sides of the Atlantic—and the publishing policies of top US journals—might be one explanation. Another is this. The exact data that positivistic designs in theory should yield are only required if rationality is at a premium. But, in practice, the more important the decision, the more likely are political rather than rational considerations to prevail (Buchanan & Badham, 2000). The more trivial the decision, the less likely is the decision maker to bother with exact information, irrespective of how rationally he/she is able to make the decision. In which case, it could be argued that positivistic designs also prosper through acting as a rhetoric for an evaluation ritual, whereby the lack of formal rationality of actual decision making and the accountability and responsibility demanded of the idealised decision maker are reconciled.

Furthermore, as Hollway (1991, p. 187) reminds us more generally about the discourses of organisational psychology, they are "conditioned by the history of the management of regulation at work... (and) through power relations and language, produce subjectivity" (read identity, "experience of work"). Writing from a Foucauldian perspective, Hollway makes the valuable point, missing from the chapters in this book, that:

> The individual at work whom work psychology is so intent on discovering (feeling that it is getting nearer to an efficacious truth as discovery succeeds discovery) is the individual that work psychology is involved, with others, in producing: the trainable hands; the fatiguable body; the individual abilities, skills and aptitudes; the sentiment; the interpersonal skills; the leadership qualities; the motivation; the boredom and satisfaction; the irrational opposition to management. The individual is all over the place, the product of diverse problems in practice not of theory, nor even of scientific experiment.*The changes in the individual over time reflect the shifting problems of regulation* (my own italics).

What we are witnessing in the mantras of "team working", "flexibility", "employee involvement", "empowerment", "lean" organisation, "business process re-engineering", "high-commitment/performance" HRM is the production of new boundaries in the frontiers of control, where commitment and control strategies are not juxtaposed (either/or), but exist side by side (both/and), if differentially applied to differently constituted groups ("core"/"periphery"; "knowledge" workers/"McDonaldized" workers). The regulation of work in a globalised economy constitutes a discourse about the "bottom line" (worker as value-adding commodity), not about QWL (worker as human being). As Hollway (1991, pp. 187–188) puts it:

> The power of work psychology is that it can reflect back the preoccupations of employers and managers in systematic, formal, apparently scientific discourses which are tied to developments in the practice of workplace regulation... They are always based on that same problematic: enhancing workplace regulation; and by reflecting back this problematic as scientific, work psychology increases the legitimacy of management practices and their justification in the workplace.

BACK TO THE FUTURE?

I will now return to the brief I began with and attempt to assess the effectiveness of new working practices, their positive/negative effects on the experience of work and to suggest ways in which the gaps in our theory and practice might be overcome.

It was often observed in the 1980s and 1990s that technical changes, such as new IT systems and CIM, took longer to disperse and to work effectively than early protagonists imagined (e.g. McLoughlin & Clark, 1988). Indeed, in spite of the prevalence of PCs in offices of the developed world, the paperless office (indeed, teleworking) is still the experience of a minority. Scarbrough's chapter on knowledge management similarly concludes that "the available evidence tends to suggest that KM's influence on management thinking has been somewhat greater than its impact on organisational practices". Further, Clegg and his colleagues, with reference to E-business, found that the majority of companies in the UK are in the "early stages" of adoption (mainly using E-mail and on-line marketing facilities) and that the impacts, not surprisingly, have been "low key". Although team working has been widely adopted in the UK, the evidence suggests that only a very small minority of initiatives involve teams with features of autonomous group working (Ackroyd & Proctor, 1998; Cully *et al.*, 1999). Again, business process re-engineering was widely adopted in the UK and USA in the 1990s, but there is little evidence that it delivers the results it promises

(Grint, 1994; Grint & Willcocks, 1995; Kinnie *et al.*, 1996; Mumford & Hendricks, 1996; Oram & Wellins, 1995; Willmott, 1994). The initiatives that are essentially about cost cutting and control (reorganising work in the context of delayering and downsizing) may deliver in the short run, but we have to question the long-term consequences in terms of potential loss of organisational memory and learning (Sparrow, 1998), work intensification, low morale, "survivor syndrome" and so on (see, Legge, 2000, for a summary of research on these issues).

An important question about effectiveness is "effectiveness for whom and on the basis of what criteria?" There is evidence, referenced throughout the chapters, that initiatives in the context of "high-commitment/performance" HRM are correlated with productivity and good financial performance, but we cannot be sure of the direction of causality. Where employees have been questioned they seem to like "high-commitment" HRM, where it has been introduced (Guest, 1999), but the evidence cited in the chapters would suggest that the "low" road (or "hard" HRM) is more prevalent. Nevertheless, it would be unwise to assume that workers' experience of "low" road practices is necessarily and uniformly negative. Much will depend on their social construction of their working experience, in the light of their expectations and situated experiences of work in general. It is popularly claimed that the neo-liberal policies of the 1980s in the UK did much to realign workers' expectations about job security and work rates. As Ron Todd (Secretary General of the TGWU at that time) is famously reported to have said in the mid-1980s, "We have 3 million unemployed and 23 million scared to death".

However, questionnaire-based research findings are often difficult to interpret. For example, the Collinson *et al.* (1998) study of TQM initiatives found that, generally speaking, it had failed to improve trust between management and workers. Nevertheless, they found that most of their respondents enjoyed working as hard as they did; that the organisations where the workers were most likely to say that they were working harder and more subject to managerial monitoring were also those where trust in management and the acceptance of quality programmes were highest; and that workers subject to output targets and most aware of the monitoring of their work were clearly the most, not the least, likely to be favourable to quality initiatives and to express trust in management. How do we interpret this finding? Collinson *et al.* (1998) conclude that employees had pragmatic expectations of TQM; that while they did not necessarily seek empowerment and retained a sense of distance from management, nevertheless they welcomed the principles of quality management and involvement in problem solving, even though this involvement was limited to immediate work tasks. Rather than being characterised in terms of "work intensification", the authors suggest that the idea of the "disciplined worker" might more appropriately describe their situation and reactions. This is a classic pluralist interpretation. However, a commentator of a unitarist persuasion might find evidence here that the more trusting workers are of management, the more positive they are about management's initiatives, do not see legitimate control systems as oppressive (cf. Delbridge's findings, this volume; Garrahan & Stewart, 1992) and are happy to give of their best (work harder). A critical theorist would be more likely to interpret the data in terms of co-optation strategies producing "docile bodies" (Foucault, 1977).

A major omission in this collection, in spite of Sparrow's chapter on the future of work and Kerrin & Icasati-Johanson's on supply chains, is a recognition of the impact of globalisation and the boundaryless organisation on *how we might approach the subject of the experience of work*. Space constraints prevent a full discussion of this issue (but see Legge, 2001b), but two points may be highlighted. First, the chapters here pay no attention to the nature of work and the experience of work among people in developing countries, to whom we increasingly sub-contract commodity production (and some knowledge work, as in the case of software programmers in India) *as a direct result of many of the initiatives discussed here*. Perhaps the Western ethnocenticism of many of the concepts and theories discussed in these chapters preclude such a consideration, although a good place to start might be in exploring the use of social and human capital theory (referred to specifically by Sparrow & Doellgast as promising avenues of research) in relation to developing countries. After all, as Handy (1979, p. 24) once remarked, whereas in the West (at that time) we tend to think of labour as a scarce resource and capital as a plentiful one, in developing countries the reverse is the case.

Secondly, in spite of reference to TQM and JIT, where the producer is conceptualised as a customer, and in spite of an interesting chapter on performance in services, there is very little attempt to consider how our experience as workers, in Western developed economies, is intimately related to the identities we seek and our expectations as customers. Our expectations about fashion, brands, quality, cost and the nature of leisure products and services are the drivers behind the design of flexible working and flexible, "hollowed-out" organisations, that, in Sennett's (1998) terms, result in "illegible" jobs, ambiguous career structures, low trust and a "corrosion of character", as employees can no longer develop a long-term, coherent narrative of their working lives.

The problem is that if we seek to achieve the meaningful identity denied to many of us at work, through the consumption of, literally, *meaningful* brands (Klein, 2000), we collude with the large, often global, corporations that have been instrumental in creating the conditions that "corrode character" in the first place. There are many ironies in this process. When we speak of shopping as "retail therapy", the implication is that it unwinds the stresses induced by the flexibalisation deemed necessary to produce the products and services we now seek to consume at a price we are prepared to pay. As producers, we may be stressed by the work intensification inherent in functional flexibility and the "contingent worker" status afforded us by numerical flexibility; as shoppers, we welcome low prices and extended opening hours. In purchasing brands we may feel we acquire a distinctive image, yet in following "fashion" we lose uniqueness. We may deplore the instabilities in our working life, yet embrace it in some of our consumption as we seek to identify and follow the latest trends. We may find no meaning in poorly paid, casualised "McJobs", but as consumers, whether of hamburgers, financial services or supermarkets, we collude with our conversion into unpaid, part-time workers, clearing tables, pushing trolleys and performing the role of bank clerks and sales assistants as we engage with call centres and cash machines. In so far as we retreat into "retail therapy" to establish identities threatened by demeaning work experiences, we perpetuate a vicious circle. And the irony is that those most in need of alternative experiences, to compensate for a "McJob" working life, are least able to afford them. What has organisational psychology to say about the producer–consumer relationship?

Finally, how may the gaps between our theory and practice be addressed? It is conventional to call for better research and certainly all the chapters have ideas here. For example, Wright and Gardner's ideas on methodological improvements in researching the HRM–performance relationship are to be welcomed. There seems to be a wide measure of agreement about the need to open up the "black box" of the processes that link HRM with organisational performance/outcomes. Guest's (1997) ideas about using expectancy theory and the psychological contract (cf. Pritchard & Payne, this volume) to explore HRM-performance linkages are promising. Purcell's (1999) approach of using in-depth case studies to explore how organisations develop successful transition management, build unique sets of competencies and distinctive organisational routines and, in situations of leanness, with greater dependency on all core workers, develop inclusiveness and trust, is yielding interesting results (Hutchinson et al., 2000).

However, in addressing the gap between theory and practice, I would urge organisational psychologists to reflect on the role of power in working lives: first, as it influences their own commitment to mainstream positivism and, second, in its role in constituting their discipline, their subjects and the world their subjects inhabit.

REFERENCES

Ackroyd, S. & Proctor, S. (1998). British manufacturing organization and workplace relations: some attributes of the new flexible firm. *British Journal of Industrial Relations*, **36**(2), 163–183.
Arthur, J. B. (1994). Effects of human resource systems on manufacturing performance and turnover. *Academy of Management Journal*, **37**, 670–87.
Bacon, N. & Blyton, P. (2000). High road and low road teamworking: perceptions of management rationales and organizational and human resource outcomes. *Human Relations*, **53**(11), 1425–1458.
Barney, J. (1991). Firm resources and sustained competitive advantage. *Journal of Management*, **17**, 99–120.
Batt, R. (1999). Work organization, technology and performance in customer service and sales. *Industrial and Labor Relations Review*, **52**, 539–564.
Batt, R. (2000). Strategic segmentation in front line services: matching customers, employees and human resource systems. *International Journal of Human Resource Management*, **11**, 540–561.
Becker, B. & Gerhart, B. (1996). The impact of human resource management on organizational performance, progress and prospects. *Academy of Management Journal*, **39**(4), 779–801.
Becker, B. & Huselid, M. (1998). High performance work systems and firm performance: a synthesis of research and managerial implications. In G. R. Ferris (Ed.), *Research in Personnel and Human Resource Management*, Vol. 16, (pp. 53–101). Greenwich, CT: JAI Press.
Boxall, P. (1992). Strategic human resource management: beginnings of a new theoretical sophistication? *Human Resource Management Journal*, **2**(3), 60–78.
Buchanan, D. & Badham, R. (2000).*The Politics of Organizational Change*. London: Sage.
Burrell, G. & Morgan, G. (1979). *Sociological Paradigms and Organisational Analysis*. London: Heinemann.
Capelli, P. & McKersie, R. B. (1987). Management strategy and the redesign of work rules. *Journal of Management Studies*, **24**(5), 441–462.
Clark, J. (1995). *Managing Innovation and Change*. London: Sage.
Clark, J. et al. (1988). *The Process of Technological Change*. Cambridge: Cambridge University Press.
Collinson, M., Rees, C. & Edwards, P. K. (with Inness, L.) (1998). *Involving Employees in Total Quality Management: Employee Attitudes and Organizational Context in Unionized Environments*. London: DTI.
Collis, D. J. & Montgomery, C. A. (1995). Competing on resources: strategy for the 1990s. *Harvard Business Review*, **73**(4), 118–128.
Cully, M., Woodland, S., O'Reilly, A. & Dix, G. (1999). *Britain at Work*. London: Routledge.
Deery, S. J., Iverson, R. D. & Walsh, J. T. (2002). Work relationships in telephone call centres: understanding emotional exhaustion and employee withdrawal. *Journal of Management Studies*, **39**(4), 471–496.
Delery, J. & Doty, H. (1996). Models of theorizing in strategic human resource management: tests of universalistic, contingency and configurational performance predictions. *Academy of Management Journal*, **39**(4), 802–835.

DiMaggio, P. J. & Powell, W. W. (1983). The iron cage revisited: institutional isomorphism and collective rationality in organizational fields. *American Sociological Review*, **48**, 147–160.
Foucault, M. (1977). *Discipline and Punish*. Harmondsworth: Penguin.
Frenkel, S., Korczyniski, M. & Shire, K. (1999). *On the Front-Line: Organization of Work in the Information Economy*. Ithaca, NY: Cornell University Press.
Gardner, T. M., Wright, P. M. & Gerhart, B. (1999). The HR-performance relationship: can it be in the mind of the beholder? Working Paper, Center for Advanced Human Resources Studies, Cornell University, Ithaca, NY.
Garrahan, P. & Stewart, P. (1992). *The Nissan Enigma*. London: Mansell.
Goodman, P. S., Devadas, R. & Griffiths-Hughson, T. L. (1988). Groups and productivity: analyzing the effectiveness of self-managed teams. In J. P. Cambell & R. J. C. & Associates (Eds), *Productivity in Organizations* (pp. 295–327). San Francisco, CA: Jossey-Bass.
Grey, C. & Mitev, N. (1995). Re-engineering organizations: a critical appraisal. *Personnel Review*, **24**(1), 6–18.
Grint, K. (1994). Re-engineering history: social resonances and business process re-engineering. *Organization*, **1**(1), 179–201.
Grint, K. & Willcocks, L. (1995). Business process re-engineering in theory and practice: business paradise regained?' *New Technology, Work and Employment*, **19**(2), 99–109.
Guest, D. E. (1987). Human resource management and industrial relations. *Journal of Management Studies*, **24**(5), 503–521.
Guest, D. E. (1997). Human resource management and performance: a review and research agenda. *International Journal of Human Resource Management*, **8**(3), 263–90.
Guest, D. E. (1999). Human resource management—the workers' verdict. *Human Resource Management Journal*, **9**(3), 263–290.
Guest, D. E. & Hoque, K. (1994). The good, the bad and the ugly: human resource management in new non-union establishments. *Human Resource Management Journal*, **5**(1), 1–14.
Guzzo, R. A. & Dickson, M. W. (1996). Teams in organizations: recent research on performance and effectiveness. *Annual Review of Psychology*, **47**, 307–338.
Hackman, J. R. (1990). *Groups that Work (and Those that Don't)*. San Francisco, CA: Jossey-Bass.
Hackman, J. R. & Oldham, G. R. (1976). Motivation through the design of work: test of a theory. *Organizational Behavior and Human Performance*, **15**, 250–279.
Handy, C. (1979). The shape of organisations to come. *Personnel Management*, June, 24–26.
Hardy, C. & Leiba-O'Sullivan, S. (1998). The power behind empowerment: implications for research and practice. *Human Relations*, **51**(4), 451–483.
Hochschild, A. (1983). *The Managed Heart*. Berkeley, CA: University of California Press.
Hollway, W. (1991). *Work Psychology and Organizational Behaviour*. London: Sage.
Huselid, M. (1995). The impact of human resource management practices on turnover, productivity, and corporate financial performance. *Academy of Management Journal*, **38**(1), 635–672.
Hutchinson, S., Purcell, J. & Kinnie, N. (2000). Evolving high commitment management and the experience of the RAC call centre. *Human Resource Management Journal*, **10**, 63–78.
Ichniowski, C., Shaw, K. & Prennushi, G. (1997). The effects of human resource management practices on productivity; a study of steel finishing lines. *American Economic Review*, **87**(3), 291–313.
Kinnie, N., Hutchinson, S. & Purcell, J. (1996). The people management implications of leaner ways of working. Report of the University of Bath. *Issues in People Management*, No. 15 (pp. 6–63). London: Institute of Personnel and Development.
Kinnie, N., Purcell, J. & Hutchinson, S. (2000). Managing the employment relationship in call centres. In Purcell, K. (Ed.), *Changing Boundaries in Employment* (pp. 163–194). Bristol: Bristol Academic Press.
Klein, N. (2000). *No Logo*. London: Flamingo.
Knights, D. & McCabe, D. (1998). 'What happens when the phones go wild?' Staff, stress and spaces for escape in a BPR telephone banking call regime. *Journal of Management Studies*, **35**, 163–194.
Knights, D. & McCabe, D. (2000). Bewitched, bothered and bewildered: the meaning and experience of teamworking for employees in an automobile company. *Human Relations*, **53**(11), 1481–1517.
Legge, K. (1984). *The Evaluation of Planned Organizational Change*. London: Academic Press.
Legge, K. (2000). Personnel management in the lean organisation. In S. Bach & K. Sisson (Eds), *Personnel Management*, 3rd Edn (pp. 41–69). Oxford: Blackwell.

Legge, K. (2001a). Silver bullet or spent round? Assessing the meaning of the "high commitment management"/performance relationship. In J. Storey (Ed.), *Human Resource Management, A Critical Text*, 2nd Edn (pp. 21–36). London: Thomson Learning.

Legge, K. (2001b). 'Why kid ourselves? Is social justice possible in global markets?' Keynote address presented at the AIRAANZ Conference, Wollongong, Australia, February.

Mabey, C., Clark, T. & Skinner, D. (Eds) (1997). *Experiencing Human Resource Management*. London: Sage.

MacDuffie, J. P. (1995). Human resource bundles and manufacturing performance; organizational logic and flexible production systems in the world auto industry. *Industrial and Labor Relations Review*, **48**, 197–221.

McCabe, D. (2000). The team dream: the meaning and experience of teamworking for employees in an automobile manufacturing company. In S. Proctor & F. Mueller (Eds), *Teamworking* (pp. 203–221). Basingstoke: Macmillan.

McLoughlin, I. & Clark, J. (1988). *Technological Change at Work*. Milton Keynes: Open University.

Morgan, G. & Smircich, L. (1980). The case for qualitative research. *Academy of Management Review*, **5**(4), 491–500.

Mumford, E. (1972). *Job Satisfaction*. London: Longman.

Mumford, E. & Hendricks, R. (1996). 'Business process re-engineering RIP'. *People Management*, **3**(9), 22–29.

Oram, M. & Wellins, R. (1995). *Re-engineering's Missing Ingredient: the Human Factor*. London: Institute of Personnel and Development.

Osterman, P. (2000). Work reorganization in an era of restructuring: trends in diffusion and effects on employee welfare. *Industrial and Labor Relations Review*, **53**, 179–196.

Pfeffer, J. (1993). Barriers to the advance of organizational science: paradigm development as a dependent variable. *Academy of Management Review*, **18**(4), 599–620.

Pfeffer, J. (1994). *Competitive Advantage through People*. Boston, MA: Harvard Business School Press.

Pfeffer, J. (1995). 'Mortality, reproducibility, and persistence of styles of theory'. *Organization Science*, **6**(6), 681–686.

Purcell, J. (1999). Best practice and best fit: chimera or cul-de-sac? *Human Resource Management Journal*, **9**(3), 26–41.

Rees, C., Scarbrough, H. & Terry, M. (1996). *The People Management Implications of Leaner Ways of Working*. Report by IRRU, Warwick Business School, University of Warwick; Issues in People Management, No. 15 (pp. 64–115). London: Institute of Personnel and Development.

Rice, A. K. (1958). *Productivity and Social Organisation*. London: Tavistock.

Rogers, E. W. & Wright, P. M. (1998). Measuring organizational performance in strategic human resource management: problems, prospects, and performance information markets. *Human Resource Management Review*, **8**, 311–331.

Sennett, R. (1998). *The Corrosion of Character*. New York: Norton.

Sparrow, P. (1998). New organizational forms, processes, jobs and psychological contracts: resolving the HRM issues. In P. Sparrow & M. Marchington (Eds), *Human Resource Management: The New Agenda* (pp. 117–141). London: Financial Times/Pitman.

Storey, J. & Sisson, K. (1993). *Managing Human Resources and Industrial Relations*. Milton Keynes: Open University Press.

Taylor, P. & Bain, P. (1999). An assembly line in the head: the call centre labour process. *Industrial Relations Journal*, **30**, 101–117.

Travic, B. (1998). Information aspects of new organizational designs: exploring the non-traditional organization. *Journal of the American Society for Information Science*, **49**, 1224–144.

Trist, E. & Bamford, K. (1951). Some social and psychological consequences of the longwall method of coal-getting. *Human Relations*, **4**(1), 3–38.

Trist, E., Higgen, G., Murray, H. & Pollock, A. (1963). *Organisational Choice*. London: Tavistock.

van Maanen, J. (1995a). Style as theory. *Organization Science*, **6**(1), 133–143.

van Maanen, J. (1995b). Fear and loathing in organization studies. *Organization Science*, **6**(6), 687–692.

Walton, R. (1985). From control to commitment in the workplace. *Harvard Business Review*, **63**(2), 77–85.

Weick, K. E. (1995). *Sensemaking in Organizations.* Thousand Oaks, CA: Sage.
Wickens, P. (1987). *The Road to Nissan.* London: Macmillan.
Willmott, H. (1994). Business process re-engineering and human resource management. *Personnel Review*, **23**(3), 34–46.

CHAPTER 21

The New Workplace: Taking Stock and Looking Forward

David Holman and **Toby D. Wall**
Institute of Work Psychology, University of Sheffield, UK

and

Ann Howard
Development Dimensions International, Tenafly, NJ, USA

The preceding contributions have focused on the nature, implications and consequences of many of the leading-edge practices, technologies and philosophies in today's workplace. Although each chapter focuses on a particular topic, collectively they cover a wide variety of contemporary initiatives and developments. The topics range from those of current concern but with a relatively long history (e.g. teamwork, total quality management) to those of more recent origin, often dependent on new technologies (e.g. call centres, teleworking, e-commerce). They also span different types and levels of analysis, from relatively specific organisational forms (e.g. supply-chain partnering, call centres), to more systemic initiatives (e.g. lean production, human resource management systems). Included as well are generic issues of contemporary significance, such as knowledge management, innovation and performance management.

This breadth of coverage reflects the diversity of practice. To facilitate drawing parallels across these diverse topics, the authors have addressed the common themes of the nature and prevalence of each development, together with its implications for employees' experience of work and for organisational performance. Our aim in this final chapter is to summarise and draw together the main issues and themes emerging from those contributions, and to identify possible ways forward. Woven within this analysis are theoretical and methodological suggestions as to how to enhance understanding of these leading-edge practices and how to best realise their potential.

THE CONCEPTUALISATION OF MODERN WORKING PRACTICES

Throughout the book, authors have sought to define the modern working practice of interest. Yet despite attempts to give them general definitions, many practices can clearly

---

The New Workplace: A Guide to the Human Impact of Modern Working Practices.
Edited by David Holman, Toby D. Wall, Chris W. Clegg, Paul Sparrow and Ann Howard. © 2003 John Wiley & Sons, Ltd.

take on different forms. For example, Cooney & Sohal (Chapter 3) noted that total quality management (TQM) "is something of a fungible concept and one that is sometimes difficult to pin down. There is not one TQM, but a range of TQMs, each dependent upon the themes and the practices that are employed in the name of TQM" (p. 38). They suggest that TQM:

> ... may be seen as a technically focused quality management program, as a philosophy of business concerned with strategic business issues or as an organizational–behavioural intervention designed to promote the more effective use of human resources (pp. 37–38).

They also distinguish the "hard" technical elements of TQM from its "soft" behavioural elements, suggesting further that the hard elements may be designed in one of two ways. One way leads to an expansion of the job role and an increase in job complexity and job control; the other creates little or no expansion of the job role and reduces job control.

Different forms of a general concept were also described in the chapters on advanced manufacturing technology, lean manufacturing, supply-chain partnering, call centres, E-business, team working, knowledge management and human resource management. That working practices do not occur in a singular form is, perhaps, unsurprising. It is also evident that practices rarely occur as singular entities existing independently from each other. Returning to TQM, Cooney & Sohal point out that:

> Quality programs may entail the development of changed approaches to employee relations to encourage greater employee participation and involvement in the business; they may entail the redesign of work to establish teams and *ad hoc* work groups; they may entail greater expenditure on training and the development of human capital ... and they may involve the review of business processes and product or service delivery systems. Many varied organizational interventions are conducted in the name of TQM, as part of the development of a quality strategy (p. 39).

Similarly, Delbridge (Chapter 2) indicates that lean manufacturing will contain TQM practices, teamwork and supply-chain partnering initiatives, while Benson & Lawler (Chapter 9) demonstrate that TQM can be an integral part of an employee involvement initiative. Even "remote" practices such as telework may be part of a supply-chain initiative or involve employees working in virtual teams. Modern working practices, therefore, can only be generally defined and tend to occur in combination (sometimes called "bundles") rather than as independent, singular entities.

There are a number of issues pertaining to bundles of practices. The first concerns which practices bundle together. At the lowest level of analysis, this is simply a question of which practices tend to co-occur. The chapters by Delbridge, Holman, Benson & Lawler, Batt & Doelgast, Wright & Gardner, and Wood, in particular, all contain descriptions of bundles of working practices. In addition, these chapters highlight bundles of human resource practices, often referred to as "high-commitment" or "high-involvement" human resource management systems.

Much as the definitions of particular working practices are less than tight, bundles also tend to differ as to their particular content. Wright & Gardner (Chapter 16) note that Dyer & Reeves (1995) counted 28 HR practices across four studies of the human resource bundle–performance link, of which only one practice, formal training, was common to all. In a similar review, Becker & Gerhart (1996) identified 27 practices, none of which was common across five studies of the human resource management-performance link.

Wright & Gardner argue that this lack of commonality is a reflection of the different research traditions of the studies reviewed. Those from a management tradition focused on practices that select, train and motivate employees, such as selection programs, job-specific training, performance management, incentive compensation and employee empowerment. Researchers from an industrial relations tradition tended to focus on practices that concern the holistic welfare of workers, such as wages, job security and decision-making authority, and other practices consistent with improving workers' physical and psychological health. Variation in bundle specification is therefore partly caused by a top-down theoretical approach.

Bundles also vary as a result of researchers' inductive strategies. Some bundles have been determined on an *a priori* conceptual or theoretical basis. Others have been specified using exploratory factor analysis, confirmatory factor analysis and latent class analysis (see Wood, Chapter 14; Wright & Gardner, Chapter 16). These inductively driven analytical strategies inevitably capture differences in the make-up of bundles that might be caused by institutional, legislative, economic or technical factors operating in different countries, sectors and industries. Indeed, it might be erroneous to assume, for example, that a "common" high-commitment HR bundle will occur across all industries, and that a "common" bundle will predict performance equally well across all sectors. Rather, the make-up of a bundle required for effective performance in one sector or industry may differ from that required in another; inductively-driven analytical strategies are necessary to establish whether or not this is the case. A problem, however, is that such diversity of specification makes it difficult to compare studies of organisational performance. A possible resolution to this dilemma is to move to a higher level of analysis and treat the overall orientation of the bundle as its key property. Studies could be compared on the basis of whether a bundle was representative of a high-performance "type" or a high-commitment "type", rather than the particular make-up of a bundle.

A second issue pertaining to bundles concerns organisational fit, i.e. the alignment between bundles of human resource practices and other organisational systems and practices. In the manufacturing sector, it has been argued that there is an organisational fit between high-commitment HR practices and bundles of "high-performance" working practices (e.g. JIT, TQM, team work). In the service sector, and in call centres in particular, bundles of HR practices do appear to be aligned with factors such as market segment and the nature of the customer interaction. This suggests that, in some organisations at least, working practices and HR practices are being designed and implemented in a systemic and integrated manner and according to an underlying managerial orientation (see Wood, Chapter 14). However, whether organisational fit is a result of strategic or pragmatic choice needs further clarification. It should also be noted that, even where a more systemic approach is taken, working practices are often designed according to a technical and economic rationale that rarely considers employee well-being.

Thus, a feature of both practice and research is a certain ambiguity around, and overlap between, the modern working practices of interest. This lack of distinctiveness is both a strength and a weakness. The strength is that it does not delimit practice or research to one particular version of a given initiative, which may ultimately not be the universally best type. The weakness is that it may impede the development of cumulative knowledge. As a remedy, finer-grained taxonomies would enable users and researchers to investigate the implications of different variants of particular practices (e.g. hard and soft TQM), different bundles of practices, or alternative models of the fit among practices and between practices and the wider organisational context. Such conceptual and empirical development may be a prerequisite for resolving the apparently inconsistent findings currently emerging. Rather than assuming an absolute truth or reality, a better approach might be to select different approaches to particular practices, and alternative bundles or systems of practices, in terms of their usefulness in explaining outcomes of interest. Although to date many alternatives have been mapped out, there is insufficient evidence about any one type to yield a coherent body of evidence. Where different findings emerge, it is unclear whether they result from differences in the practices or bundles studied or from the nature of the different contexts in which they are used. Particularly valuable for the future would be studies comparing how alternative forms of particular practices, and alternative bundles of practices, relate to key outcomes such as performance and employee well-being in the same context.

THE PREVALENCE OF MODERN WORKING PRACTICES AND THE "NEW WORKPLACE"

Most authors examining particular practices were able to provide data on their prevalence, although the available data tended to be from studies in the USA and the UK. Within the countries surveyed, there appears to be fairly widespread use (in some 40–60% of organisations) of TQM, team work, supply-chain partnering and performance management practices, particularly in manufacturing companies. Similarly, advanced manufacturing technology is used, at least to a moderate extent, by some 40% of manufacturing organisations (Clegg *et al.*, 2002). Lean manufacturing[1] appears fairly widely used in the automotive industry but less extensively in other parts of the manufacturing sector. TQM and team work are also representative of employee involvement practices. The extent of TQM and team work, plus evidence that empowerment initiatives[2] occur in about one quarter of UK, Japanese, Australian and Swiss manufacturing organisations (Clegg *et al.*, 2002), indicate that employee involvement practices are present in many organisations. However, it should also be noted that Benson & Lawler (Chapter 9) found that the use of employee involvement practices declined between 1993 and 1996 in the USA, and that employee involvement initiatives were embraced strongly by only a minority of firms.

A modern form of work that is undoubtedly on the increase is the call centre. Call centres are present in almost every sector and generally employ 1–2% of national working populations in advanced industrial economies. Less extensive are newer practices such as teleworking, knowledge management and E-business. Practices aimed at improving or capturing employee innovation, such as idea capture schemes, appear particularly rare, although if knowledge management schemes and quality circles are included as examples, then innovation practices have a greater penetration. Thus the working practices covered in this book clearly exist, but are by no means universal. There is much room for further and fuller uptake.

The chapters in this book also demonstrate a significant rise in the use of modern working practices since the early 1990s. Wood (Chapter 14), drawing on the data of Waterson *et al.* (1999), points out that of the UK manufacturing companies using TQM, team-working and empowerment, 75% had introduced the initiatives within the 5 year period preceding the 1996 survey. Similarly, 60% of companies had implemented AMT and supply-chain

---

[1] Although the main components of lean manufacturing (TQM, JIT, teamwork, SCP) are often present in manufacturing organisations, it would be unwise to suggest that their co-occurrence represents the use of lean manufacturing itself.
[2] Empowerment initiatives can be defined as practices that pass considerable responsibility for operational management to individuals or teams (Clegg *et al.*, 2002).

partnering within the same period of time. More recent follow-up evidence showed further uptake of the practices between 1996 and 2000. Equivalent increases are reported in the USA. In the service sector, there have also been rises in the use of team work, TQM, IT and call centres since 1990, although the service sector seems to lag significantly behind in its use of innovative HR practices (Batt & Doellgast, Chapter 15). Thus, the working practices on which this book is focused are indeed ones in which there is recent and increasing investment.

Given this pattern in the use of modern working practices, to what extent can it be said that a "new workplace" exists in the organisations of advanced industrial economies? One answer might be that, even though the most popular practices are hardly ubiquitous, the pace of change over the last 10 years has dramatically increased the extent of "new workplaces" within organisations. In other words, "old" Fordist, bureaucratic and inflexible workplaces are, at long last, being replaced by "new" flexible workplaces. Leaving aside the fact that a substantial proportion of organisations still have not adopted many of the new working practices, such a conclusion assumes that the form of a practice is consistent across organisations. This is clearly not the case. As the contributions to this book make clear, many of the modern practices of interest, although capable of enhancing flexibility and empowering employees, can also be applied in a bureaucratic and Tayloristic manner. By and large, existing surveys on the extent and rate of adoption of the new practices do not tell us about the form of a practice, and this implies that the spread of "flexible" modern working practices is less than surveys indicate. Few studies go beyond measuring the use of a practice to consider how or how effectively it has been implemented. This reflects the need, as mentioned above (p. 414), for consideration of alternative forms of the same general working practices (see e.g. Sitkin, Sutcliffe & Schroeder's (1994) distinction between "total quality control" and "total quality learning" forms of TQM).

A further theme in this book is that, while a focus on particular work practices is important, there is also a need to understand how practices are bundled together and how they relate to bundles of HR practices and underlying managerial orientations. The issue is particularly relevant to the question of "newness", as it has been suggested that "new workplaces" are defined by a combination of high-performance work practices, high-commitment HR practices *and* an underlying managerial orientation that views these two sets of practices as integrated and complementary (Storey, 1994; Wood, Chapter 14). At present, we simply do not know about the prevalence or co-occurrence of different bundles or the nature of managerial orientations. Claims about the extent of a "new workplace" are therefore hard to substantiate or refute.

Understanding the "new workplace" as a combination of practice and orientation also suggests that it is possible to distinguish between an "historical new" and an "experiential new". The "historical new" relates to the presence of new working practices, new types of HR practices, new bundles and new combinations of bundles. The "experiential new" relates to whether employees experience self and work in a qualitatively new manner.

Using this distinction, one can enquire whether an "historical new" is necessarily associated with an "experiential new" workplace. In other words, do modern working practices fundamentally alter the experience of self and work? Reports suggest that some managers do have a different orientation to HR and working practices, and that some employees do experience work in radically new ways (e.g. teleworking from home, communicating virtually with team members, having a flexible work orientation that stresses empathising with external customers in a supply chain). Yet most chapters in this book indicate that modern working practices are not so radical, and do not fundamentally alter the experiences of the majority of employees. Rather, there is a change in the degree but not the type of experience. In other words, as a result of a new working practice, an employee has more or fewer demands, experiences more or less control, feels less or more anxiety, performs less or more effectively, or uses more or fewer of the same skills. The experience of work is "similar but different". However, this conclusion may be due to the type of measures used to assess change, such as job satisfaction or job control, which are relatively invariant over time and context. In addition, factors are often looked at individually, and this may make it harder to ascertain more global aggregate changes.

By focusing on generic measures in a disaggregated manner, it may be difficult to assess whether modern working practices do radically change the experience of work. If other factors were assessed, or employees' perceptions examined in a more aggregated way, then qualitative shifts in the experience of work might be discerned more readily. Consider, for example, the psychological contract, which has been defined as a set of unwritten reciprocal expectations (i.e. a mental model) that act as a deep driver of motivation, career behaviour, reward and commitment (Herriot & Pemberton, 1996; Rousseau, 1995). An understanding of employees' psychological contracts has implications for the design of HR practices, such as the provision of job security, extensive training or flexible working practices. Conversely, the nature of the psychological contract might be a valuable outcome variable to consider in its own right. New forms of work, such as teleworking, for instance, might be associated with very different expectations concerning the responsibility of the employer for providing security of employment and training. Debate has focused on the extent to which organisational change, as well as economic and societal change, violates contracts and whether employees are adopting alternative psychological contracts as a result of these violations (Rousseau, 1995). Research has shown that breaches of contract in the workplace are common but often temporary, implying that the introduction of a new practice will not necessarily lead to the adoption of different types of contract (Guest et al., 1996). However, transitions in the psychological contract do occur, but there is little data on the extent to which this occurs and whether changes are due to workplace change or wider societal changes regarding work expectations (Sparrow, 1996). Further empirical research is needed, but the point here is that the psychological contract is one construct that could be used to capture qualitative changes in how employees experience work.

Identity is another construct that could capture whether employees experience work in a qualitatively different manner. Some writers have noted that modern working practices have the capacity to challenge or change an individual's identity, as they can require individuals to relate to others differently or to view themselves in a substantially different manner (Jermier, Knights & Nord, 1994). Others have expressed concern about whether the new practices allow a meaningful identity to be formed at all. Sennett (1998) has argued that modern working practices, and the flexibility that underpins them, lead to a corrosion of identity and limit the possibility of forming identities that a person can be proud of (e.g. a tradesperson, a member of a community). Whatever is the case, as Legge (Chapter 20) points out, our experience of work is intimately tied to our identity, and if our identity should change, then so too will our experience of work.

In summary, questions about the prevalence of working practices are bound up with debates about the extent and nature of the flexible, post-Fordist or "new" workplace, and these debates need to consider several points. First, it is important to consider which aspects of experience are focused on, as the aspect chosen might restrict the extent to which one can state that a working practice (or bundle) has qualitatively changed the experience of work. Second, the nature and prevalence of the "historical new" and the "experiential new" must be established. Taking that distinction further, four different types of workplace might exist: (a) "new/new" workplaces, in which modern working practices are associated with a qualitatively different or substantially changed experience of work (e.g. TQM with empowerment leading to greater self-confidence and a new orientation putting the customer first); (b) "new/old" workplaces, in which modern working practices are associated little or no change in the experience of work (e.g. just-in-time associated with no effective change or a reduction in empowerment and skill use); (c) "old/old" workplaces, in which traditional working practices are associated with a relatively unchanged experience of work; and finally (d) "old/new" workplaces in which traditional working practices are associated with a qualitatively different work experience. This last could occur, for example, where young employees, having been socialized in a different economic climate, have expectations radically different from those engendered by the traditional practices prevalent in their place of work. At present, research suggests that the first and fourth scenarios (i.e. the new/new workplace and the old/new workplace) are relatively rare within organisations, and that most workplaces conform to the second and third scenarios.

THE PSYCHOLOGICAL CONSEQUENCES OF MODERN WORKING PRACTICES

As one might expect, employees experience modern working practices in diverse ways. The constructs used to assess this experience reflect this diversity and cover areas such as well-being, emotion, performance, social relationships, fairness, creativity and innovation. The factors shown to affect these outcomes include individual characteristics, job and work design, management or team leader style, HR practices, operational uncertainty, and national and organisational culture. Again, the list of factors affecting experience is diverse and wide-ranging. As working practices are essentially different types of work design, it should come as no surprise that job and work design theories have proved to be central to understanding how a working practice affects the experience of employees.

In particular, research on job and work design has illuminated the manner in which job characteristics, contingencies and mechanisms affect the experience or outcomes of working practices. Indeed, much is known about the type of job characteristics likely to be found in modern working practices. These include job control, cognitive demands, physical demands, variety, performance monitoring, feedback, opportunity for social interaction, skill utilization, role conflict, role ambiguity, team autonomy and task interdependence. In addition, fairly firm conclusions can be drawn regarding the effects of these characteristics on well-being, although research has produced mixed findings with regard to possible synergistic effects of job characteristics (e.g. control × demand). However, there is less consistency of findings for the effects of job design on performance and very little information relating it to other outcomes such as safety, innovation and customer satisfaction (Parker, Wall & Cordery, 2001). The chapters in this book have also illuminated the cognitive and motivational mechanisms through which job characteristics have their effects, as well as a number of contingencies, such as operational uncertainty and task interdependence, that affect these relationships. So there is an argument for systematically analysing the effects of modern working practices in terms of more fundamental and established constructs and theories, such as those provided by work design theory, and many of the chapters (e.g. Cordery, Chapter 6; Holman, Chapter 7) include such a perspective. Understanding the new in terms of the old is one line to pursue.

Yet, although job design theories provide a window of understanding, they do not fully capture the "the reality and complexity" of modern working practices (Parker, Wall & Cordery, 2001, p. 433). There is a clear need for developing our understanding of how the design of jobs in a modern working practice affects employees' experience of work. Below we chart three ways in which that understanding could progress. These approaches should be seen as integrated, rather than separate, developments.

First, a general framework is needed that identifies the range of characteristics, antecedents, contingencies and outcomes that may be important. At present, the range of characteristics is fairly large, but still needs expanding. For example, job characteristics could be broadened to cover areas such as emotional demands, knowledge intensity and social and relational networks. However, what seems critical is that researchers consider which characteristics are most salient for a particular working practice or context (Holman, Clegg & Waterson, 2002). For front-line call centre workers, where procedures and response modes are closely prescribed and monitored, job control might have a significant impact on well-being; for teleworkers undertaking creative design work, where they have considerable control over both when and how to perform, level of social contact might have a stronger effect. Likewise, doctors or lawyers face ethical dilemmas that are more acute and difficult to deal with than those confronting hairdressers; ethical demands may therefore have a greater effect on well-being for doctors and lawyers than for hairdressers. Also, in knowledge management practices, managers' social and relational networks may be far more important to the development of knowledge than their level of job control. Thus the need is for meta-theory, to identify which among a potentially wide range of variables is relevant to a particular work context.[3]

Similar arguments can be made with respect to job outcomes: researchers need to expand the range of outcomes studied while also considering which outcomes are most salient in a particular context. Traditionally, outcomes have often been restricted to well-being and performance. Other outcomes include contextual performance measures (e.g. helping, citizenship behaviours), safety, errors and innovation. Work on knowledge outcomes would also benefit by assessing knowledge more directly, rather than using proxy indicators of learning such as faults, skill utilisation and self-efficacy. This may be difficult for survey-based approaches, as employees develop knowledge or skill in vastly different areas and idiosyncratic changes are hard to capture in generalisable measures. Methods such as repertory grids may need to be used in tandem with survey-based approaches. In addition, researchers need to consider how to assess global changes in understanding that may occur as a result of the working practices being implemented. This might be achieved by measuring constructs such as the psychological contract, but this assumes *a priori* that the researcher knows how an employee's experience will change. To answer questions about the presence and nature of "the new workplace", it therefore seems imperative to use measures and methodologies that are sensitive to changes in knowledge and personal experience.

The second line of development we recommend is for work to be driven by theory that posits the importance of new characteristics and outcomes and how these different facets relate. Particular attention should be paid to explicating the mechanisms through which job

---

[3] For a more comprehensive discussion see Parker, Wall and Cordery (2001).

characteristics have their effects. Indeed, a theoretically informed focus on the mechanisms of job design seems essential. For example, work on a cognitive mechanism has greatly benefited from action theory (Frese & Zapf, 1994) but could be developed further to examine the role of regulatory strategies, such as learning strategies (Holman, Epitropaki & Fernie, 2002).

It may also be time to reinvigorate our study of the motivational mechanisms of job design, a topic that has received less attention recently. In part, this lack of attention may be due to the fact that research based on the motivational assumptions of the job characteristics model "has not fared well in empirical studies" (Parker et al., 2001, p. 426), and as a consequence job design researchers have turned their attention to cognitive mechanisms. More recently, however, as Benson & Lawler note in Chapter 9, intrinsic motivation mechanisms proposed by psychological empowerment theory have provided more promising results at both the individual and group levels of analysis (e.g. Kirkman & Rosen, 1999; Liden, Wayne & Sparrow, 2000). Pritchard & Payne's theory of motivation (see Chapter 12) also provides a useful framework for exploring a motivational mechanism. In addition to providing a clear and eminently testable theory, Pritchard & Payne show how knowledge and knowledge-based processes are integral to the motivational process. Interestingly, this demonstrates how cognitive and motivational mechanisms may be interlinked. Another theory that might help in understanding the motivational basis of job design and modern working practices is the control-process theory of self-regulation (Carver, Lawrence & Scheier, 1996). Being a goal-based theory, it has many similarities to action theory but focuses on the effect of goal attainment on affect. It therefore provides a possible means of integrating two major concerns within the job design literature, namely motivation and well-being.

Also worth exploring is a "relationship" or "interaction" mechanism. Work on knowledge management, supply chains and teamwork has highlighted the importance of affective relationships (e.g. trust, care) to knowledge sharing, information flows and efficient communication. Research needs to examine how working practices affect employee relationships, networks and social groupings.

As a third and final approach, we suggest that investigations encompass more diversity—in methodology, paradigm, discipline and research population (Holman et al., 2002). This book is evidence that a multi-disciplinary approach can offer a more comprehensive understanding of an issue. There is, nonetheless, a lack of methodological and paradigmatic diversity. The empirical work described has tended to be within positivist and functionalist traditions (Burell & Morgan, 1979). Legge in Chapter 20 is particularly critical of this bias, which stems from the chapter authors' own epistemological and methodological beliefs, the general predominance of positivistic accounts in most areas, and perhaps our own editorial guidelines. We did not explicitly ask authors to report critical research, for example, or to concentrate on qualitative research. Yet qualitative and critical research is particularly useful at illuminating the specific contextual factors that affect experience, revealing the idiosyncratic nature of personal experience and showing how employees are active agents in the work process. Research has also tended to focus on Western, white, male, shop-floor employees in manufacturing organisations. More diverse samples (e.g. female, non-Western team leaders in service organisations) would broaden our understanding of how modern working practices affect employees' experience.

Drawing these three strands together will enable the development of a broad framework that integrates empirically derived models for specific domains of application. In other words, our understanding of modern working practices will be more general, more nuanced and better able to reflect the complex and diverse reality of today's workplace.

THE EFFECTIVENESS OF MODERN WORKING PRACTICES

When drawing conclusions about the effectiveness of modern working practices, it seems sensible to distinguish between two different levels of analysis: (a) studies of a single practice, or a limited set of practices, that focus on individual or team-based performance; and (b) plant- or business-level studies that cover a range of work and HR practices and focus on overall organisational performance measures, such as productivity, profit and market share. This distinction is useful, as there is stronger support for links to performance at the single practice level of analysis than there is at a plant or business level.

Studies of single practices, notwithstanding some mixed and contradictory findings, point increasingly to the positive effects of TQM, AMT and team work on measures of employee performance, such as quality, sales, productivity and customer satisfaction (see Cooney & Sohal, Chapter 3; Cordery, Chapter 6; Wood, Chapter 14; Batt & Doellgast, Chapter 15). Furthermore, the performance effects of employee involvement and lean manufacturing appear to be attributable, in part, to their use of TQM and teamwork as part of the overall package (see Delbridge, Chapter 2; Benson & Lawler, Chapter 9; Wood, Chapter 14). In addition, research on contingencies, such as operational uncertainty and task-interdependence, has added to our understanding of the conditions in which these practices are most effective. However, for other particular working practices covered in this book, including knowledge management (Scarborough, Chapter 8), supply-chain partnering (Kerrin & Icasati-Johanson, Chapter 5), E-business (Clegg, Icasati-Johanson & Bennett, Chapter 13) and teleworking (Lamond, Daniels & Standen, Chapter 11), surprisingly little is yet known about their effects on individual or team performance. This question has rarely been empirically addressed, in some cases because the practice has no specific agenda for change.

Whereas the single working practices covered in this book appear (where studied) to have generally positive effects on individual and team performance, studies of performance at the plant and business level are less compelling. Admittedly, there is mounting evidence that sets of working practices characterised as "high-involvement" or "high-commitment" human resource management are associated with better productivity, profit and market share. Nonetheless, as Wright & Gardner (Chapter 16), Benson & Lawler (Chapter 9) and Wood (Chapter 14) make clear, that evidence can at present be regarded as little more than circumstantial. This is because it is largely based on cross-sectional studies, where the direction of causality is unclear and where measures include single-source reports of practices and often self-reported organisational performance.

Given these patchy and inconclusive findings for the performance effects of modern working practices, chapter authors made a number of recommendations regarding the conduct of future research. We shall not restate these in detail, but highlight the most important themes:

1. *Conduct longitudinal studies.* There is a strong call for longitudinal studies to properly assess causality. Researchers need to establish that the use of a practice, or set of practices, is related to subsequent performance. Cross-sectional studies cannot rule out

reverse causality, that better performance leads to greater investment in the new working practices. Sonnentag (Chapter 18) proposes a variety of different ways in which better evidence can be collected through longitudinal research designs and methods.

2. *Investigate how practices relate to performance.* The nature of the relationship between practices and performance needs to be better understood. For example, do practices or bundles have direct effects, joint additive effects or synergistic effects? And are effects universal or contingent upon contextual factors? With regard to contextual contingencies, operational uncertainty, task interdependence and customer interaction appear relevant at the single-practice level of analysis, whereas strategy and fit appear important at the plant, business and corporate levels of analysis. Nonetheless, to date, evidence on these relationships can best be described as patchy.

3. *Investigate the mechanisms relating practices to performance.* There is a need to open up the "black box" and address the mechanisms through which working practices and HR practices affect performance, particularly in plant- and business-level studies. In common with job design studies, it is imperative that the possible roles of cognitive, motivational/affective and operational mechanisms are examined. It should also be remembered that practices might work through alternative mechanisms. For example, within a lean manufacturing environment, JIT and AMT might make work more efficient (i.e. through operational mechanisms reducing overhead costs and increasing speed of throughput, respectively, but with little effect on employee knowledge or motivation); team work might improve satisfaction and make employees more committed (i.e. a motivational/affective mechanism); while empowerment initiatives might improve performance through their effects on knowledge (i.e. a cognitive mechanism) or by promoting proactivity and innovation in employees (Unsworth & Parker, Chapter 10). To date, mechanisms have too often been stipulated from assumption and speculation rather than empirical evidence.

Work on cognitive mechanisms should address the role of both individuals and networks. At an individual level, the human capital of the firm, such as individual skill and knowledge, should be considered as well as employees' understanding of workplace practices (whether they see them as integrated and systemic) and their general orientation towards the firm (perhaps through assessing psychological contracts). Examining these last two issues would help to answer the question of whether the performance of modern working practices is dependent upon employees' experiencing self and work in a qualitatively different manner. In other words, is performance in the "new workplace" dependent upon "new" employee orientations? At an organisation level, research on cognitive mechanisms needs to address how intra-organisational networks affect knowledge flows within organisations; the knowledge capabilities of the firm (i.e. how knowledge is acquired, stored, used and so forth); knowledge markets within firms (e.g. transaction efficiency, intellectual capital effectiveness); the role of social capital and social networks (see Sparrow, Chapter 19); and how working practices affect knowledge flows, knowledge markets, social networks and communities of practice.

4. *Develop more reliable measures of practices.* HR practices can be measured more reliably by using more specific measures and multiple respondents within each firm (see Wright & Gardner, Chapter 16). Particularly valuable would be ratings by independent external experts, whose evaluations would be based on a wider comparative perspective. Another recommendation is to develop bundles of practices through inductive analytical techniques (e.g. exploratory factor analysis, confirmatory factor analysis, conceptual clustering, and latent class analysis) so as to capture industry- or sector-specific features.

Indeed, Wood (Chapter 14) recommends a two-stage process of analysis: a first stage to specify the relationship between practices; and a second to assess the relationship of practices to performance.
5. *Develop alternative measures of performance.* Although high-performance working practices and high-commitment HR practices may improve productivity, the extra costs of these practices may not translate into greater profits (see Benson & Lawler, Chapter 9). However, these types of practices may improve the performance of the firm in ways that are not expressed on the balance sheet or in a readily quantifiable form. The firm may become more flexible, agile, responsive to customer need and innovative, but not necessarily more profitable. These outcomes can be invaluable for a firm with an already reasonable profit profile that needs to retain its volume of business in an increasingly competitive market. Qualitative studies might offer an important means for assessing these intangible aspects of contextual performance.
6. *Determine how and why practices evolve over time.* Qualitative studies are also needed to gain a better understanding of how working practices and HR practices evolve over time and the rationales underlying this process. Such studies would contribute to understanding how the implementation of practices is related to firm success, the role of different actors in this process and how different bundles of practices emerge within different contexts.
7. *Examine social and political processes.* A final issue concerns the social and political process by which working practices are designed and introduced. The process adopted may well have as great an impact on the consequences of an initiative as the nature of the intervention itself. This is the subject of the contribution by Mumford & Axtell (Chapter 17), but few other authors in this book have addressed this question (see Holman, Chapter 7, for an exception) or even the more general question of how non-managerial employees play an active role in shaping a working practice and the rationales that inform such actions. Neither, as Legge pointed out in Chapter 20, has anything been said concerning the role of academics in legitimising and supporting an explicitly managerial agenda with regard to the study and design of working practices.

END NOTE

The contributions to this book represent the beginnings rather than the end of enquiry into new working practices. This is so for two reasons. First, the authors make quite clear that, despite the accumulation of considerable knowledge about the nature, prevalence and implications of the different practices, there is much more that is unknown. There is a long way to go before we can fully understand whether, how, when and why any given practice will affect outcomes of interest. Work to date has served to set out much of the agenda, but it has yet to supply clear answers.

The second consideration is that the practices covered are by definition time-limited. Although new now, some are destined to become established practices, others will fall by the wayside, and still others will become absorbed into more general initiatives. By the time many practices are better understood, they are likely to have receded down or even dropped off the list of priorities.

The lasting benefit of this book is not only mapping out the current domain, but also helping to set out the agenda for future work. The methods and perspectives engendered by investigation of the current new work practices will provide the intellectual fodder to more effectively address the initiatives yet to come.

REFERENCES

Becker, B. & Gerhart, B. (1996). The impact of human resource management on organizational performance: progress and prospects. *Academy of Management Journal*, **39**: 779–801.

Burrell, G. & Morgan, G. (1979). *Sociological Paradigms and Organizational Analysis*. Aldershot: Gower.

Carver, C. S., Lawrence, J. W. & Scheier, M. F. (1996). *A Control-process Perspective on the Origins of Affect* (pp. 11–52). In L. Martin & A. Tesser (Eds), *Striving and Feeling: Interactions among goals, affect and self-regulation*. Hillsdale, NJ: Erlbaum.

Clegg, C. W., Wall, T. D., Pepper, K., Stride, C., Woods, D., Morrison, D., Cordery, J., Couchman, P. Badham, R., Kuenzler, C., Grote, G., Ide, W., Takahashi, M. & Kogi. K. (2002). An international study of the use and effectiveness of modern manufacturing practices. *Human Factors and Ergonomics in Manufacturing* (in press).

Dyer, L. & Reeves, T. (1995). Human resource strategies and firm performance: what do we know and where do we need to go? *International Journal of Human Resource Management*, **6**, 656–670.

Frese, M. & Zapf, D. (1994). Action as the core of work psychology: a German approach. In H. C. Triandis, M. D. Dunnette, & L. M. Hough (Eds), *Handbook of Industrial and Organisational Psychology*, Vol. 4 (pp. 271–340). Palo Alto, CA: Consulting Psychologists Press.

Guest, D., Conway, N., Briner, R. & Dickman, M. (1996). *The State of the Psychological Contract in Employment. Institute of Personnel Development*, Report No. 16. Wimbledon: Institute of Personnel Development.

Herriot, P. & Pemberton, C. (1996). Contracting Careers. *Human Relations*, **49**, 757–790.

Holman, D. J., Clegg, C. W. & Waterson, P. E. (2002). Navigating the territory of job design. *Journal of Applied Ergonomics* (in press).

Holman, D., Epitropaki, O. & Fernie, S. (2002). Understanding learning strategies in the workplace: a factor analytic investigation. *Journal of Occupational and Organisational Psychology* (in press).

Jermier, J., Knights, D. & Nord, W. (Eds) (1994). *Resistance and Power in Organizations: Agency, Subjectivity and the Labour Process*, London: Routledge.

Kirkman, B. L. & Rosen, B. (1999). Beyond self-management: antecedents and consequences of team empowerment. *Academy of Management Journal*, **42**, 58–75.

Liden, R. C., Wayne, S. J. & Sparrowe, R. T. (2000). An examination of the mediating role of psychological empowerment on the relations between job, interpersonal relationships, and work outcomes. *Journal of Applied Psychology*, **85**, 407–416.

Parker, S. K., Wall, T. D. & Cordery, J. L. (2001). Future work design and practice: towards an elaborated model of work design. *Journal of Occupational and Organisational Psychology*, **74**, 413–440.

Rousseau, D. M. (1995). *Psychological Contracts in Organisations: Understanding Written and Unwritten Agreements*. Thousand Oaks, CA: Sage.

Sennett, R. (1998). *The Corrosion of Characters: The Personal Consequences of Work in the New Capitalism*. London: Norton.

Sitkin, S. B., Sutcliffe, K. M. & Schroeder, R. G. (1994). Distinguishing Control from Learning in Total Quality Management: a Contingency Perspective. *Academy of Management Review*, **19**(3), 537–564. 1994.

Sparrow, P. R. (1996). Transitions in the psychological contract in UK banking, *Human Resource Management Journal*, **6**, 75–92.

Storey, J. (1994). *New Wave Manufacturing Practices: Organizational and Human Resource Management Dimensions*, London: Chapman Paul.

Waterson, P. E., Clegg, C. W., Bolden, R., Pepper, K., Warr, P. B. & Wall, T. D. (1999). The use and effectiveness of modern manufacturing practices: a survey of UK industry. *International Journal of Production Research*, **10**, 2271–2292.

Author Index

Abdullah, S., 19
Abernathy, W.J., 271
Abo, T., 19
Ackers, P., 45
Ackroyd, S., 19, 397, 399, 406
Adams, M., 176
Addison, J., 164
Adler, P., 7, 32, 33, 42, 46, 161, 383, 385
Ahire, S.L., 45, 47, 48
Ahmadjian, C.L., 84, 89
Ahrentzen, S.B., 211
Aiello, J.R., 119, 125
Aiken, L.H., 293
Aiken, M., 179
Ainger, A., 132
Ajzen, I., 108
Akehurst, G., 298
Alanko, A., 355
Alavi, M., 136
Alban, B.Y., 343
Albanese, M., 273, 277
Albaum, G.S., 182
Alber, A., 60
Alder, G.S., 119, 125
Aldrich, H.E., 374
Algera, J.A., 359
Allen, J., 207, 212
Allison, D., 81, 82
Allison, G., 338
Allscheid, S.P., 302
Alper, S., 106
Alston, J., 25
Alvesson, M., 149
Amabile, T.M., 7, 177, 178, 179, 182, 183, 184, 185, 186
American Society for Training and Development, 220
Amidon, D.M., 139
Amin, A., 5
Amos, J., 169
Andersen Consulting and Investors in People UK, 256, 257
Anderson, A.H., 358
Anderson, E., 76, 79, 81, 82

Anderson, H.B., 57, 58
Anderson, J., 79, 81, 83
Anderson, L.R., 186, 235
Anderson, N.R., 186
Anderson, P., 149, 220
Andrews, F.M., 179, 184, 185
Antal, A.B., 379
Appelbaum, E., 5, 125, 127, 161, 288, 313
Appleyard, M., 161
Araujo, L., 379, 381
Argote, L., 60, 106
Argyris, C., 156
Armeli, S., 183
Arndorf, D., 63
Arnetz, B.B., 359
Arora, R., 354
Artandi, S., 58
Aryee, S., 205
Arthur, J., 318
Arthur, J.B., 49, 166, 396
Ash, M.J., 183
Ashby, W.R., 331
Ashford, S.J., 82
Ashkenas, R., 203, 375, 377
Athos, A., 19, 21
Auguste, B., 381
Aulakh, P.S., 80, 81, 82
Australian Bureau of Statistics, 197
Australian Manufacturing Council, 47
Aviram, A., 182
Axtell, C.M., 80, 84, 85, 88, 89, 87, 132, 179, 183, 185, 187, 251, 257

Ba, S., 96
Babin, B.J., 303
Babson, S., 43
Bacharach, S.B., 179
Baco, N., 395
Badham, R., 55, 59, 64, 95, 97, 257, 260, 405, 416
Bae, J., 325
Baethge, M., 294
Bailey, D.E., 96, 101, 102, 109, 298, 299, 302
Bailey, T., 161

Bain, P., 7, 117, 119, 120, 125, 128, 398
Bainbridge, L., 56
Baker, K.G., 182
Baker, W.E., 384
Bamford, K., 393
Bandura, A., 125, 237
Banker, R.D., 98, 99, 301
Banting, P.M., 81
Barker, J., 104
Barker, J.R., 97, 104
Barker, M.J., 210
Barley, S.R., 11
Barney, J.B., 79, 396
Barnes-Farrell, J.L., 352
Barrick, M.R., 102, 207
Barron, F., 182
Bartlett, C.A., 372
Bartholomew, D., 277
Baruch, Y., 198
Basadur, M., 182
Bass, A., 186
Bassi, L.J., 137, 165
Basu, R., 187
Bateman, T.S., 181
Batt, R., 5, 11, 99, 117, 118, 120, 121, 123, 124, 125, 127, 128, 129, 161, 288, 294, 296, 297, 298, 300, 303, 304, 313, 398, 399
Beaumont, P., 11, 85, 86, 88
Beaumont, P.B., 46, 47
Becker, B.E., 6, 49, 156, 161, 163, 164, 165, 167, 312, 314, 315, 319, 321, 322, 395, 414
Becker, G., 303
Beekun, R.I., 108, 300
Beer, S., 331
Beers, M.C., 142
Behling, O., 207
Behling, O.C., 40
Bejat, M., 182
Belfield, C., 164
Belt, V. 126
Benbunan-Finch, R., 353
Bennett, S., 258, 260, 261, 265
Bennett, W.R., 103
Benson, G., 155, 157, 158, 160, 161, 163
Benson, P.G., 45, 47
Berg, P., 161
Berger, H., 82
Bessant, J.R., 72
Betancourt, H., 84
Bethke, A.L., 41
Betts, A., 120, 128
Bi, S., 57, 58
Bierbaum, B., 299, 304
Bigley, G.A., 79, 105
Billsbery, J., 205

Birkinshaw, J., 169
Birnbaum, D., 303
Black, S., 161, 164
Black, S.A., 45, 47
Blackler, F., 78, 135, 137, 140
Blair, T., 176
Blanning, T., 245
Blasi, J., 156, 157, 159
Blickensderfer, E., 107
Blois, K.J., 79, 80
Bloor, R., 256
Blumberg, M., 56, 58, 59, 60, 61, 102
Blundell, R., 165
Bly, P.R., 228, 240
Blyton, P., 7, 395, 396
Boddy, D., 11, 60, 74, 77, 117
Bodker, S., 338
Boettger, R.D., 177
Bohlander, G., 166, 167
Bolden, R., 3, 55, 83, 257, 273, 416
Boles, J.S., 303
Borgatti, S., 385
Borrill, C.S., 106
Borucki, C.C., 302
Borys, B., 7, 42
Boswell, W.R., 312
Bottger, P.C., 101, 187
Bouillon, M., 165
Bourdieu, P., 383
Bourrier, M., 377
Bowen, B., 166
Bowen, D.E., 5, 38, 45, 120, 237
Bowen, D.W., 236
Bowers, C.A., 107
Bowie, N., 385
Boxall, P., 6, 124, 404
Bracken, D.W., 220
Bracker, J.S., 182
Bradach, J.L., 375
Bramer, W.L., 120
Brass, D.J., 105
Braverman, H., 7, 127
Bray, P., 258
Brazeal, D., 182
Brearly, M., 102
Breskin, S., 182
Bresnahan, T.F., 296
Bressand, A., 143
Brief, A.P., 176
Briggs, P., 26
Briner, R., 418
Brodbeck, F.C., 358
Brodner, P., 55, 57, 64
Brown, B., 322
Brown, C., 49, 161
Brown, J., 78, 293

AUTHOR INDEX

Brown, J.S., 78, 143, 144
Brown, S., 372
Brubaker, T., 166
Bruce, R.A., 190
Brynjolfsson, E., 296
Bryson, A., 34, 156, 157
Buchanan, D.A., 11, 60, 405
Budetti, P.P., 298
Budros, A., 372
Bunce, D., 185
Bunker, B., 343
Burgers, A., 129
Burke, M.J., 302
Burke, W.W., 238
Burningham, C., 186
Burawoy, M., 11
Burrell, G., 19, 399, 421
Burt, R.S., 79, 80, 82, 384, 385
Burton, P.F., 210
Butler, P., 381
Buxton, V., 302
Byham, W.C., 239
Bzdawka, A., 179

Cairncross, F., 256, 257, 258
Calingo, E., 298
Callaghan, G., 117
Camerer, C., 79, 80, 82
Cameron, J., 183
Campbell, D.J., 186, 187
Campbell, J.P., 221
Campbell, R.J., 105
Campion, M.A., 8, 97, 101, 102, 103, 104, 105, 107, 298
Cannon, J.P., 82
Cannon-Bowers, J.A., 102, 106, 107
Cantista, I., 257
Cappelli, P., 146, 156, 157, 158, 159, 164, 166, 295, 311, 314, 315, 321, 325, 372, 398
Carayon, P., 59, 60, 119, 125, 300, 303, 356
Carey, N., 337, 339, 340
Carmichael, C., 176
Carletta, J., 358
Carr, C.H., 74
Carroll, C.M., 11
Carroll, S.J., 82, 220
Carson, K., 166, 167
Carter, C., 145
Carver, C.S., 421
Cascio, W.F., 109, 198
Cassells, C., 351
Castells, M., 136, 375
Catteral, B., 338
Chadwick, C., 167, 168
Chaill, J., 33

Chalmers, N., 2
Chalykoff, J., 119, 125
Champy, J., 156, 375
Chang, L., 101, 108
Chapman, D.S., 353
Chapple, K., 148
Charles, M., 74, 77
Charles, T., 56, 63
Chase, R., 7
Chatman, J., 166
Chaudhuri, A., 117
Chebat, J., 303
Checkland, P., 337
Chee, Y., 313
Cheng, L., 300
Cherns, A., 3, 9, 116
Child, J., 372, 374, 375, 376, 379, 383
Chissick, C., 119, 120, 125, 126, 303
Choe, S., 79, 82
Choi, T.Y., 40
Christensen, P.R., 179
Christiansen, N.D., 102
Christie, A., 118
Chung, K., 162
Ciborra, C., 142, 143
Clark, A., 139, 348, 351
Clark, J., 117, 132, 393, 406
Clark, K.B., 138, 271
Clark, K.D., 305
Clark, P., 141
Clark, T., 393
Clarke, S.P., 293
Clegg, C.W., 3, 8, 9, 10, 55, 56, 58, 59, 60, 61, 62, 64, 80, 87, 95, 97, 100, 106, 132, 177, 190, 247, 251, 252, 253, 256, 257, 258, 260, 261, 273, 337, 338, 339, 340, 345, 349, 354, 355, 358, 359, 360, 416, 420
Clegg, S., 136
Clinton, R.J., 41
Cobble, D.S., 294
Coe, B., 297
Cohen, J., 361
Cohen, S.G., 9, 83, 84, 96, 97, 101, 102, 108, 109, 187, 298, 299, 300, 302
Coffey, R.J., 291
Cole, R.E., 39, 44, 46
Cole-Gomolski, B., 140
Coleman, J.S., 384
Coleman, P., 337, 339, 340
Colihan, J., 356, 361
Collett, D.N., 271
Collins, C.J., 305
Collins, H., 380
Collins, J.M., 303
Collinson, D., 7, 11
Collinson, M., 46, 49, 353, 357, 395, 407

Collis, D.J., 404
Colvin, A., 303
Compton, M., 358
Conger, J.A., 237
Connolly, T., 351
Consolini, P., 377
Conti, R.F., 33, 34, 43, 184, 186
Contu, A., 150
Conway, N., 167, 418
Cook, J.D., 359
Cook, R.I., 357
Cook, S., 78
Cooke, P., 25
Cooke, W., 155, 159, 162, 165, 168
Cooley, M., 59
Coombs, R.H., 141
Coon, H., 184
Cooper, C.L., 5, 9, 104, 208, 372, 374
Cooper, G., 11
Cooper, R., 77
Corbett, J.M., 10, 56, 58, 59, 60, 61, 62, 354, 355, 358, 359, 360
Cordery, J.L., 8, 9, 44, 78, 95, 97, 100, 104, 106, 107, 109, 257, 258, 297, 373, 374, 416, 419, 420, 421
Cornford, J., 198
Corrigan, S., 81
Cotton, J., 156
Cotton, J.L., 44, 49
Couchman, P., 95, 97, 257, 260, 416
Cowles, D., 79, 82
Cowling, A., 49
Cox, A., 76
Cox, R.S., 183
Cox, T., 210
Coyle, D., 256
Coyle-Shapiro, J.A.M., 40, 49, 356, 362
Cranfield School of Management, 141
Crant, J.M., 176, 179, 181
Cretin, S., 298
Crosby, L.A., 79, 82
Crosby, P.B., 38, 40
Cross, M., 58
Crossan, G., 210
Csikszentmihalyi, M., 182, 183
Cua, K.O., 284, 285, 287
Cully, M., 34, 156, 397, 402, 406
Cummings, A., 177, 187, 190
Cummings, T.G., 56, 59, 61, 97, 102, 239
Cunningham, C., 293
Cunningham, J.B., 300
Curkovic, S., 48
Currall, S.C., 76, 79
Currie, G., 88
Cutcher-Gershenfeld, J., 161

D'Aveni, R.D., 371
Daly-Jones, O., 352
Damodaran, L., 132, 251, 257
Daniels, K., 199, 201, 203, 208, 209, 210, 211, 212, 213, 214, 215, 385
Dankbaar, B., 9
Dauw, D.C., 177
D'Aveni, R., 377, 378
Davenport, T.H., 138, 142, 220, 380
Davidow, W.H., 375
Davids, K., 9, 59, 60, 61, 185, 353, 354, 358
Davis, G.A., 182
Davis, J.H., 105
Davis, L.E., 42, 49
Davis, M.H., 84
Davis LaMastro, V., 187
Dawson, P., 39, 40, 43, 46
Dawson, R., 348, 351
De Menezes, L., 157, 164, 274, 277, 278, 279, 285, 286, 287, 288
De Meyer, A., 47
De Ruyter, K., 128, 129
De Sitter, L., 9
Dean, J.W. Jr., 38, 45, 49, 161, 236, 271, 275, 288, 313, 315, 316, 317, 356
Dearden, L., 165
Deci, E.L., 149, 183, 185
Decktop, J.R., 312
DeCuir, A.D., 240
Dedman, R.D., 245
Dedoussis, V., 19
Deery, S.J., 125, 303, 398
Delaney, J., 159
Delbridge, R., 26, 28, 30, 31, 32, 34, 43, 76, 89, 353, 357
Delery, J., 161, 165, 296, 303, 311, 312, 313, 314, 316, 324, 325, 395, 402
Dellas, M., 182
Demarie, S.M., 46, 47, 207, 208, 213, 376
Deming, W.E., 39, 236
Den Hertog, J., 9
DeNisi, A.S., 219
Devadas, R., 99, 397
Dickman, M., 418
Dickson, M.W., 99, 101, 103, 104, 398
Diener, E., 359
Dierkes, M., 379
DiMaggio, P.J., 396
Dion, P.A., 79, 81
Dirks, K.T., 105
Distler, C., 143
Dix, G., 34, 156, 397, 402, 406
Doganis, R., 5, 291, 292, 293, 294
Doherty, N., 349
Dohse, K., 28
Doney, P.M., 82

Doran, M., 165
Dore, R.P., 72
Dormann, C., 356
Doty, H., 296, 314, 316, 325, 395, 402
Doucett, L., 129
Douglas, T.J., 298, 356, 358
Dourish, P., 139
Dow, D., 48
Dowd, M., 338
Dranove, D., 293, 294, 298
Drazin, R., 177, 178, 185, 190
Drew, S., 139
Droge, C., 48, 49
Drott, M.C., 380
Druskat, V.U., 102, 104, 107, 108
Drwal, R.L., 185
Duan, C., 84
Duarte, D.L., 96, 109
Duguid, P., 78, 143, 144
Dunphy, D., 26
Duntsch, I., 358
Dutton, J.E., 322
Duxbury, L., 206
Dwyer, R.F., 81
Dyer, J.H., 71, 76
Dyer, L., 169, 246, 258, 259, 312, 313, 414

Earl, M.J., 138
Earley, P.C., 101
Easterling, D., 79, 81
Eastman, L., 161, 165, 166
Easton, G.S., 47, 379, 381
Eccles, R.G., 118, 375
Economist Intelligence Unit, 256
Eckvall, G., 184, 185, 187
Eden, D., 322
Edge, G., 6
Edis, M., 76
Edmondson, A., 105
Edwards, H.M., 349
Edwards, P., 46, 49, 353, 357, 395, 407
Edwards, S.A., 187
Ehn, P., 337, 338, 339
Eisenberger, R., 183, 187
Eisenhardt, K., 299, 372, 377
Ekeberg, S.E., 359
Electronic Commerce Task Force, 256
Elger, T., 19, 23
Ellram, L.M., 76, 81
Emery, F., 9
Emery, M., 337, 342
Ennis, K., 295
Epitropaki, O., 421
Epstein, L.D., 97, 99
Ericksen, J., 169
Espejo, R., 332

Esser, J.K., 104
Etzioni, A., 337
European Commission, 197
Evans, J., 38
Evans, J.R., 41
Evans, K.R., 79, 82
Evenson, A., 128
Ewen, R., 186

Fagin, C.M., 293
Fairfield, K.M., 299, 304
Fairweather, N.B., 213
Farbey, B., 132, 251, 257
Farley, F.H., 182
Farmer, D.H., 72
Farr, J.L., 7, 177, 187
Farris, G.F., 185
Fasolo, P., 187
Fay, D., 176, 177, 179, 181, 183, 184, 185, 187, 190
Feigenbaum, A.V., 38
Feinberg, R.A., 128
Felstead, A., 199
Fenton, E.M., 379, 380
Ferdows, K., 47
Fernie, S., 115, 123, 127, 128, 157, 162, 163, 164, 300, 421
Ferrell, O.C., 303
Fiedler, F.E., 186
Field, J.M., 98, 99
Filipczak, B., 220
Fincham, R., 7
Finkbeiner, C.T., 182
Finklestein, S., 149, 220
Fishbein, M., 108
Fisher, C.D., 312
Fister, T., 167, 168
Fitzgerald, G., 136
Fleischer, M., 63
Florida, R., 19, 25
Flynn, B.B., 39, 47, 48, 282, 283, 284, 287
Foley, P., 247, 251, 255
Forbes, T., 77
Ford, C.M., 178, 179
Ford, K.J., 304
Ford, S., 48
Forth, J., 34, 156, 157
Foucault, M., 407
Franklin, T., 257
Fraser-Kraus, H., 74, 77
Freeman, H.E., 348
Freeman, R., 155, 164, 167, 168
Frei, F.X., 128
French, J.L., 179
Frenkel, S., 119, 120, 121, 123, 124, 126, 127, 128, 129, 187, 295, 300, 398

Frese, M., 10, 176, 177, 179, 181, 183, 184, 185, 187, 190, 235, 356, 358, 362, 421
Friedkin, N.E., 104
Frink, D.D., 103
Froggatt, K.L., 44, 49
Fromme, D.K., 183
Fruin, M., 19
Fucini, J., 19, 31
Fucini, S., 19, 31
Fujimoto, T., 19, 138
Fukuyama, F., 105

Gabriel, Y., 5
Gabrielson, G.O.S., 293
Gaier, E.L., 182
Gainey, T.W., 198
Galer, M., 338
Gall, G., 119, 124
Galper, R.E., 84
Galunic, D., 379
Gambetta, D.G., 79
Ganesan, S., 79, 82
Ganesan, V., 185
Gardner, T.M., 161, 165, 166, 167, 316, 322, 324, 403
Garey, J.G., 297, 300
Garrahan, P., 26, 31, 397, 407
Garson, B., 115
Garst, H., 184, 185, 190
Garud, 376
Garvin, D., 40
Gaucher, E.J., 291
Geber, B., 220
Gediga, G., 358
Gee, M.V., 42
Gellatly, I., 166
General Accounting Office, 47
George, J.M., 176
Gerhart, B., 49, 156, 161, 165, 301, 312, 314, 316, 317, 322, 324, 395, 403, 414
Gershenfeld, M., 236
Gerwin, D., 58
Getzels, J.W., 182
Ghoshal, S., 142, 372, 379, 385
Gibbs, W.W., 257
Gibson, C.B., 101, 105, 169
Gifford, K., 167
Giles, K., 207, 212
Gill, C., 33, 34
Gillespie, A.E., 198
Gillies, R.R., 298
Gilman, S., 298
Ginzberg, M.J., 142
Gittell, J.H., 45, 299, 301, 304, 305
Gittleman, M., 95, 155, 156, 160, 295
Giuliano, T., 106

Glosserman, B., 197
Glynn, M.A., 178, 185, 190
Gobeille, K., 156
Godard, J., 95, 99, 101
Goddard, J., 167, 302
Godfrey, A.B., 40
Godfrey, G., 41, 44
Goffin, R., 166
Goldberg, D., 359
Golden, B.R., 322, 325
Goldman, S.L., 55
Goldoftas, B., 161
Golhar, D.Y., 45, 47, 48
Goodman, J., 45
Goodman, P.S., 60, 99, 104, 397
Goodstein, L.P., 57, 58
Goodwin, G.G., 106
Gordon, A., 26
Gordon, G., 184, 210, 212
Gorman, B.S., 182
Grady, J.F. Jr., 44
Graen, G.B., 107, 298
Graham, I., 20
Graham, L., 31, 32
Grandey, A.A., 126
Granovetter, M., 78
Grant, R.A., 125
Grant, R.M., 41, 136, 137, 145, 380
Gratton, L., 319
Gray, M., 176, 210, 212
Green, S.G., 187
Greenaway, K., 379
Greenwood, M., 76
Grenier, G., 11
Greve, H.R., 384
Grey, C., 394
Grieco, A., 127
Grieves, J., 47, 49
Griffin, R., 42, 44
Griffin, R.W., 179
Griffiths, A., 210
Griffiths-Hughson, T.L., 99, 397
Grint, K., 407
Gronbaek, K., 338
Grossman, B.S., 183
Grote, G., 95, 97, 257, 260, 416
Grundy, J., 118
Gryskiewicz, S.S., 179, 182, 185
Guastello, S.J., 179
Guastello, D.D., 179
Guest, D., 156, 167, 203, 395, 402, 403, 407, 418
Guilford, J.P., 179
Guimares, T., 209
Gulati, R., 82
Gupta, N., 301, 303, 311, 312, 313

Gustafson, L.T., 46, 47
Gustafson, S.B., 177, 187
Gutek, B., 117, 118, 295
Guthrie, J.P., 103, 313, 325
Guzzo, R.A., 99, 101, 103, 104, 105, 322, 398

Haas, M.R., 381
Hackett, E.J., 44
Hackett, R., 104
Hackman, J., 8
Hackman, J.R., 8, 38, 40, 42, 46, 47, 48, 49, 78, 97, 98, 99, 101, 104, 107, 108, 109, 185, 298, 302, 358, 395, 398
Hagen, J.M., 79, 82
Hall, L., 176
Hall, T.W., 381
Hall-Mikesell, E., 186
Halpin, G., 184
Halskov Madsen, K., 339
Hamblin, H., 198
Hamborg, K.C., 358
Hamel, G., 214
Hammer, M., 156, 375
Handy, C., 408
Hanna, A.M., 381
Hansen, M.H., 79
Hansen, M.T., 146, 147, 381, 385
Hards, R., 185
Hardy C., 404
Harel, G., 297
Harker, P.T., 128
Harley, B., 157, 160, 166, 302
Harnden, R., 332
Harper, R., 206
Harrington, D., 295, 298
Harrington, D.M., 182
Harrington, E., 183, 185, 187
Harris, D., 59
Harris, M., 3
Harryson, S.J., 383
Hartline, M.D., 303
Hartman, R.I., 354
Haslam, C., 22
Hasty, R., 297
Hawkins, R., 246, 247, 251, 255
Head, W., 299, 304
Heckhousen, H., 221
Hedlund, G., 379
Heffner, T.S., 106
Heide, J.B., 76
Heimbeck, D., 353
Heller, F., 335
Helper, S., 80
Helton, B.R., 47
Hendricks, R., 407
Hendrickson, A.R., 207, 208, 213

Hendry, M., 245
Hennessey, B.A., 183
Herman, G., 245
Herriot, P., 418
Herron, M., 184
Hertel, P., 106
Hesketh, B., 359
Heskett, J., 121, 130, 291, 295, 302
Hesterly, W., 385
Hiemstra, G., 206
Higgen, G., 393
Higgins, C.A., 125, 181
Higgs, A.C., 97, 101, 103, 104, 105, 107
Hill, C.E., 84
Hill, C.W.L., 82, 385
Hill, E.J., 356, 361
Hill, G.W., 102
Hill, J.A., 198
Hill, S., 38, 44
Hillam, C.E., 349
Hillburger, T., 181
Hilligloh, S., 179
Hillthrop, J.M., 212
Hiltz, S.R., 353
Hitt, L.M., 296, 297
Hitt, M.A., 376
Hochschild, A., 398
Hodgkinson, G., 378, 380, 382
Hodson, N., 210, 212
Hofstede, G., 100
Hogg, M.A., 96
Hokama, L., 128
Holbrook, M.B., 117
Holland, W.E., 179, 182
Hollensbe, E.C., 103
Hollnagel, E., 59
Hollway, W., 405, 406
Holman, D.J., 8, 119, 120, 123, 125, 126, 127, 183, 185, 187, 252, 256, 257, 303, 420, 421
Hoque, K., 11, 156, 296, 403
Hornby, P., 337, 338, 339, 340
Horrigan, M., 95, 155, 156, 160, 295
Hoschild, A., 126
Hosmer, L.T., 6, 119
Host, V., 297
Houlihan, M., 124, 129, 130
House, E.R., 348
Houston, J.M., 236
Hout, T.M., 55
Howard, O., 292
Howell, J.M., 181
Huang, C., 298
Huemer, K.H., 359
Hueser, M., 58
Hughes, E.F.X., 298
Hughes, M., 19

Hull, R., 132, 251, 257
Hull, R.R., 141
Hunter, L., 46, 47, 85, 86, 88
Hunter, L.W., 109, 294, 295, 297
Huseslid, M.A., 6, 49, 157, 158, 161, 162, 163, 164, 165, 167, 311, 312, 313, 315, 316, 317, 318, 319, 321, 322, 325, 395
Hutchinson, S., 121, 123, 124, 398, 399, 402, 407
Huutanen, P., 362
Huws, U., 197, 210
Huxley, C., 31, 32
Hwang, L., 55, 64
Hyatt, D., 101, 107

Icasati-Johanson, B., 80, 87, 258, 260, 261
Ichniowski, C., 157, 159, 161, 162, 163, 165, 315, 325, 396
Ide, W., 95, 97, 257, 260, 416
Igbaria, M., 209
Ilgen, D.R., 95, 221, 240
Ilinitch, A.Y., 371
Imai, K., 84
Imai, M., 40
Incomes Data Services, 125
Ingham, C., 210
Inhelder, B., 83
Inness, L., 395, 407
IRS, 198, 257
Irving, R.H., 125
Isabella, L., 77
Isenberg, D.J., 104
Ishikawa, K., 38
Isic, A., 125, 126
Iverson, R.D., 125, 303, 398
Iwasawa, J., 55, 64
Iyer, A., 384

Jackson, D., 166
Jackson, P.R., 9, 10, 49, 58, 59, 60, 61, 62, 106, 183, 185, 189, 354, 355, 358, 359, 360, 361, 362
Jackson, R., 299, 304
Jackson, S.E., 11, 121
Jagger, N., 197
Janis, I.L., 104
Jarrell, S.L., 47
Jarvenpaa, S.L., 142, 354, 358
Jarvinen, K., 355
Jayaram, J., 49
Jayaratna, N., 337
Jenkins, G.D. Jr., 301, 303, 312
Jenkins, S., 138
Jennings, K.R., 44
Jensen, M.C., 79
Jermier, J., 418

Jewson, N., 199
Jick, T., 203, 375, 377
Jimmieson, N., 125
Johal, S., 22
Johannsen, G., 57, 58
John, G., 76
Johnson, J.W., 302
Johnson, R., 303
Jones, C., 385
Jones, D., 20, 21, 23, 24, 25, 27, 29, 31, 271, 286
Jones, F.E., 179
Jones, G., 137, 238
Jones, R.G., 101
Jones, R.H., 298
Jones, S.D., 359
Jones, T., 385
Joyce, M., 95, 155, 156, 160, 295
Judge, T.A., 76, 79
Judge, W.Q. Jr., 298, 356, 358
Juran, J.M., 40
Jürgens, U., 28

Kabanoff, B., 187
Kafka-Lutzow, A., 359
Kallenberg, A., 26, 161
Kanter, R.M., 177
Kanungo, R.N., 237
Kamauff, J.W. Jr., 74
Kammergaard, J., 338
Kamoche, K., 145
Kanter, R.M., 178, 187
Kantrow, A.H., 271
Karasek, R., 9, 125
Karetta, B., 355, 359
Karwowski, W., 55, 56, 58, 61, 64
Kass, T., 6
Katz, H.C., 5, 156, 291, 292, 293, 294
Katzell, R.A., 95
Katzenbach, J.R., 104
Kay, J., 145
Kayes, 102, 108
Kazanjian, R.K., 178, 185, 190
Kearney, V., 259
Keats, B.W., 376
Keefe, J., 128, 303
Keen, C., 128, 129
Keenoy, T., 19
Keita, G.P., 60
Keller, R.T., 179, 182
Kelley, D.K., 198
Kelly, M., 299, 304
Kemp, N.J., 3, 60
Kenney, M., 19, 25
Kensing, F., 339
Kerr, S., 203, 375, 377
Kerrin, M., 76, 88

Kerwin, K., 220
Kidd, P.T., 55, 56, 61, 62, 64
Kienzle, R., 297, 305
Kiggundu, M.N., 60
Kilty, J., 169
Kim, I.-K., 128
King, C.A., 297, 300
King, J., 117, 132
King, M., 349
Kinicki, A.J., 105, 166, 167, 181
Kink, N., 96
Kinnie, N., 121, 123, 398, 399, 407
Kirby, S., 157
Kirkman, B.L., 97, 100, 101, 104, 105, 106, 107, 176, 421
Kitay, J., 294
Kivimaki, M., 355
Klein, J., 6, 7, 33
Klein, J.A., 43, 59
Klein, N., 408
Klein, S.R., 187
Kleiner, M., 155, 164, 167
Kleingeld, A., 359
Kling, J., 155
Knights, D., 7, 11, 117, 120, 124, 125, 127, 398, 401, 418
Kobayashi, N., 55, 64
Koch, M., 157, 161, 162
Kochan, T.A., 10, 45, 119, 125, 155, 156, 157, 160, 161, 163, 165, 167
Kocharekar, R., 382, 383
Kofman, F., 140, 147
Kogan, N., 179
Kogi, K., 95, 97, 257, 260, 416
Kogut, B., 385
Kohn, A., 149
Kolb, K.L., 119, 125
Kolias, P., 303
Kolvenbach, T., 353
Konrad, A.M., 311
Koput, K., 385
Korcynski, M., 119, 120, 121, 123, 125, 126, 127, 128, 129, 187, 295, 398
Korunka, C., 355, 356, 358, 359, 362
Koskinen, P., 60
Kostecki, M.J., 60
Kotabe, M., 80, 81, 82
Koubek, R., 55, 56, 64
Koys, D., 16
KPMG Consultants, 147, 256, 257
Kraimer, M.L., 176, 181
Kramer, R.M., 105
Kring, W., 177, 183, 184, 185
Krishnan, R., 41, 106
Krop, H., 184
Kruse, D., 156, 157, 159

Kuchinsky, A., 353
Kuenzler, C., 95, 97, 257, 260, 416
Kumar, A., 304
Kumar, K., 5
Kumaraswamy, A., 376
Kunda, G., 149
Kwon, S., 383, 385
Kyng, M., 338

Lacity, M., 136
Lam, A., 78, 88, 145
Lam, L., 166
Lam, S.S.K., 49
Lamarsh, J., 55, 64
Lambert, S.J., 211
Lammers, J.C., 298
Lamming, R., 24, 71, 74, 76, 89
Lamond, D.A., 199, 201, 203, 207, 208, 209, 211, 212, 213, 214, 215
Landeros, R., 76, 81
Landsbergis, P., 33
Lang, T., 5
Langer, E.J., 378
Langfield-Smith, K., 76
Langfred, C.W., 298
Lank, E., 148
Lansbury, R., 156
LaPorte, T.R., 377
Lasaosa, A., 274, 277, 278, 279, 285, 286, 287, 288
Laskin, R., 299, 304
Latack, J.C., 181
Latham, W.R., 103
Lathin, D., 185
Lattin, G.W., 291, 294
Lautsch, B.A., 45
Lave, J., 78, 143, 148
Law, K., 106
Lawler, E.E. III, 3, 6, 7, 44, 95, 96, 106, 155, 156, 157, 158, 160, 161, 163, 165, 167, 220, 237, 239, 273, 274, 275, 276, 280, 281, 287
Lawler, J.J., 325
Lawrence, J.W., 421
Lawrence, P., 203
Lazear, E., 168
Lazenby, J., 184
Lea, M.T., 206
Leadbetter, C., 256, 257
Leana, C., 305
Leavitt, H.J., 97
Ledford, G., 3, 6, 7, 155, 156, 157, 158, 160, 161, 163
Ledford, G.E., 95, 96, 97, 108, 300
Ledford, G.E. Jr., 101, 108, 220, 239, 273, 274, 275, 276, 280, 281, 287, 299
Lee, M.B., 313

Lee, S.Y., 301
Lefrere, P., 137, 238
Legge, K., 400, 402, 405, 407
LeGrande, D., 60, 125
Leiba-O'Sullivan, S., 404
Leibeskind, J.P., 380
Leichner, R., 353
Leidner, D., 136
Leigh, D., 167
Leino, T., 362
Leith, G., 185
Lemons, M.A., 100
Lendrum, B., 293
Leng, K., 181
Lengnick-Hall, M.L., 44, 49
Leonard-Barton, D., 88
Lepak, D., 161, 313, 315, 316, 317
Lepak, D.P., 49
LePine, J., 177, 181, 184
Lespinger, R., 219
Lev, B., 165
Leverick, F., 77
Leviatan, U., 322
Levine, D., 157, 161, 163, 165, 167
Levitt, T., 121, 291, 295
Levy, M., 304
Lewchuck, W., 43
Lewin, A.Y., 371
Lewin, D., 159
Lewis, B.R., 293
Liang, D.W., 106
Liden, R.C., 421
Liker, J.K., 63
Likert, R., 156
Lim, S.Y., 60, 125
Lincoln, J., 26
Lincoln, J.R., 84, 89
Lindsay, W.M., 41
Lindsley, D.H., 105
Lindstrom, K., 354, 355
Lipsey, M.W., 348
Lipson, S., 299, 304
Litschauer, B., 359
Little, B.L., 105
Lloyd-Jones, R., 132, 251, 257
Locke, R., 155, 156, 160, 235
Locurto, C.M., 184
London, M., 237
Long, R.J., 354
Lorsch, J.W., 203
Loveman, G.W., 302
Lowe, J., 26, 30, 31, 32, 89, 165, 353, 357
Lubart, T.I., 179
Lubit, R., 380
Lucas, R.E., 359
Lucia, A.D., 219

Lucio, M.M., 138
Lynch, L., 161, 164
Lytle, W.O., 343

Mabey, C., 393
MacAvoy, T., 77
Macbeth, D.K., 74, 77
Maclaren, R., 337, 338, 339, 340
MacDonald, W.B., 342
MacDuffie, J., 26, 27, 29, 30, 33, 157, 161, 313, 315, 318, 325
MacDuffie, J.P., 49, 281, 287, 312, 395
MacFarlan, M., 293
MacGregor, J., 300
Madigan, R.M., 105
Maes, S., 9, 31
Maglitta, J., 138
Maguire, M., 338
Mahoney, J., 375
Mahoney, T.A., 312
Majchrzak, A., 55, 56, 57, 58, 61, 63, 66, 96
Maki, E., 355
Malhotra, A., 96
Malone, M.S., 375
Malsch, T., 28
Mangel, R., 311
Manufacturing Studies Board, 57
Manyika, J., 381
Manz, C.C., 108
March, J.G., 136, 378
Marchington, M., 5, 38, 41, 44, 45
Marchland, S., 138
Marcus, A., 377
Marks, M.A., 109
Marks, M.L., 44
Martell, R.F., 322
Martin, R., 8, 9, 10, 58, 59, 60, 61, 62, 352, 354, 355, 358, 359, 360, 361, 362
Martin, T., 55, 56
Martiny, M., 220, 238
Martocchio, J.J., 103
Mason, E., 84, 89
Masterson, S.S., 219
Mathieu, J.E., 106, 109
Matusik, S., 385
Mayer, R.C., 105
McAllistar, D.J., 82
McAulay, B., 46
McCabe, D., 46, 47, 117, 120, 124, 125, 398, 401
McCabe, D.L., 322
McCarrey, M., 187
McCauley, C., 104
McClelland, C.L., 8
McClennan, W., 209
McCloskey, L.A., 271

McCormick, M.J., 240
McCrae, R.R., 181
McDermott, R., 78
McEwan, R., 358
McGrath, R., 157, 161, 162, 372, 374, 375, 376, 379, 383
McGregor, D., 156
McHugh, D., 23
McIntire, S.A., 236
McIntosh, J., 293
McKinlay, A., 136, 142, 144
McKeen, J.D., 372, 379
McKersie, R.B., 398
McKone, K.E., 284, 285, 287
McLeod, P.L., 351
McLoughlin, I., 3, 117, 132, 406
McMahon, G., 121, 165
McMahan, G.C., 312, 313, 316, 317, 319, 324
McMurrer, D., 165
McPhee, R.D., 6
McWilliams, A., 319
Meadows, M., 120, 128
Meckling, W.M., 79
Medsker, G.J., 97, 101, 103, 104, 105, 107, 298
Meghir, C., 165
Menard, S., 325
Mendonca, L., 381
Menon, S.T., 238
Mercadal, D.E., 184
Mercadal, P.L., 184
Merril, M., 294
Merrill Lynch, 246, 253, 257, 258
Mertini, H., 125, 126
Metcalf, D., 115, 128, 157, 162, 163, 164, 300
Meyer, J., 166, 167
Milanovich, D.M., 106
Miles, R.E., 185, 187
Miles, G., 185, 187
Milgram, R.M., 182
Milkman, R., 19
Milkovich, G., 301
Miller, B.C., 356, 361
Miller, K.I., 10
Miller, S.J., 79, 81
Millward, N., 34, 156, 157
Miner, J.B., 182
Mintzberg, H., 209
Mirvis, P.H., 44
Mitev, N., 394
Mitra, A., 301
Mittal, V., 46
Mohamed, M., 187
Mohr, J., 76, 78, 81, 87
Mohrman, A.M., 97
Mohrman, A.M. Jr., 9

Mohrman, S.A., 3, 6, 7, 9, 44, 83, 84, 95, 96, 97, 155, 156, 157, 158, 160, 161, 163, 187, 220, 239, 273, 274, 275, 276, 280, 281, 287
Mokray, J., 63
Moltini, G., 127
Monden, Y., 23
Monge, P.R., 10
Monk, A., 352
Montejanon, R., 358
Montgomery, C.A., 404
Montgomery, D.C., 41
Moon, C., 213
Moore, K.R., 81
Moore, T.J., 358
Moran, T.P., 11
Moreland, R.L., 106
Morely, I.E., 118
Morgan, G., 371, 399, 401, 421
Morgan, K., 25
Morrill, C., 374
Morris, W.T., 276
Morrison, D., 95, 97, 257, 260, 416
Morrison, E., 166
Morrison, E.W., 177, 181, 183
Moses, T.P., 354
Mount, M.K., 102, 207
Moynihan, L., 125, 127, 129, 161, 165, 166, 167, 304, 316, 324
Mrela, K., 60
Mueller, F., 145
Mueller, W., 11, 30
Mukamel, D., 296
Mullane, J.V., 46, 47
Mullarkey, S., 354, 361
Mullen, B., 104
Mullen, M.R., 82
Mulvey, G., 119, 124
Mumford, E., 334, 337, 340, 342, 398, 407
Mumford, M.D., 177, 186, 187
Munday, M., 19
Munton, A.G., 181
Murray, H., 331, 393
Muscovici, S., 118
Myaskovsky, L., 106
Myhr, N., 74

Nadin, S., 176
Nadler, D., 376
Nagamachi, M., 55, 64
Nagel, R.N., 55
Nahapiet, J., 142, 379, 385
Nakamura, N., 58
Naniwada, M., 55, 64
Napier, R., 236
Nardi, B.A., 353
Narus, J., 79, 81, 83

Nash, W.R., 183
Naylor, J.C., 221, 240
Neal, A., 359
Neilsen, J.F., 297
Nelson, R.R., 187
Neubert, M.J., 102
Neuman, G.A., 102
Neumark, D., 156, 157, 158, 159, 164, 295, 311, 315, 321, 325
Newell, S., 142, 382
Newman, K., 49, 103
Newman, J., 301
Nicholl, J., 132, 251, 257
Noe, R.A., 230
Nohria, N., 118, 146, 147, 372, 381, 385
Nonaka, I., 84, 138, 140, 147, 375, 379, 380
Noon, M., 138
Noorderhaven, N.G., 82
Nooteboom, B., 82
Nord, W., 418
Nuefeld, D., 206
Nyerges, T., 358
Nystrom, H., 178
Nystrom, P.C., 42

Oakland, J., 166
Oakland, S., 166
O'Brien, G.E., 9
O'Brien, P., 338, 339
Obstfeld, D., 377, 378
Ocasio, W., 382
Occhipiati, E., 127
O'Conaill, B., 354
O'Driscoll, M.P., 9
Ody, P., 245
Office of Technology Assessment, 56
Offsey, S., 372
Oh, S., 81
Ohno, T., 21, 23
Older-Gray, M., 257
Oldham, G.R., 8, 42, 49, 78, 97, 101, 177, 185, 187, 190, 283, 302, 358, 395
O'Leary-Kelly, A.M., 103
Oliver, N., 19, 24, 26, 30, 31, 32, 76, 89, 353, 357
Olsen, S.E., 57, 58
Olson, C., 161, 163, 165
Omari, M., 205, 208, 209, 211
Oppermann, R., 358
Oram, M., 407
Orazem, P., 165
O'Regan, S., 197
O'Reilly, A., 34, 156, 397, 402, 406
O'Reilly, C.A., 98, 103, 166
Orlinowski, W.J., 11, 117, 317
Orr, J., 143, 148

Orton, J.D., 377
Osterman, P., 3, 10, 95, 96, 97, 99, 109, 155, 156, 157, 158, 159, 167, 168, 273, 274, 398
Ostroff, C., 155, 164, 167, 312, 313
O'Sullivan, D., 258
Ouchi, W., 19, 21, 25
Ouchi, W.G., 71
Oum, T.H., 291, 294
Owen, R.V., 76
Ozanne, J.L., 79

Pagel, D., 76
Palmer, G., 46
Pan, S.L., 150
Pankow, W., 60
Papper, E.M., 101, 298
Paquin, A.R., 240
Paris, M.L., 55, 56, 58
Park, H., 161, 165, 166, 167
Park, H.J., 316, 324
Parker, M., 28, 33, 46
Parker, R., 335
Parker, S.A., 49
Parker, S.K., 3, 7, 8, 9, 78, 84, 85, 88, 89, 106, 109, 130, 176, 179, 181, 183, 185, 186, 189, 190, 354, 360, 373, 374, 419, 420, 421
Parkington, J., 302
Parks, S., 156
Parnes, S.J., 184
Partnership Sourcing Ltd, 85
Pascale, R., 19, 21
Patriotti, G., 142, 143
Patterson, M., 275, 280, 286, 287, 288
Paul, M.C., 303
Paulus, P., 98
Paunonen, S., 166
Pearce, J.L., 79, 105, 166
Pearlson, K.E., 214
Peccei, R., 302
Pelz, D.C., 179, 185
Pemberton, C., 418
Pennings, J.M., 296
Pepper, K., 3, 55, 95, 97, 257, 260, 273, 416
Perry, S., 322
Pervan, G., 349
Peters, M., 5, 358
Peterson, J.M., 182
Peterson, R.B., 81
Pettigrew, A., 379, 380
Pfeffer, J., 97, 98, 314, 374, 375, 395, 405
Phelps, C.C., 177, 183
Philimore, J., 7
Piaget, J., 83
Piccolo, B., 127
Pickus, P.S., 319, 321
Pil, F., 30, 31, 157, 281

Pine, B., 295
Piore, M., 5, 155, 156, 160
Plank, R.E., 76, 81
Ploos von Amstel, R., 72
Podolny, J.K., 384
Pollitt, C., 5
Pollock, A., 393
Poole, M., 156
Poole, M.P., 6
Porac, J., 185
Porter, L.J., 45, 47, 166
Porter, M., 6
Porter, M.E., 371
Portes, A., 384
Potter, G., 301
Powell, T.C., 48
Powell, W.W., 78, 79, 385, 396
Power, T., 258
Prahalad, C.K., 214
Preiss, K., 55
Prencipe, A., 246, 247, 251, 255
Prennushi, G., 157, 161, 325, 396
Preston, J., 238, 379
Preuss, G.A., 297, 304
Price Waterhouse Cooper, 257, 258
Pritchard, R.D., 103, 220, 221, 228, 240, 359
Probst, G., 220
Probst, T., 166
Procter, S., 30, 397, 399, 406
Proquest Information and Learning Company, 197
Pruitt, S., 162
Prumper, J., 358
Prusak, L., 380
Prussia, G., 105
Purcell, J., 121, 123, 124, 396, 398, 399, 403, 404, 407
Purser, R.E., 337, 343

Quinn, J.B., 149, 220, 297
Quinn, R., 203
Quinones, M.A., 304
Quintas, P., 137, 238
Qvortrup, L., 199

Rademaker, A.W., 298
Rahimi, M., 61
Rajan, A., 148
Ramsay, D., 157, 160, 166
Ramsay, H., 302
Ramstad, P.M., 220, 221, 228
Rao, H., 374
Rasmussen, J., 57
Raub, S., 142
Raudsepp, E., 186
Ravlin., E., 104

Reardon, J., 297
Reason, J., 59
Reck, R., 76, 81
Redman, T., 38, 41, 47, 49
Redmond, M.R., 186
Rees, C., 46, 49, 353, 357, 395, 397, 407
Reeves, T., 312, 414
Regalia, I., 294
Regan, D., 84
Reger, R.K., 46, 47
Reich, M., 49
Reich, R., 136, 203
Reiterer, H., 358
Remdisch, S., 353
Renard, M.K., 219
Reynolds, K.S.E., 298
Rhodes, P., 7
Rice, A.K., 393
Rice, R.E., 96
Richardson, H., 161, 165, 166
Richardson, R., 126, 198
Richardson, S., 338, 339
Richmond, C., 258
Rickards, T., 187
Riddalls, C.E., 265
Rieke, M.L., 179
Riis, H., 65
Rinehart, J., 31, 32
Ring, P.S., 82
Ritzer, R., 7
Rizzo, J.R., 220
Roberts, K.H., 377, 378
Robertson, D., 31, 32, 43
Robertson, M., 148
Robinson, S., 23
Robsen, J., 337, 339, 340
Robson, J., 338, 339
Rochlin, G., 377
Rodin, S., 379
Rodwell, J.J., 297, 305
Rogers, E.W., 315, 317, 324, 402
Rogers, R., 167
Rogovsky, N., 166
Roitman, D., 63
Roos, D., 20, 21, 23, 24, 25, 27, 29, 31, 80, 271, 286
Roos, J., 78
Rose, H., 117, 132
Rosen, B., 97, 101, 104, 105, 106, 107, 176, 421
Rosenbloom, D., 293
Rosenfield, M., 118
Rosenthal, P., 302
Rossi, P.H., 348
Roth, P.L., 359
Rotter, J.B., 79
Rourke, J., 197

Rousseau, D.M., 79, 82, 418
Rowe, P.M., 353
Ruddy, T.M., 101, 107
Ruggles, R., 137
Ruling, C.C., 142
Rutter, D.R., 118
Rutten, M.L., 359
Ryan, A.M., 303
Ryan, R.M., 183
Rynes, S., 301

Sabel, C., 5
Sackman, S.A., 380
Safeyeni, F.R., 125
Saha, S., 104
Sahay, A., 80, 81, 82, 381
Sakakibara, S., 39, 47, 48, 276, 282, 283, 284, 287
Sako, M., 24, 72, 74, 77, 80, 83, 89
Sakolosky, G., 11
Salas, E., 102, 106, 107
Salmon, G., 207, 212
Salvendy, G., 3, 55, 56, 57, 58, 64
Salzman, H., 55, 64
Samson, D., 48
Sanchez, R., 375
Sanders, K.J., 60, 125
Sanderson, P.M., 56, 58, 59
Saraph, J.V., 45, 47
Sasser, E.W., 291, 295, 302
Saunders, C.S., 214
Sauter, S.L., 60
Sawyer, F.H., 88
Sawyer, J.E., 103, 179
Sayer, A., 24
Scarbrough, H., 139, 142, 145, 150, 238, 379, 382, 397
Schall, P., 33
Schallock, B., 55, 59, 64
Schay, B.W., 219
Scheier, M.E., 421
Schein, E.H., 177
Schilling, M.A., 375, 376, 377, 385
Schkade, D., 60
Schlesinger, L., 121, 130, 291, 295, 302
Schminke, M., 104
Schmit, M.J., 302, 303
Schneider, B., 5, 121, 302
Schneider, D., 166
Schneider, S.K., 351
Scholarios, D., 157, 160, 166, 302
Schonberger, R., 23
Schonberger, R.J., 40, 42, 45, 271
Schoonhoven, C.B., 177
Schoorman, F.D., 105
Schwarz, H., 353

Scott, S.G., 190
Schroeder, R.G., 39, 44, 45, 46, 47, 48, 98, 99, 276, 282, 283, 284, 285, 287, 288, 417
Schuler, R., 11, 121
Schurr, P.H., 79, 81
Seibert, S.E., 176, 181
Seifert, C., 125, 126
Seisfeld, T., 165
Seitsonen, S., 355
Sell, R., 132, 251, 257
Senge, P., 140, 147
Sennett, R., 408, 418
Seppala, P., 55, 60, 64
Sergeant, A., 300
Shadur, M.A., 297, 305
Shafer, R., 169
Shah, P.P., 385
Shani, R., 41
Shannon, H.S., 293
Shao, Y., 125
Shapiro, D.L., 100, 101
Sharit, J., 56
Sharma, A., 304
Shaw, J.D., 301, 303, 311, 312, 313
Shaw, K., 157, 161, 315, 325, 396
Shaw, M., 245
Shea, G.P., 105
Shepperd, J.A., 104
Sheridan, T., 55, 64
Sherman, S., 314, 318
Shingo, S., 23, 43
Shire, K., 119, 120, 121, 123, 125, 126, 127, 128, 129, 295, 398
Shire, K.A., 187
Short, J., 118
Shortell, S., 298
Sianest, B., 165
Siliski, J., 299, 304
Simon, H.A., 382
Sims, H.P. Jr., 108
Sinclair, D., 85, 86, 88
Sinclair, M.A., 57
Singh, H., 76, 146, 303
Singh, J., 117, 300
Sinha, K.K., 98, 99
Sirdeshmukh, D., 117
Sisson, K., 397
Sitkin, S.B., 44, 46, 79, 80, 82, 288, 417
Sjogren, D., 339
Skinner, D., 393
Skyrme, D.J., 139
Slack, N., 72
Slaughter, J., 28, 33, 46
Sloane, D.M., 293
Smircich, L., 401
Smith, C., 19, 23, 166, 167

AUTHOR INDEX

Smith, D.K., 104
Smith, H.L., 359
Smith, K.G., 82, 305
Smith, M.J., 59, 60, 125
Smith, N.R., 1182
Smith, R., 185
Smith-Doerr, L., 385
Smither, R.D., 236
Snape, E., 38, 41
Snell, S.A., 49, 161, 165, 271, 275, 288, 313, 315, 316, 317, 319, 321, 324, 356
Snow, C.C., 185, 187
Sochalski, J., 293
Somers, M.J., 303
Sonnentag, S., 185
Soose, A., 177, 183, 184, 185
Sparrow, P.R., 5, 208, 212, 372, 373, 374, 375, 378, 380, 382, 385, 407, 418
Sparrowe, R.T., 421
Spears, R., 206
Speckman, R.E., 74
Spector, P.E., 125
Spector, W.D., 296
Spekman, R., 76, 77, 78, 81, 87
Spencer, B.A., 39
Spender, J.C., 137, 378
Spratt, M.F., 319, 321
Sprecher, T.B., 177, 179, 182
Spreitzer, G.M., 108, 299
Sprigg, C.A., 181, 185, 190
Srinivasan, D., 301
Stahelski, A.J., 354
Stalk, G., 55
Standen, P., 199, 201, 203, 204, 205, 208, 209, 210, 211, 212, 213, 214, 215
Stanton, J.M., 119, 125, 352
Stanworth, C., 213
Staples, D.S., 379
Staw, B.M., 97, 99, 177
Steedman, H., 6
Steensma, H.K., 375, 376, 377, 385
Steiner, I.D., 102
Stephenson, G.M., 118
Stern, D., 49
Sternberg, R.J., 179
Stevens, C.K., 305
Stevens, M.J., 102, 107
Stewart, A., 245
Stewart, G.L., 95, 102, 104, 107, 108
Stewart, P., 26, 31, 397, 407
Stewart, T., 132
Stone, G.P., 84
Stoner, C.R., 354
Storey, J., 3, 7, 55, 397, 417
Stout, R.J., 106
Strader, T., 245

Strauss, G., 161, 163, 165
Streukens, S., 129
Stride, C., 95, 97, 257, 260, 416
Stuebing, K.K., 359
Sturdy, A., 7, 11, 127, 128
Subramanian, S., 185
Suh, E., 359
Sullivan, J., 81
Sun, H., 65
Sundblad, Y., 338
Sundstrom, E., 109
Susman, G., 7
Susman, G.I., 239
Sutcliffe, K.M., 44, 46, 288, 377, 378, 417
Swan, J., 142, 145, 148, 238, 379, 382
Swan, J.A., 178
Switzer, J., 145
Symon, G., 337, 339, 340, 351

Taggar, S., 104
Takahashi, M., 95, 97, 257, 260, 416
Takeuchi, H., 84, 140, 375, 380
Tam, M., 119, 120, 121, 123, 125, 126, 127, 128, 129, 187, 295
Tampoe, M., 145
Tangeberg-Andersson, Y., 185, 187
Tannenbaum, S.I., 102, 107
Tata, J., 100
Taylor, B., 337, 338
Taylor, K.M., 104
Taylor, M.S., 219
Taylor, P., 7, 117, 119, 120, 125, 128, 398
Teach, R., 186
Teachout, M.S., 304
Teng, E., 183, 184, 185
Tenkasi, R.V., 83
Tennant-Snyder, N., 96, 109
Terry, D.J., 96, 125
Terry, M., 397
Terziovski, M., 48
Tesluk, P.E., 187
Thacker, C., 176
Theorell, T., 9, 125
Thomas, J.B., 105
Thomas, P., 156
Thompson, I., 245
Thompson, J.D., 100
Thompson, P., 23, 117
Thornburg, T.H., 186
Thornhills, T., 299, 304
Thurley, K., 25
Tierney, T., 146, 147, 381, 385
Timmers, P., 245, 258
Tjosvold, D., 106
Tjosvold, M.M., 106

Todd, C., 176
Tomaney, J., 7
Tomlinson C., 132, 251, 257
Torrance, E.P., 179
Tosi, H.L., 220
Totten, J., 84
Totterdell, P., 119, 120, 125, 126, 303
Touminen, E., 60
Townsend, A.M., 207, 208, 213
Tracy, K.B., 219
Trades Union Congress, 257
Trades Union Council, 128
Travic, B., 203, 399
Tregaskis, O., 201, 212, 213
Triandis, H., 186
Tripoli, A., 166
Trist, E., 331, 393
Trist, E.L., 220
Truesdale, T.A., 74
Truss, C., 319
Tsoukas, H., 137, 375, 379
Tsui, A., 166
Tubre, T.C., 303
Tuckman, A., 46, 47
Turgoose, C., 176
Turnbull, P., 7, 24, 25, 26, 28, 43, 76
Turuch, E., 372
Tushman, M.L., 187, 376
Tyson, L., 157, 167
Tzafir, S., 297

Udell, G.G., 182
Uhl-Bien, M., 107, 298
Ulrich, D., 203, 375, 377
Unsworth, K.L., 106, 176, 177, 183, 185, 187, 190
Uzzi, B., 385

Van Buren III, H.J., 305
Van de Ven, A.H., 82
Van Den Bosch, F.A.J., 379, 382
Van Der Doef, M., 9
Van Dyne, L., 177, 181, 184
Van Maanen, J., 405
Van Ommeren, J.N., 201, 212
Van Tuijl, H.F.J.M., 359
Van Wijk, R.A., 379, 382
Vancouver, J.B., 181
Vandenberg, R., 161, 165, 166
Vandenbosch, B., 142
Vandevelde, H., 117
Vaughan, D., 377
Venkatraman, N., 82
Vickery, S., 48, 49
Virick, M., 319
Vitouch, O., 356, 358, 362

Vogt, C., 125, 126
Volberda, H.W., 375, 376
Vollrath, D.A., 44, 49
Volpe, C.E., 107
Von Hippel, E., 148
Von Krogh, G., 78
Voss, C., 23
Vroom, V.H., 221

Wacker, G.J., 42, 49
Wacquant, L.J.D., 383
Wageman, R., 38, 40, 46, 47, 48, 95, 100, 102, 103, 104, 108
Wagner, J., 157
Wagner, K., 6
Wagner, S.H., 102
Wailes, N., 156
Waldman, D.A., 44
Walker, R., 272
Wall, T.D., 3, 7, 8, 9, 10, 49, 55, 58, 59, 60, 61, 62, 78, 95, 97, 100, 106, 107, 109, 130, 183, 185, 187, 189, 257, 258, 260, 273, 275, 280, 286, 287, 288, 352, 353, 354, 355, 358, 359, 360, 373, 374, 416, 419, 420, 421
Wallach, M.A., 179
Waller, M.A., 45, 47, 48
Walley, P., 120, 128
Walsh, J.T., 125, 184, 303, 398
Walsh, S., 337, 338
Walther, J.B., 206
Walton, R., 6, 7, 395
Wang, Q., 55
Warnecke, H.J., 58
Warner, M., 43
Warr, P.B., 3, 55, 60, 209, 257, 273, 416
Warschat, J., 55, 64
Waterson, P.E., 3, 8, 55, 183, 185, 187, 252, 256, 257, 273, 416, 420
Watson, A., 119, 124
Watts, L., 352
Wayne, S.J., 421
Weaver, K.M., 182
Webb, J., 43
Weber, M., 156
Webster, J., 126
Wegner, D.M., 106
Weick, K.E., 377, 378, 401
Weiner, A., 356, 361
Weisband, S.P., 351
Weiss, A., 355, 359
Weitz, B., 76, 79, 81, 82
Weldon, E., 109
Wellins, R.S., 239, 407
Wenger, E., 78, 143, 144, 148
West, M.A., 7, 105, 106, 177, 181, 185, 186, 235, 275, 280, 286, 287, 288

Whinston, A., 245
Whitaker, A., 19
White, L., 166
White, S.S., 303
White, W.D., 293, 294
Whitfield, K., 35
Whitman, M.N., 376, 377
Whittaker, S., 353, 354
Whittington, R., 136
Whyte, G., 104
Wickens, P., 19, 25, 26, 28, 397
Wijnen, C.J.D., 183, 184, 185
Wilbur, S., 354
Wilkinson, A., 38, 40, 41, 44, 45, 46, 47
Wilkinson, B., 19, 24, 28, 43, 76
Willcocks, L., 136, 407
Williams, E., 118
Williams, J., 22
Williams, K., 22
Williams, K.Y., 103
Williamson, O.E., 72, 79, 85, 148
Williamson, S., 41
Willmott, H., 7, 11, 127, 136, 150, 407
Wilson, J.M., 239
Wilson, J.R., 56
Winfield, I.J., 76
Winslow, C.D., 120
Wobbe, W., 56, 63
Wolfe, R.A., 7
Wolff, S.B., 104, 107
Womack, J., 20, 21, 23, 24, 25, 27, 29, 31, 271, 286
Wood, R., 237

Wood, S., 7, 10, 130, 157, 164, 176, 271, 272, 273, 274, 277, 278, 279, 285, 286, 287, 288
Woodland, S., 34, 156, 157, 402, 406
Woodman, R.W., 179
Woods, D., 59, 95, 97, 257, 260
Woodward, C.A., 293
Woolcock, M., 384
Woolgar, S., 11
Wright, B., 100, 104
Wright, J., 102
Wright, P.M., 121, 161, 165, 166, 167, 246, 258, 259, 312, 313, 314, 315, 316, 317, 318, 319, 321, 322, 324, 325, 402, 403

Yang, S., 296
Yates, J., 357
Yetton, P.W., 101
Yong. J., 40, 46
Yost, P.R., 105
Youndt, M., 49, 161, 313, 315, 316, 317
Yu, C., 291, 294

Zaccaro, S.J., 109
Zaheer, A., 82
Zald, M.N., 374
Zand, D.E., 105
Zander, U., 385
Zapf, D., 10, 125, 126, 235, 356, 358, 362, 421
Zbaracki, M.J., 40, 46, 47
Zeitz, G., 46
Zempel, J., 177, 183, 184, 185
Zohar, A., 371
Zuckerman, J., 299, 304
Zuckerman, M., 185

Subject Index

Absence, 125, 302
Advanced manufacturing technology
   definition, 4, 56
   job design, 58–61
   human centred approaches, 61–3
   human resource practices, occurrence with, 275
   mechanisms in, 61
   performance, 60–1, 280
   redesign, 63–6
   role of skill in, 56–8
   stress, 60
   task allocation, 58
Anxiety, 125, 127, 185, 303
Autonomous work groups
   call centres, 121, 123
   performance management, 239
   service organisations, 294–5, 298, 300
   socio-technical theory, 9
Autonomy, 8, 9, 29, 30, 43, 44, 106, 185, 198

Call centres
   definition, 4, 116
   extent, 115
   human resource management, 121–4, 303, 304
   job design, 117, 120–1, 125–6
   performance, 128–9, 303, 304
   performance monitoring, 119–20, 125–6
   resistance, 127–8
   stress in employees, 125–8, 303, 398
   technology, 116
   types of 121–4, 127, 130, 398–9
Change
   e-business, 256–7
   economic change, organisational responses to, 372
   economic, social and political, 5, 371
   continuity and, 5–8
   organisational change and TQM, 45–7
   political dimension, 405
   tools for use in organisational change, 63–6, 336–44

Cognition
   cognitive abilities, 6
   cognitive engineering, 59
   job design, 9
   mechanisms in performance, 9–10, 165, 302, 420–1
Cognitive demands
   attention demands, 9, 59, 382
   cognitive load, 59, 77
   knowledge intensive organisations, 382
   problem-solving demands, 9, 59, 120
Consumers, 408
   relationship with producers, 408–9
Critical theories and approaches
   Foucauldian approaches, 406, 407
   in future study of working practices, 421
Customer–employee interaction, 118–19, 126, 299–300, 303

Decision-making latitude, 9, 42, 46, 156, 297–8
Depression, 127, 303
Design of modern working practices
   advanced manufacturing technology, 63–6
   political and social processes in, 11–12

E-business
   barriers to, 253–5
   definition, 4, 246–7, 258
   enablers, 253–5
   extent, 247–53
   human resource function, 259
Emotional exhaustion, 125, 126, 300, 303
Emotional labour, 126
Employee experience of work, 399–401, 417–19
   methodology and study of, 400–1, 421
   non-Western employees, 401
Employee involvement and empowerment
   call centres, 123
   cognitive mechanisms, 165
   definition, 4, 155–6
   employees, impact on, 167
   extent, 156–61
   high-performance practices, 163
   lean manufacturing, 32

Employee involvement (*cont.*)
  motivational mechanisms, 165, 166–7
  organisational performance, 161–7, 272–3, 280–1, 297
  participation in decision making, 29, 31, 32, 33, 34, 62, 101, 157, 209, 297
  performance management, 237–8
  practices involved in, 155–61
  service organisations, 297–8
  teams, 106, 160, 162
  total quality management, 43–5, 46, 158, 160, 162
Employee stress, 7
  advanced manufacturing technology, 60
  call centres, 125–8
  customer–employee interaction, 126
  human resource management, 126–7
  job satisfaction, 302
  lean manufacturing, 28, 33–4, 397
  performance, 302–3
  service organisations, 300, 303
  teleworking, 209–10
Empowerment *see* Employee involvement and empowerment
ETHICS tool for organisational redesign, 337, 340–3
Evaluation studies
  benefits, 349
  costs, 349–50
  criteria of evaluation, 348–9
  data collection methods, 357–60
  definition, 348
  experimental field studies, 352–3
  problems in design of, 360–3
  quasi-experimental studies, 353–6
  types of, 350–56

Feedback, 8, 59, 156, 233–4, 419
Flexibility, 5–6, 24, 373
Fordism
  just-in-time, 7
  lean manufacturing, 20, 24, 32
  manufacturing practice, 272
  problems with, 272
  replaced by flexible practices, 417

High-commitment approach, 7, 166, 395
  bundles of human resource practice and, 399, 414
  call centres, 121–4, 127, 130, 399
  characteristics of, 10
  contingency arguments, 10, 395–6, 399, 404
  human resource management and, 277–9
  lean manufacturing, 26–8
  service organisations, 295, 296, 299, 302, 303
  universalist argument, 10, 395–6, 404

High-involvement management (HIM)
  manufacturing practices and, 276, 277–9, 281, 286
  see also High-commitment approach
High-performance practices, 163, 164, 165, 168
  employee involvement and empowerment, 163–4, 165, 166
  see also High-commitment approach
High reliability systems
  cognitive processes in, 378
  definition, 377
HUFIT PAS toolset, 337, 338
Human capital theory, 165, 303–5
Human resource management
  bundles of human resource practices, 26–8, 123–4, 157, 312–13, 414–15
  call centres, 121–4, 123–4
  contingency arguments, 10, 164, 395–6, 399, 404
  co-occurrence with manufacturing practices, 274–9
  e-business, 259
  empirical issues in link to performance, 312–18
  innovation and creativity, 187, 188
  internal fit, 10, 121, 123–4, 312–13, 414–15
  knowledge management, 144–9
  lean manufacturing, 25–8
  measurement of, 316–17, 324, 402, 415, 423–4
  organisational fit, 10, 121, 415
  organisational performance, 10–11, 280–5, 311–12
  service organisations, 299–301
  strategic fit, 10, 121, 123–4, 313–15
  supply chain management, 85–9
  theoretical issues in study of link to performance, 318–22
  total quality management, 45, 274–9
  universalist argument, 10, 395–6, 399, 404
Hypercompetition, 371, 378, 394

Identity, 401, 408, 418
Innovation
  definition, 177–8
  individual antecedents, 179–184
  job design, 184–6
  lean manufacturing and kaizan, 21, 25, 29, 32
  proactivity and, 178
  teamwork, 186
  leadership, 186–7
Intensification, 28–9

Job characteristics
  types of, 419, 420

SUBJECT INDEX

Job control, 41, 43, 59, 120, 123, 125, 156, 209, 414, 419
Job design
  advanced manufacturing technology, 58–61
  call centres, 117, 120–1
  contingencies, 419
  flexibility, 373
  innovation and proactivity, 184–6
  job characteristics model, 8, 395
  job-demands-control model, 9
  lean manufacturing, 29, 33–4
  mechanisms, 61, 419, 420–1
  performance, 60–1, 304, 420
  redesign, 9, 394
  service organisations, 297–8
  socio-technical theories, 9
  teleworking, 209–10
  theories of, 8–10
  tools for job redesign, 65–6, 336–44
  total quality management, 41–3, 44, 48–9
Job satisfaction, 127, 167, 302, 303, 305
Job variety, 8, 58, 120, 123, 209, 396
Just-in-time *see* Lean manufacturing

Knowledge
  assets, 372, 380
  creation, 380
  competition based on, 5, 372
  definitions of, 380
  flows within organisations, 375, 379
  high-reliability organisations, role in, 378
  measuring, problems of, 420
  nature of, 137, 138, 139, 140
  know how, 383
  know who, 383
  markets, 381–3
  mechanisms in job design, 9–10
  organisations based on, 372
  relational networks, 379
  sharing and distribution, 78, 106, 136, 139, 141, 142, 143, 147–9, 375, 379, 381–3
  supply chain management, 83, 84
  teams, 106
Knowledge management
  activities involved in, 137–8
  capabilities for, 379–380
  context of, 136
  communities of practice, 143–4
  culture, role of, 149–50
  definition, 4, 136–7
  designing organisations for, 379
  discourse of, 138
  human resource management, 144–9
  human resource strategy, 146–7
  information technology, 142–3, 382–3
  performance in sales, 305

  performance management, 238
  perspectives of, 139–40
  practices, 140–1, 379–80

Lean manufacturing
  cases, 31–3
  definition, 4, 23–8, 271
  Fordist production and, 20
  human resource management, 25–8
  implications for employees, 28–31, 397
  job satisfaction and well-being, 26, 28, 33
  just-in-time, 20–22
  just-in-time, occurrence with human resource practices, 274–9
  just-in-time and organisational performance, 280, 281–5
  kaizan, 25, 29
  learning bureaucracy, 32–3
  organisational performance, 281–2, 395
  origins, 20–3
  Taylorism, 20–22
  types, 396–8
Lean production *see* Lean manufacturing

Manufacturing practices
  extent, 273–4
  human resource practices, occurrence with, 274–9
  performance, 279–86
Mass customisation, 295
Mass customised bureaucracies, 124
Mass markets
  service organisations, 296
Mass production, 5, 299
Mass service, 5
  call centres, 121–4, 127, 130
Mechanisms
  advanced manufacturing technology, 61
  cognitive, 165, 302, 420–1
  economic and sociological, 303–5
  employee involvement, 165, 166–7
  job design, 61, 419, 420–1
  manufacturing practices, 165–7, 319–22, 394
  motivational, 394, 421, 423
  organisational performance, 165–7, 273, 295–305, 319–22
  service organisations and performance, 301–5
Modern working practices
  co-occurrence with human resource practices, 274–9
  conceptualising their form, 414–16
  definitions of, 4
  evaluation studies and, 350–63
  extent, 273–4, 406–7, 416–17
  human resource management, 6–7

Modern working practices (*cont.*)
    mechanisms in performance, 165–7, 319–22, 394
    redesign, tools for, 336–44
Monitoring
    call centres, 119–20, 123, 125–6, 300, 303
    lean manufacturing, 29
    total quality management, 43
Motivation
    autonomous work groups, 239
    empowerment, 237–8
    goal setting, 325
    feedback, 233–4
    innovation, 182–4
    knowledge management, 238
    mechanism in job design, 8, 42, 394, 421
    organisational performance, 165–7, 319
    performance, 394
    performance appraisal, 234–235
    political dimension of, 405
    proactivity, 182–4
    ProMES, 240
    telework, 208–9
    theories, 221–5
    total quality management, 42–3, 236
    training, 230–3

New capitalism, 372
New workplace, 413, 418
    experiential newness, 417–18, 419
    extent of, 416–17
    historical newness, 417–18, 419
    new capitalism, the, 372
    new organisational forms
    'old' workplace in relation to
    post-fordism, 272
Non-Western employees, 401, 408

Organisational forms
    characteristics of new organisational forms, 376–7
    definition, 374–5
    different types of, 375
    high commitment approach, 7, 10, 166, 10
    high-reliability systems, 377–9
    in information-intensive economies, 374–7
    knowledge-based organisations, 372
    knowledge markets, 381–3
    mass customised bureaucracies, 124
    mass production, 5, 299
    mass service, 5 (*see also* call centres, 121–4, 127, 130)
    social capital and, 385
Organisational performance
    causal direction and human resource management, 321, 403
    e-business, 260
    evaluation studies, 350–363
    human capital theory, 303–5
    implicit performance theories, 322
    levels of analysis, 161, 315–16, 323–4, 402
    manufacturing organisations, 271–88
    measurement issues in study of, 316–18, 402
    mechanisms of performance, 165–7, 273, 295–305, 319–22
    methodology in study of, 312, 324–5, 403–4
    service organisations, 295–305
    study of, future directions, 323
Organisational scenarios tool, 337, 338–40

Participation in decision making, 29, 31, 32, 33, 34, 62, 101, 157, 209, 297
Performance management
    autonomous work groups, 239–40
    definition, 4, 219–20
    empowerment, 237–8
    extent, 220
    feedback, 233–4
    knowledge management, 238
    motivation theory, 221–5
    organisational performance, 162–299
    performance appraisal, 234–5, 162
    ProMES, 240–1
    training, 230–3
    total quality management, 236
Performance of modern working practices
    advanced manufacturing technology, 60–1, 280
    call centres, 128–9
    e-business, 260–1
    employee involvement and empowerment, 161–7, 272–3, 280–1, 311
    employee stress, 302
    just-in-time, 280, 281–5
    lean manufacturing, 281–2
    levels of analysis, 161
    manufacturing practices, 279–86
    mechanisms of performance, 165–7, 319–22, 394
    pay systems, 299–301, 311
    teamwork, 98–108, 300
    total quality management, 47–8, 280–5
Political
    dimensions of work behaviour, 393, 404–6
    processes in design, 11, 424
Post-fordism, 272
Proactivity
    definition, 176–7
    individual antecedents, 179–84
    innovation and, 177
    job design, 184–6

leadership, 186–7
teams, 106, 186
ProMES, 240–1
Psychological contract, 418
teleworking, 208–9

Quality of Working Life (QWL), 156, 394, 395, 396

Role breadth, 58, 183, 185

Search conferences, 343–4
Service organisations
business strategies, 292–5
customer segmentation, 294
economic and sociological mechanisms of performance, 303–5
economic context of, 291, 292–5
high commitment practices, 295, 296
human resource management practices, 299–301
information technology, 296–7
job design, 297–8, 304
mechanisms of performance, 301–5
models of service management, 295
pay and incentive systems, 299–301
psychological mechanisms of performance, 302–3
supervisors, effects of, 300–1
total quality management, 41, 294–5, 298
Skill
advanced manufacturing technology, 56–8
call centres, 121, 123
employee, 6, 296, 303, 304
high commitment models of service, 295–6
industrial models of service, 295
innovation, 179
lean manufacturing, 30
mechanism in performance, 319–321
proactivity, 179
skilled workforce, 6, 7
total quality management, 41–2
Social capital
definition, 383–4
information flow and, 384
new organisational forms and, 385
Socio-technical theory, 9, 332, 393
advanced manufacturing technology, 56, 61–63
call centres, 116–17
contingency and universalistic arguments, 395–6
e-business, 258–9
organisational change, 335
tools, 337
Soft-systems analysis, 337–8

Strategic flexibility
organisational forms for, 374
Strategy
performance, 312
strategic human resource management (SRHM), 311, 318, 325
Stress *see* Employee stress
Supply-chain partnering
definition, 4, 74–5
employee experiences, 77–85
extent, 76–7
human resource management, 85–9
perspective taking, 83–5, 88–9
theoretical approaches, 72–4
trust, 78–83, 86–8
Systems theory, 62, 337

Taylorism, 7, 394
call centres, 122, 398
job design, 8
lean manufacturing, 29
low commitment human resource management, 11
manufacturing job design, 272
Teamwork
characteristics of high performing teams, 101–7
definition, 4, 96, 396–7
extent, 96–8
high road team working, 396–7
innovation and proactivity, 186
lean manufacturing, 29–30, 31
low-road team working, 396–7
performance, 98–9, 299, 300
performance management, 239–40
service organisations, 295, 298–9
within-team processes, 104–6
see also Autonomous work groups
Teleworking
communication, 206–7
definition, 4, 197, 198–9
extent, 197
job design, 209–10
psychological contract, 208–9
stress, 209–10
types of, 200, 399
virtual team and, 206–7
Tools for organisational change, 63–6, 336–44
Total quality management
definition, 4, 38–9
effect on employees, 41–3, 407
employee involvement, 43–5
hard and soft, 41–3
human resource management practices, occurrence with, 274–9
management experiences of, 40–1

Total quality management (*cont.*)
　performance, 47–8, 280–5
　performance management, 236
　service organisations, 294–5, 298
　skill, 41–2
　varieties of, 38–40, 41
Trust
　control and co-ordination, role in, 375
　knowledge management, 142
　supply-chain management, 78–83, 86–8
　teams, 105

total quality management, 497
Turnover and quit rates, 127, 165, 166, 300, 302, 303, 304, 312

Uncertainty
　lean manufacturing, 24
　operational, 60–1, 100
　teams, 100
User-centred design tools, 337, 338–9

Well-being *see* Employee stress